FREEDOM FROM EXTREMES

Studies in Indian and Tibetan Buddhism

This series was conceived to provide a forum for publishing outstanding new contributions to scholarship on Indian and Tibetan Buddhism and also to make accessible seminal research not widely known outside a narrow specialist audience, including translations of appropriate monographs and collections of articles from other languages. The series strives to shed light on the Indic Buddhist traditions by exposing them to historical-critical inquiry, illuminating through contextualization and analysis these traditions' unique heritage and the significance of their contribution to the world's religious and philosophical achievements.

STUDIES IN INDIAN AND TIBETAN BUDDHISM

FREEDOM FROM EXTREMES

Gorampa's "Distinguishing the Views" and the Polemics of Emptiness

José Ignacio Cabezón *and*
Geshe Lobsang Dargyay

Wisdom Publications • Boston

Wisdom Publications, Inc.
199 Elm Street
Somerville MA 02144 USA
www.wisdompubs.org

Library of Congress Cataloging-in-Publication Data
Go-rams-pa Bsod-nams-sen-ge, 1429–1489.
[Lta ba'i san 'byed theg mchog gnad kyi zla zer. English]
Freedom from extremes : Gorampa's "Distinguishing the views" and the polemics of emptiness / José Ignacio Cabezón and Geshe Lobsang Dargyay.
p. cm. — (Studies in Indian and Tibetan Buddhism)
English translation with parallel romanized Tibetan text.
Includes bibliographical references and index.
ISBN 0-86171-523-3 (pbk. : alk. paper)
1. Madhyamika (Buddhism)—Early works to 1800. 2. Sa-skya-pa (Sect)—Doctrines—Early works to 1800. I. Cabezón, José Ignacio, 1956–- II. Lobsang Dargyay. III. Go-rams-pa Bsod-nams-sen-ge, 1429–1489. Lta ba'i san 'byed theg mchog gnad kyi zla zer. IV. Title.
BQ7454.G59713 2006
294.3'420423—dc22

2006036944

ISBN 0-86171-523-3
11 10 09 08 07
5 4 3 2 1

Cover and interior design by Gopa&Ted2,Inc. Set in DiacriticalGaramond 10.5 pt./13 pt.

Wisdom Publications' books are printed on acid-free paper and meet the guidelines for permanence and durability of the Committee for Production Guidelines for Book Longevity of the Council on Library Resources.

Printed in the United States of America

This book was produced with environmental mindfulness. We have elected to print this title on 50% PCW recycled paper. As a result, we have saved the following resources: 29 trees, 20 million BTUs of energy, 2,534 lbs. of greenhouse gases, 10,518 gallons of water, and 1,351 lbs. of solid waste. For more information, please visit our website, www.wisdompubs.org

Contents

Preface
by José Ignacio Cabezón vii

In Memoriam: Geshe Lobsang Dargyay (1935–94)
by Eva Neumaier xi

Introduction 1

DISTINGUISHING THE VIEWS OF EMPTINESS: MOONLIGHT TO ILLUMINATE THE MAIN POINTS OF THE SUPREME PATH

Thematic Subdivisions of the Text 63

Chapter 1
Three Ways of Understanding the Madhyamaka 69

Chapter 2
The Refutation of Dol po pa 97

Chapter 3
The Refutation of Tsong kha pa 115

Chapter 4
The Middle Way as Freedom from Extremes 203

Abbreviations 239

Notes 243

Bibliography 337

Index 383

Preface

José Ignacio Cabezón

In the early 1980s, I lived and studied at Sera Monastery in India while I was preparing my translation of Khedrub Jé's (Mkhas grub rje) classic of Middle Way (Madhyamaka) philosophy, the *Stong thun chen mo.* One of the great challenges I faced in my research involved identifying Khedrub Jé's unnamed opponents. This led me to read more broadly in the field of Tibetan Madhyamaka, and this, in turn, eventually led me to the work of the great Sakya scholar Gorampa Sönam Sengé (Go rams pa Bsod nams seng ge, 1429–89). In the course of reading Gorampa's writings, I came upon his *Distinguishing the Views (Lta ba'i shan 'byed),* the work translated in these pages. It immediately became clear to me why the text was considered by many scholars, both classical and contemporary, to be a work of tremendous power and, among other things, to be one of the most important critiques of Tsongkhapa's Madhyamaka views. Concise, clear, elegant in style, and powerful in its argumentation, *Distinguishing the Views* is one of Gorampa's most famous works. I had not yet finished reading the text when I decided to translate it. By the early 1990s I had a draft in hand.

I was not then aware that Geshe Lobsang Dargyay (Dge bshes Blo bzang dar rgyas), working in Hamburg, had already completed his own draft translation of Gorampa's text several years earlier. From 1994 to 1995, I had the good fortune to be a visiting research scholar at the Institut für Kultur und Geschichte Indiens und Tibets at the University of Hamburg. I first learned of Geshe Dargyay's work from my colleague in Hamburg, Prof. David Jackson. While in Hamburg, Prof. Lambert Schmithausen urged me to contact Geshe Dargyay about possibly collaborating on the translation, a suggestion that I welcomed. I soon learned, much to my regret, that Geshe-la had passed away just a short time earlier, a great loss to the field, and particularly sad news for me since I never had the opportunity to meet this fine scholar. My query, however, was answered by Prof. Eva Neumaier, the executor of Geshe Dargyay's estate, who was enthusiastic about my proposal to combine our work—mine and Geshe Dargyay's—to publish a translation of Gorampa's text under both our names. Over the many years since I first got her approval to proceed with this joint venture, Prof. Neumaier has been a model of supportiveness and patience. I also wish to thank her for contributing the brief life story of Geshe Dargyay found in these pages.

The work that you have before you is truly collaborative. While it fell on me to make the final decisions about the manuscript, I consulted Geshe Dargyay's text at every turn. In several instances, Geshe-la's translation allowed me to correct my own, and I consider myself fortunate to have had his text as a conversation partner and sounding board. Geshe Dargyay, in turn, had earlier benefited from the comments and guidance of Prof. Schmithausen. Prof. Schmithausen should therefore be seen not only as the impetus behind this cooperative undertaking but also as a contributor. However, the final responsibility for decisions fell upon me. Therefore, as the last (if not the only) scholar to work on this translation, I take responsibility for any faults and shortcomings.

Geshe Dargyay wished to thank the following individuals and institutions, the acknowledgement of which I take verbatim from his manuscript. "My deepest gratitude is due to Prof. Dr. L. Schmithausen for his readiness to take responsibility vis-à-vis the Deutsche Forschungsgemeinschaft (DFG), for checking and correcting my translation item by item, and for his many suggestions. Words of thanks to Prof. Dr. Eva Dargyay, too, are inadequate for her unfailing support of this work. I also wish to thank Prof. Dr. Leslie Kawamura for his support. Among institutions, thanks are due to the DFG, to the Social Sciences and Humanities Research Council of Canada, and also to the Calgary Institute for the Humanities. My gratitude also goes out to Mrs. Gerry Dyer for typing the first draft of the translation, and is also extended to my students who contributed to this project: Susan Hutchison, Kay Wong, Windsor Viney, and especially Donald Hamilton for his patience and readiness to spend many hours correcting my English and proofreading the text. Without their support, this work would never have been completed."

From my side, over the last decade I have had the good fortune to reread portions of Gorampa's text with students in Hamburg, Denver, and Santa Barbara. Dan Arnold helped with research on the first chapter. Most recently, two students, Michael Cox and Zoran Lasovich, have spent many hours with the English and Tibetan texts, getting them ready for publication. Several colleagues have taken time out of busy schedules to offer me feedback on the introduction or portions of the translation, among them David Jackson, Dan Martin, Gene Smith, and Tom Tillemans. Finally, the work could never have been completed without the generous support given to me by the Alexander von Humboldt Stiftung and by the Religious Studies Department of the University of California Santa Barbara. To the many individuals and institutions who have made this work possible, I express my sincere gratitude.

There is a certain irony that a work so critical of Tsongkhapa (Tsong kha pa)—the founder of the Gelug school—should have been translated and brought to the attention of a Western audience by two scholars trained in the great Gelug academies (Geshe Dargyay at Drepung and I at Sera). It is perhaps doubly ironic since the work translated here was, before 1959, actually banned by the Ganden Potrang (Dga' ldan pho brang), the Gelug-backed Tibetan government. (More on this in the introduction.) A great deal has changed since 1959. Books like *Distinguishing the Views* are no longer banned (either in Tibet or in exile). They are readily accessible and are today widely read by monks of all of the schools of Tibetan Buddhism, including Gelugpas. But the irony persists in large part because of how different things were just one generation ago.

There are many ways to engage a work like Gorampa's *Distinguishing the Views.* Because Geshe Dargyay and I were trained as exegetes and philosophers, this has been our main mode of engaging the work. We have, first and foremost, sought to understand what Gorampa himself was saying and to present Gorampa's views as accurately as possible. In the notes our goal has been to identify the works of Indian and Tibetan Buddhism that influenced our author, to find parallel passages and arguments in his other works, to find places in the works of his opponents where these same issues are addressed, and occasionally even to offer our own appraisals of Gorampa's views.

Some might think it inappropriate for scholars to make normative evaluations of the text or author they are translating. We should remember, however, that Gorampa's text is *itself* making normative evaluations of the texts and views of other authors. Rather than remaining aloof—as historians of religion are often wont to do, usually in the name of "objectivity"—aloof to the philosophical drama being played out in *Distinguishing the Views,* we have chosen to treat Gorampa's text as a living text with an intellectual agenda that calls out for assessment on the part of readers, even to this day. For better or worse, it is usually difference rather than similarity that catches the eye of the philosophically minded scholar, and thus our normative assessments are usually critical. Gorampa himself does not celebrate the points of agreement between his own tradition and that of the two figures he chooses to critique. Rather, he homes in on the differences, on the points of disagreement. That is simply the way philosophers operate, and perhaps that is as it should be, since agreement is, after all, the end of dialogue. Once you agree with someone, not much more is left to be said.

For the record—and here I (Cabezón) speak only for myself—I agree with much, perhaps even with *most* of what Gorampa has to say in *Distinguishing the Views.* From his more natural (and less tortured) interpretation of the tetralemma to his critique of the notion of "real destruction" *(zhig pa dngos po),* I find Gorampa convincing. The occasional quip against Gorampa should be seen in the context of what is a broad sympathy for his views and methods. Our main goal, as we've said, is not to assess Gorampa's views but rather to present his views as fairly and as accurately as possible, giving this great scholar the benefit of the doubt and allowing the subtlety and power of his arguments to shine through. Of course, it is up to the reader to decide whether we have succeeded in this task, just as it is up to the reader to decide whether Gorampa himself has succeeded in his.

In Memoriam: Geshe Lobsang Dargyay (1935–94)

Eva Neumaier

WITH THE WORDS "rdzogs so" and the final gesture of a *mudrā,* Geshe Lobsang Dargyay's mind began to leave his body on October 4, 1994 after a prolonged illness. His life is a testimony to the enormous changes the Tibetan people experienced during the course of the twentieth century.

Geshe-la was born in 1935 in Kartö (Kar stod), a small village in the principality of Gyalrong in Kham, part of the province of Sichuan, to parents who made a living as semi-nomads *(sa ma 'brog).* His birth name was Orgyen Hegya (O rgyan Hre rgya). He was the first of his mother's children to survive. Geshe-la had endless stories to tell about his childhood, the pranks he played, the scolding he received from his mother and, above all, the enduring love of his grandparents, to whom he was very attached. Early on, his mother and grandmother kindled in him the desire to embrace a religious life. He dreamed of becoming a *yogi,* living in a cave and emulating the life of Milarepa, the famous Tibetan poet-saint. While still a small boy, he ran away from home to seek spiritual instruction at the monastery of Rahor. This Nyingma monastery, small by traditional Tibetan standards, had a reputation as a place where the tantric practice of the Old School *(rnying ma)* was combined with the scholastic and philosophical training characteristic of the Gelug monasteries. Monastic discipline and rigorous learning were mandatory. In this monastery he received his monastic name, Blo bzang dar rgyas. Here he learned to read and write, and to memorize the basic religious texts, but he also trained in the practice of *gtum mo,* the fabled ability to increase one's body temperature.

Years later Lobsang Dargyay accompanied his cousin Rahor Rinpoche Thubten Kalsang (Ra hor Rin po che Thub bstan skal bzang), head of Rahor Monastery, Lhasa, to Drepung Monastery where they both continued their study of Buddhist philosophy. Lobsang Dargyay put all his efforts into absorbing the traditional five subjects of the scholastic training. Among his teachers one finds some of the intellectual elite of the Tibetan monastic system at that time. During the New Year's celebration of 1958, he demonstrated his competence in Buddhist philosophy during a public debate in the Jokhang temple of Lhasa. He was subsequently awarded the degree of geshe *(dge bshes)*.

His intention to further his studies at Drepung before returning to his home monastery was shattered when the political events of the late 1950s forced him (together with Rahor Rinpoche and a group of other monks and lay people from the same area) to leave Lhasa. During the winter of 1958–59 they traveled through the northern steppes *(byang thang)* before turning south to cross the Tsangpo River, heading toward Nepal and India, where they were granted asylum. There they learned about the March uprising in Lhasa and about the flight of His Holiness the Dalai Lama. The years of immersing himself in the depth of Buddhist philosophy and the joy he had experienced in exploring and understanding the intricacies of texts like the one presented here in translation came to an abrupt end. He had not only lost his native land and family but also the community of monks and the comfort it provided him, a loss that inflicted on him continuous pain.

In India he settled first in Kalimpong, in the midst of a large number of other Tibetan refugees. He continued to hope that he might return to Tibet in the near future. As he waited, he spent the days learning English and furthering his studies of Buddhist thought. As time progressed, it became clear that a return to Tibet would not happen so soon. The Tibetans started to establish themselves in India and to make their culture and Buddhist heritage known. Geshe Lobsang Dargyay was sent to Punjabi University as lecturer in Tibetan. He began to adjust to a secular life, keeping his monastic practice to himself and hidden from the eyes of those who comprised his new surroundings. As the years passed, he achieved a certain comfort by teaching Tibetan to Indian students, learning English and Hindi, and building a supportive community of colleagues and friends around him. Suddenly, Geshe-la was called to Dharamsala to see His Holiness the Dalai Lama. To his great surprise, His Holiness told him that he would be sent as religious teacher to a group of Kalmyks living as refugees in Germany. While many Tibetans would have welcomed the chance to move to a Western country, Geshe-la anticipated with anxiety this renewed disruption of his life.

Geshe-la arrived at Frankfurt airport in the late fall of 1967, dressed in cotton robes more suitable for an Indian climate than for a German winter.

German was a language unknown to him. In Ludwigsfeld, a suburb of Munich, he was offered accommodation in barracks that had housed prisoners of war during World War II. Gradually he began to sort out this new and totally unfamiliar environment. The older Kalmyks, who were devout Buddhists, spoke only their own Mongolian language and a few words of Russian; the younger ones spoke German and had little interest in a religion that seemed foreign to them. The old Kalmyk monk, known only by his title "Baksha," knew a few Tibetan words from his prayer texts. From modest beginnings, Geshe-la built a lively community of Buddhists, most of them Germans. He organized teachings, invited learned monks—for instance, Geshe Ngawang Nyima (Dge gshes Ngag dbang nyi ma), who later became abbot at the rebuilt Drepung Monastery in India—and held workshops on meditation. He joined the Department of Indian and Iranian Studies at the Ludwig Maximilians Universität in Munich as a research scholar, where his responsibilities included cataloging the *Rin chen gter mdzod.* In 1969 he was admitted as a doctoral student into the program of Buddhist and Tibetan Studies at the Ludwig Maximilians Universität. In 1974 he was the first Tibetan to receive his doctoral degree *(cum laude)* based on his dissertation, *Die Legende von den sieben Prinzessinnen (Saptakumārikā-Avadāna).* This work was subsequently published in *Wiener Studien zur Tibetologie und Buddhismuskunde,* Heft 2 (Vienna: Arbeitskreis für Tibetischen und Buddhistische Studien, Universität Wien, 1978). Geshe-la then took up a position as *Wissenschaftlicher Assistant* at the Institut für Südasien-, Buddhismus- und Tibetkunde at the University of Vienna, Austria. He worked closely with Dr. Ernst Steinkellner (University of Vienna), Dr. Michael Hahn (University of Bonn), and Dr. Dieter Schlingloff (University of Munich), who had also supervised Geshe-la's dissertation. At the University of Vienna, Geshe-la taught literary as well as modern Tibetan. Together with myself, Geshe-la conducted fieldwork in Zanskar, Ladakh, during 1978–79.

After the unexpected and premature death of Geshe Gendün Lodrö (Dge bshes Dge 'dun blo gros), Geshe-la taught at the University of Hamburg, Germany, where he started to work on Gorampa's *Lta ba'i shan 'byed.* Dr. Lambert Schmithausen provided immeasurable support and advice for this project. The Deutsche Forschungsgemeinschaft (German Research Foundation) financed the project for several years. Geshe-la's immigration to Canada in 1981 slowed the work down but did not bring it to a halt.

In Canada, Geshe-la had to adjust again to a new environment. He taught Tibetan language in the Department of Religious Studies at the University of Calgary, and became fellow at the Calgary Institute for the

Humanities. He benefited from working with Dr. Leslie Kawamura and Dr. Harold Coward, both at the University of Calgary. A group of interested students studied a number of seminal Tibetan texts under Geshe-la's guidance; some of them were published. During these years, the translation of Gorampa's work continued, with many versions being exchanged between Geshe-la and Dr. Schmithausen.

In 1990 Geshe-la visited Tibet for the first time since he had left in 1958. He returned to his birthplace in Kham. Meeting his family and his half-brother (also a monk) and seeing the rebuilt Rahor Monastery and the rebirth of religious life at this institution brought him great joy. He loved talking about the sturdy horses and the wildflowers carpeting the grassy slopes of his native place. He also relished the ease of living again among people who spoke his own tongue. Happily he conversed with old and young monks and gave advice and encouragement to his numerous nephews and nieces. He was considering returning to Tibet for good, but his karma took a different turn: in January 1991, he was diagnosed with esophageal cancer. Chemotherapy and radiation therapy slowed the disease but could not halt it. Despite his illness, which impaired his ability to swallow solid food, he returned to Kham in 1993. During the customary rainy retreat, he taught Buddhist philosophy for several months to the monks of Rahor. Although weakened by his illness, he experienced the fulfillment of his dreams when he was formally installed as abbot *(mkhan po)* for philosophical studies *(mthsan nyid grva tshang)* at Rahor Monastery. Finally, he had returned home, in both body and spirit. He selected a piece of land upon which he wanted to build his own little house, and he received permission from the Sichuan Government to settle for good in Rahor. He returned to Canada intending to prepare for his move to Tibet, but his illness worsened dramatically. He spent the last months of his life meditating and preparing himself for the great transition. When he was not meditating, he composed a history of Rahor Monastery. He passed away in Edmonton, Alberta, on October 4, 1994, comforted by friends and students. His ashes were taken back to Rahor Monastery together with some personal belongings.

Introduction[1]

THE INDIAN AND TIBETAN BUDDHIST sources tell us that the purpose of life is to attain enlightenment for the sake of others. But ignorance—the *mis*understanding of reality—stands in the way of achieving that goal of enlightenment. One of the more urgent aims of Buddhist practice, then, is to overcome ignorance by cultivating an understanding of reality, the ultimate truth, the final nature of the self and the world. The Mahāyāna sūtras use a variety of terms to designate this profound truth: *the sphere of dharma* (Skt. *dharmadhātu;* Tib. *chos kyi dbyings*), *phenomena in themselves (dharmatā; chos nyid)*, *reality* or *thusness (tathātā; de bzhin nyid)*, and of course *emptiness (śūnyatā; stong pa nyid).* The Madhyamaka *(dbu ma)*, or "Middle Way," is the name of the Buddhist philosophical tradition whose chief concern is the *view* or *theory (lta ba)* of that reality known as emptiness.[2] The Middle Way is so called because it is said to be a middle ground between two false extremes—the extremes of eternalism and nihilism. Some of the greatest minds in the history of Indian Buddhism have devoted a good deal of philosophical writing to delineating this Middle Way.

When the Tibetan court officially "adopted" Buddhism as the state religion, the Madhyamaka quickly became a part of the Tibetan intellectual landscape. Several accounts tell us that when king Khri srong lde'u btsan (eighth century) opted for the Indian over the Chinese form of Buddhism as the model of Buddhism that Tibetans would follow, he specifically mentioned the Madhyamaka as the school of thought that should be propagated.[3] Although there are some indigenous Tibetan works dealing with the subject of Madhyamaka that date from the "early dissemination period" or *snga dar* (seventh to mid-tenth centuries), it is not until the so-called "later dissemination period" or *phyi dar* (mid-tenth century onward) that Madhyamaka really emerges as a distinct field of Tibetan philosophical speculation. And even then, it is not until the fourteenth century that Middle Way philosophy becomes incorporated into the curriculum of the great monastic academies.

As was the case in India, Tibetans were not of one mind concerning the interpretation of emptiness, disagreeing—at times vehemently—over what constitutes the Middle Way. These arguments usually took place on the debate grounds of the great monasteries. As oral exchanges, these debates have been for the most part lost to us,[4] but at times the disputes made their way to the printed page. Those that did represent one of our most important sources for understanding Madhyamaka thought. *Distinguishing the Views (Lta ba'i shan 'byed)*, by the great Sa skya pa scholar Go bo Rab 'byams pa Bsod nams seng ge (or Go rams pa; 1429–89), is one of the most renowned and important works of Tibetan Madhyamaka. It is a work that highlights these differences in interpretation, and a work that therefore belongs to the genre of polemics, representing one of the highpoints in the history of this genre.[5]

On Polemics[6]

All knowledge—and this includes philosophy—is polemical by nature.

Johan Huizinga[7]

The great German Indologist Max Mueller once wrote, "To know one is to know none." For Mueller, knowledge is comparative. To know a thing—a text, a practice, a culture—it is necessary to see how the thing relates to other things. It is by understanding the nexus of relationships between things that knowledge arises. And if, as Peirce puts it, "a thing without oppositions, *ipso facto,* does not exist,"[8] then one can only conclude that knowledge not only has a positive *(cataphatic)* aspect, but also a negative *(apophatic)* one.[9] To know something requires that one understand both what a thing is and what it is *not.* Comprehension is a relational act. It requires that one be able to relate a given thing to other things that are similar, but also that one have an awareness of the way in which a given thing *differs* from other things. Knowing things in themselves—as isolates—is an incomplete form of knowledge. "To know one is to know none." If something is to be fully known, it is necessary to understand how it relates to other things. More specifically, true knowledge requires the ability not only to chart similarities, but also to notice differences and contrasts.

Just as in the field of epistemology (the theory of knowledge), so too in the field of literary studies. Some types of writing tend to approach their subject matter cataphatically, focusing on a given subject and treating it as an isolated, self-enclosed, discrete subject matter. Connections may be made to other areas, but only insofar as they contribute to understanding the thing that one is analyzing. In this mode, resemblance is the guiding principle of interpretation. Other texts may be referred to, but the emphasis is on proof texts—works that positively support the position that one is trying to defend. The goal is to get at what the thing is by charting similarities rather than by noting differences. *Expository commentary* is a good example of cataphatic literary discourse. The focus in a commentary is on a given text as a self-enclosed, discrete whole. The goal is to explain the meaning of the text by glossing words and passages using words that resemble (that is, that are synonyms of) the ones in the text itself. Commentators do look to other texts, but they are concerned with them chiefly to the extent that they support their own interpretation. The emphasis is on charting similarities. The tone is *irenic.*

Apophatic forms of literary discourse focus on differences. Here the goal is to get at the thing by contrasting it to what it is *not.* To that end, literary apophatists are more interested in the texts and traditions that *do not* resemble their own. This form of discourse must, of necessity, look outside of itself, to texts and doctrines that are different. Views that are dissimilar to one's own are carefully considered so as to create a stark contrast between self and other. The truth is arrived at through the negation of what is false/other. Apophatists are masters of negation and contrast. They have a keen eye for what is different, they are skilled in the techniques that bring out those differences, and they are accomplished in the logical strategies that repudiate what is other so as to make the self/same emerge as the only viable possibility. *Polemics* is a good example of apophatic literary discourse. In a polemical treatise, the object of analysis is the heterodox: the views (and sometimes practices) of others. These views are rhetorically constructed in a way that makes them easy (or at least possible) to refute. A variety of rhetorical strategies are used to repudiate opponents' views, and in the end the reader is left with the polemicist's own position as the only plausible alternative. The emphasis in polemical discourse is on differences. The tone is *agonistic.*

Now cataphatic and apophatic forms of literary discourse as we have just characterized them are what Max Weber would call *ideal types.* They are purely formal distinctions that exist only in the space of theory, and not in the real world of historically situated texts. No real-life literary work is purely cataphatic or apophatic. Rather, as ideal forms, the *cataphatic* and the *apophatic* occupy two poles on a spectrum; real-world literary texts always fall somewhere in between the two poles. Having said that, it is clear that some texts lie closer to the cataphatic end of the spectrum, while others are closer to the apophatic extreme. In this study, we are concerned with polemics as a form of apophatic literary discourse. Polemics is one of the most lively and interesting forms of religious-philosophical literature, and one of the most well known. Of the tens of thousands of volumes that constitute the Tibetan literary canon, the few dozen (or perhaps few hundred) works that are principally polemical are among the most popular.

What makes a polemic memorable? What makes it have an importance to a degree disproportionate to the space that works of this genre occupy within the literary canon? At least part of the reason has to do with who authored these works. Often the great luminaries of a tradition are its polemicists. Moreover, polemical works concern themselves for the most part with issues that are of central concern to a tradition. Even if polemicists sometimes get distracted by trivialities once they get going, what sets them on the path of polemics in the first place is inevitably an issue whose resolution is seen as vital, a rival's position that is seen as a threat. This fact has led some scholars to conclude that polemics—and not imitation—is the sincerest form of flattery, for why argue against someone over an issue that one deems insignificant, or—despite the rhetoric that polemicists often use—a position that one considers truly indefensible.[10] We might also add that the scholars who are the holders of these "false and dangerous" views—the polemicist's opponents—are themselves usually major players in their respective traditions. Once again, why expend energy battling an opponent one believes is incapable of influencing others? Polemics is spectacle: the greats in conversation with the greats about issues that are central to a tradition.

Just as in the contemporary Western academic world,[11] in Tibet reputations were made by attacking the views of a renowned scholar, whether on the debate ground (the professional meeting) or through the written word (the review). That Western academics have their own way of playing the game of polemics is witnessed by the way that careers are sometimes launched or buttressed on the basis of critical reviews of the work of others. In some circles this is even a rite of passage for the scholar. Of course, there is always a price to pay, for when polemicists are successful, they will always cause someone pain, even if—as they usually declare at the beginning of their works—their intentions are honorable, even if their criticism is directed at a specific view and not at the tradition as a whole, aimed at the position and not at the man, at the sin and not at the sinner. For the fact is that it is difficult—especially for philosophers, and especially when they are the target of the polemicist's pen—to think that one is not one's views. Part of it is simply human nature: our intense aversion to criticism. But it also has a lot to do with the *public* nature of polemical criticism. It is one thing to disagree with someone in the context of a private conversation, and quite another to make one's disagreement known publicly and in print. Joseph Agassi, in the introduction to his collected reviews, *The Gentle Art of Philosophical Polemics*, recounts the way in which he became estranged from his mentor, Karl Popper, precisely on these grounds:

> It must be seen that polemics is a ramification, in public, of criticism which may very well be offered in private. I report that many a time I had occasion to criticize publicly and did so privately—with the resultant gratitude, at times indicated or hinted at, at times expressed quite explicitly. I can also report that Popper's enormous annoyance at my public criticism of his ideas is rooted in his opinion that I should have offered him the criticism in private.[12]

But polemicists' estrangement from others, their regret at having caused others pain (Agassi: "to the extent my criticisms…have caused pain, I do sincerely express my genuine regret")—all of this obviously causes them distress and uncertainty (Agassi again: "Was I in error causing the pain that I caused? Was it avoidable? I do not know."). But in the end, it would seem that estrangement does not cause polemicists *so much* distress as to prevent them from continuing to write in this vein. Most polemicists publish more than one polemical work; they are "repeat offenders." (In Agassi's case, his uncertainties did not prevent him from *re*publishing his polemical reviews in the aforementioned volume!) Is polemicizing a compulsive activity? Whether or not it is pathological, it certainly appears to be an activity that causes the polemicist some anguish. Even the great Tibetan scholar Sa skya Paṇḍita Kun dga' rgyal msthan (1182–1251) feels this:

> When I announce [my views] publicly, those who do not know
> the Tantras become angry. Who is right, those angry ones or I?
> O Conquerors and their Sons, I pray that you consider [this].[13]

It is simply a fact of the matter: polemics is criticism, criticism is painful, pain causes anger and resentment, and this causes estrangement.[14] It takes a certain amount of mental fortitude and stamina on the part of the polemicist to withstand the kind of backlash that usually results from their writing, but then polemicists are strong-willed people, and they can usually stand the heat.[15] In any case, whatever rift might ensue between polemicists and their opponents is usually made up for by the status that polemicists gain within their own communities—that is, among those who are partisan to *their* views. Indeed, many religious polemicists see their work as an act of devotion (to the founders of their traditions, to their present communities, and to future generations).[16]

Yet another reason for the genre's popularity, therefore, has to do with the role that it plays in forming and nourishing a sense of identity and belonging. Polemics is both the parent and the child of sectarian identity-formation. When such an identity becomes important to a culture—as it did in Tibet during the "later propagation period"—scholars will often resort to polemics to create a sense of distinctiveness for their particular school. Followers of that school will in turn look to polemical works to give them a sense of identity: to show them how their school differs from and is superior to that of their rivals. Polemical literature is extremely effective in this regard for, as a form of apophatic discourse, its emphasis is precisely on differentiation. It makes sectarian distinctions real by introducing actually instantiated alternative views, but also safeguards sectarian identity by undercutting the alternatives that it introduces. Thus, it provides the partisans of a given theory or school with exposure to opponents' views; but because it embeds those views in a larger context that includes their refutation, it becomes a "safe haven" in which to explore alterity. All of this is to say that polemics is an important factor not only in "the invention of tradition," but also in perpetuating tradition.

It would be misleading, however, to see polemics as invariably directed *externally*—that is, outside of a given tradition. Not all polemics are *inter*-sectarian. One has only to think of the intra-disciplinary disputes that exist within the Western academy, or the schisms that have plagued the Buddhist tradition since its founding, not to mention the battles that have been waged (or are still being waged) *within* many of the schools of Tibetan Buddhism to see that polemics—and sometimes the most bitter polemics—can be *intra*-sectarian.[17] And one wonders, for example, if there are specific historical, political, and economic conditions that favor the emergence of inter- versus intra-sectarian polemics. Although it is tempting to think that intra-sectarian polemic always postdates the inter-sectarian variety, this does not seem to be the case, given that there are frequently bitter squabbles that arise in the very formation of religious sects.[18] But despite the fact that controversy is rampant within religious traditions—during, but not limited to, the time of their founding—the *occlusion* of controversy (for example, the suppression of intra-sectarian polemical texts) can also be an important strategy in the formation and preservation of sectarian identity. If there is a generalization that *can* be made here, perhaps it is that inter-sectarian polemical literature is more likely to become public and to survive as a cultural artifact than its intra-sectarian equivalent, for no other reason than that traditions are loathe to hang their dirty laundry out to dry.[19]

Let us digress for a moment to ask a question that is most urgent. Is sectarian differentiation really such a good thing? Should a literature that encourages sectarian distinction be promoted, either in its own right or indirectly, by making it into the object of the scholar's gaze? What of inter-sectarian strife? We would argue, stipulatively, that there is a difference between "sectarian differentiation" and "sectarian*ism.*" The former is simply an inevitable historical development that arises out of human beings' desire to create and nurture social and institutional structures of belonging—intellectual and spiritual homes, places where we share common goals and a common language—in a word, *traditions.* Sectarian*ism,* by contrast, is a pathological outgrowth of sectarian differentiation wherein traditions become static and reified, and wherein dogmatism prevails. Here dialogue gives way to monologue. In its more extreme form, raw forms of power (legal, military, etc.) are used to enforce the will of the hegemony. True, sectarian differentiation often gives rise to sectarianism, but the latter is not an inevitable outcome of the former. As we shall see below, Tibetan culture has seen periods where sectarian developments have been a condition for tremendous intellectual and spiritual flourishing. It has also seen periods when the society has been ravaged by sectarian violence and bloodshed. In large part due to the catholicity of the present Dalai Lama, the ethos in the Tibetan religious world today is one of relative harmony and mutual tolerance. Bon (Tibet's indigenous religion), Tibetan Islam, and the "canonical" schools of Tibetan Buddhism (Rnying ma, Bka' brgyud, Sa skya, and Dge lugs) have been relatively successful at recouping their respective cultural legacies, both in the diaspora and (to a lesser extent) in Chinese-occupied Tibet. While these traditions retain a strong sense of identity, they live side-by-side in relative harmony. Sometimes there is dialogue and cross-fertilization although, as the

Dalai Lama frequently points out, perhaps not enough. Of course, there are always occasions when the peace breaks down; but if nothing else, the present ecumenical climate shows us that strong sectarian differentiation need not always culminate in the social pathology of sectarian*ism*.

Let us grant that polemical literature is important in sectarian identity-formation. Is this the most relevant reason for the genre's popularity? In the final analysis it may be *style* more than anything else that explains the disproportionate appeal of such works. Polemical literature has glitz. It is to philosophy what action movies are to the film industry. A polemical work entices by titillating. It uses caricature, exaggerating the boundary between good and evil. It employs invective, insult, and at times even overtly violent language. And in the end the "bad guys" get reduced to dust. Is it not the case that the instinct that keeps us glued to the screen when we are watching *Mad Max* or *The Terminator* is the same instinct that also makes us enjoy a good polemical tract?

Socio-historical and psycho-analogical explanations for the popularity of the genre notwithstanding, there are good *philosophical* reasons for why polemics has been (and should continue to be) at the forefront of our study of Buddhist thought. So obvious that it may go unnoticed is the fact that polemical discourse is *dialogical.*[20] It introduces the voice of the other, and not just any other, but an other that occupies the position of challenger. Of course, not all polemical writing actually identifies the opponent by name. Keeping one's rivals anonymous is a well-known rhetorical strategy for denying them power and intellectual plausibility. (It is always easier and safer to dismiss an unattributed view than it is to reject the position of a known scholar who has a reputation.) But even when the opponent is *not* named, a polemical work by its very nature shows us that there is more than one side to a given issue, that things are not quite as simple as they appear to be on the surface, that there are others in the world who hold views different from the author's own, and that they have their reasons for doing so. True, the opponent is portrayed for the sake of being refuted, but a polemicist does not have a completely free hand in the way he depicts his adversary. Polemicists must tread a fine line, for if they caricature the opponent's stance—if they paint a picture of their opponent that is inaccurate and extreme—the intelligent reader will pick up on this. The refutation of straw men quickly turns philosophy into farce. So the position of the polemicist's opponent must always seem plausible, at least plausible enough that it appears worth refuting. Otherwise, why compose the work in the first place? Of course, polemics is also dangerous and risky. When confronted with plausible opponents, there is always the chance that readers will side *with them*, and that they will find the arguments offered by the polemicist to fall short of their mark. And this, as we know, is the one of the reasons why polemics is a *controlled* genre, why polemical works are frequently banned, why students are discouraged from reading such tracts until they are "intellectually well-formed" and until sectarian identity has been firmly inculcated in them. Polemics, therefore, is a literature that is intended "for mature audiences only."

Good philosophers are like good chess players, and much of philosophy unfolds in the way that an imaginary game of chess does. The scholar makes a move in his mind, always anticipating how an opponent will react, constructing hypothetical objections and dispatching them. But of course not every imagined countermove will be made in a real game. In the end, the imaginary game may turn out to be just that—the playing out of possibilities that will never occur in a real-life confrontation. When the game of philosophy (or chess) is played out in the mind of a single individual, there are no constraints, nothing to curb the imaginative (some would say "paranoid") impulse. It is this, in part, that has led to the charge that much of philosophy is nothing but mental masturbation. But polemics is a different kind of philosophy from the one just described. Polemics is more like playing a *real* game of chess, since it engages a real-life opponent.[21] Here the philosopher/player is responding to views/moves that are actually instantiated by a real opponent in history. And even if the polemicist's opponent/interlocutor has long since passed away, the disputant can expect a response from the latter-day followers of his adversary. This grounds polemics and gives it an air of reality that is missing from more speculative, monological forms of philosophical discourse.

The rhetoric of a polemical treatise also engages the reader in a more active fashion than simple expository and speculative prose. Polemics demands a more immediate response from the reader. It constructs a world in which there is a sense of urgency, a real need for evaluation: "You are either with us or against us. Decide now!" All of this gives it an immediacy lacking in other forms of philosophical prose.

Of course, polemicists are often given to excess. They sometimes *do* caricature their opponents' positions. They exaggerate, and at times even misrepresent, their rivals. In their exuberance to "neutralize" the views of their opponents, their logic is sometimes less than flawless. And the motives of polemicists are in many cases far from noble. A desire for reputation, patronage, power, and followers is in some cases more evident as the driving force than a desire for the truth. All of these facts—none of which, of course, can be denied—have led some scholars to paint a bleak picture of the genre. The words of Dan Martin are not atypical of the critics of polemics:

> ...polemic is extreme testimony produced under a state of duress and usually put forward to induce a state of duress. Polemic does its best to undo the background and authority of a tradition as it understands itself, and in various ways remake that background into something disreputable and unworthy of further interest. Seeing this delegitimating motive behind polemics, we may yet at times find truths in them, but they should hardly be our primary sources of truths. At best they can only occasionally, and that despite their designs, supply some useful points of secondary verification. In any case, we will keep polemics filed away in a folder clearly marked with the words "hostile testimony."[22]

Martin's somewhat hyperbolic rhetoric—his polemic against polemics, as it were—is, if nothing else, at least consistent with his view of what polemics is,[23] and of how it should be done. But the bleak picture that he paints of the genre is of course a caricature. There is obviously bad polemical literature but there is also, happily, a more noble variety. At its worst, polemics exaggerates and misrepresents. It is sophistic and at times even petulant. Instead of bringing about positive change, it causes views to become entrenched, and is therefore counterproductive.[24] It is all of the things that Martin says it is in this passage, and more. But there is also a more dignified variety of the genre: polemics that is truly motivated by the desire to know the truth, that is fair to the opponent, that is concerned with the issues and not with *ad hominem* attack, that relies on sound logic and arguments that are subtle and even convincing.[25] But in the end, perhaps the truth lies somewhere between Martin's view and my own. Idealistic portrayals of a genre (whether as good or as evil), while useful heuristically, always fall short of the mark if our goal is to understand real historical examples. And it may be that polemical literature, like all things human, probably has something of both the demon and the angel in it. But even in its more demonic forms, we would maintain, polemics is an unprecedented source for exploring religious-philosophical thought, for it is always possible, as Martin reminds us, that even in the worst of cases, "we may yet at times find truths" in these texts.[26]

Religious Polemics in Tibet[27]

As one of the world's great religious-philosophical systems, the Tibetan tradition is sufficiently rich that its literature spans the entire cataphatic-apophatic spectrum. At the cataphatic end, we find expository works epitomized by the genres of *word-commentary (tshig 'grel)* or *commentary* qua *annotations (mchan 'grel)*, which, as the names imply, provides the reader with glosses of a classical (Indian or Tibetan) text, elucidating the internal structure of a work, analyzing its terminology, providing definitions, expanding on arguments, and providing additional proof texts.[28] At the apophatic end of the spectrum are polemical works whose primary goal is to refute opponents (on which, see below).[29] And then, of course, there is much that falls in between: works that have dual agendas—to set forth one's own system, but in the process to repudiate the views of philosophical competitors, or to respond to their objections.[30] An example of this latter, mixed-genre is the so-called *Collected Topics (bsdus grwa)* literature,[31] which actually codifies both the apophatic and cataphatic elements into the very structure of the text. In Collected Topics texts, each subject is treated in three modes: through the refutation of others' positions *(gzhan lugs dgag pa)*, through the establishment of one's own position *(rang lugs gzhag pa)*, and through the rebuttal of others' objections to one's own position *(spong ba)*.[32] Despite the clearly apophatic dimension of the Collected Topics texts—the truth is partially arrived at by engaging and repudiating what is false—the genre is not, strictly speaking, polemical. In its post-fifteenth century Dge lugs form, which is the main form of this literature available to us today, it is a pedagogical genre used to teach students the art of debate. In most instances, the "others' positions" are considered not so much because they represent the positions of real opponents, but because they are heuristically useful to the overarching goal of giving students an overview of the important topics of Buddhist doctrine and of training students in the art of doctrinal disputation.

Since the text of Go rams pa translated here is a polemical work, we now turn to considering Tibetan polemics in more detail. Our purpose is to contextualize Go rams pa's work by situating it within the broader field of literature to which it belongs. We begin with a general, synchronic discussion of polemics as a genre of Tibetan literature, discussing some of the nomenclature used in the titles of these texts, as well as some of their structural features and rhetoric. In the following section we consider Tibetan polemics from a more diachronic perspective, offering a brief (and admittedly impressionistic) historical overview of the genre.

The corpus of Tibetan polemical writings appears to be relatively small. A search of the most complete digital bibliographical database of Tibetan literature yet compiled, that of the Tibetan Buddhist Resource Center (TBRC),[33] reveals that of the more than 28,000 volumes listed, less than one percent of the works can be considered overtly polemical based on their titles.[34] Of these about half are philosophical, and about one quarter deal with tantra. The rest range across all fields of Tibetan learning, from monastic discipline to medicine to grammar.[35]

Despite the relative paucity of polemical texts in the Tibetan literary corpus, however, the genre is one of the most important and popular. Some of the most significant and renowned texts in Tibetan literature are polemical. And mixed-genre works—texts that are only partially polemical—are often remembered more for their polemical than for their irenic prose. We shall consider some of the more important examples of the genre in the following section. Here, we are concerned with the more general features of such works.

Polemical passages can be found in a variety of texts of different genres. And sometimes we find an entire work of a genre that is otherwise non-polemical used for polemical ends. For example, the ordinance *(bka' shog)*,[36] the epistle *(spring yig)*,[37] and a genre known as "replies to questions" *(dris lan, zhus lan)*[38] have all been used to launch broadsides against opponents. But there *is* a class of texts in Tibetan literature that might be termed "polemics," even if Tibetan authors use a variety of different words to refer to it. The indigenous Tibetan nomenclature used to designate a literary work as polemical is twofold: (a) terms that are used to refer to works that bring forth charges (of inconsistencies, fallacies, etc.) against opponents, and that therefore initiate polemical exchanges, and (b) terms that are used to refer to works that respond to the charges made by others. As examples of the former—what we might call the accusatorial moment that initiates a polemical exchange—we find terms like "debate/dispute/argument" *(rtsod pa)*, "disputational document or record" *(rtsod yig)*,[39] "refutation" *(dgag pa)*, "record of a refutation" *(dgag yig)*, "adversarial speech" *(rgol ngag)*, and "critique/repudiation" *(sun 'byin)*. As examples of the latter terms—the terms used to designate the responsorial moments in polemical exchanges—we find words like "response to a dispute/argument" *(rtsod lan)*, "countering/overturning an argument" *(rtsod spong, rtsod bzlog)*, "response to a refutation" *(dgag lan,* honorific *gsung lan)*, and "rebuttal" *(brgal lan)*.[40] To use the analogy of warfare, the first type of text—the one that initiates an exchange—might be likened unto an offensive, while the second type is more defensive.[41] The fact that polemics as a genre is bifurcated in this way means that Tibetans view polemics chiefly as exchanges or dialogues, not unlike the exchanges that take place in oral debates. A polemicist will initiate an exchange by writing a text that is critical of a particular figure, of the texts that that figure follows, and/or the views that he holds. Later followers of the scholar being attacked will respond. Each moment in the exchange may be separated by centuries and the subsequent responses and rebuttals may go on for hundreds of years—indeed, indefinitely.

In general, the titles of indigenous Tibetan literary compositions have two parts. The first part is usually informational. It provides the reader with the gist of the subject matter of the text. The second part of a title is more poetic, a flourish that, despite its being encoded in the language of metaphor, nonetheless gives one an indication of the subject matter and genre of the work. In the case of polemical texts, the words just mentioned—"argument," "refutation," "rebuttal," "confutation," etc.—are frequently found in the informational portion of the title. For example, a polemical work on pilgrimage written in 1617 by Rig 'dzin Chos kyi grags pa (1595–1659) is known under two titles. The longer one reads *An Eloquent Disquisition Aimed at Destroying Another's Adversarial Claim: A Necklace for Those Who Preach Scripture and Reasoning (Gzhan gyi rgol ngag 'joms pa'i legs bshad lung rigs smra ba'i mgul rgyan).* The alternate title condenses the first (that is, the informational) part of the longer title, and reads *A Response to a Refutation: A Necklace for Those Who Preach Scripture and Reasoning (Dgag lan lung rigs smra ba'i mgul rgyan).* From the informational part of the title, then, the reader gleans that this is a polemical text and, more specifically, that it is a work belonging to what we are calling the second (*responsorial* or *defensive*) moment in a polemical exchange. In the informational part of a title, we often find opponents' views characterized as exemplifying ignorance *(ma rig)*, error *('khrul pa)*, evil *(ngan pa)*, falsity *(log rtog)*, and lies *(log smra).* The polemicist's text is then characterized as what overcomes *('joms)* or destroys *(tshar gcod)* that error.

The poetical or ornamental part of the title of polemical works can also be indicative of their genre, though in this case one gleans this through metaphorical allusions in which the opponent's views are likened, for example, unto darkness *(mun pa)* and the polemicists' treatise is portrayed as a lamp that clears away that darkness *(mun sel sgron me).* Throughout history, Tibetan polemicists have been fond of portraying themselves as fierce animals—lions *(seng ge)*, dragons *('brug)*, etc.—who can easily subdue their prey, and whose roar brings fear into the hearts of all who hear it. And they have used a wide variety of metaphors for their texts, calling them "diamond scepters" *(lag nyal)*, "diamond particles" *(rdo rje gzegs ma)*, "diamond weapons" *(pha lam rdo rje'i mtshon cha)*, "meteors" *(gnam lcags)*, "lightning" *(me char)*, "thunder" *('brug sgra)*, "large drums" *(rnga chen)*, and so forth—all of which are seen as having the capacity to destroy opponents' views, or to drown out their speech.[42] Take, for example, a defense of the Rnying ma tradition against its critics written by 'Gyur med tshe dbang mchog grub (1761–1829), *A Meteor that Overturns [The Views of] a Critique: The Roar of Wild Laughter of a Hundred Dragons (Rtsod bzlog gnam lcags 'brug brgya dgod pa'i nga ro)*. While the author resorts to a variety of metaphors—indeed, to more than do most texts—the reader will get a sense of how poetic images are used to convey the agonistic character of a polemical text. Of course, not all polemical works contain such metaphors. For example, the work of Go rams pa translated here is entitled *Distinguishing the Views: Moonlight [to Illuminate] the Main Points of the Supreme Path (Lta ba'i shan 'byed theg mchog gnad kyi zla zer)*. So while it is true that many polemical texts inscribe their genre into their title, we should not think that this is an invariable rule of the genre.

Turning now from the title to the body of polemical works, it is not uncommon for polemicists to begin (or end) their works by expressing a certain degree of trepidation at the task that is before them (or the task that they have just completed). They often bemoan the condition of the world in which they live. It is the degeneration *(snyigs ma)* of the present age that has caused false views to arise, they tell us, for we live in "an evil time, a time of disputatiousness" *(dus ngan rtsod pa'i dus)*.[43] While reluctant to engage in the task of refuting "false views," thereby adding to the contentiousness that already exists in the world, it is nonetheless the polemicist's duty, or burden *(khur)*, to do so. Put another way, a certain rhetorical ambivalence or hesitation is required on the part of the polemicist, lest it appear they enjoy their work. This usually gives way to a discussion of motivations. Polemicists are all too aware of the fact that not everyone who engages in controversy is operating with the best of intentions. Listen to the warning of Bu ston Rin chen grub:

> Those who, desiring one's own fame at the expense of others,
> Who with craft, deceit, harsh words and evil intentions,
> Engage in various forms of prattle that hurts the minds of others—
> Polemics of this kind are the cause [to be reborn in] hell.[44]

Is publicly challenging the views of others then worth the risk? Chag lo tsā ba believes that it is, because, as he says,

> ...there is great purpose in doing so. Not out of jealousy or pride, or to vanquish others, but so as to protect the teachings of the Buddha, so as to make the Dharma flourish, so as to repudiate false and impure doctrines, and so as to clear away the veil of misconceptions.[45]

Another author tells us that "it is out of compassion for sentient beings that we have spoken up."[46] If left unchallenged, wrong views will proliferate, especially among those of inferior intellect *(blo dman)*. Altruism is therefore the polemicists' ostensible motivation, but of course we know that there are always other motives—political, economic, etc.—also at work.[47]

Tibetan polemicists rhetorically construct their audience as being very broad—all sentient beings, all Tibetans, all "holy beings" *(skyes bu dam pa)*, and, on one occasion at least, all Buddhas and bodhisattvas[48]—but it doesn't take a great deal of discernment to see that their audiences are really much more local than their rhetoric suggests. Sometimes polemicists write to their opponents in the second person, directing their criticisms at a specific person or school: "You claim (or you do) X, but this is not right for Y and Z reasons." But as often as not, they will simply deal with issues impersonally: "X is false for Y and Z reasons." This does not mean, however, that Tibetan polemics operates with an abstract notion of truth, the way that post-Enlightenment Western philosophy does.[49] As Stephen Toulmin reminds us, a nowhere-situated reasoning that is in search of an abstract, disembodied truth is a relatively recent development, even in the history of Western thought;[50] and as Talal Asad has shown, this model of reasoning is hardly the model that is operative in all cultures.[51] Closer to the concerns of this volume, as Georges Dreyfus has observed, because the Tibetan scholastic tradition is heavily commentarial, "any philosophical elaboration must be presented as a commentary on an authoritative text" so that "views could never be presented on their own philosophical merits but only as authoritative commentary."[52] This is an important point to keep in mind, especially as we turn to the work of Go rams pa. Classical Tibetan scholars were operating with a set of assumptions—and were bound by a set of rules—that are different from those of modern Western scholars. For example, most of the Tibetan debates presume as a ground-rule the validity of Indian Buddhism, even if what Indian Buddhism *is* is often up for grabs. This is understandable, given the widespread Tibetan assumption (at least from the eighth century on) that Indian Buddhism is the *traditio franca*, the common source of all true doctrine and praxis.[53] The point is that "truth," "reasoning," and "argumentation" simply mean different things in a tradition that is committed to working within the bounds of a religious canon.[54] But this insight must be tempered through some further observations, lest it be thought that Tibetan polemics is nothing but dogmatics. First, we must bear in mind that the Tibetan canon is vast. A wide range of views are to be found within its thousands of texts. Scholars could therefore find scriptural warrant for many different positions, *and they did.* Second, the Tibetan imagination is subtle and profound. Trained exegetes could always find clever ways of creatively "interpreting" texts so as to bend them to their will, a project that has sometimes been called *eisegesis* ("reading into") as opposed to *exegesis* ("reading [the meaning] out of [the text]"). So even if truth always had to be presented in a way that was responsive (and responsible) to the tradition, there was a great deal of wiggle-room. This also allowed for innovation and, *inter alia,* for the radically divergent views that the reader will see presented in texts such as Go rams pa's. Finally, we must not forget that for Tibetans "religious experience" *(nyams pa, nyams rtogs)* came to be considered another way of legitimating innovation. While the tradition may be loathe to admit that experience is a way of injecting novelty into the system, it is nonetheless the case that Tibetan thinkers have often resorted to visionary and other forms of "mystical" experience to validate new intellectual agendas—to create theories and practices for which it would be difficult to find canonical warrant.[55] All of this is to say that while it is true that the canon serves as the rhetorical boundary for Tibetan polemical speculation, there existed mechanisms for transcending that boundary.

In the following section, the reader will get a sense of the range of topics debated by Tibetan polemicists. Here we simply note that Tibetan religious polemics has three major foci: practices, texts, and doctrines. Debates center, for example, on whether certain *practices* (both ritual and meditative) are truly Buddhist, or whether they have been "adulterated" or influenced by non-Buddhist (chiefly Bon and "Hindu") customs or traditions. *Textual disputes* are concerned with the authenticity of specific literary works (chiefly, though not exclusively,[56] tantras), and with questions of interpretation. *Doctrinal* controversies focus on the question of whether certain doctrines are consistent (internally consistent, consistent with our experience of the world, with the teachings of Buddhism, etc.).[57]

While it is true that Tibetan religious polemics is mostly issue-focused, we do not want to paint a picture of polemics as a lofty and objective exchange between two parties. Passions were involved, and not infrequently authors succumbed to the temptation to attack their opponents *ad hominem*, or to engage in any one of a number of forms of argument that in Western logic are classified under the rubric of *informal fallacies*.[58] There is plenty of unconvincing argumentation that takes place in these texts, and plenty of name-calling. In fact, there are probably few cultures that have mastered the art of the polemical insult to the extent that Tibetans have. And this undoubtedly is part of what makes the genre a spectacle, and therefore what makes it popular. Tibetan polemicists sometimes claim that their opponents are under the influence of drugs, or of various diseases, or worse, that they are possessed by demons—for why else would they be babbling nonsense. They compare them to dumb animals (sheep is the preferred species). They accuse them of pride, but too stupid to know even *how* to boast, they do their "dance" with "the decapitated head [rather than the tail] of a peacock hung from their behinds."[59] Consider these lines by one of the great masters of invective, Mkhas grub Dge legs dpal bzang (1385–1438):

> Your sophistry...has spoiled the Conqueror's vast teachings.
> It is the banner of demons, the messenger of evil spirits...
> But you, thief of the doctrine, who spread your demonic words
> in all directions,
> Cannot resist the profound doctrine, which, like a diamond,
> I now use to pierce your heart.
>
> Perpetually drunk on the evil fluids of jealousy,
> You give yourself over to the recitation of spells that harm the
> holy ones.
> Fooled by devils, mistaken are those poor beings
> Who consider such prattle to be the advice of a virtuous friend.[60]

And this is just the tip of the iceberg! Even as serious a scholar as Go rams pa cannot resist suggesting, for example, that Tsong kha pa's supposed conversations with Mañjuśrī may have been a dialogue with a demon instead. Obviously, comments like these ruffled feathers, especially when they were directed at the great saints or founding figures of a tradition. But from their years on the debate grounds of Tibet's great monasteries, Tibetan scholars also learned to take such comments in stride. All that said, if one generalization can be made about the historical development of Tibetan polemics, it is probably that there is an increasing tendency to focus on issues. This is not to say that name-calling—polemics as vilification—ever ceases. If anything, it becomes more refined and vicious over time. It *is* to say that, in the words of the old Buddhist adage, scholars increasingly "focus on the issue *(chos)* rather than on the person *(gang zag)*." As this happens, the genre becomes increasingly more rationalistic. This will become clear in the following section, as we turn to a historical overview of Tibetan religious polemics. A word of warning, however: Tibetan literature is vast, and Western scholars have barely begun to scratch the surface of this rich corpus of writings. The overview that follows, then, is of necessity impressionistic. Still, it will give the reader a general idea of the way that polemical literature has evolved over the centuries in Tibet. It is meant to provide a context for understanding Go rams pa's own work as one of the highpoints of the genre.

A Brief History of Tibetan Polemical Literature

As with most things Tibetan, the art of polemics is heavily influenced by the Indian Buddhist tradition. Polemics was a part of Buddhism from the earliest times. A variety of issues, both doctrinal and ethical, were debated in the centuries after the Buddha's death, and in some instances these led to permanent schisms in the monastic community.[61] Indian Buddhism eventually developed both a theory and a formal practice of oral disputation.[62] Some Indian Buddhist literary theories—Vasubandhu's rules for a commentator, for example—even considered the response to opponents' objections an essential aspect of more cataphatic genres like commentary.[63] And we know, of course, that Indian scholars wrote entire texts that were polemical in tone.[64] The point is that there is substantial Indian precedent for the Tibetan art of polemics within both the theory and practice of oral and literary forms of disputation.

The adoption of Buddhism by the Tibetan imperial court in the eighth century was not unproblematic. Tibet was not a religious *tabula rasa*. Bon, even if it was not yet a systematized tradition, was nonetheless a part of Tibetan life at various levels of the culture. It was also an important component of Tibetan ethnic and social identity. Even if, as Dan Martin puts it, "the internal Tibetan dialectic between Bon and Chos [i.e., Buddhism]" is already attested to in a Dunhuang text,[65] there appear to be no examples of Buddhist anti-Bon or Bon anti-Buddhist polemical (or even mixed-genre) texts dating to the early dissemination period *(snga dar)*.[66] While it seems clear that some sort of public Buddhist-Bon confrontation took place in the court of Khri srong lde'u btsan in the mid-eighth century, we have little knowledge of what, if anything, was actually debated. Indeed, the Bon po and Buddhist sources differ as to whether it was chiefly a contest of words *(ngag nus 'gran)* or of the magical abilities of each side.[67] In any case, we have no early polemical work that purports to be a record of this encounter. A Buddhist anti-Bon polemic does arise in the "later propagation period,"[68] and it continues throughout the centuries.[69] Some would argue that it is even implicit in contemporary Western academic writing on Bon.[70] The Bon anti-Buddhist polemic seems to begin only in the fourteenth century.[71]

If there is one doctrinal conflict that epitomizes the polemical impulse during the early dissemination period, it is not the Buddhist-Bon confrontation, but rather the Chinese-Indian Buddhist one or, as Seyfort Ruegg aptly puts it, the Sino-Tibetan vs. Indo-Tibetan one. In the so-called "Great Debate" that the sources tell us took place at the then newly founded monastery of Bsam yas between 792 and 794 C.E., the renowned Indian scholar Kamalaśīla is supposed to have debated the Chinese Ch'an master, Hwa shang Mahāyāna. The Tibetan sources tell us that the debate *(shags)* took place before the emperor. Kamalaśīla was the advocate of a "gradualist" *(rim gyis pa)* position, the view that enlightenment is attained through the incremental purification of the mind that takes place by the practice of the six perfections. This path, he held, requires analytical mental activity and a commitment to the intentional accumulation of merit. Hwa shang held the "simultaneist" *(cig car ba)* view—that (for advanced adepts at least) enlightenment is *not* attained gradually through the purification of the mind, that for these individuals analytical activity is a distraction and the accumulation of merit unnecessary. Instead, he claimed, enlightenment, as something that is already immanent in the individual, can immediately be accessed by directing the mind internally, by ceasing mentation, and by becoming aware of the nature of mind itself. Most of the Tibetan accounts tell us that Kamalaśīla won the debate, and this is said to have sealed the fate of Tibetan Buddhism forever. King Khri srong lde'u btsan, who served as "arbiter" or "judge" *(dpang po)* in the debate, declared that henceforth Tibetans would follow the Indian Buddhist tradition, in particular the system of Nāgārjuna. Many of the accounts also add that when he returned to China, Hwa shang left behind one of his shoes, an omen of the fact that his views would someday return to Tibet.

Western-trained scholars have been embroiled for decades in a controversy of their own conerning, among other things, whether the Bsam yas debate ever actually took place.[72] Those who deny the historicity of the debate note that the Tibetan sources that mention it date to the twelfth century or later.[73] This is true. There are no early Tibetan texts of a strictly polemical genre that give us a blow-by-blow account of the debate. That later Tibetan scholars should have written about Hwa shang Mahāyāna and his school in historical works—rather than as the object of an ongoing polemic—is not surprising, for by the time these authors were writing (post twelfth century), there were no longer any real proponents of Ch'an in Tibet, at least none that were considered a major "threat." The views of Hwa shang *are* treated more philosophically and polemically, however, when Tibetan doctrinal developments (Rdzogs chen, Mahāmudrā, and certain interpretations of Madhyamaka) come to be seen as the re-emergence of Hwa shang's views—the fulfillment of the prophecy implicit in the shoe he left behind. But in most instances, these invocations of Hwa shang represent formulaic and rhetorical moves, rather than actual philosophical engagements with real opponents. Over the centuries, Hwa shang has become the quintessential philosophical other. As Seyfort Ruegg puts it, "his teachings have come to fulfil a particularly emblematic function, one that may in fact be somewhat different from the position actually occupied by the historical *ho-shang* Mo-ho-yen."[74]

While it is true that most of our sources concerning the dispute between the gradualist and simultaneist camps at Bsam yas are historical rather than polemical, there *do* exist several early texts (or portions of texts) that deal with the doctrinal issues of the debate. Taken together, these works give us a broad picture of the controversy. Representative of the gradualist side, there is Kamalaśīla's *Bhāvanākrama* (Stages of meditation). Written in Sanskrit, and in three parts, it was translated into Tibetan. It is especially the third of these *Bhāvanākramas* that, although it never mentions Hwa shang by name, takes up what is evidently the position of Hwa shang's school with the goal of refuting it.[75] From the Chinese side, one might mention a Chinese text recovered at Dunhuang, Wang Hsi's *Ratification of the True Principles of the Great Vehicle of Sudden Awakening (Tun wu ta cheng cheng li chueh)*, a work that delineates and defends the views of Hwa shang and declares *him* the victor in the debate. Also representative of the simultaneist position are the twelfth and thirteenth chapters of the *Bka' thang sde lnga* (The narrative of the five groups),[76] a treasure text *(gter ma)*[77] that, while not compiled/discovered until the fourteenth century, appears to be derived from early traditions, so that one must agree with Tucci that the work "preserves many old fragments pieced together."[78] An exposition and defense of the simultaneist position, it states that the king opted for "the Madhyamaka," but then goes on to equate that Madhyamaka with the simultaneist view. The text clearly portrays Kamalaśīla as having the inferior philosophical/doctrinal position. These and other works like the *Eye-Lamp of Dhyāna (Bsam gtan mig sgron)*, allow us to piece together the controversy from various viewpoints.

True, none of these texts are polemical *in their entirety*. They clearly have other agendas over and above that of countering the views of the opponent—agendas that are catechetical, historical, hagiographical, and political. Moreover, two of these texts are not even of Tibetan origin. Taken together, though, they represent literary records of a polemic that was a landmark in Tibetan religious history. In particular, Kamalaśīla's *Bhāvanākramas* became for later Tibetan polemicists a model of what a sophisticated doctrinal/philosophical polemical text should look like. When doctrinal issues (rather than the authenticity of texts or practices) became the focus of disputes several centuries later, polemicists would follow the lead of Kamalaśīla in the way they formulated arguments. In many instances, they would simply quote or paraphrase him.[79] This is not to say that later Tibetan polemicists are not innovative or original, or that it is a single set of issues that are played out again and again. There is no question but that there are issues and methods of argumentation that we find in later Tibetan polemical works that are *not* presaged in the *Bhāvanākramas*. It *is* to say that just as Hwa shang becomes the paradigmatic "other," Kamalaśīla becomes in some ways the paradigmatic defender of the faith, especially when the issue has to do, as it often does, with the question of quietism. Hwa shang's shoe may continually haunt Tibet—or at least the imagination of its scholars—but so too does Kamalaśīla's spirit.

Even if it may have been written in part as a response to events that took place in Tibet, the *Bhāvanākrama* is not, as has been mentioned, an indigenous Tibetan work. What probably *does* deserve the title of the earliest polemical document in the history of Tibetan literature, the *Ordinance* of Lha bla ma Ye shes 'od, is written at the beginning of the next major period, the *later dissemination* period, or *phyi dar*. The document in some ways *defines*—at least for *us*, and in retrospect—this next period in Tibetan religious history. Let us first set the background for the writing of this work. With the murder of the emperor Glang dar ma by a Buddhist monk in the year 842, there was a resurgence of Buddhism in Tibet. But since the murder of Glang dar ma also brought with it the demise of the Tibetan empire, in the absence of unified patronage, Buddhism became decentralized and many different traditions began to flourish. The Buddhism practiced in the seats of power—in the courts of local rulers, in the houses of the nobles, and in more urbanized areas—was more "classical," which is to say more monastic and more Indian. But the *villages* were the realm of the tantric priests *(sngags pa)*, who practiced an amalgam of Indian tantra and Bon that was concerned with the enactment of practical, ecstatic—and at times, it would seem, even orgiastic—rituals: in short, with magic. We know from various hagiographical texts that a certain skepticism about the way that tantra was being practiced in Tibet at this time was growing among the elites.[80]

One of the best examples of this discontent with village religion,[81] and one of the most important documents of the early *phyi dar*, is the *Ordinance (Bka' shog)* of Ye shes 'od, the king of Pu hrangs in northwestern Tibet, who lived in the late tenth and early eleventh centuries.[82] Only a few pages long, the document is a polemic against the practices of "the priests and tantrikas who live in the villages" *(grong na gnas pa'i mkhan po sngags pa rnams)*. Various kinds of practices are condemned: sex ("union," *sbyor*), the killing of animals ("liberation," *sgrol*), ritual human sacrifice ("the offering ritual," *mchod sgrub*), as well as other magical practices like the creation of ritually empowered herbal medicines *(sman bsgrub)* and the magical manipulation of corpses *(bam sgrub)*, though of course we do not know how much the text exaggerates.[83] That the work is polemical is clear not only from its style—from its arguments and its invective tone—but also from the fact that it was considered an anti-Rnying ma polemic *(dgag yig)* by later Rnying ma pa apologists like Sog zlog pa Blo gros rgyal mtshan (1552–1624), who, even some six centuries after Ye shes 'od's document first appeared, considered it a significant enough attack on his school that he felt the need to include a response to it in his broader defense *(dgag lan)*[84] of the Rnying ma tradition.[85]

Slightly later than Ye shes 'od's *Ordinance*, and considerably more sophisticated, is *The Testament of the Pillar (Bka' chems ka khol ma)*, which is said to have been "discovered as treasure" *(gter nas bton pa)* by the Indian scholar/saint Atiśa (b. 972/982) in the Lhasa Jokhang temple. The polemical section of the work is quite short,[86] but it reiterates some of the same concerns of Ye shes 'od's *Ordinance*—to wit, the need to turn away from false practices *(log spyod)*. It also, however, departs from the *Ordinance* insofar as it is concerned not only with othropraxis, but also with proper beliefs, that is, with ortho*doxy*. Hence, it decries the proliferation of false or demonic *doctrines ('dre chos)* among "a variety of sects" *('dra min chos lugs)*—

doctrines like the "nihilism, that, grasping onto the empty aspect [of things], is especially effective at destroying the conventional truth, and at obstructing ascetic practices of body and speech [i.e., monasticism]."[87] If *The Testament* dates to the middle of the eleventh century, as many scholars believe, then it represents one of the earliest *doctrinal* polemics of the *phyi dar.*[88]

Ye shes 'od invested a great deal of capital into the reforms for which he was spokesman. He founded the monastery of Tho ling,[89] financed the translation of Sanskrit texts, and funded young Tibetans to study Buddhism in India. Among these young men was Rin chen bzang po (958–1055), who is known to have carried on the campaign of his patron. Whereas Ye shes 'od's polemic centered on the critique of tantric *practices,* however, the one initiated by Rin chen bzang po focuses on the critique of tantric *texts.*[90] Ye shes 'od's grand nephew, Pho brang Zhi ba 'od (second half of the eleventh century), who identifies himself as a Bka' gdams pa, wrote his own ordinance, which, true to this new focus, is a polemic aimed at false *texts.* It consists principally of the charge that many of the works central to what would eventually become the Rnying ma school (Zhi ba 'od's *Ordinance* is chiefly a list of these works) are apocryphal,[91] which is to say that they were not translations from Indian Sanskrit originals. The *Testament of the Pillar* calls these works "demon tantras" *('dre rgyud).* The charge that many of the texts that formed the basis for tantric practice during this time are in fact the fabrications *(rang bzo)* of Tibetans is subsequently taken up by 'Gos Khug pa lhas btsas (b. eleventh century),[92] a student of Atiśa. It is repeated in the thirteenth century by Chag lo tsā ba Chos rje dpal (1197–1264) in his *Sword of Wisdom that Refutes the False Tantras (Sngags log sun 'byin shes rab ral gri),*[93] and by Sa skya Paṇḍita in his *Differentiating the Three Vows (Sdom gsum rab dbye).*[94] When the Buddhist scriptural canon (the Bka' 'gyur) was compiled by Bu ston Rin chen grub in the fourteenth century, he excluded the vast majority of the Rnying ma tantras from the canon.[95] Such critiques, through word and (editorial) deed, of the authenticity of these tantras, and of the Rnying ma revealed *treasures (gter ma),* are found throughout the centuries,[96] down to the time of the Dge lugs apologist Pha bong kha Bde chen snying po (1878–1941).[97]

Charges that texts are apocryphal are relatively easy to make. Since the Sanskrit originals of the works that had been translated into Tibetan in the early dissemination period were for the most part no longer extant, these charges were also difficult to respond to. But sometimes the charge that a text was inauthentic simply backfired, as in the case of the *Guhyagarbha*

Tantra, a work whose authenticity was widely denied by critics of the Rnying ma pas—until, that is, the Bka' gdams ba scholar Bcom ldan rig pa'i ral gri Dar ma rgyal mtshan (1227–1305) discovered the Sanskrit original![98] And, of course, where there is a critique there is usually a response. Hence, there is a Rnying ma counter-polemical literature that addresses the charges that their tantras are apocryphal. This begins, perhaps, with Rog Shes rab 'od (b. 1166).[99] About a century later, O rgyan Rin chen dpal (1230–1309) writes a similar defense.[100] Klong chen rab 'byams pa Dri med 'od zer (1308–64) pens a defense of the Rnying ma tradition in his *Treatise to Eradicate Evil Misconceptions (Log rtog ngan pa'i bstan bcos).*[101] 'Gos lo tsā ba Gzhon nu dpal (1392–1481), in his magnum opus, *The Blue Annals (Deb sngon),* replies to Bu ston briefly by noting that the latter had included in his catalogue of authentic texts a tantra that quotes extensively from one of the tantras he refused to recognize.[102] In his treatises on the "three vows"—the *Sdom gsum rnam nges* and its autocommentary—Mnga' ris Paṇ chen Padma dbang rgyal (1487–1542) briefly responds to these same types of critics.[103] Perhaps the most extensive response from a Rnying ma scholar is found in the wide-ranging work of Sog zlog pa Blo gros rgyal mtshan (1552–1624).[104] Over a century later, 'Jigs med gling pa (1729/30–98) responds to 'Gos Khug pa lhas btsas's charge that the *Guhyagarbha* is apocryphal in his *Response to Questions Concerning the Tantric Corpus (Rgyud 'bum dri lan).*[105] In the first decade of the nineteenth century, the great Rnying ma historian Gu ru bkra shis (b. eighteenth century) shows how all of the schools of Tibetan Buddhism have adopted Rnying ma tantric practices, implying that to question the authenticity of the Rnying ma tantras is tantamount to a criticism of all schools.[106] As with the critiques, apologists who argue for the authenticity of the Rnying ma tantras are found all the way up to the twentieth century. For example, Bdud 'joms rin po che's (1904–88) *History of the Nyingma* contains an entire chapter in which he reponds to critiques of this kind.[107]

Nor is it the case that the defenders of the Rnying ma tantras and *gter ma* are exclusively Rnying ma pas. The great Dge lugs scholar Thu'u bkwan, for example, actually wrote an important defense of the Rnying ma tradition in response to an anti-Rnying ma polemic written by one of his own teachers, Sum pa mkhan po (1704–88).[108]

It is also important to realize that it was not only the Rnying ma pas who were challenged in regard to the authenticity of their texts and practices. From as early as the twelfth century, followers of the new translations *(gsar ma pa)* became the object of Rnying ma pas' polemical writings.[109] Chag lo tsā ba not only criticized the Rnying ma tantras, he also argued that (at least certain forms of) the practice of *cutting (gcod)* and *pacification (zhi byed)*, propounded in Tibet by eleventh-century Indian master Pha Dam pa sang rgyas, were "heathen" practices in Buddhist guise.[110] The Sa skya pas also faced similar challenges, for example in a work by Rngog Nyi ma seng ge (twelfth century) entitled *The Thornbush: A Treatise Refuting the Hevajra and Lam 'Bras [Traditions] (Dgyes rdor dang lam 'bras 'gog pa'i bstan bcos gze ma ra mgo)*.[111] Around this same time, Sa chen Kun dga' snying po (1092–1158) and his son Bsod nams rtse mo (1142–82) were writing a defense of tantra in general against unnamed opponents, identified only as "followers of the perfections" *(pha rol tu phin pa po)*.[112] In the first decade of the fifteenth century, the great Sa skya pa scholar Ngor chen kun bzang found himself having to write a series of apologetical defenses of the tantras in general, and of the Hevajra (the chief tantric cycle practiced in the Sa skya school) in particular.[113] As for the Bka' brgyud pas, Bdud 'joms rin po che reminds us that the Golden Doctrines of the Shangs pas were also challenged,[114] being excluded from at least one version of the commentarial portion of the Tibetan Buddhist canon, the Bstan 'gyur.[115] Even the relatively late Dga' ldan pas were not immune to criticism. For example, Ngorchen and his followers were vehement in their criticism of the Dga' ldan pa tradition of Yamāntaka.[116]

Nor was it only *texts*—for example, the Rnying ma tantras and the revealed treasures *(gter ma)*—that were an object of dispute. Starting in the mid-eleventh century, *doctrines*[117] increasingly become an object of controversy. We have already mentioned that the *Testament of the Pillar* was concerned as much with orthodoxy as with orthopraxis. In his *Ordinance*, Zhi ba 'od, almost as an afterthought, reviles the Great Perfection *(Rdzogs chen)*, claiming that "its theoretical base has been mixed up with the system of the non-Buddhists, and therefore to engage in this practice causes one to be reborn in the lower realms."[118] Many of these early condemnations of doctrines, however, are more impetuous than they are reasoned. They resort to a rhetoric of intimidation—threatening those who uphold and practice them with dire consequences in the afterlife—but they do not actually engage the doctrines that they are condemning *qua* doctrine, nor do they usually offer reasons for why they are false *(chos log, chos min)*.[119] The same might be said of those who argue for the fact that the Rnying ma is concocted *(rang bzo)* on the basis of the novel terminology found in its texts, another common charge.[120] Neither of these forms of argument are very sophisticated or philosophically interesting. In other parts of Tibet, however, things were taking a somewhat different turn.

While the debate over the authenticity of texts was taking place in western Tibet, something quite unprecedented was happening in central Tibet. There the stage was being set for a more rationalist form of polemics—one that focuses on philosophical issues rather than on questions of authenticity. In 1073, Rngog Legs pa'i shes rab,[121] a student of Atiśa (982–1054), founded Gsang phu Monastery. His nephew Rngog lo tsā ba—Rngog the translator—Blo ldan shes rab (1059–1109), often called the father of Tibetan scholasticism, continued the legacy of his uncle, and in short order Gsang phu became one of the greatest centers of textual learning in all of Tibet, with a curriculum that eventually became the model for some of the country's great monastic academies. Unfortunately, very few of the Madhyamaka works of these important figures survived, but we know that they were the founding figures of Svātantrika Madhyamaka exegesis in Tibet.[122] Recently, however, a work of another early abbot of Gsang phu, the influential Phya pa Chos kyi seng ge (1109–69), has been discovered and published.[123] Written in the first half of the twelfth century, the *Dbu ma shar gsum* is one of the earliest examples of a developed, indigenous Tibetan *philosophical* polemic that is available to us.[124] The text belongs to the field of Madhyamaka, and it is interesting not only because of its polemical character, but also because it is in large part a refutation of the Indian Madhyamaka philosopher, Candrakīrti, a figure whose work was considered (by Tibetans, at least) the quintessential example of the other major branch of the Madhyamaka, the Prāsaṅgika. This is extremely interesting because the great scholars of India rarely became the targets of Tibetan critiques, much less of full-blown polemics. So Phya pa is unusual in this regard. This does demonstrate, however, that Phya pa was an innovator, which is important to understanding his other major contribution, in the area of logic/epistemology *(tshad ma)*.

The Madhyamaka was not the only topic to become an object of polemic during the early scholastic period. The first abbots of Gsang phu were also responsible for inaugurating a new tradition of epistemological studies that focused on the works of the Indian scholar Dharmakīrti (600–660), and there developed among them an interpretation of Dharmakīrti that would have tremendous influence, extending, *inter alia,* to the Dga' ldan pas. It has recently become clear that, despite a certain degree of homogeneity in the formal structure of some of the Gsang phu works on logic—the so-called *synopses (bsdus pa)* and the works that derive from them—there was also a substantial degree of doctrinal disagreement, a fact that led to a considerable amount of polemical exchange.[125] The greatest early challenge to the Gsang phu epistemological tradition, however, is to be found in the work of the next major player in the field of philosophical polemics, Sa skya Paṇḍita (more on this figure below). Sixty years after Sa paṇ, the great Bka' gdams pa scholar Bcom ldan rig ral would enter these debates, taking on the Gsang phu tradition as well.[126] The points of contention were hermeneutical, doxographical, epistemological, and ontological: Which of Dharmakīrti's texts should be given precedence? How literally should Dharmakīrti be taken? What is the doctrinal affiliation, or *grub mtha'*, of Dharmakīrti? How should one differentiate direct from indirect cognition? Are universals real?[127]

Given the pivotal role that Sa skya Paṇḍita played in a variety of different polemical arenas,[128] a few additional words about this important figure are in order. Sa paṇ is more concerned with refuting what he considers false *views and practices* than with identifying false or apocryphal *texts.*[129] As Dreyfus shows, Sa paṇ's *Treasure of Reasoning (Rigs gter)*[130] is, *inter alia,* a critique of Phya pa and his school—a multi-faceted critique, but one that in the end really boils down to a criticism of Phya pa's innovations. Sa paṇ is a traditionalist who wishes to adhere more closely to Dharmakīrti's texts (and to Dharmakirti's *Pramāṇavārttika* in particular), and he therefore finds Phya pa's innovations problematic. Nor is Phya pa the only target of Sa paṇ's polemical quill in the field of logic. As Gene Smith has noted, 'Jig rten mgon po (1143–1217), who "tried to deny to ordinary mortals the possession of 'real' logic, defining *pramana* as the enlightened awareness *(jñāna)* of an omniscient being," is also refuted in Sa paṇ's *Rigs gter.*[131]

Nor, for that matter, did Sa paṇ limit himself to epistemological polemics. Although ostensibly written as an exposition of the pratimokṣa, bodhisattva, and tantric vows, his *Differentiation of the Three Vows (Sdom gsum rab dbye)* is a polemic against many different practices and doctrines prevalent in Sa paṇ's day. For example, his criticism of pilgrimage as it was then practiced in Tibet, though not often mentioned, is intruiguing.[132] But, as we have said, Sa paṇ is principally known as a *doctrinal* polemicist. His critique of Phya pa in the field of logic we have already mentioned, but he was also known for his critique of a certain kind of Mahāmudrā theory and practice. The Great Seal (Mahāmudrā) is of course a doctrine that has Indian roots. It became a specialty of the Bka' brgyud pa tradition founded by the great translator Mar pa Chos kyi blo gros (d. 1097) and his student Mi la ras pa (1052–1135). Sa paṇ did not direct his critique at the views of these two founding figures of the Bka' brgyud lineage, however. Instead, his polemic was principally directed at the doctrine of Mahāmudrā in its *White Panacea (dkar po chig thub)* formulation.[133] The White Panacea, or "self-sufficient white remedy," is the doctrine that "the realization of the nature of mind is sufficient in and of itself to bring about spontaneously and instantaneously the simultaneous consummation of all virtuous qualities, including Buddhahood itself."[134] Among the advocates of this view, devotion to the spiritual master, leading to his grace, was often singled out as the chief cause of that direct realization of the nature of mind. Several authors, including Sa paṇ himself, have noted the similarity between this doctrine and certain Ch'an views that were circulating in Tibet as early as the imperial era. Sa paṇ focused his critique on the formulation of the White Panacea as it was expounded by Mi la ras pa's student, Sgam po pa (1079–1153), and by the latter's disciple, Zhang Tshal pa (1123–93). David Jackson has analyzed this controversy in detail, making it unnecessary to go into details here.[135] Suffice it to say that Sa paṇ's critique of the Mahāmudrā was influential, especially among later Dge lugs scholars: for example, it influenced the Fifth Dalai Lama (1617–82),[136] 'Jam dbyangs bzhad pa Ngag dbang brtson 'grus (1648–1721), and Dbal mang Dkon mchog rgyal mtshan (1764–1853).[137]

As the *gsar ma* (or New Translation) schools developed distinct institutional identities, polemics became a vehicle through which the leading figures of these various sects differentiated their doctrines from those of their rivals. While tantra continues to be a central concern for these authors, exoteric doctrinal controversies also emerge—or re-emerge in new and more sophisticated ways—across a wide range of topics, from the character of the buddha's bodies[138] to the interpretation of the buddha-nature to the Madhyamaka.[139] Unfortunately, many of the most important Madhyamaka works written from the twelfth through fourteenth centuries have been lost to us, leaving us no choice but to glean their views from the way in which these are paraphrased in later sources.[140] This situation changes, however, when we come to the fourteenth century.

Through a rather long and circuitous route, we have finally come to the two individuals who are the objects of Go rams pa's critique in *Distinguishing the Views.* These are, of course, Dol po pa Shes rab rgyal mtshan (1292–1361) and Tsong kha pa Blo bzang grags pa (1357–1419). While these two figures held quite different philosophical views, they also shared a great deal in common. Each was the founder/systematizer of a major school of Tibetan Buddhism. Dol po pa was the chief systematizer of the Jo nang pa, Tsong kha pa the founder of the Dga' ldan pa (later called the Dge lugs pa). Both wrote extensively on a wide range of doctrinal topics—both esoteric and exoteric. Each of them showed a special interest in Madhyamaka. Their rivals held that each of the two figures was also an innovator, propounding controversial theories that were departures from the Indian and Tibetan tradition that had preceded them.[141]

Dol po pa's theory of Madhyamaka came to be known as "the emptiness of what is other" *(gzhan stong),* so-called because it maintained that the ultimate *(don dam),* while empty of all things different from itself *(rang ma yin pas stong pa = gzhan stong),* is not empty of itself *(rang stong ma yin).* In Dol po pa's view, the ultimate, which he equates with the buddha nature *(bde bzhin gshegs pa'i snying po = rigs)* and gnosis *(ye shes),* is a positive reality beyond intellectual comprehension. It is a radiant, permanent, stable unity that is self-sufficient. It can never be understood in terms of the deconstructionist and reductive dialectic of the negationist *(chad pa'i)* branch of the Madhyamaka tradition epitomized in the *rationalist* works *(rigs tshogs)* of Nāgārjuna. Rather, says Dol po pa, it is the positivist tradition found, for example, in Nāgārjuna's "corpus of hymns" or "praises" *(bstod tshogs)* that is the best source for understanding the ultimate.

Tsong kha pa's Madhyamaka theory has come to be known simply as the *Prāsaṅgika.* Like many of the luminaries of Tibetan scholasticism before him, Tsong kha pa saw the great texts of Indian Buddhism as the foundation for Buddhist theory and practice. As regards the doctrine of emptiness, he cast his lot with Indian Mādhyamika thinkers like Buddhapālita, Candrakīrti, and Śāntideva, claiming that it was *their* interpretation of Nāgārjuna, and their interpretation *alone,* that constituted the correct theory *(yang dag pa'i lta ba)* of the nature of things. Tsong kha pa maintained that emptiness, the ultimate truth, was an absolute negation *(med dgag)*—the negation of inherent existence—and that nothing was exempt from being empty, including emptiness itself. The ultimate truth, he claimed, could be understood conceptually, and while that conceptual understanding needed to be transformed through meditation into a deeper and more transformatively efficacious mode of cognition (the gnosis of the āryan, the direct realization of emptiness; *'phags pa'i mnyam bzhag ye shes = stong nyid mngon sum du rtogs pa'i blo*), he believed that the object of the conceptual understanding of the ultimate and the object of gnosis *were no different.* Moreover, he believed that since emptiness is a truth that is not evident, it could only be approached (at least initially) through the path of reasoning, that is, through the Madhyamaka dialectical strategies. The logic of the Madhyamaka, he felt, was not fundamentally inconsistent with the theories of Buddhist logicians like Dharmakīrti.[142]

Now Dol po pa and Tsong kha pa are important in the history of Tibetan Madhyamaka polemics not because they were themselves major polemicists, but because they were the *object of others' polemics.* Not that Dol po pa and Tsong kha pa completely refrained from criticizing other scholars—far from it—but these criticisms occur more in the context of other agendas than they do in major, independent polemical works. Dol po pa *did* write at least two clearly polemical minor works in the field of Madhyamaka, about which we will have more to say below. Tsong kha pa, on the other hand, usually treated the theories of his philosophical rivals in passing, leaving the defense of his tradition to a later generation of scholars.[143] Go rams pa mentions some of the critics of Dol po pa in *Distinguishing the Views,* among them his own teacher, Rong ston Shes bya kun rig (1367–1450), and another great master of the Sa skya school, Red mda' ba Gzhon nu blo gros (1349–1412), who was also a teacher of Tsong kha pa. And of course it is well-known that Tsong kha pa himself criticized the views of Dol po pa in such works as *The Essence of Eloquent Discourse (Legs bshad snying po).* The great Dge lugs textbook author 'Jam dbyangs bzhad pa Ngag dbang brtson 'grus (1648–1721) also devotes several pages of his *Great Treatise on the Philosophical Schools (Grub mtha' chen mo)* to a critique of Dol po pa.[144]

The most famous classical critics of Tsong kha pa were Stag tshang lo tsā ba Shes rab rin chen (b. 1405),[145] the Eighth Karma pa Mi bskyod rdo rje (1507–54),[146] Shākya mchog ldan (1428–1507),[147] Mi pham rgya mtsho (1846–1912),[148] and of course Go rams pa.[149] These figures, in turn, were responded to by later generations of Dge lugs polemicists. Stag tshang lo tsā ba was responded to, for example, by the First Paṇ chen bla ma Blo bzang chos kyi rgyal mtshan (1570–1662), by 'Jam dbyangs bzhad pa Ngag dbang brtson 'grus (1648–1721), and by Phur lcog Ngag dbang byams pa (1682–1762).[150] Rje btsun Chos kyi rgyal mtshan (1469–1544/6) responded to the Eighth Karma pa in his *Ornament to the Intention of Nāgārjuna: A Response to Honorable Speech (Gsung lan klu sgrub dgons rgyan).*[151] 'Jam dbyangs dga' ba'i blo gros (1429–1503)[152] and Lcang lung paṇḍita (1770–1845)[153] both wrote apologetical works responding to Go rams pa's attack on Tsong kha pa. The most extensive and detailed critiques of Go rams pa and Shākya mchog ldan, however, are the two parts of a single work called *Eliminating the Darkness of Bad Views (Lta ba ngan pa'i mun sel),* more colloquially known as *The Reply to Go* and *The Reply to Shāk (Go lan, Shāk lan).*[154] 'Ju Mi pham rgya mtsho was responded to by a variety of Dge lugs apologists such as Dpa' ri(s) Blo bzang rab gsal (b. 1840),[155] Brag dkar sprul sku (1866–1928),[156] and Ldan ma Blo bzang chos dbyings (b. nineteenth century).[157]

One final thought before moving on: the discussion up to this point makes it seem as though the various polemical texts, responses, and counter-responses mentioned in this section were written and disseminated in a free society where the expression of views was always tolerated and freedom of speech was the norm. But we know this to be far from true in Tibet throughout much of its history. For example, after the victory of the Fifth Dalai Lama's Dge lugs school and the rise of the Dga' ldan pho brang as the government of central and western Tibet in the mid seventeenth century, there was a concerted effort to control religious institutions that had previously opposed the Dge lugs pas or that were seen as rivals. Many monasteries in central and western Tibet—especially Bka' brgyud and Jo nang ones—were forcibly converted into Dge lugs institutions. And as with institutions, so too with the written word: texts critical of Dge lugs views and practices were suppressed—their copying and printing were banned, and the copies of the texts that already existed were either destroyed or sealed in storerooms. Many important works—sometimes the entire collected works of renowned scholars, and even the works of Dge lugs scholars who were seen to diverge from the Dge lugs mainstream—simply stopped circulating in central and western Tibet from the beginning of the eighteenth century as the result of censorship. But because the government of the Dalai Lamas was always weaker in some of the eastern frontier regions of Khams and A mdo, many of these persecuted schools and texts managed to survive in these regions. Such was the fate, for example, of the Jo nang school and of the works of the great Jo nang masters Dol po pa and Tāranātha (1575–1634). Suppressed for all intents and purposes in their homeland in Gtsang, Jo nang pas came to flourish in places like 'Dzam thang in eastern Tibet, where they preserved and transmitted the collected works of their most famous lineage lamas. We have them today thanks in large part to their preservation in these remote regions.

While Sa skya monasteries were not, on the whole, subject to the same degree of persecution as the Jo nang pas, individual Sa skya authors *were* targeted for censorship. The works of Go rams pa—principally because of his critique of Tsong kha pa—were banned and probably circulated only secretly in areas controlled by the Dga' ldan pho brang. The situation in eastern Tibet was different, however. Manuscript copies of Go rams pa's works must have been in circulation in eastern Tibet for centuries, and it seems that reading transmissions *(lung)* of his collected works exists to the present day.[158] It is a tribute to the scholars of the Sa skya tradition that they were able to preserve the texts of Go rams pa and to propagate their formal transmission for centuries in a milieu of censorship, without access to blockprinted works. The blocks for Go rams pa's collected works, the source of the earliest edition of *Distinguishing the Views* available to us, were only carved in Sde dge in the first decade of the twentieth century.[159]

The suppression of the works of Go rams pa and of his erudite contemporary Shākya mchog ldan meant that Sa skya institutions in central Tibet were denied access to works that today are seen as the very core of Sa skya scholastic studies. This lack of access to Go rams pa's works, combined with fear of reprisals from Dga' ldan pho brang officials, probably goes a long way to explaining the dearth of Sa skya polemical replies to those Dge lugs scholars who wrote against Go rams pa. It was a risky business to defend the views of a banned author, especially one who had taken on the founder of the Dge lugs school. Defending Go rams pa in print was risky; defending his views on the debate courtyard was probably something that happened with greater frequency. One wonders, for example, how often the views of Go rams pa became the object of discussion at institutions like Rgyal rtse Dpal 'khor chos sde in western Tibet, where Dge lugs, Sa skya, and Zha lu pa monks lived and studied side by side in the same monastery (as they do to this day). It appears that the views of scholars like Go rams pa also made their way into the debate courtyards of eastern Tibet. David Jackson recounts the story of a Sa skya scholar, Lama Gendun, who challenged the monks of Ra nyag, a Dge lugs pa institution, to debate:

> At the debate he [Lama Gendun] defeated one of the monastery's best geshes, and in victory he rode around the courtyard on the shoulders of his disgraced opponent. He said, "This being able to ride on the nape of a first-class geshe from the Central Tibetan seminaries is due to the grace *(bka' drin)* of Go rams pa!"[160]

If nothing else this story shows us that in certain areas of Khams, Dge lugs and Sa skya monks felt free to engage each other and to debate controversial subjects. It also tells us the extent to which Sa skya pas associated the name of Go rams pa with doctrinal victory over Dge lugs pas.

Go rams pa may be the most famous of Tsong kha pa's classical critics, but his most famous contemporary critic of Tsong kha pa is the brilliant Amdo eccentric Dge 'dun chos 'phel (1903–51), whose work represents one of those relatively rare instances in the history of Tibetan philosophical speculation in which a scholar overtly critiques the views of the founder of the school in which he was trained.[161] Dge 'dun chos 'phel, in turn, was responded to by another renowned Dge lugs scholar of the modern period, Dge bshes Shes rab rgya mtsho (1884–1968),[162] and more recently by Dze smad rin po che Blo bzang dpal ldan bstan 'dzin dar rgyas (1927–68).[163]

Go rams pa, as far as we know, never experienced reprisals against his person because of the views he held or because of the writings he published. The same cannot be said of Dge 'dun chos 'phel, who spent years in a Lhasa prison—perhaps because of his critique of Tsong kha pa, perhaps because of his left-leaning policitcal views, or perhaps for both reasons. Even in twentieth-century Tibet, being an anti-Dge lugs polemicist carried with it substantial risk.

The nineteenth and twentieth centuries have seen the writing of a tremendous amount of polemical literature in all branches of Tibet's religious and secular sciences. Even the nonsectarian *(ris med)* movement that began in Khams in the nineteenth century,[164] known for its inclusivistic views and for its appreciation of the teachings of all of the schools of Tibetan Buddhism, had its apologists.[165] So vast is the literature of the modern period, however, that it is impossible to analyze it within the scope of this introduction. Suffice it to conclude by simply noting that the genre of Tibetan polemics is very much alive and well. While polemical monographs continue to be written on religious subjects,[166] the last decade has begun to see Tibetan-language periodicals as a venue for polemical exchanges, where the topics debated range from politics to poetry.[167] A great deal more could be said regarding the history of polemics in Tibet, but perhaps this brief overview is sufficient to see that Go rams pa is part of a very long and honorable tradition.

The Life and Works of Go rams pa[168]

Go rams pa was born in 'Bom lung mda' in the Go bo area of Khams, eastern Tibet, in 1429. His father's name was Ru tsha Zhang skyabs, and his mother's name was Rgyal ba sman. The tradition considers him the reincarnation of the famed Sa skya hierarch, Rje btsun Grags pa rgyal mtshan (1147–1216), though it is not clear that anything like a formal recognition ever took place in his lifetime. At the age of ten, Go rams pa took novice ordination from his tutor, Kun dga' 'bum, the monk responsible for his initial training.[169] It was at this time that Go rams pa received the monastic name of Bsod nams seng ge. During these early years, he also studied under and received empowerments from other teachers like Go bo rab 'byams pa Shes rab dpal and Bka' bcu pa Sbyin bzang. The biographies tell us that his teachers were impressed with his intellectual abilities, and it appears that it was during this time that he began to be called *rab 'byams pa*—literally "[a master of] a vast array [of scriptures]," but actually a formal title.[170]

In 1447, at the age of nineteen, Go rams pa traveled to Nalendra Monastery in Central Tibet to study under the great Rong ston Shes bya kun rig,[171] who was the teacher of several of his teachers in Khams. By the time he arrived, however, Rong ston pa was seriously ill. He in fact died the following year, and although Go rams pa is sometimes considered "Rong ston pa's last student," one wonders how much interaction there actually was between Go rams pa and Rong ston pa in this, the final year of his life.

The year after Rong ston pa's death, Go rams pa traveled first to Lhasa and then to the recently founded monastic college of 'Bras yul Skyed tshal[172] to study under Byams chen rab 'byams pa Sangs rgyas 'phel (1411–85),[173] "the best of the learned." Under him Go rams pa studied many of the classical subjects of scholastic learning: Prajñāpāramitā, Vinaya, Abhidharma, etc., all of which he is said to have quickly mastered. For some of his contemporaries, this is said to have further confirmed the idea that he was the reincarnation of a great former lama.

Four years later, at age twenty-five, Go rams pa decided to do a "monastic debate tour" *(grwa skor)* of some of the more important monastic centers of central and western Tibet, but illness prohibited him from doing so. It appears that it was in part to counteract the illness that he decided to more seriously pursue the study of tantra. And so in the winter of 1453 he went to the famous monastery of Ngor E vam chos ldan to pursue tantric studies.[174] Under Ngor chen Kun dga' bzang po (1382–1456),[175] the founder of that monastery, he twice received the instructions on the *Path and Its Result (lam 'bras),* the main practice tradition of the Sa skya school. This took almost four years. During this time he also pursued other tantric studies related to the deities Cakrasaṃvara, Guhyasamāja, and Red Yamāntaka, receiving initiations into each of these tantric cycles, along with instructions *(khrid)* on the sādhanas *(sgrub thabs).* At age twenty-six, Go rams pa became a fully ordained monk under Ngor chen.[176] While Ngor chen was his main teacher during this period, Go rams pa also studied under several of Ngor chen's senior students. For example, he pursued more intensive tantric study under Mus chen Dkon mchog rgyal mtshan (1388–1469),[177] who gave him initiations and oral transmissions *(dbang dang lung).* During his stay at Ngor Monastery, he also received many profound instructions from Mkhan chen Kha phyar ba and from Gung ru Shes rab bzang po (1411–75). Gung ru ba was one of the main students of Rong ston, Ngor chen, and Mus chen, and the person whom Go rams pa credits with motivating him to compose *Distinguishing the Views.*[178]

After Ngor chen passed away in 1456 *(me pho byi ba'i lo)* Go rams pa continued to study various tantric practices under Mus chen, receiving many initiations and teachings during this period. He also broadened his knowledge of the Sa skya tradition by studying the collected works of the "five great lords of the Sa skya school" *(Rje btsun gong ma lnga)*[179] and listened to lectures on the collected works of Rgyal sras Thogs med pa (1295–1369)[180] and the works of Ngor chen.

When Go rams pa was thirty-two, at the prodding of his half-brother, he decided to return to Khams. On his way back home, he visited 'Bras yul Skyed tshal, where he had studied eleven years earlier. After seeing his tremendous mastery of the texts, his former teacher, Byams chen rab 'byams pa, the abbot of this monastery, asked Go rams pa to stay to assist him in teaching the younger monks. One source tells us that during his periods of teaching he taught ten classes every day![181] While at Skyed tshal, however, he also spent time in meditation and writing. It was during this time, for example, that he wrote his major commentaries on the *Abhisamayālaṃkāra,* the *Yum don rab gsal,* and his two most important commentaries on Sa paṇ's *Sdom gsum rab dbye.* After several years, Byams chen rab 'byams pa retreated to Mus, and Go rams pa replaced him as head of the monastery. In his new position as abbot, he taught Prajñāpāramitā, Pramāṇa, Vinaya, and Abhidharma, in each case starting with the great commentaries on these subjects and progressing to the root texts. His students advanced in knowledge, and this added to his already increasing fame. Go rams pa left 'Bras yul Skyed tshal after some time and went to Mus to see his teacher, from whom he received teachings, particularly on Cakrasaṃvara.

At age thirty-eight, Go rams pa accompanied Mus chen on his trip to Byang Ngam ring, which the latter undertook at the invitation of the local ruler Rnam rgyal grags pa and his son. While at Ngam ring, Go rams pa taught about forty students and his fame grew. Shortly after this time, in the year 1466, Go rams pa founded Rta nag gser gling Monastery.[182] Go rams pa appears to have been in residence at Gser gling most of the time for the next seven years, although the colophons to several of the texts he composed during this time attest to the fact that he travelled to other monasteries as well.[183] It was during these travels that he saw his teachers Mus chen and Gung ru ba for the last time, and it was perhaps at this, his last meeting with Gung ru ba, that he was instructed by him to compose *Distinguishing the Views.* In any case, as far as writing is concerned, it is clear that this was one of his more productive periods. For example, *Distinguishing the Views* was written during this time, as were other important works on Prajñāpāramitā and Pramāṇa philosophy. In the construction of the monastery, Go rams pa received support from aristocrats affiliated with the Rin spungs court.[184]

In 1473 Go rams pa founded another monastery in Rta nag, Thub bstan rnam rgyal. After construction was completed, he established a curriculum of sūtra and tantric studies. Just the exoteric subjects and texts that he taught constitute an impressive list:[185]

- *Prajñāpāramitā Saṃcayagāthā*
- *Abhisamayālaṃkāra* together with *Sphuṭārtha,* and the remaining works of Maitreya
- *Abhidharmakośa*
- *Abhidharmasamuccaya*
- The five Madhyamaka treatises of Nāgārjuna
- *Catuḥśataka*
- *Madhyamakāvatāra*
- *Bodhicaryāvatāra*
- *Vinayasūtra*
- *Pramāṇavārttika,* together with Sa paṇ's *Rig gter,* and
- The *Sdom gsum rab dbye,* also of Sa paṇ

Of course Go rams pa also taught tantra extensively at his new monastery. It appears that he remained at Thub bstan rnam rgyal for almost a decade after founding the monastery.

Because we know that Go rams pa wrote one of his *Prajñāpāramitā* commentaries at Ngor Monastery in 1481, it would appear that he had already left Rta nag sometime before this point.[186] In any case, we know for certain that in 1483 Go rams pa became the sixth abbot of Ngor, replacing another of his teachers, Dpal ldan rdo rje (1411–82). Go rams pa remained at Ngor until 1486, teaching in great detail the Lam 'bras system as well as other topics of both sūtra and tantra.[187] He then enthroned Dkon mchog 'phel (1445–1514) as his successor at Ngor and returned to his own monastery in Rta nag. There he instructed his disciples in many different subjects. In his spare time, he performed empowerments *(dbang),* permissions *(rjes gnang),* blessings *(rab gnas),* and burnt offering rituals *(sbyin sreg).* He also composed many treatises during this time. His writings are known for their excellent style and lucidity. His major exoteric works, listed below, basically fall into seven categories:

(1) ***Middle-Way (Madhyamaka; Dbu ma) works***

- *Dbu ma rtsa ba'i shes rab kyi rnam par bshad pa yang dag lta ba'i' 'od zer* (incomplete), a commentary on Nāgārjuna's *Mūlamadhyamakakārikā*
- *Rgyal ba thams cad kyi dgongs pa zab mo dbu ma'i de kho na nyid spyi'i ngag gis ston pa nges don rab gsal,*[188] also known as the *Dbu ma'i spyi don,* a general, synthetic exposition of the Madhyamaka with a strong polemical element[189]
- *Lta ba'i shan 'byed theg mchog gnad kyi zla zer,* his polemic against Dol po pa and Tsong kha pa (translated in this volume), written at the beginning of 1469
- *Dbu ma la 'jug pa'i dkyus kyi sa bcad pa dang gzhung so so'i dka' ba'i gnas la dpyad pa lta ba ngan sel,*[190] a quasi-polemical commentary that focuses on the difficult points of Candrakīrti's *Madhyamakāvatāra,* taking issue with many of Tsong kha pa's interpretations

(2) ***Perfection of Wisdom (Prajñāpāramitā; Phar phyin) works***

- *Shes rab kyi pha rol tu phyin pa'i man ngag gi bstan bcos mngon par rtogs pa'i rgyan 'grel pa dang bcas pa'i dka' ba'i gnas rnam par bshad pa yum don rab gsal,* a commentary on the *Abhisamayālaṃkāra,* with an emphasis on its difficult points, written in 1464 at Skyed tshal
- *Shes rab kyi pha rol tu phyin pa man ngag gi bstan bcos mngon par rtogs pa'i rgyan gyi gzhung snga phyi'i 'grel dang dka' gnas la dpyad pa sbas don zab mo'i gter gyi kha 'byed,* another commentary on the *Abhisamayālaṃkāra* with an emphasis on the views of earlier and later commentators and on its difficult points, written in 1470 at Rta nag
- *Grel pa don gsal gyi ngag don,* a commentary on Haribhadra's *Sphuṭārtha,* written in 1481 at Ngor E vam chos ldan
- *Shes rab kyi pha rol tu phyin pa'i man ngag gi bstan bcos mngon par rtogs pa'i rgyan gyi mtshon byed kyi chos rnams kyi yan lag khyad par bshad pa sbas don rab gsal,* a commentary on some ancillary points in the *Abhisamayālaṃkāra,* written in 1472 at Rta nag
- *Zhugs gnas kyi rnam gzhag skyes bu mchog gi gsal byed,* a treatise on those who "enter and abide" in the different fruits of the path (stream-enterer, etc.), written in 1470 at Rta nag
- *Mthar gyi gnas pa'i snyom par 'jug pa'i rnam bshad snyoms 'jug rab gsal,*[191] a treatise on the advanced meditative states of the form and formless realms, written in 1470 at Rta nag

- *Rten 'brel gyi rnam par bzhag pa 'khor 'das rab gsal,* a treatise on dependent arising, written in 1470 at Rta nag

(3) ***Epistemo-Logical (Pramāṇa; Tshad ma) works***

- *Rgyas pa'i bstan bcos tshad ma rnam 'grel gyi rnam par bshad pa kun tu bzang po'i 'od zer,* an extensive commentary on Dharmakīrti's *Pramāṇavārttika,* composed in 1474[192]
- *Rgyas pa'i bstan bcos tshad ma rnam 'grel gyi ngag don kun tu bzang po'i nyi ma,* a shorter commentary on the *Pramāṇavārttika,* written at Rta nag
- *Sde bdun mdo dang bcas pa'i dgongs pa phyin ci ma log par 'grel pa tshad ma rig[s] pa'i gter gyi don gsal bar byed pa,* a commentary on the seven treatises of logic in connection with an elucidation of Sa paṇ's *Tshad ma rigs gter*
- *Tshad ma rigs pa'i gter gyi dka' gnas rnam par bshad pa sde bdun rab gsal,* a commentary on Sa paṇ's *Tshad ma rigs gter* that emphasizes the difficult points of the text, composed in 1471 at Dga' ba tshal Monastery

(4) ***Vinaya ('Dul ba) works***

- *'Dul ba mdo rtsa'i rgyas 'grel* (no longer extant), an extensive commentary on the *Vinaya Sūtra* of Guṇaprabhā
- *Rab tu byung ba rnams kyi bslab bya nyams su blang ba'i chos 'dul ba rgya mtsho'i snying po,* advice to monks, written in 1481 at Rta nag

(5) ***Abhidharma (Mdzod) works***

- *Chos mngon pa mdzod kyi bshad thabs kyi man ngag ngo mtshar gsum ldan* (incomplete), a commentary to the *Abhidharmakośa*
- *Phung khams skye mched kyi rnam gzhag ji snyed shes bya'i sgo 'byed,* a treatise on the aggregates, elements, and spheres, written in 1472 at Rta nag

(6) ***Works having to do with the three vows (Sdom gsum skor)***

- *Sdom pa gsum gyi rab tu dbye ba'i rnam bshad rgyal ba'i gsung rab kyi dgongs pa gsal ba,* an extensive commentary on Sa paṇ's *Sdom gsum rab dbye,* written in 1463 at Skyed tshal

- *Sdom gsum rab dbye'i spyi don yid bzhin nor bu,* a general, synthetic treatise on the *Sdom gsum rab dbye,* written in 1461 at Skyed tshal
- *Sdom pa sgum gyi bstan bcos la dris shing rtsod pa'i lan sdom gsum 'khrul spong,* a polemical work defending the *Sdom gsum rab dbye,* written in 1476 at Rta nag
- *Sdom pa gsum gyi rab tu dbye ba'i kha skong legs bshad 'od kyi snang ba,*[193] a supplement to the *Sdom gsum rab dbye* that is in large part polemical, written in 1478 at Rta nag
- *Sdom gsum kha skong gi bsdus don,* an abbreviated version of the supplement to the *Sdom gsum rab dbye,* written at Rta nag

(7) ***Miscellaneous texts***

- *Blo sbyong zhen pa bzhi bral byi khrid yig zab don gnad kyi lde'u mig,* a commentary on the famous short text, *Abandoning the Four Attachments*
- *Rgyud bla'i 'grel pa rtsom 'phro,* an incomplete commentary on the *Uttaratantra*

In addition to these works, in the thirteen volumes of his collected works, there are many expository works on tantra, as well as liturgical and devotional texts.

Like many of the great scholars of his day, Go rams pa was also a visionary. For example, he had vivid dreams of Mus chen instructing him in the doctrine while he was composing one of his polemical texts, the *Gzhan phan 'od zer gyi rtsod spong.*[194] Such visionary dreams were frequent in Go rams pa's life, especially when he was about to begin a new writing project. The wrathful protector Four-Faced Mahākāla *(Gdong bzhi pa)* played a role on more than one occasion. Go rams pa also had the gift of foretelling future events. In the eyes of his biographers these are, of course, also considered signs of his holiness.

In 1488, Go rams pa decided to make a trip to Sa skya, but his trip was initially blocked by some nobles who spread rumors that he was going to engage in "rituals of propitiation and exorcism for the gZhi-kha-ba [Rin-spungs-pa]."[195] Go rams pa responds that his trip was "not aimed merely at doing ritual propitiations and supportive practices to aid the ruler [Rin-spungs-pa]," but rather "aimed at helping in general the doctrine and sentient beings, and in particular I am going there to offer prayers for the pacification of the political disturbances and the happiness of the domain because my mind cannot bear the great political disturbances that are existing nowadays."[196] In the end, Go rams pa was given permission to visit Sa skya. This episode shows us the extent of Go rams pa's affiliation (or perhaps others' perceptions of his affiliation) to the Rin spungs court. It also shows us the role that magic played in the politics of the day, and the power that Go rams pa was seen to have in this regard. When he finished his work at Sa skya, Go rams pa set out for Thub bstan rnam rgyal, but had to first stop at the monastery in Sngon mo rdzong at the request of its monks. He took ill at Sngon mo rdzong and his condition quickly got worse. He died on the twenty-first day of the *cho 'phrul* month of the Earth-Bird year of the eighth *rab byung* (1489). His body was transported to Thub bstan rnam rgyal, where it was eventually cremated. His remains were partially made into funerary clay tablets, and partially housed inside a large Buddha statue that was created in his memory. Sadly, the monastery of Rta nag and all of its art, including the statue that contained the relics of Go rams pa, were destroyed during the Cultural Revolution.

After Go rams pa's death his "spiritual son," Kong ston Dbang phyug grub (b. fifteenth century), became his successor at Rta nag.[197] Of course, given Go rams pa's reputation, he had vast numbers of students. Many of them went on to become abbots of some of Tibet's most important monasteries, including Dpal 'khor bde chen, Ngam ring, Nalendra, Ngor E vam chos ldan, the Gling stod and Gling smad colleges of Gsang phu, and many others. The following disciples, perhaps, are especially worthy of mention:[198]

- Yongs 'dzin Dkon mchog 'phel, who succeeded Go rams pa on the throne of Ngor
- 'Bum phrag gsum pa (1432/33–1504), the author of a commentary on the *Tshad ma rigs gter*
- 'Jam dbyangs kun dga' chos bzang (1433–1503), the author of an important work on the Vinaya, and of a commentary on the *Pramāṇavārttikam*
- Mus chen Sangs rgyas rin chen (1450–1524), the author of a recently discovered biography of Go rams pa,[199] of several liturgical works, and of a Lam 'bras instructional manual
- Mus chen Thugs rje dpal bzang (b. fifteenth century), the author of three major commentaries—on the *Abidharmakośa*, on the *Abhisamayālaṃkāra*, and on the *Tshad ma rigs gter;* he was also the founder of

the monastery of 'Jad Thub bstan yangs pa can in central Tibet. Thugs rje dpal bzang's *supplements (kha skong)* to Go rams pa's texts are used in Sa skya pa educational institutions to this day.

Glo bo mkhan chen Bsod nams lhun grub (1456–1532), though not a student of Go rams pa, was influenced by him and was the author of many important works, including a biography of Go rams pa.[200]

Given his vast literary output, Go rams pa has had a tremendous influence on the Sa skya tradition up to the present day. The curriculum of studies at the philosophical college of Sa skya, for example, apparently followed the curriculum set up by Go rams pa at Rta nag,[201] and even today his works are extensively used at many Sa skya pa monastic institutions, like the Sa skya College in Dehra Dun, India.[202] Go rams pa must therefore be counted as one of the great systematizers of the Sa skya pa exoteric tradition. Following in the steps of his teacher, Rong ston, he has provided countless generations of Sa skya pa scholars with sources that form the basis for their curriculum of scholastic study, without a doubt the reason that he came to be known among the Sa skya pas as one of the six "Ornaments of Tibet." Unlike Rong ston, however, Go rams pa is also known as one of the tradition's greatest polemicists, composing polemical works in many fields, from logic and epistemology to tantra. Among these, *Distinguishing the Views* is undoubtedly his most important and influential work.

Distinguishing the Views

The Socio-Political Background

Distinguishing the Views [of Emptiness]: Moonlight [To Illuminate] the Main Points of the Supreme Path (Lta ba'i shan 'byed theg mchog gnad kyi zla zer)—*Distinguishing the Views* for short—is one of Go rams pa's most famous works. Its subject is the philosophy of the Middle Way. Before we turn to the text itself, it may be worth rehearsing something of the conditions under which it was written. Go rams pa's opponents in this text are, as we have mentioned, two of the most important figures in the history of Tibetan religious thought: Dol po pa Shes rab rgyal mtshan, the first great systematizer of the Jo nang pa school, and Tsong kha pa Blo bzang grags pa, the founder of the Dga' ldan pa school. The fact that the Jo nang pas and Dga' ldan pas were relative newcomers to the Tibetan religious scene at this point in time is important for understanding the dynamics of the exchange that takes place in Go rams pa's text.

In Tibet, as elsewhere, the success of new religious institutions depended upon a variety of factors: spiritual, intellectual, economic, and of course political. The financial support of patrons was essential, but this, in turn, depended upon other factors: the charisma and vision of the founding figure; the commitment, persistence, and intellectual abilities of his successors; the public perception of the order's monks; their perceived ability to enact rituals that brought about the goals of patrons, and so forth. These were some of the factors that attracted not only patrons but also prospective monks to newly founded monasteries. It is clear that Dol po pa and Tsong kha pa had at the very least created the infrastructure for highly successful institutions. And at the time that Go rams pa was writing, both the Jo nang pa and Dga' ldan pa schools were flourishing.

By the mid-fifteenth century, the major Dga' ldan pa monastic universities had all been founded. The three great monasteries of the order in central Tibet—Dga' ldan (founded in 1409), 'Bras spungs (in 1416), and Se ra (in 1419)—although still fledgling institutions, were by all accounts thriving. The Dga' ldan pas also had a new seat in Gtsang, in Western Tibet—the monastery of Bkra shis lhun po, founded in 1447 by one of Tsong kha pa's disciples, Dge 'dun grub (1391–1474). Moreover, the monastic university of Gsang phu ne'u thog, where Go rams pa actually stayed for a period of several months in 1453, had become factionalized in such a way that a large portion of the institution had aligned itself with the new Dga' ldan pa tradition.[203] What is more, several of Tsong kha pa's disciples had by this time already established monasteries in Khams, Go rams pa's home region. Finally, it is perhaps no accident that during Go rams pa's lifetime a young boy *from his own village of Rta nag* was identified as the reincarnation of the first Dalai Lama, Dge 'dun grub.[204] Go rams pa was undoubtedly aware of all of these developments.

On the intellectual front, some of Tsong kha pa's most influential students—Mkhas grub rje and Dge 'dun grub among them—were attempting to create a separate identity for their new school, which involved distancing themselves from their Sa skya roots. Mkhas grub rje, in fact, had already attempted (apparently unsuccessfully) to engage Go rams pa's teacher, Rong ston pa, in debate. In "inventing tradition," early Dga' ldan pas were following in the footsteps of Tsong kha pa, who had already begun the process of breaking with the Sa skya pas philosophically by repudiating, for example, their theory of Madhyamaka.[205]

Although Dol po pa had died more than a century earlier, his school was still basking in the glory it had achieved under its charismatic founder.[206] Like Tsong kha pa, Dol po pa also wrote against the Sa skya pa interpretation of the Madhyamaka (on which, see below). And as with the Dga' ldan pas, the Jo nang pas had *their* apologists—the brilliant Sa bzang Ma ti pan chen (1294–1376) and, a generation later, the erudite Nya dbon Kun dga' dpal (1345–1439)—each of whom would take up the challenge of defending the views of Dol po pa. Clearly, then, both the Dga' ldan pas and Jo nang pas were attempting to create identities for themselves apophatically—by distinguishing themselves from their rivals, and among those rivals were the Sa skya pas.[207] Although the debates between these various schools covered many different topics, one of the most important sets of debates took place in the field of Madhyamaka.

There were many great scholars among the Sa skya pas in the generation just prior to Go rams pa, but none appear to have emerged as the great defender of the Sa skya tradition in the face of critics. Rong ston pa, a great scholar and a prolific writer, produced very learned students like Byams chen rab 'byams pa Sangs rgyas 'phel, but neither Rong ston pa nor Byams chen pa was a polemicist.[208] The great Sa skya pa scholar Red mda' ba (1349–1412) was in his maturity known as a staunch critic of the Jo nang pas, but it is not clear how widely his polemical texts circulated—no polemical work of Red mda' ba is extant.[209] The time was therefore ripe for a committed Sa skya pa intellectual to step up and offer a defense of the classical Sa skya tradition as a whole.[210] Go rams pa had all the qualifications: he had received a classical Sa skya pa education at the feet of some of the greatest teachers in the tradition; he was a brilliant thinker whose knowledge of the philosophical tradition was both broad and deep; and he was a renowned debater who possessed that important critical edge that makes for a good polemicist. Go rams pa took up the challenge, and responded to critics of his tradition across the entire range of Tibetan religious studies, from tantra to epistemology to Madhyamaka.

The hundred years prior to the writing of *Distinguishing the Views* was a period of great political upheaval in Tibet. The middle of the fourteenth century saw the decline and eventually the end of the Mongol Yuan dynasty in China, and with it, the end of a hundred-year period of Sa skya pa hegemony over Tibet. In 1350, Tai situ Byang chub rgyal mtshan (1302–64) was able to wrest power from the Sakyapas, thereby establishing the Phag mo gru pas as the rulers of Tibet, a situation that would last for the next hundred years. By the time that Go rams pa arrived in central Tibet in 1447, however, things were changing. While the Phag mo gru pas still had control over most of central Tibet, the so-called Rin spungs princes, although relatives of the Phag mo gru pas, had established independent power over major regions of Gtsang."[211] We know from Go rams pa's biographies and other documents that the Rin spungs pa hierarch Nor bu bzang po (d. 1466)[212] and his son Don grub rdo rje[213] acted as Go rams pa's patrons. They provided him and one attendant with a lifelong stipend, and later with the funds to build the monastery of Rta nag gser gling.

Bsod nams grags pa's (1478–1554) *New Red Annals (Deb ther dmar po gsar ma)* recounts an interesting meeting between Nor bzang pa and Go rams pa's teacher, Ngor chen Kun dga' bzang po, the founder of Ngor Monastery, a confrontation that took place just a few years prior to Go rams pa's arrival at Ngor. The account begins by informing us that Nor bzang pa "had faith in the Sa skya pas and in the bKa' brgyud pas," but that "he also looked kindly upon the dGe ldan pas."[214] Once, when Nor bzang pa requested instruction from Ngor chen, the latter replied that he would grant the ruler's wish only on the condition that he increase his financial support for Ngor Monastery, and, more important, only if "all the dGe ldan pas under his [Nor bzang pa's] rule were converted to Sa skya pas, *and* if he stopped the bKa' bcu pa dGe 'dun grub pa from building his monastery."[215] Nor bzang pa refused. The monastery in question could be none other than Bkra shis lhun po (built by Dge 'dun grub pa in 1447). There is reason to question the veracity of Bsod nams grags pa's account of this episode,[216] but even if a politically motivated exaggeration, it tells us something of the perceived tensions that existed between Sa skya pas and Dge lugs pas in the mind of an author writing just forty years after Go rams pa. It also gives us some socio-political perspective on why Go rams pa should have seen fit to polemicize against Tsong kha pa, the founder of a school that by this time was seen as presenting a major challenge to Sa skya pa doctrinal views.

To summarize, Go rams pa was writing in the wake of the loss of Sa skya pa political hegemony in Tibet, in a period in which rival schools were vying with one another for the support of patrons, and at a time of great political instability, where an institution's affiliation with one political faction could cause retaliation from others.[217] He was writing at a time when new sects like the Jo nang pas and the Dga' ldan pas were gaining in popularity, and at a time when Sa skya pa philosophical views were coming under increasing attack from these new sects. None of the Sa skya pa scholars of his day appear to have offered a full-scale defense of the tradition (at least none that have survived), creating an intellectual vacuum in Sa skya pa philosophical literature that Go rams pa had all the qualifications to fill. Finally, we must remember that Go rams pa wrote *Distinguishing the Views* just as his new monastery of Rta nag gser gling was being built. The text was therefore written at a time when he must have been trying to bring greater attention to himself as the great defender of the Sa skya faith, and greater visibility to his new institution as a bastion of Sa skya pa orthodoxy. With this by way of background, we turn finally to the text.

Intertextuality

Distinguishing the Views[218] is ostensibly written as an assault against the Madhyamaka views of Dol po pa and Tsong kha pa. As such, it seems at first glance to be a work of the first type described above: a text that initiates a polemic, an offensive move against opponents. Since Dol po pa and Tsong kha pa had already penned refutations of Sa skya pa Madhyamaka views, however, there is reason to believe that *Distinguishing the Views* is also a text of the second type—a defense of the tradition in the wake of other scholars' prior challenges. Tsong kha pa, as we have mentioned, never wrote a philosophical work that was polemical in its entirety, but he did write critiques of Sa skya pa views in several of his Madhyamaka treatises. Although he rarely mentions his opponents by name, we know, for example, that it is the Sa skya pas that Tsong kha pa has in mind when he refutes what he calls the "view that things are neither existent nor nonexistent" *(yod min med min gyi lta ba).*[219] In his *Great Treatise on the Stages of the Path (Lam rim chen mo)*, for example, Tsong kha pa lays out this position in some detail, and then attempts to show how it is in contradiction to both "scripture and reasoning." For Tsong kha pa, the view represents a faulty understanding of emptiness, one that "goes too far" *(khyab che ba)* in its negation of the "object to be refuted" *(dgag bya).*[220] By denying existence altogether, he claims, it falls into the extreme of nihilism. Because it repudiates *the law of double negation (dgag pa gnyis kyi rnal ma go ba)*, he says that it flies in the face of our ordinary understanding of the workings of language, wherein the negation of the existence of something necessarily implies the affirmation of its *non*existence. This is but one example of the ways in which Tsong kha pa takes on the Sa skya pas. There are others as well. Taken together, they constitute a critique of the mainstream Sa skya pa interpretation of the Middle Way.

Because they were suppressed by the Dga' ldan pho brang, the collected works of Dol po pa have only been available to Western scholars for about a decade, and it is for this reason that his writings have yet to be fully explored. But thanks to the work of Matthew Kapstein, both the collected works and a catalogue are currently available.[221] And it is now possible to say that, unlike

Tsong kha pa, Dol po pa *did* write at least two short Madhyamaka works that are polemical in their entirety. The first is entitled *Clearing Away the Darkness of Bad Views.*[222] The second work, though shorter, is arguably more relevant to the present study if for no other reason than that the first portion of its title is *identical* to that of Go rams pa's *Distinguishing*. Dol po pa's text is called *Distinguishing*[223] *the Views: Clearing Away Mental Darkness.*[224] That the Sa skya pas are the object of Dol po pa's critique in his *Distinguishing the Views* is clear from several passages. Consider, for example, this passage, in which Dol po pa contends with an opponent:

> An opponent takes the *gotra* [i.e., the buddha nature] *qua* support
> To be [identical to] the ultimate of the Madhyamaka *qua* freedom from extremes,
> Which is known to be neither existent nor non-existent,
> Neither permanent nor annihilated,
> And neither true not false.
> But if the ultimate does not exist,
> Neither could it be understood.[225]

Dol po pa then goes on to say that if the ultimate is not understood, then there could be no gnosis, since gnosis is, by definition, the understanding of the ultimate. If there is no gnosis, then there could be no buddhahood, and if there is no buddhahood, then those who claim to have realized such a state would have to be mistaken.[226]

Go rams pa in fact calls his version of the Madhyamaka "the Middle Way *qua* freedom from extremes" *(mtha' bral dbu ma)*, and, just like the opponent being portrayed here, he claims that the real ultimate truth *(don dam mtshan nyid pa)* of this Madhyamaka view is ineffable—beyond predication, and beyond characterization as either *existent, nonexistent,* and so forth. It seems clear, therefore, that it is the Sa skya pa theory of the Madhyamaka (or something very close to it) that is being represented and "refuted" here. Another passage sheds more light on the identity of Dol po pa's opponent:

> If even [the Madhyamaka] does not exist [as you claim],
> Then, once again, it follows, absurdly, that the Madhyamaka [is tantamount to] the extreme of nihilism,
> For nothing exists, whether in the extremes or in the middle *(dbu ma)*,
> And it is *you* who ends up "cycling the three cycles," [a fault that you accused us of].[227]

And [if you claim that] these [i.e., the Madhyamaka and the
extremes] are not nonexistent, [then I reply:]
Based on your [claim] that they are not nonexistent and not [not
nonexistent],
Is there a negation of non-existence or not?
If so, then they are not nonexistent,
Which means that they must exist, no?
Doesn't the law of double negation apply?
The negation of a negation yields an affirmation,
And the negation of an affirmation, a negation,
This is the way existence functions.
It is a tradition among scholars.[228]

Once again, it is essentially the type of view espoused by Go rams pa—a theory that Go rams pa says is the Sa skya pa mainstream view—that Dol po pa is arguing against here. What is perhaps most interesting about this passage is that the argument that Dol po pa makes against the Sa skya pa position is precisely the type of argument that Tsong kha pa will make decades later. Since Tsong kha pa was familiar with the writings of Dol po pa, it is not inconceivable that he borrowed these arguments from the Jo nang pa tradition.[229] Equally interesting is the fact that Go rams pa uses arguments like those found in Tsong kha pa against Dol po pa, arguments that Tsong kha pa, in turn, may have borrowed from one of *his* Sa skya pa teachers, Red mda' ba. When we remember that Go rams pa calls his text by the same name that Dol po pa uses for his—*Distinguishing the Views*—then the irony is all the more striking, for we have one scholar (Go rams pa) borrowing the name of the text that critiques his own school to name the text that responds to that very critique. Jo nang pas critique Sa skya pas. Dga' ldan pas use arguments popular among Jo nang pas to critique Sa skya pas, and arguments popular among Sa skya pas to critique Jo nang pas. And Sa skya pas possibly borrow arguments from Dga' ldan pas (who might have borrowed them from Sa skya pas) to critique the Jo nang pas. Western scholars have come to refer to this type of mutual textual referencing as *intertextuality*. "Any text is constructed as a mosaic of quotations; any text is the absorption and transformation of another," Julia Kristeva says.[230] Tibetan philosophical polemics is obviously a fine example of this phenomenon.

The Structure and Contents of Go rams pa's Text

Distinguishing the Views[231] is a middling-size work that Go rams pa says was influenced by the Madhyamaka teachings he received from Byams chen rab 'byams pa, and by the oral commentary on the texts of the founders *(gong ma)*[232] of the Sa skya school he received from the "great Mus pa," who, from the language that Go rams pa uses, may have been ill at the time of composition of the work. (We know that Mus chen died that same year.) Go rams pa was urged to write the work by another of his teachers, Gung ru Shes rab bzang po. Gung ru ba had a reputation as a polemicist, and so it is not surprising that he should have been the force behind the composition of *Distinguishing the Views.*[233] The work was completed within a short timespan in late January or early February of 1469 at Go rams pa's home monastery of Rta nag gser gling in the midst of a phase of tremendous literary activity that coincided with the period during which the monastery was being constructed.[234] The scribe was Chos rje Dgon po dbang phyug, whom Gdong thog Bstan pa'i rgyal mtshan lists as one of Go rams pa's twelve chief students.[235]

The text is lucid and structurally very simple, with little complexity in its subdivisions *(sa bcad).* It can roughly be divided into seven parts: three short sections that describe, respectively, Dol po pa's, Tsong kha pa's, and Go rams pa's own views, followed by three much longer sections in which he refutes each of the first two views and sets forth his own position in more detail, responding to possible objections along the way. The seventh and last section of the work consists of 36 stanzas summarizing his arguments. Since these verses—probably meant as a mnemonic device to help students retain the gist of the arguments—add little to what is found in the already lucid prose text, we do not translate them here.

Go rams pa uses as a structural device the widely accepted Buddhist notion that in philosophy, as in ethics, one should follow a middle way *(madhyamaka, dbu ma)* between extremes.[236] *Distinguishing the Views* is then structured so as to demonstrate how Go rams pa's interpretation of the Indian Madhyamaka, which he calls the "Madhyamaka *qua* freedom from proliferations" *(spros bral kyi dbu ma)* or "Madhyamaka *qua* freedom from extremes" *(mtha' bral dbu ma),* is the true middle way between two extremist views prevalent in his day: the *eternalistic* view of the Jo nang pas, and the *nihilistic* view of the Dga' ldan pas. The expression "freedom from proliferations" or *spros bral (niṣprapañca)* has a long history in the Madhyamaka literature of both India and Tibet.[237] Go rams pa, however, uses the term as much denominatively as descriptively, which is to say that he uses the term to designate his particular brand of Madhyamaka—that is, as an appellation or trademark for a lineage of Madhyamaka philosophical speculation that includes, but is not limited to, the Sa skya pas—in much the same way as *emptiness of what is other (gzhan stong)* came to be the trademark of the Jo nang pas, and *Prāsaṅgika* that of the Dge lugs pas.[238]

It is clear that Go rams pa believes that his theory of emptiness represents the orthodox Sa skya pa interpretation. This does not mean that Go rams pa relies only on Sa skya pa sources. The lineage of the Madhyamaka that he describes in the text is exceedingly eclectic but, he says, quite old, including both the Rngog (eleventh century) and Pa tshab (b. 1055) lineages, and even Mar pa and his student Mi la ras pa. Although he mentions Rngog's Gsang phu lineage,[239] Go rams pa calls Pa tshab Nyi ma grags "the one who introduced the Madhyamaka as freedom from extremes [into Tibet]," indicating his greater allegiance to Pa tshab, and therefore to the tradition of Candrakīrti.[240] Despite his proclivity for Pa tshab's lineage—that is, for the Prāsaṅgika view—Go rams pa is reticent to identify himself as exclusively Prāsaṅgika, and there are probably several reasons for this. First, Tsong kha pa had already co-opted this term, and Go rams pa obviously wished to distance his interpretation of the Madhyamaka from that of the Dga' ldan pas. Secondly, Go rams pa's unequivocal adherence to the "freedom from extremes" doctrine precludes advocating any strong duality, even the Svātantrika/ Prāsaṅgika one.

> Both the grasping at duality and at nonduality must be negated, so that any object that is grasped in terms of the four extremes cannot be found. It is the non-grasping [of things] in those [terms] that we call "the realization of the Madhyamaka view." But if there arises a one-sided grasping of the form "this is the Madhyamaka view," then whether one grasps things as empty or as not empty, one has not gone beyond grasping at extremes, and this is not the Middle Way.

Finally, Go rams pa has a wide-ranging and holistic view of the Madhyamaka that permits his reliance on Indian texts usually classified in Tibet as Svātantrika—for example, Jñānagarbha's *Satyadvayavibhaṅga*—making it difficult for him to side with Candrakīrti's Prāsaṅgika to the exclusion of other Madhyamaka systems of thought.

Go rams pa's interpretation of Madhyamaka is committed to a more literal reading of the Indian sources than either Dol po pa's or Tsong kha pa's, which is to say that it tends to take the Indian texts at face value. For example, Go rams pa believes that the fourfold negation found in the tetralemma or *catuṣkoṭi*—not x, not non-x, not both, and not neither—is to be taken literally as a repudiation of, for example, existence, nonexistence, both, and neither *without the need for qualification.* Hence, contra Tsong kha pa, existence *itself* is an object of negation for him, there being no need to add the qualifier "ultimate" (as in "ultimate existence") to make this negation palatable.

To explain how existence can be repudiated, Go rams pa resorts to a theory that bifurcates the ultimate truth into two parts. Emptiness for him is therefore of two kinds: the emptiness that is the endpoint of rational analysis, and the emptiness that yogis fathom by means of their own individual gnosis.[241] The first of these—the emptiness that is arrived at rationally—is of two kinds: the selflessness of persons and the selflessness of phenomena. Emptiness as the byproduct of rational analysis—that is, the emptiness of truth—is not the real ultimate truth, but only an analogue *(rjes mthun)* thereof, or, put another way, it is the ultimate truth in name only *(rnam grangs pa).* Since the cognition of this quasi-ultimate requires that the mind entertain the empty/nonempty dichotomy, where the first element of the pair is privileged, the conceptual understanding of emptiness must eventually be negated in order to achieve an understanding of the highest form of emptiness that is the object of yogic gnosis. This latter form of emptiness—the emptiness that is mystically fathomed—is the real ultimate truth *(don dam dngos, don dam mtshan nyid pa).* Being ineffable, it cannot be expressed in linguistic terms, since it is beyond all proliferative dichotomizing. Nonetheless, for Go rams pa understanding emptiness rationally is a necessary prerequisite to understanding it in its true, nonanalytical form.

The style of *Distinguishing the Views* is quasi-formal and philosophical.[242] As a scholastic, Go rams pa shares a great deal in common with his opponents—both doctrinally and methodologically—making it unnecessary for him to prove petty points on which he knows there is bound to be agreement. Where there *is* disagreement, Go rams pa gives reasons—reasons for why his opponents' views are implausible and for why his views are superior. In some instances, he shows how a view subscribed to by his opponent is internally inconsistent. In other cases, he argues that a view is contradictory to the positions of texts that are considered authoritative (the texts of Indian Buddhism—that is, scriptures or the writings of the great Indian philosophers). Much of *Distinguishing the Views* is in fact concerned with arguments of this kind, and so it is as much a polemic over the interpretation of texts as it is a polemic over tenets.

The Refutation of Dol po pa

Go rams pa makes it clear that his refutation of Dol po pa's theory of emptiness is based on Red mda' ba's critique of the Jo nang pas. His goal is to demonstrate that the Jo nang pa view is non-Buddhist:[243]

> It is not the purport of any of the sūtra traditions, whether Mahā or Hīna yānist. It is incompatible with all of the four [Buddhist] philosophical schools, and it is not accepted by any Mahāyānist, whether Indian or Chinese. Hence, it cannot but fall outside of the [bounds of the] Buddhist tradition.

Dol po pa's theory of emptiness is not consistent with the view of the Hīnayāna schools, says Go rams pa, because Hīnayānists do not accept the fact that conventional things are empty of their own nature. Hīnayānists would thus reject Dol po pa's claim that some things are "empty of themselves" *(rang stong).* Dol po pa's theory is not consistent with the views of Nāgārjuna, Go rams pa claims, because by exempting the ultimate from the same negative dialectic that deconstructs conventional reality, Dol po pa's theory implies that there is a form of emptiness that is different from any of the three forms explained above.[244] Finally, he says, it is not consistent with the views of Maitreya, Asaṅga, and Vasubandhu because it insists that the dependent is empty of its own nature, whereas the Cittamātra maintains that the dependent exists substantially. Go rams pa then invokes the opinion of his teacher Rong ston pa to the effect that the Jo nang pa is a "system that, while having strong affinities to the Cittamātra, never manages to reach the Middle Way." This section concludes with Go rams pa's jibes at what is perhaps the position of his rival, Shākya mchog ldan, a scholar who, while never abandoning his Sa skya pa affiliation, is known to have had strong affinities for the *emptiness of what is other* perspective of the Jo nang pas:

> Certain persons of coarse mental faculty, holding the eternalistic view [of the Jo nang pas] secretly in their hearts, take sides with the philosophical views of others for the sake of diplomacy, and claim that the Sa skya and Jo nang pa schools are not incompatible as regards their philosophical views.

Go rams pa sees this as a sellout of the Sa skya tradition, and in support of his position he cites Rje btsun Grags pa rgyal tshan so as to demonstrate that even the great founders of the tradition were aware of Jo nang pa-like views, and rejected them.

The Refutation of Tsong kha pa

Go rams pa was not the first critic of Tsong kha pa in the field of Madhyamaka. Five years prior to the composition of *Distinguishing the Views,* the founder of Dga' ldan had already been the object of a polemical attack by Stag tshang lo tsā ba in his famous *Grub mtha' kun shes* (written in 1463).[245] But even if it is not the first Madhyamaka polemic directed at Tsong kha pa, *Distinguishing the Views* is arguably the more wide-ranging. Go rams pa's refutation of Tsong kha pa is extensive—much more extensive than his treatment of Dol po pa, for example. It is also very detailed and complex. It would be beyond the scope of this introduction to discuss it in its entirety. Suffice it to mention some highlights of the argument, using Go rams pa's own outline as a basis.

Go rams pa accuses Tsong kha pa of holding a nihilistic interpretation of the Madhyamaka. This is somewhat ironic, given that this is precisely the charge that Tsong kha pa levels against the *neither existence nor nonexistence (yod min med min)* view to which Go rams pa subscribes. In one sense at least, Go rams pa's accusations of nihilism are puzzling, for his central thesis is that Tsong kha pa and his followers *do not go far enough* in their negation. While agreeing with the Dga' ldan pas concerning the need to repudiate true existence, Go rams pa maintains that both the emptiness that is that very negation and its apprehension/conceptualization must also be negated, a view that is anathema to Tsong kha pa. But according to Go rams pa it is precisely this—Tsong kha pa's grasping at emptiness—that makes him a nihilist. As Go rams pa says, "Those who grasp at emptiness have not gone beond falling into the extreme of nihilism."

For Tsong kha pa, the object of the analytical/rational/conceptual understanding of emptiness is the real ultimate truth. For Go rams pa it is a conventional (and *not* an ultimate) truth. Put another way, for Tsong kha pa, both inference and yogic gnosis understand the same object—emptiness—albeit in different ways. For Go rams pa only yogic gnosis, which is nonanalytical and nonconceptual, is capable of perceiving the true *(mtshan nyid pa)* ultimate. In Go rams pa's view, the dichotomizing tendency of the mind that culminates in extremist proliferations (existence/nonexistence, and so forth) is built into the very structure of conceptual thought and, as such, any object of conceptual thought, even emptiness, is of necessity contaminated with the type of dualistic proliferation that is the Madhyamaka's object of negation. That is why emptiness as the object of conceptual thought cannot be the real ultimate truth:

> In brief, if one accepts that the direct object of the conceptual thought that apprehends things as truthless...is the real ultimate truth, then one would have to accept that the generic image *(don spyi)* of the ultimate truth is the ultimate truth. It would be like accepting the generic image of the pot to be the pot.

Hence, everything, including emptiness *qua* object of conceptual thought, is an object of the Madhyamaka critique, and this means that it must be negated—not simply negated as lacking mere inherent existence (as Tsong kha pa maintains), but negated *in toto* through the fourfold dialectic.

Go rams pa is astute in anticipating the Dge lugs objection to this view. Like Go rams pa, Tsong kha pa also believes that emptiness is the object of the Madhyamaka critique, not because it is itself to be negated, but because its *true existence* is to be negated. Go rams pa, however, calls this "the deceptive blithering of individuals of little intelligence and merit, the demonic words that slander the 'freedom from proliferations view,' which is the heart of the teachings." His reason for leveling this invective against Tsong kha pa is interesting. Why should the Madhyamaka texts claim that *all* views and conceptual constructs are to be abandoned if there is one—emptiness—that should not? Go rams pa implies that Tsong kha pa's view makes the fourfold structure of the *catuṣkoṭi* meaningless because it subsumes the entire Madhyamaka critique into a qualified first *koṭi* (the negation of *true* existence), making the other three *koṭis* (the negation of nonexistence, both, and neither) pointless. For Go rams pa, the truth of things comes to be negated (and their illusory nature understood) not through the negation of true existence, but through the negation of *all four* extremes—existence, nonexistence, both, and neither—*without the need for any qualification.* For Tsong kha pa, the problem of ignorance lies in the fact that the mind improperly reifies objects, imputing real or inherent existence to things that lack it. For Go rams pa, the chief problem lies in the fact that the mind operates through a dichotomizing filter that continuously splits the world into dualities (existent/nonexistent, permanent/impermanent, and so forth). Put another way, for Tsong kha pa the problem lies with the false quality that the mind attributes to objects, whereas for Go rams pa it lies with the very proliferative character of the conceptual mind itself, an aspect of mental functioning that cannot be entirely eliminated through the selective negation of a specific quality (true existence), requiring instead the use of a method (the complete negation of all extremes) that brings dualistic thinking to a halt.

Given this view, it is not surprising that Go rams pa should repudiate the *law of double negation,* for clearly the negation of existence does not for him imply the acceptance of nonexistence. He also rejects the Dga' ldan pa charge that the *yod min med min* view is tantamount to the view of Hwa shang—that is, to quietism—claiming that this charge "comes about due to the blessing of demons for the purpose of degenerating the essence of the doctrine." His defense against this charge is, again, quite interesting:

> The Chinese H[w]a shang [believes] that, without analyzing the object, reality, one should negate ordinary conceptual thoughts and think of nothing whatsoever, and this he accepts to be the realization of the ultimate view... We, on the other hand, set forth reality as an object using the reasoning that is explained in the Madhyamaka textual tradition. In so doing, we individually repudiate each of the conceptions [of the various thoughts] that grasp at extremes, and at the end [of this process] we reserve the term *realization of the Madhyamaka view* to refer to precisely that not-finding of any of the extremes of proliferation, such as existence and nonexistence.

Hence, the Hwa shang view repudiates the very process of analysis, while Go rams pa sees analysis as a necessary prerequisite, but one that must be transcended through such techniques as the *catuṣkoṭi.*

These are some of the main points of Go rams pa's critique of Tsong kha pa's theory of emptiness, but Go rams pa's critique does not end here, for he also finds fault with Tsong kha pa's views *of the conventional.* For example, Go rams pa criticizes Tsong kha pa

- for not properly understanding the meaning of the Madhyamaka claim that conventional things are *mere labels;*
- for accepting the *destruction of things* to be a real entity *(zhig pa dngos po ba),* a tenet that he says is more heterodox than Buddhist;
- and for his theory of perception across world spheres, the controversial

Dge lugs claim that in order to account for the fact that different types of beings in different realms (humans, hungry ghosts, gods, etc.) perceive the same object differently, a vessel full of liquid must be said to contain actual water, actual pus and blood, actual nectar and so forth.

Finally, Go rams pa criticizes Tsong kha pa in regard to what he calls the *five ancillary points,* the majority of which are subsumed within what the Dge lugs pas call the *eight great difficult points (dka' gnad chen po brgyad)* of the Madhyamaka.[246] On almost every count, Go rams pa's views stand counter to those of Tsong kha pa. For example, Go rams pa maintains:

- that grasping at the truth of phenomena is an "obscuration to omniscience" *(shes sgrib),* and not an "afflicted obscuration" *(nyon sgrib),* as Tsong kha pa claims;[247]
- that Tsong kha pa reifies the "mere I," making it into a real entity that is found when the self is rationally analyzed;
- that not all grasping at the self of phenomena *(chos kyi bdag 'dzin)* involves grasping at truth *(bden 'dzin),* as Tsong kha pa claims;
- that, contra Tsong kha pa, śrāvakas and pratyekabuddhas, while they understand the emptiness of true existence *(bden pas stong pa),* do not understand the *ultimate* truth that is the freedom from proliferations, which, as has been noted, involves more than just the negation of true existence;
- that the Dga' ldan pas err in their understanding of the existence of external objects, and in their repudiation of the foundation consciousness *(kun gzhi)* and of self-reflexive cognition *(rang rig);*
- that, contra Tsong kha pa, the Svātantrikas and Prāsaṅgikas *do not* differ as regards the subtlety of their object of negation; and, finally,
- that Tsong kha pa has misunderstood the Prāsaṅgika repudiation of autonomous *(rang rgyud kyi)* syllogisms *(rtags)* and theses *(dam bca').*

Entire essays could be devoted to each of these various topics, making it foolish to attempt any detailed treatment of them here. Suffice it to conclude by observing that Go rams pa's critique of Tsong kha pa is extensive, detailed, and provocative. That it was seen as a major response to the Dga' ldan pa tradition is witnessed by the fact that it has been responded to by some of the Dge lugs tradition's most important apologists. Two of them in particular are worthy of note: Rje btsun Chos kyi rgyal mtshan (1469– 1544/46) and 'Jam dbyangs bzhad pa Ngag dbang brtson 'grus.[248] Each of these figures was a writer of textbooks *(yig cha)*—the works used as the basis for the curriculum of Dge lugs monastic universities to this day—and it would not be an understatement to say that each is also considered the greatest Dge lugs intellectual of his respective generation. We know of no Sa skya pa counter-polemical work that responds to the critiques of Rje btsun pa and 'Jam dbyangs bzhad pa, though given the risks involved in attempting such a response, at least in those portions of central and western Tibet under dGe lugs rule, one cannot consider this particularly surprising.

Go rams pa's work has continued to exert a major influence in Tibetan Madhyamaka exegesis up to the twentieth century, even outside the Sa skya tradition. For example, the reviver of Rnying ma scholastic studies in Khams, Gzhan phan mtha' yas (b. 1800), held Go rams pa's work in high esteem. And a later important figure in this same tradition, Mi pham rgya mtsho (1846–1912), was also greatly influenced by the work of Go rams pa,[249] as were other later figures in Mi pham's lineage like Bod pa sprul sku (1900/1907–59), whose most important work, *Distinguishing the Views and Practices (Lta sgrub shan 'byed)*, makes an allusion to Go rams pa's work in its very title.

Conclusion

In an article entitled "Books, Canons and the Nature of Dispute,"[250] G. Thomas Tanselle bemoans the fact that contemporary literary criticism should have become so enmeshed in disputes—in particular, in the dispute over authorial intent, a polemic that consumed so much of the field in the late 1980s. But he bemoans this state of affairs not so much because it has distracted the discipline from other more important questions, but because of its very character as a polemic. Tanselle believes that dispute and confrontation make human beings less rational, and perhaps even less human:

> The impulse to have one's own way and to deny the distasteful conclusions of others is apparently so strong as to suppress in many instances whatever desire human beings have to be coherent.[251]

Perhaps the greatest irony about Tanselle's essay is that the plausibility of its premise—that polemic is less than desirable as a form of discourse—rests on his ability as a polemicist. As we have already noted, polemic can sometimes be exaggerated and grotesque. It polarizes viewpoints, people and schools. But it is precisely this type of polarization—this "differentiation"—that brings great clarity to issues. In fact, it does this for Tanselle himself, as he analyzes the two options (social textual criticism vs. intentionalist criticism) in an attempt to come to his own literary-critical middle way. Could Tanselle have achieved such critical insight if the polemic had never occurred? Did it not crystallize for him the issues, options, and pitfalls in ways that less contentious prose could not have? It is precisely because of the polemic over authorial intention that Tanselle's essay, and its concomitant insights, were possible.

The same is true, of course, of Tibetan Madhyamaka polemical literature. It is at times filled with crass name-calling, misrepresentation, and overstatement. But even then it can act as a source of insight, as critical scholars—traditional or modern—are forced to work their way through the morass. Studying a text like *Distinguishing the Views* allows us to better understand the views of three great Tibetan scholars in their own right. But more important, it allows us to glean the most significant issues of the Madhyamaka within the context of the broader conversation to which all three figures contributed so significantly. This is the virtue of turning our attention to the polemical literature of Tibetan Madhyamaka, and to the work of Go rams pa in particular. *Du choc des opinions jaillit la vérité.* And now let the clash of opinions begin!

Distinguishing the Views of Emptiness:

Moonlight to Illuminate the Points of the Supreme Path

Lta ba'i shan 'byed theg mchog gnad kyi zla zer

NOTE: To download a PDF file of Gorampa's text in Tibetan script with matching pagination, go to the *Freedom from Extremes* page on Wisdom Publication's Web site, wisdompubs.org.

THE PRESENT TIBETAN EDITION of the *Lta ba'i shan 'byed* has been compiled on the basis of three previously published texts:

1. That found in *The Complete Works of Go ram bsod nams seng ge* (vol. 3) in *Sa skya pa'i bka 'bum: The Complete Works of the Great Masters of the Sa skya Sect of Tibetan Buddhism* (vol. 13), compiled by Bsod nams rgya mtsho (Tokyo: The Tōyō Bunko, 1968), 47 folios. This is a reproduction of the Sde dge xylograph carved in the first decade of the twentieth century and already mentioned in the introduction. **Abbrev. = K**

2. *Lta ba'i shan 'byed theg mchog gnad kyi zla zer (Distinguishing the Views by Gorampa Bsodnams sengge)*, published together with *Rtags kyi rnam bzhag rigs lam gsal ba'i sgron me* of Mkhan chen Bsod nams lhun grub (Sarnath: Sakya Students' Union, 1988—date of preface), pp. 1–154. **Abbrev. = S**

3. An unidentified mechanical reproduction of a handwritten text in the collection of the library of the Institut für Kultur und Geschichte Indiens und Tibets, Hamburg (access number MIV 345/6, catalogued 1968?), most likely printed in Buxa Duar, India in the early 1960s, 42 folios. **Abbrev. = B**

In the present edition, the names of texts appear in italics, and the names of agents (persons and deities) are underlined. The pagination of the Sa skya bka' 'bum (K) and Sarnath (S) texts—the two versions of the text most widely available—have been provided in parentheses within the present edition. For the sake of clarity, we have taken some liberties with the thematic subdivisions *(sa bcad)* of the text—for example, repeating previously mentioned subtitles at their proper place within the text and adding new ones when it seemed necessary or helpful. When this is done, the newly added material appears in square brackets [ ]. For ease of reference, the Tibetan text has been subdivided into paragraphs that follow the formatting of the translation.

Variants between K, B, and S have been given in footnotes. Unless there is an ambiguity of some kind, *only* the variant readings are noted. Hence, if the Tibetan text here reads *rigs,* and the note states "KB *rig,*" one can assume that S reads *rigs.* Go rams pa's citations of sūtra and śāstra works have been compared to existing editions (e.g., those found in the canon, or in modern critical editions), and differences between K/B/S and these editions have been given in the notes to the Tibetan edition that follows. Bibliographical references to the works cited by Go rams pa, however, are given in the notes *to the translation,* and not in the notes to the Tibetan edition.

Thematic Subdivisions of the Text
sa bcad

[SKOR 'GO DANG PO]
[dbu mar smra ba'i lugs gsum] 68

[mngon brjod] 68

1.1.0.0.0 rtag mtha' la dbu mar smra ba 70
1.2.0.0.0 chad mtha' la dbu mar smra ba 76
1.2.1.0.0 don dam stong nyid kyi rnam bzhag 78
1.2.2.0.0 kun rdzob snang ba'i rnam bzhag 82
1.2.3.0.0 de dag las 'phros pa'i don 84
1.2.3.1.0 sgrib gnyis kyi ngos 'dzin 84
1.2.3.2.0 bdag gnyis kyi ngos 'dzin 86
1.2.3.3.0 theg pa che chung gi spang rtogs kyi khyad par 86
1.2.3.4.0 kun gzhi dang rang rig mi 'dod pas phyi don khas len pa'i tshul 88
1.2.3.5.0. rang rgyud kyi rtag dang dam bca' med pa'i tshul 90
1.3.0.0.0 mtha' 'bral la dbu mar smra ba 92

Thematic Subdivisions of the Text

[Chapter One]
The Three Systems of Those Who Claim to Be Mādhyamikas 69

[Introduction] 69

1.1.0.0.0 Those Who Claim that the Extreme of Eternalism Is the Madhyamaka 71
1.2.0.0.0 Those Who Claim that the Extreme of Nihilism Is the Madhyamaka 77
1.2.1.0.0 [Tsong kha pa's] Exposition of Emptiness, the Ultimate 79
1.2.2.0.0. [Tsong kha pa's] Exposition of Appearances—That Is, of the Conventional [World] 83
1.2.3.0.0 Some Points that Remain [to Be Discussed] in the Wake of These [Points Just Raised] 85
1.2.3.1.0 [How Tsong kha pa] Identifies the Two Obscurations 85
1.2.3.2.0 [How Tsong kha pa] Identifies the Two Selves 87
1.2.3.3.0 [How Tsong kha pa Propounds] the Differences between What the Hīna- and Mahā-yānas [Accept as] the Objects to Be Abandoned and Realized 87
1.2.3.4.0 How [Tsong kha pa] Accepts External Objects *(phyi don)*, Given that [He] Does Not Believe in the Foundation [Consciousness] or in Reflexive Awareness 89
1.2.3.5.0. What It Means for There to Be No Autonomous Reasons *(rang rgyud kyi rtags)* and No Theses 91
1.3.0.0.0. Those Who Claim that the Freedom from Extremes Is the Madhyamaka 93

[SKOR 'GO GNYIS PA]
[rtag mtha' la dbu mar smra ba'i lugs dgag pa] 96

[SKOR 'GO GSUM PA]
[chad mtha' la dbu mar smra ba'i lugs dgag pa] 114

[3.1.0.0.0 don dam gyi rnam bzhag la dpyad pa] 114
[3.2.0.0.0 kun rdzob kyi rnam bzhag la dpyad pa] 132
[3.2.1.0.0 las kyis 'bras bu bskyed pa'i tshul la brtags pa] 136
[3.2.2.0.0 rigs drug gi mig shes kyis mthong snang la dpyad pa] 138
[3.3.0.0.0 'phros don la dpyad pa] 142
[3.3.1.0.0 sgrib gnyis kyi ngos 'dzin la dpyad pa] 142
[3.3.2.0.0 bdag gnyis kyi ngos 'dzin la dpyad pa] 148
[3.3.3.0.0 theg pa che chung gi spang rtogs kyi khyad par la dpyad pa] 156
[3.3.4.0.0 kun gzhi dang rang rig mi 'dod cing phyi don khas len pa'i tshul la dpyad pa] 172
[3.3.5.0.0 rang rgyud kyi rtags dang dam bca' med pa'i tshul dpyad pa] 176
3.3.5.1.0 dam bca'i khyad par 190
3.3.5.2.0 'thad pa'i khyad par 192
3.3.5.3.0 bden gnyis gang gi steng du 'byed pa 192

[Chapter Two]
[The Refutation of the System that Advocates that the Extreme of Eternalism Is the Madhyamaka = The Refutation of Dol po pa] 97

[Chapter Three]
[The Refutation of the System that Advocates that the Extreme of Nihilism Is the Madhyamaka = The Refutation of Tsong kha pa] 115

[3.1.0.0.0 An Examination of (Tsong kha pa's) Exposition of the Ultimate] 115
[3.2.0.0.0 An Examination of (Tsong kha pa's) Exposition of the Conventional] 133
[3.2.1.0.0 An Examination of the Way that Karma Gives Rise to Its Effects] 137
[3.2.2.0.0 An Analysis of (Tsong kha pa's View Concerning) How the Eye Consciousnesses of the Six Classes of Beings Perceive (Objects)] 139
[3.3.0.0.0 The Analysis of Some Ancillary Points] 143
[3.3.1.0.0 The Analysis of (Tsong kha pa's Views Concerning) the Identification of the Two Obscurations] 143
[3.3.2.0.0 An Examination of (Tsong kha pa's) Identification of the Two Selves] 149
[3.3.3.0.0 An Examination of (Tsong kha pa's) Views Concerning the Differences Between What the Mahā- and Hīna-yāna [Believe] Ought to Be Abandoned and Realized] 157
[3.3.4.0.0 An Examination of (Tsong kha pa's View that Prāsaṅgikas) Accept External Objects Despite the Fact that They Do Not Believe in the Foundation (Consciousness) and in Reflexive Awareness] 173
[3.3.5.0.0 An Examination of (Tsong kha pa's Views) Concerning Why There Are No Autonomous Reasons and Theses] 177
3.3.5.1.0 The Differences (Between Prāsaṅgikas and Svātantrikas) with Respect to Theses 191
3.3.5.2.0 The Difference (Between Prāsaṅgikas and Svātantrikas) As Regards Adequate Argumentation 193
3.3.5.3.0 The Basis for Distinguishing Between the Two Truths 193

[SKOR 'GO BZHI PA]
[mtha' bral la dbu mar smra ba'i lugs bsgrub pa] 202

4.1.0.0.0. gnas lugs bstan pa'i snod ngos bzung ba 202
4.1.1.0.0 grub mthas blo bsgyur ba 204
4.1.2.0.0 grub mthas blo ma bsgyur ba 204
4.2.0.0.0 bstan bya gnas lugs kyi rang bzhin 206
4.2.1.0.0 gzhi dbu ma bden gnyis zung 'jug 206
4.2.1.1.0 kun rdzob kyi rnam bzhag 206
4.2.1.2.0 don dam gyi rnam bzhag 210
4.2.1.2.1 rigs pas dpyad pa'i don dam rjes mthun pa 210
4.2.1.2.2 'phags pa'i mnyam bzhag la spros pa dang bral ba'i tshul gyis snang ba'i don dam mtshan nyid pa 216
4.2.2.0.0 lam dbu ma tshogs gnyis zung 'jug 218
4.2.2.1.0 spang bya sgrib gnyis ngos bzung ba 218
4.2.2.2.0 spong byed kyi gnyen po ngos bzung ba 220
4.2.3.0.0 'bras bu dbu ma sku gnyis zung 'jug 226
4.3.0.0.0 yid ches pa'i lung dang sbyar ba 228
4.3.1.0.0 rnam grangs dang rnam grangs min pa'i don dam bden pa gnyis su phye ba 228
4.3.2.0.0 mtha' bzhi'i spros bral lung dang sbyar ba 230

[mjug byang] 236

[Chapter Four]
[Those Who Claim that the Freedom from Extremes Is the Madhyamaka = Go rams pa's Own System] 203

4.1.0.0.0. Identifying the Vessel [That Is, the Student,] to Whom Reality Is to Be Taught 203
4.1.1.0.0 Those Who [First Adhere to Any One of the Philosophical Positions of the Realists—Whether Buddhist or Non-Buddhist—and Subsequently] Change Their Philosophical Outlook [to the Madhyamaka] 205
4.1.2.0.0 Those Who Do Not Change Their Minds Philosophically, [but Who from the Very Beginning Exert Themselves at Understanding Reality through the Power of the Awakening of Their Mahāyāna Lineage] 205
4.2.0.0.0 What Is to Be Taught: The Nature of Reality 207
4.2.1.0.0 The Madhyamaka *Qua* Basis: The Union of the Two Truths 207
4.2.1.1.0 The Exposition of the Conventional 207
4.2.1.2.0 The Exposition of the Ultimate 211
4.2.1.2.1 The Quasi-Ultimate, Which Involves Analysis 211
4.2.1.2.2. The Real Ultimate, Which Is What Appears to the [Meditative] Equipoise of Āryans in a Way that Is Devoid of the Proliferations 217
4.2.2.0.0 The Madhyamaka *Qua* Path, Which Is the Union of Method and Wisdom 219
4.2.2.1.0 The Identification of the Two Obscurations, the [Objects] to Be Eliminated 219
4.2.2.2.0 The Identification of the Antidotes that Eliminate Those [Two Obscurations] 221
4.2.3.0.0 The Madhyamaka *Qua* Result: The Union of the Two Bodies 227
4.3.0.0.0 Bringing Trustworthy Scriptural [Evidence] to Bear [on These Questions] 229
4.3.1.0.0 The Division of the Ultimate Truth into Two—[The Ultimate Truth] in Name Only and [the Ultimate Truth] Not in Name Only 229
4.3.2.0.0 The Scriptural Sources for the Freedom from the Proliferations of the Four Extremes 231

[Colophon] 237

(K1b) (S1) lta ba'i shan 'byed theg mchog gnad kyi zla zer zhes bya ba/

[1.0.0.0.0 skor 'go dang po: dbu mar smra ba'i lugs gsum]

[mngon brjod]

bla ma dang mgon po 'jam pa'i dbyangs la phyag 'tshal lo//

ye shes dkyil 'khor thugs rje'i rta ljang gis//
gdul bya'i ri la ci ltar 'os pa bzhin//
rim par drang ba'i phrin las gzi 'od can//
sang rgyas nyi ma de la bdag cag dad//

gang zhig rtogs na blo yi rim pa bzhin//
theg pa gsum gyi byang chub sbyin byed pa'i//
rtag chad mtha' spang dbu ma'i lam 'di la//
gangs can 'di na rtogs pa tha dad gyur//

de la klu sgrub snying po'i bzhed pa yi//
yang dag lta ba'i de nyid 'di yin zhes//
dam pa rnams kyi gsung rab la brten nas//
(S2) rnam par dbye ba 'di ni (K2a) kho bos smra//

1. Three Ways of Understanding the Madhyamaka

[The Three Systems of Those Who Claim to Be Mādhyamikas]

[Introduction]

HOMAGE to the spiritual master and to the protector Mañjuśrī.

We place our trust in the Buddha, the sun,
Who possesses the brilliance of enlightened actions *(phrin las)* that guide us, systematically:
The great horse of (his) compassion *(thugs rje)* drawing the sun-disk of (his) gnosis *(ye shes)*
Over the mountains, his disciples, in appropriate fashion.[1]

The path of the Middle Way (Madhyamaka) eliminates the extremes of eternalism and nihilism.
When it is realized, it bestows upon one the enlightenment of the three vehicles *(theg pa gsum gyi byang chub)*
According to one's level of mental [development].
[But the Madhyamaka] has been understood variously in this Land of Snows.[2]

So I will distinguish [between these various interpretations][3]
Based upon the treatises of the holy ones,
[The texts that] identify the nature of the true view [of emptiness] *(yang dag lta ba)*
That is the essential purport of Nāgārjuna.

de la spyir grub mtha' smra ba bzhi po thams cad kyang rang rang gi grub mtha' nas bshad pa'i lam de nyid rtag chad spangs pa'i dbu ma'i lam du 'dod cing/ de'i tshe dngos por smra ba dag gis grub mtha' bzhi'i phyi ma la dbu ma zhes mi brjod par ngo bo nyid med par smra ba zhes brjod do/ /'on kyang/

> rnal 'byor pa yang blo khyad kyis//
> gong ma gong ma rnams kyis gnod//

zhes pa'i tshul gyis dbu ma pa rnams kyis ni/ grub mtha' 'og ma dag gis rtag chad kyi mtha' ci ltar spangs kyang dngos po ngo bo nyid kyis yod par smra bas/ rtag chad kyi mtha' gang rung las ma 'das la/ des na byang chub gsum po gang rung bsgrub pa la rtag chad kyi mtha' spong ba'i tshul 'di ltar dgos so zhes rang gi grub pa'i mtha' las rtag chad kyi (K2b) mtha' spong tshul dang/ de'i sgo nas byang chub gsum (S3) sgrub tshul gyi gzhung 'dzug par mdzad do//

de la yang 'phags yul gyi dbu ma pa chen po rnams kyis ni gzhung gi 'chad tshul dang/ tha snyad kyi rnam bzhag la mi 'dra ba'i khyad par mang du mdzad kyang mthar thug gi lta ba'i gnad la mi 'dra ba'i khyad par mdzad pa mi snang ngo/ /gangs ri'i[1] khrod 'dir ni dbu ma'i lta ba khas len bzhin du mthar[2] thug gi lta ba'i gnad la mi 'dra ba gsum du snang ste 'di ltar/

[1] rtag mtha' la dbu mar smra ba dang/
[2] chad mtha' la dbu mar smra ba dang/
[3] mtha' bral la dbu mar smra ba'o/

[1.1.0.0.0 rtag mtha' la dbu mar smra ba] lugs dang po ni/

mkhyen rab dang thugs rje phul du byung zhing nyams dang rtogs pa'i dbang phyug kun mkhyen dol bu ba[3] shes rab rgyal mtshan gyi bzhed pa la/

1 S *re'i.*
2 KB *mtha'.*
3 All three editions use this epithet, as opposed to Dol po pa.

In general, all of the advocates of the four philosophical schools *(grub mtha' smra ba)*[4] believe that the path they set forth in their own philosophical *(grub mtha')* system is the middle way that brings an end to eternalism *(rtag)* and nihilism *(chad)*. This being the case, the realist schools *(dngos por smra ba dag)* do not call the last of the four philosophical schools "the Madhyamaka" [that is, "the Middle Way School"], but instead refer to it as the "Niḥsvabhāvavāda" ["the School that Advocates Essencelessness"]. Nevertheless, in accordance with the passage that states:

> And with yogis too, because of the differences in their intellects,
> The higher trump the lower.[5]

the Mādhyamikas [claim that], even though the lower philosophical schools eliminate their [own] versions of the extremes of eternalism and nihilism, since they advocate that things exist by virtue of their nature *(ngo bo nyid kyis yod pa)*, they fail to go beyond either the extreme of eternalism or that of nihilism.[6] That is why they say that [the Madhyamaka] method of eliminating the extremes of eternalism and nihilism is essential to the attainment of any of the three enlightenments,[7] why they set about the task [of composing] texts [that demonstrate] how their own philosophical position eliminates the extremes of eternalism and nihilism, and how through this [method] the three enlightenments are obtained.

Furthermore, even though the great Mādhyamikas of the Noble Land [of India] have a multitude of different ways of explaining texts and using terms, there do not appear any differences in their ultimate philosophical point of view.[8] But in this abode of snow mountains [Tibet], though [people] profess the Madhyamaka view, it seems that their fundamental philosophical theories are of three kinds:

1. Those who claim that the extreme of eternalism is the Madhyamaka
2. Those who claim that the extreme of nihilism is the Madhyamaka
3. Those who claim that the freedom from extremes is the Madhyamaka

The First System [The Views of Dol po pa]

This is [the position advocated by] the omniscient Dol bu ba Shes rab rgyal mtshan,[9] who is the epitome of knowledge *(mkhyen rab)* and compassion, a lord of spiritual practice *(nyams)* and realization *(rtogs pa)*.

stong pa nyid ni rnam pa gnyis te/ rang gi ngo bos stong pa nyid dang/ gzhan gyi (S4) ngo bos stong pa nyid do/ bden pa yang gnyis te/ kun rdzob bden pa dang/ don dam pa'i bden pa'o/ ngo bo nyid kyang rnam pa gsum ste/ kun brtags[4] dang/ gzhan dbang dang/ yongs grub bo/

de la kun brtags[5] dang gzhan dbang ni kun rdzob bden pa yin la/ kun rdzob bden pa gang yin pa de ni/ rmi lam dang/ sgyu ma la sogs pa bzhin du gdod ma nas rang gi ngo bos stong pa'i phyir/ de dag gi stong pa nyid de ni rang gi ngo bos stong pa nyid ces bya la/ de yang med par dgag pa tsam gyi ngo bo nyid yin pas chad pa'i stong pa nyid dang/ bem po'i stong pa nyid dang/ nyi tshe ba'i stong pa nyid yin gyi yang dag par phyin ci ma (K3a) log pa'i stong pa don dam pa'i bden pa min no//

kun rdzob rang stong yin pa 'di la dgongs nas/ sher phyin gyi mdo las/ gzugs nas rnam mkhyen gyi bar gyi chos thams cad rang gi (S5) ngo bos stong pa nyid du gsungs pa yin la/ de'i dgongs 'grel klu sgrub zhabs kyi rigs tshogs rnams las kyang rang stong med dgag chad pa'i stong nyid de gtso bor bstan pa yin gyi/ mdo dang bstan bcos de dag gis kyang don dam bden pa rdzogs pa dang gsal por[6] bstan pa ni med do/ sher phyin gyi mdo las gzugs nas rnam mkhyen gyi bar gyi chos thams cad med do/ /[7]zhes gsungs pa kun brtags[8] dang/ sgyu ma dang/ rmi lam la sogs pa bstan pa ni/ gzhan dbang la dgongs nas gsungs pa yin gyi/ yongs grub don dam pa'i bden pa med pa dang/ rdzun pa sogs su ston pa ni min te/ *brgyad stong don bsdus* las/

> med ces bya ba'i tshig gis ni//
> rtags pa thams cad 'gog pa ste//
> sgyu ma la sogs dpe yis ni[9]//
> gzhan gyi dbang ni yongs su bstan//
> rnam par dag pa bzhir bstan nas//
> yong su grub pa bstan pa yin//[10]
> ces gsungs pas so// (S6)

4 KB *btags.*
5 KB *btags.*
6 K *bor.*
7 KB second / omitted.
8 KB *btags.*
9 S *na.*
10 *Prañāpāramitāpiṇḍārtha* = *Prañāpāramitāsaṅgraha,* vv. 28a–29b. P vol. 146, 170: *med ces bya la sogs tshig kyis/ brtags pa thams cad 'gog pa ste/ sgyu ma la sogs dpe rnams kyis/ gzhan gyi dbang ni yang dag bstan/ rnam par byang ba bzhi yis ni/ yong su grub pa rab tu bsgrag.*

Emptiness *(stong pa nyid)*, [according to him,] is of two kinds: the emptiness of own nature *(rang gi ngo bos)*, and the emptiness of other nature *(gzhan gi ngo bos)*. Truth *(bden pa)* is also of two kinds: conventional *(kun rdzob kyi)* truth and ultimate *(don dam pa'i)* truth. Nature *(ngo bo nyid)* is of three kinds: the imagined *(kun brtags)*, the dependent *(gzhan dbang)*, and the real *(yongs grub)*.[10]

The imagined and the dependent are conventional truths. Anything that is a conventional truth is, like a dream and an illusion, from time immemorial, empty of its own nature; that is why the emptiness of these [conventional truths] is called "emptiness of own nature."[11] Moreover, since [this form of emptiness] is, by nature, but a simple absolute negation *(med par dgag pa tsam)*,[12] it is a nihilistic emptiness *(chad par stong pa nyid)*, an inanimate emptiness *(bem po'i stong pa nyid)*, and a partial emptiness *(nyi tshe ba'i stong pa nyid)*.[13] It is not the ultimate truth—the perfect, unmistaken emptiness.

It is intending the fact that *the conventional* is empty of its own [nature] that the Perfection of Wisdom sūtras say that all phenomena, from form up to omniscience, are empty of their own nature.[14] The commentaries on the purport of those [sūtras], the philosophical works *(rigs tshogs)* of the Venerable Nāgārjuna,[15] chiefly teach this self-emptiness, this nihilistic emptiness *qua* simple negation. But those sūtras and the treatises [of Nāgārjuna] do not give a complete and clear exposition of the ultimate truth. When the Perfection of Wisdom sūtras state that all phenomena, from form up to omniscience, are nonexistent *(med)*, they intend that teaching—that [things] are imaginary, illusory, and dreamlike—[to refer to] the dependent. They do not teach the real, the ultimate truth, to be nonexistent, false *(rdzun pa)*, and so forth,[16] for the *Aṣṭasāhasrikāpiṇḍārtha* states:

> The word "nonexistent"
> Repudiates all that is imaginary;
> And the examples of the illusion and so forth
> Illustrate [the nature of] the dependent.
> Through the teaching that purification is fourfold,[17]
> It teaches the real.[18]

chos nyid yongs grub don dam pa'i bden[11] pa ni rang gi ngo bos stong pa min gyi kun brtags[12] gzhan dbang gi ngo bo 'dus byas kyi chos kun rdzob kyi ngo bos stong pa'i phyir na gzhan gyi ngo bos stong pa yin la/ de ni yang dag pa phyin ci ma log pa'i stong nyid don dam pa'i bden pa dang/ chos kyi sku dang/ (K3b) yang dag pa'i mtha' dang/ de bzhin nyid dang/ rnam pa thams cad kyi mchog dang ldan pa'i stong pa nyid yin no/ de la stobs dang mi 'jigs pa dang/ mtshan dang dpe byad la sogs pa 'dus ma byas pa'i yon tan dpag tu med pa gdod ma nas gnas pa yin te/ *phal po che'i mdo* las/ stong gsum dar yug chen po'i dpe dang bcas te gsungs pa dang/ *de bzhin gshegs pa'i snying po'i mdo* las/ dpe dgu dang sbyar te rgyas par gsungs pa'i phyir ro/ /gzhan yang de ni rtag pa brtan pa ther zug pa mi 'gyur ba'i chos can gtsang ba bde ba rtag pa (S7) bdag dam pa'i pha rol tu phyin pa yin no//

de lta bu'i gzhan stong don dam pa'i bden pa 'di yang/

[1] *'phags pa gzungs kyi dbang phyug rgyal po'i mdo* dang/
[2] *lhag bsam bstan pa'i le'u'i mdo* dang/
[3] *dpal phreng seng ge'i nga ro'i mdo* dang/
[4] *de bzhin gshegs pa'i snying po'i mdo* dang/
[5] *'phel 'grib med par bstan pa'i mdo* dang/
[6] *rnga bo che'i mdo* dang/
[7] *ye shes snang ba rgyan gyi mdo* dang/
[8] *gtsug na rin po che'i mdo* dang/
[9] *sor mo'i phreng ba'i mdo* dang/
[10] *mya ngan 'das pa chen po'i mdo*/

la sogs pa bka' tha ma don dam rnam par nges pa'i mdo rnams las gsal por gsungs shing/ de dag gi dgongs 'grel *theg pa chen po rgyud bla ma* sogs byams chos phyi ma rnams dang/ <u>thogs med sku mched</u> kyi bstan bcos rnams dang/ <u>'phags pa klu sgrub</u> kyi *dbu ma chos dbyings bstod pa* sogs bstod tshogs rnams las gsal bar (K4a) bstan to// (S8)

de la kun rdzob bden pa ni rang rang gi ngo bos stong pa'i phyir dang/ de dag kyang chos nyid don dam pa'i bden pa la gdod ma nas ma grub pa'i

Toh no. 3809, Sher phyin *pha*, f. 293b, reads exactly the same as P, with the exception of the last word, which reads *bsgrags* instead of *bsgrag*.

11 K *bdan*.

12 K *btags*.

Reality *(chos nyid)*, the real *(yongs grub)*, the ultimate truth *(don dam bden pa)*, is not empty of its own nature.[19] It is, however, empty of [everything that is] by nature imaginary or dependent, that is, of all compounded *('du byas)* phenomena that are by nature conventional.[20] This [reality] is the perfect, unmistaken emptiness, the ultimate truth, the *dharmakāya (chos kyi sku)*, the perfect end *(yang dag pa'i mtha')*, thusness *(de bzhin nyid)*, the emptiness that possesses the best of every quality *(rnam pa thams cad kyi mchog dang ldan pa)*.[21] It contains, from time immemorial, infinite good qualities that are noncompounded, such as the powers *(stobs)*,[22] the fearlessnesses *(mi 'jigs pa)*,[23] the marks *(mtshan)*,[24] signs *(dpe byed)*[25] and so forth, for the *Avataṃsaka Sūtra* explains it using the example of the great silk cloth of the three thousand [worlds] *(stong gsum dar yug chen po)*,[26] and the *Tathāgatagarbha Sūtra* explains it extensively by employing the nine examples.[27] Moreover, it is something that possesses the qualities of permanence *(rtag pa)*, stability *(brten pa)*, eternality *(ther zug)*, and unchangeability *(mi 'gyur ba'i chos can)*;[28] it is limpid *(gtsang ba)*, blissful *(bde ba)*, permanent *(rtag pa)*, and it is the perfection of the higher self *(bdag dam pa'i pha rol tu phyin pa)*.[29]

This ultimate truth that is empty of what is other is clearly spoken of in the later sermons [of the Buddha] *(bka' tha ma)*—that is, in the ultimate definitive sūtras *(don dam pa rnam par nges pa'i mdo)*,[30] such as:

1. the *Āryadhāraṇīśvararāja Sūtra*[31]
2. the *Dṛdhādhyaśayaparivarta Sūtra*[32]
3. the *Śrīmālā[devī]siṃhanāda Sūtra*[33]
4. the *Tathāgatagarbha Sūtra*[34]
5. the *Anūnatvāpurṇatvanirdeśa Sūtra*[35]
6. the *Mahābherī Sūtra*[36]
7. the *Jñānālokālaṃkāra Sūtra*[37]
8. the *Ratnacūda Sūtra*[38]
9. the *Aṇgulimāliya Sūtra*,[39] and
10. the *Mahā[pari]nirvāṇa Sūtra*,[40] etc.

The commentarial literature on these [scriptures] clearly teaches [this doctrine of the emptiness of other] in such texts as the last [three] works of Maitreya,[41] such as the the *Mahāyānottaratantra*, in the treatises of Asaṅga and his brother [Vasubandhu],[42] and in the ārya Nāgārjuna's devotional works *(bstod tshogs)*, such as the *Madhyamakadharmadhātustava*.[43]

In this [system of Dol po pa], it is because conventional truths are empty of their own natures, and because they have never, from time immemorial, existed in reality, that is, as the ultimate truth, that [this position considers

phyir/ rtag pa'i mtha' las grol la/ chos nyid yongs grub ni nam yang med pa min pas gdod ma nas bden pa dang rtag pa sogs su grub pa'i phyir chad pa'i mtha' las grol bas de'i phyir/ 'di ni mtha' bral dbu ma chen po'i lam yin te/ *kun btus* su/

> gang la gang med pa de ni des stong pa[13] yang dag par mthong[14] ste/ 'di la lhag ma gang yin pa de ni 'dir yod pa'o/ /zhes[15] yang dag pa ji[16] lta ba bzhinṬ du rab tu shes so/ /'di ni stong pa nyid la 'jug pa yang dag pa[17] ji[18] lta ba ste/ phyin ci ma log pa

zhes dang/

> 'di la[19] dgongs nas bcom ldan 'das kyis yod pa yang yod par[20] med pa yang med par yang dag par ji[21] lta ba bzhin du rab tu shes so//

zhes sogs 'byung ba'i phyir/

de'i (S9) phyir lugs 'di ni nges pa'i don gyi mdo sde rnams kyis bstan pa/ shing rta chen po rnams kyis bkral ba grub pa brnyes pa'i rnal 'byor pa rnams kyis bsgom pa bstan pa'i snying po dam pa yin gyi/ rang stong tsam gyis chog par 'dzin pa dag gis ni bstan pa'i snying po stong pa nyid kyi don legs par rtogs pa ma yin no/ /zhes bzhed do//

[1.2.0.0.0 chad mtha' la dbu mar smra ba]

lugs gnyis pa ni/ legs par dpyod pa'i blo gros kyis gsung rab kyi dgongs pa rang stobs kyis 'grel zhing snying rje dang/ sems bskyed la sogs pa'i yon tan gyi rgyan gyis (K4b) mdzes pa shar tsong kha pa blo bzang grags pa'i dpal kyi zhal snga nas/ *dbu ma rtsa 'jug gi rnam bshad* dang/ *drang nges rnam 'byed* la sogs pa rnams su 'phags yul gyi rang rgyud pa'i slob dpon chen po rnams dang/ (S10) bod yul du sngar byon pa'i dbu ma pa rnams kyis ma rtogs pa'i

13 *Chos mngon pa kun las btus pa.* N no. 4049, vol. 80, f. 823: *par.*
14 N, f. 823: *rjes su mthong.*
15 N, f. 823: *yod pa'i zhes.*
16 KBS *ci;* N, f. 823: *ji.*
17 N, f. 823: *pa'i.*
18 KBS *ci;* N, f. 823: *ji.*
19 N, f. 823: *las.*
20 N, f. 823: *par/.*
21 KBS *ci;* N, f. 823: *ji.*

itself to be] free from the extreme of eternalism. It is because reality, the real, has never *not* existed, that it is primordially true, permanent, and so forth; and it is because of that that [this position considers itself to be] free from the extreme of nihilism.[44] That is why [according to Dol po pa] this is the path of the Great Madhyamaka free from the extremes, as confirmed by such [passages] as this one from the *[Abhidharma]samuccaya:*

> [To notice] the absence of something in something else is to see the fact [that the former] is empty of [the latter], but what remains in [the former] does exist therein. This [is what it means] to understand things exactly as they are. It is called "the nonerroneous"—that is, the perfect and exact—entrance into emptiness.[45]

And also:

> It is with reference to this that the Lord understood things exactly as they are—that is, what exists as existent, and what does not exist as nonexistent.[46]

Therefore, this system is taught in the sūtras of definitive meaning, and it represents the quintessence *(snying po dam pa)* of the teachings, commented on by Mahāyāna [scholars], and meditated on by accomplished yogis. On the other hand, those who content themselves simply with the emptiness of self [-nature] do not properly realize the meaning of the emptiness that is the essence of the teachings. This is what [Dol po pa] believes.

The Second System [That of Tsong kha pa]

[These are the views of] the easterner, Tsong kha pa Blo bzang grags pa [1357–1419],[47] a man who beautified himself with the ornaments of such good qualities as compassion and altruism *(sems bskyed)* and who, with his fine analytical intellect, commented, on his own *(rang stobs kyis)*,[48] on the purport of the scriptures. From his glorious lips have emerged [such texts as] his expositions of the *Mūlamadhyamaka[kārikas]*[49] and the *Avatāra,*[50] as well as the *Elucidation of the Definitive and Provisional.*[51] [In these works] there seem to be many unique philosophical tenets and interpretations,[52] such as when he says that the main point of the Prāsaṅgika Madhyamaka

dbu ma thal 'gyur ba'i gnad 'di yin no/ /zhes thun mong ma yin pa'i grub mtha'i 'jog tshul dang/ gzhung gi bshad tshul mang po zhig snang ba la/ 'dir nye bar mkho ba rags[22] rim tsam zhig brjod na/

[1.2.1.0.0] don dam stong nyid kyi rnam bzhag dang/
[1.2.2.0.0] kun rdzob snang ba'i rnam bzhag dang/
[1.2.3.0.0] de dag las 'phros pa'i don/ gsum las/

[1.2.1.0.0 don dam stong nyid kyi rnam bzhag]

dang po ni/ *stong nyid bdun cu pa* las/ dngos po la bden par 'dzin pa'i bden 'dzin las yan lag[23] bcu gnyis 'byung bas 'khor ba'i rtsa bar gyur pa'i ma rig pa yin par gsungs pa dang/ *bzhi brgya pa* las/

> srid pa'i sa bon rnam shes te//
> yul rnams de yi spyod yul lo//
> yul la bdag med mthong nas[24] ni//
> srid pa'i sa bon 'gag par 'gyur[25]//

ces dang/ yang gti mug bcom pas nyon mongs thams cad bcom par 'gyur zhing/ rten 'brel mthong bas (S11) gti mug 'byung bar mi 'gyur bar gsungs pa dang/ de dag gi 'grel pa rnams las kyang/ bden 'dzin gyi ma rig pa ni 'khor ba'i rtsa ba yin par gsungs pas/ dbu ma'i dgag bya ni gang zag dang chos la bden par 'dzin pa'i bden 'dzin kho na yin la/ de 'gog pa la de'i zhen yul bden pa ngos bzung nas de sun phyung dgos pas/

bden (K5a) pa'i tshad la rang rgyud pa rnams kyis blo la ma ltos par yul rang gi sdod[26] lugs kyi ngos nas grub pa zhig yod na/ bden par[27] grub pa dang/ don dam par grub pa dang/ yang dag par grub pa zhig yin pas/ de dag dgag bya yin la/ rang gi mtshan nyid kyis grub pa dang/ rang bzhin gyis

22 KB *rag.*
23 K *yag.*
24 *Cathuḥśataka* (XIV, 25). Lang, *Āryadeva's Cathuḥśataka,* 134: *na.*
25 KB *gyur.* Lang, *Cathuḥśataka: 'gyur.*
26 S *srod.*
27 KB *pa.*

has not been understood either by the great Svātantrika scholars of the Noble Land [of India],[53] or by the Mādhyamikas who preceded him in Tibet. Let me here give just a rough overview [of Tsong kha pa's view] under three headings:

1. His exposition of emptiness, the ultimate
2. His exposition of appearances, the conventional
3. Some points that follow from those [first two]

[Tsong kha pa's Exposition of Emptiness, the Ultimate]

The *Śūnyatāsaptati* states that since the twelve links [of dependent arising] arise from the grasping at truth—that is, from grasping at things *(dngos po)* to be true—this [form of grasping] is the ignorance that is the root of cyclic existence.[54] The *Catuḥśataka* states:

> Consciousness is the seed of existence,
> And its domain is all objects.
> When objects are seen to be selfless,
> The seed of existence is eliminated.[55]

[That same text] also states that destroying delusion *(gti mug)* destroys all of the afflictions *(nyon mongs)*, and that seeing interdependence *(rten 'brel)* stops the emergence of delusion.[56] The commentaries to these [texts] state that the ignorance that grasps [things as] true is the root of cyclic existence;[57] therefore, the grasping at truth—that is, the grasping of persons and phenomena to be true—is the sole "Madhyamaka object-to-be-negated" *(dbu ma'i dgag bya)*.[58] To negate it, it is necessary to [first] identify the "truth" that is the object constructed *(zhen yul)* within that [ignorance], and then to repudiate *(sun phyung)* it.[59]

As regards the measure *(tshad)* of the "truth" [that is the object-to-be-negated, Tsong kha pa says] that the Svātantrikas believe that [it refers to] the existence of objects in their own right,[60] without their depending on the mind *(blo la ma ltos par yul rang gi sdod lugs kyi ngos nas grub pa)*; if something has such existence, then it must be truly existent *(bden par grub pa)*, ultimately existent *(don dam par grub pa)*, and perfectly existent *(yang dag par grub pa)*. Hence, all of these are objects-to-be-negated. But because [things] exist *nominally (tha snyad du)* by virtue of their own characteristic *(rang gi mtshan nyid kyis grub pa)*,[61] because they exist inherently *(rang bzhin*

grub pa dang/ ngo bo nyid kyis grub pa ni tha snyad du yod pas/ dgag bya min par bzhed do//

thal 'gyur ba rnams kyis ni/ rang rgyud pa'i dgag byar byed pa de dag ni dgag bya rags[28] pa yin la/ phra (S12) ba ni/ btags don btsal ba'i tshe rnyed pa zhig yod na bden par grub pa'i tshad yin pas/ de nyid dgag bya phra ba yin la/ de ni rang rgyud pa rnams kyis dgag byar mi 'dod pas thal 'gyur ba'i lugs kyi gnad thun mong ma yin pa'o//

de lta bu'i bden pa de/ dbu ma'i gzhung las bshad pa'i rigs pa rnams kyis[29] btsal ba'i tshe ma rnyed pa'i bden pa bkag tsam gyi stong nyid med dgag de nyid dbu ma'i lta ba mthar[30] thug pa yin zhing/ don dam bden pa mtshan nyid pa yin la/ chos rnams kyi gnas lugs mthar thug pa'ang yin no/ /de ltar bden pa bkag zin nas bden pa bkag pa'i stong nyid der mngon par zhen pa ni dgag tu mi rung ste/ de yul gyi gnas lugs rtogs pa'i blo yin pa'i phyir dang/[31] dbu ma'i dgag bya ni bden pa kho na yin la des bden par ma bzung ba'i phyir/

'o na/

> yod min med min yod med min/
> gnyis ka'i bdag nyid min (S13) pa'ang min//

ces sogs (K5b) yul gyi gnas lugs mtha' bzhi char gyi spros pa dang bral bar gsungs pa dang/ blos mtha' bzhi gang du yang gzung du mi rung bar gsungs pa rnams dang 'gal lo snyam na

de'i don ni/ don dam du yod pa yang ma yin/ kun rdzob tu med pa yang ma yin pa'i phyir/ blos kyang de ltar 'dzin du mi rung zhes pa'i don yin gyi yod min med min sgra ji bzhin du khas len du mi rung ste/ dgag pa gnyis kyi rnal ma go bas/ yod pa ma yin na med dgos shing/ med pa min na yod

28 KB *rag.*
29 K *kyi.*
30 KB *mtha'.*
31 S / omitted.

gyis grub pa), and exist naturally *(ngo bo nyid kyis grub pa)* [at the conventional level], these [latter ways of existing] are not [for the Svātantrikas] objects-to-be-negated.[62]

[According to Tsong kha pa,] the Prāsaṅgikas believe that what the Svātantrikas take to be objects-to-be-negated are [only] rough *(rags pa)* objects-to-be-negated and that the subtle one is [as follows]:[63] the measure [of something] being truly existent is that it is found when the object labeled [by a certain name] is searched for *(btags don btsal ba'i tshe rnyed pa)*.[64] That is itself the subtle object-to-be-negated, and because the Svātantrikas do not accept that as an object-to-be-negated, it is a doctrine that is specific to the Prāsaṅgika system.

The simple negation of such "truth"—[that is, the truth] that is not found when it is searched for by means of the reasoning that is explained in the Madhyamaka texts—*is* emptiness; it is a non-affirming negation *(med dgag)*, and it is the ultimate philosophical viewpoint of the Madhyamaka; it is the real *(mtshan nyid pa)* ultimate truth *(don dam bden pa)* and the ultimate reality *(gnas lugs mthar thug pa)* of phenomena. Once "truth" has been negated in this way, the [concomitant] conceptualization *(mngon par zhen pa)* of emptiness as the negation of truth *should not* be negated,[65] for (a) it is a mental state *(blo)* that understands the reality of that object and (b) the object-to-be-negated in the Madhyamaka is "truth" alone, and that [conceptualization of emptiness] does not grasp [things] as true.

[Objection:] Does this not contradict the passage that states:

> [Things] do not exist, nor are they nonexistent, nor [both] existent
> and nonexistent
> Nor are they by nature neither.[66]

for such [passages] state that the reality of objects is the freedom from the proliferations of *all four* extremes, and that the mind should not grasp things in terms of *any* of the four extremes?

[Tsong kha pa replies:] The meaning of that passage is as follows. [Things] do not exist ultimately, nor are they nonexistent conventionally. Hence, the mind should not apprehend them in those ways. This is what it means.[67] [The claim] that things are neither existent nor nonexistent should not be taken literally, for, according to the law of double negation *(dgag pa gnyis kyi rnal ma go bas)*,[68] if something does not exist, it must be nonexistent, and if it is not nonexistent, it must exist. Therefore, those who believe that the Madhyamaka view consists of the mind's nonapprehension of any the

dgos pa'i phyir/ blos mtha' gang du yang mi 'dzin pa dbu ma'i lta bar 'dod pa ni rgya nag hwa shang gi lta ba dang mtshungs pas/ bden pa bkag zin nas bden pas stong pa'i stong nyid kho nar bzung ba ni gnas lugs rtogs pa'i blo yin no// de ltar bden 'dzin legs par ngos zin na bden 'dzin gnyis min pa'i rtog pa du ma zhig (S14) yod par shes par 'gyur bas/ rtog pas gang bzung gi yul thams cad de kho na nyid la dpyod pa'i rigs pas dgag par 'dod pa'i log rtog thams cad zlog par 'gyur ro//[32]

[1.2.2.0.0 kun rdzob snang ba'i rnam bzhag]

gnyis pa kun rdzob snang ba'i rnam bzhag ni/ dbu ma rang rgyud pa rnams kyis tha snyad du rang gi mtshan nyid kyis grub pa'i chos khas len gyi[33] 'dir de khas mi len pas gang zag dang chos tha snyad du 'jog pa'i tshul ni/ 'di ni lha sbyin no 'di ni lha sbyin gyi rna ba'o zhes sogs tha snyad btags pa'i tshe na/ tha snyad de'i dbang gis lha sbyin dang/ lha sbyin gyi rna ba la sogs pa yod par 'jog gi de las gzhan pa'i 'jog byed (K6a) med pa ni tha snyad du yod pa'i don no/ /de dag la tha snyad des btags pa'i don gang yin btsal ba'i tshe na ma rnyed kyang tha snyad btags pa tsam la rgyu 'bras la sogs pa 'jog ces pa ni lugs 'di pa'i thun mong min (S15) pa'o//

kun rdzob kyi nang tshan gyi 'jog tshul la kun gzhi med kyang las 'bras 'jog pa'i tshul ni/ las byas ma thag tu 'gag pas las de 'bras bu'i bar du yang mi 'gro na las 'gag nas yun ring po lon pa des 'bras bu ci ltar bskyed ce na/

'di la bye brag smra bas las 'gag pa na las kyi chud mi za skye zhing des 'bras bu bskyed par 'dod do/ /mdo sde pas las kyi thob pa skye zhing des 'bras bu bskyed par 'dod do/ /sems tsam pas kun gzhi'i rnam shes la bag chags bzhag nas bag chags des las 'bras bskyed par 'dod pa[34] rnams ni las 'bras

32 This line is taken directly from Tsong kha pa's *Dbu ma dgongs pa rab gsal, Collected Works,* Lhasa Zhol ed., vol. *ma,* f. 79b. The words/syllables in bold are words that vary from Go rams pa's text: *de ltar bden 'dzin legs par ngos zin na/* ***bdag*** *'dzin gnyis min pa'i rtog pa du ma* ***cig*** *yod* ***pa*** *shes par 'gyur bas/ rtog pas gang bzung gi yul thams cad de kho na nyid la dpyod pa'i rigs pas* ***'gog*** *par 'dod pa'i log rtog thams cad* ***ldog*** *par 'gyur ro.*
33 KB *gyis.*
34 K *par.*

[four] extremes hold a view similar to that of the Chinese Hwa shang.[69] Hence, the mind that understands reality is the apprehension of emptiness alone—that is, of the emptiness of truth [that is arrived at] after having negated truth. If one properly identifies [what it means] to apprehend [things] as true *(bden 'dzin)*, one will come to understand that there are many conceptual thoughts that are neither of the two forms of the grasping at truth [of self and phenomena].[70] This counteracts all of the mistaken views *(log rtog)* that believe that every object that is apprehended by a conceptual thought is negated by means of the reasoning that analyzes reality.[71]

[Tsong Kha Pa's Exposition of Appearances—that Is, of the Conventional World][72]

The Svātantrika Mādhyamikas accept that nominally *(tha snyad du)*, phenomena exist by virtue of their own characteristic and, since [Tsong kha pa believes that] this is not accepted in the [Prāsaṅgika Madhyamaka system], how then *does* [the Prāsaṅgika, according to Tsong kha pa,] posit persons and phenomena nominally *(tha snyad du)*? When one employs terms *(tha snyad)* such as "This is Devadatta," or "This is Devadatta's ear," and so forth, Devadatta and Devadatta's ear, etc., are posited as existing by virtue of those terms. There is no process of positing [their existence] apart from that one; and this is what we mean [when we—i.e., Tsong kha pa and his followers—say that they] nominally exist. When one searches for what it is that is labeled by the terms in those [expressions], nothing is found. Nonetheless, causality and so forth [can be] posited as simply labeled by terms. This is a unique [tenet] of this system.[73]

Even though the foundation [consciousness] *(kun gzhi)* is not a part of [Tsong kha pa's] exposition of the conventional,[74] this does not preclude [his attempts to] account for karma and its effects. Given that a karmic action ceases immediately after it has been created, the karmic action does not survive up to the time of the effect. If this is so, how can a karmic action that has long since ceased give rise to an effect?[75]

In this regard, the Vaibhāṣikas believe that when the karmic action ceases, there arises [an intermediate entity called] "karmic inexhaustibility" *(las kyi chud mi za ba)*, and that it is *this* that gives rise to the effect.[76] The Sautrāntikas believe that there arises [something called] "karmic attainment" *(las kyi thob pa)*, and that it is *this* that gives rise to the effect.[77] The Cittamātras believe that "latent traces" *(bag chags)* [are deposited] in the foundation consciousness, and that it is these traces that give rise to karma and its

ngo bo nyid kyis grub pa'i gzhan du 'dod pa'i lugs yin la/ de dag bkag nas 'dir las kyis zhig pa dngos po ba bskyed nas de las kyi 'bras bu bskyed pa ni thun mong min pa'i gnad yin no//

chu phor gang gi go sa na rigs drug gis chu dang/ rnag khrag la (S16) sogs pa'i mthong snang drug 'byung ba'i tshe mig shes de dag la 'khrul ma 'khrul gyi khyad par med pas chu'i rdzas cha yod pa bzhin du dngos po gzhan rnams kyi rdzas cha yod pa'ang mtshungs pa yin no//

[1.2.3.0.0] de dag las 'phros pa'i don

[1.2.3.1.0] sgrib gnyis kyi ngos 'dzin/
[1.2.3.2.0] bdag gnyis kyi ngos 'dzin/
[1.2.3.3.0] theg pa che chung gi (K6b) spang rtogs kyi khyad par/
[1.2.3.4.0] kun gzhi dang rang rig mi 'dod pas phyi don khas len pa'i tshul/
[1.2.3.5.0] rang rgyud kyi rtags dang dam bca' med pa'i tshul/

[1.2.3.1.0 sgrib gnyis kyi ngos 'dzin]

dang po ni/ dbu ma pa gzhan gyis shes sgrib tu khas blangs pa'i chos kyi bdag 'dzin ni 'di pa'i lugs kyi nyon sgrib yin te/ yan lag bcu gnyis kyi nang tshan du gyur pa'i ma rig pa yin pa'i phyir ro/ /shes sgrib ni *'jug pa'i rang*

effects.[78] But these are systems that accept things differently [from the Prāsaṅgika], insofar as they believe karma and its effects to exist by virtue of their very nature *(ngo bo nyid kyis grub pa)*. Having refuted those [other views], it is the unique position of [Tsong kha pa's interpretation of the Prāsaṅgika system] that karmic action gives rise to "destruction *qua* entity" *(zhig pa dngos po ba)*, and it is this, in turn, that gives rise to the effect of the karmic action.[79]

At the site of a cup full of water there appear six [different things] to the six classes [of sentient beings]:[80] [humans] see water, [pretas] see pus and blood, and so forth. When this occurs, the eye consciousnesses [of these various beings] cannot be distinguished as to whether or not they are in error *('khrul pa)* [since they are all accurate in regard to their object, the fluid]. Therefore, just as [that fluid] has a portion of water-substance within it, it has portions of the other substances within it as well, [and each being is witnessing that portion of the liquid that it has a karmic propensity to see].[81]

Some Points that Remain to Be Discussed in the Wake of These Discussions]

This has five [subdivisions]:

1. [How Tsong kha pa] identifies the two obscurations *(sgrib pa)*
2. [How Tsong kha pa] identifies the two selves *(bdag)*
3. [How Tsong kha pa propounds] the differences between what the Hīna- and Mahā-yānas [accept as] the objects to be abandoned and realized *(spang rtogs)*
4. How [Tsong kha pa] accepts external objects *(phyi don)*, given that [he] does not believe in the foundation [consciousness] *(kun gzhi)* or in reflexive awareness *(rang rig)*
5. What it means for there to be no autonomous reasons *(rang rgyud kyi rtags)* and no theses *(dam bca')*

[How Tsong kha pa Identifies the Two Obscurations (sgrib pa)*]*[82]

What other Mādhyamikas accept as an obscuration to omniscience *(shes sgrib)*—namely, the grasping at the self of phenomena *(chos kyi bdag 'dzin)*—is for this [Prāsaṅgika] system an afflicted obscuration *(nyon sgrib)*, for it is a form of ignorance that is [contained] among the twelve links.[83] The *Avatārabhāṣya* states that the obscurations to omniscience are the latent traces of the afflictions *(nyon mongs pa'i bag chags)*.[84] Therefore, [the obscurations to

'grel las nyon mongs pa'i bag chags yin par gsungs pas/ nyon mongs pa'i bag chags dang de'i 'bras bu gnyis snang (S17) 'khrul pa'i cha'o//

[1.2.3.2.0 bdag gnyis kyi ngos 'dzin]

gnyis pa/ slob dpon legs ldan 'byed kyis yid kyi rnam par shes pa gang zag tu 'dod cing/ 'di pa'i lugs kyi ngar 'dzin lhan skyes kyis nga'o snyam du bzung ba de la dmigs pa'i yul ni nga tsam yin zhing/ 'dzin stangs kyi bzung bya ni bden par grub pa yin pas/ dang po ni gang zag kyang yin zhing/ bdag kyang yin la/ phyi ma ni gang zag gi bdag yin no/ /chos kyi bdag ni dngos po rnams la gzhan la rag ma las par rang dbang du grub pa zhig yod na de nyid la 'jog go//

[1.2.3.3.0 theg pa che chung gi spang rtogs kyi khyad par]

gsum pa ni/ theg pa che chung thams cad kyis kyang sngar bshad pa ltar gyi bden pa bkag tsam gyi stong nyid de rtogs par mtshungs shing de las lhag pa'i rtogs bya med pas lta ba la khyad par med pa kho na'o//

'o na shes sgrib spong nus mi nus kyi khyad par med par 'gyur ro snyam na/ goms pa yun ring thung dang snying rje dang sems (S18) bskyed la sogs pa spyod pa'i grogs kyi khyad (K7a) par gyis shes sgrib spong nus mi nus kyi khyad par byung ba yin gyi/ shes sgrib kyi gnyen po la yang sngar gyi stong nyid rtogs pa'i lta ba las lhag pa'am gzhan pa'i gnyen po ni med do//

spong ba'i khyad par la/ nyan thos dgra bcom pas nyon sgrib ma lus pa spangs pas bden 'dzin ma lus par spong ba yin la/ theg chen gyis ni sa brgyad pa ma thob kyi bar du bden 'dzin ma spangs pas ma dag sa bdun gyi skabs

omniscience] consist of (a) the latent traces of the afflictions and (b) their effect, which is the aspect that causes error [by making things] appear dualistically *(gnyis snang 'khrul pa'i cha)*.[85]

[How Tsong kha pa Identifies the Two Selves][86]

The [Svātantrika] master Bhāvaviveka believes that the mental consciousness *(yid kyi rnam par shes pa)* is the person *(gang zag)*.[87] This [Prāsaṅgika] system [instead maintains] that the referent object *(dmigs pa'i yul)* of the thought "I" as it is apprehended by the innate form of self-grasping *(ngar 'dzin lhas skyes)* is the "mere I" *(nga tsam)*;[88] how it appprehends it—that is, the mode of apprehension—is as truly existent. The first of these [that is, the mere "I"] is the person, and the self. The latter [that is, the true existence of the person] is the self of the person. The self of phenomena [Tsong kha pa] posits as a kind of independent existence *(rang dbang du grub pa)*—that is, as a lack of dependence on anything else, which, if it existed, would constitute the reality *(de nyid)* [of phenomena].[89]

[How Tsong kha pa Propounds the Differences between What the Hīna- and Mahā-yānas Accept as the Objects to Be Abandoned and Realized (spang rtogs)*]*[90]

All [branches] of the greater and lesser vehicles are similar in that they all realize *(rtogs pa)* emptiness, the mere negation of truth, as explained above. Since there is nothing greater than this to be realized, there is not the slightest difference in regard to their view [of the ultimate].[91]

Is there then no difference [in the two vehicles] as regards their ability to eliminate the obscurations to omniscience? The difference in their ability to eliminate the obscurations to omniscience [that is, that the Mahāyāna can, and that the Hīnayāna cannot, do so,] is due to the difference in the length of their [respective] meditations, and in [the extent to which] they are aided *(grogs)* by practices like compassion *(snying rje)* and altruism *(sems bskyed)*. But there is no antidote to the obscurations to omniscience that is different from, or greater than, that previously [explained] view that is the realization of emptiness.

As regards the difference in the [*process* of] eliminating [the obscurations], since the śrāvaka arhats must have eliminated every afflicted obscuration *(nyon sgrib)*, they must have eliminated all grasping at [things as] true *(bden 'dzin)*. The Mahāyāna does not eliminate the grasping at [things as]

su bden 'dzin mngon gyur ba 'byung ba yin pa'i phyir ro/ /des na ma dag sa bdun gyi gnas skabs su nyon sgrib kho na spong ba yin gyi/ bden 'dzin sa bon dang bcas pa ma bcom gyi bar du/ shes sgrib spong ba mi srid pas shes sgrib spong ba'i ma mtha'i sa mtshams sa brgyad pa nas 'dzin pa yin no//

des na lugs 'di la bden 'dzin shes sgrib tu 'jog pa'i lugs kyis/ de la shes (S19) sgrib chung 'bring chen po dgur byas nas sa gnyis pa sogs sgom lam dgus spong ba'i rnam bzhag khas mi len te da dung 'chad par 'gyur ro//

theg pa gsum po gang gi yang mthong lam ma thob par bden bzhi mi rtag la sogs bcu drug mngon sum du rtogs zin rgyun ldan du goms par byas pas khams gsum gyi nyon mongs mngon gyur pa spangs pa'i gang zag gcig yod la des chos kyi bdag med ma rtogs pas bden 'dzin nyon mongs su byas pa'i nyon mongs mngon gyur ba tsam yang spong mi nus la/ mngon pa nas bshad pa'i dmigs rnam can gyi nyon mongs mngon gyur ba tsam spong ba yin no/ /zhes dang/ *spyod 'jug* las/ (K7b) bstan rtsa dge slong nyid yin na/ /zhes pa nas/ des na stong nyid sgom par bya/ /zhes sogs kyi tshigs bcad lnga po yang/ gang zag 'di la sbyar te 'chad par byed do// (S20)

[1.2.3.4.0 kun gzhi dang rang rig mi 'dod pas phyi don khas len pa'i tshul]

bzhi pa ni/ dbu ma pa gzhan gyis kun gzhi med cing/ phyi don khas len pa yang yod la/ 'ga' zhig phyi don khas mi len par kun gzhi khas len pa'ang yod

true until the attainment of the eighth bhūmi, since throughout the seven impure bhūmis the grasping at the truth [of things] arises in a manifest *(mngon gyur ba)* way. Therefore, only afflicted obscurations are eliminated during the seven impure bhūmis. It is impossible to eliminate the obscurations to omniscience until the grasping at the truth [of things] and its seeds have been overcome. That is why the threshold—or the point from which—the obscurations to omniscience are eliminated is taken to be the eighth bhūmi.[92]

Therefore, [Tsong kha pa's interpretation of the Prāsaṅgika] does not find acceptable the claims of those who believe that the grasping at the truth [of things] is an obscuration to omniscience—claims like the one that maintains that obscurations to omniscience are divided into nine [gradations: three in each of the three categories of] small, medium and large, with each being eliminated during one of the nine [stages of the] path of meditation *(sgom lam)*, the second bhūmi and so forth; but this has yet to be explained.[93]

There is, [according to Tsong kha pa,] one [type of] individual who, without obtaining the path of seeing *(mthong lam)* of any one of the three vehicles,[94] eliminates the *manifest* afflictions *(nyon mongs mngon gyur pa)* of the three worlds *(khams gsum)*[95] by directly realizing *(mngon sum du rtogs pa)*, and then continuously meditating on, the sixteen aspects of the four [noble] truths,[96] such as impermanence and so forth. But since that [individual] has not understood the selflessness of phenomena, he/she cannot eliminate even the manifest [portion, let alone the seeds] of the affliction that grasps at the truth [of things]. They can only eliminate the [relatively more trivial] manifest afflictions whose objects and aspects *(dmigs rnam)* are explained in the Abhi[dharma]. That is what [Tsong kha pa] says. The five *[Bodhi]caryāvatāra* verses from "Even though monkhood is the root of the teachings," up to "Therefore, one should meditate on emptiness," he explains as referring to such an individual.[97]

[How Tsong kha pa Accepts External Objects **(phyi don)**, *Given that He Does Not Believe in the Foundation Consciousness* **(kun gzhi)**, *or in Reflexive Awareness* **(rang rig)***]*[98]

There are other Mādhyamikas who reject the foundation [consciousness] and accept external objects;[99] and there are some who reject [the existence of] external objects and accept a foundation [consciousness].[100] Nonetheless, [since these are both subschools of the Svātantrika school, they are] systems

mod kyi/ de dag ni yod na rang gi mtshan nyid kyis yod dgos la rang gi mtshan nyid kyis med na med dgos par 'dod pa'i lugs yin la/ 'dir ni kun gzhi med kyang las 'bras kyi 'brel ba 'jog shes pas kun gzhi khas mi len zhing/

phyi don dang shes pa sher phyin gyi mdo las/ rang bzhin gyis[35] stong par[36] gsungs par mtshungs shing mngon pa las rang spyi'i mtshan nyid yod mnyam du bshad pa ltar bya dgos pas don shes gnyis ka la tha snyad btags[37] pa'i btags[38] don yod tshul dpyad na mi rnyed par mtshungs la de ltar na'ang tha snyad kyi dbang gis kun rdzob tu yod par 'jog pa'ang khyad par med pa'i phyir ro//

[1.2.3.5.0 rang rgyud kyi rtags dang dam bca' med pa'i tshul]

lnga pa ni rang gi mtshan nyid kyis grub par 'dod na ni nges par (S21) rang rgyud bya dgos te/ rang sde dngos por smra ba dang legs ldan 'byed la sogs pa bzhin no/ /tha snyad du yang rang gi mtshan nyid kyis grub pa'i chos mi 'dod na ni rang rgyud khas mi len par gdon mi za bar bya dgos pas 'di dgag bya phra mo nas 'gog pa 'di la thug go//

des na legs ldan 'byed la sogs pas rang gi mtshan nyid kyis grub pa'i chos khas (K8a) blangs pas de bsgrub pa'i phyir du rang rgyud kyi gtan tshigs khas blang dgos la/ slob dpon zla ba la sogs pas rang gi mtshan nyid kyis grub pa'i chos khas ma blangs pas rang rgyud kyi rtags dang dam bca' khas len pa'i don med do/ /*tshig gsal* las

35 KB *gyi.*
36 B *pa.*
37 K *btag.*
38 K *btag.*

that believe that if these [things] exist, then they must exist by virtue of their own characteristic and that if they do not exist by virtue of their own characteristic, then they must be nonexistent. This [interpretation of the Madhyamaka, that is, Tsong kha pa's,] rejects the foundation [consciousness], for it maintains that it is possible to posit a connection between karma and its effects without [having to assume the existence of] a foundation [consciousness].[101]

Both external objects and consciousness must be [equally] operative [as existent things], since the Perfection of Wisdom sūtras state that they are equally empty of essence *(rang bzhin gyis stong pa)*; and the Abhidharma explains that [their] specific and general characteristics *(rang dang spyi'i mtshan nyid)* are equally existent. But [external] objects and consciousness are similar insofar as neither [exist ultimately, since neither] is found when their mode of existence as labeled objects—[as objects] labeled by terms—is analyzed. Likewise, there is no difference [between the two in so far as] they can both be posited as conventionally existing, that is, [as existing only] by virtue of the terms [used to designate them].

[What It Means for There to Be No Autonomous Reasons **(rang rgyud kyi rtags)** *and No Theses* **(dam bca')***]*[102]

[Tsong kha pa believes that] if one accepts existence by virtue of own characteristic, then one must definitely accept autonomous [syllogisms] *(rang rgyud)*, like our own [Buddhist] realists, and like Bhāvaviveka, and so forth. If one does not believe that phenomena exist by virtue of their own characteristic even nominally, then one must, without a doubt, reject [the notion of] autonomous [syllogisms]. Hence, [the issue of whether or not one accepts autonomous syllogisms] boils down to [whether or not one] negates the subtle object-to-be-negated.[103]

Therefore, because Bhāvaviveka and [other Svātantrikas] accept that phenomena exist by virtue of their own characteristic, they must accept autonomous syllogisms in order to prove that [thesis]; and because the Master Candra[kīrti] and [other Prāsaṅgikas] do not accept that phenomena exist by virtue of their own characteristic, it makes no sense for them to accept autonomous reasons and theses.

[Tsong kha pa] believes that the *Prasannapadā* [passage] that states that,

> dbu ma pa yin na ni rang gi rgyud kyi rjes su dpags par bya ba rigs pa min te/ phyogs gzhan khas blangs pa med pa'i phyir/

zhes gsungs pas kyang rang rgyud khas mi len pa'i shes byed du rang gi mtshan nyid kyis grub pa'i chos khas len pa (S22) med pa bkod pa yin no zhes bzhed do//

[1.3.0.0.0 mtha' 'bral la dbu mar smra ba]

lugs gsum pa ni/ gangs ri'i khrod kyi thub pa'i rgyal tshab rngog lo chen po la sogs pa gsang phu ba'i dge ba'i bshes gnyen gong ma rnams dang/ bshad sgrub gnyis kyi sgo nas rgyal ba'i bstan pa 'dzin pa la 'gran zla dang bral ba rje btsun sa skya pa yab sras rnams dang/ sgrub rgyud bstan pa'i rgyal mtshan 'dzin pa mar pa dang/ mi la la sogs pa'i skyes chen rnams dang/ mtha' bral dbu ma'i srol 'byed lo tsā[39] ba pa tshab nyi ma grags dang/ de'i dngos slob zhang thang sag pa ye shes 'byung gnas la sogs pa dang/ rma bya byang chub brtson 'grus dang/ de'i rjes 'brang gzad pa ring mo dang/ rtogs pa nang nas rdol bas nges don gyi dgongs pa rang dbang du 'chad pa lce sgom shes rab rdo rje la sogs pa nas bzung ste dpal ldan sa (S23) skya pa'i mkhas pa g.yag gzhon gnyis kyi bar du byon pa'i bod yul gyi mkhas grub mtha' bral dbu ma'i lta ba rang gis sgom zhing/ gzhan la 'chad pa (K8b) thams cad mgrin gcig dbyangs gcig tu 'di ltar gsung ste/

dbu ma'i don ni yod med dang yin min la sogs pa'i mtha' thams cad dang bral ba yin pas/ mthar 'dzin pa dang mtshan mar 'dzin pa thams cad spong dgos la/ de la thog mar bden par 'dzin pa'i yul gyi bden pa ma bkag na mthar 'dzin phyi ma rnams dgag tu med pas/ gcig dang du bral la sogs pa'i rigs pa rnams kyis phyi nang gi dngos po thams cad bden med du gtan la

39 KBS *tsa.*

> Mādhyamikas should not engage in autonomous inferences, for they do not accept the other's position,[104]

[should be interpreted to mean] that the non-acceptance of phenomena as existing by virtue of their own characteristic is posited [by Prāsaṅgikas] as a reason for not accepting autonomous [syllogisms].[105]

[Those Who Claim that the Freedom from Extremes Is the Madhyamaka]

The third system is the view of the Madhyamaka as Freedom from Extremes *(mtha' bral dbu ma'i lta ba)*, a view that has been cultivated and then explained to others as the unanimous opinion and the single melody of the scholar-practitioners of the Tibetan nation up to the time of the glorious Sa skya pa scholars G.yag and Gzhon[106] from [the time of] the spiritual friends of former times [belonging to the monastery of] of Gsang phu,[107] like the great translator Rngog,[108] the Conqueror's regent within this Abode of Snow Mountains, and [from the time of] the Lord of Sa skya and his sons,[109] who have no equal in taking up the teachings of the Victor, both in terms of explanations and practice, and great beings, like Mar pa and Mi la,[110] who have taken up the banner of the teachings of the practice lineage *(sgrub (b)rgyud)*, and the translator Pa tshab Nyi ma grags,[111] the one who introduced *(srol 'byed)* the [system of the] Madhyamaka as Freedom from Extremes [into Tibet], and his direct disciples, Zhang Thang sag pa Ye shes 'byung gnas, etc.,[112] and also Rma bya Byang chub rtson 'grus,[113] and their followers, Gzad pa ring mo,[114] Lce sgom Shes rab rdo rje,[115] and so forth, who explained in an independent manner *(rang dbang du)* the purport of the definitive meaning *(nges don gyi dgongs pa)* [of the scriptures] as it emerged from their own understanding.

Madhyamaka [literally, "the Middle Way"] refers to the freedom from all extremes, like existence and nonexistence, and *is* and *is-not (yod med dang yin min)*.[116] That is why it is necessary to eliminate all grasping at extremes and all grasping at signs *(mtshan ma)*. Furthermore, since the subsequent grasping at extremes *(mthar 'dzin phyi ma rnams)* will not be eliminated unless one first negates "the truth" that is the object of the grasping at truth, it *is* necessary to set forth the truthlessness of all things, both external and internal, by means of such reasoning as "being devoid of being one and many" *(gcig dang du bral la sogs pa'i rigs pa)*.[117] This is the rough

dbab par bya dgos/ 'dir[40] dgag bya rags pa yin zhing 'khor ba'i rgyu'i gtso bo yang yin pas/ gzhung rnams las/ de'i zhen yul bden pa 'gog byed kyi rigs pa rgyas par gsungs pa yin la/ de bkag nas bden pas (S24) stong pa nyid du bzung ba/ dper na rta la zhon pa g.yas phyogs su ma lhung yang/ g.yon phyogs su lhung ba ltar chad pa'i mthar lhung ba las ma 'das pas de yang dgag par bya ba yin no/ /de'i phyir gnyis 'dzin dang gnyis min du 'dzin pa yang bkag dgos pas mtha' bzhi gang du yang bzung ba'i yul ma rnyed pas/ der 'dzin pa med pa la dbu ma'i lta ba rtogs zhes tha snyad 'dogs pa yin gyi/ dbu ma'i lta ba 'di'o zhes mtha' gcig tu 'dzin pa byung na[41] stong mi stong sogs gang du bzung yang mthar 'dzin las ma 'das pas dbu ma'i lta ba min no zhes bzhed do//

tsong kha pa'i *'jug pa'i ṭī kar/*

> de ltar bden 'dzin legs par ngos zin na bdag 'dzin gnyis min pa'i rtog pa du ma zhig yod pa shes par 'gyur bas rtog pas gang bzung gi (K9a) yul thams cad de kho na nyid la dpyod pa'i rigs pas 'gog par 'dod (S25) pa'i log rtog thams cad zlog[42] par 'gyur ro//[43]

zhes gsungs pa yang grub mtha' 'di la dgongs par snang ngo//

lugs 'di mtha' chod pa'i rigs pa dang/ yid ches pa'i lung gis zhib tu gtan la dbab pa ni/ 'og rang lugs kyi skabs su 'chad do//

40 S *'di.*
41 K *'dzin pa gcig byung na.*
42 S *bzlog.*
43 See above, n. 32.

object-to-be-negated, and it is also the main cause of cyclic existence; and that is why the texts give extensive explanations of the forms of reasoning to negate the "truth" that is the object conceptualized *(zhen yul)* in that [ignorance]. But having negated that, [there is then a tendency to] grasp at that very emptiness of "truth" [as if *it* were a real thing]. Just as someone mounted on a horse may not fall off on the right side, but may still fall off on the left side; likewise, those [who grasp at emptiness] have not gone beyond falling into the extreme of nihilism *(chad pa'i mtha');*[118] and that is why even [the grasping at emptiness] must be refuted. And since grasping at [things] as if they were both *(gnyis 'dzin)* [empty and non-empty], and neither *(gnyis min)* must also be refuted, no object grasped in terms of the four extremes is found. It is the nongrasping [of things] in [any of those four ways] that we call "the realization of the Madhyamaka view." But if there arises a one-sided grasping of the form, "this is the Madhyamaka view," then whether one grasps thing as empty [as Tsong kha pa does] or as non-empty [as Dol po pa does], since one will not have gone beyond a grasping at extremes, this is not the Madhyamaka view. This is what we believe.

Tsong kha pa appears to have in mind this tenet [that grasping at emptiness is not improper, that holding a fixed view of the Madhyamaka is necessary] when he states in his *ṭīkā on the Avatāra:*

> When one properly identifies the grasping at "truth" in this way, one will come to understand that there are exceedingly many conceptual thoughts that are neither of the two forms of self-grasping. And [this understanding enables one] to repudiate all of the mistaken views that maintain that any object grasped by a conceptual thought is refuted by means of the reasoning that analyzes reality.[119]

The detailed exposition of this [Freedom from Extremes] system in terms of decisive reasoning and trustworthy testimony will be explained in the section [describing] our own system below.

[2.0.0.0.0. skor 'go gnyis pa:
rtag mtha' la dbu mar smra ba'i lugs dgag pa]

de ltar lugs gsum las/ dang po la mkhas pa'i dbang po red[44] mda' bas dgag pa 'di ltar mdzad de/ 'di ni theg pa che chung gi mdo sde gang gi yang dgongs pa min la/ grub mtha' smra ba bzhi po gang dang yang mi mthun zhing/ rgya bod kyi shing rta chen po su gang gi yang bzhed pa min pas/ chos 'di pa las phyi rol du gyur pa kho na yin pas/ de'i phyir sangs rgyas kyi bstan pa la gces spras su byed pa rnams kyis dgag pa bya ba kho na yin pas/ 'dir yang cung zad[45] mdor bsdus te smra bar bya'o// (S26)

de la bye brag tu smra ba dang/ mdo sde pa dag gis ni stong nyid ces pa gang zag gi bdag gis stong pa tsam la 'dod la/ de yang gang la gang med pa de ni des stong ngo[46] zhes pa'i tha snyad du ji skad bshad pa ltar rtag sogs kyis khyad par du byas pa'i bdag med la/ des stong pa'i phung po chos tsam zhig grub par 'dod la/ de yang mi rtag sdug bsngal sogs kyi rang bzhin yin gyi/ rtag sogs kyis khyad par du byas pa'i stong nyid ni cung zad kyang mi 'dod do/ /de'i phyir lugs snga ma de ni theg pa chung ngu'i mdo rnams kyi dgongs pa yang min no zhes bya bar (K9b) yang grub pa yin no//

theg pa chen po'i mdo sde'i dgongs pa 'grel bar byed pa la/ tshad ma'i skyes bur gyur pa ni 'phags pa klu sgrub dang/ 'phags pa thogs med gnyis las/ klu sgrub kyi gzhung lugs las byung ba'i stong nyid ni rnam pa gnyis te/ [1] rigs pas dpyad pa'i stong (S27) nyid dang/ [2] rnal 'byor pas so so rang gis rigs par bya ba'i stong nyid do/ /dang po ni/ gang zag gi bdag gi stong pa nyid dang/ chos kyi bdag gi stong pa nyid do//

44 KB *re.*
45 BS *zad* omitted.
46 S *nga.*

2: The Refutation of Dol po pa[120]

[The Refutation of the System that Advocates that the Extreme of Eternalism Is the Madhyamaka]

THE FIRST OF THE THREE SYSTEMS was refuted by Red mda' ba,[121] the lord of scholars, as follows. [He states that] it is not the purport of any of the sūtra traditions, whether Maha- or Hīna-yāna; that it is not compatible with any of the four philosophical schools; and that it is not accepted by any Mahāyānist, whether Indian or Tibetan.[122] Hence, it cannot *but* fall outside of the [Buddhist] Dharma and, therefore, anyone who holds the Buddha's teachings dear should do nothing but refute it. This [view of Red mda' ba] will now be briefly expanded upon here.

The Vaibhāṣikas and Sautrāntikas believe that the term "emptiness" refers only to the emptiness of the self of persons. Moreover, in accordance with what has been explained [in the scriptures], namely, that whenever *x* is lacking in *y*, then *y* is said to be empty of *x*,[123] they believe that there is no self that has the qualities of permanence and so forth; but they believe that the aggregates that are empty [of qualities like permanence] exist as mere *dharmas (chos tsam zhig grub pa)*.[124] These [aggregates], in turn, are by nature impermanent, painful, and so forth. But [the Vaibhāṣikas] do not in the least believe in an emptiness that possesses the quality of permanence and so forth. Therefore, that former system—[that is, the system of Dol po pa]—does not represent the purport of the sūtras of the Hīnayāna. This is how he [Red mda' ba] proves [his first point].

[Nor is such a view, according to Red mda' ba, the intention of the Mahāyāna.] The trustworthy *(tshad ma'i)* commentators on the purport of the Mahāyāna sūtras are the ārya Nāgārjuna and the ārya Asaṅga. There are two kinds of emptiness found in the treatises of Nāgārjuna: (1) the emptiness that is rationally analyzed *(rigs pas dpyad pa'i stong nyid)*, and (2) the emptiness that is to be intuited by yogis themselves *(rnal 'byor pas so sor rang gis rig par bya ba'i stong nyid)*.[125] The first of these [is further subdivided into] the emptiness of the self of persons and the emptiness of the self of phenomena.

de la dang po ni re zhig phung khams skye mched rnams la 'jig rten pa dang phyi rol pa rnams kyis kun brtags pa'i gang zag dang/ bdag dang skyes bu sogs yul la longs spyod pa po'i rang bzhin bkag nas phung sogs chos tsam du sgrub par byed pa yin te/ ji skad du *'jig rten las 'das par bstod pa* las/

> phung po tsam las grol ba yi//
> sems can med par khyod bzhed lags[47]//

zhes gsungs pa ltar ro//

gnyis pa ni/ phyi nang gi khams skye mched rnams la rang gzhan gyi grub mtha' smra ba rnams kyis[48] kun brtags[49] pa'i[50] rtag mi rtag yod med/ skye mi skye sogs thams cad bkag nas rten cing 'brel bar 'byung ba sgyu ma tsam zhig tu zad par ston par byed do/ /(S28) de nyid las/

> blo ldan khyod kyis phung po de'ang[51]//
> sgyu ma smig rgyu dri za yi//
> grong khyer rmi lam ji bzhin[52] du//
> blo ldan rnams la khyod kyis[53] bstan//

ces gsungs so// 'di dag ni rigs pa'i rjes su 'brang ba'i thos bsam gyi shes pas dpyad nas stong par bzhag pa yin pa'i phyir/ rnam grangs pa'i (K10a) stong pa nyid ces bya'o//

gnyis pa ni/ 'phags pa rnams kyi so so rang gis rig pa'i ye shes kyis brjod du med pa'i tshul du rtogs par bya ba'i stong pa nyid don dam pa'i bden pa zhes tha snyad du btags pa gang yin pa de ni yod med/ rtag chad stong mi stong sogs spros pa'i mtha' gang du yang tshig gi lam nas bstan par mi nus pa tha snyad thams cad kyi yul las 'das pa zhig yin no//

de lta bu'i chos nyid stong pa nyid de yang ci ltar snang ba'i rten cing

47 *Lokātītastava,* v. 2. Lindtner, *Nagarjuniana,* 128: *la.*
48 K *kyis* omitted.
49 KB *brtag.*
50 K *ba.*
51 KBS *phung po de'ang. Lokātītastava,* v.3. Lindtner, *Nagarjuniana,* 128: *phung de 'ang.*
52 KBS *'jig rten.* Lindtner, *Nagarjuniana,* 128: *ji bzhin.*
53 KBS *khyod kyis.* Lindtner, *Nagarjuniana,* 128: *rab tu.*

[Let us consider] the first of these [latter two forms of emptiness]. Worldly beings *('jig rten pa)* and non-Buddhists *(phyi rol pa)* [have a notion of] a person *(gang zag)*, a self *(bdag)*, a being *(skye bu)*, and so forth, which they impute, at times onto the aggregates *(phung)*, and at other times onto the elements *(khams)* or onto the sense spheres *(skye mched)*. [The emptiness of the self of the person] is the negation of [the fact that such a self] is by nature the agent that utilizes [or possesses] objects *(yul la longs spyod pa po)* [such as the aggregates], so that [in the wake of that negation] the aggregates, etc., come to be established as mere phenomena *(chos tsam du grub pa)*. As the *Lokātītastava* states:

> You [the Buddha] yourself accept that there is no sentient being
> That is different from the mere aggregates.[126]

The second, [that is, the emptiness of the self of phenomena,] is the negation of all [distinctions like] permanent/impermanent, existence/nonexistence, arising/nonarising, and so forth, that are imputed by philosophers, both Buddhist and non-Buddhist, in regard to the internal and external elements *(khams)* and onto the sense spheres *(skye mched)*, so that [in the wake of that negation] they are demonstrated as nothing but mere illusions that arise interdependently.

That very [text] states:

> You, oh Wise One, have taught this
> To [other] wise ones:
> That *even the aggregates* are like illusions, mirages,
> Fairy cities, and dreams.[127]

Because these are forms of emptiness [that are arrived at] through an analysis based on rational *(rigs pa'i rjes su 'brang ba'i)* study and contemplation *(thos bsam)*, they are called "emptinesses in name only" *(rnam grangs pa'i stong pa nyid)*.[128]

The second [principal form of emptiness] is labeled "emptiness as the ultimate truth that is realized ineffably by āryans' own intuitive gnosis" *('phags pa rnams kyis so so rang gi rig pa'i ye shes)*.[129] This cannot be taught linguistically—that is, in terms of any of the proliferative extremes *(spros pa'i mtha')* like existence/nonexistence, eternalism/nihilism, empty/nonempty, and so forth; it is beyond being the referent of any term.[130]

Such a reality—that is, such an emptiness—is the essence *(rang bzhin)* of

'brel bar 'byung ba sgyu ma lta bu 'di'i rang bzhin yin gyi 'di las logs su grub pa ni (S29) cung zad kyang med do//

gsum po 'di las gzhan pa'i stong gzhi don dam par grub pa la/ dgag bya kun rdzob bkag pa'i stong pa nyid ces bya ba cung zad kyang bzhed pa min te/ *rtsa ba shes rab* las/

> gal te stong min cung zad yod//
> stong pa cung zad yod par 'gyur//
> mi stong cung zad yod min na//
> stong pa'ang yod par ga la 'gyur//

zhes stong gzhi ma grub pas/ stong pa yang ma grub par gsungs la/ yang de nyid las/ rgyal ba rnams kyis stong pa nyid// ces sogs stong nyid la bden par 'dzin pa rnams gsor mi rung ba'i lta ba can du gsungs pa'i phyir ro//

gal te rigs tshogs dag las rang stong tsam las ma bstan la/ bstod tshogs las gzhan stong don dam pa'i bden pa bstan pa yin no zhe na/ bstod tshogs las kyang de bzhin du don dam par grub par ston pa'i tshig cung zad kyang med kyi rigs tshogs dang mthun par spros pa'i (S30) mtha' (K10b) thams cad 'gog par mdzad do// de'i phyir gzhan stong smra ba'i lugs 'di ni 'phags pa klu sgrub kyi lugs las phyi rol du gyur pa yin no//

byams chos phyi ma gsum dang/ thogs med sku mched kyi gzhung las byung ba'i stong pa nyid ni rnam pa gsum ste/

- rang gi mtshan nyid kyi stong pa nyid dang/
- de bzhin du yod pa min pa'i stong pa nyid[54] dang/
- rang bzhin gyi stong pa nyid do//

dang po ni kun brtags[55] / gnyis pa ni gzhan dbang/ gsum pa ni yongs grub

54 KSB *nyid* omitted.
55 K *brtag*.

this interdependent [world] of appearances, which is like an illusion. Nothing whatsoever exists in any other way; [that is, there is nothing that is not empty].

[The Mahāyāna sources] do not in the least accept, [as Dol po pa does,] an emptiness different from the three [just mentioned][131]—one that negates the conventional as its object-to-be-negated [and that posits] the empty basis *(stong gzhi)* as an ultimately existent thing—for the *Prajñāmūla [madhyamaka kārikas]* states:

> If there were some thing that were not empty,
> Then the empty [quality of things] might exist;
> But because there is nothing whatsoever that is not empty,
> How can the empty [quality] exist?[132]

This is stating that because the empty basis *(stong gzhi)* does not exist, the [quality of being] empty also does not exist. Again, in that same [text, the verse that begins] "The Victors have said that emptiness..."[133] states that those who grasp emptiness as [if it were a] true [thing, as Dol po pa does,] have a view that is incurable.

[It is wrong] to claim, [as Dol po pa does,] that the philosophical works *(rigs tshogs)* [of Nāgārjuna] only teach the emptiness of self *(rang stong)*[134] and that the compendium of praises *(bstod tshogs)* teaches the ultimate truth, the emptiness of what is other *(gzhan stong)*.[135] There is not a single line even in the compendium of praises that teaches [anything] to exist ultimately, as [Dol po pa claims]. Instead, the latter [compendium] is consistent with the philosophical works in its negation of all proliferative extremes. Therefore, this system that advocates the emptiness of what is other falls outside of the system of the ārya Nāgārjuna.

[Nor is the interpretation of Dol po pa in accord with the works of Maitreya and Asaṅga.] The emptiness found in the last three works of Maitreya and in the texts of Asaṅga and his brother [Vasubandhu] is of three kinds:

1. the emptiness of own characteristic *(rang gi mtshan nyid kyi stong pa nyid)*,
2. the empti[ness] [that is the fact that things] do not exist as [they appear] *(de bzhin du yod pa min pa'i stong pa)*, and
3. the emptiness *qua* essence *(rang bzhin gyi stong pa nyid)*.[136]

The first [is a quality] of the imaginary *(kun brtags)*, the second of the dependent *(gzhan dbang)*, and the third is [itself] the real *(yongs grub)*.[137]

bo/ /de las gzhan dbang rang gi mtshan nyid kyis grub cing/ de la kun brtags[56] kyis stong pa'i stong nyid yongs grub don dam par yod pas rtag chad dang bral bas dbu ma'i lam du bzhed de/ *dbus mtha'* las/

yang dag ma yin kun rtog yod//
de la gnyis po yod pa min//
stong pa nyid ni 'di la yod//
de la yang ni de yod do//

stong pa yang min mi stong min//
yod pas med (S31) pas yod pas na//
de lta bas na thams cad bshad//
'di ni dbu ma'i lam yin no//

zhes gsungs so/ /de ltar na gzhan dbang dang/ kun brtags kyis stong pa'i yongs grub gzhan stong bden par grub bo/ zhes pa'i tshul 'di ni/ 'phags pa byams pa dang/ thogs med sku mched kyi gzhung dang mi mthun te/ de dag gi ltar na kun brtags[57] bzhin du gzhan dbang yang rang gi mtshan nyid kyis ma grub pa 'gyur dgos na/ gzhung 'di dag tu ni gzhan dbang ni sgyu ma'i sprul gzhi ltar yang dag par rdzas su grub par[58] bshad pa'i phyir/

de'i phyir (K11a) 'di ni theg pa chen po'i mdo sde rnams kyi dgongs pa dang de'i dgongs 'grel rnam rig pa dang/ dbu ma'i grub mtha' las kyang phyi rol du gyur pa yin no/ /zhes bya ba legs par grub pa yin no/ /'di rnams ni kho bos grub mtha' ngan pa 'di'i mtshang[59] rags[60] pa cung zad cig smos par zad kyi/ zhib (S32) mor dpyad na/ mdo sde la mi 'jug/ 'dul bar mi snang/ mngon pa'i chos nyid dang 'gal ba sogs lung dang/ rigs pa'i gnod byed du ma zhig yod mod kyi 'dir ni dkyus ma 'chad pa'i gegs su 'gyur ba'i phyir ma spros so/ /zhes pa'i dgag pa mdzad do//

56 KB *btags.*
57 K *brtag.*
58 KBS *pa.*
59 K *mchang.*
60 KB *rag.*
61 B / omitted.

From this [one can infer that Asaṅga and Vasubandhu] believe that the dependent exists by virtue of its own characteristic and that the real—that is, emptiness, the emptiness of the imaginary in the [dependent]—ultimately exists *(don dam par yod pas)*. It is for this reason that [they consider their view to be] free from eternalism and nihilism, and therefore [to be] the Middle Way, because, as the *Madhyāntavibhāga* states:

> That which is imperfectly conceived, [that is, the dependent,]
> does exist,
> But there is no duality within it.
> Emptiness does exist within it,
> And, as regards that [emptiness], it [too] exists.
>
> That is why everything is explained to be
> Neither empty nor non-empty:
> Because of existence, nonexistence and existence.
> This is the Middle Way.[138]

[But Dol po pa's] method of interpreting [these texts] such that the real, being empty of what is other—that is, empty of the dependent and the imaginary—truly exists is incompatible with the texts of the ārya Maitreya, Asaṅga, and his brother [Vasubandhu]. Why? Because like the imaginary, the dependent too could not exist by virtue of its own characteristic. But in those texts [of Maitreya and Asaṅga,] the dependent is explained to really exist as a substance *(yang dag par rdzas su grub pa)*, just like the basis of an illusory manifestation *(sgyu ma'i sprul gzhi)*.[139]

Therefore, this [view] falls outside the purport of the Mahāyāna sūtras, outside of the Vijñapti[mātra] and Madhyamaka philosophical schools, and outside of their commentarial traditions. This is how [Red mda' ba's position] is correctly established. These [above lines] represent just a brief overview on our part of the grossest errors found in these evil philosophical tenets. If these were analyzed in more detail, they would be found to miss [the point of] the sūtras, to not appear in the vinaya, and to contradict the abhidharma;[140] but despite the fact that there are many scriptural and logical refutations [of this position], I will not go into them here for fear that this might act as an obstacle to the continuity of my explanation. This is how [Red mda' ba] refutes [Dol po pa].[141]

'on kyang 'di'i phyogs snga phyi rnams la brtags na 'di ltar mthong ste/

phyogs snga ma'i lugs de theg pa che chung gang gi lugs min pas chos 'di pa las phyi rol du gyur pa'o/ /zhes pa ni skur pa ches pa'i skyon te/ bka' phyi ma byams chos phyi ma dang/ thogs med sku mched kyis bkral ba'i lugs nges don du byas nas yongs grub don dam pa'i bden pa ma gtogs pa'i chos gzhan thams cad bden med du gtan la phab zin pas/ dngos smra ba gzhan rnams las khyad par du 'phags shing/ dbu ma'i lta ba skye ba la tshegs med pa'i lugs yin pa'i (S33) phyir/

sems tsam pa'i grub mtha' min pa'i shes byed du gzhan dbang bden grub tu mi 'dod pa'i phyir/ ces pa yang ma nges te/ *dbus mtha'* dang/ *theg bsdus* la sogs pa sems tsam pa'i gzhung phal cher du/ gzhan dbang rang gi mtshan nyid kyis grub par gsungs kyang/ de ltar du khas len pa'i sems tsam pa de dbu (K11b) ma par blo sbyong ba'i tshe gzhan dbang bden med du gtan la phab zin nas/ chos nyid yongs grub la bden 'dzin gyi lhag ma lus pa gcig nges par 'dod dgos pa'i phyir/

gzhan dbang dang bden med kyi gzhi mthun khas blangs pa tsam gyis sems tsam pa min par mi 'gyur te/ rnam bden rdzun rtsod pa'i gzhir gyur pa'i rnam pa de/[61] gzhan dbang las ma 'das pas/ sems tsam rnam rdzun pa yang sems tsam pa min par 'gyur ba'i skyon yod pa'i phyir ro/ /gal te[62] de yang kun brtags yin no snyam na/ 'o na de sems tsam rnam bden (S34) pas bden par khas blangs par mi 'thad par 'gyur te/ kun brtags yin pa'i phyir/

'o na ji ltar snyam na/ rje btsun shes bya kun rig gi zhal snga nas lugs 'di sems tsam pa'i lta ba drag shos dbu mar cung zad ma slebs pa zhig yin gsungs pa de nyid don la gnas te/

[a] gzhan dbang bden med du gtan la phab zin nas yongs grub la bden 'dzin gyi lhag ma lus pa'i phyir dang/

62 K *da.*
63 S *khas* omitted.

Nonetheless, if one were to investigate this further [by framing it as a conversation] between a proponent [of Dol po pa's views] and an opponent [i.e., Red mda' ba], this is how I imagine that it might proceed:

[Defender of Dol po pa:][142] To say that, since it is neither a Mahāyāna nor a Hīnayāna system, the system of the proponent [i.e., of Dol po pa] falls outside of the Buddhist tradition, is to excessively slander [this view]. Why? [The followers of Dol po pa] take the final [turning of the wheel of the Buddha's] word,[143] the last [three] works of Maitreya, and the commentarial tradition of Asaṅga and his brother to be of definitive meaning. Having done so, they posit all phenomena except for the real—that is, the ultimate truth—to be truthless. Hence, [their view] is superior to that of other realists, and it is a system that leads effortlessly to the generation of the Madhyamaka view.[144]

Nor is it definitely the case that *not* accepting the dependent to be truly existing can be taken as proof for the fact that [a view] is not Cittamātra in its philosophical stance. Why? Most Cittamātra texts, like the *Madhyānta-[vibhāga]* and the *Mahāyānasaṃgraha,* state that the dependent exists by virtue of its own characteristic. Nonetheless, when the Cittamātras who accept this [position—that the dependent exists by virtue of its own characteristic—] train their minds as Mādhyamikas, they [eventually come to] consider the dependent as truthless. But having done so, it must be accepted that they still have a slight trace of true grasping left in regard to reality, that is, in regard to the real.[145] Simply accepting that there is something that is both dependent and truthless does not disqualify one from being a Cittamātra, for that would mean that the Cittamātras who believe in false aspects *(rnam rdzun)* are not Cittamātras, since the "aspects" that are the locus of controversy between "those who accept true aspects" and "those who accept false aspects" can be none other than the dependent.[146] And if you think that [those aspects do not refer to the dependent, but rather to the] imaginary *(kun brtags)*, then it would not be fitting for the Cittamātras who accept true aspects to accept [those aspects] as true, for they would be imaginary.

Well, what are we to make of this? The remarks of the Lord [Rong ston] Shes bya kun rig are relevant here.[147] He says that this system [of Dol po pa] represents the most refined view of the Cittamātra, falling just short of the Madhyamaka. How so?

a. Having posited the dependent to be truthless, there remain [within this view] traces of grasping at the truth of the real;

[b] *mdo sde dgongs pa nges 'grel* gyi dngos bstan nges don du khas blangs pa'i phyir dang/

[c] thogs med sku mched dang/ phyogs glang chos grags rnams la dbu ma pa chen po zhes pa'i tha snyad mdzad nas/ de dag gi gzhung lugs la dbu ma'i gzhung lugs su khas blangs pa'i phyir dang/

[d] gsung rab kyi dgongs pa 'grel bar byed pa'i sgo yang/ kun brtags gzhan dbang yongs grub gsum gyi sgo nas gtso bor mdzad pa'i phyir ro//

rjes (S35) 'brang dag na re/ sems tsam pa'i lugs min te/ de ni dngos smra ba yin la/ dngos smra ba yin na/ dngos (K12a) po dang bden grub kyi gzhi mthun khas len dgos pa las 'dir dngos po yin na bden par med pas khyab par khas[63] blangs pa'i phyir/ zhes zer ba mi 'thad de/ 'gal ba lhag po khas blangs pa ma gtogs pa don la khyad par mi snang ba'i phyir te/ shes pa dang bden grub kyi gzhi mthun khas blangs pa'i phyir/

gal te/ 'phags pa klu sgrub kyi gzhung lugs tshad mar khas blangs pas/ dbu ma pa yin no snyam na yang/ 'di ni ma nges te/ klu sgrub la brgal ma nus pas de'i gzhung lugs 'khyog por bshad nas/ rang gi grub mtha' la sbyar ba'i phyir/ klu sgrub kyi dgongs pa gtan nas min te/ *rtsa ba shes rab* las/

skye dang gnas dang 'jig pa dag/
ma grub phyir na 'dus byas med/
'dus byas rab tu ma grub pas/
'dus ma byas (S36) ni ji ltar grub/

ces bden par grub pa yod na/ bden par grub pa'i 'os su gyur pa 'dus byas yang bden par ma grub na 'dus ma byas ci'i phyir bden par[64] grub ces gsungs la/ khyod 'dus ma byas yongs grub bden grub tu 'dod pa'i phyir/

gal te skyon med de/ gzhung 'di dang/ *rtsod zlog* las/

64 KB *pa.*

b. it accepts the actual teachings *(dngos bstan)* of the *Saṃdhinirmocana Sūtra* to be of definitive meaning [as the Cittamātra does];[148]
c. [the followers of Dol po pa] call Asaṅga and his brother, as well as Dignāga and Dharmakīrti, [all classical Cittamātras,] "Great Mādhyamikas," and having done so, they consider their textual traditions to be the textual tradition of the Madhyamaka School; and
d. they consider the key to the exegesis of the scriptures to be principally the three [natures: that is,] the imaginary, the dependent, and the real.

The claim made by some followers—namely that this system [of Dol po pa] is *not* Cittamātra [in its orientation], for those [Cittamātras] are realists and realists must accept that there are entities that truly exist, whereas in this system *all* entities are [considered] truthless—is not correct. Why? All they have done is to accept an additional contradiction. Aside from that, there does not appear to be anything new here. [Whence the additional contradiction? Cittamātras] accept that there are consciousnesses [and hence entities] that truly exist.

However, it is not true, [as some defenders of Dol po pa claim,] that anyone who accepts the textual tradition of the ārya Nāgārjuna as authoritative [as Dol po pa does] must necessarily be a Mādhyamika. There is no certainty to this, for there are those who, unable to oppose *(brgal)* Nāgārjuna, amalgamate [his views] to their own [faulty] philosophical views by rapidly glossing over his texts. That this [view of Dol po pa] is not at all what Nāgārjuna had in mind is witnessed by the following lines from the *Prajñāmūla:*

> Because arising, abiding, and ceasing
> Are not established, there are no composite entities *('dus byas).*
> And when composite entities are not established,
> How could noncomposite entities *('dus ma byas)* be established?[149]

This is saying that if there were such a thing as true existence, then composite entities should be the best candidates for being truly existent. If, on the other hand, [the latter] are not truly existent, then how could noncomposite [phenomena] be truly existent? But you [Dol po pa's followers] believe that the real, which is non-composite, truly exists.

[Defender of Dol po pa:] There is no fault [here], for this passage and the following one from the *Vigrahavyāvartanī* that teach the freedom from the

gal te ngas dam bca'[65] 'ga' yod//
des na nga la skyon 'di[66] yod//
nga la dam bca' med pas na//
nga ni[67] skyon med kho na yin//

ces pa dang/ stong ngo zhes kyang mi brjod de/ zhes sogs mtha' bzhi'i spros bral gsungs pa rnams ni/ mnyam bzhag la zlo'i gnas skabs yin gyi rjes thob shan 'byed gnas skabs min no/ mnyam bzhag la zlo'i don ni/ 'phags (K12b) pa'i mnyam bzhag ngor 'dus byas dang/ 'dus ma byas kyi chos gang yang bden par mi[68] snang zhing/ yod med sogs mtha' bzhi gang du (S37) yang mi 'dzin pa'i don yin pas/ mnyam bzhag zag med kyi blo'i 'dzin stangs 'chad pa yin la/ rjes thob shan 'byed kyi don yang rjes thob yul gyi gnas lugs la dpyod pa'i tshe/ 'di ni bden par grub/ 'di[69] ni bden par ma grub ces so sor 'byed pa'o zhes smra'o//

de shin tu mi 'thad de/ 'dus ma byas ma grub par gsungs pa[70] de mnyam bzhag la zlo'i gnas skabs yin na/ 'dus byas ma grub par gsungs pa de yang mnyam bzhag la zlo'i skabs yin par 'dod dgos shing/ 'dod pa'ang yin la/ de ltar na mtshan nyid skye gnas 'jig gsum rigs pas dpyad nas 'gog pa don med du thal ba'i phyir ro//

des na 'di ni rjes thob shan 'byed kyi gnas skabs yin te/ bden 'dzin ni 'dus byas phung po lnga la zhugs pa shas che bas/ 'dus byas bden med du gtan la phab pa'i rigs pa rgyas par gsungs nas/ 'dus (S38) ma byas la bden 'dzin ches chung bas de bden med du sgrub pa'i rigs pa[71] rgyas par[72] ma gsungs

65 KBS *bcas*. *Vigrahavyāvartanī*, v. 29. Lindtner, *Nagarjuniana*, 80: *bca'*.
66 KBS *'di*. Lindtner, *Nagarjuniana*, 80: *de*.
67 KBS *ni*. Lindtner, *Nagarjuniana*, 80: *la*.
68 K *min*.
69 K *'da*.
70 K *par*.
71 KB *par*.
72 S *pa*.

proliferations of the four extremes apply only within the context of equipoise *(mnyam bzhag la zlo)*,[150] and not within the context of the aftermath state, where distinctions [once again] arise [in the mind]. [The passage is:]

> If I had any thesis *(dam bca')*,
> Then I would suffer from this fault.
> But as I have no theses,
> It is I alone who am without fault.[151]

As well as the passage that [begins], "I do not claim [that things are] 'empty'..."[152] What does "in the context of equipoise" mean? No phenomenon—whether composite or noncomposite—appears to be true within the equipoise of āryans; and there is no grasping [at things] in terms of the four extremes—like existence, nonexistence, and so forth—[when one is in such a meditative state]. This is what [these passages] mean. Hence, [Nāgārjuna is here] explaining how it is that the stainless mind of equipoise apprehends things. But as regards the aftermath state, wherein distinctions *are* made, when the aftermath [cognition] analyzes the nature of its object, it does make distinctions: "This truly exists" or "This does not truly exist."

[Reply:] This is utterly incorrect. Why? If the [passage that] states that the non-composite is not established were referring to the context of equipoise, you should accept that the passage that states that the composite is not established is also referring to the period of equipoise; and, in fact, you do accept that. But if that were so, it would follow, absurdly, that the analysis and subsequent negation of the three characteristics of [composite phenomena]—arising, abiding, and cessation—would be purposeless [since the nonexistence of these three things would also have to be occurring in the context of equipoise, where their emptiness is already being understood directly].

Therefore, this [negation of the true existence of the noncomposite refers] to the period of the aftermath state during which distinctions are made. Why? The grasping at truth focuses primarily on the five composite aggregates, and it is because of this that there are extensive reasons given to establish the truthlessness of composite [things]. Given that grasping at the truth of the non-composite is much more rare, [the text] does not extensively teach the reasoning that establishes the truthlessness of that [i.e., of the non-composite] and instead teaches the latter in a brief way, stating, "if

par/ dgag bya 'dus byas bden par ma grub pas/ de bkag pa'i 'dus ma byas bden par ma grub ces bsdus te gsungs pa'i phyir ro//

'di ni 'phags yul gyi mkhas pa chen po rnams kyi 'chad tshul rmad du byung ba ste/ dpal ldan chos kyi grags pas/ dngos po'i yul can gyi sgra rtog sel 'jug tu sgrub pa'i rigs pa rgyas par gsungs nas/ dngos med kyi yul can gyi sgra rtog sel 'jug (K13a) tu sgrub pa'i rigs pa tshigs su bcad pa gcig gis bsdus pa bzhin no//

rtsod zlog gi lung don/ mnyam bzhag la zlo'i skabs la sbyar na dbu ma pas dngos smra ba'i rtsod pa bzlog pa de mnyam bzhag gi skabs yin gyi/ rjes thob kyi gnas skabs min par khas blangs dgos pas gad pa la thug kyang phyir ldog mi shes pa'o//

des na yul gyi gnas lugs (S39) bden par grub kyang 'phags pa'i mnyam bzhag la bden pa mi snang bar 'dod pa la ni/ rje btsun grags pa rgyal mtshan gyis/

> rnal 'byor spyod pa pa rnams kyang dbu ma par 'dod/ sangs rgyas kyi ye shes spros pa thams cad dang bral bar 'dod pa yin mod kyi/ khyed rang gi 'dod pa dang nang 'gal bas de ltar 'dod pa ni mi grub bo zhes sun phyung ste rnam par[73] 'jog go//

zhes gsungs pa 'di nyid btegs nas mgo bo'i thog tu bzhag par bya ste/ yul gyi gnas lugs bden par grub na gnas lugs rtogs pa'i blo la bden pa mi snang ba 'gal ba'i phyir ro//

gang dag rtag lta phugs su 'tshang zhing spyod lam bde ba'i phyir gzhan gyi grub mtha' la kha g.yar ba'i blo rtsing dag gis sa jo gnyis lta ba'i gnad la mi mthun pa med do/ /zhes zer ba ni/ rje btsun grags pa rgyal mtshan gyis/

> gal te don dam par yod do zhe na/ 'o (S40) na yod pa'i mthar[74]

73 KB *pa.*
74 KB *mtha'.*

the composite, the object to be negated, does not truly exist, then the noncomposite, which is its negation, cannot truly exist."

This is the amazing explanatory method of the great scholars of the Noble Land [of India]. It is just like [the case in which] the glorious Dharmakīrti extensively teaches the reasoning that establishes [the fact that] speech and conceptual thoughts *(sgra rtog)* that possess entities as their objects *(dngos po'i yul can)* engage [their objects] in a negative way *(sel 'jug du)*, whereas he condenses into a single verse the reasoning that establishes [the fact that] speech and conceptual thought that possess *nonentities* as their objects *(dngos med kyi yul can)* engage [their objects] in a negative way.[153]

If the *Vigrahavyāvartanī* passage were to be interpreted as referring to the period of equipoise, then the Madhyamaka's refutation of the realists' arguments would also have to be accepted as applying to the period of equipoise and not to that of the aftermath state. So even when you have come up to a cliff, you do not know how to turn back.

That is why the Lord Grags pa rgyal mtshan (1147–1216) has directed the following lines to [the likes of you] who accept that, despite the fact that reality truly exists, truth does not appear to the equipoise of āryans, [the individuals who are in intimate contact with such a reality]:

> You accept that Yogācāras are Mādhyamikas, and you also accept that a buddha's gnosis is free from all proliferations. But this is internally contradictory to your own beliefs [i.e., that a buddha's gnosis cognizes an ultimate truth that is real]. Hence, to accept things as you do is like repudiating something by saying, "it is not established," and then [turning around] and positing it.

You should take this passage and lift it to the top of your head [as a sign of respect], for if the reality *(gnas lugs)* of objects truly exists, it contradicts the fact that truth does not appear to the mind that understands reality.

Certain persons of unrefined mental faculty, who harbor within themselves an eternalistic view and who take sides with the philosophical views of others for the sake of diplomacy, claim that the Sa [skya] and Jo [nang pa] schools are not incompatible as regards their philosophical view.[154]

[It is obvious] that those who claim this have not even seen, [much less understood,] what the Lord Grags pa rgyal mtshan has said:

> *[Opponent:]* There is ultimate existence.

> lhung ba'i phyir dbu ma pa'i lam min par 'gyur ro/ /'o na khyod don dam du med par 'dod pa'i phyir khyed kyang med pa'i mthar lhung bar 'gyur ro zhe na/ kho bo cag don dam par yod par ma grub (K13b) pa'i phyir med par ni mi 'dod do/ /'o na khyed gang du 'dod ce na kho bo cag kun rdzob tu ji ltar gnas pa de ltar 'dod de/ kun rdzob tu chad pa'i mtha' las grol la don dam par gang du yang 'dod pa med pas mtha' thams cad las grol bas dbu ma zhes bya'o//

zhes gsungs pa 'di tsam yang ma mthong bar zad do//

des na bden pa la/ mya ngan 'das pa bden gcig pu/ zhes gsungs pa ltar[75] mi bslu ba la bden par byas pa dang/ don dam par ma grub par gsungs pa'i/ dgag bya la bden grub tu byas pa gnyis[76] las/ dang po ni/ dbu ma pa rnams kyang tha snyad du yod par 'dod la/ phyi ma la ltos pa'i (S41) bden pa/ ji srid khas len gyi bar du dbu ma par 'gyur ba'i go skabs med do//

de dag gis ni lugs dang po la sgro skur dang bral ba'i rab dbye bstan zin to//

75 BS *lta bu.*
76 K *gnyas.*

[Reply:] Well then, [you] are not [a follower of] the Madhyamaka, for [you] have fallen into the extreme of existence.

[Opponent:] Well then, since you accept [that things] do not ultimately exist, *you* have fallen into the extreme of nonexistence.

[Reply:] We do not accept things to be nonexistent simply because we accept that [they] do not ultimately exist.

[Opponent:] Well then, what *do* you accept [about the nature of things]?

[Reply:] We accept things just as they are conventionally. This frees us from the extreme of nihilism in regard to the conventional [world]. But because we have no beliefs at all at the ultimate level, we are free from all extremes. That is [why our view is the true] "Middle Way."[155]

Therefore, as regards "truth," there is a sense of [the word] "truth" in which it refers to what is nondeceptive *(mi slu ba)*, as in the expression "Nirvāṇa is the sole truth." Then there is a second [sense] in which it refers to true existence *qua* object-to-be-negated, [as] in the expression "[things] do not ultimately [or truly] exist." Even Mādhyamikas believe that the first [notion of truth] exists nominally. But to the extent that one accepts the notion of truth in the second [sense of the term], to that extent is one impeded from the possibility of being a Mādhyamika.

With these [reflections]—an analysis that is free of both under- and overestimating *(sgro skur)* the first system [that is, the system of Dol po pa]—we conclude our exposition.

[3.0.0.0.0 skor 'go gsum pa: chad mtha' la dbu mar smra ba'i lugs dgag pa]

da ni lugs gnyis pa la lung rigs kyis[77] dpyad pa cung zad brjod par bya ste/

[3.1.0.0.0 don dam gyi rnam bzhag la dpyad pa]

de la dngos po la bden par 'dzin pa'i bden 'dzin nyes pa thams cad kyi rtsa ba yin pas de'i zhen yul sun phyung dgos pa shin tu 'thad kyang/ [a] rigs pas btsal ba'i tshe ma rnyed pa'i bden pa bkag tsam gyi stong nyid med dgag de nyid don dam bden pa mtshan nyid pa yin par 'dod pa dang/ [b] stong nyid der mngon par zhen pa dgag bya ma yin par 'dod pa dbu ma'i gzhung lugs las 'das te/ *bden gnyis rang 'grel* du *mdo* drangs pa las/

> de la kun rdzob kyi bden pa gang zhe na/ ji snyed 'jig rten gyi (S42) tha snyad gdags pa dang/ yi ge dang/ (K14a) skad dang/ brda bstan pa dag go//[78]don dam pa'i bden pa ni gang la sems kyi rgyu ba yang med na/[79] yi ge rnams lta smos kyang ci dgos

zhes gsungs shing/ de'i don *bden gnyis* las/

> yod med dngos po mkhyen pa yi//

77 KBS *kyi.*
78 KBS: *gdags pa dang yi ge dang/ skad dang/ brda bstan pa dag go/. Satyadvayavibaṅgha-vṛtti,* Eckel, ed., *Jñānagarbha's Commentary,* 159: *gdags pa dang/ yi ge dang skad dang rda bstan pa dag go//.*
79 KBS *sems kyi rgyu ba yang med na/. Satyadvayavibaṅghavṛtti,* Eckel, ed., *Jñānagarbha,* 159: *sems rgyu ba yang med na* (/ omitted).

3: The Refutation of Tsong kha pa[156]

[The Refutation of the System that Advocates that the Extreme of Nihilism Is the Madhyamaka]

I WILL NOW OFFER a brief analysis of the second system, using scripture and reasoning.

[An Examination of Tsong kha pa's Exposition of the Ultimate]

It is perfectly correct [for Tsong kha pa and his followers] to maintain that since the grasping at truth—that is, the grasping at the truth of entities—is the root of all faults, it is necessary to negate *(sun phyung)* the object that it constructs *(zhen yul)*. However, they believe (a) that emptiness as an absolute negation *(med dgag)*—that is, as the mere negation *(bkag tsam)* of truth, the not finding [of something] when it is searched for by means of reasoning—is the real *(mtshan nyid pa)* ultimate truth, and (b) that thought constructions *(mngon par zhen pa)* in regard to emptiness are *not* to be negated.[157] [Both of these views] fall outside of the textual tradition of the Madhyamaka. Why? The *Satyadvayavṛtti* cites the following sūtra passage:

> What is the conventional truth? It is that which is labeled by the terminology of the world, that which is revealed by letters, language, and symbols. As for the ultimate truth, it is that in regard to which the mind becomes immobile, in which case what need is there to speak of [it being inexpressible by] letters?[158]

And as regards the meaning of that [passage], the *Satyadvaya* states:

> It is something that even the Omniscient One,

kun mkhyen pas kyang gang ma gzigs//[80]
de yi dngos po ci 'dra zhig//
shin tu zhib pa'i lta bas dpyod//

zhes don dam bden pa mtshan nyid pa ni/ so so skye bo'i blo'i yul las 'das pa 'phags pa'i mnyam bzhag zag pa med pa'i ye shes kyis kyang gnyis su snang ba nub cing/ yod med rtag chad la sogs pa'i mtha' gang du yang ma mthong ba nyid don dam bden par gsungs pa'i phyir/

gal te de ni rang rgyud pa'i lugs yin no snyam na/

thal 'gyur pa[81] rnams kyang 'di dang khyad par med de/ dpal ldan zla bas/

dngos kun yang dag rdzun pa mthong ba yis//[82]
dngos rnyed[83] ngo bo gnyis ni (S43) 'dzin par 'gyur//
yang dag mthong yul gang de de nyid[84] de//
mthong ba rdzun pa'ang[85] kun rdzob bden par gsung//

zhes dang/ *spyod 'jug* las/

don dam blo yi spyod yul min//
blo ni kun rdzob yin par 'dod[86]//

ces gsungs pa'i mthong ba yang dag pa ni/ 'phags pa'i mnyam bzhag zag pa med pa yin la/ 'jig rten pa'i blo thams cad ni mthong ba rdzun pa yin pas/

bden pa brtsal nas ma rnyed pa'i rigs shes/ rjes dpag gi dngos kyi bzung byar gyur pa'i stong nyid med dgag de kun rdzob tu 'jog dgos pa'i phyir ro//

'o na skabs 'ga' zhig tu (K14b) bden pa bkag tsam gyi stong nyid med dgag de don dam bden par gsungs pa dang/ slob dpon zla bas *rigs pa drug cu pa'i 'grel par* bden pa gnyis su 'jog pa ni 'jig rten pa'i blo la ltos nas 'jog go[87]/ /zhes gsungs pa dang 'gal lo snyam na/

80 *Satyadvayavibangha,* verse 7ab. C, vol. 28, Dbu ma *sa,* f. 2b: *yod med dngos po mkhyen pa po// kun mngon mkhyen pas gang ma gzigs;* Eckel, ed., *Jñānagarbha,* 158: *yod med dngos po mkhyen pa po// kun mnkhyen pas kyang gang ma gzigs//.*

81 K ba.

82 *Madhyamakāvatāra* (VI, 23a). P no. 5261, vol. 98, 94: *dngos kun yang dag mthong ba'i 'khrul ba yis.*

83 MA, 94: *snyed.*

84 KBS *gang de de nyid.* MA, 94: *gang yin de nyid.*

85 KBS *mthong ba rdzun pa'ang.* MA, 94: *mthong ba 'khrul ba'i.*

86 BCA, 185: *yin par brjod.*

87 These exact words are not found anywhere in Candrakīrti's text.

> Who knows all entities, both existent and not, does not perceive.
> Using the extremely detailed view, analyze
> What its nature is like.[159]

This is stating that the real ultimate truth is beyond the mental objectification of ordinary beings; it [occurs in the state in which there is] a waning of dualistic appearances *(gnyis su snang ba)* within the stainless equipoised gnosis of āryans; it is the not-seeing of [things] in terms of any of the extremes, like those of existence and nonexistence, and eternalism and nihilism.

[Opponent:] Isn't that [the definition given by] the Svātantrika system?

[Reply:] Even the Prāsaṅgikas share this [definition], for the glorious Candra[kīrti] states:

> All entities are apprehended in terms of their two natures,
> Depending upon whether they are perceived by correct or false perception.
> The object of the correct perception is reality,
> And what is seen falsely is the conventional truth.[160]

Also, the *Bodhicaryāvatāra* states:

> The ultimate is not an object of the mind.
> The mind is accepted as conventional.[161]

"Correct perception" refers to the stainless equipoise of āryans; all worldly minds are [examples of] false sight. Hence, emptiness as utter negation—that is, as the direct object *(dngos kyis gzung bya)* of inference, of the rational consciousness *(rigs shes)* that does not find truth when it searches for it—must be posited as conventional.[162]

[Opponent:] Does that not contradict the fact that emptiness as utter negation—as the mere negation of truth—is occasionally said to be the ultimate truth [in the Madhyamaka sources]; and does it not contradict the fact that the master Candra[kīrti] states in his *Yuktiṣaṣṭikāvṛtti* that positing truth to be twofold [conventional and ultimate] is done in dependence upon a worldly understanding *('jig rten pa'i blo)*?[163]

de ni bden par 'dzin pa'i blo la ltos (S44) nas bden med rtogs pas/ de'i yul la don dam par 'jog pa rnam grangs pa'i[88] don dam bden pa zhes btags pa bar 'jog go/ /'dogs pa'i rgyu mtshan ni bden pa 'dzin pa'i blo la ltos nas gnas lugs rtogs pa'i blo'i yul yin pa'i phyir/ btags pa'i dgos pa ni don dam bden pa mtshan nyid pa rtogs pa la thog mar 'di nyid rtogs dgos so/ zhes shes pa'i ched yin pa'i phyir/ dngos la gnod byed ni/ stong mi stong sogs kyi mtha' gang rung du gzung ba'i rtog pa'i dngos yul yin pa'i phyir ro//

mdor na rigs pas bden pa bkag nas bden med du bzung ba'i rtog pa'i dngos yul don dam bden pa mtshan nyid par 'dod pa ni[89]/ don dam bden pa'i don spyi la don dam bden par 'dod pa yin pas/ bum pa'i don spyi la bum par 'dod pa dang 'dra'o/ /di ni *spyod 'jug* las/

> rnal 'byor kun rdzob nyes[90] med de// (S45)
> 'jig rten la ltos de nyid mthong//

zhes dang *'jug grel* las kyang/

> zag pa med pa'i ye shes dang bral ba so so skye bo rnams kyi shes pas kyang gzigs pa zag pa med pa la gnod pa min[91] pas rnam pa de lta bu'i yul la 'jig rten gzhan[92] gyis gnod pa min[93] no//

zhes dang/ *bden gnyis* las/ (K15a)

> de bas 'di ni kun rdzob ste//
> yang dag par na[94] skye ba med[95]//

ces bya ba la sogs pa'o/ /zhes gsungs pa thams cad dgongs pa gcig par snang ngo//

88 K *ba'i.*
89 S *na.*
90 KB *nyis;* S *nyes.* BCA, 186: *nyes.*
91 *Madhyamakāvatārabhāṣya,* Toh no. 3862, Dbu ma *'a,* f. 254b: *ma yin.*
92 MABh, f. 254b and MA, 106: *gzhan* omitted.
93 MABh, f. 254b and MA, 106: *ma yin.*
94 BS *ni.*
95 *Satyadvayavibhaṅgha* (10cd). This line of the verse in Go rams pa's text varies considerably from the canonical versions. Eckel, ed., *Jñānagarbha,* 161: *yang dag don yin yang dag min//.*

[Reply:] That [passage is stating] that one understands truthlessness based upon a mind that apprehends [things] to be true; hence, [the *Yuktiṣaṣṭikāvṛtti*'s] claim that the object of that [worldly understanding] is an ultimate [truth] is done in an informal way *(btags pa ba)*, [such that the "ultimate" being referred to is] "an ultimate truth in name only *(rnam grangs pa)*." What is the *reason* for calling it that? It is because [the object of the understanding of truthlessness] is the object of a mind that understands reality based upon a mind that grasps [things] as true. What is the *purpose* of calling it that? It is because it must first be understood before one can understand the real *(mtshan nyid pa)* ultimate truth. This is how [this passage] is to be understood.[164] How would this contradict reality [if it were taken literally—that is, if the object of the conceptual cognition of truthlessness *were* the ultimate truth]? It is because it is the direct object *(dngos yul)* of a conceptual thought *(rtogs pa)* that apprehends [things] in terms of extremes, such as empty/nonempty [that it would contradict reality, since conceptual thoughts, which are by nature dualistic, cannot cognize the real ultimate truth].

In brief, take the direct object of the conceptual thought that apprehends [things] as truthless after it has negated truth through reasoning: if one accepts *this* [object] to be the real ultimate truth, then one would have to accept the generic image *(don spyi)* of the ultimate truth to be the ultimate truth. It would be like accepting the generic image of a pot to be a pot. That this [cannot be the case] is something that emerges as the common purport of each of the following passages. The *Bodhicaryāvatāra* states:

> A yogi's [use] of the conventional is faultless,
> [For] compared to the world, they see reality.[165]

And the *Avatārabhāṣya* states:

> The consciousness of an ordinary being, since it is devoid of stainless wisdom, cannot challenge [the validity of] the stainless vision [of those who see reality]. Therefore, others' [mode of perception]—that is, worldly [beings' mode of seeing things]—poses no threat to such an object [as it is perceived in āryan gnosis].[166]

And the *Satyadvaya* states:

> Therefore, that is conventional,
> But it does not really *(yang dag par)* arise.[167]

bden pa bkag zin nas de bkag pa'i stong nyid du mngon par zhen pa bkag tu mi rung bar 'dod pa ni dbu ma'i gzhung lugs kyi gnad chen po 'chug pa ste/ *mdo sdud pa* las/

phung 'di stong zhes rtog na'ang byang chub sems dpa' ni//
mtshan ma la spyod skye med gnas la dad ma yin//

ces dang/ *yum bar ma* las/

gzugs stong (S46) zhes bya bar spyod na mtshan ma la spyod do/
gzugs mi stong zhes bya bar spyod na mtshan ma la spyod do//

zhes sogs gnyis 'dzin mtha' dag dgag byar gsungs pa'i phyir dang/ de dag gi don *mngon rtogs rgyan* las/

gzugs sogs phung po stong nyid la[96]/[...]
spyod pa'i 'du shes mi mthun phyogs/

zhes dang/ theg pa chen po'i sbyor lam gyi skabs su/ rtag mi rtag sogs kyi mtha' so gnyis la zhen spyod bkag nas bsgoms pas mthong lam gyi gnas skabs su sgro 'dogs so gnyis dang bral ba mngon du 'gyur bar gsungs pa dang/ 'phags mchog klu sgrub kyis/

rgyal ba rnams kyis stong pa nyid//
lta kun nges par 'byung bar gsungs[97]//
gang dag stong pa nyid lta ba//
de dag bsgrub tu med par gsungs//

zhes dang/

stong ngo zhes kyang mi brjod do[98]//
mi stong zhes kyang mi bya zhing//

96 *Abhisamayālaṃkāra* (III, 3ad). Stcherbatsky and Obermiller, *Abhisamayālaṃkara,* Tib., 29: *nyid dang.*
97 BS *gsung.*
98 MMK (XXII, 11), Toh no. 3824, Dbu ma *tsa,* f. 13b: *de.*

To accept that, once one has negated truth, the [resulting] conceptualization of emptiness that is that negation should not *[itself]* be negated is to err in regard to one of the most important points of the textual tradition of the Madhyamaka. How so? The *Samcaya[gatha]* states:

> Bodhisattvas who understand these aggregates to be empty
> Are preoccupied with signs, and have not [attained] true faith in the realm of the unarisen.[168]

The *Intermediate Mother [Perfection of Wisdom Sūtra]* states:

> To be preoccupied with "the emptiness of form" is to be preoccupied with signs. To be preoccupied with "the non-emptiness of form" is to be preoccupied with signs.[169]

These passages are stating that all dualistic grasping is to be negated. The [same] point [made by] those [texts] is expressed by the *Abhisamayālaṃkāra,* when it says:

> The recognition that is preoccupied with the emptiness of the aggregates, such as form...
> Belongs to the side discordant [to omniscience].[170]

It also states that abandoning conceptual preoccupation with the thirty-two extremes, such as permanence and impermanence, and meditating on this during the Mahāyāna path of preparation *(sbyor lam)* leads, during the path of seeing *(mthong lam),* to the actualization of [insight] devoid of the thirty-two reifications *(sgro 'dogs).*[171] The supreme ārya Nāgārjuna has said:

> The Victors have said that emptiness
> Is the renunciation of all views.
> Those who have a view of emptiness
> Will accomplish nothing.[172]

And also:

> I do not claim that [things are] empty;
> Nor do I claim [that they are] non-empty.

gnyis dang gnyis min mi bya ste//
gdags pa'i (S47) don du brjod par bya//

zhes dang/ (K15b)

kun rtog thams cad spong ba'i[99] phyir//
stong nyid bdud rtsi ston mdzad na//
gang zhig de la zhen gyur pa//
de ni[100] khyod kyis shin tu smad//

ces dang/

gang gis thugs brtses nyer bzung pas[101] //
lta ba thams cad spong[102] ba'i phyir//
dam pa'i chos ni ston mdzad pa//
go tam de la phyag 'tshal lo//

zhes dang/ dpal ldan zla bas/

gnyis su med pa'i blo ni dngos po dang/ dngos po med pa la sogs pa'i mtha' gnyis dang bral ba'i shes rab bo//[103]

zhes dang/ de'i phyir/[104] de kho na nyid la de'i yul can ni[105] dngos po dang dngos po med pa dang/ zhes pa nas de'i rang gi ngo bo mi[106] dmigs pa'i phyir ro/ /zhes[107] pa'i bar du gsungs pa dang/ *bden gnyis* las/

yang dag nyid du gnyis med[108] de//
de nyid phyir na de stong min[109]//

99 *Lokātītastava,* v. 23. Lindtner, ed., *Nagarjuniana,* 136: *spangs pa'i.*
100 Lindtner, ed., *Nagarjuniana,* 136: *nyid.*
101 KS *pas;* B *nas.* MMK (XXVII, 30). Toh no. 3824, Dbu ma *tsa,* f. 18b: *thugs brtse nyer bzung nas.*
102 MMK, f. 18b: *spang.*
103 MABh. Toh no. 3862, Dbu ma *'a,* f. 22b: *gnyis su med pa'i blo ni/ dngos po dang dngos po med pa la sogs pa mtha' gnyis dang bral ba'i shes rab po//.*
104 MABh, Toh no. 3862, Dbu ma *'a,* f. 256a: / omitted.
105 MABh, f. 256a: *ni* omitted.
106 MABh, f. 256a: *ma.*
107 K *zhas.*
108 K *mad.*
109 KBS *med. Satyadvanavibhaṅga,* Eckel, ed., *Jñānagarbha,* 162: *min.*

> Neither both nor neither is the case.
> [These distinctions] should be spoken of only in a nominal sense
> *(gdags pa'i don du)*.[173]

And also:

> When the nectar of emptiness is taught
> For the purpose of eliminating all discursiveness *(kun rtog)*,
> Whoever becomes attached to it
> Is denounced by you.[174]

And also:

> Out of empathy,
> You taught this holy Dharma
> So as to eliminate all views.
> I bow down to you, Gautama.[175]

The glorious Candra[kīrti] has also said:

> The nondual mind is the wisdom that is devoid of dualistic extremes like entity *(dngos po)* and non-entity.[176]

And also, there is the passage that goes from [the line], "Therefore, [the mind] that takes reality it as its object, [that is beyond the duality] of entity and non-entity..." up to, "for its own nature is not perceived."[177] Also, the *Satyadvaya* states:

> From the perspective of reality, it is nondual
> That is why the Lord has said

mi stong ma yin yod med min//
mi skye ma yin skye min zhes[110]//
de la (S48) sogs pa bcom ldan gsungs//

zhes sogs dbu ma'i gzhung lugs khung thub thams cad nas stong mi stong la sogs pa gnyis 'dzin thams cad dgag byar gsungs par[111] mthun no//

gal te sngar gyi lung de dag gi don/ stong nyid la bden par bzung ba dgag byar gsung ba yin gyi/ bden pa bkag pa'i stong nyid du gzung[112] ba dgag byar ston pa min no/ /zhes smra ba ni/

bstan pa'i snying po spros bral nyams par byed pa'i bdud tshig blo gros dang bsod nams chung ba rnams bslu bar byed pa'i gtam ste/ de ltar na lta kun ces dang/ kun rtog thams cad ces dang/ lta ba thams cad ces mang tshig gsungs pa don med par 'gyur te/ (K16a) chos can la bden par bzung ba dang/ de'i stong nyid la bden par 'dzin pa gnyis ka yang mthar 'dzin bzhi'i nang nas dang po gcig pur 'dus pa'i phyir/ des na mthar 'dzin bzhi (S49) char bsdu ba'i phyir du mang tshig gsungs pa yin gyi/ chos can so so ba'i steng gi mthar 'dzin gcig kho na dgag bya yin na mang tshig gsungs pa don med par shes par bya'o/ /bden pas stong pa'i stong pa kho nar bzung ba dbu ma'i lta ba mthar thug[113] rtogs par byas nas/ de dgag tu mi rung bar[114] 'dod pa ni gsang sngags kyi rgyud sde rnams las rnam grangs du mas smad cing/ rnal 'byor chen po'i skabs su rtsa ltung bcu gcig par 'gyur bar gsung ba sogs rab tu mang po yod kyang skabs 'dir[115] ni ma spros so//

yod min med min gyi don/ don dam du yod pa min/ kun rdzob tu med pa min/ ces pa la 'chad pa ni shin tu mi 'thad de/ yod min med min mtha' bzhi'i spros bral mtshan nyid pa ni/ 'phags pa'i mnyam bzhag zag pa med pa'i ye shes kyi gzigs ngo yin la/ rjes mthun pa ni so so skye bo'i gnas skabs su mthar thug dpyod (S50) pa'i rigs[116] shes kyi blo ngor rtogs[117] dgos shing/ de'i tshe chos can bum pa lta bu kun rdzob tu med pa min na rigs[118] shes

110 KBS *ces.* Eckel, ed., *Jñānagarbha,* 162: *zhes.*
111 K *pa.*
112 KS *bzung.*
113 B *thug* omitted.
114 BS *ba.*
115 K *di.*
116 KBS *rig.*
117 KB *rtog.*
118 KBS *rig.*

That it is neither empty nor nonempty,
Neither existent nor nonexistent,
Neither unarisen nor arisen.[178]

In this way, all the sources of the Madhyamaka textual tradition agree in their teaching that all forms of grasping at duality, such as empty and nonempty, should be negated.

[Opponent:] All those previously [cited] texts [should be interpreted as] meaning that the apprehension of emptiness *as something true* is to be negated.[179] They do not teach that apprehending the emptiness that is the negation of truth is to be negated.

[Reply:] This is the deceptive blithering of [individuals] of little intelligence and merit, the demonic words that slander the Freedom from Proliferations [doctrine], which is the heart of the teachings. If this were so, then the use of the pluralizing [adjectives] in expressions like "*all* views [should be abandoned]," and "*every* conceptualization *(kun rtog)*," and "*every* view [should be abandoned]" would be purposeless. Why? Because [for you] grasping at the truth of a certain phenomenon *(chos can)* and grasping at the truth of its emptiness are both subsumed within the first of the four [forms of] grasping at extremes *(mthar 'dzin bzhi)*.[180] Therefore, it is for the purpose of [ensuring] that *all* four [forms of] the grasping at extremes get included that the plural is used. Were it the case that only one [form of] grasping at an extreme were to be negated in regard to each phenomenon, then the use of the plural would be purposeless. Please understand this. Thinking that the apprehension of emptiness alone—that is, of the emptiness of truth—is the ultimate view of the Madhyamaka, and then further believing that this should *[itself]* never be negated is [a stance that is] repudiated by many passages in the tantras of the Secret Mantra [Vehicle]. In the context of the "Great Yoga," this is said to constitute the eleventh root downfall.[181] Even though there are many such points [that could be brought up in this regard], I will not proliferate [the discussion].

It is also quite wrong to take "neither existence nor nonexistence" as referring to the fact that [things] are not ultimately existent and not conventionally nonexistent. Why? The real *(mtshan nyid pa)* freedom from the proliferations of the four extremes, "neither existence nor nonexistence," is what is perceptually confronted *(gzigs ngo)* in the stainless equipoised gnosis of āryans. [But there is an] analogue *(rjes mthun)* [to that real ultimate truth in the form of a quasi-ultimate,[182] and it is this latter kind of ultimate "in name only" that] ordinary beings must understand within the mental purview of

de'i ngor bum pa kun rdzob tu yod par 'gyur te/ kun rdzob tu med pa min pa'i phyir/ rtags khyab gnyis char khas blangs/ 'dod na thal 'gyur ba rnams kyis myu gu bdag las skye ba med par bsgrub pa la rang rgyud bya mi rigs[119] pa'i shes byed du/ de'i tshe chos can myu gu tshad mas (K16b) grub pa med pa 'di nyid gtso bor bkod pa tshig gsal las gsungs pa dang 'gal mi 'gal legs par soms shig/

yang yod min med min gyi don yod pa yang bden par ma grub/ med pa yang bden par ma grub ces sogs la 'chad pa ni/ spros bral blo yul du ma shar ba'i gtam ste/ spyir

> 'dus byas rab tu ma grub pas//
> 'dus ma byas ni ci[120] ltar 'grub[121]//

ces dang/

> dngos po yod pa ma yin na//
> dngos med gang gis[122] yin par 'gyur// (S51)

zhes pa lta bu/ 'dus byas 'dus ma byas dngos po dngos med gnyis ga dgag gzhir byas nas/ de'i steng du bden pa bkag pa yang yod mod kyi chos can bzung 'dzin gnyis stong gi shes pa lta bu'i steng du mtha' bzhi'i spros pa bkag par *ye shes snying po kun las btus pa* las gsungs pas/ de'i tshe yod pa dang med pa sogs bzhi po chos can du byas nas/ de'i steng du bden pa bkag pa la 'brel ci yod soms[123] shig/

gal te de'i don gzung 'dzin gnyis stong gi rnam par shes pa don dam du yod pa min/ kun rdzob tu med pa min/ ces sogs la sbyar ba yin no snyam na/

gzung 'dzin gnyis stong gi rnam shes chos can/ don dam du yod pa dang/ kun rdzob tu med pa gnyis ka yin par thal/ de gnyis ka min pa ma yin pa'i

119 BK *rig.*
120 MMK (VII, 33). Toh no. 3824, Dbu ma *tsa,* f. 5b, *ji.*
121 MMK, f. 5b, *'grub.*
122 MMK (V, 6); Toh no. 3824, Dbu ma *tsa,* f. 4a: *gi.*
123 K *sams.*

the reasoning consciousness *(rig shes)* that analyzes the ultimate. Now when [ordinary beings are engaged in such an analysis], if, say, a pot is not conventionally nonexistent, that means that within the purview of that reasoning consciousness the pot would (according to you, Tsong kha pa,) have to conventionally exist, for it is not conventionally nonexistent. You accept both the reason *(rtags)* and the pervasion *(khyab)*.[183] If you accept [the premise], then give some thought to whether or not you are contradicting the *Prasannapadā*'s claim that the chief [reason] the Prāsaṅgikas give to explain that it is incorrect to use autonomous [syllogisms] to prove that the sprout does not arise from itself lies in the very fact that at such a time the sprout *qua* subject [of the syllogism] is not established by means of a valid cognition.[184]

To explain [the doctrine of] "neither existence nor nonexistence" to mean that neither existence nor nonexistence truly exist is also the blithering of someone who has no idea of the Freedom from Proliferations [doctrine].[185] Why? It is true that in passages like this:

> If the composite is not established,
> How can the non-composite be established?[186]

and also:

> When entities do not exist,
> How can non-entities exist?[187]

both composite and noncomposite—entities and non-entities—are taken as the basis of the negation *(dgag gzhir byas nas)* and then, with that as the basis, there is a negation of truth. But even though [there is such a negation], based then on a new subject *(chos can)* such as "a consciousness that is devoid of subject/object duality *(gzung 'dzin gnyis stong gi shes pa)*," the proliferations of the four extremes are eliminated. This is stated in the *Jñānasārasamuccaya*.[188] This being the case, ask yourself what sense it makes to [do what you suggest and to] take the four [extremes]—existence, nonexistence, and so forth—as the subject, and then to negate their truth.

[Opponent:] The [passages that teach "neither existence nor nonexistence"] should be taken as referring to the fact that "the consciousness devoid of subject/object duality" is neither ultimately existent nor conventionally nonexistent.

[Reply:] It follows, absurdly, that the consciousness devoid of subject/object duality is both ultimately existent and conventionally nonexistent,

phyir/ rtags gsal 'bru gnon gyi thog tu dngos 'gal yin la/ khyab pa dgag pa gnyis kyi rnal (S52) ma go ba la dngos 'gal yin pas gangs ri'i khrod kyi dge sbyong thams cad 'di la lan gang 'debs bka' gros mdzod cig/ (K17a)

dbu ma'i lta ba la dpyod pa'i gnas skabs su/ dgag pa gnyis kyi[124] rnal ma go ba 'di la 'phags mchog klu sgrub kyis/

gal te yod pa sun phyung bas//
ci ste med pa par gyur na//
de phyir med pa sun phyung bas//
ci phyir yod pa par mi 'gyur//[125]

ces ched du gtad pa'i dgag pa gsungs pa 'di yang dran par gyis shig/

mthar thug dpyod pa'i rigs[126] shes kyi ngor yod min med min gyi lta ba khas blangs pa la/ rgya nag hwa shang gi lta ba yin no zhes brtags dpyad ma byas pa'i tshig rang dga' ba 'jig rten gyi khams su 'phangs pa ni bstan pa'i snying po spros bral nyams pa'i ched du bdud rigs kyis[127] byin gyis rlabs nas bkye bar byed pa ste/ rgya nag hwa shang gis ni gnas lugs (S53) kyi don la brtags dpyad ma byas par rtog pa[128] rang dgar bkag nas ci yang yid la mi byed pa tsam la/ lta ba mthar thug rtogs par 'dod pa yin zhing/ de nyid mkhas pa ka ma la shiḥ[129] las lung dang rigs pas sun phyung ba yin la/ 'di ni dbu ma'i gzhung lugs las bshad pa'i rigs pa rnams kyis yul gyi gnas lugs gtan la dbab pa na/ mthar 'dzin rnams kyi zhen yul re re nas sun phyung ste/ mthar yod med la sogs spros pa'i mtha' gang yang ma rnyed pa tsam la dbu ma'i lta ba rtogs zhes pa'i tha snyad tsam zhig mdzad pa yin pas/ de gnyis mtshungs par 'dod pa ni/ mkhas pa sbyangs par rlom pa rnams kyang brtag dpyad cung zad kyang ma byas pa'am/ yang na thabs la bslu ba'i bdud kyis (K17b) zin par nges so//

124 K *kyi* omitted.
125 Go rams pa is apparently quoting from Nāgārjuna's *Ratnāvalī* (I, 59). However, Go rams pa's wording differs from that found in C, vol. 93, f. 118a, as well as from that found in the Hahn ed. (= Rat). C and Rat both read: *gal te yod pa sun phyung bas/ don gyis 'di ni med par bslan/ de bzhin med pa sun phyung bas/ yod par ci yi phyir mi bslan/.*
126 KB *rig.*
127 K *gyi.*
128 KB *par.*
129 KBS *shi.*

because it is not neither.[189] Based on a careful reading *('bru gnon gyi thog tu)*[190] of this debate *(rtags sal),*[191] [you will see that you are confronted with] a direct contradiction, and given as well that [to challenge] the pervasion [requires you to] directly contradict the principle of double negation *(dgag pa gnyis kyi rnal ma go ba)* [which you accept], please discuss with all of the monks of this Abode of Snow Mountains what response could be offered to this [predicament, even though it will be to no avail].

As regards [whether or not] the law of double negation [is applicable] when one is analyzing the Madhyamaka view, the supreme ārya Nāgārjuna has said:

> If by repudiating existence
> [We] become nihilists,
> Then why does repudiating nonexistence
> Not make one an eternalist?[192]

Give some thought to what precisely the refutation in [this passage] is getting at.[193]

[We] believe that the view of "neither existence nor nonexistence" exists within the purview of the reasoning consciousness that analyzes the ultimate. For you to claim that this belief is the view of the Chinese Hwa shang[194] and to spread this rumor in the world without analyzing [what you are saying] is to unleash the curse of demons so as to degenerate the Freedom from Proliferations, the essence of the doctrine. The Chinese Hwa shang [believes that] devoid of any analysis of the meaning of reality, one should simply eliminate ordinary conceptual thoughts and think of nothing whatsoever; and this he believes to be the realization of the ultimate view. This [position] has been repudiated by the scholar Kamalaśīla using scripture and reasoning.[195] When in this, [our own system,] we set forth reality *qua* object *(yul gyi gnas lugs)* using the reasoning that is explained in the textual tradition of the Madhyamaka school, we repudiate each of the objects constructed *(zhen yul)* by [the various thoughts that] grasp at extremes. And at the end [of this process], we reserve the term "the realization of the Madhyamaka view" to refer only to the "not finding" of any of the extremes of proliferation, such as existence and nonexistence. Hence, those who accept that these two views [ours and that of the Hwa shang] are similar must be either individuals who [merely] pride themselves on their scholarly training without in fact having the slightest analytical [capabilities], or else must be possessed by demons who deceive them as to what is [proper] method *(thabs).*

des na bden pas stong pa tsam du bzung nas/ yod min med min gyi spros bral 'gog pa 'di ni/ bla ma dbu ma pa[130] la 'jam dbyangs (S54) kyis bstan pa'i grub mtha' yin gyi/ 'phags mchog klu sgrub yab sras kyi gzhung dang 'gal ba kho na yin no/ /ji ltar[131] bstan na/ de nyid kyi *gsang ba'i rnam thar* las/

> kho bo'i rgyud la yod pa'i dbu ma'i lta ba 'di thal rang gang gi lta ba yin ces bla ma dbu ma pa[132] brgyud nas 'jam dbyangs la zhus pas/ 'jam dbyangs kyi zhal nas de ni thal rang gang gi 'ang lta ba min no[133]

zhes gsungs/ de la *rnam thar rtsom pa po* na re/ de'i tshe rje 'di nyid kyi thugs rgyud la zhang thang sag pa nas brgyud pa'i yod min med min gyi lta ba de yod pas de skad du gsungs pa yin par 'dug ces bris snang ngo/ /thar pa don gnyer[134] rtog dpyod dang ldan pa rnams kyis 'di la bag zon mdzod cig/

gal te stong nyid du mngon par zhen pa yang 'gog dgos na/ [a] bden pa bkag nas stong nyid rigs pas bsgrub pa don med par 'gyur zhing/ [b] stong nyid rtogs pa'i blo (S55) de yul gyi gnas tshul la zhugs pa ma yin par 'gyur ro zhe na skyon med de/ [a] thog mar bden pa ma bkag na/ bden stong du zhen pa dgag tu med pas stong nyid rigs pas sgrub dgos la/ [b] bden pas stong pa tsam rtogs[135] pa'i blo ni/ bden 'dzin nyid la ltos nas yul gyi gnas lugs rtogs par[136] 'jog pa'i phyir ro//

dbu ma rang rgyud pas rang gi mtshan nyid kyis grub pa'i chos khas blangs pa la/ sgrub byed du bkod pa rnams ni sgrub byed ltar (K18a) snang ba[137] yin tshul dang/ rang rgyud pa'i gzhung khung thub rnams las/ kun rdzob gcig pur ma brtags nyams dga' ba nyid du gsungs kyi/ rang gi mtshan

130 K *pa'i.*
131 K *ltang.*
132 KBS *pas.* See the following note.
133 This is not a direct quote, but rather a paraphrase of Tsong kha pa's *Gsang ba'i rnam thar* by Mkhas grub rje, in *The Collected Works of rJe-tsong-kha-pa,* vol. *ka,* ed. Gelek Demo (New Delhi, n.d.), 171: *nged kyi lta ba 'di thal rang gang yin zhus pas gang yang min gsung/ de dus rje 'di'i thugs la yang khas len ci yang med cing/ gang du'ang bzung mi nyan par lta ba de thugs la bde ba tsam yod par 'dug go/.* Similar lines are also found in Mkhas grub rje's other biography, the *Dad pa'i 'jug ngog,* in Tsong kha pa's *Collected Works,* vol. ka, ACIP S5259, f. 31a: *de'i tshe rje 'di'i thugs yul na yang khas len ci'ang med cing gang yang rang lugs la bzhags med par gzhan ngo 'ba' zhig la skyel ba'i dbu ma'i lta ba de cung thugs la bde bar yod pas/ bdag gi dbu ma'i lta ba 'di thal rang gang gi lta ba yin zhus pas/ gang gi'ang min zhes gsung zhing.*
134 K *gnyir.*
135 BS *rtog.*
136 K *pa.*
137 KS *par;* B *bar.*

[That one should] apprehend only the emptiness of truth and then refute the Freedom from Proliferations [as expressed in] the "neither existence nor nonexistence [doctrine]" is, [according to the followers of Tsong kha pa,] a tenet taught by Mañjuśrī to Bla ma Dbu ma pa;[196] but this is in fact nothing more than to contradict the texts of the supreme ārya Nāgārjuna and his spiritual son. How was this [supposedly] taught? [Tsong kha pa's] Secret Biography *(gsang ba'i rnam thar)* states:

> I asked Mañjuśrī, through Bla ma Dbu ma pa, whether the Madhyamaka view that I had in my mind belonged to the Prāsaṅgika or to the Svātantrika [school], and Mañjuśrī replied that it was a view that belonged to neither the Svātantrika nor to the Prāsaṅgika school.[197]

Now it appears that the author of the biography has written that it was because the Lord [Tsong kha pa] had within his mindstream at that time the view of "neither existence nor nonexistence" that came from the lineage of Zhang Thang sag pa[198] that [Mañjuśrī] said what he did.[199] So let those individuals who possess analytical insight and the desire for emancipation beware of this [view]!

[Opponent:] Were it necessary to bring an end to the conceptualization *(mngon par zhen pa)* of emptiness, then it would be pointless to establish emptiness by means of reasoning through the negation of truth. Also, it would follow that the mind that understands emptiness could not be abiding in the way things are *(yul gyi gnas tshul)*.

[Reply:] There is no problem here. Why? Without first negating truth, there can be no negating the conception *(zhen pa)* of the emptiness of truth. Hence, it is necessary to establish emptiness by means of reasoning.[200] The mind that understands the mere emptiness of truth is posited [by us] to be an understanding of the way things are, [but one which is] based on a grasping at truth.

What [Tsong kha pa] offers as his reasons [for believing] that the Svātantrikas accept phenomena to exist by virtue of their own characteristics are faulty *(ltar snang)*. I [intend to compose] an extensive explanation [demonstrating] how this is so and to [explain that] authentic Svātantrika texts do *not* teach [things] to exist by virtue of their own characteristics and, instead, teach that conventional [things exist] only to the extent that one remains content not to analyze them *(ma brtags nyams dga' ba nyid du)*.

nyid kyis grub par gsungs pa med pa sogs kyi rnam bzhag rgyas par ni/ gzhan du 'chad par 'dod pas 'dir ma spros so//

[3.2.0.0.0 kun rdzob kyi rnam bzhag la dpyad pa]

da ni kun rdzob kyi rnam bzhag la brjod par bya ste/ de la kun rdzob thams cad 'di ni lhas byin (S56) no/ 'di ni lhas sbyin gyi mig go zhes sogs ming gi tha snyad btags pa thams cad/ ming gi tha snyad de'i dbang gis[138] yod par bzhag pa ma gtogs pa 'jog byed gzhan med par 'dod pa ni/ kun rdzob tha snyad kyi dbang gis bzhag pa'i don gtan min te/ *chos yang dag par sdud pa'i mdo* las/

> rigs kyi bu 'jig rten gnas pa na skye ba dang/ 'gag pa la mngon par zhen pa yin pas/ de la de bzhin gshegs pa thugs rje chen po can gyis/[139] 'jig rten skrag pa'i gnas yongs su spong ba'i phyir/ tha snyad kyi dbang gis skye'o[140]/ 'gag go zhes gsungs kyi/ rigs kyi bu 'di la[141] chos 'ga' yang skye ba ni med do//[142]

zhes gsungs shing[143]/ *bden gnyis rang 'grel* du mdo drangs pa las kyang/

> de la kun rdzob kyi bden pa gang zhe na/ ji[144] snyed 'jig rten gyi tha snyad btags pa dang/ yi ge dang skad dang brdar[145] bstan pa dag go//[146]

zhes dang/ (S57) *stong nyid bdun cu pa* las/

138 B *gi.*
139 B / omitted.
140 B *bo.*
141 KBS *las;* see following note.
142 This passage from the *Dharmasaṅgīti sūtra* is cited in *Śikṣāsamuccaya,* Toh no. 3940, Dbu ma *khi,* f. 145b: *rigs kyi bu 'jig rten gnas pa skye ba dang 'gag pa la mngon bar chags pas de la de bzhin gshegs pas thugs rje chen pos 'jig rten dang nga ba'i gnas bsal ba'i phyir tha snyad kyi dbang gis skye'o 'gag go zhes gsungs te/ 'di la chos gang yang skye ba dang 'gag pa med do.*
143 KB *zhing.*
144 KBS *ci.* See also note 146.
145 K *brda'.* See also the following note.
146 *Satyadvayavibhaṅgavṛtti,* Eckel ed., *Jñānagarbha,* 154: *de la kun rdzob kyi bden pa gang zhe na/ ji snyed 'jig rten gyi tha snyad gdags pa dang/ yi ge dang skad dang bdra bstan pa dag go//.* See also above note 78.

However, wishing to [deal with these points] elsewhere, I will not expatiate on them here.[201]

[An Examination of Tsong kha pa's Exposition of the Conventional][202]

Now we should say something [about Tsong kha pa's] position concerning the conventional. [Mādhyamikas believe] that all conventional [truths] are established by virtue of conventional linguistic usage *(kun rdzob tha snyad).* [But Tsong kha pa believes that this means] that there is no other way to posit [conventional entities as existing] other than to posit them as existing by virtue of those linguistic conventions as found in expressions like "This is Devadatta," or "This is Devadatta's eye." But this is definitely not the case.[203] Why? The *Dharmasaṃgīti Sūtra* states:

> Son of good family, those who live in the world conceptualize [or are attached to] arising and cessation. That is why the Tathāgata, who possesses great compassion, so as to eliminate their fear of the world, has taught them [that things] "arise" and "cease" by means of [linguistic] conventions. But, son of good family, [in reality] there are no phenomena that arise in this [way/world].[204]

The *Satydvayavṛtti* also cites a sūtra:

> What then is the conventional truth? It is the designations of worldly convention—what is taught in terms of letters, language, and signs.[205]

The *Śūnyatāsaptati* also states:

> gnas pa'am skye 'jig yod med dang[147]//
> dman pa'am mnyam dang khyad par can//
> sangs rgyas 'jig rten bsnyad[148] dbang gis// (K18b)
> gsungs kyi[149] yang dag dbang gis min//

zhes kun rdzob tha snyad kyi dbang gis gzhag par gsungs pa'i don la *bden gnyis rang 'grel* las/

> 'jig rten gyi tha snyad gdags pa ni/ 'jig rten gyi 'jug pa ste/ shes pa dang shes bya'i mtshan nyid yin gyi/ rjod par byed pa'i mtshan nyid ni min[150] te/ de ni 'og nas[151] brjod pa'i phyir ro//

zhes 'jig rten pa'i blo la snang ba'i dbang gis bzhag pa dang/ de la brten nas ming gi tha snyad kyis bzhag pa sogs thams cad kyang tha snyad kyi dbang gis bzhag pa'i don du gsungs kyi/ ming gi tha snyad kho na la 'dod pa bkag pa'i phyir/

gal te de ni rang rgyud pa'i lugs yin no snyam na/
dpal ldan zla ba yang 'di kho na bzhin du bzhed de/ *'jug pa* las/

> de (S58) blo la ltos gnyis char bden pa ste//
> don gsal mthong la gnyis ka'ang rdzun[152] pa yin//

ces dang

> 'di na ji[153] ltar sad bzhin ji[154] srid du//
> ma[155] sad de srid de la gsum po yod//

ces dang/ rab rib mthu yis skra shad la sogs pa'i/ zhes pa'i *'grel bar*

> de bzhin du ma rig pa'i rab rib kyis gnod pa byas pas[156] de kho na

147 *Śūnyatāsaptati* v.1; Lindtner, ed., *Nagarjuniana,* 34: *dam. Śūnyatāsaptativṛtti,* Toh no. 3831, Dbu ma *tsa,* f. 110a: *dam.*
148 Lindtner, ed., *Nagarjuniana,* 34: *snyad. Śūnyatāsaptativṛtti,* f. 110a: *bsnyad.*
149 Lindtner, ed., *Nagarjuniana,* 34: *gsung gyi. Vṛtti,* f. 110a: *gsung gyi.*
150 *Satyadvayavibhaṅgavṛtti.* Eckel, ed., *Jñānagarbha,* 158: *ma yin.*
151 Eckel, ed., *Jñānagarbha,* 158: *mas.*
152 MA, Toh no. 3861, Dbu ma *'a,* f. 206b: *brdzun.*
153 KBS *ci.* MA, f. 206b: *ji.*
154 KBS *de.* MA, f. 206b: *ji.*
155 KBS *ma.* MA, f. 206b: *mi.*
156 KBS *pa'i.* MABh, Toh no. 3862, Dbu ma *'a,* f. 255b: *pas.*

> The Buddha spoke of abiding, arising, ceasing,
> Existence, nonexistence, inferior, equal, and superior
> [Using] only worldly conventions,
> And not from the viewpoint of reality.[206]

What it means to say that the conventional is posited by virtue of [linguistic] conventions is explained in the *Satyadvayavṛtti:*

> [In the above sūtra quotation] "Labeling by worldly conventions" [refers to] "worldly activity," and it has a cognitive character. It does not have a linguistic character, for this is explained below.[207]

Hence, "things being posited by [linguistic] conventions" means that "things are posited by virtue of the way they appear to the *mind* of [beings] in the world," and that based on that [cognitive act] "things are posited by means of language." It refutes the belief that [things] are *only* linguistic conventions.[208]

[Opponent:] That is a Svātantrika [and not the Prāsaṅgika] view.[209]

[Reply:] The glorious Candra[kīrti] also accepts things in exactly this same way. He states, in the *Avatāra:*

> From the perspective of that mind, both [types of optical illusions] seem true,
> But for those who perceive the object clearly, both are false.[210]

and also:

> [It no longer exists] when one awakens.
> But so long as one has not awakened, the three exist.[211]

and also, the commentary to the line that goes "the hair [perceived] due to an eye disease..."[212] states:

> Likewise, those who do not see reality because they are

> nyid ma mthong ba dag gis[157] phung po dang/[158] khams dang/[159] skye mched la sogs pa'i rang gi ngo bo dmigs pa gang yin pa de ni[160] de dag gi ngo bo kun rdzob pa'o//

zhes 'jig rten pa'i blo la snang ba'i dbang gis yul de dang/ der bzhag pa thams cad kun rdzob tha snyad kyi dbang gis bzhag pa'i don du gsungs pa'i phyir ro//

[3.2.1.0.0 las kyis 'bras bu bskyed pa'i tshul la brtags pa]

tha snyad btags pa'i don btsal ba'i tshe na mi rnyed ces pa'i sgra tsam smras kyang don la btsal (K19a) nas rnyed par byas 'dug ste/ las kyis 'bras bu bskyed (S59) pa'i tshul la rigs pas brtags shing dpyad pa'i tshe na/ las 'bras kyi rten du gyur pa'i zhig pa dngos po ba khas blangs pa'i phyir/ 'di thun mong min pa'i grub mtha' byed pa rnams la 'di 'dri ste/ las kyis zhig pa dngos po ba bskyed nas zhig pa dngos po bas 'bras bu bskyed pa de rig ngor khas len pa yin nam/ tha snyad du khas len pa yin/ dang po ltar na don go bas kho bo ni ci yang mi smra 'o//

phyi ma ltar na tha snyad du las dang 'bras bu gzhan yin par thal/ tha snyad du de gnyis kyi bar du zhig pa dngos po bas chod pa'i phyir/ dper na chus bar du chod pa'i ri phan tshun bzhin no/ /'dod na tha snyad du sngar gyi shing gi sa bon dang/ phyis kyi shing sdong gnyis gzhan yin par thal lo/ /de yang 'dod na/ gang phyir 'jig rten sa bon tsam btab nas/ /zhes pa rtsa 'grel gyi skabs su/ tha snyad du gzhan skye med pa'i shes byed du/ tha (S60) snyad du sngar gyi shing gi sa bon dang/ phyis kyi shing sdong gzhan ma yin pa'i phyir/ ces bkod pa 'di dran par gyis shig/

rang sde dngos smra ba dag gis las 'bras kyi rten du chud mi za ba dang/ thob pa dang/ kun gzhi'i rnam shes khas len pa dang/ khyed zhig pa dngos

157 BS *gi.* K and MABh, f. 255b: *gis.*
158 MABh, f. 255b: / omitted.
159 MABh, f. 255b: / omitted.
160 KBS *ni/.* MABh, f. 255b: / omitted.

afflicted by the [spiritual] "eye disease" of ignorance focus on the self-nature *(rang gi ngo bo)* of the aggregates, the elements, and the spheres. That which is focused on in this way is by nature conventional.[213]

[The passage] is stating that the fact that "the conventional is posited by virtue of [linguistic] conventions" means that it is by virtue of the fact that they appear to a worldly mind *('jig rten pa'i blo la snang ba'i dbang gis)* that everything—this object and that—is posited.

[An Examination of the Way that Karma Gives Rise to Its Effects]

Even though you pay lip service to the [doctrine] that "when one searches for the referent labeled by [a certain term], it is not found," in fact, there *is* something that you find when you search for the referent. How so? When you examine and analyze through reasoning how it is that the effects of karma arise, you accept "destruction *qua* real entity" *(zhig pa dngos po ba)*[214] to be the basis for karma and its effects. And now, to you who make this into a special tenet [of the Prāsaṅgikas, I argue] as follows. [According to you,] karma gives rise to destruction *qua* real entity, and then destruction *qua* real entity gives rise to the effect. Now do you accept this to [be true] within the purview of knowledge *(rig ngor)* [that analyzes the ultimate] or do you accept it [only] as a convention *(tha snyad du)*?

In the first case, since an object *is* understood, [it is therefore "found," and] there is nothing [more] for me to say. In the latter case, it follows, absurdly, that karma and its effects are different since at the level of conventions, they are set off from one another by an intermediary, namely "destruction *qua* real entity," just like two mountains that face each other are set off from one another by the river [that runs between them]. If you accept [the premise—that karmic cause and effect are different at the level of conventions—] then it follows, absurdly, that at the level of conventions the earlier tree seed and the later tree are different. If you accept *that,* then think back to the root text and commentary on the line that goes, "When a worldly being plants a seed,"[215] where the fact that the earlier tree seed and the later tree are *not* different at the level of conventions is cited as the reason that proves that there is no arising [of one thing] from another even at the level of conventions.[216]

Buddhist realists who accept "[karmic] inexhaustibility" *(chud mi za ba),*[217] "attainment" *(thob pa),*[218] and the "foundation consciousness" *(kun*

po ba[161] khas len pa rnams dbu ma thal 'gyur ba'i ngos nas 'khrul ba yin pa mnyam po la/ snga ma gsum ni sangs rgyas pa'i grub mtha' smra ba re re'i (K19b) lugs yin la/ zhig pa dngos po ba[162] ni chos 'di pa las phyi rol du gyur pa mu stegs bye brag pa'i grub mtha' yin gyi/ nang pa'i grub mtha' la med pas shin tu mi 'thad pa'i gnas so//

dpal ldan zla bas/ kun gzhi las 'bras kyi rten yin pa 'gog pa'i rigs[163] pa de zhig pa dngos po la yang mtshungs te/

> gang phyir rang bzhin gyis de mi 'gag pa//
> de phyir zhig dngos med kyang 'dir nus phyir//[164]

zhes 'don pa bsgyur bas chog pa'i (S61) phyir/ gzhan du na kun gzhi'i rnam par shes pas[165] mi rigs pa ci zhig byas nas chad pa bcad/

des na kun gzhi sogs las 'bras kyi rten du med kyang las 'gag nas yun ring po lon kyang/ 'bras bu 'byung ba mi 'gal ba'i shes byed du/ las rang bzhin gyis mi 'gag pa'i phyir/ ces bkod cing/ *rtsa shes*[166] las kyang de ltar gsungs pas tha snyad du gzhan skye med pa'i tshul go na/ mi go ba'i don med kyang rang gi rtog pa la gang shar tshad mar byed pa dag gis 'di ma go bar snang ngo/ /zhib par gzhan du 'chad cing ngag las shes so//

[3.2.2.0.0 rigs drug gi mig shes kyis mthong snang la dpyad pa]

yang chu phor pa gang gi go sa na/ rigs drug gi mig shes drug gis bltas pa'i tshe/ mig shes drug po ma 'khrul par mtshungs pas de'i yul drug po yod

161 K *pa.*
162 K *pa.*
163 K *rig.*
164 The actual *Madhyamakāvatāra* line (Toh no. 3861, Dbu ma *'a,* f. 206a), of course, reads: *de phyir kun gzhi med kyang 'di nus phyir//.*
165 S *bas.*
166 K *she.*

gzhi'i rnam shes) as the basis for karma and its results, and [you who accept] "destruction *qua* real entity," from a [so-called] "Prāsaṅgika Madhyamaka" viewpoint, all suffer from the same error. But [at least] the first three are each of them doctrines that belong to [recognized] Buddhist philosophical schools, whereas this "destruction *qua* real entity" falls outside of the [Buddhist] Dharma, being instead a tenet of the heterodox Vaiśeṣika [school]. Since it is not a Buddhist tenet, it is utterly inappropriate [for you to advocate it].[219]

The reasoning that the glorious Candra[kīrti] has used to refute the fact that the foundation [consciousness] is the basis of karma and its effects applies, *mutatis mutandis,* to "destruction *qua* real entity." Why? Because [the *Madhyamakāvatāra* lines that repudiate the foundation consciousness] could be modified to [apply to your notion of destruction *qua* real entity], so that they read:

> Since that [karma] does not inherently cease,
> Even though there is no real destruction, it [karma] can function.[220]

Otherwise, [tell us] what kind of mistake is implied by the [doctrine of] the foundation consciousness that should cause it to be singled out for punishment.

Therefore, "the fact that karma does not inherently cease" is taken as the reason for the fact that even though the foundation [consciousness] and [the other stipulated metaphysical entities like "inexhaustibility," etc.] are not the basis of karma and its effects, that does not contradict the fact that effects arise from the cessation of karma, no matter how much time elapses. The *Prajñāmūla*[221] makes the same point. Hence, the mystery [of how karma functions] becomes resolved *(mi go ba'i don med)* if one understands how it is that [one thing] does not arise from another [even] at the level of conventions. Nonetheless, it seems that those who make valid cognitions *(tshad ma)* out of whatever pops into their heads *(rang gi rtog pa la gang shar)* have not understood this. I will explain this in more detail elsewhere, and it can [also] be understood from the oral [tradition] *(ngag las shes).*[222]

[An Analysis of Tsong kha pa's View Concerning How the Eye Consciousnesses of the Six Classes of Beings Perceive Objects]

Moreover, [Tsong kha pa claims] that when the six eye consciousnesses of the six classes of beings look at [the object found] at the site occupied by a

mtshungs su 'dod pa ni/ dbu ma thal 'gyur ba'i lugs las 'das shing/ dngos stobs kyi rigs pa dang yang 'gal te/ thal (S62) 'gyur ba'i lugs la mi'i mig shes la ltos te/ mig shes de nyid ma 'khrul bas/ de'i yul chu yod pa yin (K20a) gyi/ mig shes gzhan lnga 'khrul bas/ de 'i yul lnga po yang 'jig rten nyid la ltos nas log pa'i kun rdzob tu 'dod pa yin la/ yi dvags kyi mig shes la ltos nas mig shes de nyid ma 'khrul pas de'i yul rnag khrag yang 'jig rten nyid la ltos nas bden pa yin cing/ mig shes gzhan lnga 'khrul pa yin pa sogs thams cad la sbyar bar bya ba yin no//

gal te mi'i mig shes dang yi dvags kyi mig shes sogs la ltos nas ma bzhag par/ spyir mi'i mig shes 'khrul lam ma 'khrul zhe na/

'dir kun rdzob thams cad blo la de ltar snang ba'i dbang gis bzhag par khas blangs pa yin gyi/ yul can gyi blo la ma ltos pa'i don bzhag mi shes pa ni/ kun rdzob tha snyad kyi dbang gis bzhag pa'i don yin par gong du bshad (S63) ma zin nam/ 'on kyang deng sang gi byis pa rnams kyis 'di ma go bas grub mtha'i gnad 'chug par snang ngo/ /don 'di nyid/

> rab rib dang ldan dbang po can mtshungs la[167]//
> chu 'bab klung la yi dvags[168] rnag blo yang//

zhes pa rtsa 'grel gnyis kyi don la dpyad na mi rtog pa'i don med do//

dngos stobs kyi rigs pa dang ji ltar 'gal na/ shakya thub pa'i gzugs gcig la mdzes mi mdzes kyi rdzas gnyis yod par thal/ de la lta ba'i 'od srung gi mig shes dang/ rdzogs byed kyi mig shes gnyis ma 'khrul bar mtshungs pa'i phyir/ chu phor gang la rigs drug gi mig shes drug gis bltas[169] (K20b) nas

167 S *ba.* MA, Toh no. 3861, Dbu ma *'a,* f. 207b: *la.*
168 MA, f. 207b: *dag.*
169 S *bltas;* KB *ltas.*

full cup of water,[223] all six eye consciousnesses are equally nonerroneous *(ma 'khrul pa)*, and that hence their six objects must be accepted as equally existent [therein]. [But this] is a belief that falls outside of the Prāsaṅgika system. It also contradicts factually based [inferential] reasoning *(dngos stobs kyi rigs pa)*.[224] The Prāsaṅgika system maintains that from the perspective of the eye consciousness of humans, the object [of that eye consciousness]—i.e., the water—does exist, since the eye consciousness [that perceives water] is nonerroneous. Since the other five eye consciousnesses [of the other types of sentient beings] are erroneous, however, the five objects of those [consciousnesses] are, from the perspective of the [human] world, mistaken [or false] conventionalities *(log pa'i kun rdzob)*.[225] From the perspective of a preta's eye consciousness, that same [that is, the preta's] eye consciousness is nonerroneous. Hence, *its* object—pus and blood—is true from the perspective of that same [preta] world, while the other five eye consciousnesses are erroneous, and so forth, where the [same thing can be said] to apply to each [of the other cases—that of hell beings, etc.].

[Opponent:] [Well then, isn't it possible to determine] whether or not the eye consciousness of humans is *in general* erroneous without positing [a context]—that is, independent [of stating a reference point] such as the human eye consciousness, the preta eye consciousness, and so forth?

[Reply:] [We] accept that all conventional things are posited [as existing] by virtue of the fact that they appear to the mind in a certain way. We know of no way to posit [the existence] of an object that does not depend upon the mind *qua* subject. Haven't I already explained earlier that this is what is meant by saying that the conventional is posited by virtue of [linguistic] conventions? Nevertheless, it seems that the infantile of this day and age have not understood this and, because of that, their philosophical doctrines are confused. The point is that there is nothing mysterious [in all of this] if we analyze the meaning of both the root text and commentary on the lines:

> When a preta's mind sees pus where a river flows,
> It is the same as the case of someone who possesses a diseased
> eye organ.[226]

How [does Tsong kha pa's position] contradict factually based [inferential] reasoning? It follows, absurdly, [from his view] that the body of Śākyamuni, which is one, contains two substances—one beautiful and one ugly—because the eye consciousness of [his disciple] Kaśyapa and the eye consciousness of [the heterodox ascetic] Purāṇa were both nonerroneous

chu phor gang mi kho nas btung ba'i tshe na mi des bdud rtsi dang rnag khrag sogs kyi rdzas drug car btung bar 'gyur te/ chu phor gang gi go sa na[170] rdzas drug cig car yod pa'i phyir/ des na thogs[171] bcas kyi dngos rdzas so so ba[172] drug go sa gcig tu gnas (S64) pa 'di ni dbang gis phyug pa dag ma gtogs gzhan su zhig smra bar[173] nus/

rjes 'brang dag skyon de spang bar 'dod nas/ chu phor gang gi go sa na bdud rtsi phor gang/ rnag khrag phor gang sogs yod par mi 'dod kyi/ phor pa gang po de nyid la rigs drug gi mig shes drug gis bltas pa'i tshe/ chu'i rdzas drug cha dang/ bdud rtsi'i rdzas drug cha sogs yod par smra'o/ /'di ni gyi na ste/ de'i tshe chu phor gang de mi yis btung ba na rdzas drug char btung bar thal ba'i skyon so na gnas shing/ chu phor gang btung rgyu med pa'i nyes pa lhag po gnas te/ chu'i rdzas drug cha las med pa'i phyir ro/

/des na mi'i mig shes kyis bltas pa'i tshe 'gro ba gzhan gyi mig shes kyis bltas pa dang ma bltas pa gang yin rung/ mig shes de'i ngor tha snyad du chu las gshan ma dmigs shing don dam par ni chu nyid kyang ma dmigs pa la/ khyod rdzas drug car tshang (S65) bar byed pa ni dngos 'dzin lhag po bsnan pa'o/ des na kun rdzob ma dpyad pa'i blo ngor 'jog dgos zhes pa'i 'ud sgrog[174] mang yang don la rigs[175] pas dpyad nas 'jog par snang bas/ dbu ma thal 'gyur ba'i lugs kyi kun rdzob kyi rnam bzhag las nyams pa yin no//

[3.3.0.0.0 'phros don la dpyad pa]

'phros don la yang rim pa bzhin dpyad par bya ste/

[3.3.1.0.0 sgrib gnyis kyi ngos 'dzin la dpyad pa]

dbu ma pa gzhan gyis shes sgrib tu khas blangs (K21a) pa'i chos kyi bden

170 B *na* omitted.
171 KB *thog.*
172 KB *so so pa.*
173 KB *pa;* S *ba.*
174 KBS *gog.*
175 KB *rig.*

when they looked at it.[227] It would also follow that a human [being] drinks all six substances—ambrosia, pus and blood, and so forth—when it is only the human drinking a cup full of water, so long as that cup of water is being watched by the six eye consciousnesses of the six classes of beings, for all six substances would exist in the space of that cup of water [at that time]. Therefore, who but those who have an inflated sense of their own powers would dare maintain that six separate, real, and tangible substances exist in a single location?[228]

Some of [Tsong kha pa's] followers, wishing to avoid this fault, claim that they do not accept that in the location occupied by a cup full of water there exists a *full* cup of ambrosia, a *full* cup of pus and blood, and so forth. Instead, they claim that when that full cup is perceived by the eye consciousnesses of the six classes of beings, one-sixth [part] is water-substance, one-sixth is ambrosia-substance, and so forth. Let us assume this is so. They *still* suffer from the fault of [having to accept] the absurdity that when a human being drinks that cup full of water, he or she is drinking all six substances. Not only that, but they [now] suffer from the additional fault that [for them] there is no such thing as drinking a cup full of water, since only one-sixth [of the liquid] is [ever] water-substance.

Therefore, when human beings are looking at it with their eye consciousnesses—whether or not other beings are looking at it with *their* eye consciousnesses—within those [human] eye consciousnesses nothing but water is perceived at the level of conventions; and, ultimately, not even the water is perceived. But your [insistence that] all six substances be complete is just a superfluous hypostatization.[229] So it appears that even though you broadcast the fact that the conventional must be posited within the purview of a nonanalytical mind, in point of fact you [*do* have some notion that the conventional can be] posited after analyzing it by means of reasoning.[230] Hence, you have fallen away from the way in which the Prāsaṅgika Madhyamaka system sets forth the conventional.

[The Analysis of Some Ancillary Points]

The ancillary points must now be examined in their proper order.

[The Analysis of Tsong kha pa's Views Concerning the Identification of the Two Obscurations]

It is definitely *not* the purport of the ārya Nāgārjuna[231] that the grasping at

'dzin nyon sgrib yin pa 'phags pa klu sgrub kyi dgongs pa gtan min te/ *rtsa ba shes rab* las/

> las dang nyon mongs zad pas thar[176]/
> las dang nyon mongs rnam rtog las/

zhes pa'i rnam rtog ni chos kyi bden 'dzin yin la/ de nyon sgrib yin na/ skabs 'dir[177] nyon mongs su thal ba'i skyon yod pa'i phyir ro//

yang chos la bden par[178] 'dzin pa'i bden 'dzin ni/ yan lag bcu gnyis kyi nang tshan du gyur pa'i ma rig pa yin (S66) pas/ stong nyid bdun cu pa las/

> rgyu rkyen las skyes dngos rnams la[179]//
> yang dag par[180] ni rtog pa[181] gang//
> de ni ston pas ma rig gsungs//
> de las yan lag bcu gnyis 'byung//

zhes pa'i gzhung gis bstan par 'dod pa ni blo gros shin tu rtsing[182] ba'i rnam thar ste/ gzhung des chos la bden par 'dzin pa'i bden 'dzin yan lag bcu gnyis kyi rgyur bstan gyi yan lag bcu gnyis kyi nang tshan du ma bstan pa'i phyir ro//

gal te gzhung des de lta bu'i bden 'dzin de ma rig pa[183] yin par bstan pa yin no snyam na/

skyon med de/ ma rig pa la shes sgrib tu gyur pa'i[184] ma rig pa dang/ nyon sgrib tu gyur pa'i ma rig pa gnyis yod pa las/ dang po ni/ yan lag bcu gnyis kyi rgyu dang/ phyi ma yan lag bcu gnyis kyi nang tshan du gzhung de nyid kyis bstan pa'i phyir ro//

des na[185] chos la bden par 'dzin pa'i bden 'dzin shes sgrib yin (S67) kyang/ *bzhi brgya pa* las/ srid pa'i sa bon du bshad pa ni/ yan lag bcu gnyis kyis (K21b) bsdus pa'i ma rig pa'i rgyu byed pa la dgongs pa yin gyi/ nyon sgrib yin pa'i don ni min no/ /chos kyi bden 'dzin shes sgrib yin pa la/

176 KB *mthar.* MMK, Toh no. 3824, Dbu ma *tsa,* f. 11a: *thar.*
177 K *'di'i.*
178 KB *pa.*
179 *Śūnyatāsaptati,* Lindtner, ed., *Nagarjuniana,* 62: *rgyu rkyen las skyes dngos po rnams/.*
180 KBS *pa.* Lindtner, ed., *Nagarjuniana,* 62: *par.*
181 Lindtner ed., *Nagarjuniana,* 62: *par.*
182 K *brtsing.*
183 KB *par.*
184 KB *ba'i.*
185 KBS *ni.*

the truth of phenomena *(chos kyi bden 'dzin)*—which other followers of the Madhyamaka school consider to be an obscuration to omniscience *(shes sgrib)*—is an afflicted obscuration *(nyon sgrib)*. Why? The *Prajñāmūla* states:

> Emancipation [comes about] through the exhaustion of karma and afflictions;
> And karma and the afflictions [arise] from misconception[232]

"Misconception" *(rnam rtog)* in this passage refers to the grasping at the truth of phenomena. Were [the "misconception" being referred to here] an afflicted obscuration, then there would occur the fault—that is, the absurdity—that it would *be* an affliction [rather than the cause of affliction, as is stated] in the context of [the first line].

[Opponent:] It is because "the grasping at truth *qua* grasping at the truth of phenomena" is [the kind of] ignorance that is to be found among the twelve links, [i.e., ignorance *qua* afflicted obscuration], that the *Śūnyatāsaptati* states:

> Conceiving as real the things
> That are taught by the Teacher to be ignorance;
> It is from this that the twelve links arise.[233]

[Reply:] Anyone who believes that this text demonstrates [that the grasping at truth is an afflicted obscuration] has the personal trait of having the coarsest of intellects. Why? That text is teaching that the grasping at truth *qua* grasping at the truth of phenomena is the *cause* of the twelve links. It is not teaching that it is *one of* the twelve links.

[Quandary:] But that text is teaching that such a grasping at truth *is ignorance.*

[Reply:] There is no problem, for ignorance is of two kinds: the ignorance that is an obscuration to omniscience, and the ignorance that is an afflicted obscuration. The first is the cause of the twelve links, whereas the latter is *one of* the twelve links. This is what the text itself teaches.

Therefore, even though "the grasping at truth qua grasping at the truth of phenomena" is an obscuration to omniscience, [it is true that] the *Catuḥśataka* explains it to be the seed of existence.[234] In so doing, it means to imply that it [i.e., the grasping at the truth of phenomena] acts *as the cause* of the ignorance that is part of the twelve links, and not that it is an afflicted obscuration [which would make it *one of* the twelve links]. The fact that

mgon po byams pa dang klu sgrub gnyis dgongs pa gcig tu snang ste/ gnyis char gyis kyang/ yan lag bcu gnyis kyis bsdus pa'i 'bras bu'i rten 'brel bdun po/[186] rgyu'i rten 'brel lnga las 'byung zhing/ rgyu'i rten 'brel ni chos kyi bden 'dzin du gyur pa'i rnam rtog las 'byung bar gsungs pa'i phyir ro/ /ji ltar na/

[1] *rtsa shes* las/ las dang nyon mongs rnam rtog las/ /zhes pa'i rnam rtog dang/

[2] *rin chen phreng ba* las/ ji srid phung por 'dzin yod pa/ /de srid de la ngar 'dzin yod/ /ces pa'i phung por 'dzin pa dang/

[3] *stong nyid bdun cu pa* las/ sngar drangs pa'i tshig rkang dang po gsum gyis bstan (S68) pa'i ma rig pa dang/

[4] *bzhi brgya pa* las/ srid pa'i sa bon rnam shes te/ /zhes pa'i rnam shes dang/

[5] *mngon rtogs rgyan* las bshad pa'i chos kyi dbang du byas pa'i rdzas 'dzin rtog pa dang/ bden 'dzin gyi dbang du byas pa'i gzung rtog rnams dang/

[6] *rgyud bla ma* las/

> de bzhin[187] phung po khams dbang rnams//
> las dang nyon mongs dag la gnas//
> las dang nyon mongs tshul bzhin min//
> yid la byed la rtag tu gnas//

zhes pa'i tshul min yid byed rnams don gcig tu snang la/ de'i ngos 'dzin *rgyud bla mar*/

> 'khor gsum rnam par[188] rtog pa gang//
> de ni shes bya'i sgrib par 'dod//

ces shes sgrib tu bshad pa'i phyir ro//

(K22a) de lta bu'i shes sgrib de ji srid dbu ma'i lta ba rgyud la ma skyes kyi bar du dngos po la bden par 'dzin pa'i bden 'dzin kho na yin la/ dbu ma'i

186 S //.
187 KBS *de ni. Uttaratantra,* Toh no. 4024, Sems tsam *phi,* f. 57a: *de bzhin.*
188 KB *pa. Uttaratantra,* f. 72b: *par.*

grasping at the truth of phenomena is an obscuration to omniscience is something that is agreed upon by both the protectors Maitreya and Nāgārjuna, for both state that the seven resultant interdependencies[235] that are part of the twelve links arise from the five causal interdependencies,[236] and the [five] causal interdependencies arise from the misconception that is the grasping at the truth of phenomena. How so? All of the following:

1. the "misconception" in the *Prajñāmūla* line that states "And karma and the afflictions [come from] misconception";
2. the "grasping at the aggregates" *(phung por 'dzin pa)* that is spoken of in the *Ratnāvalī* lines that go, "To the extent that one grasps at the aggregates/ To that extent is there a grasping at the 'I'";[237]
3. the "ignorance" spoken of in the first three lines of the previously cited passage from the *Śūnyatāsaptati;*
4. the "consciousness" that is mentioned in the *Catuḥśataka* line that goes, "Consciousness is the seed of existence";[238]
5. the "conceptualization directed at a substantial subject [that takes place] with reference to phenomena" *(chos kyi dbang du byas pa'i rdzas 'dzin rtog pa)* and the "conceptualization directed at objects [that takes place] with reference to the grasping at truth" *(bden 'dzin dbang du byas pa'i gzung rtog)* explained in the *Abhisamayālaṃkāra;*[239] and
6. the "improper cogitation" *(tshul min yid byed)* mentioned in the *Uttaratantra* passage that goes:

   Likewise, the aggregates, elements, and organs
   Are based upon karma and the afflictions;
   And karma and the afflictions
   Are always based on improper cogitation[240]

[All of these terms—misconception, grasping, ignorance, conceptualization, improper cogitation—] are synonyms, and the *Uttaratantra* identifies them, explaining them to be obscurations to omniscience. This it does in the lines:

> Any of the three misconceptions
> Is considered an obscuration to omniscience.[241]

Until such time as the Madhyamaka view is generated within one's [mental] continuum, such obscurations to omniscience are precisely the grasping at truth—that is, the grasping at the truth of things. From [the time]

lta ba rgyud la skyes nas/ mthong lam ma thob kyi bar du yul gyi phyogs (S69) su zhen pa yin na/ gzung rtog dang/ yul can gyi phyogs su zhen na mos pa yid byed kyi btags 'dzin rtog pa yin la/ chos rang bzhin med par rtogs pa'i mthong lam skyes phyin chad bden 'dzin med pa'i gzung rtog dang/ de kho na nyid yid byed kyi btags 'dzin rtog pa yin no/ /des na shes sgrib la bden 'dzin yod pa dang/ med pa gnyis las/ snga ma yan lag bcu gnyis kyis bsdus pa'i ma rig pa'i rgyu yin pas nyon mongs kyi ming gis btags pa yod la/ phyi ma la yang yul la mngon par zhen pa'i cha nas nyon mongs kyi ming gis btags pa yang yod de/ byang chub sems dpa' rnams kyi nyon mongs ni rnam par rtog pa'o/ zhes pa ltar ro//

klu sgrub kyi gzhung las/ chos kyi bden 'dzin nyon mongs su bshad pa mi snang zhing/ dpal ldan zla bas/ chos la bden par 'dzin pa'i bden 'dzin nyon mongs can gyi mi shes par[189] (S70) bshad pa ni/ sngar ltar btags pa ba[190] la dgongs pa yin gyi/ gzhan du llu sgrub kyi dgongs par 'gro ba dka' 'o/ /chos kyi bdag 'dzin yin na/ bden 'dzin yin pas ma khyab pa yang snga ma la dpag ste shes nus shing/ 'og tu 'chad par yang 'gyur ro/ /des na bden 'dzin yin na/ nyon (K22b) sgrib yin pas khyab pa ni klu sgrub dang byams pa gnyis char gyi dgongs pa min no//

[3.3.2.0.0 bdag gnyis kyi ngos 'dzin la dpyad pa]

bdag gnyis kyi ngos 'dzin la/ slob dpon legs ldan 'byed kyis/ yid kyi rnam par shes pa bdag gi gdags gzhir 'dod pa yin gyi/ bdag dang gang zag tu 'dod

189 KB *pa*.
190 KB *pa*.

the Madhyamaka view *is* generated in one's [mental] continuum until one obtains the path of seeing, [obscurations to omniscience are twofold]: (a) when thought construction/attachment *(zhen pa)* is directed at objects *(yul)*, [it is] "object-conceptualization" *(gzung rtog)*,[242] and (b) when thought construction/attachment is directed at subjects *(yul can)*, [it is] "conceptualization that, while attending to faith, grasps the [subject] as a [mere] label" *(mos pa yid byed kyi btags 'dzin rtogs pa)*.[243] From the time that *the path of seeing* is generated—[a path] that realizes phenomena to be essenceless—[there are obscurations to omniscience that are twofold:] (a) object-conceptualizations that lack any grasping at truth *(bden 'dzin med pa'i gzung rtog)* and (b) conceptualizations that, while attending to reality, grasp [the subject] as a [mere] label *(de kho na nyid yid byed kyi btags 'dzin rtog pa)*. Therefore, obscurations to omniscience [are of two types]: those that possess a grasping at truth, and those that do not. Because the former is the cause of the ignorance that is part of the twelve links [and because that ignorance is itself an affliction, that first form of obscuration to omniscience is occasionally] called an "affliction" [even though it is not actually a true affliction]. As for the latter, there are also instances when even this [more subtle obscuration to omniscience] is called an "affliction," and this is in view of the fact that, [even at this more advanced stage, the mind is still] attached to objects *(yul mngon par zhen pa)*, [something that is evident from] the line "the afflictions of bodhisattvas are the misconceptions."

The texts of Nāgārjuna never claim that the grasping at the truth of phenomena is an affliction. The glorious Candra[kīrti] does explain that "the grasping at truth *qua* grasping at the truth of phenomena" is an afflicted form of unknowing *(nyon mongs can gyi mi shes pa)*,[244] but, as was [explained] earlier, he intends this only in an informal *(btags pa ba)* way, [and not because the grasping at truth *is* an actual affliction]. Otherwise, it would be difficult for [him to be seen as] being true to the purport of Nāgārjuna. Not all forms of grasping at the self of phenomena *(chos kyi bdag 'dzin)* are forms of grasping at truth, and this is something that can be known—that is, inferred—from what was [stated] earlier. I will explain it again below. Therefore, that all forms of grasping at truth are afflicted obscurations [as Tsong kha pa maintains] is the purport of *neither* Nāgārjuna nor Maitreya.

[An Examination of Tsong kha pa's Identification of the Two Selves]

The identification of the two selves [is as follows]. The master Bhāvaviveka believes that the mental consciousness *(yid kyi rnam par shes pa)* is the basis

pa ni min te/ rnam par shes pa de chos dang gang zag gnyis su phye ba'i tshe chos su bzhed pa'i phyir ro/ /*rtog ge 'bar ba* las/

> 'di ltar kho bo cag kyang tha snyad du rnam par shes pa la bdag gi sgra dngos su 'dogs te/ 'di ltar rnam par shes pa ni yang srid pa len pa'i (S71) phyir bdag yin no zhes lus dang dbang po'i[191] tshogs dag la nye bar 'dogs pa'i phyir te/

zhes gsungs so//

ngar 'dzin lhan skyes kyis nga'o snyam du bzung ba'i dmigs yul gyi nga tsam tha snyad du yod pa dbu ma thal 'gyur ba'i lugs yin kyang de nyid phung po dang/ gcig dang tha dad gang du grub btsal ba'i tshe gcig dang gzhan gnyis gang du yang ma rnyed kyang nga tsam tha snyad du yod par 'dod pa ni shin tu mi 'thad de/ de ltar btsal ba'i tshe nga tsam nyid kyang med par bya dgos pa'i phyir ro//

kha cig dbu ma thal 'gyur ba'i lugs la nga tsam tha snyad du yod pa 'gog pa la brtson pa ni/ gzhan gyis khas blangs pa'i[192] rgyu mtshan gyis 'gog pa'am/ yang na rang nyid kyis *'jug pa rtsa 'grel* ma mthong bar zad de/ ji skad du/

> de bzhin 'jig rten grags pa'i phung po dang//
> khams dang de bzhin skye mched drug brten nas//
> bdag kyang nye bar len (S72) po nyid du 'dod//

ces dang de'i *'grel par*[193] / (K23a)

> bdag kyang kun rdzob kyi bden par 'jig rten gyi tha snyad kun tu[194] mi bcad par bya ba'i phyir shing rta ltar nye bar len pa por 'dod pa yin/

191 KBS *dang/ dbang po'i. Tarkajvālā,* Toh no. 3856, Dbu ma *dza,* f. 80b: *dang dbang po'i* (/ omitted).
192 KBS *ba'i.*
193 KB *bar.*
194 KBS *kun tu tha snyad.* MABh, Toh no. 3862, Dbu ma *'a,* f. 307a: *tha snyad kun tu.*

onto which the self is labeled *(bdag gi gdags gzhi);* he does not believe that [that consciousness] *is* the self or the person,[245] for he believes that when we divide [the world up into] the two [categories of] persons and phenomena, mental consciousness [falls into the category of] phenomena. The *Tarkajvālā* states:

> At the level of worldly conventions, even *we* apply the word "self" to consciousness, for [the world claims] "consciousness is the self, since it is what takes rebirth." [Likewise, there are instances when] the body and the collection of organs are labeled [as the self].[246]

The Prāsaṅgika Madhyamaka school does maintain the nominal existence of the mere "I" that is the referent object *(dmigs yul)* that is grasped when the innate grasping at the "I" *(ngar 'dzin lhan skyes)* thinks "I"; but, having searched for [the "I" by asking oneself] whether it is the same as or different from the aggregates, and finding it to be neither the same as nor different [from them], to accept that the mere "I" exists nominally even though [it is not found during this search] is utterly incorrect, for at the time of that search, even the mere "I" must of necessity disappear.

Those who attempt to refute the fact that the Prāsaṅgika Madhyamaka school accepts the existence of the mere "I" at the level of conventional usage must either engage in such a refutation by means of reasoning accepted by some other [school[247]—in which case, what force would this have?]—or else, [if they propose to resort to Prāsaṅgika sources,] they have not seen what the root text and commentary on the *Avatāra* [have to say on this matter]:

> As acknowledged by the world,
> We accept the self to be the possessing agent *(nye bar len po)*
> [of the parts]
> Upon which it is based: the aggregates, elements, and six spheres[248]

And the commentary [on these lines] states:

> We believe the self to be the possessing agent, just as the chariot [possesses *its* parts; and we maintain this] so as not to contradict the convention that in the world as a whole, [this is considered] to be a conventional truth.[249]

zhes gsungs pa'i don la rtog dpyod mdzod cig/

rje btsun shes bya kun rig gi zhal snga nas kyang/ zla ba'i bzhed pa la/ phung po la brten nas ngar 'dzin lhan skyes kyis gzhi med la nga'o snyam du bzung ba'i yul du gyur pa'i nga tsam tha snyad du yod par gsungs shing[195]/ *'jug pa rtsa 'grel* las kyang shin tu gsal bas kho bo ni 'di 'gog pa la brtson par mi byed do//

nga tsam de nyid tha snyad du las byed pa po[196] dang/ rnam smin myong ba po yang yin te/ lugs 'di la kun rdzob rang gi yul can gyi blo la snang ba'i dbang gis bzhag pa yin zhing/ 'jig rten[197] pa'i blo la ngas las byas so/ /ngas 'bras bu myong zhes nga tsam las byed pa po dang 'bras bu myong ba por snang ba'i (S73) phyir ro/ /'o na las byed pa po dang 'bras bu myong ba po gcig dang gzhan gang yin/ rtag pa yin nam/ mi rtag pa yin/ dngos po yin nam/ dngos med yin zhes dpyod na de dag gang du'ang ma grub pas/ de ltar dpyod pa'i tshe nga tsam mi rnyed pa ni/ bdag rigs pas dpyad bzod du ma grub pa'i don no/ /gzhan dag de ltar dpyad pa'i tshe nga tsam khas len pa ni bdag rigs pas dpyad bzod du khas len pa las mi 'da'o[198]/ /de skad du *'jug 'grel* las/

> 'di'i las dang byed pa po'i rnam par bzhag[199] pa yang shing rta ltar khas blang bar bya'o/ /[200]nyer len las yin 'di ni byed pa po yang yin/ /[201]nye (K23b) bar len pa zhes bya ba phung po la sogs pa dag ni las nyid dang bdag ni byed po'o[202] zhes bya bar rnam par bzhag go//

zhes dang/

> de rnams shing rta'i rnam dpyad byas pas rnam bdun yod min[203] zhing/ /de las gzhan du gyur par[204] 'jig (S74) rten grags pa'i sgo nas yod pa yin/

zhes gsungs so//

195 KBS *zhing.*
196 K *pa ba.*
197 K *rtan.*
198 S *'di'o.*
199 MABh. Toh no. 3862, Dbu ma *'a,* f. 307a: *gzhag.*
200 MABh, f. 307a: *bya'o zhes bshad pa/.*
201 K *po'ang yin/.* BS *po yang yin/.* MABh, f. 307a: *po yang yin/ /.*
202 MABh, f. 307a: *pa po.*
203 KBS *yod pa min.* MABh, f. 309a: *yod min.*
204 KB *pa.* MABh, f. 309a: *par.*

Analyze what this means!

Take the mere "I" that is the object of the thought "I" as this is apprehended by the innate grasping at the "I" on the basis of the aggregates without any [real] support *(gzhi med)*: The Lord Shes bya kun rig has stated that according to Candra[kīrti] such an "I" exists nominally.[250] Since this is also very clear [from the wording] in the root text and commentary of the *Avatāra*, we take no pains to refute it.

That same mere "I" is nominally the doer *(byed pa po)* of karma and the one who experiences *(myong ba po)* the ripening [of karma]. Why? In this system, the conventional is posited by virtue of the fact that it appears to the mind that takes it as its object, and the mere "I" appears to the worldly mind as the doer of karma and the one who experiences its ripening, [as witnessed by such expressions as] "I perform an action (karma)" and "I am experiencing [its] effect." Nonetheless, when the doer of karma and the experiencer of its effects are analyzed in terms of whether they are the same or different, permanent or impermanent, entities or nonentities, and so forth, they [are found] not to exist in any of these ways. Hence, when analyzed in these ways, [even] the mere "I" is not found, and this is what it means to say that the self cannot withstand rational analysis *(rigs pas dpyad bzod du ma grub)*. Those others who accept that the mere "I" [*is* found] when it is analyzed in that way have not gone beyond the belief in a self that withstands rational analysis.[251] This same point is expressed in the following lines from the *Avatārabhāṣya:*

> The positing of karma and its doer should be accepted [as it is in the world,] just as the chariot is. "The appropriated *(nyer len)* is karma,[252] and the [self] is the doer, [i.e., the appropriator of that karma]." "The appropriated" refers to the aggregates and so forth, and that is precisely karma. The self is the doer [or appropriator of the aggregates/karma]. That is how they are posited [in accordance with worldly convention].[253]

And also:

> These do not exist when they are analyzed in the seven ways in the manner of the chariot.[254] Contrariwise [i.e., so long as they are *not* analyzed], they *do* exist from the viewpoint of what the world recognizes [as being true].[255]

des na brjod du med pa'i bdag khas len pa'i nyan thos 'ga' zhig ma gtogs pa'i rang sde dngos por smra ba rnams dang/ dbu ma pa rnams bdag rigs pas dpyad bzod du ma grub cing/ btags pa tsam zhig khas len par 'dra yang/ dbu ma pa'i lugs la/ btags pa tsam la las byed pa po dang rnam smin myong ba po rung zhing/ dngos smra ba la de mi rung bas/ snga mas bdag las byed pa po dang/ rnam smin myong ba por 'dod cing/ phyi mas bdag med pa'i phung po tsam zhig der 'dod pa ni gnad kyi don no/ /dbu ma pa'i lugs la/ phung po las byed pa po dang rnam smin myong ba por mi rung ste/ rigs pas dpyad pa'i tshe bdag phung gnyis ka yang der[205] ma grub par mtshungs shing/ tha snyad du bdag der snang gi phung po der mi snang ba'i phyir ro/ /gnad 'di blo (S75) yul du shar ba nyung bar snang ngo//

chos kyi bdag dngos po rnams la gzhan la rag ma las pa'i ngo bo zhig yod na de nyid la 'jog pa ni/ *bzhi brgya pa'i 'grel par*/ de ltar gsungs kyang de kho na la 'jog pa ni rtsa 'grel gnyis kyi dgongs pa min te/

de dag spros las spros pa ni//
stong pa nyid kyis 'gags par 'gyur//

zhes pa'i spros pa de nyid la chos kyi bdag dang/ (K24a) der 'dzin pa'i mtshan 'dzin la chos kyi bdag 'dzin[206] du 'jog pa ni klu sgrub kyi dgongs pa yin zhing/ mtshan 'dzin de la bden pa 'i mtshan mar 'dzin pa dang/ bden pas stong pa'i mtshan mar 'dzin pa sogs bzhi yod pas/ de'i yul gyi spros pa de la mtha' bzhi'i spros pa bzhi yod pa'i bzhi char la chos kyi bdag tu 'jog dgos pa'i phyi ro/ /des na *bzhi brgya pa'i 'grel ba'i* dgongs pa ni/ spros pa dang po la dgongs par gsal zhing/ chos kyi bdag (S76) 'dzin yin na bden 'dzin yin pas ma khyab pa'i gnad kyang 'di nyid yin la/ zhib par ngag las shes pa'am gzhan du 'chad par 'gyur ro//

205 BS *yang der* omitted.
206 K *'dzan.*

Therefore, except for a few śrāvakas who accept the self to be inexpressible,[256] Buddhist realists and the followers of the Madhyamaka school are alike in accepting the fact that the self cannot withstand rational analysis, and that it is a mere label *(btags pa tsam zhig)*. Nonetheless, in the Madhyamaka system it is possible for someone to engage in the doing of karma and in the experiencing of the ripening [of that karma] in a merely nominal [way], whereas for the realists this is impossible. Hence, the former [i.e., the Mādhyamikas] believe that the self is the doer of karma and the experiencer of its ripening, whereas the latter believe that it is "the mere aggregates that lack a self" that is the [entity that accumulates karma and experiences its results]. That is the point. In the Middle Way system, the aggregates *cannot* be the doer of karma and the experiencer of its ripening. Why? When they are analyzed using reasoning, neither the self nor the aggregates can be established, and at the level of [worldly] conventions the aggregates that appear to be the self do not appear to be the [doer of karma and the experiencer of its results]. It seems that those who have understood this point are few indeed.

Now the *Catuḥśatakavṛtti*[257] does state that the self of phenomena refers to the [impossible] "fact" that things have a nature [that makes them] independent of other [things].[258] But that this is *all* [the self of phenomena] is is not the purport of either the root text or the commentary. Why? The "proliferations" spoken of in this passage [from Nāgārjuna's *Mūlamadhyamakakārikas*]:

> [Misconceptions][259] proliferate on the basis of mental proliferations,
> But emptiness extinguishes the proliferations.[260]

refer to the self of phenomena. That the grasping at the self of phenomena is to be posited as the grasping at signs *(mtshan 'dzin) qua* grasping in terms of those [proliferations spoken of in the just cited passage]: this is the purport of Nāgārjuna. The "grasping at signs" is of four kinds—grasping at true signs, grasping at signs that are empty of truth, and so forth. Hence, proliferation *qua* object [of those forms of grasping] is also fourfold, [corresponding] to existence [in terms of] the four proliferative extremes, and all four must be considered "the self of phenomena." Therefore, it is clear that the *Catuḥśatakavṛtti* is referring [only] to the first [of these] proliferations [when it claims that the grasping at the self of phenomena is a grasping at true or independent existence], and so not all forms of grasping at the self of phenomena are forms of grasping at truth. That is the point. For more detail, one can either consult the oral tradition *(zhib par ngag la shes pa)*, or else [consult the treatment of this point as] I explain it elsewhere.[261]

[3.3.3.0.0 theg pa che chung gi spang rtogs kyi khyad par la dpyad pa]

theg pa che chung gi spang rtogs kyi khyad par la yang dpyad par bya ste/ theg pa che chung gnyis char la bden pa bkag tsam gyi stong nyid rtogs pa'i lta ba de las gzhan pa'i lta ba'i khyad par mi 'dod pa ni/ theg chen gyi lta spyod zab cing rgya che ba la skur pa btab pa ste/ theg chen gyi tshogs lam gnas skabs su mtshan med thos bsam gyis gtan la phab/ sbyor lam gyi gnas skabs su mi rtag la sogs bcu drug la yang mngon zhen bkag/ mthong lam gyi skabs su bsam gyis mi khyab pa la sogs pa'i chos nyid mngon sum du rtogs pa'i sgo nas theg dman las khyad par du 'phags pa *mngon rtogs rgyan* las gsungs pa'i phyir ro//

gal te de nyid 'dir khas mi len no zhe na/

de'i rgyu (S77) mtshan dris nas 'og tu 'gog cing/ klu sgrub yab sras kyi dgongs pa yang 'di kho na yin te/ (K24b)

[1] *bstod tshogs* las/

> mtshan ma med pa ma rtogs par//
> khyod kyis thar pa med par gsungs//
> de[207] phyir khyod kyis theg chen las//
> de[208] ni tshang bar bstan pa lags//[209]

ces dang/

[2] *rin chen phreng bar*/

> mu stegs gzhan dang rang nyid kyi'ang[210] //
> gnas min skrag pas ma mnyangs pa'o[211] //

[3] zhes dang/

207 K *de'i.*

208 K *'di.*

209 *Lokātītastava,* v. 65. P vol. 46, 34, and Lindtner, ed., *Nagarjuniana,* 138: *mtshan ma med la ma zhugs par/ thar pa med ces gsungs pa'i phyir/ de phyir khyod kyis theg chen rnams/ ma lus par ni de nyid bstan/.*

210 *Ratnāvalī* (I, 79). Rat, 33: *rang gi yang.*

211 BS *pa;* K *ba.* Rat, 33: *gnas med 'jigs pas ma myangs pa'o.*

[An Examination of Tsong kha pa's Views Concerning the Differences Between What the Mahā- and Hīna-yāna Believe Ought to Be Abandoned and Realized]

Now we must examine the differences between what the Mahā- and Hīnayāna [believe] ought to be abandoned and realized. To claim that both the Mahā- and Hīna-yāna [advocate] the view that understands emptiness, the mere negation of truth, and that apart from that they do not differ philosophically, is to cast doubt upon the breadth and depth of the theory and practice of the Mahāyāna.[262] Why? During the Mahāyāna path of accumulation *(theg chen tshogs lam)*, signlessness (*mtshan med*, i.e., emptiness) is established by means of hearing and thinking *(thos bsam)*. During the path of preparation *(sbyor lam)*, one eliminates conceptions/attachments *(mngon zhen)* even in regard to the sixteen aspects [of the four noble truths], such as impermanence, and so forth. During the path of seeing *(mthong lam)*, one directly *(mngon sum du)* understands reality [in its various forms, such as] "the inconceivable" and so forth;[263] and through this [direct understanding], one surpasses the Hīnayāna. This is stated in the *Abhisamayālaṃkāra.*

[Opponent:] I do not accept this in the [way you have set it forth].

[Reply:] I will refute you through cross-examination below, but [for now, let me simply show you] that this, and this alone, is the purport of the father Nāgārjuna and his spiritual son.[264] How so?

(1) In the compendium of praises, we find the lines:

> You have said that without understanding signlessness,
> There is no emancipation;
> That is why in the Mahāyāna
> You have taught [signlessness] in a complete form.[265]

(2) and in the *Ratnāvalī* [there are the lines]:

> Others—that is, the heterodox[266]—and even some [members of our own [religion—that is, Buddhists—]
> Fearing nonexistence *(gnas min)*, have not experienced it.[267]

(3) and also:

> zab mo khu 'phrig[212] can 'jigs pa/

zhes dang/

[4] dpal ldan zla bas *'jug 'grel* las/

> mi dmigs pa ni 'jig rten las' das pa'i phyir la/ dmigs pa ni tha snyad kyi bden pas bsdus pa nyid kyis[213] 'jig rten pa nyid yin pa'i phyir ro/ /de ni byang chub sems dpa'i gnas skabs ma thob pa dag gis shes par mi nus so//

[5] zhes dang/

> theg pa chen po bstan pas ni chos la bdag med pa tsam 'ba' zhig ston par byed pa ni[214] ma yin (S78) gyi/[215] 'o na ci zhe na/ byang chub sems dpa' rnams kyi sa dang pha rol du phyin pa dang[216] smon lam dang snying rje la sogs pa[217] dang yongs su bsngo ba dang/[218] tshogs gnyis dang bsam gyis mi khyab pa'i chos nyid kyang yin no//

zhes gsungs pa'i phyir ro//

[1A] de la lung [219] dang po'i don ni spyir[220] mtshan med bzhi po gang rung cig ma rtogs par thar pa thob pa med de/ nyan thos kyi byang chub thob pa la bden pa'i mtshan ma med par[221] rtogs dgos/ theg chen gyi byang chub thob pa la mtshan med bzhi char rtogs dgos pa'i phyir ro/ /des na nyan thos kyi theg[222] par[223]/ gzugs ni dbu ba[224] brdos pa 'dra/ zhes sogs bden pa'i mtshan med tsam las ma bstan zhing theg (K25a) pa chen po las mtshan med bzhi

212 *Ratnāvalī* (IV, 96). Rat, 131: *'phrigs.*
213 MABh, Toh no. 3862, Dbu ma *'a,* f. 230b: *nyid kyi phyir.*
214 MABh, f. 227b: *ni* omitted.
215 MABh, f. 227b: //.
216 MABh, f. 227b: *dang/*
217 MABh, f. 227b: *snying rje chen po la sogs pa.*
218 MABh, f. 227b: / *omitted.*
219 K *lugs.*
220 S *pyar.*
221 K *phar.*
222 K *thag.*
223 B *pa.*
224 KB *bar.*

Those who are apprehensive about the profound [doctrine of emptiness] fear it...[268]

(4) and also, the glorious Candra[kīrti] has stated in his *Avatārabhāṣya:*

...for [on the one hand] not perceiving *(mi dmigs pa)* [the gift, the giver, etc.] is beyond the world, and [their] perception, being subsumed within the truth of conventions *(tha snyad kyi bden pa)*, is a worldly thing. Those who have not attained the bodhisattva context cannot understand this.[269]

(5) and also:

It is not the case that the teachings of the Mahāyāna expound only the selflessness of phenomena. How so? [Taught are] also the bodhisattvas' stages *(sa)*, their perfections, their prayers *(smon lam)*, and their compassion, and so forth; and also their dedication *(bsngo ba)* [of merit], the two accumulations *(tshogs gnyis)*, and the inconceivable reality *(bsam gyis mi khyab pa'i chos_nyid)*.[270]

[1A] Let us consider the meaning of the first passage. In general, one cannot attain emancipation without understanding one of the four forms of signlessness, for to attain the enlightenment of the śrāvakas, it is necessary to understand the nonexistence of the sign of truth *(bden pa'i mtshan ma)*, and to attain the enlightenment of the Mahāyāna it is necessary to understand all four signlessnesses. Therefore, in the Śrāvakayāna, such passages as "form is like a lump of foam" are teaching only the nonexistence of the sign of truth,

char tshang bar bstan/ ces pa'i don yin pas/ 'di yang lta ba la[225] khyad par yod pa'i lung yin no//

[2A] lung gnyis pa'i don ni/ mu stegs gzhan dang zhes pa'i don ni/ phyi rol mu (S79) stegs byed yin la/ rang nyid kyi 'ang zhes pa ni/ nyan thos dang rang sangs rgyas yin pas/ 'di yang lta ba la khyad par yod pa'i lung yin no//

[3A] lung gsum pa'i don ni/ zab mo zhes pa ni/ mtha' bzhi'i spros pa dang bral ba'i stong nyid yin la/ de khu 'phrig can te/ bag chags sad pa rnams kyis rtogs la/ khu 'phrig med pa rnams la 'jigs pa ste skrag pa bskyed par byed ces pa'i don yin pas/ 'di yang lta ba la khyad par yod pa'i lung yin no/ /khu 'phrig can ji lta bu zhe na/ *'jug pa* las/

> so so'i[226] skye bo'i dus na'ang stong pa nyid thos nas//
> nang du rab tu dga' ba yang dang yang du 'byung//
> rab tu dga' ba las byung mchi mas mig brlan zhing//
> lus kyi ba spu ldang bar gyur pa[227] gang yin pa//
> de la rdzogs pa'i sangs rgyas blo yi sa bon yod//

zhes gsungs pa lta bu yin pas/ gzhung 'dis bstan pa'i stong (S80) pa nyid/ de dag spros las spros pa ni/ /stong pa nyid kyis 'gag par 'gyur/ /ces pa'i[228] stong nyid dang/ rgyal ba rnams kyis[229] stong pa nyid/ ces pa'i stong nyid sogs phal cher mtha' bzhi char gyi spros pas stong pa'i stong nyid yin la/ nyan thos kyis rtogs par gsungs pa'i stong nyid ni bden pas stong tsam gyi stong nyid (K25b) yin pas khyad par shin tu che ste/ 'di la dgongs nas/ *'jug 'grel* las/ chos la bdag med pa tsam ces gsungs so//

de ltar ma yin par stong nyid thams cad bden pas stong pa tsam la byas nas theg pa che chung la khyad par med pa yin na/ stong nyid kyi sgra thos pas[230] mig nas mchi ma 'khrugs pa dang/ lus kyi ba spu ldang ba tsam gyis

225 K *la* omitted.
226 *Madhyamakāvatāra* (VI, 4). Toh no. 3861, Dbu ma *'a*, f. 204a: *so so skye bo.*
227 MA, f. 204a: *'gyur ba.*
228 KBS *pa'i* omitted.
229 KBS *kyi.*
230 BS *pa.*

whereas in the Mahāyāna all four signlessnesses are taught in their entirety. This is what [the passage] means; and hence, it is a passage [that shows] that there is a difference in the philosophical view [of the two vehicles].

[2A] Now let us consider the meaning of the second passage. "Others, the heterodox" refers to the non-Buddhist heterodox. "Some of our own" refers to the śrāvakas and pratyekabuddhas. Hence, this is a passage [that shows] that there is a difference in the philosophical view [of the two vehicles].

[3A] As for the meaning of the third passage, the "profound [doctrine]" refers to emptiness *qua* absence of the fourfold extremist proliferations. "Those who are apprehensive" *(khu 'phrig can)*[271] realize it through the awakening of their latent potentialities. Those who are not timid *(khu 'phrig med pa rnams)* are the ones who fear it, that is, [those in whom] it causes fear to arise.[272] Hence, this is also a passage that [demonstrates] a difference in the philosophical view [of the two vehicles]. How should "those who are apprehensive" be understood? As it is explained in the *Avatāra:*

> Even when they are [still] ordinary individuals, some hear [the doctrine of] emptiness
> And repeatedly experience great joy internally.
> That joy elicits tears
> And the standing on end of the hairs of their body.
> These [individuals] possess the seed of the mind of perfect buddhahood.[273]

Hence, the emptiness taught in these passages—that is, the "emptiness" [spoken of] in such passages as "[Misconceptions] proliferate on the basis of mental proliferations, but emptiness extinguishes the proliferations"[274] and "The Victors have said that emptiness..."[275]—refers for the most part to the emptiness of the proliferation of all four extremes. And given that the emptiness that the śrāvakas are said to understand is just the emptiness of truth, there is an enormous difference [between the emptiness realized in the Hīna- and Mahā-yānas].[276] It is with this intention that the *Avatāra-bhāṣya* says "[It is not the case that the Mahāyāna teachings set forth] only the selflessness of phenomena."[277]

Let us suppose, however, that [as you, Tsong kha pa, maintain] this is not the case, and all forms of emptiness refer only to the emptiness of truth, so that there is no difference between the Mahā- and Hīna-yānas [in regard to their understanding of emptiness]. How then do you avoid the contradictions that follow [from this]—utter contradictions, such as the fact that, on

theg chen gyi[231] rigs sad par rjes su dpag nus/ nyan thos dgra bcom pas stong nyid mngon sum du rtogs pa'i mi slob lam thob nas kyang theg chen gyi rigs ma sad pa ni shin tu 'gal bas 'di (S81) dag gi 'gal spang ci ltar byed/

[4A] *'jug 'grel* gyi lung dang po'i don ni/ sbyin pa'i 'khor gsum la btags pa tsam du yang mi dmigs pa ni/ 'jig rten las 'das pa yin la/ dmigs pa ni 'jig rten pa yin no/ /des na sbyin pa'i 'khor gsum mi dmigs pa ni byang chub sems dpa'i gnas skabs sa dang po ma thob pa dag gis shes par mi nus zhes pa'i don yin pas/ 'di yang lta ba la khyad par yod pa'i lung yin no/ /gal te mi dmigs pa'i don bden par mi dmigs pa la 'chad na ni/ dmigs pa yang bden pa la 'chad dgos pas/ tha snyad kyi bden pas/[232] zhes pa dang yang 'gal zhing/ byang chub sems dpa'i gnas skabs ma thob pa dag gis shes par mi nus zhes pa dang yang 'gal te/ bden par mi dmigs pa ni nyan thos la yang yod par khas blangs pa'i phyir//

[5A] lung gnyis pa'i don ni/ nyan thos kyi theg par[233] (K26a) dngos po rang bzhin med (S82) pa'i chos la bdag med par bstan na/ theg pa chen po bstan pa don med par 'gyur ro zhe na mi 'gyur te/ theg pa chen po las dngos po rang bzhin med pa'i chos la bdag med pa tsam 'ba' zhig ston par byed pa min te/ sa dang pha rol tu phyin pa la sogs pa yang bstan pa'i phyir/ zhes pa'i don yin la/

de la sa bcu'i chos dbyings kun tu 'gro ba'i tshul gyis rtogs pa sogs dang/ phar phyin drug gi shes rab kyi pha rol tu phyin pa dang/ smon lam dang/ yongs su bsngo ba la mtshan mar mi 'dzin pa dang/ snying rje chen po la dmigs pa med pa'i snying rje dang/ tshogs gnyis las ye shes kyi tshogs dang/ bsam gyis mi khyab pa'i chos nyid rnams ni/ theg chen thun mong ma yin pa'i lta ba yin pas/ 'di yang lta ba la khyad par yod pa'i lung yin no//

231 KB *gyis.*
232 KBS *bden pas dang/.*
233 K *par /.*

the one hand, one can infer that someone has awakened their Mahāyāna lineage *(theg chen gyi rigs sad pa)* based simply on the fact that hearing the word "emptiness" brings tears to their eyes and causes the hairs on their body to stand on end, while [on the other hand] the śrāvaka arhat who has attained the path of no more learning and who has [therefore] directly understood emptiness has yet to awaken his or her Mahāyāna lineage?[278]

[4A] Let us now consider the meaning of the first citation from the *Avatārabhāṣya.* Not perceiving the "three cycles of giving" even as merely nominal things *(btags pa tsam)* is what is beyond the world.[279] Perceiving [them] is a worldly [activity]. Therefore, [the passage must be understood] to mean that the nonperception of the three cycles of giving cannot be understood by those who have not obtained the first bhūmi of the bodhisattva state. Hence, this passage also [demonstrates] that there is a difference in philosophical view [between the two yānas]. Now if you take the words "not perceiving" to mean "not perceiving [things] *as true,*" then one would also have to explain "perceiving" as referring to [the perception of] truth, which contradicts [the fact that the passage states that perceiving things in this way is] "a truth of the conventional [world]."[280] [Glossing "perception" as "the perception of truth"] also contradicts the portion of the passage that says, "Those who have not attained the bodhisattva state cannot understand this." Why? Because [you, Tsong kha pa,] accept that even śrāvakas do not perceive [things] as true.

[5A] The meaning of the second *[Avatārabhāṣya]* citation [is as follows]. *[An opponent asks:]* If in the Śrāvakayāna there are teachings to the effect that "essenceless phenomena lack a self," does this make the teachings of the Mahāyāna pointless?[281] *[Reply:]* No, for the Mahāyāna does not teach *only* the selflessness within phenomena—that is, their lack of an inherent nature—since it *also* teaches about the stages, the perfections, and so forth. That is the meaning [of the passage].

In this regard, the expansive method of realizing reality *(chos dbyings kun tu 'gro ba'i tshul gyis rtogs pa)* of the tenth stage, etc., the perfection of wisdom [found among] the six perfections, the nongrasping at signs *(mtshan mar mi 'dzin pa)* during prayer and dedication, the objectless compassion *(dmigs pa med pa'i snying rje)* [that is a part] of great compassion,[282] the accumulation of gnosis [that is one] of the two accumulations, and the inconceivable reality *(bsam gyis mi khyab pa'i chos nyid):* all of these are special philosophical views of the Mahāyāna. Hence, this passage also [teaches] that there is a difference in [the two yānas'] philosophical views.

des na dbu ma pa rang gi lugs la theg pa gsum po bdag med rtogs (S83) par mtshungs kyang/ spros bral dang/ tshogs gnyis dang/ chos nyid dang/ gnas lugs mthar thug rtogs ma rtogs kyi khyad par yod pa ni/ dbu ma'i gzhung lugs kun las gsal zhing/ don 'di la klu sgrub yab sras dang/ mgon po byams pa dgongs pa gcig kho nar snang ngo/ /*'jug 'grel* las/

> chos kyi bdag med pa gsal bar bya ba'i phyir/[234] theg pa chen po bstan pa yang rigs pa nyid de[235] rgyas par bstan pa brjod par 'dod pa'i phyir/[236] nyan thos kyi theg (K26b) pa las ni chos kyi bdag med pa mdor mtshon pa tsam zhig tu zad do/

zhes pa'i don yang kho bos sngar bshad pa ltar yin te/ mtha' dang po bkag pa ni bsdus pa yin la/ mtha' bzhi char bkag pa ni rgyas pa yin pa'i phyir ro//

gang dag lung 'di'i don bsgrub bya bden pas stong pa'i stong nyid gcig pu la/ sgrub byed kyi rigs pa[237] rgyas bsdus kyi don du 'chad (S84) pa ni theg pa che chung gnyis dbang po rno rtul go log par 'dod dgos te/ bsgrub bya gcig nyid sgrub byed bsdus pa'i sgo nas rtogs pa ni dbang po rno ba yin cing/ sgrub byed rgyas pa dgos pa ni[238] dbang po rtul ba yin pa'i phyir ro//

gal te skyon med de/ sgrub byed kyi rigs pa rgyas pa'i sgo nas rtogs pa de/ spang bya spong ba la nus pa che ba yin pa'i phyir snyam na/

'o na spang bya bden 'dzin gcig nyid nyan thos brtson 'grus myur bas tshe gsum gyis spong bar nus shing/ theg pa chen pos[239] bskal pa grangs med pa gnyis kyi bar du spong mi nus pa 'di dang mi 'gal lam/ 'jig rten pa thams cad kyis bzhad gad bya bar 'os so//

nyan thos dgra bcom gyis bden 'dzin ma lus par spangs nas/ theg chen gyis sa brgyad pa ma thob kyi bar du bden 'dzin ma spong bar 'dod pa ni/

234 MABh, Toh no. 3862, Dbu ma *'a*, f. 228a: /omitted.
235 MABh, f. 228a: *de/*.
236 MABh, f. 228a: *phyir ro//*.
237 K *ba*.
238 S *na*.
239 KBS *po'i*.

Therefore, according to the Madhyamaka school, all three vehicles are similar in their realization of selflessness. But there *is* a difference as to whether or not they understand the freedom from proliferations, the two accumulations, reality *(chos nyid)*, and the ultimate nature *(gnas lugs mthar thug pa)* [of things]. The entire Madhyamaka textual tradition is clear on this point, and in this regard Nāgārjuna, the father, his spiritual son/s, and the protector Maitreya are completely unanimous in their opinion. The *Avatārabhāṣya* also states:

> It is because [the Mahāyāna] wishes to elucidate the selflessness of phenomena that it is fitting for the Mahāyāna teachings to set forth that very reasoning in an extensive manner. And it is for this reason that the Śrāvakayāna offers only a brief exposition of the selflessness of phenomena.[283]

The meaning [of this passage] is to be explained as I have [suggested] above—the refutation of one extreme being the brief [exposition], and the refutation of all four extremes being the extensive one.

Those who interpret this passage as referring to the extensiveness or brevity of the formal reasoning used to prove only one kind of emptiness[284]—the emptiness of truth qua *probandum (bsgrub bya)* [of a syllogism]—must be considered to have inverted the acuity of the intellectual capacities of the [followers of] Mahā- and Hīna-yānas. How so? [In actuality, and in contrast to Tsong kha pa's position], those who understand that single *probandum* through an abbreviated proof have a sharper intellect, whereas those who require an extensive proof have an intellect that is more dull.[285]

[Tsong kha pa's] Objection: There is no problem, since the understanding [of emptiness] by means of extensive probative reasoning represents a greater ability to abandon those [obscurations] that are to be abandoned.

[Reply:] Well then, does this not contradict the fact that śrāvakas who [move through the path] quickly due to their effort *(brtson 'grus myur bas)* can abandon that self-same apprehension of truth *qua* object to be abandoned in three lifetimes, whereas the Mahāyāna cannot eliminate this for two countless eons?[286] [A view such as yours] should therefore be an object of ridicule for the entire world!

[Tsong kha pa:] We believe that the śrāvaka arhat has eliminated all of the grasping at true [existence], whereas in the Mahāyāna the grasping at true [existence] is not eliminated until one obtains the eighth [bodhisattva] stage *(sa brgyad pa)*.

theg chen gyi spangs rtogs zab cing rgya che ba rnams la skur 'debs (S85) 'ba' zhig ste/ rtogs bya stong nyid gcig spang bya bden 'dzin kho na spong bar mtshungs pa la/ nyan thos mthong chos zhis/ stong nyid mngon sum du rtogs zin rgyun ltan du sgom (K27a) pas tshe gcig gis spang bya de spong nus la/ theg pa chen pos spang bya de spong ba la/ stong nyid mngon sum du rtogs te/ bskal pa grangs med gcig dgos par khas blangs pa'i phyir/

> 'di la'ang rjes su brjod pa yod//
> des na ngan pa'i mun pas khyab//

zhes gsungs pa yang dran par bya'o//

ma dag sa bdun gyi gnas skabs su bden 'dzin yod na/ las dang/ nyon mongs pa'i dbang gis skye ba len pa yod par 'gyur te/ bden 'dzin de las ngar 'dzin 'byung/ des las bsags[240]/ de las skye ba 'byung ba'i phyir ro/ /gsum char khas blangs soms shig/

gzhan yang sa bdun pa man chad du shes grib spong ba mi srid na/ nyan thos dgra bcom theg chen lam du zhugs pa'i tshe sa bdun (S86) pa man chad du spang bya gang spong ba yin/ zhes zhus na ber thul gyis dbu btums nas bzhugs dgos par 'gyur ro//

kha cig de'i skyon spong bar 'dod nas nyan thos dgra bcom sa brgyad pa nas 'jug pa yin ces smra ba ni shin tu smad pa'i gnas te/ de ltar na sangs rgyas bsgrub pa la dang po nyid nas theg chen kyi lam du 'jug pa las/ nyan thos kyi lam du 'jug pa shin tu myur bar 'gyur te/ snga mas sa brgyad pa ma thob kyi bar du bskal pa grangs med gnyis 'gor la/ phyi mas brtson 'grus

240 K *bsag*.
241 K *ba*.

[Reply:] This is tantamount to disparaging *(skur ba 'debs)* the depth and breadth of the Mahāyāna's [methods] for eliminating [obscurations] and realizing [insight]. Why? [According to you, both yānas] are similar (a) insofar as what is to be realized [in both of them] is the one [form of] emptiness, and (b) insofar as [they both] eliminate what is to be abandoned—namely, that very grasping at true [existence]. The śrāvakas who will attain peace in this life *(nyan thos mthong chos zhis)* can eliminate those objects to be abandoned in a single lifetime by [first] directly realizing emptiness, and then meditating on it in a continuous fashion; whereas for the [followers of the] Mahāyāna, to eliminate the objects to be abandoned, they need one countless eon after the direct understanding of emptiness. Think about the passage that states:

> There are followers even of [an evil doctrine the likes of this]!
> That is why [the world] is pervaded by the darkness of evil.[287]

If [as you, Tsong kha pa, claim], there is grasping at truth during the seven impure stages *(ma dag sa bdun)*, there would also have to be [the kind of] rebirth that occurs under the influence of karma and the afflictions, since (1) the grasping at truth gives rise to the grasping at the "I" *(ngar 'dzin)*, (2) [which in turn gives rise to] the accumulation of karma, (3) [which in turn] gives rise to rebirth. Think about what is claimed in all three [statements and you will see that for you there is no way out]!

Moreover, if it is not possible to eliminate obscurations to omniscience before the seventh stage, then consider the case of the śrāvaka arhat who enters the Mahāyāna path [after becoming an arhat and removing all afflictions]. What objects are there for [that arhat] to abandon before the seventh stage [since they have already eliminated the afflicted obscurations, and, according to you, they cannot begin to eliminate the obscurations to omniscience until they reach the seventh stage]? When posed with this question, [those who hold these views] must remain with their heads buried in their robe *(ber thul gyis dbu btums nas bzhugs)* [in shame].

One individual, wishing to avoid the problems with this [position], claims that the śrāvaka arhat enters [the Mahāyāna path directly] at the eighth [bodhisattva] stage, but this is an utterly disgraceful position. Why? It would imply that it would be much faster to obtain buddhahood by [first] entering the śrāvaka path [and then switching to the Mahāyāna], rather than by entering the Mahāyāna path directly, since it takes two countless aeons to obtain the eighth stage in the latter case, whereas in the former, myur na tshe gsum gyis dgra bcom thob cing/ de nas sa brgyad pa la 'jug pas[241] chog pa'i phyir/ 'di yang theg chen gyi lam la skur pa 'debs pa'i snyad du snang ngo//

mngon rtogs (K27b) *rgyan* las sa dgu dang sgom spang shes sgrib dgu spang gnyen du sbyar ba 'dir khas mi len pa de/ [1] drang don yin pas khas mi len pa (S87) yin nam/ [2] rang rgyud pa man chad kyi lugs yin pas khas mi len pa yin nam/ [3] *dbu ma 'jug pa* dang mi mthun pas khas mi len pa yin nam/ [4] rgyu mtshan gzhan smra rgyu yod pas khas mi len pa yin/

[1] dang po ltar na skabs der drang don yin nam/ *mngon rtogs rgyan* ril po drang[242] don yin/ dang po ltar na/ gsal bar dbang phyug spyod pa kho na yin no/ /phyi ma ltar na/ slob dpon dbyig gnyen la sogs pas sems tsam du 'grel ba tsam[243] ma gtogs/ gzhan du na rgya bod gang na yang de skad du smra ba su yang ma byung zhing/ zab mo sher phyin gyi sbas don *mngon rtogs rgyan* gyi rim pa mgon po byams pas 'grel pa'i bstan bcos 'dzam bu'i gling gi theg pa chen po'i[244] bstan pa'i snying po drang don du byas nas de dang mi mthun pa'i grub mtha' bcas te/ 'di ni thun mong min pa'i gnad yin no/ /zhes sgrog cing/ blun po ma bslabs pa rnams de la (S88) 'jug pa bden kyang/ mkhas par rloms zhing rtog dpyod dang ldan pa dag gis kyang 'di kho na bzhin du 'dzin pa ni shin tu 'jigs shing ya nga ba'i gnas su mthong bas rtog dpyod ldan pa dag gis bag zon mdzod cig/

[2] gnyis pa ltar na/ dngos smra ba'i gzhung yin nam/ ran rgyud pa'i gzhung yin ces dpyad na dpyad mi bzod pas dor bar bya ba kho na yin no//

242 K *dang.*
243 K *tsa.*
244 K *chan pa'i.*

those who, due to their effort, [move through the path] quickly obtain arhatship in three lifetimes, and from there enter the eighth [bodhisattva] stage [directly]. This [position therefore] appears to be a pretext for slandering the Mahāyāna path.

[You, Tsong kha pa,] do not accept the *Abhisamayālaṃkāra's* [teaching that] the nine stages [of the bodhisattva path] are correlated with the antidotes to the nine [degrees of] obscurations to omniscience that are to be abandoned during the path of meditation *(sgom spang shes sgrib dgu)*.[288] Now do you not accept this (1) because it is a provisional [teaching] *(drang don)*? Or is it because (2) [it represents the view of a philosophical] system that is at or below that of the Svātantrikas? Or (3) do you not accept it because it is not in accordance with the *Madhyamakāvatāra?* Or, finally, (4) do you have some other reason to offer for not accepting it?

[1] In the first case, is it that this [particular] section [of the *Abhisamayālaṃkāra*] is of provisional meaning, or is the entire *Abhisamayālaṃkāra* of provisional meaning? In the former case, your analysis [of what is and what is not provisional is] clearly [frivolous, like that of a petulant] god *(gsal bar dbang phyug spyod pa kho na)*.[289] And what of the latter case [that is, that the *entire* AA is provisional]? The master Vasubandhu, and others, have commented [on the AA[290]] from an exclusively Cittamātra perspective, but except for them there is no one in either India or Tibet who makes such a claim—[namely, that the entire text is of provisional meaning]. The stages of the *Abhisamayālaṃkāra (Mngon rtogs rgyan gyi rim pa)*—the implicit meaning *(sbas don)* of the profound Perfection of Wisdom [sūtras][291]—are the essence of the teachings of the Mahāyāna of [our world,] Jambudvīpa, [taught] by the protector Maitreya in his commentarial treatise [the AA]. [For you] to then take this [text] to be of provisional meaning is a philosophical position that is inconsistent with the [lofty status of the AA just explained]. And yet [you] boast that this is a special doctrine [of your system]. Even though it is true that untutored fools have subscribed to this [position, it is also the case that] even some who fancy themselves scholars and who possess analytical abilities have adopted such a position. Seeing it to be an utterly terrifying and dangerous [view], those who possess analytical abilities should beware [of it].

[2] In the second case, [that is, if you do not accept it because it represents the view of a philosophical system that is at or below the Svātantrikas, then we argue as follows]. Is [the AA] a treatise of the realists, or is it a Svātantrika treatise? Since upon examination it can be considered neither, [this position] can only be rejected.[292]

[3] gsum pa ltar na/ *'jug pa* dang mi mthun pa nyid ma grub par gong du bshad (K28a) zin la/ gal te grub na rgyu mtshan des *mngon rtogs rgyan* 'dor bar 'dod kyang/ phugs kyis *'jug pa* 'dor 'dod pa'i snyad du snang ngo//

[4] bzhi pa ltar na rgyu mtshan de smra dgos shing/ smras kyang rang bzo min pa lung dang mthun pa khyed la med do//

theg pa gsum po gang gi 'ang mthong lam ma thob par bden bzhi mi rtag la sogs bcu drug mngon (S89) sum du rtogs zin rgyun ldan du goms par byas nas khams gsum kyi nyon mongs mngon gyur pa spangs pa'i gang zag yod pa ni sangs rgyas pa'i grub mtha' smra ba bzhi po gang gi lugs la yang med la/ phyi rol pa rnams kyis kyang mi smra zhing/ grub mtha' la ma zhugs pa rnams kyis kyang mi smra bas 'di ni shar tsong kha pa blo bzang grags pa'i dpal kho na'i grub mtha' 'o//

spyir grub mtha' 'di 'dra'i rigs can la dgag sgrub byed pa la dgos pa cher mi snang yang/ 'ga' zhig 'di la yang bden par 'dzin par snang bas/ de la 'di 'dri ste/ de lta ba'i gang zag de so so skye bo las 'os med pas [1] lam du ma zhugs pa yin nam/ [2] theg dman so skye yin nam/ [3] theg chen so skye yin/

[1] dang po ltar na lam la ma zhugs kyi gang zag gis[245] bden pa mngon sum du mthong pa ngo mtshar che zhing/ [2] gnyis pa ltar na/ tshe de nyid la spangs pa de las ma (S90) nyams bzhin du shi 'phos nas khams gang du skye ston dgos la/ [3] gsum pa ltar na/ des chos kyi bdag med rtogs par 'gyur ro//

gzhan (K28b) yang gang zag des mngon sum du rtogs pa'i lam rigs pa sgrub pa nges 'byin bzhi dang/ 'gog pa/ zhi ba gya noms nges 'byung bzhi

245 K *gi.*

[3] In the third case, [if this doctrine is rejected because it is not in accord with the *Madhyamakāvatāra*], we have already explained that there is no basis for [claiming that there are] inconsistencies [between the AA] and the *Avatāra.* But even if [these two texts] *are* [inconsistent], though you claim this to be the reason for rejecting the *Abhisamayālaṃkāra,* in point of fact it appears as though in the final analysis this is just a pretext for rejecting the *Avatāra.*

[4] In the fourth case, [that is, if there is another reason,] you must state that reason; but even if you do, it will be something of your own fabrication, something that is not consistent with scripture.

[Tsong kha pa] maintains that there is an individual who, without having obtained the path of seeing of any of the three vehicles, has abandoned the manifest afflictions of the three worlds by means of his or her direct realization of—and subsequent continuous meditation on—the sixteen [aspects] of the four noble truths, such as impermanence and so forth. But this is not [a position] that is to be found in any of the four Buddhist philosophical schools; nor is it advocated by any [non-Buddhist] outsider; nor is it advocated by non-philosophers. Hence, this is a philosophical tenet of the Easterner, the glorious Tsong kha pa Blo bzang grags pa, and his alone.[293]

Even though I see no great need to engage in polemics in regard to those who belong to the lineage of this philosophical tenet, since it seems as though there are some who hold onto it as if it were the gospel truth, I will ask the following questions. Since such individuals [who have rid themselves of the manifest afflictions without having obtained the path of seeing] cannot but be ordinary individuals *(so so skye bo),* (1) do they not abide in a path *(lam du ma zhugs)*; (2) are they ordinary individuals [who abide in one of the] Hīnayāna [paths]; or (3) are they ordinary individuals [who abide in a] Mahāyāna [path]?

[1] In the first case, it would be utterly amazing for individuals who do not abide in a path to directly perceive the truth *(bden pa mngon sum du mthong ba).* [2] In the second case, when such [individuals]—who, having eliminated [those manifest afflictions] in this life, still keep [this accomplishment] intact *(ma nyams pa bzhin du)*—die, it is necessary [for you to] show us into which of the realms they are born *(khams gang du skye ston dgos).* [3] In the third case, [such individuals] would have to understand the selflessness of phenomena.

Moreover, what if one were to ask, "Which of the four [aspects of the third noble truth of cessation] is it that is directly realized by such an individual? Is it [the aspect of] deliverance *(nges 'byin),* of cessation *('gog pa),* of

gang yin/ zhes dris na 'phags pa rta thul gyis tshangs pa chen po la 'byung ba bzhi po 'di gang du 'gag/ ces dris pa'i lan de nyid gsungs dgos par 'gyur zhing/ *'jug 'grel* las/ 'gog pa'i bden pa ni don dam pa'i bden pa'i[246] rang gi ngo bo zhes gsungs pa 'di'i 'og nas kyang mi thar ro//

spyod 'jug gi lung gi don gtan min pa'i rgyu mtshan gzhan du 'chad cing/

> sred 'di nyon mongs can min yang//
> kun rmongs bzhin du ci ste med//

ces pa'i lung dang yang dngos su 'gal te/ de lta bu'i gang zag de'i yang srid len pa'i rgyur gyur pa'i sred pa de nyon (S91) mongs can du khas blangs pa'i phyir ro//

[3.3.4.0.0 kun gzhi dang rang rig mi 'dod cing phyi don khas len pa'i tshul la dpyad pa]

kun gzhi dang/ rang rig mi 'dod cing/ phyi don khas len pa'i tshul la yang dpyad par bya ste/ dbu ma pa gzhan gyis yod na rang gi mtshan nyid kyis yod dgos la/ rang gi mtshan nyid kyis med na med dgos par 'dod ces pa ni/ 'phags yul gyi mkhas grub chen po rnams la 'di tsam gyis skur pa btab pa la dgos pa ci zhig 'grub ste/ *dbu ma rgyan gyi 'grel par* dngos po rnams[247] ma brtags gcig pu nyams[248] dga' ba/ ma lus pa gzugs brnyan la sogs pa lta bur ces dang/ *bden gnyis* las/

> gal te rigs pa'i stobs kyis na//
> kun rdzob tu yang mi skye zer[249]//
> de bden de yi phyir na 'di//
> ji ltar snang ba yin par gsungs[250]//

zhes dang/ yang de nyid las/ (K29a)

246 KBS *pa.* MABh, Toh no. 3862, Dbu ma *'a,* f. 243b: *pa'i.*
247 *Madhyamakālaṃkāra.* Ichigoḥ, ed., 14: *po'i rnam pa.*
248 *Madhyamakālaṃkāra.* Ichigoḥ, ed., 14: *na.*
249 *Satyadvayavibhaṅga,* v. 20. Eckel, ed., *Jñānagarbha,* 174: *mi skye dang.*
250 Eckel, ed., *Jñānagarbha,* 174: *ji ltar snang bzhin yin par gsungs.*

peace *(zhi ba)*, or of the sublime *(gya nom)*?"[294] In such a case, it is necessary for [Tsong kha pa] to give the same response that Mahābrahma gave to Ārya Aśvajit *('Phags pa rta thul)*[295] when the latter asked him how the four elements cease [namely, the response of befuddled silence]. Nor [can Tsong kha pa] escape the implications of the *Avatārabhāṣya* passage that states "the truth of cessation is the ultimate truth's own nature."[296]

I will explain elsewhere the reasons for why [Tsong kha pa's view] is not what is meant by the passages from the *Bodhicāryavatara*.[297] [His position] is also in direct contradiction to the passage that states:

> Even though this craving *(sred pa)* is not afflicted
> Why should it not exist, [just] like delusion *(kun rmongs)*?[298]

How so? Because he accepts that the craving that is the cause for the rebirth of such an individual *is* afflicted.[299]

[An Examination of Tsong kha pa's View that Prāsaṅgikas Accept External Objects Despite the Fact that They Do Not Believe in the Foundation Consciousness and in Reflexive Awareness]

We should also examine how it is that [Prāsaṅgikas] accept external objects despite the fact that they do not believe in the foundation [consciousness] *(kun gzhi)* and reflexive awareness *(rang rig)*. [Tsong kha pa claims that] other followers of the Middle Way, [that is, Svātantrikas,] believe that if something exists, it must exist by virtue of its own characteristic, and that if it does not exist by virtue of its own characteristic, then [according to them] it cannot exist. But what need is there to slander the scholar-practitioners of the Noble Land [of India] in this peculiar way? The *Madhyamakālaṃkāravṛtti* states, "[When one understands] that things are satisfactory so long as they are not analyzed, and that like a reflection [they are in reality essenceless]..."[300] And the *Satyadvaya* states:

> *[Opponent:]* When [things] are subjected to analysis,
> They are not [seen to] arise even in a conventional sense.
> *[Reply:]* That is true, and it is why
> The [Buddha] taught that things are as they appear.[301]

And again, that same [text states]:

> ji ltar snang bzhin ngo bo'i phyir//
> 'di la dpyad pa mi 'jug go//
> kun rdzob[251] ni ji ltar snang bzhin yin (S92) te[252]/ 'di la[253] ji skad bshad pa'i dpyad pa'i gnas med pa nyid do//

zhes dang/ slob dpon legs ldan 'byed kyis/ 'ba' zhig pa zhes bya ba ni ngo bo nyid kyi dri tsam gyis kyang ma gos pa'o//[254] zhes dang/ slob dpon seng ge bzang pos/ ma brtags[255] gcig pur nyams dga' ba nyid du rgyu dang 'bras bur 'brel pa zhes pa zhes sogs[256] rang rgyud pa'i gzhung lugs khung thub rnams las/ 'di bzhin du bshad pa tshad ma yin la/ 'di las lhag pa'i kun rdzob kyi 'jog lugs thal 'gyur ba[257] rnams la yang mi snang ba'i phyir ro//

las 'bras kyi rten du gyur pa'i kun gzhi rigs pas dpyad bzod thal 'gyur ba rnams kyis khas mi len kyang spyir kun gzhi khas len dgos te/ *byang chub sems 'grel* las/ kun gzhi yod par dngos su gsungs pa'i phyir ro//

phyi don khas len pa thal 'gyur ba'i lugs thun mong min pa yin na/ slob dpon (S93) legs ldan 'byed kyis kyang/ phyi don khas blangs pa dang 'gal zhing/

gal te khas len lugs la khyad par yod de/ rang gi mtshan nyid kyis grub pa khas len mi len gyi khyad par yod pa'i phyir snyam na/

rang gi mtshan nyid kyis grub pa'i don/ [1] rigs pas dpyad bzod la byed dam/ [2] rang mtshan dang spyi mtshan gyi ya gyal du gyur pa'i rang mtshan la byed dam/ [3] thun mong min pa'i 'jog byed la byed/ (K29b)

[1] dang po ltar na/ rang rgyud pas bden grub khas len par 'gyur zhing/ de yang 'dod na dbu ma pa ma yin par 'gyur ro/ /de yang 'dod na/ *drang nges rnam 'byed* kyi shog bu[258] zhe brgyad pa'i nang logs su/

> mkhas pa de dag kyang chos bden par yod pa'i grub mtha' rigs

251 Eckel, ed., *Jñānagarbha,* 175: *ci ste kun rdzob.* KBS *ci ste* omitted.

252 Eckel, ed., *Jñānagarbha,* 175: *snang ba bzhin yin te.*

253 Eckel ed., *Jñānagarbha,* 175: *de la ni.*

254 Bhāvaviveka, *Prañāpradīpamūlamadhyamakavṛtti* on MMK (XXII, 8ab). Toh no. 3842 Dbu ma *tsha,* f. 221b: *'ba' zhig ces bya ba ni ngo bo nyid med pa ste / ngo bo nyid kyi dri tsam gyis kyang ma bsgos pa dag yin no//.*

255 KB *rtags.* S and Haribhadra, *Sphuṭārtha,* Toh no. 3793, Sher phyin *ja,* f. 118: *brtags.*

256 KB *'bras bur 'brel pa zhes pa zhes sogs;* S *'bras bur 'brel ba zhes ba zhes sogs.* Haribhadra, *Sphuṭārtha,* f. 118: *'bras bu 'brel pa'i stobs kyis...*

257 B *pa.*

258 BS *gu.*

> Because its nature is just as it appears to be,
> We do not subject it to analysis.[302]
> [Given then that] the conventional is just as it appears to be,
> it is not a locus for the kind of analysis just explained.[303]

The master Bhāvaviveka has also said, "'isolated' means that it is not stained even with the trace-odor of essentialism *(ngo bo nyid kyi dri tsam gyis)*";[304] and the master Haribhadra states, "only when one is satisfied with not analyzing it [can one can speak of] 'a relationship between cause and effect.'"[305] Passages like these from the Svātantrika textual tradition are valid explanations of how [the conventional exists], and there is no Prāsaṅgika method of positing the conventional that is superior to that found in those [Svātantrika sources].

[True,] the Prāsaṅgikas do not accept the foundation [consciousness] as the basis for karma and its effects [when this is conceived of as something] that can withstand rational analysis. But [as followers of Nāgārjuna], they must in general accept the foundation [consciousness],[306] for the *Bodhicittavivaraṇa* explicitly states that the foundation [consciousness] exists.[307]

[Your claim] that accepting external objects is a unique tenet of the Prāsaṅgika system is contradicted by the fact that the Master Bhāvaviveka [a Svātantrika] also accepts external objects.

[Objection:] There is a difference in the way in which he accepts them, since there is a difference [between Svātantrikas and Prāsaṅgikas] as regards whether or not [external objects] exist by virtue of their own characteristics.[308]

[Reply:][309] What do you mean by [the expression] "exist by virtue of their own characteristics" *(rang gi mtshan nyid kyis grub pa)*? (1) Does this refer to "withstanding rational analysis" *(rigs pas dpyad bzod)*; (2) does it refer to the "specific characteristic" *(rang mtshan = svalakṣaṇa)* that is part of the pair [of terms] "specific characteristic and general characteristic" *(rang mtshan/spyi mtshan = svalakṣaṇa/sāmānyalakṣaṇa)*; or (3) does it refer to the special [distinguishing quality] that makes things what they are?

[1] In the first case, it would [mean that] Svātantrikas would accept true existence, and if they believe in that, it [means that] they could not be followers of the Middle Way. If you accept that [they accept true existence], moreover, remember what you [Tsong kha pa] have written, in a separate instance, on the reverse side of the forty-eighth folio of [your] *Elucidation of the Provisional and Definitive:*[310]

> These scholars refute through many rational methods *(rigs pa'i sgo*

pa'i sgo du ma nas 'gog cing bden med du legs par[259] zhal gyis bzhes pas dbu ma pa ni yin no//

zhes bris pa de dran par gyis shig/ [2] gnyis pa ltar na/ phung po lnga po (S94) mngon pa las rang spyi'i mtshan nyid yod mnyam du bshad pa ltar 'dod par bya dgos pas/[260] zhes pa dang 'gal lo/ /[3] gsum pa ltar na dpal ldan zla bas/ gzugs nas rnam mkhyen gyi bar gyi chos thams cad kyi 'jog byed gsungs pa dang 'gal lo//

[3.3.5.0.0 rang rgyud kyi rtags dang dam bca' med pa'i tshul dpyad pa]

rang rgyud kyi rtags dang dam bca' med pa'i tshul la yang dpyad par bya ste/

rang rgyud kyi dgos pa ni/ rang gi mtshan nyid kyis grub pa'i chos bsgrub pa'i ched yin pas rang gi mtshan nyid kyis grub pa'i chos khas len na/ rang rgyud dgos shing/ de khas mi len na rang rgyud mi dgos zhes 'dod pa ni

dngos smra ba dang/ dbu ma thal rang[261] gang gi yang lugs min te/ dngos smra ba rnams kyis spyi dngos med du bsgrub pa la rang rgyud kyi gtan tshigs mang du bkod pas/[262] gtan tshigs[263] de dag gis chos can spyi dang/ chos dngos med dang sgrub bya de gnyis (S95) kyi tshogs don gang rang gi mtshan nyid kyis grub pa bsgrub pa yin smra dgos pa la smra rgyu med pa'i phyir ro//

rang rgyud pas rang gi mtshan nyid kyis grub pa'i chos bsgrub pa'i ched du rang rgyud khas (K30a) blangs[264] pa yin ces pa ni/ dbu ma *tshig gsal* las/ rang rgyud yod med kyi dgag sgrub mang du gsungs pa rnams kyi don cung zad kyang ma rtogs pa'am/ yang na rtogs bzhin du phyin ci log tu gsungs

259 B *du bar* (*legs* omitted).
260 Tsong kha pa, *Legs bshad snying po, Collected Works,* Lhasa Zhol ed., vol. *pha,* f. 78a: *phung po lnga ga khyad med par rang bzhin gyis stong par bstan zhing mngon pa las lnga ga'i rang spyi'i mtshan nyid yod mnyam du bshad pa ltar 'dod par bya ste.*
261 K *dbu mtha' rang.*
262 BS / omitted.
263 KB *tshig.*
264 S *lan;* B *len.*

> *du ma)* the philosophical tenet that [maintains] that phenomena truly exist; and they correctly accept [phenomena] to be truthless. Hence, they are followers of the Middle Way.[311]

[2] In the second case, it contradicts [the passage that states], "It is necessary to accept the way in which the Abhi[dharma] explains the five aggregates—namely, as having both specific [characteristics] and general characteristics."[312] [3] In the third case, [for you to claim that Prāsaṅgikas reject this form of self-characteristic] contradicts the glorious Candra[kīrti]'s teachings that all phenomena—from form up to omniscience—have such [distinguishing attributes].[313]

[An Examination of Tsong kha pa's Views Concerning Why There Are No Autonomous Reasons and Theses]

We must also analyze what it means for there to be no autonomous reasons *(rang rgyud kyi rtags)* and theses *(dam bca').*[314]

[Tsong kha pa:] What purpose do autonomous *(svatantra)* [reasons] serve [in the Svātantrika school]? They function to establish [or to prove, *bsgrub pa*] phenomena/attributes *(chos)* that exist by virtue of their own characteristic.[315] Hence, if one accepts [that there are] phenomena that exist by virtue of their own characteristic, autonomous [reasons] are necessary; and if one does not accept this, then autonomous [reasons] are not necessary.

[Reply:] This is not [representative of] the views of the realists, of the Prāsaṅgikas, or of the Svātantrika followers of the Middle Way. Why? The realists repeatedly use autonomous reasons *(rang rgyud kyi gtan tshigs)* to establish the nonreality [lit. nonthingness] of universals *(spyi dngos med).*[316] Hence, [according to you] they would have to advocate that those reasons establish (1) the subject, "generally [characterized phenomena]," (2) the predicate, "unreal" *(dngos med)*, and (3) the *probandum,* the combination *(tshogs don)* of those [latter] two, as existing by virtue of their own characteristic, but they *do not* advocate this.[317]

Those who claim that the Svātantrikas accept autonomous [syllogisms] for the sake of [establishing that phenomena] exist by virtue of their own characteristic have either completely misunderstood the meaning of the many [passages of the] *Madyamakaka Prasannapadā,* in which [Candrakīrti] discusses proofs for the nonexistence[318]—and refutations of the existence—of autonomous [reasons], or else, having understood those [passages], they teach them incorrectly. How so? In the section on the refutation of [the fact

par snang ste/ 'di ltar bdag skye 'gog pa'i skabs su/ slob dpon sangs rgyas bskyangs kyis

> dngos po rnams bdag las skye ba mi 'thad de/ de dag gi skye ba don med pa nyid du 'gyur ba'i phyir dang/ shin tu thal bar 'gyur ba'i phyir ro/ /dngos po bdag gi bdag nyid du yod pa rnams la ni yang skye ba la dgos pa med do/ /ci ste yod kyang skye na ni nam yang mi skye bar mi 'gyur ro//[265]

zhes gsungs pa la/ slob dpon legs ldan 'byed kyis/

> de ni rigs pa min te/ gtan (S96) tshigs dang dpe ma brjod pa'i phyir dang/ gzhan gyis smras pa'i nyes pa ma bsal ba'i phyir/

zhes sogs kyi skyon brjod mdzad do//

de la zla bas skyon spang mdzad pa ni/ gtan tshigs dang dpe ma brjod pa'i phyir/ zhes pa'i don [1] rang rgyud kyi gtan tshigs dang dpe ma brjod pa'i phyir dang/ de la gzhan gyis smras pa'i nyes pa ma bsal ba'i phyir zhes zer ba yin nam/ [2] gzhan la grags kyi gtan tshigs dang dpe ma brjod pa'i phyir dang/ de la gzhan gyis smras pa'i nyes pa ma bsal ba'i phyir zhes zer/

[1] dang po ltar na rang rgyud kyi gtan tshigs dang dpe brjod mi dgos te/ [i] slob dpon sangs rgyas bskyangs kyi ngag des grangs can pas bdag skye khas blangs pa la 'bras bu rgyu'i du na yod pa de nyid slar skye ba dang/ (K30b) yod pa slar skye ba la dgos pa med par khas blangs pa ni 'gal ba yin no/ /zhes bstan pa yin la/ khas blangs nang 'gal bstan (S97) pas pha rol po'i log rtog 'gog nus pas/ rang rgyud kyi gtan tshigs dang dpe brjod pa la dgos pa med pa'i phyir dang/ [ii] khas blangs nang 'gal bstan pas kyang log rtog mi bzlog[266] na/ rang rgyud kyi gtan tshigs dang dpe brjod pas kyang mi bzlog[267] pa'i phyir ro//

265 The passage in Buddhapālita's *Mūlamadhyamakavṛtti*, Toh no. 3842, Dbu ma *tsa,* f. 161b, reads: *dngos po rnams bdag gi bdag nyid las skye ba med de/ de dag gi skye ba don med pa nyid du 'gyur ba'i phyir dang/ skye ba thug pa med par 'gyur ba'i phyir ro/ /'di ltar dngos po bdag gi bdag nyid du yod pa rnams la yang skye ba dgos pa med do/ /gal te yod kyang yang skye na nam yang mi skye bar mi 'gyur bas.* But the passage quoted here in Go rams pa's text more closely resembles (and is therefore probably derived from) Candrakīrti's paraphrase of Buddhapālita in the latter's *Prasannapadā*, Toh no. 3860, Dbu ma *'a,* f. 5b: *dngos po rnams bdag las skye ba med de/ de dag gi skye ba don med pa nyid du 'gyur ba'i phyir dang/ shin tu thal bar 'gyur ba'i phyir ro/ /dngos po bdag gi bdag nyid du yod pa rnams la ni yang skye ba la dgos pa med do/ /ci ste yod yang skye na nam yang mi skye bar mi 'gyur ro.* The same applies to the quotation from Bhāvaviveka that follows.

266 K *gzlog.*

267 K *gzlog.*

that things] arise from themselves, the master Buddhapālita [refutes the arising of something from itself] as follows:

> It is not possible for phenomena to arise from themselves, because that would make their arising purposeless *(don med pa nyid)*, and because it would entail extreme absurdities *(shin tu thal ba'i phyir)*. Things that exist in and of themselves do not need to arise again. If something that already existed were to arise [again], then it would never *not* arise [that is, the arising of that thing would repeat itself endlessly].[319]

Against this, [Bhāvaviveka] points out errors [in Buddhapālita's formulation]—errors like:

> This is not a correct [formulation of the critique of self-arising], because [you, Buddhapālita,] state no reason *(gtan tshigs)* and no example, and because [you] do not rebut the fault that the other party claims [exists in our position].[320]

Candra[kīrti] then engages in a defense [of Buddhapālita]. [He asks] whether [Bhāvaviveka's claim that Buddhapālita] states no reason and no example means (1) that [Buddhapālita] states no *autonomous* reason and example, and that he does not eliminate the faults advocated by the other [party against that reason and example] *or* (2) that he does not state a syllogism and example understandable to the other [party] *(gzhan la 'grags kyi gtan tshig dang dpe)*,[321] and that he does not eliminate the faults advocated by the other [party against *this* type of reason and example].

[1] In the first case, it is unnecessary to cite an autonomous reason and example. Why? The master Buddhapālita's argument is [pointing out] the contradiction inherent in the Sāṃkhya belief that [things] arise from themselves[322]—namely, the belief [on the one hand] that an effect that exists at the time of its cause [nonetheless still] arises again and, [on the other,] that what exists need not arise again.[323] This is what he teaches. This demonstration of the internal contradiction [in the opponent's] beliefs *does*—[*contra* what Bhāvaviveka believes]—have the ability to refute the opponent's mistaken conceptions *(log rtog)*. Hence, it is not necessary to state an autonomous reason and example. If [the opponents'] mistaken conception can*not* be overturned by demonstrating that their beliefs are internally contradictory, then it will not be overturned even by stating an autonomous reason and example.[324]

dbu ma pa yin na ni/ nang gi skye mched rnams bdag las skye ba med par rang rgyud kyi dam bca' byas nas/ de sgrub pa'i rang rgyud kyi gtan tshigs rigs pa min te/ nang gi skye mched rnams bdag las skye ba las phyogs gzhan bdag las skye ba med pa yang rang rgyud du khas blangs pa med pa'i phyir/ de'i shes byed du bzhi brgya pa dang rtsod bzlog gi lung gnyis drangs pa yin pas/ 'di dag gi don/ rang rgyud med pa'i shes byed du rang gi mtshan nyid kyis grub pa'i chos khas blangs pa med pa bkod pa yin ces pa la ni 'brel cung zad kyang med pa yin no// (S98)

'di la shes bya kun rig gi zhal snga nas/

> dbu ma pa yin na bdag skye bkag nas gzhan skye sgrub pa'i rang rgyud kyi gtan tshigs bya mi rigs te/ bdag skye las phyogs gzhan gzhan skye khas blangs pa med pa'i phyir/

ces gsungs kyang/ 'dir bdag skye med par sgrub pa'i rang rgyud yod med rtsod pa'i skabs yin pas mi 'thad par sems so/

/des na nang gi skye mched rnams bdag las skye ba med pa'i rang rgyud kyi dam bca' med pas/ de la gzhan gyis smras pa'i (K31a) nyes pa 'bras bui'i[268] bdag nyid las skye ba med pa yin na/ grub pa la sgrub[269] pa yin la/ rgyu'i[270] bdag nyid las skyes pa yin na/ gtan tshigs 'gal ba'i don nyid du 'gyur ro zhes pa'i nyes pa bsal mi dgos te/ de lta bu'i nyes pa ni bdag skye med pa'i rang rgyud kyi dam bca' la nye bar gnas pa yin no//

[2] gal te gtan tshigs dang dpe ma brjod pa'i phyir/ ces pa'i don gzhan (S99) la grags pa'i gtan tshigs dang dpe ma brjod pa'i phyir zhes zer ba yin na/ de yang mi 'thad de/ 'dir gzhan grags kyi rjes dpag brjod dgos pa'i nges

268 KBS *rgyu'i.* The text of the *Lta ba'i shan 'byed* is corrupt at this point, reversing *rgyu'i* and, in the next line, *'bras bu'i.* This becomes clear by comparison to *Prasannapadā,* Tib., Bhopal ed., 12: *gang gi tshe de ltar dbu ma pas rang gi rgyud kyi rjes su dpag pa mi brjod pa nyid yin pa de'i tshe/ dam bca' ba'i don di gang yin/ ci bdag las shes bya ba 'bras bu'i bdag nyid las sam/ 'on te rgyu'i bdag nyid las yin grang/ de las cir 'gyur/ gal te 'bras bu bdag nyid las yin na ni grub pa la sgrub pa yin la rgyu'i bdag nyid las yin na ni 'gal ba'i don nyid du 'gyur te/.*

269 K *bsgrub.*

270 KBS *'bras bui'i.* See note 268.

If one is a Madhyamaka, it is incorrect to [assert] that the internal sense-fields *(nang gi skye mched)* do not arise from themselves in such a way that one turns this into an autonomous thesis and, having [taken up such a thesis autonomously, to then posit] an autonomous reason to prove that [thesis]. Why [is it incorrect for Mādhyamikas to posit autonomous theses and reasons]? [Mādhyamikas] have no autonomous beliefs—[not] even [the belief] in the fact that the internal sources do not arise from themselves, which is the position opposite to that [of the opponents], that they *do* arise from themselves. Candrakīrti cites two passages—one from the *Catuḥśataka* and one from the *Vigrahavyāvartanī*[325]—as proofs of this [point]. It makes no sense, however, [to take these passages] to mean that it is the lack of a belief in phenomena that exist by virtue of their own characteristic that is to be posited as the reason for why there are no autonomous [theses and reasons].[326]

In this regard, (Rong ston) Shes bya kun rig has said:

> If one is a Mādhyamika, it is incorrect to resort to an autonomous reason to establish the arising [of one thing] from another once self-arising has been refuted. This is because [Mādhyamikas] do not believe in the arising [of one thing] from another, which is the position opposite to that of self-arising.[327]

Despite [his having said this], I think that it is incorrect,[328] since in the present context we are dealing with a dispute concerning whether or not there exist autonomous [reasons] that prove the lack of *self*-arising.[329]

Therefore, it is because [Mādhyamikas] have no autonomous thesis [that advocates] the lack of the arising of the internal sources from themselves that it is not necessary for them to rebut the faults [urged upon them] by others, namely the faults (a) "If there is no arising [of a thing] from its own self *qua* effect, you are proving what has already been proven," and (b) "If there is no arising [of a thing] from its own self *qua* cause, then the reason would have implications exactly opposite [to those you desire] *('gal ba'i don nyid du 'gyur)*."[330] Such faults [only apply to someone] who holds the autonomous thesis that there is no arising [of a thing] from itself.

[2] To claim that the phrase "because [Buddhapālita] states no syllogism and example" means "because [he] states no syllogism and example acceptable to the other [party]" *(gzhan la 'grags pa'i gtan tshigs dang dpe)* is also incorrect. In this case there is no certainty as to the fact that it is necessary to state an inference acceptable to others. But whether or not it is necessary to state [such

pa yang med cing/ cis kyang brjod dgos na/ sangs rgyas bskyangs kyi ngag des brjod pa yin te/ de dag gi zhes pa ni/ bdag gi bdag nyid du yod pa zhes pa'i don yin pas gtan tshigs bstan la/ skye ba don med pa nyid du 'gyur ba'i phyir ces pas ni sgrub bya'i chos bstan pa yin la/ dpe shugs la bstan pas 'di ltar 'gyur te/ gang rang gi bdag nyid du yod na/ slar skye ba don med pas khyab/ dper na mdun du gnas pa'i mngon gsal gyi bum pa bzhin/ 'jim dus kyi bum pa yang rang gi bdag nyid du yod pa yin no/ /zhes slob dpon sangs rgyas bskyangs kyi ngag des bstan pa'i phyir ro//

'di la *tshigs gsal* las/ rang gi rjes su dpag pa zhes pa dang/ (S100) skabs 'ga' zhig tu gzhan la grags kyi rjes dpag/ ces pa'i tha snyad gnyis gsungs pa ni/ snga ma ni phyi rgol dang/ phyi ma ni snga rgol la[271] ltos nas gsungs pa yin pas don (K31b) gcig tu shes par bya'o//

des na gzhan grags kyi rjes dpag gi don ni/ chos can gnyis[272] dang/ gtan tshigs dang khyab pa thams cad phyir rgol kho nas khas blangs pa yin gyi/ snga rgol gyis khas blangs med pa zhig[273] dgos la/ de dag snga rgol phyi rgol gnyis ka'i mthun snang du grub pa zhig[274] dgos/ zhes mkhas pa'i mdun sar ngo tsha bor ba'i gtam ni kho bo mi smra'o//

o' na de sus smras na/ *drang nges rnam 'byed* kyi shog gu zhe brgyad pa'i phyi logs su

> des na gzhan grags rtags[275] kyis bsgrub bya sgrub[276] pa la pha rol pos khas blangs pa tsam gyis mi chog gi chos can gnyis dang rtags la sogs pa rang ngos nas gzhal na tshad mas kyang grub la kho rang yang nges par 'dod dgos pa'am (S101) 'dod pa gcig dgos te/ de med par zhen yul la 'khrul na des de kho na nyid rtogs pa'i lta ba skyed[277] par mi nus pa'i phyir ro//

271 KBS *la* omitted.
272 This should be understood as an abbreviation for *chos dang chos can gnyis*. See Pras, Tib., Bhopal ed., 19. See also below, where the same expression occurs in the citation from Tsong kha pa's text.
273 KBS *cig*.
274 KBS *cig*.

an inference], Buddhapālita *does in fact* state it in his argument. How so? The [word] "their" *(de dag gi)* [in his text] refers to "existing in [their] own nature" *(bdag gi bdag nyid du yod pa)*, and this is his expression of the reason *(gtan tshigs)* [of the inference]. Through the [words] "because arising becomes purposeless" *(skye ba don med pa nyid du 'gyur ba'i phyir)* he expresses the *probandum (bsgrub bya'i chos)*. The example is implicitly *(zhugs la)* taught. Hence, the master Buddhapālita's argument teaches [the full inference] as follows: "If something exists in its own nature, then it follows that its further arising is purposeless, as is the case, for example, with the pot that is evident before one. Now the pot at the time it is still raw clay *('dzim dus kyi bum pa)*, [according to you], also exists in its own nature, [and so its arising *too* is purposeless]."

As regards this [type of syllogism], the *Prasannapadā* sometimes refers to it as "[their] own inference" *(rang gi rjes su dpag pa)* and sometimes as "an inference acceptable to the other [party]" *(gzhan la 'grags kyi rjes dpag)*, depending upon whether the point of reference is the opponent *(phyi rgol)*[331]—in which case the former [expression is used]—or whether it is the proponent *(snga rgol)*[332]—in which case the latter [expression is used]. Hence, [both terms] should be understood to be synonyms.[333]

Therefore, an "inference acceptable to the other [party]," refers to [a syllogism] in which the subject, the predicate, the reason, and the pervasion are all accepted only by the opponent, and is not accepted by the proponent. The claim that they must be established in common by both proponent and opponent is something that should cause shame in the presence of scholars; we do *not* advocate this.

Well then, who *does* claim this? This has been advocated [by Tsong kha pa, who] has written on the reverse side of folio 48 of his *Elucidation of the Provisional and Definitive:*

> Therefore, as regards the [way in which] a reason acceptable to the other [party] proves the *probandum*, it is not sufficient that it be merely accepted by the opponent. The subject, the predicate, the reason and so forth must be established also by means of a valid cognition from our/their own perspective.[334] [101] [In other words,] they themselves must accept them as certainties—that is, these must be their beliefs. Why? In the absence [of such beliefs], error could occur in regard to the object that is the focus *(zhen yul)* [of inquiry], which would make it impossible for there to arise the view that understands reality.[335]

zhes bris pas smras so/ gzhan la grags kyi gtan tshigs la khyod 'dod pa de ltar dgos na/ gong du kho bo'i smras pa de gzhan la grags kyi rjes dpag gi mtshan gzhir dngos su *tshig gsal* las gsungs pas/ khyed nyid grangs can gyi grub mtha'i mthil khas blangs pa ste[278] / chos can 'jim dus kyi bum pa dang/ gtan tshigs rang gi bdag nyid du yod pa khas blangs pa'i phyir ro/ /rang rgyud pa dang dngos smra ba gang gi lugs la yang/ rang rgyud kyi gtan tshigs kyi don la khyed 'dod pa'i gzhan grags kyi rtags kyi don las lhag pa byas pa med pas/ gzhan grags kyi rtags la rang rgyud (K32a) kyi gtan tshigs byas/ rang rgyud kyi gtan tshigs la rang gi mtshan nyid kyis grub pa'i chos bsgrub byar (S102) byas pa ni/ thal rang gnyis kyi gzhung 'grel gang nas kyang bshad pa med pas gdul bya mgo rmongs pa'i phyir du sbyar bar[279] snang ngo//

des na slob dpon legs ldan 'byed kyis/ dngos po bdag las skye ba med par bsgrub pa la/ rang rgyud kyi gtan tshigs khas blangs pa yin pas/ de'i tshe rang gi mtshan nyid kyis[280] grub pa'i chos bsgrub pa yin na/ [1] chos can myu gu lta bu'i dngos po de rang gi mtshan nyid kyis grub par bsgrub pa yin nam/ [2] bsgrub chos bdag las skye ba med pa rang gi mtshan nyid kyis grub par bsgrub pa yin nam/ [3] de gnyis tshogs pa'i tshogs don der bsgrub pa yin/ [1] dang po ltar na shin tu mi 'thad de/ myu gu skye med du bsgrub pa'i skabs yin pa'i phyir ro/ /[2–3] gnyis pa dang gsum pa yang mi 'thad de[281]/ skabs 'dir 'brel med pa'i phyir ro//

des na nang gi skye mched bdag las skye ba med par bsgrub pa'i (S103) skabs su rang rgyud kyi gtan tshigs mi rigs pa'i shes byed[282] du/ rang rgyud kyi gtan tshigs yin na/ chos can rgol phyi rgol gnyis ka'i mthun snang du grub pa gcig dgos pas/ de'i tshe chos can mthun snang du grub pa med pa'i phyir ro/ /zhes pa 'di nyid rigs pa'i gtso bor bkod par snang ngo//

slob dpon zla bas/ rang rgyud 'gog pa'i skabs su mig sogs kun rdzob pa chos can du bzung na snga rgol la ma grub cing/ mig sogs don dam pa (K32b) chos can du bzung na phyi rgol la ma grub pa zhes bkag nas/ gal te

275 *Legs bshad snying po, Collected Works,* Lhasa Zhol ed., vol. *pha*, f. 90b: *gzhan 'grags kyi rtags.*
276 KBS *bsgrub.* Zhol ed., f. 90b: *sgrub.*
277 KBS *bskyed.* Zhol ed., f. 90b: *skyed.*
278 KB *de.*
279 KBS *ba.*
280 B *kyi.*
281 KBS *de.*
282 K *phyed.*

[What are the implications of your position] that the reasons acceptable to the other [party have the property] you believe they have [namely, that they are established in common for both parties]? The [syllogism] as formulated by us above is explicitly taught in the *Prasannapadā* as an example of an inference acceptable to the other [party]. Hence, you have sunk to the level of accepting Sāṃkhya tenets, for you accept that pots [exist] when they are still raw clay, and you accept the reason, "existence through own nature." Both the Svātantrika and realist systems believe that "autonomous reasons" are defined exactly as you define "reasons acceptable to the other [party]." Hence, you turn "reasons based on what is acceptable to the other [party]" into "autonomous reasons," and you turn autonomous reasons into [logical forms] that prove phenomena/properties *(chos)* that exist by virtue of their own characteristic.[336] But there is no such explanation in the commentarial traditions of either the Svātantrikas or Prāsaṅgikas. Hence, this appears to be something you have invented to confuse your disciples!

When the master Bhāvaviveka proves that things do not arise from themselves, he is, [according to you,] accepting an autonomous syllogism. Hence, [according to you] he is, at that point in time, proving a phenomenon/property that exists by virtue of its own characteristic. If this is so, (1) is he proving that the subject *(chos can)*, something like the sprout, exists by virtue of its own characteristic, or (2) is he proving that the property to be proved—the nonexistence of self-arising—exists by virtue of its own characteristic, or (3) is he proving that the conjunction *(tshogs don)* of those two [the non-arising of the sprout from itself] is this? The first [alternative] is utterly incorrect, since this is an instance in which the sprout is being proved to be unarisen.[337] The second and third [alternatives] are also incorrect because they are unrelated [to the present context].

Therefore, the reason [given in the *Prasannapadā*] for why autonomous reasons are inappropriate when one is proving that the internal sources do not arise from themselves is as follows. If an autonomous reason [were used], then the subject [of the syllogism] would have to be established in common for both the proponent and opponent, but at that point in time there is no establishment of the subject in common.[338] This is what appears to be posited as the main reason [for why autonomous syllogisms are invalid].

When the master Candra[kīrti] refutes [the notion of] an autonomous [syllogism], he does so by refuting [the possibility of a subject that is established in common for both parties]: if the eye, etc. *as conventionalities,* are

sgra mi rtag par sgrub pa la rtag mi rtag gang gis kyang khyad par du ma byas pa'i sgra tsam chos can du 'dzin pa bzhin du 'dir yang bden rdzun gang gi[283] kyang khyad par du ma byas pa'i mig sogs tsam chos can du 'dzin pa yin no zhe na/ de'i lan du/ skye ba bkag pa bsgrub bya'i chos su byed pa'i tshe/ chos can mig sogs nyams par/ (S104) legs ldan 'byed rang nyid kyis khas blangs pa dang 'gal zhing/ mig sogs skye med du rtogs pa'i blo ni phyin ci ma log pa'i blo yin pas de'i ngor mig sogs tsam yang mi snang ste/ mig sogs ni phyin ci log gi blo'i rnyed don yin pa'i phyir ro/ /zhes pa'i rigs pa[284] gnyis gsungs ste/ de ltar yang *tshig gsal* las/

> 'dir skye[285] ba bkag pa bsgrub bya'i chos[286] su 'dod pa de'i tshe kho nar[287] de'i rten chos can phyin ci log tsam gyis bdag gi dngos po rnyed pa ni nyams par 'gyur bar[288] 'dis rang nyid kyis khas blangs pa nyid do[289]

ces dang/

> gang gi phyir de ltar phyin ci log pa dang/[290] phyin ci ma log pa dag tha dad pa de'i phyir phyin ci ma log pa'i gnas skabs na phyin ci log yod pa min pa'i[291] phyir na/ gang zhig gi chos can[292] nyid du 'gyur ba'i[293] mig kun rdzob pa ga la[294] yod/ de'i phyir gzhi ma grub pa'i phyogs kyi skyon dang/ gzhi ma grub pa'i (S105) gtan tshigs kyi skyon ldog pa med pas[295] 'di lan ma yin pa nyid do/ /dpe la yang 'dra ba yod pa ma yin no/[296] de[297] ni sgra'i spyi dang mi rtag pa nyid kyi spyi khyad par brjod par mi 'dod pa gnyis ka[298]

283 BS *gis.*
284 K *rigs la.*
285 K *skya.*
286 Pras, Toh no. 3860, Dbu ma *'a,* f. 9b: *bsgrub par bya ba'i chos.*
287 Pras, f. 9b: *de'i tshe de kho nar.* KBS *de'i tshe kho nar* (*de* omitted).
288 KBS *gyur pa.* Pras, f. 9b: *'gyur bar.*
289 KBS *de.* Pras, f. 9b: *do*
290 Pras, f. 9b: / omitted.
291 Pras, f. 9b: *ma yin pa'i.*
292 K *zhi gi chos can;* BS *zhig gi chos can.* Pras, f. 9b: *zhig chos can.*
293 Pras, f. 9b: *'gyur ba.*
294 Pras, f. 9b: *lta ga la.*
295 Pras, f. 9b: *ldog pa med pa nyid pas.*
296 Pras, f. 9b: *//.*
297 Pras, f. 9b: *der.*
298 Pras, f. 9b: *gnyi ga.*

taken as the subject, [the subject would] not be established for the proponent [in this case, the Sāṃkhyas];[339] and if the eye, etc. *as ultimates* are taken as the subject, [the subject would] not be established for the opponent [i.e., for the Mādhyamikas].[340] Then, [Candrakīrti has an opponent raise the following] objection: "Just as, when one [is attempting to prove that] sound is impermanent, one takes as the subject [of the syllogism] mere sound that is not qualified as being either permanent or impermanent, likewise, in this case, one can take as the subject the mere eye, etc., not qualified as being either true or false." In response to that, [Candrakīrti] offers two arguments: (1) [the proposition that there is an unqualified or unspecified subject] contradicts the fact that when the refutation of arising is taken as the property to be proved *(bsgrub bya'i chos)*, Bhāvaviveka himself [believes that the] the subject—the eye, etc.—wanes *(nyams par)*;[341] and (2) the thought *(blo)* that understands the eye, etc., to be unarisen is an unmistaken *(phyin ci ma log pa'i)* thought and hence the mere eye, etc., do not appear within its purview, since the eye, etc., are objects found [only] by a mistaken thought. The *Prasannapadā* clearly expresses this as follows:

> [Bhāvaviveka] himself accepts that it is only when the refutation of arising *qua* probandum is accepted that there is a waning of its support *(rten)*, the subject, *qua* something that a mistaken [thought] finds to be [imbued with] self-existence.[342]

and also as follows:

> It is because the mistaken and the unmistaken are different that when the unmistaken [is operative], the mistaken cannot exist. Hence, how can the eye *qua* conventionality be the subject [of the syllogism]? Therefore, since there is [for you] no avoiding the fault that the thesis *(phyogs)* is not established, and the fault that the reason *(gtan tshigs)* is not established, [yours] is no response at all. Even the example [you give concerning the proof of the impermanence of sound] has no analogy [to the present situation, for in the case of the proof of the impermanence of sound], both [parties] have [some notion of] generic sound *(sgra'i spyi)* and generic impermanence *(mi rtag pa nyid kyi spyi)* without wishing to assert any qualifications [about the ontological status of the sound or impermanence they are discussing]. But since [such an unqualified] generic eye is not accepted as a conventionality, either by

> la yang yod na[299] de bzhin du mig gi (K33a) spyi ni stong pa nyid dang/[300] stong pa nyid ma yin[301] par smra ba dag gis kun rdzob tu yang khas ma blangs[302] la/ don dam par yang ma yin pas[303] dpe la yang[304] 'dra ba yod pa ma yin no//

zhes gsal bar gsungs pa'i phyir ro//

'di dag gi don la/ drang nges rnam 'byed kyi shog bu zhe lnga pa dang zhe drug pa'i nang du/ rang gi grub mtha' dang ma mthun pa'i dbang gis bshad tshul ngo mtshar ba byas 'dug pa ni/ des nye bar dpag na 'chad tshul[305] gzhan rnams la yang skrag pa skye ba'i gnas su snang ngo//

zla bas rang rgyud 'gog pa la/ rang rgyud pa phyi ma rnams kyis skyon spang mdzad pa mi snang zhes gsungs pa ni/ *bden gnyis rang 'grel* ma (S106) gzigs par snang ste/ de nyid las/

> rjes su dpag pa dang rjes su dpag par bya ba'i[306] tha snyad ni[307] rgol ba dang[308] phyir rgol ba dag gi blo'i bdag nyid la snang ba'i chos can dang chos dang dpe nyid du rnam par bzhag pa la[309] 'byung gi/ chos can dang chos la sogs pa gnyis ka[310] la ma grub pa nyid kyis rjes su dpag pa 'byung bar mi rung ngo/ /[311]gzhan ni[312] min te[313]/ gzhung lugs tha dad pa la gnas pa rnams ni gang la yang blo mtshungs pa nyid med pa'i phyir ro/ /chos can de lta bu la gnas pa rnams ni gtan tshigs la sogs pa de lta bu[314] kho nas yang dag par na[315] yod dam med ces sems par byed par khas

299 Pras, f. 9b: *na/.*
300 Pras, f. 9b: / omitted.
301 KBS *stong pa nyid dang mi ldan par.* Pras, f. 9b: *stong pa nyid ma yin par.*
302 KBS *khas ma blangs pa la.* Pras, f. 9b: *khas ma blangs la* (*pa* omitted).
303 KBS *min pa'i.* Pras, f. 9b: *ma yin pas.*
304 KBS *dpe la yang* omitted. Pras, f. 9b: *dpe la yang*
305 K *chul.*
306 *Satyadvayavibhaṅgavṛtti.* Eckel, ed., *Jñānagarbha,* 173: *ba.*
307 Eckel, ed., *Jñānagarbha* , 173: *tha snyad kyi.*
308 Eckel, ed., *Jñānagarbha,* 173: *dang/.*
309 Eckel, ed., *Jñānagarbha,* 173: *bzhags par.*
310 Eckel, ed., *Jñānagarbha,* 173: *gnyi ga.*
311 Eckel, ed., *Jñānagarbha,* 173: *'byung ba mi rung ba'i phyir;* and // omitted.
312 K *gzhan na ni;* BS *gzhan ni* (*na* omitted). Eckel, ed., *Jñānagarbha,* 174: *gzhan na ni.*
313 K *gzhan min te;* BS *gzhan ni min te.* Eckel, ed., *Jñānagarbha,* 174: *gzhan na ni ma yin te.*
314 KBS *lta bur.* Eckel, ed., *Jñānagarbha,* 174: *lta bu.*
315 KBS /. Eckel, ed., *Jñānagarbha,* 174: / omitted.

> those who advocate emptiness or by those who advocate non-emptiness, since it is also not an ultimate, therefore, there is no similarity of the example [to the present case] either.[343]

On folios 45 and 46 of the *Elucidation of the Provisional and Definitive,* [Tsong kha pa] resorts to explaining [these passages] in a strange way—strange because it does not accord with his own tenets. If one fathoms this, it makes one wonder whether there might not be cause to fear his other explanations as well.[344]

Those who claim that later Svātantrikas do not appear to engage in a rebuttal of the faults raised by Candra[kīrti] in his refutation of autonomous [syllogisms] have not, it would seem, seen what the *Satyadvayavṛtti* states:

> "Inference" and "what is to be inferred" *(rjes su dpag par bya ba)* consist of the subject, the predicate, and the example which appear to the minds of the proponent and opponent in the discussion. When the subject, the predicate, and so forth are not established for both [parties], an inference cannot arise. It cannot be otherwise because [without these things appearing in common, individuals] belonging to different scriptural traditions would lack agreement in regard to anything. Those who hold to such a subject [can then]—through precisely such a reason [and example], etc.—contemplate whether or not [the subject] really exists, and in this way come to accept [that it does

> blang bar bya'o/ /de lta bas na[316] rigs pa[317] smra ba yang de ltar rjes su dpag pa[318] 'byung bar byed na/ su zhig 'gog par 'gyur/ 'di ni mtshungs pa nyid du grub par gtan la phab pas[319] 'dir ni[320] rgya ma bskyed do//

zhes gsungs (K33b) pa 'di la gzigs (S107) mdzod cig/

des na thal rang gi khyad par ni/ 'grel pa *tshigs gsal* las/ gsal ba dang/ rgyas pa med pas/ de'i lugs bzhin rgyas par ni gzhan du 'chad par 'gyur zhing/ 'dir mdor bsdus pa tsam zhig gzu bor gnas pa'i blos brjod pa 'di la rna ba blag ste nyon cig/ 'di la

[3.3.5.1.0] dam bca'i khyad par/
[3.3.5.2.0] 'thad pa'i khyad par/
[3.3.5.3.0] bden pa gnyis gang gi steng du 'byed pa (s.3.3.5.3.0)

dang gsum las/

[3.3.5.1.0 dam bca'i khyad par]

dang po ni/ phyi nang gi dngos po rnams bdag las skye ba med de/ zhes sogs dam bca' bzhi po/ dam bca' tsam du khas len pa thal rang gnyis po khyad par med kyang/ rang rgyud pas ni rang rgyud kyi dam bca'[321] 'dod pa dang/ thal 'gyur bas thal 'gyur gyi dam bcar 'dod pa ni khyad par ro/ /'o na de gnyis kyi khyad par gang zhe na/ chos can rgol ba gnyis kyi mthun snang du grub pa'i steng du/ snga rgol (S108) gyis khyad par gyi chos la dpag 'dod zhugs nas/ tshad mas grub pa'i gtan tshigs kyis bsgrub par[322] bya ba ni rang rgyud kyi dam bca' yin la/ chos can mthun snang du grub pa'i steng du khyad par gyi chos la dpag 'dod zhugs pa med kyang ldog[323] phyogs la gnod byed gyi rigs pa mthong nas re zhig der dam bca' ba ni thal'gyur gyi dam bca' 'o//

316 KBS *na /.*
317 Eckel, ed., *Jñānagarbha,* 174: *pas.*
318 KBS *par.* Eckel, ed., *Jñānagarbha,* 174: *pa*
319 Eckel, ed., *Jñānagarbha,* 174: *pas /.*
320 Eckel, ed., *Jñānagarbha,* 174: *'dir ni 'di'i.* KBS *'di'i* omitted.
321 S *bcar.*
322 KBS *pa.*
323 K *ldag.*

> not]. Therefore, when philosophers *(rigs pa smra ba)* make such an inference arise [among themselves], who can refute them?
>
> Because I have already explained this [point] in regard to [other] similar cases, I will not expand upon it here.[345]

Give [this passage] a glance!

Since the difference between the Prāsaṅgikas and Svātantrikas is neither clearly nor extensively [explained] in the *Prasannapadā,* I will explain this extensively in accordance with this system elsewhere. Here, [I will give] just a brief [explanation]. Lend me your ear, then, and listen with an impartial mind to what I have to say.

This [explanation] has three parts: (1) the differences [between Prāsaṅgikas and Svātantrikas] with respect to theses *(dam bca');* (2) the differences as regards adequate [argumentation] *('thad pa);* (3) [the differences concerning] that on the basis of which the two truths are to be distinguished.

[The Differences Between Prāsaṅgikas and Svātantrikas with Respect to Theses]

[Both schools] accept the four theses—that external and internal things do not arise from themselves, [from other things], and so forth—as *mere* theses *(dam bca' tsam).* [On this point] there is no difference between the two [schools]: Prāsaṅgikas and Svātantrikas. However, there *is* a difference [in another respect]: Svātantrikas believe in *autonomous* theses, whereas Prāsaṅgikas believe in *reductio* theses. And what is the difference between these two? An "autonomous thesis" is what is proven by a reason that is established by means of a valid cognition in such a way that the proponent has a desire to infer the specific predicate based upon a subject that is established in common for both parties. A "*reductio* thesis" is one that is provisionally asserted [by the proponent] after he or she witnesses that there are arguments [that can be leveled] against the opponent's position; [in a *reductio,* such arguments are asserted] even though [the proponent] has no desire to infer the specific predicate based upon a subject that is established in common [for both parties].[346]

[3.3.5.2.0 'thad pa'i khyad par]

gnyis pa ni/ chos can mthun snang du grub pa'i steng du khyad par gyi chos 'ga' zhig bsgrub pa'i ched du/ tshul gsum tshad mas grub pa'i gtan tshigs bkod pa ni rang rgyud kyi 'thad pa yin te/ *bden gnyis* las/ (K34a)

> rgol ba gnyis ka'i[324] shes pa la//
> ci[325] tsam snang ba'i cha yod pa//
> de tsam de la brten nas ni//
> chos can chos la sogs par rtogs[326] //
> de tshe rjes su dpag pa 'byung//

zhes gsungs pa'i phyir ro/ /dam bca' de nyid bsgrub pa la/ ldog phyogs kyi dam bca' la khas blang nang 'gal gyi (S109) thal 'gyur 'ba' zhig brjod nas/ tshul gsum tshang ba'i gtan tshigs mi 'god pa ni/ thal 'gyur gyi 'thad pa ste/ *tshig gsal* las/

> de'i phyir khyed cag gi rtsod pa ni 'thad pa dang bral ba dang/ rang gis khas blangs pa dang 'gal ba[327] yin no/[328] zhes pha rol po bdag las skye bar 'dod pa la 'dri bar byed pa yin te/ gang las gtan tshigs dang dpe bkod pa 'bras bu dang bcas par 'gyur ba 'di dag tsam zhig gis brtsad pa na ci pha rol pos[329] khas len par mi byed dam/

ces gsungs pa'i phyir ro//

[3.3.5.3.0 bden gnyis gang gi steng du 'byed pa]

gsum pa ni/ tha snyad kyi rnam bzhag la/ thal rang gi khyad par 'byed pa ni min te/ tha snyad kyi rnam bzhag la rang rgyud kyi gtan tshigs thal 'gyur ba rnams kyis kyang khas len pa'i phyir te/ *'jug pa* las/

> rang sha ster la'ang gus par byas pa yis[330]//

324 *Satyadvayavibhaṅga*. Eckel, ed., *Jñānagarbha*, 173: *gnyi ga'i*.
325 Eckel, ed., *Jñānagarbha*, 173: *ji*.
326 Eckel, ed., *Jñānagarbha*, 173: *rtog*.
327 K *pa*.
328 Pras, Toh no. 3860, Dbu ma *'a*, f. 5b: / omitted.
329 KBS *rtsod pa ni pha rol po*. Pras, f. 5b: *brtsad pa na ci pha rol po*.
330 K *ya;* B *yi;* S and MABh, Toh no. 3862, Dbu ma *'a*, f. 228a: *yi*. MA: *yis*.

[The Difference Between Prāsaṅgikas and Svātantrikas As Regards Adequate Argumentation]

An "autonomous argument" is (a) the positing of a reason to prove some specific property in such a way that (b) the trimodal criteria are established by means of a valid cognition, and (c) [the predicate and reason are] based upon a subject that is established in common [for both parties]. How so? The *Satyadvaya* states:

> The subject, property, and so forth are understood
> Only to the extent that there exists
> A common aspect to what appears
> In the minds of both parties.
> It is [only] then that an inference occurs.[347]

A *reductio* argument is one that does not posit a reason with full trimodal criteria *(tshul gsum)*, and that instead expresses only a *reductio* that [points out to the opponents] that they suffer from an internal contradiction in what they believe—[an internal contradiction that arises from simultaneously believing] in the very thesis that they uphold and [simultaneously] in the opposite thesis. How so? The *Prasannapadā* states:

> Therefore, this is the inquiry one should direct at those opponents who maintain that things arise from themselves: "Your argument is unreasonable, and is [in fact] contradictory to your own beliefs." Why should [only] the positing of [a formal] reason and example bear fruit? What kind of an opponent refuses to accept an argument unless [it contains] those two [formal] elements?[348]

[The Basis for Distinguishing Between the Two Truths]

There is no distinguishing between the Prāsaṅgikas and Svātantrikas on the basis of the [way in which they] posit the conventional *(tha snyad kyi rnam bzhag)*, since even the Prāsaṅgikas accept autonomous syllogisms when positing the conventional. How so? The *Avatāra* states:

> Their dedication [to giving]—even the giving of their own flesh—

snang du mi rung dpog pa'i rgyu ru 'gyur[331]//

de'i tshe byang chub sems dpa' de'i yon tan snang du (S110) rung ba min pa'i[332] rtogs pa la sogs pa[333] gang dag yin pa de dag kyang phyi dang nang gi bdag nyid kyi dngos po gtong[334] ba'i khyad par gyi rjes su dpag[335] pa nyid las gsal bar dpog pa yin te[336]/ du ba la sogs pa las (K34b) me la sogs pa bzhin no[337]//

zhes dang/ sngar bshad pa ltar lus ngag gi mtshan ma las theg chen gyi rigs sad pa dpog par gsungs shing/ de yang *mdo sde sa bcu pa* las/

du ba las ni mer shes dang[338]//
chu skyar las ni chur shes bzhin[339]//
byang chub sems dpa' blo ldan gyi[340]//
rigs ni mtshan ma dag[341] las shes//

zhes pa'i don du mdzad par snang ba'i phyir ro//

mngon rtogs rgyan las bshad pa'i phyir mi ldog pa'i gtan tshigs bzhi bcu zhe bzhi po thams cad kyang rang rgyud kyi gtan tshigs kho na yin pa'i phyir ro/ /gal te de dag rang rgyud kyi gtan tshigs[342] min na/ du bas du ldan la la me sgrub pa'i gtan tshigs de yang rang rgyud kyi gtan (S111) tshigs min par 'gyur te/[343] sngar gyi mdo 'grel gnyis las khyad par med par gsungs pa'i phyir ro//

de'i phyir zhang thang sag pa ye shes 'byung gnas 'od kyis/ don dam dpyod pa'i skabs min pas rang rgyud byas kyang 'gal ba med/ ces gsungs pa dang/ rong ston chos kyi rgyal pos kyang/ tha snyad rnam bzhag la thal 'gyur bas kyang rang rgyud khas len par gsungs pa ni 'di'o zhes ston rgyu yod pas don la gnas pa de kho na'o//

331 MA and MABh, f. 228a: *rgyur yang 'gyur.*
332 MABh, f. 228a: *snang rung ma yin pas.*
333 KBS *la sogs pa* omitted.
334 MABh, f. 228a: *stong.*
335 KB *dpags.*
336 MABh, f. 228a: *dpog par byed pa yin te.*
337 MABh, f. 228a: *du ba la sogs pa khams me la sogs pa dag bzhin no.*
338 *Daśadharmaka Sūtra,* LK, vol. 36, f. 274a: *shing.*
339 *Daśadharmaka Sūtra,* f. 274a: *ltar.*
340 *Daśadharmaka Sūtra,* f. 274a: *blo ldan byang chub sems dpa' yi.*
341 *Daśadharmaka Sūtra,* f. 274a: *rnams.*
342 KB *tshig.*
343 KBS / omitted.

> Serves as the cause for adducing [attributes] that are not yet evident
> [in the bodhisattvas].
>
> The attributes of the bodhisattva that are not yet evident at that time—i.e., their understanding, and so forth—are clearly adduced through the inference [based on witnessing] the quality of their generosity in regard to things both internal and external, just as fire, etc., [is deduced] from smoke, and so on.[349]

As explained previously, this is claiming that [one can] adduce the fact of the awakening of the Mahāyāna lineage on the basis of bodily and verbal signs. This [point in the *Madhyamakāvatāra*] appears to be a gloss [on the following passage] from the *Daśabhūmikasūtra:*

> Just as one can know [that there is] fire from [seeing] smoke,
> And know [that there is] water from [seeing] herons,
> [It is possible] to know [that someone belongs] to the lineage of
> discerning bodhisattvas
> On the basis of [certain] signs.[350]

Also, all of the *Abhisamayālaṃkāra's* forty-four reasons concerning [the bodhisattva's] "irreversibility" are nothing but autonomous reasons.[351] If they were *not* autonomous reasons, then the reasoning that proves, by [the presence of] smoke, [that there is] fire on the smoke-filled mountain pass could also not be an autonomous syllogism, since both the previously [cited] sūtra and commentary treat [the two instances] as identical.

We can also point to [other works] that make precisely this same point. [For example, there is] a passage of Zhang thang sag pa Ye shes 'byung gnas in which he states, "Because this is not an instance in which the ultimate is being analyzed, there is no contradiction in resorting to autonomous [syllogisms],"[352] and one in which the Dharma king Rong ston states, "This is [the point]: it is stating that even Prāsaṅgikas accept autonomous [syllogisms] when positing the conventional."[353]

des na thal rang gi khyad par ni gnas lugs la dpyod pa'i skabs su rang rgyud khas len pa dang mi len pa la 'jog pa ni gnad kyi don yin te/ mtha' bzhi'i skye ba bkag pa'i skabs su rang rgyud 'thad mi 'thad kyi dgag sgrub dngos su gsung zhing/ de nyid tha snyad kyi rnam bzhag ston pa'i tshigs su bcad pa 'ga' zhig ma gtogs pa/ *rtsa ba shes rab* kyi (K35a) gzhung thams cad kyi skabs su sbyar bar bya ba (S112) yin pas/ gnas lugs la dpyod pa'i skabs kyi tshigs su bcad pa re re'i skabs su yang/ thal rang gi khyad par 'byed dgos pa'i phyir ro//

gnas lugs la dpyod pa'i skabs su rang rgyud pas rang rgyud kyi gtan tshigs khas len ces pa'i don yang/ myu gu bdag las skye mi skye dpyod pa'i skabs su myu gu bdag las skye ba med par bsgrub pa'i rang rgyud kyi gtan tshigs khas len ces pa'i don yin gyi/ rang rgyud kyi gtan tshigs rang ldog nas gnas lugs dpyod pa'i rig ngor grub pa'i don la 'khrul par mi bya'o/ /myu gu bdag las mi skye bar bsgrub pa'i skabs su/ thal 'gyur bas rang rgyud khas mi len pa'i gnad kyang de'i tshe chos can myu gu snang tsam nyid kyang ma grub pa'i phyir ro zhes pa 'di nyid bkod pa yin no//

rang rgyud med na phyi rgol gyi rgyud la myu gu bdag las skye[344] med du rtogs pa'i nges shes bskyed mi nus so snyam na/ (S113)

skyon med de/ myu gu bdag las skye ba la khas blang nang 'gal mthong ba na myu gu bdag las skye ba med par nges pa'i nges shes skye ba ni rigs pa smra ba'i lugs yin la/ 'di'i phyi rgol ni rigs pa smra ba yin pa'i phyir snyam du dgongs so//

rang rgyud pa rnams[345] kyis thal 'gyur gyis log rtog bcom zin pa'i rjes su rang rgyud kyi gtan tshigs ma bkod na bsgrub bya nges pa'i rjes dpag mi skye ste/ rjes dpag ni/ gtan tshigs yang dag la brten dgos pa'i phyir snyam du dgongs so//

thal 'gyur (K35b) bas myu gu bdag las skye mi skye dpyod pa'i skabs su/ chos can myu gu snang tsam yang khas mi len na de'i tshe dam bca' dang/

344 K *skya*.
345 K *rnam*.

Therefore, the essential point is that Prāsaṅgikas and Svātantrikas are differentiated on the basis of whether of not they accept autonomous [syllogisms] *in the context of the analysis of reality (gnas lugs la dpyad pa'i skabs su).*[354] How so? [Candrakīrti] explicitly states his arguments against autonomous [syllogisms] in the context of [MMK (I, 1), on the] refutation of arising by means of the four extremes, [which is an analysis of the final nature—the reality—of causation]. With the exception of a few verses that deal with how the conventional is to be posited, the *Prajñāmūla* as a whole [also deals with the analysis of reality]. Hence, it is necessary to make the distinction between Prāsaṅgikas and Svātantrikas only in the context of those individual verses that deal with the analysis of reality.

What does it mean to say that Svātantrikas accept autonomous reasons in the context of the analysis of reality? It means that in the context of the analysis of whether or not a sprout arises from itself, they accept an autonomous reason that proves that a sprout does not arise from itself. But be not confused, this does *not* mean that [they believe that] an actual autonomous reason *itself (rang rgyud kti gtan tshigs rang ldog nas)*[355] exists within the purview of the cognition that analyzes reality. And as regards the fact that the Prāsaṅgikas do *not* accept autonomous [syllogisms] in the context of proving that the sprout does not arise from itself, [Candrakīrti] posits this on the basis of the fact that, at that time, even the mere appearance of the subject—the sprout—does not exist.

A quandary [posed by a Svātantrika]: "Without an autonomous syllogism, an ascertaining consciousness *(nges shes)* that understands that the sprout does not arise from itself cannot emerge in the mental continuum of the opponent."

[Reply:] There is no problem [here]. Why? It is a general principle among reasonable people *(rigs pa smra ba)* that when one sees an internal contradiction in [a position, like the one that] believes that a sprout arises from itself, there arises an ascertaining consciousness that ascertains that the sprout *does not* arise from itself; and the opponent [in this case] is a reasonable person. This is what [the Prāsaṅgikas] believe.

The Svātantrikas, [on the other hand,] believe that after [the opponent's] misconceptions have been overcome through the use of *reductio* arguments, they do not generate an inference that ascertains the *probandum* unless they are presented with an autonomous reason, since [for them] an inference necessarily depends upon a valid reason *(gtan tshigs yang dag pa).*

[Objection:] If it is the case that in the context of analyzing whether or not the sprout arises from itself, Prāsaṅgikas do not accept that there is even

thal 'gyur dang rgol phyi rgol yang med par 'gyur bas rtsod pa byed pa yang med par 'gyur ro zhe na/

de'i lan du/ rong ston chos kyi spyan dang ldan pa'i zhal snga nas/

> de'i tshe myu gu'i gnas lugs la dpyod pa yin gyi/ dam (S114) bca' dang/ thal 'gyur sogs kyi gnas lugs la dpyod pa med pas skyon med la/ de dag gi gnas lugs la dpyod pa'i tshe de dag snang tsam yang khas mi len pa ni snga ma dang 'dra'o/

zhes gsungs pa ni/ blo gros kyi spyi bor gser gyi cod pan bzhin du bcings par bya ba yin te/ rtog pa sel 'jug yin pas myu gu'i gnas lugs la dpyod pa'i tshe/ thal 'gyur gyi gnas lugs la ma dpyad pa'i phyir ro/ /mngon sum ni sgrub 'jug yin pas/ myu gu'i gnas lugs mngon sum du rtogs pa'i tshe chos thams cad kyi gnas lugs mngon sum du rtogs pa'i phyir ro//

des na rang rgyud pas mtha' bzhi'i skye ba bkag pa'i skabs su/ rang rgyud khas blang pa yin pas/ de'i tshe rang gi mtshan nyid kyis grub pa'i chos bsgrub pa la rang rgyud dgos pa yin ces pa ni log rtog zhugs pa'i gzhi tsam yang mi 'dug kyang/ rjes 'jug gi (S115) gdul bya rnam dpyod dang ldan pa dag gis kyang brtag dpyad mi byed par 'dzin pa 'di ni ci yin mi shes so//

lugs[346] gnyis pa 'di ni rje tsong kha pa sngar yongs (K36a) 'dzin dam pa la brten nas gsung rab kyi don la sbyangs pa byas pa'i dus su ma byung la/ dus phyis bla ma dbu ma pas/ mdo khams nas gdan drangs pa'i[347] 'jam dbyangs dang mjal phyin chad dbu ma'i gnad la yang thun mong ma yin pa'i dam bca' 'di tsam dang/ gsang sngags rdo rje theg pa'i gnad la yang/ thun mong ma yin pa'i grub mtha' rab tu mang po bcas pa yin la/ de dag rang nyid kyis kyang sngon gyi mkhas pa sus kyang ma thon pa'i grub mtha' yin par sgrogs shing/ gzhan gyis kyang de ltar du mthong ngo/ /'on kyang yi dam gyi lhas

346 K *lugs* omitted.
347 K *ba*.

the mere appearance of the subject, the sprout, then at that time there can also be no thesis, no *reductio,* and even no proponent and opponent. And so [for them] the process of argumentation itself ceases to exist.

Here is the reply, from the lips of Rong ston, who possesses the Dharma-eye:

> There is no problem, since at that time it is the reality *of the sprout* that is being analyzed, and not the reality of the thesis, of the *reductio,* and so forth. And when it is the reality of *these* [latter entities—the thesis, *reductio,* etc.—] that becomes [the object of] investigation, we do not accept that they appear in the least either; [in the context of *their own* ultimate analyses,] they are like the former [case of the sprout that disappears].[356]

These words should be worn on the crown of those who are wise, as if they were a golden diadem. Why? Since conceptual thought *(rtog pa)* engages [its object] in a negative way *(gsal 'jug),*[357] during the analysis of the reality of the sprout there can be no analysis of the reality of "thesis." [On the other hand,] since perception *(mngon sum)* engages [its object] in a positive way *(sgrub 'jug),*[358] when the reality of the sprout is being understood *directly,* one understands directly the reality of all [its] properties.[359]

Therefore, there is not the slightest basis for [Tsong kha pa's] misconception that since Svātantrikas accept autonomous [syllogisms] in the context of the refutation of arising via the four extremes, at that time they need an autonomous [syllogism] so as to prove a phenomenon/property *(chos)* that exists by virtue of its own characteristic. [So Tsong kha pa is simply mistaken here], but I do not know why it is that [his] erudite later disciples hold onto [this view] without examining it.

This second system [of Madhyamaka exegesis in Tibet] did not come about during the time that the Lord Tsong kha pa was studying the meaning of the scriptures in reliance upon his earlier holy tutors.[360] It came about later, after the time of his visions of Mañjuśrī and of his invitation to Mdo khams by Bla ma Dbu ma pa.[361] It was then that he came to possess these peculiar theses concerning the doctrine of the Madhyamaka, as well as a plethora of peculiar tenets in regard to the doctrines of the Secret Mantra Vajra Vehicle. [Tsong kha pa] himself then proclaimed these [tenets] as being tenets that no previous scholar had ever noticed, and others [also came to] see things in this way. Now if these tenets—[derived from] the religious practice of a tutelary deity *(yi dam)*—were in accordance with the

bstan pa'i grub mtha' de mdo rgyud kyi gnad dang mthun na yi dam gyi lha mtshan nyid pas bstan pa yin pas gang zag de gang du bzhugs pa'i (S116) sa phyogs kyang mchod par 'os shing rjes 'jug gi gdul bya rnams kyang sgrub thag nye ba yin la/ mdo rgyud kyi gnad dang mi mthun na thabs la bslu ba'i bdud yi dam gyi gzugs su brdzus nas chos log ston par gsungs te/ ji skad du *mdo* las/

> 'di skad smra[348] te 'di ni[349] khyod kyi[350] pha ma dang/
> khyod kyi bdun mes rgyud kyi bar gyi ming yin zhing/
> gang tshe khyod ni sangs rgyas 'gyur ba'i ming 'di yin/
> sbyangs sdom rnal 'byor ldan pa ci 'dra 'byung 'gyur la/
> khyod sngon yon tan tshul yang 'di 'dra'o zhes brjod de/
> de skad gang thos rlom sems[351] byang chub sems dpa' ni/
> bdud kyis yongs su bslus shing[352] blo chung rig par[353] bya/

zhes (K36b) sogs theg pa chen pa'i mdo rgyud rnams las mang du gsungs pas dpyad dgos so//

348 *Prajñā-pāramitā-ratna-guna-samcaya-gatha.* Yuyama, ed., 179: *smras.*
349 BS *'di ni* omitted.
350 *Prajñā-pāramitā,* Yuyama, ed., 179: *khyod dang.*
351 K *sams.*
352 *Prajñā-pāramitā,* Yuyama, ed., 179: *bslang zhing.*
353 KSB *pa.*

doctrines of the sūtras and tantras, [this would be indicative of the fact that the practitioner] had been relying on a *real* tutelary deity. [In such a case,] the place where that person sits should be worshipped, and [that person's] followers should also be close to spiritual accomplishments. But if [these tenets] are *not* in accordance with the doctrines of the sūtras and tantras, then they must be proclaimed to be what they are: the false doctrines *(chos log)* taught by a demon who, skilled in deception, has taken the form of a tutelary deity. As the *[Saṃcayagāthā]* sūtra states:

> [The demon Māra] will say [to the bodhisattva], "These are the names of your parents, and the names of your ancestors down to seven [generations]; and when you become a buddha, your name will be this." And [to that bodhisattva] who follows the yoga that binds him/her to purification, he says, "In your previous [life] your good qualities were also like this." The bodhisattva who, hearing this, becomes conceited, has been fooled by demons and should be understood to have little by way of intellect.[362]

Given that there are many [cautionary] passages like this in the Mahāyāna sūtras and tantras, [the positions of those who claim to have had teachings revealed to them by deities] must be [carefully] examined.

[4.0.0.0.0. skor 'go bzhi pa: mtha' bral la dbu mar smra ba'i lugs brgrub pa]

da ni lugs gsum pa sangs rgyas thams cad (S117) kyi dgongs pa/ gzhung lugs thams cad kyi bstan don/ grub thob thams cad kyi gshegs shul/ mkhas pa thams cad kyi bzhed pa'i don de nyid rang lugs su byas nas 'chad pa la/

[4.1.0.0.0] gnas lugs bstan pa'i snod ngos bzung ba/
[4.2.0.0.0] bstan bya gnas lugs kyi rang bzhin/
[4.3.0.0.0] yid ches pa'i lung dang sbyar ba

gsum las/

[4.1.0.0.0. gnas lugs bstan pa'i snod ngos bzung ba]

dang po ni/ dbu ma'i grub mtha' bstan pa'i yul gyi gdul bya de la/[354]

[4.1.1.0.0] phyi nang gi dngos por smra ba'i grub mtha' gang rung la zhugs pa grub[355] mthas blo bsgyur pa gcig dang/
[4.1.2.0.0] grub mthas blo ma bsgyur bar theg chen gyi rigs sad pa'i stobs kyis gnas lugs rtogs pa don du gnyer ba gnyis yod pa las[356]/

354 KB *las.*
355 K *zhugs mthas* (*pa grub* omitted).
356 KBS *la.*

4: The Middle Way as Freedom from Extremes

[Those Who Claim that the Freedom from Extremes Is the Madhyamaka]

THIS THIRD SYSTEM is the purport of all of the buddhas; it is the essential point of the teachings of every textual tradition, the path followed by all of the siddhas and the truth accepted by all scholars. Taking up [this tradition] as my own system, I will now explain it in three subdivisions:

1. Identifying the vessel [that is, the student,] to whom reality is to be taught,
2. What is to be taught: the nature of reality, and
3. Bringing trustworthy scriptural evidence [to bear on the topic].

[Identifying the Vessel (That Is, the Student) to Whom Reality Is to Be Taught]

The disciples who are [fit] recipients for the teachings of the Middle Way philosophy are of two types:

1. Those who [first] adhere to any one of the philosophical positions of the realists—whether Buddhist or non[Buddhist]—and subsequently change their philosophical outlook [to the Madhyamaka], and
2. Those who never change their minds philosophically, but who [from the very beginning] exert themselves at understanding reality through the power of the awakening of their Mahāyāna lineage.[363]

[4.1.1.0.0 grub mthas blo bsgyur pa]

dang po la phyi rol pa'i grub mthas blo bsgyur ba rnams la ni dbu tshad kyi gzhung las bshad pa'i rigs pa rnams kyis log rtogs sun phyung ba na rang rang gi grub mtha' 'dor ba rnams ni dbu ma'i lta ba bstan pa'i snod (S118) yin no/ /rang sde dngos por smra ba'i grub mtha' la zhugs pa yin na/ nyan thos sde gnyis kyis rdul phran bden par 'dod pa ni/ sems tsam pa'i gzhung las bshad pa'i rigs pa rnams kyis sun phyung ste/ shes pa la bden 'dzin gyi lhag ma lus pa de yang gcig du bral la sogs pa'i rtags kyis bkag pa na/ de dag kyang dbu ma'i lta ba bstan pa'i snod (K37a) yin no//

des na phyi nang gi dngos por smra ba rnams la dbu ma'i lta ba ston pa la thal 'gyur ba ltar na/ thal 'gyur gyi sgo nas khas blangs nang 'gal brjod pa dang/ rang rgyud pa ltar na de'i 'og tu rang rgyud kyi gtan tshigs kyis sgrub bya rtogs pa'i rjes dpag bskyed dgos par bzhed de/ gzhung las bshad pa'i rigs pa phal che ba 'di la dgongs so//

[4.1.2.0.0 grub mthas blo ma bsgyur ba]

gdul bya gnyis pa la ni/ dang po nyid nas gang zag gi bdag med dang chos kyi bdag med sgom tshul dmigs thun re re bzhin du khrid (S119) kyi tshul gyis bstan pas chog pa yin gyi/ snga rgol dang phyi rgol gyi rnam bzhag byas nas rtsod pa bya ba ni don med do// gdul bya gnyis pa 'di ni/ so so skye bo'i dus na'ang stong pa nyid thos nas/ ces[357] sogs dang/ zab mo khu 'phrig can

357 B *zhes.*

[Those Who First Adhere to Any One of the Philosophical Positions of the Realists—Whether Buddhist or Non-Buddhist—and Subsequently Change Their Philosophical Outlook to the Madhyamaka]

The first [category consists of] those who convert from non-Buddhist philosophical schools. When their misconceptions *(log rtog)* are eliminated by means of the rational arguments explained in the Madhyamaka and Pramāṇika texts, they abandon their own philosophical positions and become vessels for the teachings of the Middle Way view. Now from among those who subscribe to the tenets of the Buddhist realists, the two śrāvaka schools believe in the truth of atoms.[364] [This belief] is repudiated by means of the rational arguments explained in the Cittamātra texts.[365] [But Cittamātras, despite their refutation of the externality of objects *qua* atoms,] possess a residual grasping at the truth *of consciousness,* and this is refuted by means of [Madhyamaka] reasons such as "being devoid of being one and many."[366] When [this occurs], they too become fit vessels for the teachings of the Middle Way view.

Teaching the Middle Way view to the Buddhist and non-Buddhist realists, according to the Prāsaṅgika, involves showing them, by means of *reductio* arguments, the internal contradictions that they accept. According to the Svātantrikas, even after [they have realized the contradictory nature of their own beliefs], they must [still] generate an inference *(rjes dpag)* that understands the thesis *(bsgrub bya)* by means of an autonomous syllogism, and most of the rational arguments explained in [Svātantrika] texts are intended [to function so as to generate such inferences in their opponents].

Those Who Do Not Change Their Minds Philosophically, [but Who from the Very Beginning Exert Themselves at Understanding Reality through the Power of the Awakening of Their Mahāyāna Lineage]

As regards the second type of disciple [who enter the Madhyamaka directly], it is permissible from the outset to teach them by leading them systematically through each of the steps involved in meditating on the selflessness of the person and on the selflessness of phenomena. It is purposeless to make them engage in forms of argumentation involving the exposition of the [positions] of proponents and opponents. This second type of disciple is also [the one] mentioned in such lines as "Even when they are [still] ordinary individuals, some hear [the doctrine of] emptiness..."[367] and "The profound doctrine that terrifies the mind..."[368] If these [more astute disciples] do not

'jigs pa zhes sogs kyis ston la/ de dag gis kyang bsgom par bya ba'i dmigs pa ma go na gzhung las bshad pa'i rigs[358] pas zhib tu bshad dgos pa yin no//

[4.2.0.0.0 bstan bya gnas lugs kyi rang bzhin]

gnyis pa la sngon gyi mkhas pa rnams/

[4.2.1.0.0] gzhi dbu ma bden gnyis zung 'jug/
[4.2.2.0.0] lam dbu ma tshogs gnyis zung 'jug/
[4.2.3.0.0] 'bras bu dbu ma sku gnyis zung 'jug

ste gsum du bsdu bar gsung pa ltar bshad na/

[4.2.1.0.0 gzhi dbu ma bden gnyis zung 'jug]

dang po la

[4.2.1.1.0] kun rdzob kyi rnam bzhag dang/
[4.2.1.2.0] don dam gyi rnam bzhag

gnyis las/

[4.2.1.1.0 kun rdzob kyi rnam bzhag]

dang po ni/ [1] nyan thos sde gnyis kyi grub mtha' sngon du song nas sems tsam gyi lta ba ma skyes kyi gong du/ (S120) dbu ma par 'gyur ba yin na/ tha snyad du phyi don khas len yang (K37b) rigs pas dpyad bzod ni khas len pa mi srid do/ / [2] sems tsam pa'i lta ba sngon du song nas dbu ma par 'gyur ba yin na/ tha snyad du snang ba sems kyi bdag nyid du khas len pa yin yang/ rigs pas dpyad bzod ni khas len pa min no/ / [3] dngos por smra ba'i grub mtha' sngon du ma song bar dang po nyid nas dbu ma par 'gyur ba yin na/ tha snyad kyi rnam bzhag dpal ldan <u>zla ba'i</u> bzhed pa bzhin du 'jig rten na ji ltar grags pa ltar ma brtags par khas len pa yin no//

ma brtags pa'i don yang gnas lugs dpyod pa'i rigs pas ma brtags pa yin gyi/ tha snyad pa'i tshad mas ma brtags pa ni min te/ tha snyad pa'i tshad

358 KB *rig*.

understand the object to be meditated upon, then it *is* necessary to explain it in a detailed way through the reasoning explained in those texts.

[What Is to Be Taught: The Nature of Reality]

Previous scholars have said that [the Madhyamaka doctrine] is subsumable into three [categories], and I shall explain it likewise:

1. The Madhyamaka *qua* basis *(gzhi)*: the union of the two truths *(bden gnyis zung 'jug)*,
2. The Madhyamaka *qua* path *(lam)*: the union of the two accumulations *(tshogs gnyis zung 'jug)*, and
3. The Madhyamaka *qua* result *('bras bu)*: the union of the two bodies *(sku gnyis zung 'jug)*.

[The Madhyamaka **Qua** *Basis* **(gzhi)**: *The Union of the Two Truths]*

The first of these has two subdivisions:

1. The exposition of the conventional, and
2. The exposition of the ultimate.

[The Exposition of the Conventional]

(1) Individuals who start [their training] in either of the two śrāvaka philosophical schools and then become followers of the Madhyamaka *before* they generate the Cittamātra view will accept external objects nominally, but [since they are Mādhyamikas] it is impossible that they accept that [things] withstand rational analysis. (2) Those who have first generated the Cittamātra view and then become followers of the Madhyamaka accept that conventional appearances *(tha snyad du snang ba)* are of the nature of mind, but they [too] do not accept that [things] can withstand rational analysis. (3) Those who have not previously advocated realist tenets, but who become followers of the Madhyamaka from the start, explain the conventional just as the glorious Candra[kīrti] does—that is, by accepting [things] just as they are known in the world, that is, without analyzing them.[369]

As regards the words "without analyzing them" *(ma brtags pa)*, they mean that [in coming to an understanding of the conventional world,] things are not to be analyzed by means of the reasoning that analyzes reality. [This

mas yin min yod med la sogs pa ji ltar gzhal ba ltar rnam bzhag so sor phye nas khas blang dgos pa'i phyir ro/ /de'i phyir snga rabs pa (S121) 'ga' zhig gis tha snyad kyi rnam bzhag la'ang yod min med min khas len pa ni gzhung gi dgongs pa min te/ tha snyad kyi skabs su sa lu'i sa bon las sa lu'i myu gu ske/ nas kyi myu gu mi skye ba'i khyad par dang/ me tsha zhing sreg pa yin la/ chu tsha zhing sreg pa min pa'i khyad par khas len dgos pa'i phyir ro/ /gnas lugs la dpyod pa'i skabs su de gnyis khyad par med pa ni gzhan skye 'gog pa'i rigs pas shes so//

kun rdzob jig rten na ji ltar grags pa bzhin 'jog pa'i don yang glo bur gyi 'khrul rgyus ma slad pa'i 'jig rten rang 'ga' ba'i blo la snang zhing/ snang ba ltar rjes kyi tha snyad 'di 'di (K38a) yin no/ /'di 'di min no zhes tha snyad ji ltar byed pa tsam zhig khas len pa yin gyi/ de las gzhan gyi sgrub byed mi 'tshol ba'o/ /dper na sa bon las myu gu skye bar khas blangs pa la sgrub byed ci ltar ce na/ sa bon las myu gu skye (S122) bar blo la snang zhing snang ba ltar rjes su tha snyad byed pa tsam zhig bkod pa yin gyi/ sgrub byed gzhan bdag skye dang/ gzhan skye la sogs pa bkod pa na/ de dag la rigs pa'i gnod byed yod pas/ sa bon las myu gu skye ba mi rnyed pa ni gnad kyi don to// des na las kyis 'bras bu bskyed pa'i tshul la'ang/ blo la de ltar du snang ba las sgrub byed gzhan med la/ sgrub byed gzhan btsal ba na phrad nas bskyed[359] dam/ ma phrad nas bskyed pa gnyis las ma 'das pas/

dang po ltar na las rtag par 'gyur zhing/ phyi ma ltar na thams cad kyis thams cad bskyed par thal ba'i nyes pa mthong nas/ dngos smra ba rnams kyis nyes pa phyi ma spang ba'i phyir du las 'bras kyi rten khas len pa yin la/ zhig pa dngos po ba las 'bras kyi rten du 'dod pa'ang 'di las ma 'das pas/ kho bo ni phrad ma phrad kyi dpyad pa byas pa'i tshe na las kyis 'bras bu

359 KB *skyed.*

phrase] does not mean that things should not be analyzed by means of conventional valid cognitions *(tha snyad pa'i tshad ma)*, for it is necessary to accept [things] only after they have been critically set forth, in accordance with the way they are apprehended by conventional valid cognitions: "It is [this way] and not [that way]," "It exists [in such a way] and not [in another]," and so forth. Therefore, those few former scholars who accept that the [doctrine of] "neither existence nor nonexistence" applies even to the conventional [world] go against the purport of the texts. How so? In the context of the conventional *(tha snyad kyi skabs su)* we must accept the distinction that *salu* sprouts, and not barley sprouts, arise from *salu* seeds; and also that fire is hot and burns, whereas water is *not* hot and does *not* burn. That these two distinctions do not exist in the context of the analysis of reality *(gnas lugs dpyod pa'i skabs su)* can be known through [Candrakīrti's explanation of] the reasoning that refutes the arising from another.[370]

What do we mean when we say that we posit the conventional in accordance with how it is understood in the world? [The conventional is what] appears to an ordinary worldly mind that has not been affected by some adventitious source of error [like cataracts]. In the wake of that appearance, and in accordance with it, conventional expressions are used: "This is this way," "This is not that way." Things are to be accepted precisely in accordance with those expressions, without searching for [speculative] justifications *(sgrub byed)*[371] over and above [what is found in the mere conventional use of language]. For example, if someone asks, "What justification is there for accepting that seeds give rise to sprouts?" Our response would be as follows: That seeds give rise to sprouts is something that appears to the mind, and subsequent [to that appearance] we resort to using only those conventional expressions that *accord with* that appearance. [That is how] we posit [the arising of sprouts from seeds]. Since [other speculative theories or] justifications [for accepting that seeds give rise to sprouts]—such as "[sprouts] arise from themselves," or "they arise from something else," and so forth—can all be logically refuted, one concludes that the arising of sprouts from seeds cannot be found.

[The same is true of] the way in which karma gives rise to its effects. There is no justification [for the workings of karma] over and above the fact that it appears in that way to the mind. To search for some other [speculative] proof would involve determining whether, [for example, the effect] arises *after* it has come into contact with the [cause] or without coming into contact with it. In the first case, karma would be permanent.[372] In the latter case, there is witnessed the absurd fault that everything would arise from

(S123) bskyed pa nyid kyang mi 'dod pas las 'bras kyi rten khas len pa'i[360] don med do/ /'di dpal ldan zla ba'i dgongs par song ma song skyo ma snga btsan gyi sgros rnams bor nas 'jug pa rtsa 'grel la gzu bor gnas pa'i blos dpyod par mdzod cig//

de bzhin du chu phor gang la (K38b) mi'i mig shes kyis bltas[361] pa'i tshe chu yod de/ chu[362] mig shes la snang ba'i phyir ro/ /rnag khrag med de/ rnag khrag mi snang ba'i phyir ro/ /'o na yi dvags[363] kyis[364] rnag khrag tu mthong ba'i tshe na rnag khrag de ji ltar yod snyam na/ mig shes de'i ngor rnag khrag yod cing/ chu med pa ni snga ma dang 'dra la/ de gnyis las gzhan pa'i shes pa'i ngor ni gnyis ka med par shes par bya'o//

[4.2.1.2.0 don dam gyi rnam bzhag]

gnyis pa don dam pa'i rnam bzhag la/

[4.2.1.2.1] rigs pas dpyad pa'i don dam rjes mthun pa dang/
[4.2.1.2.2] 'phags pa'i mnyam bzhag la spros pa dang bral ba'i tshul gyis (S124) snang ba'i don dam mtshan nyid pa gnyis las/

[4.2.1.2.1 rigs pas dpyad pa'i don dam rjes mthun pa]

dang po ni/ *spyod 'jug* las/

> 'di[365] ni sdug bsngal rgyur gyur pa'i[366]//
> bden par zhen[367] pa bzlog bya yin/

ces dang/ *chos dbyings bstod pa* las/

> bdag dang bdag gir zhes 'dzin pas[368]//
> ji srid phyi rol rnam brtags pa[369]//

360 K *pa'ang.*
361 KB *ltas.*
362 BS *chu* omitted.
363 K *dags.*
364 KB *kyi.*
365 KBS *'di.* BCA (IX, 26), 191: *'dir.*
366 BCA, 191: *pa.*
367 BCA, 191: *bden par rtogs.*
368 KBS *'dzin ces pa'i. Dharmadhātu stava,* v. 64; P vol. 46, f. 32: *zhes 'dzin pas.*
369 BS *brtags pa'i.* K and P ed., f. 32: *btags pa.*

everything else.[373] It is so as to avoid this latter fault that the realists accept a "basis" *(rten)* [as an intermediary between] karma and its effects.[374] Nor is one any better off by accepting "destruction *qua* real entity" to be the basis of karma and its effects. Therefore, it is pointless to accept that karma gives rise to its effects when it is being analyzed as to whether or not they [karma and its effect] come into contact. So abandon [the method] that settles on what is the purport of the glorious Candra[kīrti] based on what is historically prior,[375] and just examine with an open mind the root text of the *Avatāra* and its commentary [and you will see the truth for yourself]!

In a similar fashion, [one can conclude that] there is water in the cup full of water when it is being perceived by a human's eye consciousness because the water *appears* to the eye consciousness. There is *no* pus and blood because the pus and blood *do not appear* [to the human being]. Well then, why do pus and blood exist [in the cup] when pretas are perceiving it as pus and blood? As in the previous case, [when pretas are looking at it] there exists pus and blood—and no water—within the purview of their eye consciousnesses. And in the purview of a consciousness different from those two, one should understand that neither [water nor pus and blood] exist.[376]

[The Exposition of the Ultimate]

The exposition of the ultimate has two parts:

1. The quasi-ultimate *(don dam rjes mthun pa)*, which involves rational analysis, and
2. The real ultimate *(don dam mtshan nyid pa)*, which is what appears to the [meditative] equipoise of āryans in a way that is devoid of the proliferations.

[The Quasi-Ultimate, Which Involves Analysis]

As regards the first [type of ultimate], the *Bodhicaryāvatāra* states:

> [Ignorance] is the cause of suffering, and so here
> Conceiving things as true is to be eliminated.[377]

and the *Dharmadhātustava* states:

> They imagine an external world
> By grasping at "I" and at "mine."

bdag med rnam pa gnyis mthong nas//
srid pa'i sa bon 'gag par 'gyur//

ces gsungs pa ltar/ chos la bden par 'dzin pa'i bden 'dzin las skyes pa'i/ gang zag la bden par 'dzin pa'i bden 'dzin de nyid nyes pa thams cad kyi rtsa ba yin pas/ bden 'dzin de gnyis kyi zhen yul rigs pas sun phyung dgos la/ de'i tshe gang zag dang chos bden par med pa re zhig khas blangs shing rtog pas kyang de ltar du zhen pa las ma 'das te/ de lta bu'i bden med rtogs pa'i blo de sgra don 'dres 'dzin gyi rtog pa yin pa'i (K39a) phyir ro//

de la chos kyi bdag med (S125) sgrub[370] pa'i rigs pa la/ dbu ma' gzhung lugs rnams las/

- rdo rje'i gzegs ma/
- yod med skye 'gog/
- mu bzhi skye 'gog/
- gcig du bral/
- rten 'brel gyi rigs pa ste/

lnga gsungs shing de dag rang rgyud pa rnams kyis rang rgyud kyi gtan tshigs su 'dod la/ thal 'gyur ba rnams kyis[371] gzhan la grags kyi rtags su 'dod do//

gang zag gi bdag med sgrub[372] pa'i rigs pa ni/ *'jug pa* las/ phung po dang gcig dang tha dad la sogs pa rnam pa bdun gyis btsal na mi rnyed par gsungs pa 'di nyid rgyas shos su snang ngo//

de ltar bden pa bkag pa'i tshe/ rtog pas bden med du zhen pa las ma 'das kyang/ de'i 'og tu bden med du mngon par zhen pa nyid kyang dgag dgos pas/ bden pas stong pa nyid gnas lugs su bzung du mi rung ste/ dgag bya bden pa med pas de bkag pa'i bden stong nyid kyang ma grub pa'i phyir ro/ /de (S126) dag gi mtha' dpyod pa'i yan lag tu bden pas stong mi stong gnyis kar yang bzung du mi rung ste/ re re bar bzung du mi rung ba'i phyir ro/ /gnyis ka min par yang bzung du mi rung ste/ gnyis ka min pa ma grub pa'i phyir ro/ /des na gnas lugs dpyod pa'i rig ngor ma grub na der bzung du mi

370 KBS *bsgrub*.
371 K *kyas*.
372 KBS *bsgrub*.

But when they see the two forms of nonself,
They eliminate the seed of existence.[378]

As these works state, "the form of the grasping at truth that grasps at the truth of *phenomena*" gives rise to "the form of the grasping at truth that grasps at the truth of the *person*" and *that*, in turn, is the root of all faults. That is why the conceived object *(zhen yul)* of those two forms of grasping at truth must be repudiated using reasoning. During [the process of rational analysis,] the truthlessness of persons and phenomena is only provisionally *(re zhig)* accepted, and conceptual thought simply cannot transcend that kind of conceptual construction. This is because the thought that understands truthlessness in that way is a conceptual thought that mixes up words and their meaning.[379]

In this regard, the Madhyamaka textual tradition speaks of five forms of reasoning that prove the selflessness of phenomena.[380] They are:

1. the diamond-sliver *(rdo rje'i gzegs ma)*,[381]
2. the refutation of the arising of existent and nonexistent things *(yod med skye 'gog)*,
3. the refutation of arising via the four alternatives *(mu bzhi skye 'gog)*,
4. being devoid of being one/many *(gcig du bral)*,
5. the reasoning of dependent arising *(rten 'brel gyi rigs pa)*.

The Svātantrikas accept these to be autonomous syllogisms, while the Prāsaṅgikas accept them to be "reasons acceptable to others" *(gzhan la grags kyi rtags)*.

The most extensive exposition of the reasoning that proves the selflessness *of the person* is to be found in the *Avatāra*,[382] where it says that the self is not found when searched for in seven ways—[involving an analysis of] whether it is the same as the aggregates, different from them, and so forth.

When truth is refuted in this way, one does not go beyond constructing *(zhen pa)* truthlessness conceptually *(rtog pas)*.[383] Afterwards, that very conceptual construction *(mngon par zhen pa)* of truthlessness must itself be negated. Hence, the emptiness of truth cannot be considered reality *(gnas lugs)*. Why? Since the object to be negated—truth—does not exist, neither does the emptiness of truth that is the negation [of that truth]. Nor is it appropriate to then apprehend things as being *both* empty and nonempty of truth as the [next] step in those determinations, for it is inappropriate to apprehend [things as being] each individually. Nor is it appropriate to apprehend [things] as being neither, for they are not established as neither.

rung ba ni/ bden pa bkag pa'i rigs pas shes la/ rig ngo der mtha' bzhi gang du yang ma grub pas mtha' bzhir 'dzin pa thams cad bkag (K39b) dgos pa'i gnad kyang 'di nyid yin no//

gal te gnas lugs dpyod pa'i rig ngor bden pa grub par thal/ de'i ngor bden stong ma grub pa'i phyir/ zhes smra ba ni/

'phags pa klu sgrub kyi phyogs snga rig ngor dgag pa gnyis rnal ma go ba'i lugs yin pas gong du bkag zin to//

'o na *rigs pa drug cu pa* las/

> rang bzhin med pa nyid zlog[373] na//
> rang zhin nyid du rab grub 'gyur[374]// (S127)

ces pa dang 'gal lo snyam na/

de ni tha snyad du rang bzhin med pa min na/ rang bzhin yod dgos ces pa'i don yin la/ tha snyad kyi skabs su yod min med min khas len pa min pas 'gal ba ci zhig yod/

mdor na gnas lugs la dpyod par byed pa'i blo ni sgra don 'dres 'dzin gyi rtog pa las ma 'das pas/ mtha' bzhi'i spros pa gang rung du bzung bas bzhi po cig char du bkag pa mi srid kyang/ res 'jog gi tshul du spros pa bzhi char yang 'gog pa yin la/ de dag gi dngos yul du gyur pa'i mtha' bzhi'i spros bral ni/ bden 'dzin can gyi blo la ltos te/ don dam bden par[375] bshad kyang/ 'phags pa'i mnyam bzhag zag med la ltos te kun rdzob bden pa yin pas/ rnam grangs pa'i don dam bden pa'am/ don dam pa rjes mthun pa yin par bshad do//

373 Go rams pa identifies the *Yuktiṣaṣtika* as source of this quotation, but the passage is actually found in the *Vigrahavyāvartanī,* v. 26. Lindtner, ed., *Nagarjuniana,* 79: *log.*
374 KBS *phyir.* Lindtner ed., *Nagarjuniana,* 79: *'gyur.*
375 KB *pa.*

Therefore, the essential point is this. If something does not exist within the purview of the reasoning consciousness that analyzes the ultimate, it should not be apprehended. This is something that is understood by means of the reasoning that negates truth. Now since [things] do not exist in any of the four extreme ways within the purview of that reasoning consciousness, it is necessary to negate all of the forms of apprehending [things] in terms of the four extremes.

[Opponent:] [According to your logic,] truth *must* exist within the purview of the reasoning consciousness that analyzes reality, for the emptiness [or negation] of truth does not exist in its purview.

[Reply:] This has already been refuted, for it represents the views of an opponent of the ārya Nāgārjuna who believes that in the purview of that reasoning consciousness the law of double negation is operative, [when it is not].

[Opponent:] Well then, [by repudiating the law of double negation] you are contradicting the passage from [Nāgārjuna's] *Yuktiṣaṣṭikā* that says:

> If one repudiates essencelessness,
> One will be affirming essentialism.[384]

[Reply:] The meaning of this passage is this: if, on the level of conventions, essences were not nonexistent, they would have to exist. What contradiction is there, then, given that *in a conventional context* we do not accept the "neither existence nor nonexistence" [doctrine]?[385]

In brief, the thought that engages in the analysis of reality is nothing but a conceptual thought that mixes up words and their meanings. Hence, since it only focuses on *one* of the fourfold extremist proliferations, it cannot eliminate *all four* simultaneously *(cig char du)*. Nonetheless, [conceptual thought] *does* eliminate all four proliferations *one at a time.* Now the freedom from the proliferations of the four extremes that is the direct object *(dngos yul)* of those [various negations individually], by comparison with a mind that possesses a grasping at truth *(bden 'dzin can gyi blo)*, is explained to be an ultimate truth, but compared to the stainless equipoise of āryans, it is only a conventional truth. That is why it is called "an ultimate truth in name only" *(rnam grangs pa'i don dam bden pa)*[386] or a "quasi-ultimate" *(don dam pa rjes mthun pa)*.

[4.2.1.2.2 'phags pa'i mnyam bzhag la spros pa dang bral ba'i tshul gyis snang ba'i don dam mtshan nyid pa]

gnyis pa don dam bden pa mtshan nyid pa ni/ (S128) de ltar so so'i skye bo'i gnas skabs su/ mtha' bzhi'i spros pa res 'jog tu bkag nas bsgoms pas/ theg chen gyi (K40a) mthong lam skyes pa'i tshe/ mtha' bzhi'i spros pa cig char du 'gags nas rtog bya'i chos nyid dang rtogs byed kyi blo gnyis so sor mi snang bar/ blo de nyid spros bral dang dbyer med par mngon du gyur pa'i yul de nyid la/ don dam bden pa zhes pa'i tha snyad btags pa yin gyi/ de'i tshe yang don dam bden pa 'di'o zhes cung zad kyang bzung bar bya ba med do/ /'di la dgong nas bka' dang bstan bcos dri ma med pa rnams las/ ma mthong ba'i tshul gyis mthong/ ma gzigs pa'i tshul gyis gzigs zhes sogs mang du gsungs so//

'o na stong nyid de la don dam bden par gsungs pa dang 'gal lo snyam na/ spyir stong nyid ces pa'i tha snyad tsam la mang du yod de/

[1] nyan thos sde gnyis kyis gang zag gi bdag (S129) gis stong pa la stong nyid kyi tha snyad byed de/ *rnam 'grel* las/ stong nyid lta dang de 'gal phyir// ces so//

[2] sems tsam pas ni gzung 'dzin rdzas gzhan gyis stong pa la stong nyid kyi tha snyad byed de/ de nyid las/ de phyir gnyis stong gang yin pa// de ni de yi de nyid[376] yin// ces so//

[3] dbu ma pa rnams kyis/ [a] bden pas stong pa tsam la stong nyid kyi tha snyad mdzad[377] pa dang/ [b] mtha' bzhi char gyi spros pas stong pa la stong nyid kyi tha snyad mdzad pa gnyis yod de/ dang po ni/ theg pa gsum char gyi thun mong du rtogs par bya ba yin la/ phyi ma ni theg chen kho na'i thun mong min pa'i rtogs bya yin no/ /gnyis po de re re la (K40b) yang sngar ltar rjes mthun pa dang/ mtshan nyid pa gnyis gnyis yod pa las phyi ma gnyis char don dam bden pa mtshan nyid par bzhed de/ lugs 'di la theg dman 'phags pas kyang don dam bden pa rtogs par bzhed pa'i (S130) phyir ro/ /chos nyid dang/ chos dbyings dang/ spros bral dang/ zung 'jug yin na mtha' bzhi char gyi spros bral yin pa zhig[378] dgos te/ de dag ni theg dman gyis cung zad kyang ma rtogs pa'i phyir ro//

376 B *de ni de'i de nyid. Pramāṇavārttika* (III, 213d). E. Steinkellner, *Verse Index of Dharmakīrti's Works (Tibetan Versions)* (Wien: Arbeitskreis für Tibetische und Buddhistische Studien Universität Wien, 1977), 95: *de ni de yi'ang de nyid.*
377 K *mjad.*
378 KS *cig.*

[The Real Ultimate, Which Is What Appears to the Meditative Equipoise of Āryans in a Way that Is Devoid of the Proliferations]

While one is still an ordinary being, one eliminates each of the proliferations of the four extremes one at a time, and then meditates [on each of these individually]. This leads to the emergence of the Mahāyāna path of seeing. At that time, the proliferations of all four extremes are eliminated simultaneously *(cig char du)* in such a way that the reality that is to be realized and the mind that realizes it do not appear as two distinct things. The object that manifests itself without proliferations and indivisibly from that mind is given the name "the ultimate truth"; but at that time, there is no apprehension whatsoever of the fact, "This is the ultimate truth." It is intending this that the stainless word [of the Buddha] and its commentarial tradition repeatedly urge us to "see things through the method of not seeing, and perceive things through the method of nonperception."

[Opponent:] Well then, aren't you contradicting the fact that [in those same texts] emptiness is *called* "the ultimate truth"?

[Reply:] In general, there are many [uses] of the term "emptiness."

[1] The two śrāvaka schools use the term "emptiness" to refer to the emptiness of the self of the person, as in the *Pramāṇavārttika* line that goes, "Because it contradicts the view of emptiness."[387]

[2] The Cittamātras use the term "emptiness" to refer to the emptiness of the fact that subject and object are empty of being different substances, when that same text says, "Therefore, its nonduality is its reality."[388]

[3] The followers of the Madhyamaka [use the term "emptiness"] in two ways: (a) they use the term "emptiness" to refer to the mere emptiness of truth, and (b) they also use the term "emptiness" to refer to the emptiness of the proliferations of the four extremes. The first [kind of emptiness] is [an object] that is understood in common [by the followers] of all three vehicles *(theg pa gsum char)*.[389] The latter [—that is, emptiness *qua* negation of all four extremes—is an object] that is *not* understood in common, but [is understood] only in the Mahāyāna. Each [of these kinds of emptiness], as before, has two subdivisions: quasi *(rjes mthun pa)* and real *(mtshan nyid pa)*. The latter two[390] are accepted as real ultimate truths, for this system accepts that even Hīnayāna āryans understand the ultimate truth.[391] Reality *(dharmatā, chos nyid)*, the sphere of reality *(dharmadhātu, chos dbyings)*, the freedom from proliferations *(niṣprapañca, spros bral)*, and the union *(yuganadha, zung 'jug)*—each one of these must be a form of freedom from *all four* extremes, for Hīnayanists have not the slightest understanding of any of them.

[4.2.2.0.0 lam dbu ma tshogs gnyis zung 'jug]

gnyis pa lam dbu ma thabs shes zung 'jug la/

[4.2.2.1.0] spang bya sgrib gnyis ngos bzung ba/
[4.2.2.2.0] spong byed kyi gnyen po ngos bzung ba

dang gnyis/

[4.2.2.1.0 spang bya sgrib gnyis ngos bzung ba]

dang po ni/ sngar bshad pa[379] ltar phung po la dmigs nas bden par 'dzin pa'i blo ni chos kyi bdag 'dzin yin pas shes sgrib yin la/ chos kyi bdag 'dzin yin na bden 'dzin yin pas ma khyab ste/ mtha' bzhi'i spros pa[380] phyi ma gsum du 'dzin pa'i blo de la yang chos kyi bdag 'dzin yin par bshad pa'i phyir dang/ bden 'dzin gyi sgro 'dogs chod nas btags pa tsam du mngon par zhen pa'i blo de yang chos kyi bdag 'dzin du gsungs pa'i phyir ro//

chos la bden (S131) par 'dzin pa'i bdag 'dzin de nyid/ gang zag gi bdag 'dzin gyi dngos rgyu nus pa thogs med yin pas skabs 'ga' zhig tu nyon mongs pa'i ming gis brtags pa yang yod la/ yang *rgyud blar* byang chub kyi le'u skabs su nyon mongs kyi bag chags la shes sgrib tu bshad cing/ *'jug 'grel*[381] las kyang/ de ltar du gsungs pas de yang shes sgrib tu khas (K41a) blang bar bya'o/ /*rgyud blar* phan yon gyi le'u skabs/ 'khor gsum rnam par rtog pa'i blo shes sgrib tu bshad pas/

bsdu na 'di ltar 'gyur te/ shes sgrib la rnam rtog mngon 'gyur ba dang/ bag chags gnyis/ dang po la bden 'dzin yod pa dang med pa gnyis/ phyi ma

379 KBS *par.*
380 K *ba.*
381 K *'grol.*

[The Madhyamaka Qua *Path* (lam), *Which Is the Union of Method and Wisdom* (thabs shes zung 'jug)][392]

This has two subdivisions:

1. The identification of the two obscurations, the [objects] to be eliminated *(spang bya sgrib gnyis)*, and
2. The identification of the antidotes that eliminate those [two obscurations] *(spong byed kyi gnyen po)*.

[The Identification of the Two Obscurations, the Objects to Be Eliminated][393]

As explained previously, the thought that focuses on the aggregates and grasps them as true is [a form of] the grasping at the truth of phenomena *(chos kyi bdag 'dzin)*, and that is why it is an obscuration to omniscience *(shes sgrib)*. But not every [instance] of the grasping at the self of phenomena is a grasping at truth. This is because the thoughts that grasp [things] in terms of the latter three proliferations of the four extremes are explained to be forms of grasping at the self of phenomena, and the thought that, having broken through the reification of the grasping of truth, conceptualizes [things] to be mere imputations *(btags pa tsam)* is also said to be [a form of] grasping at the self of phenomena, [but neither of these two are examples of the grasping at truth].

The "grasping at the self *qua* grasping at the truth of phenomena" *(chos la bden par 'dzin pa'i bdag 'dzin)* is the ever-present power that is the direct cause of the grasping at the self of the person, and that is why in some instances it is also called an "affliction." Also, in the "Enlightenment" chapter of the *Uttaratantra*,[394] the latent potentialities of the afflictions *(nyon mongs pa'i bag chags)* are explained to be obscurations to omniscience; and the *Avatārabhāṣya* also teaches this in the same way.[395] Hence, [these latent potentialities of the afflictions] must also be accepted as being obscurations to omniscience. The "Benefits" chapter of the *Uttaratantra* explains that the thought that conceptualizes the three cycles *('khor gsum rnam par rtogs pa'i blo)* is also an obscuration to omniscience.[396]

Therefore, when we combine [all of these sources], we find that obscurations to omniscience are of two kinds: manifest *(mngon 'gyur ba)* and latent *(bag chags)*.[397] The first of these [i.e., the manifest obscurations to omniscience,] are twofold: those that include grasping at truth *(bden 'dzin)* and those that lack it. The latter [i.e., the latent obscurations to omniscience]

la shes sgrib kyi rnam par rtog pa'i bag chags dang/ nyon mongs pa'i bag chags gnyis so//

nyon sgrib ni *rgyud blar* ngos 'dzin tshul gnyis byung ba[382] ni don gcig tu snang zhing/ klu sgrub yab sras kyi gzhung rnams (S132) las kyang/ gang zag la bden par 'dzin pa'i bden 'dzin dang/ de'i 'bras bur gyur pa'i[383] rtsa nyon dang nye[384] nyon rnams la gsungs pa rnams don gcig tu snang bas nyon mongs pa sa bon dang bcas pa rnams la nyon sgrib tu 'jog pa la ni byams pa dang/ klu sgrub gnyis dgongs pa gcig tu snang ngo//

[4.2.2.2.0 spong byed kyi gnyen po ngos bzung ba]

gnyis pa spong byed kyi gnyen po ngos bzung ba ni/ nyan thos sde gnyis kyis phung po bden med du ma rtogs kyang/ phung po'i steng du gang zag gi bdag bkag pa'i stong nyid rtogs pas/ theg pa gsum char gyi byang chub thob par 'dod pas theg pa gsum la lta ba'i khyad par mi bzhed do//

sems tsam pas lta ba des nyan thos dang/ rang sangs rgyas kyi byang chub thob kyang theg pa chen po'i byang chub thob pa la gzung 'dzin gnyis stong gi de bzhin nyid rtogs dgos pas/ theg pa che chung la lta ba'i khyad par yod kyang nyan thos dang rang sangs (S133) rgyas la lta ba'i (K41b) khyad par mi bzhed do//

dbu ma pa'i lugs la/ byams pa dang/ klu sgrub gnyis char dgongs pa mthun par theg[385] pa gsum char gyi byang chub thob pa la/ phung po bden med du rtogs dgos shing/ theg chen kyi byang chub thob pa la mtha' bzhi'i spros pa dang bral ba'i spros bral rtogs dgos pas/ theg pa che chung la lta

382 K *pa.*
383 KB *ba'i.*
384 S *nyon dang nye* omitted.
385 K *thag.*

are also twofold: the latent potentialities of the conceptualizations that are obscurations to omniscience *(shes sgrib kyi rnam par rtog pa'i bag chags)* and the latent potentialities of the afflictions *(nyon mongs pa'i bags chags)*.

The *Uttaratantra* has two ways of identifying the afflicted obscurations *(nyon sgrib)*,[398] but it seems that they amount to the same thing. The texts of Nāgārjuna, the father, and his spiritual son[s] also state [that the afflicted obscurations consist of] "the grasping at true [existence] *qua* grasping at the true existence of the person" *(gang zag la bden par 'dzin pa'i bden 'dzin)*, and the root and secondary afflictions that are the result of that [grasping at the true existence of the person];[399] [the explanation in these texts] too appears to amount to the same thing. Hence, it is the afflictions together with their seeds *(sa bon)* that must be considered [to make up the category of] "afflicted obscurations." On this point, Maitreya and Nāgārjuna appear be in agreement.

[The Identification of the Antidotes That Eliminate Those Two Obscurations]

Even though the two śrāvaka schools do not understand the aggregates to be truthless,[400] they *do* understand the emptiness that is the negation of the self of the person based on the aggregates. Because they believe that [this understanding] brings about the attainment of the enlightenment of each of the three vehicles—[śrāvaka, pratyekabuddha, and bodhisattva vehicles]—they do not accept that there are differences in the philosophical view of the three vehicles.

The Cittamātras [maintain that] one can obtain the enlightenment of the śrāvakas and pratyekabuddhas by means of that philosophical view, but [claim that] to obtain the enlightenment of the Mahāyāna, one must understand reality *qua* emptiness of the duality of subject and object. Hence, even though there is [for them] a difference in the philosophical view between the Mahā- and Hīna-yānas, they do not accept that there is a difference between the philosophical views of the śrāvakas and pratyekabuddhas.[401]

As regards the system of the Madhyamaka, both Maitreya and Nāgārjuna are in agreement as to the fact that in order to obtain the enlightenment of any of the three vehicles, one must understand the aggregates to be truthless; and that to obtain the enlightenment of the Mahāyāna, one must [additionally] understand the freedom from proliferations—that is, the freedom from the proliferations of the four extremes. Hence, [for them] there is

ba'i khyad par shin tu che zhing/ nyan thos kyis gzung ba phyi rol gyi don btags pa tsam yang mi dmigs par ma rtogs la/ rang sangs rgyas kyis de rtogs pas/ de gnyis la yang lta ba'i khyad par yod do//

'o na nyan thos kyi bar chad med lam des phung po la bden par 'dzin pa'i bden 'dzin spang nus par 'gyur ro snyam na/

phung po bden med 'dzin stangs kyi gtso bor mi byed par/ gang zag bden med 'dzin stangs gtso bor byed pas skyon med do/ /de bzhin du rang rgyal gyi mthong lam bar chad med (S134) lam gyis kyang gzung ba phyi rol gyi don bden par med pa dzin stangs kyi gtso bor byed pas/ bzung ba ba phyi rol gyi don la bden par 'dzin pa'i bden 'dzin spong nus pa yin gyi de las gzhan pa'i shes sgrib spong mi nus so/ /theg chen mthong lam bar chad med pa'i lam gyis mtha' bzhi char gyi spros bral 'dzin stangs kyi gtso bor byed pas/ shes sgrib mtha' dag spong nus pa'i gnad kyang de nyid yin no//

nyan rang gis bden med rtogs pa ni/ klu sgrub yab sras kyi gzhung las lan mang du bshad cing/ *mngon rtogs rgyan* gyi dbu zhabs na (K42a) theg pa che chung gi lta ba'i khyad par bshad pa mang du yod kyang/ bden med rtogs ma rtogs kyi khyad par 'byed pa ni cung zad kyang mi snang bas/ de gnyis dgongs pa gcig tu mngon no//

gal te dngos por mngon par zhen pa yod med kyi khyad par bshad pas bden med rtogs ma rtogs kyi khyad par yod do (S135) snyam na

de ni ma nges ste/ btags pa'i dngos por mngon par[386] zhen pa ni/ dngos

386 KB *pa*.

a *great* difference between the philosophical views of the Mahā- and Hīna-yānas. [Mādhyamikas also claim that] śrāvakas do not understand even in a nominal way *(btags pa tsam yang)* that external objects *(gzung ba phyi rol gyi don)* are not perceived [or established], and since pratyekabuddhas *do* understand that, [they maintain] that there is a difference in philosophical view between these [i.e., between śrāvakas and pratyekabuddhas].[402]

Objection: Well then, it would follow that the śrāvaka's uninterrupted path *(bar chad med lam)* can eliminate the grasping at truth that grasps at the truth of the aggregates.[403]

[Reply:] There is no problem [here], for they do not chiefly focus on the truthlessness of the aggregates, but instead chiefly focus on the truthlessness of the person. Likewise, the pratyekabuddha's *(rang rgyal)*[404] uninterrupted path of the path of seeing also focuses chiefly on the truthlessness of external objects, and that is why they can eliminate the [form of the] grasping at truth that grasps at the truth of external objects, and why they are *not* able to eliminate the obscurations to omniscience that are different from those. The uninterrupted path of the path of seeing of the Mahāyāna focuses chiefly on the freedom from the proliferations of all four extremes, and that is why it can eliminate all of the obscurations to omniscience. This is the point.

The texts of Nāgārjuna, the father, and of his spiritual son[s] repeatedly explain that śrāvakas and pratyekabuddhas understand truthlessness. And even though throughout the *Abhisamayālaṃkāra* there are many explanations concerning the difference in the philosophical view of the Mahā- and Hīna-yānas, there is not a single instance of [the AA's] differentiating between [śrāvakas and pratyekabuddhas on the one hand, and bodhisattvas on the other] as regards their understanding of truthlessness. Hence, it is evident that these two [figures, that is, Nāgārjuna and Maitreya,] are in agreement [on this point].

Objection: Since [the AA] explains that there is a difference [between these two groups] as regards whether or not they conceptualize [things] in terms of entitiness *(dngos por mngon par zhen pa)*, there is a difference as regards whether or not they understand truthlessness.

[Reply:] There is no certainty [in this regard—that is, this is not an unambiguous way of differentiating between the two groups], for [the AA's claim that śrāvakas conceptualize things in terms of their entitiness] does not mean that they do not realize truthlessness. Why? Because the conceptualization of things in terms of their *imputed* entitiness *(btags pa'i dngos por mngon par zhen pa)* [is a form of understanding that, while understanding the

po'i gnas tshul spros bral ma shes pa'i don yin pas bden med ma rtogs pa'i don min no//

mtshungs med chos rje'i zhal snga nas/ nyan rang gis[387] phung po bden med ma rtogs pa'i shes byed du/

> rtag tu khams gsum bdag med rdzas med cing//
> byed po rang dbang med par rnam ltas nas//
> rjes su mthun pa'i bzod pa gang bsgom pa//
> de dag 'gro ba kun las thar bar 'gyur//

ces gsungs pa 'di drangs kyang/ lung 'di bden med rtogs pa'i lung du rje nyid kyang bzhed dgos pa 'dra ste/ lung 'dis khams gsum rdzas med rtogs par bstan cing/ rdzas 'dzin rtog pa bden 'dzin yin par zhal gyis bzhes pa'i phyir ro//

mdor na nyan thos kyi rtogs bya'i gtso bo ni gang zag gi bdag med yin la/ de rtogs pa la (S136) phung po la bden par 'dzin pa[388] bkag dgos te/ phung po la bden par 'dzin pa'i bden 'dzin ni gang zag gi bdag 'dzin gyi dngos rgyu nus pa thogs med yin pa'i phyir ro/ /rang rgyal gyi rtogs bya'i gtso bo ni/ bzung ba (K42b) phyi rol gyi don bden par med pa yin la/ theg chen gyi rtogs bya'i gtso bo ni gnyis 'dzin gyi spros pa mtha' dag dang bral ba yin pas lta ba'i[389] khyad par shin tu che'o//

gal te *mdo sde sa bcu pa* las/ sa bdun pa ma thob bar du nyan rang dgra bcom blo'i stobs kyis zil gyis gnon mi nus par bshad pa dang 'gal lo zhe na/ de'i don kho bos bshad pa 'di kho na[390] ltar snang ste/

> byang chub sems dpa'i sa bdun pa 'di la gnas pa'i byang chub sems dpa' ni rang gi yul shes pa'i che ba la gnas pas kyang nyan thos dang rang sangs rgyas kyi bya ba thams cad las shin tu 'das pa yin no[391]

387 KB *gi*.
388 K *pal*.
389 BS *ba*.
390 K *nar*.
391 The canonical versions of the sūtra differ slightly from Go rams pa's, but the passage in Go rams pa corresponds exactly to the sūtra passage as it is found in MABh, Toh no. 3862, Dbu ma *'a*, f. 226b.

truthlessness of things,] does not understand their final reality as devoid of proliferations.

True, the incomparable Lord of the Dharma *(mtshungs med chos rje)* [has cited the following verse] as proof of the fact śrāvakas and pratyekabuddhas *do not* realize truthlessness:

> Constantly perceiving the three spheres [of existence]
> As selfless, substanceless, and as lacking an independent creator,
> And then cultivating a corresponding receptivity [to this],
> This is how [they are] liberated from all of the transmigratory [realms].[405]

Nonetheless, it seems to me that even the Lord [Rong ston pa] himself must accept this passage as one [that proves] that they *do* understand truthlessness. Why? This passage teaches that they understand the three spheres [of existence] to be substanceless, and he accepts that the conceptual thought that apprehends substance is [a form of] the apprehension of truth.

In brief, the chief thing that śrāvakas must realize is the selflessness of the person. To understand that, they must eliminate grasping at the aggregates as true [things]. This is because "grasping at truth *qua* grasping at the truth of the aggregates" is the ever-present power that is the direct cause of the apprehension of the self of the person. The chief thing that pratyekabuddhas must realize is the truthlessness of external things *qua* objects. The chief thing that Mahāyānists must realize is the freedom from all dualistic proliferations *(gnyis 'dzin gyi spros pa mtha' dag dang bral ba)*. Hence, there is a very great difference in the philosophical view [understood by these three types of adepts].

Objection: This contradicts an explanation in the *Daśabhūmikasūtra* to the effect that until they obtain the seventh level, *(sa bdun pa)* [bodhisattvas] cannot surpass śrāvaka and pratyekabuddha arhats by virtue of their intellectual prowess *(blo'i stobs kyis)*.[406]

[Reply:] The meaning [of this passage] is, in fact, consistent only *with our own* explanation [of this],[407] [for the sūtra] states:

> The bodhisattva who abides in the seventh bodhisattva stage utterly supercedes all of the actions of śrāvakas and pratyekabuddhas because of the greatness of his understanding of his own object as well.[408]

zhes gsungs la/ de'i don ni/ rang (S137) gi yul ni theg dman la med pa'i theg chen thun mong min pa'i yul sngar bshad pa ltar gyi spros bral de nyid yin la/ de shes pa la don spyi'i tshul gyis shes pa ni theg chen gyi tshogs sbyor na yang yod la/ de'i sgo nas nyan rang las khyad par du 'phags pa ni/ rnam pa mngon zhen la sogs 'gog ces pa'i skabs su bstan la/ de mngon sum du shes pa ni/ theg chen gyi mthong lam du yod la/ de'i sgo nas khyad par du phags pa ni/ gang gis[392] lam ni gzhan dag las/ khyad du 'phags pas khyad par lam/ zhes pa'i skabs su bstan/ de'i che ba ni mtshan 'dzin mtha' dag 'gog pa'i nus pa yin la/ de'i sgo nas nyan rang zil gyis[393] gnon pa ni/ sa bdun pa'i gnas skabs su thob ste/ sa brgyad pa yan chad du mtshan 'dzin mngon du 'gyur ba mi srid pa'i phyir ro//

de yang rang gi yul dang/ de shes pa dang/ de'i che ba dang/ kyang dang/ shin (S138) tu zhes pa'i tshig lnga'i nus pa shes na/ lung 'di la brten nas theg pa che chung lta ba'i khyad par med pa'i log rtog mi (K43a) 'byung ngo//

kho bos ni *sher phyin kyi mdo* dang/ *mdo sde sa bcu pa* dang/ *mngon rtogs rgyan* dang/ 'phags pa klu sgrub kyi gsung gnad gcig tu go zhing dgos pa'i dbang gis tha snyad cung zad mi 'dra ba mdzad pa ni yod de/ *mngon rtogs rgyan* gyi skabs su theg chen thun mong min pa'i lam gtso bor 'chad pas/ spros bral rtogs pa la chos kyi bdag med rtogs par byas nas/ de nyid nyan rang la med par gsungs la/ 'phags mchog klu sgrub kyis theg pa gsum char gyis rtogs bya'i skye med gtan la dbab pas de tsam la chos kyi bdag med rtogs par byas nas de theg pa gsum char la yod par gsungs so//

[4.2.3.0.0 'bras bu dbu ma sku gnyis zung 'jug]

gsum pa 'bras bu dbu ma sku gnyis zung 'jug ni/ gzhan du rgyas par 'chad (S139) par 'gyur ro//

392 KBS *gi.* AA (IV, 26). Stcherbatsky ed., 39: *gis.*
393 KB *gyi;* S *gyis.*

The meaning [of this passage] is as follows. "His own object" is precisely the previously explained freedom from proliferations, an object that is unique to the Mahāyāna and lacking in the Hīnayāna. The knowledge of that [object] through a generic image *(don spyi'i tshul gyis)* already exists in the Mahāyāna paths of accumulation and preparation; their superiority to śrāvakas and pratyekabuddhas from this point of view is taught in the *[Abhisamayālaṃkāra]* section that states: "the cessation of conceptualization and so forth."[409] The direct perceptual knowledge *(mngon sum du shes pa)* of that [object] occurs in the Mahāyāna path of seeing; and their superiority from *this* point of view is taught in the section that states: "Hence, because their path supercedes that of others [in this way], it is a special path."[410] Their "greatness" refers to their ability to eliminate all apprehension of signs *(mtshan 'dzin)*. Their surpassing of śrāvakas and pratyekabuddhas from this point of view is obtained during the seventh stage, since from the eighth stage on it is impossible for the apprehension of signs to manifest [within their minds] *(mtshan 'dzin mngon du 'gyur ba)*.[411]

If one understands the power *(nus pa)* of the five [pivotal sets of] words [of the above passage]—namely, "his own object," "understanding of [that object]," "their greatness," "as well," and "utterly"—there cannot arise the misconception that, based on this passage, [one can claim that there is] no difference between the Mahā- and Hīna-yānas in regard to their view [of emptiness].

We understand the *Prajñāpāramitāsūtras*, the *Daśabhūmikasūtra*, the *Abhisamayālaṃkāra*, and the texts of Nāgārjuna to be doctrinally unanimous *(gnad gcig)*; but we acknowledge that, for some specific purpose, they do [on occasion] use terminology in slightly different ways. Since, in the context of the *Abhisamayālaṃkāra*, it is the special [structure of the] path *of the Mahāyāna* that is chiefly taught, it takes the understanding of the freedom from proliferations to be the understanding of the selflessness of phenomena, and states that śrāvakas and pratyekabuddhas lack it. [On the other hand,] the supreme ārya Nāgārjuna states that it is non-arising that is the object to be realized by [the followers of] all three vehicles; taking only *that* [i.e., non-arising] to be the selflessness of phenomena, he states that it [the selflessness of phenomena] exists in all three vehicles.

[The Madhyamaka Qua *Result: The Union of the Two Bodies]*

This will be explained extensively elsewhere.[412]

[4.3.0.0.0 yid ches pa'i lung dang sbyar ba]

gsum pa yid ches pa'i lung dang sbyar ba ni/ rang lugs mdor bsdus pa 'di dag ni/ re re bzhin du gzhung khung thub rnams dang sbyar bar bya dgos kyang/ mang bas 'jigs nas 'dir ma spros la/ nye bar mkho ba/

[4.3.1.0.0] rnam grangs pa dang/ rnam grangs min pa'i don dam bden pa gnyis su phye ba dang /

[4.3.2.0.0] mtha' bzhi'i spros bral gnyis lung dang sbyar na/

[4.3.1.0.0 rnam grangs dang rnam grangs min pa'i don dam bden pa gnyis su phye ba lung dang sbyar ba]

dang po ni/ slob dpon ye shes snying pos/

> gang gi phyir
> skye ba la sogs bkag pa yang//
> yang dag par skye ba la sogs par[394] rtog pa'i dngos po bkag pa'i gtan tshigs kyis[395]
> yang dag pa dang mthun pa'i phyir/[396]
> don dam pa yin par kho bo cag kyang[397] 'dod do/ /gzhan dag ni yang dag pa kho nar 'dzin pas/ yang zhes (K43b) bya ba ni bsdu ba'i don to/ /de yang rigs pas dpyad na kun rdzob kho na ste/ ci'i phyir zhe na/[398]
> dgag bya yod (S140) min pas//
> yang dag tu na bkag med gsal//

zhes dang/ zhi ba mtshos[399]/

> skye ba med pa la sogs pa yang/ yang dag pa'i[400] kun rdzob tu gtogs pa yin du zin kyang/

394 K *par;* BS *pa. Satyadvayavibhaṅgavṛtti.* Eckel, ed., *Jñānagarbha,* 161: *par.*
395 KBS *kyi.* Eckel, ed., *Jñānagarbha,* 161: *kyis/.*
396 Eckel, ed., *Jñānagarbha,* 161: *mthun phyir 'dod//.*
397 Eckel, ed., *Jñānagarbha,* 161: *kyang* omitted.
398 KBS / omitted.
399 BS *'tshos.*
400 KBS *la sogs pa yang dag. Madhyamakālaṅkāravṛtti,* Toh no. 3885, Dbu ma *sa,* f. 73a: *la sogs pa yang/ yang dag pa'i.*

[Bringing Trustworthy Scriptural Evidence] to Bear on These Questions]

Even though I should cite individual proof texts for each of the brief points [in this exposition of] our own system, fearing that this will be excessive, I will not here expand [my text in this way]. Instead, I will focus on what is most crucial, and bring scriptural evidence to bear on just two points:

1. The division of the ultimate truth into two—[the ultimate truth] in name only *(rnam grangs pa)* and [the ultimate truth] not in name only *(rnam grangs min pa),* and
2. The freedom from the proliferations of the four extremes.

[The Division of the Ultimate Truth into Two—The Ultimate Truth in Name Only and the Ultimate Truth Not in Name Only]

The master Jñānagarbha has said:

> How so? Even we accept that "the negation of arising *also*" is an ultimate "because it is in accordance with reality"[413]—i.e., [with the reality established] by means of the logical reasoning that has negated the object of conceptual thoughts like, "[Things] really arise." Others take it to be [a form of] reality exclusively, [and so we have added] the word "also" [in the first line, which] has the function of including it *(bsdu ba)* [within an *additional* category—the ultimate—given that it is also conventional]. But when it is analyzed using reasoning, it is *only* conventional. Why? Since the *object* of negation [in this case, that is, arising,] does not exist, it is clear that the negation cannot exist [either].[414]

Moreover, Śāntarakṣita has said:

> Even nonarising, etc., have already been classified as real conventionalities *(yang dag pa'i kun rdzob).* Nonetheless,

> dam pa'i don dang mthun pa'i phyir//
> 'di ni dam pa'i don ces bya//
> yang dag du na spros pa yi//
> tshogs rnams kun las de grol yin//

> don dam pa ni dngos po dang dngos po med pa[401] dang/[402] skye ba dang mi skye ba dang/[403] stong pa dang mi stong pa la sogs pa spros pa'i dra[404] ba mtha' dag spangs pa'o/ /skye ba med pa la sogs pa ni[405] de la 'jug pa dang mthun pa'i phyir don dam pa[406] zhes nye bar 'dogs so//

zhes dang/ dpal ldan zla bas *rigs pa drug cu pa'i 'grel par*/ bden pa gnyis su 'jog pa ni 'jig rten pa'i blo la ltos nas 'jog go//[407] zhes gsungs shing/

'di rnams la dgongs nas/ rje btsun grags pa rgyal mtshan dang/ lce sgom shes rab rdo rje dang/ (S141) mkhas pa red[408] mda' ba la sogs pa rnams kyis kyang/ 'di bzhin du mdzad par snang ngo//

[4.3.2.0.0 mtha' bzhi'i spros bral lung dang sbyar ba]

gnyis pa spros bral gyi lung ni/ rigs tshogs dang bstod tshogs rnams las/ mang du gsungs pa rnams ni 'dir ma bris la/ *'phags pa bden pa gnyis la 'jug pa* las/

> lha'i bu gal te don dam par na don dam pa'i bden pa lus dang/ ngag dang/[409] yid kyi yul gyi[410] rang bzhin du gyur[411] na ni/ de don dam bden pa zhes[412] bya ba'i grangs su mi 'gro ste/[413] (K44a) kun rdzob kyi bden pa nyid du 'gyur ro/ /'on kyang lha'i bu don dam pa na[414] don dam pa'i bden pa ni tha snyad thams cad las 'das

401 K *ba.*
402 KBS / omitted; *Madhyamakālaṅkāravṛtti,* f. 73a: *dang /.*
403 KBS / omitted; *Madhyamakālaṅkāravṛtti,* f. 73a: *dang /.*
404 KBS *drwa.*
405 KBS *ni/. Madhyamakālaṅkāravṛtti,* f. 73a: / omitted.
406 BS *pa* omitted.
407 See above n. 87.
408 KBS *re.*
409 Cited in MABh. The variants in the notes that follow are with reference to the passage as found in this text. Toh no. 3862, Dbu ma *'a,* f. 255b: / omitted.
410 KBS *yul gyi* omitted. MABh, f. 255b: *lus dang ngag dang yid kyi yul gyi.*
411 MABh, f. 255b: *'gyur.*
412 K *zhas.*
413 MABh, f. 255b: / omitted.
414 S *don dam par* (*na* omitted). MABh, f. 255b: *don dam par na.*

> Since they accord with the ultimate,
> They are called "ultimates."[415]
> They free one from all of the accumulations
> Of the proliferations [that conceive of things] as real.

> The ultimate eliminates the entire net of proliferations, such as entity and nonentity, arising and nonarising, and empty and nonempty. It is because nonarising, etc., are in accordance with [i.e., aid one] to enter into [that more profound realization] that they are called "ultimate."[416]

And also the glorious Candra[kīrti] states, in his *Yuktiṣaṣṭikāvṛtti,* "The positing of the two truths is based upon the thought of the world."[417]

It seems to me that it is intending [the same message as is expressed] in these [passages] that the Lord Grags pa rgyal mtshan, Lce sgom Shes rab rdo rje, the sage Red mda' ba, and so forth put forward [a position] just like [the one I have explained in these pages].

[The Scriptural Sources for the Freedom from the Proliferations of the Four Extremes]

I will not write here all of the multitudinous texts [that support this view found] in the philosophical and devotional works [of Nāgārjuna]. The *Āryasatyadvayāvatāra* states:

> Oh Divine One,[418] if the ultimate truth were, on the ultimate [level], by nature an object of the body, speech, and mind,[419] it could not be reckoned as what we call "ultimate truth," but would instead be a conventional truth. Rather, Divine One, the ultimate truth is, on the ultimate [level], beyond all terminology.

pa[415]/ bye brag med pa/ ma skyes pa/ ma 'gag pa/ smra bar bya ba dang/ smra ba dang/ shes par bya ba dang/ shes pa dang bral ba'o/ /lha'i bu don dam pa'i bden pa ni rnam pa thams cad kyi mchog dang ldan pa thams cad mkhyen pa'i ye shes kyi yul gyi bar las 'das (S142) pa yin te/ ji ltar don dam pa'i bden pa'o zhes brjod pa ltar ni min[416] no//

zhes pa dang/ *'od srung gis zhus pa'i mdo* las/

'od srung gang[417] zag gi bdag tu lta ba ni ri rab tsam la gnas kyang bla'i/[418] mngon pa'i nga rgyal can stong pa nyid du lta ba ni de ltar min no/ /de ci'i phyir zhe na/ lta bar gyur pa thams cad las nges par 'byin pa ni/ stong pa nyid yin kyang/ stong pa nyid kho nar lta ba de ni gsor mi rung zhes ngas bshad do//[419]

zhes dang/ *nyi khri las*

gzugs stong zhes bya bar mngon par chags shing gnas te 'du shes pa dang/ tshor ba dang/ 'du shes dang/ 'du byed dang/ rnam par shes pa stong zhes bya bar mngon par chags shing gnas te 'du shes pa ni[420] byang chub sems dpa' sems dpa' chen po'i mthun pa'i chos la sred pa ste/ skyon du 'gyur ro[421]//

415 B *pa na.*
416 MABh, f. 255b: *ma yin.*
417 B *ging.*
418 See the following note.
419 Go rams pa's version differs from the Peking edition of the *Kaśyapaparivarta Sūtra,* P vol. 24: *'od srung gang zag tu lta ba ri rab tsam la gnas pa ni* ***bla'i*** *mngon pa'i nga rgyal can stong pa nyid du lta ba ni de lta ma yin no/ de ci'i phyir zhe na 'od srung lta bar gyur ba thams cad las 'byung ba ni stong pa nyid yin na 'od srung gang stong pa nyid kho nar lta ba de ni gsor mi rung ngo zhes ngas bshad do/.* The same passage is also cited in Candrakīrti's *Prasanna-padā,* Toh no. 3860, Dbu ma *'a,* f. 84a: *od srungs gang zag tu lta ba ri rab tsam la gnas pa ni* ***bla'i/*** *mngon pa'i nga rgyal can stong pa nyid du lta ba ni de lta ma yin no/ /de ci'i phyir zhe na/ 'od srungs lta bar gyur pa thams cad las byung ba ni stong pa nyid yin na/ 'od srungs gang stong pa nyid kho nar lta ba de ni gsor mi rung ngo zhes ngas bshad do/.* A portion of the passage is also cited by Go rams pa in *Lta ngan mun sel,* 588, where it reads: *'od srung gang zag gi bdag tu lta ba ri rab ni sla'i stong pa nyid du lta ba mngon pa'i nga rgyal can can ni de lta ma yin no/.*
420 *Pañcaviṃśatisāhasrikā-prajñāpāramitā,* Toh no. 9, Nyi khri *ka,* f. 164b adds the clause *[ni]/ tshe dang ldan pa sh'a radva ti'i bu/.*
421 *Pañcaviṃśatisāhasrikā-prajñāpāramitā,* f. 164b: *'gyur ba'o.*

> It has no distinctions, it is unarisen, unceasing, free from the spoken and from the act of speaking, from the known and from the act of knowing. Divine One, the ultimate truth is even beyond being the object of the gnosis of the omniscient, the [state] that possesses the highest of all good qualities. It is not even as it is spoken [in the expression] "ultimate truth."[420]

Also, the *Kaśyapaparivarta* states:

> Kaśyapa, a view of the self of the person that is as large as Mount Meru would be better than the view of emptiness [entertained by] those who are proud. How so? I have explained that even though emptiness is the way out of *(nges par 'byin pa)* all views, those whose view is emptiness itself cannot be cured.[421]

The *Twenty-[Five]-Thousand [Line Prajñāpāramitāsūtra]* states:

> Those who recognize but remain attached to the claim that "form is empty," those who recognize but remain attached to the claim that "feeling, recognition, compositional factors, and consciousness are empty," are [beings who] hanker after [doctrines] that are [only] analogues to the Dharma of the bodhisattva, the great being. This is a fault.[422]

zhes dang/ *'bum* las/ stong pa nyid ces bya bar yang ma grub bo/ (S143) /stong pa nyid ces bya bar yang ma 'dzin cig/ ces so//

chad lta yin na kun rdzob tu med par 'dzin pas ma[422] khyab pa'i lung ni/ *rta skad byang chub sems dpas zhus* (K44b) *pa'i mdo* las/

> bcom ldan 'das thams cad stong pa lags na/ chad par[423] thal bar mi 'gyur lags sam/ bcom ldan 'das kyis bka' stsal pa/ rigs kyi bu chad par lta ba ni/ rgyu mtshan gsum gyis chad par lta bar 'gyur ro/ / [1] las rgyu 'bras la sogs pa kun rdzob nyid du yang yod pa 'gog pa dang/ [2] med pa'i phyogs 'ba' zhig tu zhen pa dang/ [3] zab mo'i chos kyi don ma rtogs par stong pa'o zhes tshig tu zhen pa'o//

zhes so//

des na gnad kyi don ni/ dbu ma pa'i lugs la theg pa gsum char la mtha' gnyis spangs pa'i dbu ma'i lam re yod dgos pa las/ theg dman la ni don dam du ma grub pas rtag pa'i mtha' las grol/ kun rdzob tu las rgyu 'bras la bskur (S144) ba mi 'debs pas chad pa'i mtha' las grol dgos pa *rin chen phreng bar* bshad la/ theg pa chen po la de'i steng du yang [1] gnas lugs rang gi ngo bo la yod med la sogs pa'i gnyis 'dzin mtha' dag dang bral ba'i lta ba khyad par can dang/ [2] sems can la dmigs pa'i snying rje dang/ [3] theg pa chen po'i sems bskyed gsum zung 'brel du byas nas bsgoms pas 'bras bu mthar thug pa'i tshe/ chos dbyings spros bral gyi ngang las ma g.yos bzhin du nam mkha'i mthas khyab pa'i sems can gyi don 'bad med lhun grub tu 'byung bar 'gyur ro//

[The thirty-six–verse summary occurs here in all three editions. It is not included in this edition.]

422 KBS *mi.*
423 KBS *pa.*

And also, the *[Prajñāpāramitā in] One-Hundred-Thousand [Lines]* states: "Even 'emptiness' is not established. Do not even apprehend 'emptiness.'"[423]

A passage [proving] that nihilistic views *(chad lta)* do not necessarily apprehend [things] to be conventionally nonexistent [is the following one] from the *Rta skad byang chub sems dpa'i zhus pa'i mdo*:[424]

> "Lord, if everything is empty, then does there not follow the absurdity of nihilism?"
>
> The Lord said, "Son of good lineage, a nihilistic view becomes a nihilistic view due to three reasons: (1) because it denies the fact that karmic causes and effects exist even conventionally; (2) because it is attached only to the side of nonexistence; and (3) because it is attached to the word "empty" without understanding the meaning of this profound doctrine.

So the essential point is as follows. According to the Madhyamaka school, each of the three vehicles must possess a middle path that avoids the two extremes. [For example,] the *Ratnāvalī* has explained that, for the Hīnayāna, [it is the fact that things] do not ultimately exist that frees one from the extreme of eternalism,[425] and [it is the fact that] conventionally karmic cause and effect are not denied that frees one from the extreme of nihilism. The Mahāyāna, based on that [Hīnayāna interpretation of the meaning of "middle way," then goes on to teach] (1) a special philosophical view in regard to the nature of reality that is the freedom from all dualistic thoughts, such as exists/does-not-exist; (2) compassion focused on sentient beings *(sems can la dmigs pa'i snying rje)*; and (3) the generation of the Mahāyāna attitude *(theg pa chen po'i sems bskyed)*. Joining these three together and meditating on them, one ultimately attains the result, which is this: that, while immersed in the *dharmadhātu*—the freedom from proliferations—there emerges, effortlessly and spontaneously, the welfare of sentient beings that are as pervasive [in number] as the very limits of space.[426]

[The thirty-six–verse summary occurs here in all three editions. It is not included in this translation.]

[mjug byang]

lta ba'i shan 'byed theg mchog gnad kyi zla zer zhes bya ba 'di ni/ thog mar[424] bka' drin mnyam med kun mkhyen sangs rgyas 'phel gyi drung du dbu ma'i gzhung lugs mnyan cing/ rje btsun gong ma rdo rje 'chang dang mi gnyis pa'i thugs mnga' ba de dag gi gsung rab kyi steng du mtshan brjod par dka' ba rje mus pa chen po'i gsung gis brda sprad pa'i sgron me bzung ste/ 'phags mchog klu sgrub yab sras kyi gzhung la bltas tshe gnas lugs kyi don la nges shes skyes nas gzhan la ston pa'i yi ge bya bar[425] 'dod pa na/ bdag cag gi dpal ldan bla ma dam pa mdo rgyud rgya mtsho'i pha rol du son pa gung ru shes rab bzang po'i zhal snga nas/ thog (S154) mar lta ba'i shan 'byed mdor bsdus pa gcig gyis zhes bka' gnang ba la brten nas shākya'i dge slong bsod nams seng ges/ sa pho byi ba lo'i (dgung lo bzhi bcu tham pa'i dus[426]) rgyal zla'i[427] tshes bcu bdun (bcu gsum zhes pa'ang snang ngo[428]) la dbu btsugs te nyi shu'i nyin rta nag gser gling gi dgon par sbyar ba'i yi ge pa ni mgon po dbang phyug go//

'dis kyang rgyal ba'i bstan pa dar rgyas su byed nus par gyur cig/ dge'o/ /sarba mangga lam/[429]

thub bstan gser gyi me tog bzang//
'jig rten dbyar gyi dpal mo'i rgyan//
legs bshad dbyangs kyis 'bod mkhas pa//
kun mkhyen ngag gi dbang po'i gsung//
blo gsal blo yi nyin byed shar//
blo gros pad mo kha bye shog//
spar du sgrub po dhyā nas smras// //.

424 KB *ma.*
425 KB: *ba.*
426 KB This parenthetical remark "*(dgung lo bzhi bcu tham pa'i dus)*" is found in S at this point in the text. In K and B it occurs a few lines below; see note 427.
427 B *rgyal zla'i* omitted.
428 KB This parenthetical remark "*(bcu gsum zhes pa'ang snang ngo)*" is found in S at this point in the text. In K and B, it occurs a few lines below; see the next note.
429 The above two parenthetical remarks are given together in KB at this point in the text: *dgung lo bzhi bcu tham pa'i dus/ bcu gsum zhes pa'ang snang ngo/*

[Colophon]

This *Distinguishing the Theories [of Emptiness]: Moonlight [to Illuminate] the Main Points of the Supreme Vehicle* is, first of all, [the result of my] having studied the textual system of the Madhyamaka under the omniscient Sangs rgyas 'phel,[427] the incomparably kind one. I then illuminated the scriptures of the founding lords [of the Sa skya school], whose minds are inseparable from Vajradhara, with the lamp of exegesis of the teachings of the great Lord Mus pa,[428] whose name [so fills me with emotion] that it is difficult to pronounce. Then, having studied the texts of the supreme ārya Nāgārjuna, the father, and his spiritual son [Āryadeva], I generated an ascertaining consciousness *(nges shes)* of the meaning of reality, and wishing to put this in written form so as to teach it to others, [I,] the Śākya monk Bsod nams seng ge, [composed this text] following the orders of Gung ru shes rab bzang po, our glorious and holy spiritual master, who has traversed the ocean of sūtra and tantra, and who said, "At the outset [compose] a brief [text] distinguishing the views." Beginning [the work] on the seventeenth day[429] of the Month of Victory [i.e., the twelfth lunar month] in the Earth Male Rat year,[430] [I completed it] on the twentieth at the monastery of Rta nag gser gling. The scribe was Mgon po dbang phyug.

May this [work] become a force for the spread of the teachings of the Victor. Virtue!

> The beautiful golden flowers of the Conqueror's teachings,
> Act as ornaments of the glory of summer in this world.
> The music of eloquence is what skillfully proclaims [its arrival].
> May the speech of the omniscient lord of speakers
> Cause the mind-sun of clearmindedness to shine!
> May it cause the the lotus of erudition to unfold!
> Dhyāna, the one responsible for the woodblocks, makes this prayer.

Abbreviations

AA	*Abhisamayālaṃkāra.* Edition specified in text.
B	Go rams pa, *Lta ba'i shan 'byed,* cyclostat in the collection of the library of the Institut für Kultur und Geschichte Indiens und Tibets, Hamburg (access number MIV 345/6, catalogued 1968?), most likely printed in Buxador, India in the early 1960s, 42 folios.
BA	Roerich, George N. *The Blue Annals,* Parts I and II (Delhi: Motilal Banarsidass, 1988).
BB	Shākya mchog ldan, *Dbu ma'i byung tshul rnam par shes pa'i gtam yid bzhin lhun po.* In *Collected Works,* reprint of the Pha jo sdings 'og ma gnyis pa edition (Delhi: Ngawang Tobgyal, 1988), vol. 4 *(nga),* 209–48.
BCA	Śāntideva, *Bodhicaryāvatāra.* V. Bhattacharya, ed. (Calcutta: The Asiatic Society, 1960).
BJN	Rong ston Shes bya kun rig, *Dbu ma la 'jug pa'i rnam bshad nges don rnam nges,* in *Two Controversial Madhyamaka Treatises* (New Delhi: Trayang and Jamyang Samten, 1974).
BPD	Go rams pa, *Rgyal ba thams cad kyi thugs kyi dgongs pa zab mo dbu ma'i de kho na nyid spyi'i ngag gis ston pa nges don rab gsal = Dbu ma'i spyi don.* In Bsod nams rgya mtsho, ed., *The Complete Works of the Masters of the Sa skya Sect of Tibetan Buddhism = Sa skya pa'i bka' 'bum* (Tokyo: Toyo Bunkyo, 1968), vol. 12, 348–51.
BRKT	Rong ston Shes bya kun rig, *Dbu ma rigs tshogs kyi dka' ba'i gnad bstan pa rigs lam kun gsal.* (Photoreproduction of a xylograph with no bibliographical information).
BTN	Rong ston Shes bya kun rig, *Dbu ma rtsa ba'i rnam bshad zab mo'i de kho na nyid snang ba* (Sarnath: Sakya Students' Union, 1988).

C Cone ed. of the Bstan 'gyur. (The Institute for Advanced Studies of World Religions, microfiche ed.).

DN 'Gos lo tsa ba Gzhon nu dpal, *Deb ther sngon po,* 2 vols. (consecutive pagination) (Si khron: Mi rigs dpe skrun khang: 1985).

DSG Red mda' ba Gzhon nu blo gros, *Dbu ma la 'jug pa'i rnam bshad de kho na nyid gsal ba'i sgron me* (Sarnath: Sakya Students' Union, 1983).

DZGG Sgra tshad pa Rin chen rnam rgyal. *Bde bzhin gshegs pa'i snying po'i mdzes rgyan gyi rgyan.* In *The Collected Works of Bu ston,* vol. 28. (New Delhi: International Academy of Indian Culture, 1965–71).

GJL Don rdor and Bstan 'dzin chos grags, compilers, *Gangs ljongs lo rgyus thog go grags can mi sna* (Lha sa: Bod ljongs mi dmangs dpe skrun khang: 1993).

GR Tsong kha pa, *Bstan bcos chen po dbu ma la 'jug pa'i rnam bshad dgongs pa rab gsal,* in *Tsong kha pa'i gsung 'bum* (Collected Works), vol. *ma* (New Delhi: Ngawang Gelek Demo, 1983).

JIABS *Journal of the International Association of Buddhist Studies.*

K Go rams pa, Sa skya bka' 'bum ed. of *Lta ba'i shan 'byed,* in *The Complete Works of Go rams bsod nams seng ge* (vol.3), in *Sa skya pa'i bka 'bum: The Complete Works of the Great Masters of Sa skya Sect of the Tibetan Buddhism* (vol. 13), compiled by Bsod nams rgya mtsho (Tokyo: The Toyo Bunkyo, 1968), 47 folios.

KDZP Dol po pa Shes rab rgyal mtshan, *Bka' bsdu bzhi pa,* in *The Collected Works (gSung 'bum) of Kun-mkhyen Dol-po-pa Ses-rab-rgyal-mtshan (1292–1361),* reproduced from eye copies of prints from the Rgyal-rtse Rdzong blocks preserved at Kyichu Monastery (Paro, Bhutan: 1984), vol. 1.

LK Lhasa ed. of the Bka' 'gyur (The Institute for Advanced Studies of World Religions ed.).

LNMS Mkhas grub rje, *Lam ngan mun sel sgron ma,* in *Collected Works* (Dharamsala), vol. *ta.*

LRCM Tsong kha pa, *Byang chub lam rim che ba* (Zi ling: Mtsho sngon Mi rigs dpe skrun khang, 1985).

LSN Tsong kha pa, *Drang ba dang nges pa'i don rnam par phye ba'i bstan bcos legs bshad snying po.* In *Tsong kha pa gsung 'bum,* vol. *pha* (New Delhi: Ngawang Gelek, 1975–81).

LSN-mi Tsong kha pa, *Drang ba dang nges pa'i don rnam par phye ba'i bstan bcos legs bshad snying po.* In *Rje Tsong kha pa chen po'i gsung 'bum,* vol. *pha* (Zi ling: Mtsho sngon mi rigs dpe skrun khang, 1987).

MA Louis de la Vallée Poussin, ed., *Madhyamakāvatāra par Candrakīrti* (St. Petersbourg: Imprimerie de l'Academie des Sciences, 1912).

MA-Fr Louis de la Vallée Poussin, *Madhyamakāvatāra: introduction au traité du milieu de l'ācārya Candrakīrti, avec le commentaire de l'auteur* (Paris: *Le Muséon,* 1907–11). In three parts. Avant Propos, MA (I-V) = *Le Muséon* 8: 249–317; MA (VI, 1–80) = *Le Muséon* 11:271–358; MA (VI, 81–165) = *Le Muséon* 12: 235–328.

MABh *Madhyamakāvatārabhāṣya.* The edition found in MA.

MABh (Bhopal) *Dbu ma la hjug pa ran hgrel* (Bhopal: The Tibetan Publishing House, 1968).

MMK Nāgārjuna, *Mūlamadhyamakakārikā.* Edition specified in text.

MVy *Mahāvyutpatti.* R. Sakaki, ed. (Tokyo: Suzuki Gakujutsu Zaidan, 1962; repr. of the Kyoto ed.), 2 vols.

N *The Nyingma Edition of the sDe-dge bKa'-'gyur and bsTan-'gyur.* Oakland: Dharma Publishing, 1980.

P Peking ed. of the Tibetan canon.

Pras Candrakīrti, *Prasannapadā,* ed. by Louis de la Vallée Poussin, in *Mūlamadhyamakakārikās de Nāgārjuna avec la Prasannapadā Commentaire de Candrakīrti,* Bibliotheca Buddhica IV (St. Petersburg: The Imperial Academy of Sciences, 1913).

PV Dharmakīrti, *Pramāṇavārttika.* Edition specified in text.

Rat *Nāgārjuna's Ratnāvalī, Vol. 1, The Basic Texts (Sanskrit, Tibetan, Chinese),* ed. by Michael Hahn (Bonn: Indica et Tibetica Verlag, 1982).

RCNG Dol po pa Shes rab rgyal mtshan, *Ri chos nges don rgya mtsho* (Delhi: Dodrup Sangyey, 1976).

RGV *Ratnagotravibhāga Mahāyānottaratantraśāstra,* ed. by E. H. Johnston and T. Chowdhury (Patna, Bihar Research Society, 1950).

S Go rams pa, *Lta ba'i shan 'byed theg mchog gnad gyi zla zer (Distinguishing the Views by Gorampa Bsodnams sengge),* published together with *Rtags kyi bzhag rigs lam gsal ba'i sgron me* of Mkhan chen Bsod nams lhun grub (Sarnath: Sakya Students' Union, 1988–date of preface), pp. 1–154.

TBRC Tibetan Buddhist Resource Center (W = Work, P = Person)

TN-CW Go rams pa, *Dbu ma la 'jug pa'i dkyus kyis sa bcad pa dang gzhung so so'i dka' ba'i gnas la dpyad pa lta ba ngan sel = Lta ba ngan sel,* in Sherab Gyaltsen Lama, ed., *The Collected Works of Kunmkhyen Go-rams pa bSod-nams-seng-ge* (Kangra: Dzongsar Institute, n.d.) vol. 5 *(ca)*: 511–751.

TN-SK Go rams pa, *Dbu ma la 'jug pa'i dkyus kyis sa bcad pa dang gzhung so so'i dka' ba'i gnas la dpyad pa lta ba ngan sel,* in Bsod nams rgya mtsho, ed., *The Complete Works of the Masters of the Sa skya Sect of Tibetan Buddhism = Sa skya pa'i bka' 'bum,* 3 (Tokyo: Toyo Bunkyo, 1968), vol. 13.

Toh Tohoku edition of the Sde dge Canon. Catalogued in Hakuju Ui, Munetada Suzuki, Yenshō Kanakura, and Tōkan Tada, eds. *Chibetto Daizōkyō Sōmokuroku/A Complete Catalogue of the Tibetan Buddhist Canons (Bkaḥ-ḥgyur and Bstan-ḥgyur).* Sendai: Tōhoku Imperial University, 1934.

TSTC Tsong kha pa, *Dbu ma rtsa ba'i tshig le'ur byas pa shes rab ces bya ba'i rnam bshad rigs pa'i rgya mtsho = Rtsa shes ṭīk chen.* In *Tsong kha pa'i gsung 'bum* (Collected Works), vol. *ba* (New Delhi: Ngawang Gelek Demo, 1983).

TT Mang thos Klu grub rgya mtsho, 'Dar stod Dgra 'dul dbang po, et al., eds., *Bstan rtsis gsal ba'i nyin byed tha snyad rig gnas lnga'i byung tshul blo gsal mgrin rgyan* (Lha sa: Bod ljong mi dmangs dpe skrun khang: 1987).

WZKSO *Wiener Zeitschrift für kunde Sud-und Ostasiens.*

Notes to the Introduction

1 JIC: Because statements are made in this introduction that I am not sure would have been acceptable to my co-author, I should make it clear that most of the introduction is my own work. The sections on Go rams pa's life and oeuvre, however, draw heavily from Geshe Dargyay's manuscript.

2 For a brief overview of Madhyamaka philosophy in India, see Paul Williams, *Buddhist Thought: A Complete Introduction to the Indian Tradition* (London: Routledge, 2000). For an overview of Tibetan Madhyamaka philosophy, see Tom J. F. Tillemans's 1998 article, "Tibetan Philosophy," parts 1 and 2, *Routledge Encyclopedia of Philosophy,* found online at http://www.rep.routledge.com/article/F003. For a history of Madhyamaka thought, see D. Seyfort Ruegg, *The Literature of the Madhyamaka School of Philosophy in India* (Wiesbaden: Harrassowitz, 1981) and *Three Studies in the History of Indian and Tibetan Madhyamaka Thought,* Studies in Indian and Tibetan Madhyamaka Thought, Part 1 (Wien: Arbeitskreis für Tibetische und Buddhistische Studien, Universität Wien, 2000).

3 See below for a more detailed account of the "Great Debate" that was supposedly the occasion for this pronouncement.

4 Of course, many of these debates probably made their way indirectly into the writings of the great scholars of the twelfth to fifteenth centuries. There is, however, evidence that in at least some cases records or transcripts *(rtsod yig)* of these oral debates were kept. But to my knowledge none of these "records" have yet come to light. The term *rtsod yig* has various meanings in different fields of Tibetan cultural sciences. In the realm of ecclesiastical polity, since the eighteenth century at least, the term *rtsod yig* came to refer to documents that explained the rules for monastic debate. In this latter sense the term was shorthand for *rtsod grwa'i sgrig yig* or *rtsod grwa'i bca' yig,* "the rules that governed the debate ground." Karmay discusses *rtsod yig* as a genre of medical polemical texts; see Samten G. Karmay, *The Arrow and the Spindle: Studies in History, Myths, Rituals and Belief in Tibet* (Kathmandu: Mandala Book Point, 1998), p. 232. *Rtsod yig* is also the name of a type of legal document. In the next section the reader will see that the term was used to refer to religious polemical writings as well.

5 I use the term *genre* when referring to Tibetan polemical literature with some trepidation, for while there is a fairly well circumscribed body of literature—for example, the *refutations (dgag pa)* and *response to refutations (dgag lan)*—that do have the characteristics of a relatively uniform genre, there are also a host of Tibetan polemical works that also belong to other (e.g., epistolary) genres.

6 While our admiration for polemics as a genre will quickly become evident in this section, the discussion that follows is more of a description than it is a defense of the genre. For a more intentional and sustained defense, see Paul J. Griffiths, *An Apology for Apologetics: A Study in the Logic of Interreligious Dialogue* (Mayknoll: Orbis, 1991). The subject of religious polemics has not received sufficient scholarly attention by scholars of comparative religious thought. For example, the entries "polemics" and "apologetics" found in Eliade's *Encyclopedia of Religion* focus principally on Christianity, and make no substantial reference to Asian religions. Many studies treat *specific* examples of religious polemics, especially among the Abrahamic monotheisms; see, for example, Frank E. Talmage, *Apples of Gold, Settings of Silver: Studies in Medieval Jewish Exegesis and Polemics,* ed. Barry Dov Walfish (Toronto: Pontifical Institute of Mediaeval Studies, 1999). However, there are, to my knowledge, no truly comparative works on the topic of religious polemics. The Leiden project on religious polemics, "Thinking Differences," described at http://website.leidenuniv.nl/~hettematl/Onderzoek/thinkdif-pap.html, while focused principally on Western sources, nonetheless recognizes polemics as an important comparative category.

7 *Homo Ludens: A Study of the Play Element in Culture* (Boston: Beacon Press, 1955), p. 156.

8 Charles Sanders Peirce, *Collected Papers,* ed. Charles Hartshorne, et al. (Cambridge, MA: Harvard University press, 1931), I:457.

9 The Greek-derived words *cataphatic* and *apophatic* have been brought to prominence as technical terms in recent years by scholars who work in the fields of Christian theology and mysticism. See Michael A. Sells, *Mystical Languages of Unsaying* (Chicago: University of Chicago Press, 1994). In the Christian tradition, apophatic discourse about God is language that attempts to come to an understanding of God (or God's attributes) through negative means—that is, by the negation of what God is not. The tradition to which this gave rise—sometimes called "negative theology"—is a corollary of the belief that God in God's self is unknowable, and that the only way in which to approach the divine is through negation. Recently, David Seyfort Ruegg has used these terms more broadly to characterize two streams within Buddhist thought. In what follows it will become clear that I am using the words *cataphatic* and *apophatic* neither in the Christian theological sense nor in Seyfort Ruegg's, instead modifying the meaning of these terms to suit my own purpose, and giving them an even broader semantic range that allows me to use them as the basis for constructing ideal-typical categories of literary discourse. Other nomenclatures might have served equally well. We might have borrowed, for example, *simulacrum* and *resistance* from the work of Mark C. Taylor; *Nots* (Chicago: University of Chicago Press, 1993), chap. 4. But in the end, whatever terms we might have used would have required a considerable amount of manipulation and "defamiliarization" in order to serve our purposes here.

10 Walter Ong goes even further, suggesting that "all verbal abuse attests some attraction between interlocutors as well as their hostility. Even in the formalized all-out verbal hostility of standard epic flitting...through all their contention the disputants manifest simultaneously some reluctant or wry attraction"; Walter J. Ong, *The Presence of the Word* (New Haven: Yale University Press, 1967), p. 207. For Ong, hostility becomes most extreme not at the stage when opponents resort to verbal abuse or name-calling, but at the point when "speech is simply broken off entirely."

11 On the "agonistic heritage of academia," see Walter J. Ong, *Fighting for Life: Context, Sexuality, and Consciousness* (Amherst: The University of Massachusetts Press, 1981), chap. 4. While there is much that one might take exception to in Ong's work, it is, if nothing else, a stimulating and broad-ranging discussion of this important issue.

12 Joseph Agassi, *The Gentle Art of Philosophical Polemics: selected reviews and comments* (La Salle, IL: Open Court, 1988), pp. 5–6.

13 Trans. by David P. Jackson, *Enlightenment by a Single Means: Tibetan Controversies on the "Self-Sufficient White Remedy" (Dkar po chig thub)* (Wien: Verlag der Österreichischen Akademie der Wissenschaften, 1994), p. 188. The Tibetan text that follows this passage is missing the last line in Jackson's transcription.

14 As Sa skya Paṇḍita says elsewhere, "The wise are satisfied only with what is true, but fools are content with whatever accords with their views" *(dam pa bden pa smras pas mgu/ blun po rang dang mthun pas mgu/)*. Truth is a hard pill to swallow.

15 The following, culled from various traditions and time periods, are given as examples of the self-assurance of some of Tibet's greatest scholars, most of whom are renowned polemicists. A word of warning is in order, however. One should not understand these as signs of egomania, as one would be tempted to do if one were to take them at face value. For even if it is not quite *de rigueur* among the great figures of a tradition to express this kind of self-assurance, it is not an unusual structural/rhetorical feature of Tibetan scholastic literature to find proclamations of the vastness of one's learning.

(1) Sa paṇ, the scholar already mentioned in note 14, states:

I am the grammarian. *I* am the dialectician.
Among the vanquishers of sophists, peerless am *I*.
I am learned in metrics. *I* stand alone in poetics.
In explaining synonymics, unrivaled am *I*.
I know celestial calculations. In exo- and esoteric science,
I have a discerning intellect equaled by none.
Who can this be? Sa skya alone!
Other scholars are my reflected forms.

Cited in Matthew Kapstein, *The Tibetan Assimilation of Buddhism: Conversion, Contestation, Memory* (Oxford: Oxford University Press, 2000), p. 120.
(2) A later Sa skya pa, G.yag ston Sangs rgyas dpal (1350–1414), in a polemical exchange on the subject of logic, states, "Those who know should speak having unerringly realized the meaning of those points…Nowadays in this Land of Snows I am the only [such informed speaker]." Cited in Georges B. J. Dreyfus, *Recognizing Reality: Dharmakīrti's Philosophy and Its Tibetan Interpretation* (Albany: State University of New York Press, 1997), p. 24.
(3) Rong ston Shes bya kun rig (1367–1449), a student of G.yag ston, after completing an intensive period of lecturing in which he taught eleven major texts in a six-month span of time, is reported to have concluded his series of teachings with these words: "Hey there! Those of you studying the Dharma, arise and dance! You are very fortunate to meet such an excellent person as me. Do you think I'm just a decrepit (?) Khams pa?" Cited in David P. Jackson in collaboration with Shunzo Onoda, *Rong-ston on the Prajñāpāramitā Philosophy of the Abhisamayalaṃkara: His Sub-commentary on Haribhadra's "Sphuṭarthā"* (Kyoto: Nagata Bunshodo, 1988), p. xi. Jackson also

cites a passage in which Rong ston says, "If I die, even my skin and pus will be transformed into relics"; Jackson, *Rong-ston,* p. xiii.
(4) One of Rong ston's chief rivals, the Dga' ldan pa (or Dge lugs pa) scholar Mkhas grub Dge legs dpal bzang (1385–1438), is said to have portrayed himself to Rong ston using these words:

I live in the gorge of a snow mountain,
My mane heavy with the weight of a thousand scriptural traditions.
Possessing the power of the inexhaustible claws of reasoning,
I alone am the supreme sage, the king of beasts.

Cited in José Ignacio Cabezón, *A Dose of Emptiness: An Annotated Translation of the sTong thun chen mo of mKhas grub dGe legs dpal bzang* (Albany: State University of New York Press, 1992), p. 14.
(5) The "holy madman," Gtsang smyon Heruka (1452–1507), uses various metaphors to describe the vastness of his activities, something that he implies his challengers, some Dge lugs dge bshes, cannot fathom:

The ant cannot see the mountain.
The frog in the well cannot find the end of the sea.
The hand of a child cannot cover the sky.

In this passage, it is Gtsang smyon who is the mountain, the sea and sky; cited in E. Gene Smith, *Among Tibetan Texts: History and Literature of the Himalayan Plateau* (Boston: Wisdom Publications, 2001), p. 69.
(6) Finally, the third Karma pa Pakshi (1204–83) begins his autobiography:

I am Rangjung Dorje
The vajra-king, one of great might…

Cited in Kapstein, *The Tibetan Assimilation of Buddhism*, p. 120.

16 The words of the great Tibetan historian Bu ston Rin chen grub (1290–1364) resonate here. In the introductory verses to his *History of Buddhism,* he carefully crafts a representation of himself (and of his work) that is at once humble and yet self-assured, which acknowledges the profundity of the Buddha's teachings and the difficulty of gaining expertise in the scriptures while reassuring his readers that, notwithstanding the difficulties, he has indeed managed to fathom the scriptural tradition. While recognizing that his views are disputed, he nonetheless proceeds stridently forward for the greater glory of the religion, not quite confident (but at least hopeful) that there are individuals who will rise to the challenge of taking up his tradition: *de ltas bdag kyang shākya'i mtsho/ gting mtha' yas par rgal bar 'dod pa yin/ de yi gting mtha' rtogs par ma nus kyang/ ngo mtshar don gyi rin chen cis mi rnyed/ rnyed kyang 'bul po'i lag gi rin chen ltar/ bdag gi legs bshad dri ma med pa 'di/ 'gren 'dod phrag dog dang sems kyis bsgribs nas/ gzur gnas yid ches gnas su su zhig len/ len pa med kyang dam chos bdud rtsi yis/ rang gi yid kyi zig rngu cis mi sel/ gal te 'ga' zhig len na de dag gi/ gdung ba'i rims nad 'joms par mi 'gyur ram/ de phyir rang blo'i dbul ba bsal ba dang/ chos ldan don gnyer skye bo rnams la yang/ rgya chen chos kyi dga' ston spel slad du/ gsung rab rin chen mdzod kyi sgo dbye'o/*; *Bu ston chos 'byung* (Mtsho sngon: Krung go bod kyi shes rig dpe skrun khang, 1988), p. 2. "I am someone who wishes to traverse the limitless ocean of Śākya[muni's scriptural tradition], and even though I may be unable to fathom its breadth and depth [completely], shouldn't I be able to extract from it the jewel of its amazing meaning? But though I have found [this jewel], who is there that can accept it [from me] as an object of faith and in a spirit of impartiality? A shadow has fallen over my

stainless and eloquent words due to the rivalry and jealousy [of others, and to entrust *them* with my insights] would be like putting a jewel into a beggar's hand. But even if there is no one to take up [my tradition], this nectar of the holy doctrine clears away my own mental anguish, and *if* there are some others who take it up, will it not also destroy the disease that afflicts *them*? That is why I open the door to this *Precious Treasury of Scripture:* so that it may eliminate my own mental poverty, and so that it may increase the banquet that is this expansive Dharma for those individuals who are faithful and diligent." See also E. Obermiller, *History of Buddhism (Chos-hbyung) by Bu-ston,* part I (Heidelberg: O Harrassowitz, 1931), p. 7. There are clear rhetorical similarities between Bu ston's portrayal of hesitancy in this passage, a hesitancy that he overcomes in the course of these lines, and the hesitancy that the Buddha is said to have experienced before he launched his teaching career. Such hesitancy is also to be found in the introductory lines of Indian treatises like Dharmakīrti's *Pramāṇavārttika.* This is also a typical structural feature of Tibetan (especially polemical) literature, related (but not quite identical) to another common Indo-Tibetan rhetorical device known as the "expression of humility" *(khengs skyung brjod pa).* On the latter, see José Ignacio Cabezón, *Buddhism and Language: A Study of Indo-Tibetan Scholasticism* (Albany: State University of New York Press, 1994), p. 76.

17 The Shugs ldan affair among the Dge lugs pas, and the Karma pa controversy among the Kar ma Bka' brgyud pas come to mind.

18 Certainly this was the case in Tibet. One has only to think of the debates that existed between rival factions in the early formation of the Dge lugs school, debates whose existence were eventually squelched by the winning side—that of Mkhas grub rje and his heirs—with the goal of portraying Tsong kha pa's tradition as a seamless whole. This was the subject of a paper, Cabezón, "Toward A History of Sera Monastery: The Early Years," presented at the meeting of the International Association of Tibetan Studies, Oxford, 2003 (unpublished).

19 The intra/inter distinction is always relative. For example, while it is true that the fifteenth century Sa skya polemics against Tsong kha pa (of which Go rams pa's text is an instance) represents a case of inter-sectarian conflict, it might be argued that the banning of these texts by the Fifth Dalai Lama (if this in fact happened) is as much a case of the intra-traditional occlusion of divergent opinion, for the Fifth Dalai Lama and his regent were at that time engaged in the invention of a tradition—that of Tibet as a unified culture and polity under Dga' ldan pa hegemony—with respect to which the texts of the Sa skya pa masters represent internal disagreements (*lege* "dirty laundry"). What is inter from one vantage point (Sa skya and Dge lugs as distinct traditions) can be intra from another (Tibet as a cultural-political whole).

20 A similar point has been made by Mikhail Bakhtin as regards the novel, a genre that he believes is intrinsically tied to dialogicality. See *The Dialogic Imagination: Four Essays by M. M. Bakhtin,* ed. Michael Holquist, trans. Caryl Emerson and Michael Holquist (Austin: University of Texas Press, 1981); and Michael Gardiner, *The Dialogics of Critique: M.M. Bakhtin and the Theory of Ideology* (London: Routledge, 1992), p. 175.

21 This is not to say that polemicists do not *also* engage in imaginative acts of philosophizing, but the point of departure for the polemicist is always the views of a real other (regardless of how these views may end up being contorted), and the polemicist always places herself in the position of awaiting a response.

22 Dan Martin, "Beyond Acceptance and Rejection? The Anti-Bon Polemic in the Thirteenth-Century *Single Intention* (Dgongs-gcig Yig-cha) and Its Background in Tibetan Religious History," *Journal of Indian Philosophy* 25 (1997): 263–64.

23 It is also consistent with the type of polemic he is considering, since Martin explicitly excludes the more strictly philosophical types of polemic, which are not his concern.

24 Consider, for example, the words of the seventeenth-century British divine, Richard Baxter: "...nothing so much hindreth the Reception of Truth, as urging it on men with too harsh Importunity, and falling too heavily on their errors: For hereby you engage their honour in the business, and they defend their errors as themselves...In controversies it is fierce Opposition which is the bellows to kindle a resisting Zeal; when if they be neglected, and their opinions lie in a while despised, they usually cool and come again to themselves." Cited in N. H. Keeble, "The Autobiographer as Apologist: Reliquiae Baxterianae (1696)," in *The Literature of Controversy: Polemical Strategies from Milton to Junius,* ed. Thomas N. Corns (Totowa, NJ: Frank Cass, 1987), p. 105.

25 And, in fact, this is the view of polemics that we find expounded in texts like Dharmakīrti's *Vādanyāya,* a view that represents the Buddhist approach to polemics as being grounded in facts and on the inferences that one can draw from those facts *(vastubalapravṛttānumāna, dngos stobs rjes dpag),* rather than on, say, tricks of logic and word-play. This same view of polemics is put forward by later Tibetan scholars like Sa skya Paṇḍita—in the last chapter of his *Treasury of Valid Reasoning (Tshad ma rigs gter),* for example. None of this is to say that either Indian or Tibetan scholars always exemplify this lofty view of polemics *in practice,* but this at least is the theory of polemics that in principle undergirds their work. And, of course, this Buddhist theory of polemics, we must remember, is itself a kind of polemics, given that it is a response to the theory and practice of argumentation espoused by Indian Buddhists' classical opponents in the field of logic, the Naiyāyikas. I am grateful to Tom Tillemans for provoking me to think about the points raised in this note.

26 In all fairness, I should point out that Martin never advocates that we give up on the study of polemics altogether. "I do not agree with the position that polemic should be left entirely out of account; in the first place and at the very least because, historically speaking, polemics have had their own impact on the very sectarian formulations we might wish to understand. I would like to suggest, even though there may be many who will disagree with me on this point, that polemicists are worthy of our compassionate interest if we are ever to be able to gain some insight into their thoughts or at least begin to understand their intentions"; Martin, "Beyond Acceptance and Rejection," p. 264. While I think that the study of polemics has something more to offer us than mere access to the polemicist's intentions, it is gratifying that Martin chooses not to give up on the genre altogether.

27 On polemics as a Tibetan literary genre, see Donald S. Lopez, "Polemical Literature *(dGag lan),*" in *Tibetan Literature: Studies in Genre,* ed. José I. Cabezón and Roger R. Jackson (Ithaca: Snow Lion, 1996), pp. 217–28, which focuses chiefly on the work of Se ra Rje btsun Chos kyi rgyal mtshan (1469–1546) as an example of the genre. The following sources treat specific examples of Tibetan polemical literature, and/or specific controversies. Three major articles dealing with Sa skya Paṇḍita's rejection of the White Panacea doctrine (on which, see below), with Sa paṇ's sources and polemical strategies, and with a Bka' bgryud pa rebuttal, should be considered

together: (1) Roger Jackson, "Sa skya Paṇḍita's Account of the bSam yas Debate: History as Polemic," *JIABS* 5 (1982): 89–99; (2) Michael Broido, "Sa-skya Paṇḍita, the White Panacea and the Hva-shang Doctrine," *JIABS* 10 (1987): 27–68; (3) David Jackson, "Sa skya Paṇḍita the 'Polemicist': Ancient Debates and Modern Interpretations," *JIABS* 13.2 (1990): 107–16.

Other scholars have considered various other controversies. For example, Samten Gyaltsen Karmay, *The Great Perfection: A Philosophical and Meditative Teaching of Tibetan Buddhism* (Leiden: E. J. Brill, 1988), chap. 5, discusses the critics and defenders of the doctrine of the Great Perfection in the eleventh century. Matthew Kapstein dicusses the controversy over the authenticity of the Rnying ma tantras in "The Purifactory Gem and Its Cleansing: A Late Tibetan Polemical Discussion of Apocryphal Texts," *History of Religions* 28.3 (1998): 217–44; an updated version is to be found in *The Tibetan Assimilation of Buddhism,* pp. 121–37. Other examples of these more focused studies include Martin, "Beyond Acceptance," pp. 263–305; and by the same author, *Unearthing Bon Treasures: Life and Contested Legacy of a Tibetan Scripture Revealer* (Leiden: Brill, 2001); Robert Mayer, "Were the Gsar-ma-pa Polemicists Justified in Rejecting Some Rnying-ma-pa Tantras?" in *Tibetan Studies,* ed. Helmut Krasser, et. al. (Wien: Verlag der Osterreichichen Akademie der Wissenschaften, 1997), II: 618–32; E. Gene Smith, *Among Tibetan Texts* (Boston: Wisdom, 2001), chap. 16: "Mi pham and the Philosophical Controversies of the Nineteenth Century"; Ronald M. Davidson, "Reflections on the Maheśvara Subjugation Myth: Indic Materials, Sa-skya-pa Apologetics, and the Birth of Heruka," *JIABS* 14.2 (1991): 197–235; and by the same author, "Gsar ma Apocrypha: The Creation of Orthodoxy, Gray Texts, and the New Revelation," in *The Many Canons of Tibetan Buddhism,* PIATS 2000, ed. Helmut Eimer and David Germano (Leiden: Brill, 2002), pp. 203–24.

28 An example, taken from Go rams pa's own collected works, is his commentary *(rnam bshad)* on Nāgārjuna's *Mūlamadhyamakakārikā,* the *Rtsom phro.*

29 An anthology of such works (mostly on the topic of Madhyamaka, and all by Dge lugs authors) is Rinchen Tshering, ed., *Dgag lan phyogs bsgrigs* (Kheng tu'u: Si khron mi rigs dpe skrun khang, 1997). A defense against attacks made throughout history contra the Rnying ma school is (Sog bzlog pa) Blo gros rgyal mtshan, *Gsang sngags snga 'gyur la bod du rtsod pa snga phyir byung ba rnams kyi lan du brjod pa nges pa don gyi 'brug sgra* (Kheng tu'u: Si khron mi rigs dpe skrun khang, 1998). For references to other examples, see Lopez, "Polemical Literature."

30 Given that there is no such thing as a purely apophatic/polemical or purely cataphatic/expository work, one expects most literature to fall in between. Examples of works that are to be found approximately midpoint in the spectrum include Go rams pa's own *General Exposition of Madhyamaka (Dbu ma'i spyi don);* or, again, a mixed genre work by the Rnying ma apologist Bod pa sprul sku Mdo sngags bstan pa'i nyi ma (1900/1907–59), the *Lta grub shan 'byed* (Kheng tu'u: Si khron mi rigs dpe skrun khang, 1996).

31 For an overview of the genre, see Shunzo Onoda, "Bsdus grwa Literature," in Cabezón and Jackson, *Tibetan Literature,* pp. 187–201. A more detailed, historical study of the Bsdus grwa literature is Onoda's *Monastic Debate in Tibet: A Study of the History and Structures of Bsdus grwa Logic* (Wien: Arbeitskreis für Tibetische und Buddhistische Studien Universität Wien, 1992). See also Christopher Beckwith, "The Medieval Scholastic Method in Tibet and the West," in *Reflections on Tibetan Culture: Essays in memory of Turrell V. Wylie,* Studies in Asian Thought and Religion

12, ed. Lawrence Epstein and Richard F. Sherburne (Lewiston: The Edwin Mellen Press, 1990), pp. 307–13. Dan Martin informs me that the *dgag gzhag spong gsum* structure is known to Bon po authors as early as the twelfth century.

32 See Daniel E. Perdue, *Debate in Tibetan Buddhism* (Ithaca: Snow Lion, 1992), p. 222 et passim. In that work, Perdue translates the famous Bsdus grwa text of Phur lcog Blo bzang tshul khrims byams pa rgya mtsho (1825–1901), the *Tshad ma'i gzhung don 'byed pa* (Lan kru'u: Kan su'u mi rigs dpe skrun khang, 1982). A very similar structure—"presenting first objections to the answer, then the answer with proof, then responses to objections"—is to be found in Thomas Aquinas' *Summa Theologiae;* see Walter Ong, *Fighting for Life,* p. 126.

33 See www.tbrc.org.

34 This is a very rough calculation, and the estimate is undoubtedly on the low side, for the reasons given below. Moreover, the works found in the TBRC database may represent only a fraction of the literary works that existed in Tibet prior to 1959. Still, it is perhaps a useful first approximation, and is only meant as such. The figure was arrived at by searching the titles of works for keywords that typically are found in the titles of polemical texts—words like *brgal lan, gsung lan, dgag pa, dgag lan, rtsod yig, rtsod lan*—as well as for nomenclature that often signals a work as polemical—nomenclature like *ngan sel, gcod pa,* etc. The titles were then examined to weed out works that were clearly *not* polemical. There is bound to be some repetition in the titles, and of course there are *many* works that such a search will not catch. For example, Dge 'dun chos 'phel's famous Madhyamaka polemical work, the *Ornament to the Purport of Nāgārjuna (Klu grub dgongs rgyan),* contains none of these keywords in its title. The same is true of Sa paṇ's *Distinguishing the Three Vows (Sdom gsum rab dbye),* which is perhaps best known for its polemic portions. Moreover, because the TBRC database does not always break down the collected works of authors into their individual titles, there will also be many works that will be missed for this reason. The breakdown of the works found to be polemical is as follows:

Philosophical works: 56
Tantra: 25
Vinaya: 1
History: 1
Medicine and Astrology: 5
Grammar: 1
General and Miscellaneous (pilgrimage, anthologies, lam rim, etc.): 10
Unknown genre: 24
TOTAL: 123

Since the determination of the subgenre (philosophical work, tantra, etc.) was made on the basis of the title, and not from examination of the work itself, this breakdown too must be considered tentative.

35 A perusal of the dates of the authors of the works suggests that about 80 percent of the texts in question belong to the seventeenth, nineteenth, and twentieth centuries, with about equal numbers in each of these three centuries. But we should be wary of drawing from this any definitive historical conclusion (for example, that polemicists were most active in the last four centuries) since, among other things, we have no idea what portion of the *entire* literary canon was written when.

36 See the next section for a discussion of the ordinances of Ye shes 'od and Zhi ba 'od.

37 For example, Chag lo tsā ba mentions several critiques of the Rnying ma tantras, all of which he knows as *spring yig*. These include the epistles of 'Gos, Pho brang Zhi ba 'od, and Tsa mi; see *Sngags log sun 'byin kyi skor* (Thimpu, Bhutan: Kunsang Topgyel and Mani Dorje, 1979), p. 17. Chag lo tsā ba's own polemic against apocryphal texts is also known under the name *spring yig;* see also Derek Frank Maher, "Knowledge and Authority in Tibetan Middle Way Schools of Buddhism: A Study of the Gelukba (dGe lugs pa) Epistemology of Jamyang Shayba ('Jam dbyangs bzhad pa) in its Historical Context" (Ph.D. Diss., University of Virginia, 2003), p. 619. Sa skya Paṇḍita also wrote polemical works in this genre, most notably *An Epistle to the Holy Beings (Skyes bu dam pa rnams la spring yig),* and *A Letter Offered to All of the Buddhas and Bodhisattvas of the Ten Directions (Phyogs bcu'i sangs rgyas dang byang chub sems pa rnams la phul ba'i yi ge);* see Jackson, *Enlightenment by a Single Means,* pp. 169–75, 187–88.

38 Chag lo tsā ba mentions the *zhus lan* of Paṇḍita Śākyaśrī (1127–1251) in his *Sngags log sun 'byin;* see *Sngags log sun 'byin kyi skor,* p. 17. Other examples include the *Dris lan nges don 'brug sgra* of Sog bzlog pa, the *Padma bka' thang las brtsams pa'i dris lan* of Rtse le Sna tshogs rang grol, and the *Dris lan yang gsal sgron me lung gi rnga chen* of Dge rtsa paṇ chen.

39 The word *rtsod pa* often refers to oral debate—what monks do in the debate courtyards of monastic educational institutions. Likewise, *rtsod yig* sometimes refers to the written record of such oral debates. Both terms, however, are also used in polemical literature to refer especially to the written accusation that initiates a polemical exchange. For example, Stag tshang lo tsā ba is said to have composed a *rtsod yig* against Tsong kha pa. The term *rtsod yig* has a broad semantic range, referring to a variety of texts—from the record of an important oral debate to a legal document. On the former, see Cabezón, *Dose,* pp. 397–98, n. 25. See also above note 4.

40 The term *rebuttal* is a translation of a Sanskrit compound, *codyamparihāra,* literally "the removing/confuting of questions/objections." The fourth century Indian scholar Vasubandhu states in his *Vyākhyāyukti (The Science of Exegesis)* that commentators *must* respond to the objections of opponents as part of the commentarial task. This effectively inscribes polemics into one of the most fundamental Indo-Tibetan literary practices: exegesis. No matter how otherwise cataphatic a commentary is, therefore, it is not complete without the negative moment constituted by the rebuttal of opponents. (In Tibet, however, the term *brgal lan* came to characterize an independent genre of text whose chief task was to respond to the objections of others.) This reminds us, once again, that there is no purely apophatic or cataphatic discourse, and that these two categories are ideal types. Skt. *Vyākhyāyukti,* Tib. *Rnam bshad rigs pa,* Toh no. 4061, sems tsam *si,* folio 30b; P no. 5562, sems tsam *si,* folio 33b: *mdo don smra ba dag gis ni/ dgos pa bsdus pa'i don bcas dang/ tshig don bcas dang mtshams sbyor bcas/ brgal lan bcas par bsnyad par bya/:*

> Those who would preach on the meaning of sūtras
> Must state the purpose *(prayojana, dgos pa)* [of their work], they must offer a synopsis of it *(piṇḍārtha, bsdus pa'i don),*
> They must give the meaning of the words [of the sūtra] *(padārtha, tshig don),* [they must identify] the boundaries (of the different sections) *(anu/pratisaṁdhi, mtshams sbyar)*
> And they must rebut opponents' arguments *(codyamparihāra, brgal lan).*

See Richard Nance, "Models of Teaching and the Teaching of Models: Contextualizing Indian Buddhist Commentary," PhD Dissertation, University of Chicago, 2004, where the first chapter of the *Vyākhyāyukti* is translated and discussed. See also his translation of the portion of the *Abhidharmasamuccayabhāṣya* dealing with *rejection (pratikṣepamukha)*, pp. 323–24, in the same work. Bu ston, in *Bu ston chos 'byung*, p. 4, paraphrases the *Vyākhyāyukti* to the effect that soteriological knowledge *(blang dor gyi gnas shes pa)* comes about as the result of the knowledge of both Buddhist and non-Buddhist theories *(phyi nang gi grub mtha')*.

41 In this introduction, we reserve the word "apologetics" for this more defensive type of work, realizing that in some ways this goes counter to the way that the term is used in a Christian theological context.

42 Other images are also used: for example, arrows *(mda')*, and, more scatologically, emetics *(skyug sman)*, a medicinal substance whose function is to purge—in this case, to purge the reader or the society of the disease that is the opponent's view. These violent metaphors were sometimes more than mere metaphors. Occasionally, scholars relied not on words but on killing rites to destroy opponents. See, for example, the discussion of Ra lo Rdo rje grags's confrontations with opponents in Ronald M. Davidson, *Tibetan Renaissance: Tantric Buddhism in the Rebirth of Tibetan Culture* (NY: Columbia University Press, 2005), p. 137.

43 See Atiśa (as treasure revealer), *Bka' chems ka khol ma* (Lan Chou: Kan su'u: mi rigs dpe skrun khang, 1989), p. 282. Also Stearns, *Buddha from Dolpo;* and Kapstein, *The Tibetan Assimilation of Buddhism,* chap. 6.

44 Cited in *Skyabs rje pha bong kha pa chab mdor bzhugs skabs snyan sgron du gsol zer ba'i yig rdzus kyi dpyad don mchan bus bkrol ba dpyod ldan bzhin 'dzum dgod pa'i thal skad rnga chen bskul ba'i dbyu gu,* in Ldan ma Blo bang rdo rje, et. al., *Three Texts Reflecting the Views of Pha-bong-kha-pa Bde-chen-snying-po on the Questions of Heresies and Intersectarian Relations in Tibet* (New Delhi: Ngawang Tobgay, 1977), p. 11: *rang nyid grags 'dod pha rol dma' dbab 'dod/ g.yo sgyu'i spyod pa tshig rtsub ngan sems can/ ngag 'khyal sna tshogs smra zhing gzhan rgyud sreg/ de lta rtsod pa 'di yang dmyal ba'i rgyu/.*

45 Chag lo tsā ba, in *Sngags log sun 'byin kyi skor,* p. 17: *'di ni don chen po zhig ste/ phrag dog dang/ nga rgyal dang/ gzhan zil gyis gnon pa'i phyir ma byas shing/ sangs rgyas kyis bstan pa bsrung ba'i phyir dang/ dam pa'i chos dar bar bya ba dang/ chos log dri ma can sun 'byin pa dang/ log rtog kyi sgrib g.yogs bsal ba'i phyir.* Chag lo may well borrow these lines from his predecessor 'Gos Khug pa lhas btsas, who states that he composed his work "so as to differentiate false Dharma from flawless Dharma, so as to bring [others] to the right path, so as to [entice] wise scholars to investigate the Dharma...Not out of anger or pride or jealousy, but so as to benefit those tantrikas and monks who are abiding in erroneous Dharma." It should be mentioned that it is unclear whether these are the actual words of 'Gos and Chag, since the editor(s) of the *Sngags log sun 'byin kyi skor* are not precise in telling us where the actual texts begin, and where their own comments have been added.

46 The passage is found in a text attributed to Bu ston, *Chos log sun 'byin,* in *Sngags log sun 'byin kyi skor,* p. 36: *...sems can la/ rjes su rtse ba'i tshul 'di smras.* See also Sakya Pandita, *A Clear Differentiation,* pp. 178–80.

47 See below for a discussion of those other motivations in the case of Go rams pa. See also Maher, "Knowledge and Authority," p. 259, where the author mentions that the Fifth Dalai Lama was known to have encouraged Dge lugs apologists to defend

Tsong kha pa's Madhyamaka views vis-à-vis rival views. Since the Fifth Dalai Lama was at this time also engaged in a political campaign to consolidate Dge lugs power, it is not a stretch to see, as Maher does, a political agenda as at least partially motivating his encouragement of apologetics.

48 This is the intended audience of Sa paṇ's *Phyogs bcu'i sangs rgyas dang byang chub sems dpa' thams cad la phul ba'i yi ge.*

49 A qualification is in order here. As has been noted above (see n. 25), the Indian Buddhist *theory* of argumentation does appeal to something like the power of a nowhere-situated rationality, but *in practice,* actual argumentation (and especially polemics) often operates in very different ways—for example, appealing to the views of authoritative texts and persons as proofs of specific doctrines.

50 See Stephen Toulmin, *Cosmopolis: The Hidden Agenda of Modernity* (Chicago: The University of Chicago Press, 1990); and Thomas Nagel, *The View from Nowhere* (NY: Oxford University Press, 1986).

51 Talal Asad, *Genealogies of Religion: Disciplines and Reasons of Power in Christianity and Islam* (Baltimore: The Johns Hopkins University Press, 1993), chap. 6. Asad is there principally concerned with analyzing a form of contemporary Islamic criticism called "advice" *(nasīha)*, which appears to be less adversarial, more personal and perhaps more oral than another form of discourse called "criticism" *(naqd)*. Notwithstanding, his insights are relevant to the point being made here.

52 Dreyfus, *Recognizing Reality,* p. 40.

53 This is not to say that Tibetans did not sometimes argue against Indian scholars or Indian doctrines. For example, Davidson, "Gsar ma Apocrypha," p. 209, mentions Sa paṇ's rejection of the Indian in favor of the Khotanese dating of the Buddha's death. Also, in the field of Madhyamaka, Phya pa is known for his critique of the Indian scholar Candrakīrti, on which see below. But these instances are very infrequent in the history of Tibetan thought.

54 By *canon* here I mean not just the "official" canon—the collection of scriptures that are said to be the Buddha's word and their Indian commentaries, the *Bka' Bstan*—but also the secondary canon of Tibetan indigenous writings: for example, the collected works *(gsung 'bum)* of the great scholar/saints of the tradition that in many instances came to have a greater power over adherents' lives and thought than the official canon. I use words like *canon* and *scripture,* therefore, in this broader sense.

55 These experience-based traditions—often transmitted privately in the form of secret oral instruction (*bka' gdams, man ngag, gdams ngag,* etc.)—have in some instances come to constitute a new canon. See, for example, Matthew Kapstein's discussion of the "Treasury of Instructions" *(Gdams ngag mzod)* in "gDams ngag: Tibetan Technologies of the Self," in Cabezón and Jackson, *Tibetan Literature,* pp. 275–90. The "experiential canon" sometimes achieves a higher status than the classical canon. When it is a vision of a Buddha, tantric deity, or *siddha* that is the source of a new doctrine, because of its proximity to a source of sacred power/knowledge, the new doctrine comes to be designated by a variety of terms that are meant to show its greater relevance or accessibility. For example, many such doctrines or practices come to be known as constituting a *close lineage (nye brgyud)*, compared to which the classical sources are considered *far (ring)*.

56 For example, there was a dispute in Tibet over the authenticity of the *Akutobhayā,* a commentary to the *Mūlamadhyamakakārikā,* that is attributed to Nāgārjuna; see

LMS, pp. 47–48; and C. W. Huntington, Jr., "A Lost Text of Early Indian Madhyamaka," *Asiatische Studien/Études Asiatiques* 59.4 (1999): 693–767.

57 While the Bon-Buddhist polemic operates with a different set of presuppositions, even here one frequently finds that authors appeal to Buddhist presuppositions.

58 For a brief but excellent summary of these forms of argument, which derive principally from the discussion in Aristotle, see Robert Audi, General Ed., *The Cambridge Dictionary of Philosophy* (Cambridge, U.K.: Cambridge University Press, 1999), pp. 373–76.

59 See Maher, "Knowledge and Authority," p. 240.

60 This is a slightly edited version of stanzas found in his *Stong thun chen mo;* see Cabezón, *Dose,* p. 184.

61 Of course, at this point in time Buddhism has yet to become a literary tradition, so that *polemics* must here be understood in a broader sense that includes oral disputation. These early oral controversies, however, have been preserved in later literary sources. See *Kathāvatthu,* trans. Shwe Zan Aung and Mrs. Rhys Davids, *Points of Controversy,* Pali Text Society Translation Series no. 5 (1915; repr., Oxford: The Pali Text Society, 1993); and also Keishō Tsukamoto's translation from the Chinese of Vasumitra's *The Cycle of the Formation of Schismatic Doctrines* BDK English Tripiṭitaka 61-VI (Berkeley: Numata Center for Buddhist Translation and Research, 2004), p. 76-I. In the introductory verses to the latter work, Vasumitra sees the divergence of opinion as a sign of the degenerate times and calls the factionalism "a disaster." And yet he believes that from "the various worldly views that were whirling round and round" it was still possible "to pick up the truth as if gathering gold from heaps of sand." This ambivalence toward religious controversy is a theme throughout the history of Buddhist thought.

62 Vasubandhu's *Vādavidhi* and Dharmakīrti's *Vādanyāya* are examples of Indian Buddhist texts that deal with the art of disputation.

63 See above, n. 40.

64 Of course, many Indian Buddhist philosophical texts were of a mixed polemical genre. Much of the work of Buddhist Pramāṇikas, for example, was devoted to the constructive act of creating a system of Buddhist logic and epistemology, while at the same time replying to opponents like the Naiyāyikas. But there were also texts of a wholly polemical nature, one of the most famous perhaps being Nāgārjuna's *Vigrahavyāvartanī;* for the literature on this text, see Cabezón, *Dose,* p. 431, n. 190.

65 Dan Martin, *Unearthing Bon Treasures,* p. 40, n. 1.

66 Karma Phuntsho, "The Position of Mipham in the Indo-Tibetan Debate on Emptiness" (Ph.D. diss., University of Oxford, 2003), n. 285, mentions an early Bon-Buddhist debate similar to the Indian-Chinese debate that took place at Bsam yas but gives no source. But see Martin, *Unearthing Bon Treasures,* pp. 193–94, for the translation of a passage that mentions an event in the imperial court that began as a debate and ended as a contest of magical powers.

67 See the discussion of this debate in Per K. Sørensen, *Tibetan Buddhist Historiography: The Mirror Illuminating the Royal Genealogies, An Annotated Translation of the XIVth Century Tibetan Chronicle: rGyal-rabs gsal-ba'i me-long* (Wiesbaden: Harrassowitz Verlag, 1994), pp. 366–67, 601–6.

68 See Martin, *Unearthing Bon Treasures;* and Samten G. Karmay, *The Arrow and the Spindle,* chap. 9.

69 Martin has discussed another thirteenth-century Buddhist anti-Bon polemic in his "Beyond Acceptance and Rejection?" Many writers have also seen Thu'u bkwan's (1737–1802) "Bon" chapter as being polemical; see Thu'u bkwan Blo bzang chos kyi nyi ma, *Thu'u bkwan grub mtha'* (Lan kru'u: Kan su'u mi rigs dpe skrun khang, 1985), pp. 378–90.

70 Zeff Bjerken has argued that the Buddhist anti-Bon polemic, including that found in Thu'u bkwan's text, has been unselfconsciously assimilated into the Western rhetoric of Bon as a form of "Shamanism"; see his "Exorcising the Illusion of Bon Shamanism: A Critical Genealogy of Shamanism in Tibetan Religions," *Revue d'études tibétains* 6 (2004): 4–60. Gene Smith has communicated to me that Thu'u bkwan's arguments are derived from the works of Spyan snga Blo gros rgyal mtshan (1402–72), a late student of Tsong kha pa, who takes on both Bon and Rnying ma in his *Rnying ma dang bon gyi rnam gzhag.*

71 One of the most interesting examples of this kind of polemic is a defense of Bon attributed (Gene Smith believes spuriously) to the Sa skya pa scholar Rong ston Shes bya kun rig (1367–1449), a teacher of Go rams pa. It is unclear when this text was written, but we know that Rong ston pa was a Bon po in the early part of his life. Mkhas grub rje, one of Tsong kha pa's chief disciples, uses Rong ston pa's past as a Bon po to polemical advantage in verses he composed challenging Rong ston pa; see Cabezón, *Dose,* p. 389, where Rong ston pa is described as "taking up the banner of the teachings of gShen rab." Rong ston pa's (or pseudo-Rong ston pa's) *Chos kyi bstan pa shan 'byed (Distinguishing the Teaching of Dharma)* is a polemical treatise that argues for the fact that Bon represents true, uncorrupted *Buddhist* teachings. If nothing else, this work shows us how complex the Buddhist-Bon polemic can sometimes be. A synopsis of the texts is found in Martin, *Unearthing Bon Treasures,* chap. 12. I have Dan Martin to thank for bringing this to my attention. See also Dudjom Rinpoche, Jikdrel Yeshe Dorje, *The Nyingma School of Tibetan Buddhism: Its Fundamentals and History* (Boston: Wisdom, 1991), pp. 936–37, for remarks concerning why there are similarities between the Bon po and Buddhist teachings. His answer is that "these [Bon works] were written so as to resemble the Buddhist doctrine." Dudjom Rinpoche does not, however, rule out the possibility that the similarities exist because (the beneficial) aspects of the Bon religion "may have been revealed by the enlightened activities and emanations of the Buddhas." He concludes by stating that "so long as other traditions do not harm the teachings, we should just let them be."

72 For an overview of the literature, and a sober assessment of the arguments on both sides, see David Seyfort Ruegg's Jordan Lectures, *Buddha-Nature, Mind and the Problem of Gradualism in a Comparative Perspective: On the Transmission and Reception of Buddhism in India and Tibet* (London: School of Oriental and African Studies, 1989). G. W. Houston has translated many of the later Tibetan historical documents that treat the debate in his *Sources for a History of the bSam yas Debate* (Sankt Augustin: VGH Wissenschaftverlag, 1980). Still a classic because of its treatment of many sources, including Chinese ones, is Paul Demiéville, *Le Concile de Lhasa: une controverse sur le quiétisme entre bouddhistes de l'Inde et de la Chine au VIII. siècle de l'ère chrétienne* (Paris: Impr. nationale de France, 1952).

73 Yoshiro Imaeda, "Documents Tibétains de Touen-houang Concernant le Concile du Tibet," *Journal Asiatique* (1975): 125–46, has examined two Dunhuang Tibetan

manuscripts that he claims further support the view that the debate was "not a historical fact, but a legend invented by later Tibetan historians." Seyfort Ruegg, who is himself a partisan of the view that the event probably did take place, concedes that with the exception of the history of Nyang Nyi ma 'od zer (1136–1204), "Sa skya Paṇḍita appears to be the oldest securely datable Tibetan source discussing Hwa shang Mahāyāna's teachings now available"; *Buddha-Nature,* p. 101; see also p. 71.

74 Seyfort Ruegg, *Buddha-Nature,* p. 6; Seyfort Ruegg deals with many of the later philosophical critiques of the positions ascribed to Hwa shang in *Buddha-Nature,* chap. 2.

75 For the relevant literature, see Joseph F. Roccasalvo, "The debate at bsam yas: religious contrast and correspondence," *Philosophy East and West* 30.4 (1980): 505–20.

76 O rgyan gling pa, *Bka' thang sde lnga* (Pe cin: Mi rigs dpe skrung khang, 1986). The relevant chapters have been edited and translated by Giuseppe Tucci, *Minor Buddhist Texts,* Part II (Rome: IsMEO, 1958), pp. 68–102. Tucci's work also contains a translation of Kamalaśīla's first *Bhāvanākrama,* and a great deal of interesting information on the debate as well.

77 On the *gter ma* literature, see Janet Gyatso, "Drawn from the Tibetan Treasury: The gTer ma Literature," in Cabezón and Jackson, *Tibetan Literature,* pp. 170–86; Tulku Thondup Rinpoche, *Hidden Teachings of Tibet: An Explanation of the Terma Tradition of the Nyingma School of Buddhism,* ed. Harold Talbott (London: Wisdom Publications, 1986); and Andreas Doctor, *The Tibetan Treasure Literature: Revelation, Tradition and Accomplishment in Visionary Buddhism* (Ithaca: Snow Lion, forthcoming).

78 Tucci, *Minor Buddhist Texts,* Part II, p. 64.

79 For example, Sa paṇ states that, as regards his refutation of the doctrine of the White Panacea: "I too have explained this following the ācārya Kamalaśīla"; *bdag gis kyang/ slob dpon ka ma la shī la'i rjes su 'brangs nas bshad/; Skyes bu dam pa rnams la spring yig,* in Jackson, *Enlightenment by a Single Means,* pp. 169, 173. See also his paraphrase of Kamalaśīla's arguments against the Hwa shang in *Thub pa'i dgongs gsal* in Jackson, *Enlightenment by a Single Means,* pp. 178–79, 183–84. These examples could be multiplied manyfold in the history of Tibetan Buddhist polemics.

80 For example, the Sa skya pa hagiographical literature maintains that the father of 'Khon Dkon mchog rgyal po (1034–1102), the founder of the Sa skya school, urged him to find a purer form of tantra than what was being practiced in Tibet at the time. Hence, the founding narrative of the Sa skya school includes an appeal to the need for reform.

81 The association of the rural with lowly and degenerate views and practices is of course not unique to Tibet. In what is usually considered the Buddha's first sermon, the *Dhammacakkapavattana Sutta,* the Buddha characterizes the extreme of sensual indulgence as a way of life that "belongs to the village" *(gammo),* usually glossed as "vulgar"; see T. W. Rhys Davids and William Steade, *Pali-English Dictionary* (Delhi: Motilal Banarsidass, 2003), p. 245.

82 Samten Karmay has edited and translated this text in *The Arrow and The Spindle,* chap. 1.

83 It seems clear that Ye shes 'od questioned not only the specific practices of Tibetan village priests, but the tantras in general. Bu ston, for example, states that Ye shes 'od

had no doubts that the "vehicle of philosophy" *(mtshan ngyi theg pa)* was the word of the Buddha, but that he questioned whether the tantras were *buddhavacana.* See Obermiller, *History,* II, p. 212.

84 (Sog bzlog pa) Blo gros rgyal mtshan, *Gsang sngags snga' 'gyur la bod du rtsod pa phyir byung ba rnams kyi lan du brjod pa nges don gyi 'brug sgra,* pp. 179–204.

85 It has been pointed out by Karmay that there is a certain anachronism in the fact that Sog bzlog pa considers Ye shes 'od's ordinance to be an attack on the Rnying ma school, for of course there was at this point "no question of the rNying-ma-pa as such, for the *sngags gsar ma* (the New Tantras) had hardly begun"; Karmay, *Arrow and Spindle,* p. 5. But he goes on to add that what is clearly under attack are tantric works that would become central to the Rnying ma school, especially the *Guhyagarbha.*

86 For a discussion of Atiśa as treasure revealer, see *Bka' chems,* pp. 281–85. Since the text was supposed to have been written by Srong bstan sgam po, this section is written as a prophecy of events to come. The passage is also quoted in a text attributed to a certain Bla ma Byams pa, the *Lta log sun 'byin,* in *Sngags log sun 'byin* (Thimpu), pp. 37–42.

87 *Bka' chems,* p. 282: *med par lta ba stong pa'i phyogs bzung nas/ kun rdzob bden pa khyad du gsod byed cing/ lus ngag dka' thub byed pa 'gog byed pa/.*

88 That there were others engaged in doctrinal controversies at this time in Western Tibet is evidenced by some of the work of the great Rnying ma scholar Rong zom Chos kyi bzang po (b. eleventh century). Karmay has discussed Rong zom Chos kyi bzang po's apologetical treatise, entitled *Introduction to the Mahāyāna Method (Theg pa chen po'i tshul la 'jug pa)*; see Karmay, *The Great Perfection,* pp. 125–33. In addition, his *Great State of the Buddha (Sangs rgyas kyi sa chen po)* has a long section in which he defends his views on the nature of the Buddha's gnosis, and on the way that the Buddha's bodies function; see *Rong zom chos bzang gi gsung 'bum* (Kheng tu'u: Si khron mi rigs dpe skrun khang, 1999), II, pp. 69–87, and especially 74ff. See also his *Note on Seeing the Resultant State of Great Self-arisen Gnosis as Maṇḍalic Display (Rang byung ye shes chen po'i 'bras bu rol pa'i dkyil 'khor du blta ba'i yi ge),* in *Gsung'bum,* II, pp. 111–30. And also Karmay, *The Great Perfection,* chap. 5. Seyfort Ruegg has discussed early *phyi dar* Madhyamaka controversies involving different authors in *Three Studies,* passim.

89 See Roberto Vitali, *Records of Tho.ling: A Literary and Visual Reconstruction of the "Mother" Monastery in Gu.ge* (Dharamsala: High Asia, 1999).

90 Rin chen bzang po's *Critique of the False Tantras (Sngags log sun 'byin)* is no longer extant, but it is mentioned in a variety of sources, including Chag lo tsā ba's own work by the same name; see *Sngags log sun 'byin kyi skor,* p. 17. See also Bu ston, Obermiller, *History,* II, p. 214; and Martin, *Unearthing Bon Treasures,* p. 108.

91 This work is edited and translated in Karmay, *The Arrow and the Spindle,* chap. 2; see also Davidson, *Tibetan Renaissance,* pp. 153–54. Sog bzlog pa responds to these charges in his apologetic work, *Gsang sngags,* pp. 204–17. Rin chen bzang po, as is well known, was an influential figure in the Pu 'rangs court, so it may be that Zhi ba 'od's list derives from Rin chen bzang po's work; see the discussion in Georges N. Roerich, *The Blue Annals* (Delhi: Motilal Banarsidass, 1976), p. 417, n. 4. Davidson, "Gsar ma Apocrypha," p. 207, has conjectured that the Tibetan concern with

the critique of apocryphal texts was inherited from the Chinese, who had already been debating these issues for centuries.

92 On this figure and his *Refutation of False Tantras,* see Davidson, *Tibetan Renaissance,* 152f, and the note that follows. It is interesting that 'Gos himself is later charged not with composing new tantras, but with plagiarism; see Davidson, *Tibetan Renaissance,* p. 205.

93 Both of the works of 'Gos and Chag (as well as others in the same vein) are found in *Sngag log sun 'byin kyi skor,* though it is not clear how much of their texts are actually contained in this work, which at times reads more like a paraphrase of these various authors' works than an anthology. Both of these figures have been responded to by Sog bzlog pa, *Gsang sngags,* 217ff. Khug pa lhas btsas, it seems, also composed a text that "differentiated the true from the false doctrine" *(chos dang chos min rnam par dbye ba),* which, unfortunately, is no longer extant; see Ko shul Grags pa 'byung gnas and Rgyal ba Blo bzang mkhas grub, *Gangs can mkhas grub rim byon ming mdzod* (Lan zhou: Kan su'u Mi rigs dpe skrun khang, 1992), p. 346. The portion of 'Gos's *Refutation* excerpted/paraphrased (?) in *Sngags log sun 'byin kyi skor* is little more than a list of which tantric works are "pure word" *(bka' dri ma med pa),* and which are "false and impure doctrines" *(chos log dri ma can),* interspersed with some historical remarks, like that concerning the punishment that Rma Rin chen mchog experienced when he was caught composing tantric works. Chag's work is more detailed, providing us with a kind of etiology of how the false texts were derived from authentic ones. Besides mentioning texts, Chag also mentions several individuals by name in his work. These include Gu ru Chos dbang (1212–70), Pha dam pa sangs rgyas (b. 11th century), La stod Dmar po, and Bla ma Ras chung pa (= Rdo rje grags pa?, 1085–1161).

94 See Sakya Pandita Kunga Gyaltsen, *A Clear Differentiation of the Three Codes,* trans. by Jared Rhoton (Albany: SUNY Press, 2002), pp. 166–67, 175, 180, 196–98.

95 For references concerning Bu ston's views on the canonicity of these texts, see Kapstein, "The Purificatory Gem," pp. 253–54, n. 35. The *Chos log sun 'byin* attributed to Bu ston, and anthologized in *Sngags log sun 'byin kyi skor,* pp. 25–36, is widely considered to be a forgery. This polemical text, written in verse, contains short chapters on *treasures (gter),* on the Rnying ma school, on the White Example/Four Sons *(dpe dkar bu bzhi),* and on Bon. In the *Bu ston chos 'byung,* p. 313, Bu ston mentions the ordinances of Ye shes 'od and Zhi ba 'od, though he knows both of them by the title *Refutation of the False Tantras (Sngags log sun 'byin pa).* He also mentions the work of Rin chen bzang po by the same title, and *Distinguishing the Philosophical Tenets (Grub mtha'i rnam dbye)* by Byang chub 'od (eleventh century). But Bu ston's main discussion of this issue is found in his *Catalogue (Dkar chag)* to the canon. See also E. K. Neumaier-Dargyay, *The Sovereign All-Creating Mind: The Motherly Buddha* (Albany: State University of New York Press, 1992), pp. 25–26.

96 The list of figures whom Sog bzlog pa mentions in his *dgag lan* include Bu ston rin chen grub (1290–1364), Sa skya Paṇḍita (1182–1251), the Bka' gdams pa scholar Bcom ldan rig ral (b. thirteenth century), Shākya mchog ldan (1428–1507), Bri gung pa Dpal 'dzin, and Rgyan ro Byang chub 'bum, although it is clear that not all of these figures are equally skeptical about the authenticity of all of the Rnying ma scriptures and teachings; see Sog bzlog pa, *Gsang sngags,* p. 231ff.

97 'Dan ma Blo bzang rdo rje, et. al., *Three Texts,* p. 26ff.

98 This is all the more remarkable, given that Bcom ldan rig ral was otherwise himself a critic of the Rnying ma. See Sog bzlog pa, *Gsang sngags,* p. 232; Karmay, *The Arrow and the Spindle,* p. 7, and n. 35; Karmay, *The Great Perfection,* p. 140, and n. 23; and Davidson, *Tibetan Renaissance,* p. 153.

99 See the important passage of his *Grub mtha' so so'i bzhed gzhung chos 'byung,* discussed in Davidson, *Tibetan Renaissance,* pp. 232–33.

100 O rgyan pa is quoted in Bdud 'joms rin po che's *Chos 'byung,* but neither he nor the translators identify the source. See (Bdud 'joms rin po che) 'Jigs bral ye shes rdo rje, *Snga 'gyur rnying ma'i chos 'byung* (1999, published anonymously in India, perhaps from the Chinese ed.), pp. 572–73; translated by Gyurme Dorje, with the collaboration of Matthew Kapstein, in Dudjom Rinpoche and Jikdrel Yeshe Dorje, *The Nyingma School,* I, p. 891. The great Rnying ma pa scholar Rong zom Chos kyi bzang po mentions that "charlatan translators of the present day made various reforms in the ancient translations... [and] compose their own doctrines," but he never addresses the charge that the tantras are apocryphal, probably because these charges were just beginning to surface during his own time; see Bdud 'joms rin po che, *Chos 'byung,* p. 572; Dudjom Rinpoche, *The Nying ma school,* pp. 890–91. See also Dan Martin, *Unearthing Bon Treasures,* p. 116, for the translation of a "polemic-like statement" by a follower of the Rnying ma *Bka' ma* tradition, Rog Bande Shes rab 'od (1166–1244).

101 Klong chen pa at times also goes on the polemical offensive in an attempt to show the superiority of the Great Perfection over its Gsar ma rivals. For a discussion of some polemical passages in Klong chen pa's writings that take aim at specific Gsar ma tantric practices—for example, the practice of intentionally placing the energy into the central channel—see David Germano, "Architecture and Absence in the Secret Tantric History of the Great Perfection (rdzogs chen)," *JIABS* 17.2 (1994): 315–24.

102 See Smith, *Among Tibetan Texts,* p. 16.

103 Smith, *Among Tibetan Texts,* p. 17.

104 See Sog bzlog pa, *Gsang sngags;* Karmay summarizes some of Sog bzlog pa's replies to Zhi ba 'od in *The Arrow and the Spindle,* chap. 2.

105 See Dudjom Rinpoche, *The Nyingma School,* II, p. 89, n. 1274.

106 See *Gu bkra'i chos 'byung* (Mtsho sngon: Mi rigs dpe skrun khang, 1990), p. 977ff.

107 Bdud 'joms rin po che, *Chos 'byung,* chap. 7, part I, p. 567ff; Dudjom Rinpoche, *The Nyingma School,* I, pp. 887–95.

108 On this exchange, see Kapstein, "The Purificatory Gem."

109 See Davidson, *Tibetan Renaissance,* pp. 232–35, 419.

110 See Chag, *Sngags log sun 'byin kyi skor,* p. 14. See also Davidson, "Gsar ma Apocrypha," p. 215.

111 This work is mentioned in Lokesh Chandra, *Materials for a History of Tibetan Literature* (Kyoto: Rinsen Book Co., 1981), no. 12442, p. 695. Access to Dan Martin's list of Tibetan polemical works has brought this to my attention.

112 Of course, we cannot assume that opponents like this were real, living opponents, since Tibetans were fond of entertaining positions and then refuting them simply as part of the task of exegesis. See Davidson, *Tibetan Renaissance,* pp. 314, 363.

113 Ronald M. Davidson, "Reflections on the Maheśvara Subjugation Myth," pp. 221–22: "Ngor-chen's hagiographies speak of his defending the Sa-skya-pa position in central Tibet against vociferous critics." As Bdud 'joms rin po che mentions, 'Gos Lhas btsas also criticized the path and its result *(Lam 'bras)*, the chief tantric system of the Sa skya pas, because "he was jealous of its propagator, the translator Drokmi"; Dudjom Rinpoche, *The Nyingma School,* I, p. 930.

114 Dudjom Rinpoche, *The Nyingma School,* I, p. 929.

115 Dudjom Rinpoche, *The Nyingma School,* II, p. 91, n. 302.

116 Gu ru bkra shis, Ngag dbang blo gros Stag sgang mkhas mchog, *Gu bkra'i chos 'byung* (Pe cin: Krung go'i bod kyi shes rig dpe skrun khang, 1990), p. 992: *ngor chen rdo rje 'chang slob tshogs dang bcas pas dge ldan pa'i 'jigs byed 'di lung rigs 'du mas bkag.* "The Great Ngor Vajradhāra and his circle of disciples repudiated the Dge ldan pa [tradition] of Yamāntaka, using many scriptural citations and forms of reasoning." In this case, however, it appears that what was at stake was not so much the authenticity of texts as their interpretation and ritual enactment.

117 I take the term *doctrine* to refer to more than just the verbal expression of tenets, meaning also to include in the semantic range of the word the broader system that encodes those tenets in certain (e.g., meditational) practices as well.

118 Karmay, *The Arrow and the Spindle,* p. 40: *khyad par du rdzogs pa chen poi'i lta ba mu stegs kyi rim pa dang sres pas/ 'di byas na ngan song gi lam du 'gro bar 'gyur zhing/.*

119 The *Testament of the Pillar* is no exception to this rule. Although it mentions some examples of the "demonic doctrines"—to wit, "having no position, impartiality, inactivity, the exhaustion of causes, the exhaustion of conditions, spontaneity" *(phyogs med ris med byar med zer ba dang/ rgyu zad rkyen zad lhun sgrub zer ba dang)*—it does not analyze them in any extensive way, nor does it give reasons for why they are "scripturally baseless views" *(lung ma bstan pa'i lta ba).*

120 See, for example, Karmay's discussion of 'Bri gung Dpal 'dzin's (c. fourteenth century) critique of Rdzogs chen in *The Great Perfection,* pp. 140–42.

121 Bcom ldan rig ral, it seems, suggested a different periodization of history, believing that there was an intermediate stage between the *dnga dar* and the *phyi dar,* with Rngog Legs pa'i shes rab representing the beginning of the true *phyi dar.* This opinion is criticized by Bu ston; see Obermiller, *History,* II, pp. 211–12.

122 See Seyfort Ruegg, *Literature of the Madhyamaka School;* Seyfort Ruegg, *Three Studies,* Section I; and Georges Dreyfus and Sara McClintock, *The Svātantrika/Prāsaṅgika Distinction: What Difference Does a Difference Make?* (Boston: Wisdom Publications, 2003).

123 Phya pa chos kyi seng ge, *Dbu ma shar gsum gyi stong thun,* ed. by Helmut Tauscher (Wien: Arbeitskreis für Tibetische und Buddhistische Studien Universität Wien, 1999). On Phya pa and his status as one of the Tibetan tradition's most independent thinkers, see Leonard W. J. van der Kuijp, *Contributions to Tibetan Buddhist Epistemology* (Wiesbaden: Franz Steiner, 1983), chap. 2; on his refutations of the Prāsaṅgika, see van der Kuijp, *Contributions,* p. 63 and n. 228. See also L. W. J. van der Kuijp, "Phya-pa Chos-kyi Seng-ge's Impact on Tibetan Epistemological Theory," *Journal of Indian Philosophy* 5 (1978): 355–69.

124 Another early *phyi dar* text with a strong polemical content is the *Bstan rim chen mo* of Gro lung pa Blo gros 'byung gnas (eleventh century), whose Madhyamaka section takes on various types of "wrong views"; Dge bshes Gro lung pa Blo gros 'byung gnas, *Bstan rim chen mo* (Mundgod: The Library of His Eminence Trijang Rinpoche, 2001).

125 See, for example, Pascale Hugon, "Continuity and Rupture in the Development of Tibetan Espistemology" (paper presented at the 2005 Princeton Graduate Student Conference). As Hugon makes clear, Phya pa refuted several of the views of Rngog Lo tsā ba. Phya pa was then refuted by his student Gtsang nag pa (late twelfth century), who was, in turn, refuted by Chu mig pa (thirteenth century).

126 See Peter A. Schwabland, "Direct and Indirect Cognition and the Definition of Pramāṇa in Early Tibetan Epistemology," *Asiatische Studies/Études Asiatiques* XLIX.4 (1995): 793–816.

127 See Dreyfus, *Recognizing Reality.*

128 See Roger R. Jackson, "Sa-skya Paṇḍita's Account," pp. 89–99; and David Jackson, "Sa-skya Paṇḍita the 'Polemicist'," pp. 17–116.

129 Although, as has been already noted, he is one the figures who disputes the authenticity of some of the Rnying ma tantras.

130 On this text, see also Z. Horvath, "Structure and Content of the Chad-ma rigs-pa'i gter, an Epistemological Treatise of Saskya Paṇḍita," *Tibetan and Buddhist Studies,* Bibliotheca Orientalis Hungarica, 29.1 (1984): 267–302.

131 See Smith, *Among Tibetan Texts,* p. 114. See also Leonard W. J. van der Kuijp, "An Early Tibetan View of the Soteriology of Buddhist Epistemology: The Case of 'Bri-gung 'Jig-rten mgon-po," *Journal of Indian Philosophy,* 15 (1987): 57–70.

132 Sa paṇ considers pilgrimage to be a dangerous thing, something to be practiced only after one has attained a certain level of spiritual maturity. He also disputes the identification of certain sites in Tibet with some of the classical sites of tantric Buddhist pilgrimage. See Sa skya Paṇḍita, *A Clear Differentiation of the Three Codes,* pp. 135–41, 310–14.

133 David Jackson has discussed both the White Panacea doctrine and the Sa skya pa critiques of it in his *Enlightenment by a Single Means.* See also Michael Broido, "Sa-skya Paṇḍita," pp. 27–68.

134 David Jackson, *Enlightenment by a Single Means,* p. 155.

135 Here are the main points of Sa paṇ's claims/argument:

1. Mahāmudrā is a valid Buddhist doctrine, but only as it is formulated in the classical Indian tantra. Any formulation of the doctrine that purports to transcend or replace doctrines like the generation and completion stages of the tantra can only be considered a later invention.
2. True Mahāmudrā does not contradict, surpass or make moot the Madhyamaka as the philosophical underpinning of the tantras, as the White Panacea purports to do.
3. Practicing Mahāmudrā does not replace the necessity of accomplishing the "two accumulations"—those of merit and wisdom.
4. Any form of Mahāmudrā that does not accord with the sūtras and tantras

is false. Sa paṇ invests a great deal of energy trying to convince his readers that the White Panacea contradicts scripture: for example, by showing how the gradualist/simultaneist distinction made by the proponents of this form of Mahāmudrā falls outside the bounds of the scriptures.

5. The advocates of the White Panacea use their charisma to trick the untutored into believing that "a slight reduction in their conceptual thought" *(rtog pa cung zad 'gags pa)* is the real Mahāmudrā.
6. Since the White Panacea is tantamount to "the Great Perfection of the Chinese tradition" *(rgya nag lugs kyi rdzogs chen)*—that is, to the simultaneist view—Kamalaśīla's arguments apply to it as well. He rehearses many of those arguments.
7. Enlightenment cannot be attained through a single cause, nor is it instantaneous, nor is it easy to achieve. When the scriptures reduce all practices to a single one, they are speaking allegorically.
8. In general, recognizing the nature of mind is necessary, but this form of meditation is effective only after one has prepared oneself spiritually by the practice of *means (thabs kyis yon tan rdzogs nas)*. For beginners, trying to recognize the nature of mind is a waste of time.
9. The White Panacea's espousal of keeping the mind at ease *('bol te)*, relaxed *(lhug pa)* and "loose" *(shig ge)* is a form of deluded meditation *(rmongs pa'i sgom pa)*.
10. It is internally contradictory to maintain, on the one hand, that one is practicing a form of meditation that requires no effort and, on the other, to strive to overcome what the advocates of the White Panacea call "the four lapses" *(shor sa bzhi)*.

136 See Maher, "Knowledge and Authority," pp. 259–60.

137 See below, n. 136.

138 Little work has been done in the West on the controversies in the field of Prajñāpāramitā *(phar phyin)* studies in Tibet. One of the chief controversies in this area appears to be that related to what John Makransky has called "buddhology"; see his *Buddhahood Embodied: Sources of Controversy in India and Tibet* (Albany: SUNY Press, 1997), chap. 12, for a discussion of Tsong kha pa's and Go rams pa's views on this issue.

139 See, for example, David Seyfort Ruegg, *Le traité du tathāgatagarbha de Bu ston Rin chen grub: traduction du De bźin gsegs pa'i sñiṅ po gsal źin mdzes par byed pa'i rgyan* (Paris: École française d'Extrême-Orient, 1973).

140 Seyfort Ruegg canvases the views of various figures with respect to the question of whether or not the Madhyamaka have theses in *Three Studies*, p. 156ff. As this book is going to press a cache of early Bka' gdams texts—including several important works on Madhyamaka—is being published in Lhasa by the Dpal brtsegs bod yig dpe rnying zhib 'jug khang.

141 On the Indian precedents for Dol po pa's theory, however, see Cyrus Stearns, "Dol-po-pa Shes-rab rgyal-mtshan and the Genesis of the gzhan-stong Position in Tibet," *Asiatische Studien/Études Asiatiques* XLIX.4 (1995): 829–52.

142 On Tsong kha pa's synthesis of Madhyamaka and Pramāṇika thought, and the problems that this raises, see Seyfort Ruegg, *Three Studies*, section III.

143 Among his direct disciples, it is Mkhas grub Dge legs dpal bzang who is best known as the defender of the faith. A generation later, the gauntlet is taken up by Se ra Rje btsun Chos kyi rgyal mtshan (1469–1544/46). Mkhas grub rje defended his master's views in many of his more expository works. For example, in the field of Madhyamaka, the *Stong thun chen mo* is a synthetic work whose goal is to give a general overview of the theories of emptiness in Mahāyāna Buddhism. This does not keep Mkhas grub rje from devoting large portions of the work to a critique of alternative views, however; for a translation of the work see Cabezón, *Dose.* Mkhas grub rje did, however, write other univocally polemical works. On the subject of Madhyamaka, his most famous polemical text is *The Lamp that Dispels the Darkness of Bad Views (Lam ngan mun sel sgron ma),* Collected Works, vol. *ta;* and in the field of tantra, it is *The Wheel of Thunderbolts (Phyin ci log gi gtam gyi sbyor ba la zhugs pa'i smra ba ngan pa rnam par 'thad pa'i bstan bcos gnam lcags 'khor lo)* in Rin chen tshe ring, ed., *Dgag lan phyogs bsgrigs,* pp. 1–68. On Rje btsun pa, see Lopez, "Polemical Literature." Another later Dge lugs polemicist, Dbal mang Dkon mchog rgyal mtshan (1764–1853), wrote an interesting text that takes on each of the most important theories of the major schools of Tibetan Buddhism, the Sa skya pas' Not Grasping Clarity and Emptiness *(gsal stong 'dzin med),* the Rnying ma pas' Great Perfection *(rdzogs chen),* the Bka' brgyud pas' Mahāmudrā *(phyag chen),* and what he calls "the system of the followers of the Bka' gdams, like Zhang thang sag pa, etc." The work is part of a larger work called *A Compassionate Lake of Straightforward Speech (Bden gtam snying rje'i rol mtsho)*; the relevant section *(Sa rnying bka brgyud sogs kyi khyad par 'go smos tsam mu to'i rgyangs 'bod gyi tshul du bya gtong snyan sgron bdud rtsi'i bsang gtor),* is found in Rin chen tshe ring's anthology, *Dgag lan phyos bsgrigs,* pp. 647–743. See also Chizuko Yoshimizu, "The Madhyamaka Theories Regarded as False by the dGe lugs pas," WZKSO 37 (1993): 201–27.

144 See Jeffrey Hopkins, *Maps of the Profound: Jam-yang-shay-ba's Great Exposition of Buddhist and non-Buddhist Views on the Nature of Reality* (Ithaca, NY: Snow Lion Publications, 2003), p. 513ff; and Maher, "Knowledge and Authority," p. 241. Of course, there were earlier non-Dge lugs critics of Dol po pa as well. Dan Martin, in his list of polemical texts, mentions the work of Dka' bzhi 'dzin pa Rin chen rdo rje (fourteenth century), the *Man ngag mnyam med dbang po'i rdo rje lta bu,* which goes with two other earlier related works by the same author entitled, *Rdo rje thog chen* and *Rdo rje tho ba,* which were criticized by Nya phrug Kun dga' dpal (d. 1379?).

145 This takes place principally in a short text known simply as the "Polemical Document" *(Rtsod yig),* and at greater length in his *Knowledge of All Philosophical Systems (Grub mtha' kun shes).* The first of these texts is but a list of the so-called "eighteen great burdens of contradiction" *('gal khur chen po bco brgyad)*; it is translated in Cabezón, *Dose,* Appendix I, and discussed further in Cabezón, "On the *sGra pa Rin chen pa'i rtsod lan* of Paṇ chen bLo bzang chos rgyan," *Asiatische Studien/Études Asiatiques* 49.4 (1995): 643–69. See also Hopkins, *Maps of the Profound,* 527ff; and Shirō Matsumoto, "sTag tshang pa no Tsong kha pa Hihan ni tsuite" (On Stag tshang pa's Criticism of Tsong kha pa), *Report of the Japanese Association for Tibetan Studies* 28 (1982): 11–14. For further references in Western language sources, see Seyfort Ruegg, *Three Studies,* pp. 68–69, n. 156. E. Gene Smith translates a humorous passage from a work of the Fifth Dalai Lama wherein the Bka' brgyud pas get scolded for meddling in the Dge lugs pa/Stag tshang debate, *Among Tibetan Texts,* p. 244.

146 Mi bskyod rdo rje, Eighth Karma pa, *Dbu ma la 'jug pa'i rnam bshad dpal ldan dus gsum mkhyen pa'i zhal lung dwags brgyud grub pa'i shing rta,* in Gsung'bum (Collected

Works) ed. by Karma bde legs (Lhasa: Tsadra, 2004), v. 14. See also Seyfort Ruegg, *Three Studies,* pp. 70–71 and n. 160.

147 On Shākya mchog ldan's critique of Tsong kha pa, see Komarovski Iaroslav, *Three Texts on Madhyamaka* (Dharamsala: Library of Tibetan Works and Archives, 2000), passim. See also Yoshimizu, "The Madhyamaka Theories Regarded as False," p. 207; and David Seyfort Ruegg, *Three Studies,* p. 36.

148 Mi pham engages Tsong kha pa's views, for example, in his commentary to the Wisdom chapter of the *Bodhicaryāvatāra,* the *Brgal lan nyin byed snang ba,* and in his *Nges shes rin po che sgron me,* a work that, incidentally, has been influenced by Go rams pa's *Lta ba'i shan 'byed.* See the translation of the latter in John Whitney Pettit, *Mipham's Beacon of Certainty: Illuminating the View of Dzogchen, the Great Perfection* (Boston: Wisdom Publications, 1999). Concerning Mi pham's refutations of Tsong kha pa and his exchanges with Dge lugs apologists, see also Smith, *Among Tibetan Texts,* chap. 16. See also Seyfort Ruegg, *Three Studies,* pp. 6–7, 206.

149 This of course does not exhaust the list of those who polemicized against Tsong kha pa. To name but one additional example, 'Brug pa Pad ma dkar po (1527–92) was also a critic of Tsong kha pa who was in turn responded to by Dge lugs author Sgom sde Nam mkha' rgyal mtshan (1532–92) in his *Reply to 'Brug ('Brug lan).*

150 On the first Paṇ chen bla ma's critique of Stag tshang lo tsā ba, see Cabezón, "On the *sGra pa rin chen pa'i Rtsod lan.*" On 'Jam dbyangs bzhad pa's critique, see David Seyfort Ruegg, "Thesis and Assertion in the Madhyamaka/dBu ma" in *Tibetan and Buddhist Studies Commemorating the 200th Anniversary of the Birth of Alexander Csoma de Koros,* ed. Ernst Steinkellner and Helmut Tauscher (Budapest: Akademias Kiado, 1984), II, pp. 205–41; and Maher, "Knowledge and Authority," chap. 5, esp. p. 240ff. Phur lcog's response has yet to be studied by Western scholars; the Tibetan text is to be found in *Stag tshang lo tstsha ba'i brgal lan rdo rje'i gzegs ma,* in *Collected Works (Gsung'bum) of Phur-bu-lcog Nag-dbang-byams-pa reproduced from a set of tracings from the prints from the Phur-bu-lcog Hermitage blocks* (New Delhi: Ngawang Sopa, 1973), I, pp. 272–353. The *A khu dpe tho* also mentions responses to Stag tshang by the Li thang abbot Blo bzang chos grags (b. seventeenth century), and by Rgyal rong Nam mkha' lhun grub (b. seventeenth century).

151 The work is found in Rin chen tshe ring, *Dgag lan phyogs bsgrigs,* pp. 70–173. Rje btsun pa's usage of the honorific, both in the title and in the body of his work, is not meant sarcastically. Rather, Rje bstun pa's deference to the Karma pa's work is probably due (a) to the fact that the Karma pa is a recognized incarnation, and (b) to the fact that the Karma pa approached his polemical subject matter with a certain amount of humility, from the outset asking scholars to correct him wherever he might have gone wrong. Rje btsun pa paraphrases this invitation as follows: *dpyod ldan rnams kyis dgag bsgrub legs par gyis shig ces pa'i bka' stsal pheb pa zlog par ma nus par/ rje karma pa gang gi gsung la 'di 'thad/ 'di ma 'thad ces pa'i dgag sgrub zhu bar,* etc. See also Paul Williams, "A Note on Some Aspects of Mi bskyod rdo rje's Critique of dGe lugs pa Madhyamaka," *Journal of Indian Philosophy* 11 (1983): 125–45; and David Seyfort Ruegg, "A Kar ma bKa' brgyud work on the Lineages and Traditions of the Indo Tibetan Dbu-Ma (Madhyamaka)," in *Orientalia Iosephi Tucci Memoriae Dicata,* Serie Orientale Roma, LVI, volume 3, ed. G. Gnoli and L. Lanciotti (Rome: IsMEO, 1988), pp. 1249–80.

152 *Lta ba ngan pa thams cad tshar gcod pa'i bstan bcos gnam lcags 'khor lo zhes bya ba go bo bsod nams seng ge zhes bya ba'i dge ba'i bshes gnyen la gdams pa: Wheel of Thunderbolts, A Treatise to Put an End to All Evil Views: Advice to the Spiritual Friend Go bo rab 'byams pa Bsod nams seng ge,* in Rin chen tshe ring, *Dgag lan phyogs bsgrigs,* pp. 519–605.

153 *A Refutation of Those Who Boast of Being Accomplished Ones and Yogis (Grub pa dang rnal 'byor par rlom pa rnams kyi de nyid gsal byed),* a short text of three folios described in TBRC no. W6783.

154 *Zab mo stong pa nyid kyi lta ba la log rtog 'gog par byed pa'i bstan bcos lta ba ngan pa'i mun sel,* part I, *Chen po Shāk mchog pa'i rtsod lan,* pp. 178–385, and part II, *Go bo rab 'byams pa'i rtsod lan,* in Rin chen tshe ring, ed., *Dgag lan phyogs bsgrigs,* pp. 385–514. The *Lta ba ngan pa'i mun sel* was begun by Se ra Rje btsun Chos kyi rgyal mtshan and completed by his student Paṇ chen Bde legs nyi ma (b. sixteenth century).

155 In his *Brilliance of Reasoning: An Ornament to the Purport of Mañjuśrī; 'Jam dbyangs dgongs rgyan rigs pa'i gzi 'bar* (Beijing: Krung go'i bod kyi shes rig dpe skrun khang, 1991), pp. 354–412.

156 On this work of Brag dkar sprul sku, see Pettit, *Mipham's Beacon,* p. 467, n. 54.

157 See his *Rtsod lan blo dman snying gi gdung sel ga bur thig pa'i spun zla* (Mundgod: Drepung Loseling Library Society, 1985).

158 In contemporary times this transmission lineage was preserved and passed down by, for example, Dezhung Rinpoché and Kenpo Appé; see David P. Jackson, *A Saint in Seattle: The Life of the Tibetan Mystic Dezhung Rinpoche* (Boston: Wisdom Publications, 2003), p. 128 passim.

159 On the printing of Gorampa's Collected Works, and role of Kenpo Shenga (Mkhan po Gzhan dga' = Gzhan phan chos kyi snang ba, 1871–1927), Ga Lama Jamgyal Rinpoche (Sga bla ma 'Jam rgyal rin po che, 1870–1940), and Jamyang Loter Wangpo ('Jam dbyangs blo gter dbang po, 1847–1914) in this undertaking, see Jackson, *A Saint in Seattle,* pp. 28, 57–58.

160 Jackson, *A Saint in Seattle,* p. 586, n. 119.

161 *Dbu ma'i zab gnad snying por dril ba'i legs bshad klu grub dgongs rgyan,* in Hor khang Bsod nams dpal 'bar, ed., *Dge 'dun chos 'phel gyi gsung rtsom,* vol. II (Lhasa: Bod ljongs bod yig dpe snying dpe skrun khang, 1990), pp. 271–376. Donald Lopez's translation of this work is in press.

162 *Rtsod yig rigs pa'i gad rgyangs la rnam par dpyad pa bskal pa'i me dpung,* in *Rje btsun shes rab rgya mtsho 'jam dpal dgyes pa'i blo gros kyi gsung rtsom* (Mtsho sngon: Mi rigs dpe skrun khang, 1982), I, pp. 137–309.

163 The work is usually referred to simply as *The Response to the Refutation of Dge 'dun chos 'phel (Dge 'dun chos 'phel gyi dgag lan),* in Dze smad rin po che's *Collected Works, Gsung'bum,* ed. Geshe Thubten Jinpa (Mundgod: Zemey Labrang, 1997), III, pp. 1–270.

164 See E. Gene Smith, *Among Tibetan Texts,* chap. 17.

165 Most notably, Mi pham, but also Bod pa sprul sku.

166 One has only to think of the texts in the last couple of decades that have focused on the contoversy surrounding the practice of the protector deity Rdo rje shugs ldan, a dispute that has had both inter and intra-sectarian implications, on which see Georges B. J. Dreyfus, "The Shuk-Den Affair: Origin of a Controversy," originally published in the *JIABS* 21.2 (1998): 227–70. For a revised version, see http://www.tibet.com/dholgyal/shugden-origins.html#_ftn1.

167 See, for example, a variety of examples in the journal *Jangzhon*. Rakra Rinpoche, "The Consequential Dispute Caused Either by Zurkharpa Lodoe Gyalpo's Failure in Conducting Proper Analysis on the Root text of Tibetan Poetry or His Upholding Other's Misinterpretation," *Jangzhon* 3: pp. 1–23; Sampe Dondrub, "A Dispute of Jangzhon," *Jangzhon* 4: pp. 1–4; and Zurmang Drungpa Tulku Choekyi Gyatso, "A Letter of Criticism," *Jangzhon* 7: pp. 41–42.

168 The discussion of Go rams pa's life that follows is based on the following sources: T. G. Dhongthog Rinpoche, *Byang phyogs thub pa'i rgyal tshab dpal ldan Sa-skya-pa'i bstan pa rin po che ji ltar byung ba'i lo rgyus rab 'byams zhing du snyan pa'i sgra dbyangs zhes bya ba bzhugs so: A History of the Sa-skya-pa Sect of Tibetan Buddhism* (New Delhi: Dhongthog, 1977); the biography of Go rams pa by his disciple and successor, Kong ston Dbang phyug grub, *Rje bla ma'i rnam par thar pa ngo mtshar rin po che'i phreng ba = The biography of Kun-mkhyen Go-rams-pa Bsod-nams Sengge,* ed. by T. G. Dhongthog (Delhi: Dhongthog, 1973); and *A history of Buddhism: Being the Text of Dam pa'i chos kyi byung tshul legs par bshad pa bstan pa rgya mtshor 'jug pa'i gru chen zhes bya ba rtsom 'phro kha skong bcas,* begun by Dkon mchog lhun grub Ngor chen (1497–1557) and completed by Ngor chen Sang rgyas phun sthogs (1649–1705), the twenty-fifth abbot of Ngor Monastery (New Delhi: Ngawang Topgey, 1973). Brief biographies are to be found in *Ming mdzod,* pp. 260–62; and in Dung dkar Blo bzang 'phrin las, *Bod rig pa'i tshig mdzod chen mo = Dung dkar tshig mdzod chen mo* (Beijing: Krung go'i bod rig pa dpe skrung khang, 2002). In the Western literature, Go rams pa's life has been discussed by van der Kuijp, *Contributions,* pp. 116–24; and by Ngawang Jorden, "Buddha-Nature: Through the Eyes of Go rams pa Bsod nams seng ge in Fifteenth-Century Tibet" (Ph.D. Diss., Harvard University, 2003), who relies on nine biographies in his compilation of the details of Go rams pa's life; see Jorden, "Buddha-Nature," p. 42, n. 85, for a list of these texts, seven of which have been collected by Ngag dbang kun dga' bsod nams into a work entitled *Kun mkhyen bsod nams seng ge'i rnam par thar pa dad pa rgya mtsho'i rlabs phreng rnam par g.yo ba.* A one-page account of Go rams pa's life is also to be found in Kunkhyen Gorampa Sonam Seng-ge, *Zhugs gnas kyi rnam gzhag skyes bu mchog gi gsal byed, Illuminating the Holy Saints: Stages of Entrance and Attainment* (Sakya Centre, nd); see also Chobgye Trichen Rinpoche, *The History of the Sakya Tradition: A Feast for the Minds of the Fortunate,* trans. Jennifer Scott (Bristol: Ganesha Press, 1983), p. 32.

169 *Ming mdzod* states that he received *lay* or *upāsaka* ordination from Kun Dga' 'bum at age eight, and that he then dedicated himself to memorizing the five works of Maitreya, the complete *ṭīkās* of Rong ston, and the entirety of G.yag ston's great commentary on the Prajñāpāramitā, though one wonders whether this might be hyperbole.

170 For a history of this title and its relationship to other scholastic titles, see Georges B.J. Dreyfus, *The Sound of Two Hands Clapping* (Berkeley: University of California Press, 2003), pp. 144–45.

171 A short biography of Rong ston (with a discussion of his written work) is found in the foreword to Jackson and Onoda, eds., *Rong-ston on the Prajñā-pāramitā Philosophy,* pp. i–xxii. See also Dhongthog, *Byang phyogs,* folios 113b–117a; and *Ming mdzod,* pp. 1628–29. A brief mention in English of Rong ston's life is also found in the Foreword to the Sarnath edition of his commentary to the *Madhyamakakārikā,* the *Dbu ma rtsa ba'i rnam bshad bzab mo'i de kho na nyid snang ba* (Sarnath: Sakya Students' Union, 1988), pp. 3–4. See also Jorden, "Buddha-Nature," p. 34.

172 Alfonsa Ferrari, *mKhyen brTse's Guide to the Holy Places of Central Tibet,* Serie Orientale Roma, vol. XVI (Rome: IsMEO, 1958), p. 70 and n. 635. Byams chen rab 'byams pa founded this monastery in 1449, and it seems that Go rams pa's own monastery would eventually have some affiliation to Skyed tshal, which acted as the "mother" institution to five monasteries in all; see van der Kuijp, *Contributions,* pp. 120–21.

173 Ferrari, *mKhyen brTse's Guide,* p. 163. *Ming mdzod,* pp. 1122–24. See also van der Kuijp, *Contributions,* p. 120.

174 Dongthog, *Byang phyogs,* folio 107b; Ferrari, *mKhyen brTse's Guide,* n. 468.

175 Ferrari, *mKhyen brTse's Guide,* p. 158. *Ming mdzod,* pp. 449–50.

176 The *Ming mdzod,* p. 261, states that he was ordained at age twenty-seven, with Mus chen as abbot. Jorden, "Buddha-Nature," p. 50, states that the ordination took place in 1454, with Ngor chen as abbot, Mus chen as *slob dpon,* and Sangs rgyas dpal grub as *gsang slob.*

177 Ferrari, *mKhyen brTse's Guide,* p. 158. Go rams pa wrote three short biographical works on this figure. *Ming mdzod* states that it was from this lama that Go rams pa received the *lam 'bras* teachings.

178 On Gung ru Shes rab bzang po, the sixth throne holder of Nalendra, the monastery founded by Rong ston, see David P. Jackson, *The Early Abbots of 'Phan-po Ne-len-dra: The Vicissitudes of a Great Tibetan Monastery in the 15th Century* (Wien: Arbeitskreis für Tibetische und Buddhistische Studien Universität Wien, 1989), pp. 15–16, 45, n. 47.

179 See David P. Jackson, "Madhyamaka Studies among the Early Sa-skya-pas," *The Tibet Journal* 10.2 (1985): 20–34.

180 See Ferrari, *mKhyen brTse's Guide,* p. 158.

181 *Ming mdzod,* p. 261.

182 Ferrari, *mKhyen brTse's Guide,* p. 68, and n. 586. The monastery has been destroyed, but its site is located in present day Danapu (Rta nag phu) county, west of Lhasa, in the TAR. Jorden (*Buddha-Nature,* p. 58) quotes the *bca' yig* of the monastery, written by Go rams pa himself, which gives the date of the founding as 1466. Chobgye Trichen Rinpoche, *History of the Sakya,* p. 20, states that Go rams pa "restored" the monastery at Rta nag.

183 For example, we know that Go rams pa was at Mdo mkhar Chos rdzong in 1469, and at Dga' ba tshal in 1471.

184 Jorden, "Buddha-Nature," pp. 47–48, 58–59, mentions Drung chen Nor bu bzang po as the chief lifelong patron of Go rams pa. Jorden translates the section of the *bca' yig* document for Rta nag gser gling written by Go rams pa, where Go rams pa mentions

a *sprul sku,* Bsod nams chos kyi kun dga' bkra shis rgyal mtshan dpal bzang po, as having procured funding for the building of Gser gling. Jorden explains that this figure was a "scholar of Byams chen" who met Go rams pa at Mus and who acted as an intermediary, requesting that Nor bzang pa fund Go rams pa's building project. Nor bzang pa died in 1466, and given that the work on Rta nag would not be completed for another six or seven years, we must assume that Go rams pa continued to enjoy the patronage of Nor bzang pa's son Don grub rdo rje; see *Dung dkar tshig mdzod,* p. 525. On Nor bu bzang po and his son Don grub rdo rje, see below, and also Giuseppe Tucci, *Deb ther dmar po gsar ma: Tibetan Chronicles by bSod-nams-grags-pa,* vol. I, Serie Orientale Roma, XXIV (Rome: IsMEO, 1971), pp. 221–23, 239. Go rams pa's biographer Kong ston, *rJe'i bla ma rnam par thar pa,* pp. 24–25, also mentions the Rin spungs pa general of Mdo mkhar, G.yung pa tshe dbang, as a patron during this time.

185 Compare to the list of "texts of great renown" *(grags chen bco brgyad)* mentioned in Jackson, *Entrance Gate,* vol. 1, pp. 138, 158.

186 *Ming mdzod,* p. 262, states that he left for Ngor when he was fifty-three, and that he remained there for five years. Jorden, *Buddha-Nature,* pp. 55–56, states that he was inivited in 1481 and actually went in 1482.

187 The colophons of several of his works on the *Hevajra Tantra* tell us that they were written in this period, but they give the place of composition as Rta nag (and not Ngor). Perhaps Go rams pa was travelling back and forth between the two institutions during his tenure as abbot of Ngor, or perhaps he gave lectures on topics related to Hevajra at Ngor, lectures which where then processed into written documents by his scribe, Gzhon nu bzang po, at Rta nag. Moreover, *Dung dkar tshig mdzod,* p. 525, states that he remained on the throne of Ngor for four (as opposed to three) years.

188 The colophon to the text does not mention the date of composition, although it does state that it was written by Go rams pa at Thub bstan rnam rgyal. The printer's colophon states that it was published at Sde dge Lhun grub steng in the earth-monkey year of the fifteenth *rab tses,* that is, 1908.

189 This work forms the basis for much of the discussion of Go rams pa in Peter Della Santina, *Madhyamaka Schools in India* (Delhi: Motilal Banarsidass, 1986).The *Lta ba'i shan 'byed* and the *Dbu ma'i spyi don* are not listed under these titles in the list of Go rams pa's works found in the biography by Kong ston, *Rje'i bla ma'i rnam thar,* p. 38ff., although they might be the texts referred to (p. 39) as the "greater and lesser Madhyamaka digests" *(dbu ma'i stong thun che chung gnyis).*

190 The colophon to the text states that it was composed by Go rams pa at Thub bstan rnam rgyal, but no date for the composition is given. Dzongsar Khyentse Rinpoche has used this text as the basis for a recent series of lectures, a portion of which have been published on the web at http://www.khyentsefoundation.org/publica tions.html.

191 Jorden, "Buddha-Nature," p. 201, knows this text under a slightly different title: *Bsam gzugs 'gog snyoms thod rgal rnams ston pa snyoms 'jug rab gsal.*

192 For an analysis of this text, see van der Kuijp, *Contributions,* p. 122ff.

193 The first chapter of this work has been studied and translated by Jorden in "Buddha-Nature."

194 Jorden, "Buddha-Nature," pp. 205–6.

195 Jackson, *The Early Abbots,* p. 20: a translation from a portion of one of Go rams pa's biographies.

196 Jackson, *The Early Abbots,* p. 20.

197 Kong ston is perhaps best remembered as Go rams pa's biographer although, interestingly, he also composed introductory logic texts—a *blo rig* and *rtags rigs.* Since Go rams pa himself never composed texts of this type, perhaps they were written so as to serve the needs of the then newly established Rta nag gser gling. Kong ston also wrote two synthetic commentaries *(spyi don)*—one on Vinaya and one on pramāṇa.

198 A more extensive list is found in Jorden, "Buddha-Nature," pp. 64–65.

199 See Jorden, "Buddha-Nature," p. 43.

200 This important figure is not usually counted among Go rams pa's students, but we know, for example, that Glo bo mkhan chen was writing at Go rams pa's monastery of Rta nag in 1481; see Smith, *Among Tibetan Texts,* pp. 112–13.

201 See Shing bza' Paṇḍita, *Bod sog chos 'byung,* p. 679: *dpal sa skya'i lha khang chen mo'i mtshan nyid grwa tshang yang 'di'i bshad rgyun las byung/.* Chobgye Trichen Rinpoche, *History of the Sakya,* p. 32, states that Go rams pa actually founded a philosophical college at Sa skya.

202 As David Jackson states, "During his lifetime he had a strong Sa skya pa rival in Shākya mchog ldan; but in the subsequent centuries it was his and not his rival's views that were accepted as definitive"; David P. Jackson, "Commentaries on the Writings of Sa skya Paṇḍita," *Tibet Journal* 8.2 (1983): 15.

203 See Sde srid Sangs rgyas rgya mtsho, *Dga' ldan chos 'byung baiḍurya gser po* (Pe cin: Krung go'i bod kyi shes rig dpe skrun khang, 1991), p. 146ff.

204 Dge 'dun rgya mtsho, the Second Dalai Lama, was born in Rta nag 1475/6. He was believed locally to be the reincarnation of Dge 'dun grub from a very young age, even if he was not formally ordained and admitted to Bkra shis lhun po until he was ten or eleven. See Amy Heller, "The Second Dalai Lama Gendün Gyatso," in Martin Brauen, ed., *The Dalai Lamas: A Visual History* (Zurich: Ethnographic Museum of the University of Zurich, 2005), pp. 43–50.

205 See, for example, Shirō Matsumoto, "Chibetto no Chūgan Shisō—Toku ni 'rihen chūgan setse' wo chūsin ni shite," ("Tibetan Mādhyamika thought, with a special focus on the theory of 'freedom from extremes as the middle view'") *Tōyō Gakujutsu Kenkyū* 21.2 (1982): 161–78.

206 See Stearns, *The Buddha From Dol po,* p. 64.

207 Obviously it was not only the Sa skya pas who were the object of the Jo nang pa and Dga' ldan pa polemical pen. Tsong kha pa and his followers also wrote against the Jo nang pas. We also know that a certain Bka' bzhi pa Rin chen rdo rje, who considered himself a disciple of Tsong kha pa, wrote an important early polemical treatise against the Jo nang pas that was chiefly directed at Nya dbon; see Stearns, *The Buddha from Dolpo,* p. 204, n. 49. From among the theorists of the *emptiness of what is other (gzhan stong)* perspective, it is not a Jo nang pa, but, ironically, a Sa skya pa convert to the gzhan stong view, Shākya mchog ldan, who is remembered for his critique of Tsong kha pa.

208 This is not to say that Rong ston pa was completely silent as regards either Dol po pa or Tsong kha pa. For example, Rong ston pa was known as a critic of the *emptiness of what is other* theory of the Jo nang pas, a fact known to Go rams pa, who cites Rong ston pa in his own critique of Dol po pa in *Distinguishing the Views.* Rong ston pa is also known to have criticized some of the views of Tsong kha pa, although there is more overlap between the views of these two figures than is commonly thought; see José I. Cabezón, "Rong ston Shā kya rgyal msthan on Madhyamaka Thesislessness," in *Tibetan Studies, Proceedings of the International Conference on Tibetan Studies* (Graz, Austria), ed. Helmut Krasser, et. al. (Wien: Verlag der Österreichischen Akademie der Wissenschaften, 1997), pp. 97–105.

209 Dan Martin, citing Cyrus Stearn, mentions three Red mda' ba titles in his list of polemical works—the *Nor bu 'phreng ba,* the *'Gal spong,* and the *Nges don gsal byed.* He also mentions his polemic concerning the Kālacakra, the *Garland of Jewels: An Open Letter to the Holders of the Teachings (Dus kyi 'khor lo'i spyad pa las brtsams te bstan 'dzin rnams la 'phrin du gsol ba nor bu'i phreng ba).*

210 Stag tshang lo tsā ba, usually considered a Sa skya pa, was, despite his tremendous erudition and skill as a polemicist, something of a rogue figure, and it appears that his philosophical views were never accepted as representative of the Sa skya mainstream. His Madhyamaka polemical work, the *Omniscience in Tenets (Grub mtha' kun shes)* appears to be more an offense against the views of opponents (i.e., Tsong kha pa) than a real defense of the Sa skya tradition. Go rams pa's teacher, Gung ru Shes rab bzang po, also had a reputation as a polemicist (on which, see Jackson, *The Early Abbots,* p. 15), but we have no knowledge of any *exoteric* polemical works authored by him. The works of Gung ru ba mentioned in Khenpo Appey's *Sa skya pa'i dkar chag,* for example, are almost all tantric, and among these is one polemical work on Guhyasamāja; see Jackson, *The Early Abbots,* p. 45, n. 47, where the list is given. Finally, Go rams pa's contemporary, the great Shākya mchog ldan (1428–1507), partially filled the role of defender of the Sa skya tradition in areas like epistemology and logic, but perhaps because Shākya mchog ldan adopted Jo nang pa-like Madhyamaka views, he was never seen as truly representative of the Sa skya pa mainstream over all.

211 Giuseppe Tucci, *Tibetan Painted Scrolls* (Kyoto: Rinsen, 1980), p. 254, n. 69, tells us that already in 1435 Don drub rdo rje of the Rin spungs clan, one of Go rams pa's patrons, shifted from being the Phag mo gru pa governor *(dpon chen)* of Bsam grub rtse (i.e., Gzhis ka rtse) to being its ruler. The same thing happened in several other major areas of Gtsang, where Rin spungs pa aristocrats gained de facto independence from the Phag mo gru pas.

212 See Tucci, *Deb ther,* p. 223; and also *Ming mdzod,* pp. 1615–16. See also Tucci, *Tibetan Painted Scrolls,* p. 254, n. 69.

213 See *Ming mdzod,* pp. 1612–13. The Fifth Dalai Lama's history of Tibet states, however, that the patron who was responsible for the building of Thub bstan rnam rgyal, Go rams pa's monastery, was not Don grub rdo rje, but rather another son of Nor bzang pa, namely, Kun tu bzang po; see Ṅag-dBaṅ Blo-bZaṅ rGya-mTSHo, Fifth Dalai Lama, *A History of Tibet,* trans. Zahiruddin Ahmad (Bloomington: Indiana University Research Institute for Inner Asian Studies, 1995), p. 162.

214 *chos lugs sa dkar la mos kyang dge ldan pa la'ang dag snang mdzad/;* Tucci, *Deb ther,* p. 99a, 239.

215 *mga' zhabs kyi sde ldan pa nams sa skya par sgyur ba dang/ dka' bcu pa dge 'dun grub dgon pa 'debs pa'i mkhar las 'di 'gog pa/;* Tucci, *Deb ther,* pp. 99a, 239–40.

216 Bsod nams grags pa, the author of the *Red Annals*, is, of course, a partisan Dga' ldan pa, which would argue in favor of caution when it comes to accepting his account of this meeting between Nor bzang pa and Ngor chen. However, there are other non-Dge lugs historians to whom a rivalry between Ngor chen and Dge 'dun grub pa is known. For example, Gu ru bkra shis, *Chos 'byung*, p. 992, tells us: *rje dge 'dun grub pas bkra shis lhun po btab dus ngor nas chags sdang gi rnam pa byung ba.* "When the Lord Dge 'dun grub pa founded Bkra shis lhun po, attachment and anger arose in Ngor." The Fifth Dalai Lama, relying on Bsod nams grags pa as a source, also mentions this episode. See Ṅag-dBaṅ Blo-bZaṅ rGya-mTSHo, Fifth Dalai Lama, *A History of Tibet*, p. 162. However, the Dalai Lama gives this no credence, calling it "loose talk (based on) false tradition." He does so largely because it was Hor Dpal 'byor bzang po, and not Nor bzang pa, who had control of Bsam grub rtse at this time.

217 It appears that Go rams pa would not have to worry tremendously about the shifting tide of political power struggles as regards the fate of Rta nag, since his monastery remained well within the borders of Rin spungs controlled territory from the time of its founding until well after his death. The same cannot be said of Rong ston's monastery of Na len dra, which was much closer to Lhasa; on which see Jackson, *The Early Abbots*, p. 18ff.

218 The title, "Distinguishing the Views" or "Differentiating Between the Views"—*Lta ba'i shan 'byed*—has parallels to the titles of both earlier and later works of a doxographical (or mixed polemical/doxographical) genre whose goal it was to distinguish between different philosophical (especially, though not exclusively, Madhyamaka) views. The earliest of these is Ye shes sde's *Lta ba'i khyad par*; see D. Seyfort Ruegg, "Autour du *Lta ba'i khyad par* de Ye shes sde (version de touen-houang, Pelliot Tibetain 814)," *Journal Asiatique*, 269 (1981): 207–29. Whether or not the *Lta ba'i khyad par* is the same as a certain *Lta ba'i shan 'byed* of the same author (Ye shes sde) characterized by Shākya mchog ldan as the "first treatise ever composed by a Tibetan," we do not know; see Karmay, *The Great Perfection*, p. 150, n. 66. A later Sa skya pa scholar, Ngag dbang chos grags (1572–1641), attempted a more general and extensive overview of Tibetan philosophical theories in his *Pod chen drug gi 'bel gtam*, full title: *Bod kyi mkhas pa snga phyi dag gi* ***grub mtha'i shan 'byed*** *mtha' dpyod dan bcas pa'i 'bel ba'i gtam skyes dpyod ldan mkhas pa lus rgyan rin chen mdzes pa'i phra tshom bkod pa* (Thim-phu: Kunsang Tobgyel and Mani Dorje, 1979); the same author also composed a work of much narrower scope entitled *Dbu ma thal rang gi* ***shan 'byed*** (TBRC W10279), dealing with the specific issue of the distinction between the Svātantrika and Prāsaṅgika Madhyamaka. A much later example of a work bearing a similar name is to be found among the works of the Rnying ma pa scholar Bod pa sprul sku (1900/1907–59): *Lta grub shan 'byed* (Kheng tu'u: Si khron mi rigs dpe skrun khang, 1996), "Distinguishing Between [the Different Positions Regarding] View and Practice," a work that examines the philosophy of all four schools of Tibetan Buddhism. To my knowledge, there are only two works with the words *Lta ba('i) shan 'byed* in the title: (1) Dol po pa Shes rab rgyal mtshan's (1292–1361) *Lta ba shan 'byed yid kyi mun sel*, on which see below, and (2) a work on the differences between the Sa skya pa and Jo nang pa views on emptiness by a certain Dpal ldan rdo rje, the *Sa jo gnyis kyi* ***lta ba shan 'byed*** *don la rang gi rtogs pa brjod pa* (see TBRC W24129). As the title implies, this latter work is devoted to an examination of the differences between the Sa skya pa and Jo nang pa views.

219 In *Distinguishing the Views*, Go rams pa sees Tsong kha pa's critique of the *yod min med min* view as a critique of his own tradition.

220 See Tsong kha pa, *Byang chub lam rim che ba* (Zi ling: Mtsho sngon mi rigs dpe skrun khang, 1985), 580ff; Tsong kha pa, *The Great Treatise on the Stages of the Path to Enlightenment,* trans. Joshua Cutler, et. al., 3 vols. (Ithaca: Snow Lion, 2002), III, p. 126ff, especially pp. 146, 151, 189, 211, and 216.

221 See Matthew Kapstein, *The 'Dzam thang Edition of the Collected Works of Kun-mkhyen Dol-po-pa Shes-rab rgyal-mtshan: Introduction and Catalogue* (Delhi: Shedrup Books, 1992).

222 *Lta ngan mun sel.* The work occupies 40 folios in volume 2 (*e*), pp. 841–921, of the 'Dzam thang edition (Kapstein catalogue, no. 5). I have yet to compare this text with a work called *Lta ba ngan gsal* found in the one volume ed. of *The Collected Works (gSuṅ 'bum) of Kun-mkhyen Dol-po-pa Ses-rab-rgyal-mtshan (1292–1361),* reproduced from eye copies of prints from the Rgyal-rtse Rdzoṅ blocks preserved at Kyichu Monastery (Paro, Bhutan: 1989), vol. 1. (Kapstein enumeration, no. 7), 37 folios long, pp. 287–361. This latter work may be identical to the *Lta ba mun sel.*

223 For a discussion of Dol po pa's use of the term *shan 'byed,* see Dol po pa's *Bka' bsdu bzhi pa,* in *The Collected Works (Gsung 'bum),* p. 403; Stearns, *Buddha from Dolpo,* pp. 161, 265, n. 118.

224 *Lta ba shan 'byed yid kyi mun sel.* The text is found in vol. 5 (yā) of the 'Dzam thang edition (Kaptsein catalogue, no. 40), and is 21 folios in length, pp. 789–810. Cabezón is planning a more extensive study of this text in the near future.

225 Dol po pa, *Lta ba'i shan 'byed yid kyi mun sel,* p. 791: *de la kha cig rten pa'i rigs/ mtha' bral dbu ma'i don dam byed/ yod pa min zhing med pa'ang min/ rtag pa min zhing chad pa'ang min/ bden min rtzun [rdzun] pa'ang min par grags/ don dam yod pa min na ni/ de nyid rtogs pa'ang yod min 'byung/.*

226 An astute reader will have noticed that Dol po pa's argument rests on his assertion that to claim that the ultimate does not exist means that it is nonexistent. This, of course, would be rejected by the Sa skya pas.

227 That is, it is you, the opponent, who suffers from the contradiction that you accused us of suffering from.

228 Dol po pa, *Lta ba shan 'byed yid kyi mun sel,* pp. 792–93: *de yang yod pa min zhe na/ slar yang dbu ma med mthar thal/ mtha' dbus gang na'ang med pa'i phyir/ 'khor gsum de yang khyod la 'khor/ med pa dag kyang min zhe na/ khyod kyi med min min pa steng/ med pa dag ni khegs ma khegs/ khegs na med pa min par'gyur/ des na yod pa cis mi 'gyur/ dgag gnyis rnal ma go min nam/ dgag pa bkag pas bsgrub pa dang/ bsgrub pa bkag pas dgag pa dag/ 'grub pa don gyi byas lugs dang/ mkhas pa'i gsung lugs dag la 'byung/.*

229 Of course, one cannot simply assume that Tsong kha pa borrowed this argument directly from a text like Dol po pa's *Lta ba'i shan 'byed.* As likely is the scenario in which views like the ones here expressed by Dol po pa were in wide circulation. In a culture where scholars had extensive face to face contact—such as in the debate courtyards of the great monasteries—it is as plausible to see arguments like this circulating orally and being picked up promiscuously by anyone who found them convincing.

230 Julia Kristeva, "Word, Dialogue, and the Novel," in *The Kristeva Reader,* ed. Toril Moi (New York: Columbia University Press), p. 37. Roland Barthes, in "Theory of the Text," puts it this way: "Any text is a new tissue of past citations. Bits of code,

formulae, rhythmic models, fragments of social languages, etc. pass into the text and are redistributed within it, for there is always language before and around the text. Intertextuality, the condition of any text whatsoever, cannot, of course, be reduced to a problem of sources and influences." Cited in Corns, *The Literature of Controversy,* p. 2.

231 For an insightful analysis of the role that differentiation or distinction plays in philosophical argumentation, see David Goodwin, "Distinction, Argumentation and the Rhetorical Construction of the Real," *Argumentation and Advocacy* 27 (1991): 141–58.

232 These are Sa chen Kun dga' snying po (1092–1158), Bsod nams rtse mo (1142–82) and Rje btsun Grags pa rgyal mtshan (1147–1216), Sa paṇ and 'Phags pa Blo gros rgyal mtshan (1235–80); see David Jackson, "Madhyamaka Studies Among the Early Sa-skya-pas," *Tibet Journal* 10.2 (1985): 21.

233 See Jackson, *The Early Abbots of 'Phan-po Na-len-dra,* p. 15.

234 Of course, once the construction was completed, we know that Go rams pa had many duties: instituting the new curriculum of studies and then teaching it, creating a liturgical schedule for the monastery, blessing all of the new images, and so forth.

235 van der Kuijp, *Contributions,* p. 120.

236 James M. Jasper, "The Politics of Abstractions: Instrumental and Moralist Rhetorics in Public Debate," *Social Research* 59.2 (1992): 315–44, discusses what he calls "God-terms," that is, the "universal trump cards plunked down to win an argument." These are theories/principles/concepts so fundamental to a culture or worldview that they are axiomatic, as it were. When an argument can be cast so that one's own side becomes the upholder of the "God-term," then victory is guaranteed. Clearly, the notion of *middle way* was for Buddhists such a God-term.

237 Only a thorough study of the work of Go rams pa's predecessors can tell us the extent to which the term was used in this way prior to him, and therefore the extent to which Go rams pa's use of the term as an appellation for a unique interpretive tradition is or is not innovative. Jackson, for example, cites a passage from Sa skya Paṇḍita that uses the term *spros bral* in a way that seems central to the latter's vision of the Madhyamaka; see Jackson, "Madhyamaka Studies," p. 27. The term was also used widely by non-Sa skya pas, and not only in sūtra contexts but in tantric ones as well; see, for example, Dung dkar rin po che, *Tshig mdzod,* p. 1312, where "the lack of proliferations" *(spros bral)* is defined as follows: "From among the four yogas, the second is the yoga without proliferations. This is the realization that one's own mind lacks the proliferation of the three—arising, cessation, abiding. The Lord Rgod tshang pa claimed that it corresponded to the sūtra system's path of seeing, and to the 'extremely joyful,' the first of the ten bhūmis" (my translation); see also Dung dkar Rin po che's definition of "resting in a state of nonconceptuality that is without proliferations" *(spros med mi rtog ngang la sdod), Tshig mdzod,* p. 1312.

238 Concerning the Sa skya pas' Madhyamaka outlook, see Jackson, "Madhyamaka Studies." The later Dge lugs doxographer Thu'u bkwan Blo bzang chos kyi nyi ma (1737–1802) has a great deal to say on the question of the Sa skya pa's philosophical view *(lta ba),* though Go rams pa is never mentioned by name in his discussion. Regarding doctrinal affiliation, Thu'u bkwan identifies Sa skya Paṇḍita and Rong ston pa as being primarily Svātantrika in their viewpoint, while the lord Red mda'

ba he considers a Prāsaṅgika. However, David Jackson, "Madhyamaka Studies," pp. 27–28, has argued that although Sa paṇ studied both Svātantrika and Prāsaṅgika sources, his philosophical outlook is closer to the Prāsaṅgika. Jackson, however, also points out that Sa paṇ upholds a form of *tantric Madhyamaka* theory that appears to be a third option, different from either the Svātantrika or Prāsaṅgika. Thu'u bkwan also states that Shākya mchog ldan began as a Madhyamaka, became a Cittamātra, and eventually became a Jo nang pa. He continues that many other Sa skya pas have been attracted to the Rdzogs chen view, but adds that the Sa skya pas' own special philosophical outlook is the *nongrasping of clarity and emptiness (gsal stong 'dzin med)* or the *indivisibility of samsara and nirvana ('khor 'das dbyer med)*. This view, in turn, has sūtra and tantra versions. The sūtra version, he states, has a tradition based on Nāgārjuna's instructions and one based on Maitreya's. Regardless of the accuracy of Th'u kwan's exposition of Sa skya pa doxography, it is clear that Go rams pa's exposition of the Madhyamaka in the *Lta ba'i shan 'byed* is very close to the Nāgārjuna version of the sūtra branch mentioned in Thu'u bkwan's text, implying of course that Go rams pa's view would fall squarely within (what Thu'u bkwan, at least, understands to be) the Sa skya pa mainstream. See *Thu'u bkwan grub mtha'* [Lan kru'u: Kan su'u mi rigs dpe skrun khang, 1984], p. 199ff. See also Chab spel Tshe brtan phun tshogs and Nor brang O rgyan, *Bod kyi lo rgyus rags rim g.yu yi phreng ba* (Lhasa: Bod ljongs dpe rnying dpe skrung khang, 1989), p. 707, which gives the same general divisions found in Thu'u bkwan. An unattributed verse cited in the latter text—a verse that is said to encapsulate the Sa skya pa sūtra "view"—is worth mentioning here because, as the reader will see, it is very much in accord with Go rams pa's own views. The verse reads: *bsod nams min pa dang por zlog// bar du bdag ni zlog pa dang// tha mar lta zhig kun zlog pa// gang gis shes de mkhas pa yin//;* "At the beginning, when one is without merit, one overturns [attachment to the world]. In the middle, one overturns the self. At the end, one overturns all views. Those who understand this are scholars." The authors of the *Bod kyi lo rgyus* gloss the last line as follows: *tha mar lta ba kun bzlog pa la bden 'dzin gyi spros pa gcod pa dang/ bden med kyi spros pa gcod pa gnyis so;* "To overturn all views at the end [means] both to do away with the proliferations that are the grasping at truth, and to do away with the proliferation of truthlessness."

239 As David Jackson shows, several of the early Sa skya pa masters either studied Madhyamaka at Gsang phu or else studied under teachers who were affiliated with Gsang phu; see Jackson, "Madhyamaka Studies," pp. 21–23.

240 Aside from the Sa skya pa scholars mentioned in the colophon, and aside from Dol po pa and Tsong kha pa, his chief opponents in this work, Go rams pa additionally either mentions, paraphrases or cites Zhang Thang sag pa Ye shes 'byung gnas (b. eleventh century), Rma bya Byang chub brtson 'grus (d. 1185), Gzad pa ring mo, Lce sgom Shes rab rdo rje, G.yag ston Sangs rgyas 'phel (1348–1414), Red mda' ba Gzhon nu blo gros (1349–1412), Shes bya kun rig (i.e., Rong ston pa), Rje btsun Grags pa rgyal mtshan (1147–1216), and (with obvious disapproval) Bla ma Dbu ma pa (fifteenth century). Thu'u bkwan, *Grub mtha'*, p. 189, makes a cryptic remark concerning the area of Thang sag. Citing Karma dkon gzhon, he says that there was nothing but the corpse of a Madhyamaka left in Thang sag before Red mda' ba resuscitated it, and that the fact that scholars and fools alike have a Madhyamaka to talk about at all, something to label with different names—X Madhyamaka, Y Madhyamaka—is due to the kindness of Red mda' ba.

241 This distinction is also known to Shākya mchog ldan, who uses it to doxographical ends in his *History of the Madhyamaka (Dbu ma'i byung tshul).*

242 Although *Distinguishing the Views* employs formal *consequence-reason (thal phyir)* arguments, it is not as dense or abstract as other works that consist exclusively of strings of such formal arguments. An example of that latter, more formal and logically dense type of literature is the genre of monastic textbooks known as *Critical Analyses (mtha' dpyod).*

243 On the actual genealogy of Dol po pa's views, see Cyrus Stearns, "Dolpo-pa Shes-rab rgyal-mtshan and the Genesis of Gzhan stong in Tibet," *Asiatische Studien/Études Asiatiques* 49.4 (1995): 829–54.

244 That is, the two rational forms (the selflessnesses of person and of phenomena) and the true ultimate that is the freedom from extremes.

245 Only a detailed comparison of Stag tshang pa's and Go rams pa's works will allow us to determine the overlap between the two views. Clearly there are similarities, but there appear to be divergences as well. It is significant that Go rams pa never mentions Stag tshang lo tsā ba in the *Lta ba'i shan 'byed,* perhaps because of the Stag tshang pa's extremist views concerning the nature and function of valid cognitions *(tshad ma).* See Hopkins, *Maps,* p. 527ff.

246 See Cabezón, *Dose,* p. 397, n. 23. D. Seyfort Ruegg, *Two Prolegomena to Madhyamaka Philosophy: Candrakīrti's Prasannapadā Madhyamakavṛttih on Madhyamakakārikā I.1, and Tsong kha pa bLo bzang Grags pa/ Rgyal tshab Dar ma rin chen's dKa' gnad/gnas kyi zin bris, Annotated translations,* Studies in Indian and Tibetan Madhyamaka Thought, Part 2 (Wien: Arbeitskreis für Tibetische und Buddhistische Studien Universität Wien, 2002).

247 For a comparative analysis of this issue among a variety of Indian and Tibetan philosophers, see Alex Berzin, "Eliminating the Two Sets of Obscurations in Sutra and Highest Tantra According to the Nyingma and Sakya," http://www.berzin-archives.com/tantra/eliminating_2_sets_obscurations.html.

248 See Hopkins, *Maps,* p. 516ff.

249 See Pettit, *Mipham's Beacon of Certainty,* pp. 136–40.

250 G. Thomas Tanselle, "Books, Canons, and the Nature of Dispute," *Common Knowledge* 1.1 (1992): 78–91.

251 Tanselle, "Books, Canons and the Nature of Disputes," p. 80.

Notes to the Translation

1 This verse employs several classical Indian mythological motifs in a metaphorical elaboration of the Buddha's relationship to humanity. The Buddha is the sun; his enlightened activity, its rays; his gnosis, the actual orb of the sun; his compassion, the horses, the active force that pulls the chariot on which the sun is said to ride; and the mountains, each of different heights, the hosts of disciples, each with their own level of spiritual maturity. Similar images are to be found in the RGV (IV, 58–66); Jikido Takasaki, *A Study of the Ratnagotravibhāga (Uttaratantra), Being a Treatise on the Tathāgatagarbha Theory of Mahāyāna Buddhism* (Rome: IsMEO, 1966), pp. 369–71. In BRKT, 1b, Rong ston pa begins his text with an almost identical verse.

2 In the classical system of Buddhist textual exegesis as expounded in such works as the *Vyākhyāyukti* of Vasubandhu, this verse, and the next one, constitute what is called the "motivation for" or "necessity of" (Tib., *dgos pa*, Skt., *prayojana*) the composition. It is the need to decide between the diversity of Madhyamaka interpretations that leads Go rams pa to compose the present text. See José I. Cabezón, "Vasubandhu's *Vyākhyāyukti* on the Authenticity of the Mahāyāna Sūtras," in *Texts in Contexts: Traditional Hermeneutics in South Asia,* ed. J. Timm (Albany: SUNY Press, 1992), pp. 221–43; and Michael M• Broido, "A Note on dGos-'brel," *The Journal of the Tibet Society* 3 (1983): 5–19. See also BRKT, 1b–2a.

3 This line can be seen as constituting what is called in traditional Tibetan oral exegesis the "commitment to compose (the text)" *(rtsom par dam bca' ba)*. Explicitly stating the intention to compose the text at the outset is said to create the karmic cause for seeing the composition through to the end—the commitment of the sage, once made, being like writing on stone.

4 These are the Vaibhāṣika, Sautrāntika, Cittamātra (i.e., Yogācāra), and Madhyamaka (the last being understood here as the philosophical school that was systematized by Nāgārjuna and his followers). The first two schools are considered Hīnayāna philosophical schools, and the latter two, Mahāyāna schools. From the viewpoint of the Madhyamaka, the first three are considered *realist (dngos por smra ba)* schools, since they advocate the real or true existence of phenomena. The Madhyamaka is a *non-realist (dngos po ma yin par smra ba)* or *anti-essentialist (ngo bo nyid med par smra ba)* school because it repudiates the fact that things exist by virtue of their own nature. See Katsumi Mimaki, ed., "Le *Grub mtha' rnam bzag rin chen phreṅ ba* de Dkon mchog 'jigs med dbaṅ po (1728–1791)," *Zinbun*, 14 (1977): 55–112; as well as his *Blo gsal grub mtha'* (Kyoto: Zinbun Kagaku Kenkyusyo, Université de Kyoto, 1982); also, Geshe Lhundub Sopa and Jeffrey Hopkins, *Cutting Through Appearances: Practice and Theory of Tibetan Buddhism* (Ithaca: Snow Lion Publications, 1990); and José I. Cabezón, "The Canonization of Philosophy and the Rhetoric of *Siddhānta* in Indo-

Tibetan Buddhism," in *Buddha Nature,* ed. Paul Griffiths and John Keenan (Reno, NV: Buddhist Books International, 1991), pp. 7–26.

5 *Bodhicaryāvatāra* (IX, 4ab). See Vidushekhara Bhattachārya, ed., *Bodhicaryāvatāra* (BCA), Bibliothetca Indica, no. 280 (Calcutta: The Asiatic Society, 1960), p. 185; Louis de la Vallée Poussin, trans., *Bodhicaryāvatāra: Introduction a la Practique des Futurs Bouddhas* (Paris: Librarie Bloud et Cie, 1907), p. 111; Ernst Steinkellner, *Śāntideva: Entritt in das Leben zur Erleuchtung* (Dusseldorf: Diederichs, 1981), p. 114; Kate Crosby and Andrew Skilton, *Śāntideva's Bodhicaryāvatāra* (Oxford and New York: Oxford University Press, 1995), p. 115.

6 It is interesting that Go rams pa should accuse the realists of falling not only into the extreme of eternalism, which is to be expected, but into the extreme of nihilism as well. Rong ston pa (BRKT, 3a) explains that they fall into the latter extreme by virtue of the fact that they repudiate emptiness or, in his words, because "they consider the repudiation of essentialism to be nihilism"; see also José I. Cabezón, *A Dose of Emptiness* (Albany: State University of New York Press, 1992), pp. 107–8.

7 The enlightenment of a śrāvaka, of a pratyekabuddha, and of a buddha. For Tibetan scholastics, the *locus classicus* for the doctrine of the three forms of enlightenment is the *Abhisamayālaṃkāra* and its commentaries; Ramaśaṅkaratripāṭhi, ed., *Abhisamayālaṃkāravṛttiḥ Sphuṭārtha* (Sarnath: Central Institute for Higher Tibetan Studies, 1977). For a translation of the root text, see Edward Conze, *Abhisamayālaṃkāra: Introduction and Translation from Original Tibetan Text with Sanskrit-Tibetan Index,* Serie Orientale Roma 6 (Rome: IsMEO, 1954); and for a translation of the first seven chapters of Haribhadra's commentary, see Alex Naughton, *The Buddhist Path to Omniscience* (Ph.D. diss., University of Wisconsin—Madison, 1989). See also E. Obermiller, and T. Stcherbatsky, *Abhisamayālaṃkāra-Prajñāpāramitā-upadesa-śāstra, The Work of the Bodhisattva Maitreya* (1929; repr., Delhi: Sri Satguru Publications, 1992); and E. Obermiller, *The Doctrine of the Prajñāpāramitā as Exposed in the Abhisamayālaṃkāra of Maitreya,* Acta Orientalia 11 (1932), pp. 1–133, 334–54.

8 Go rams pa, unlike Tsong kha pa, believes that the distinction between Svātantrika Mādhyamikas and Prāsaṅgika Mādhyamikas is more a difference in style/emphasis than in substance. According to Go rams pa, who follows his teacher Rong ston pa on this point, the differences between Svātantrikas and Prāsaṅgikas is one of emphasis in regard to logical strategy. For both of these scholars, *svatantra* forms of reasoning *(rang rgyud kyi rtags)* are accepted at the nominal or conventional level, and repudiated at the ultimate level, by both the Svātantrikas *and* Prāsaṅgikas. This, as we shall see, goes counter to the position of Tsong kha pa and his followers. For Rong ston pa's treatment of this issue see, e.g., BTN, 31–41, but especially 40: *thal rang gnyis su g.yes par bshad pa'i don ma rtogs par lta ba bzang ngan gyi bye brag gis 'byed pa ni 'phags pa yul gyi dbu ma smra ba chen po dag gi lta ba la sgro 'dogs bskur 'debs su smra ba yin pas/ mchil ma'i thal ba bzhin du dor bar bya'o/ gzhung gi bshad tshul cung zad mi 'dra ba tsam gyis kyang khyad par phyed pa ma yin;* see also BRKT, 97. Mkhas grub rje attacks this view at several points in his *Stong thun chen mo;* see, e.g., Cabezón, *Dose of Emptiness,* p. 153, where he states that those who hold such a view "have had their minds and eyes affected by the poisonous waters of jealousy," and especially pp. 173–80, 266. The view being espoused by Go rams pa—that doxographical distinctions among the great Mahāyāna scholars of India exist only on the surface—has led Cabezón to classify Go rams pa and his teacher Rong ston pa as "soft doxographers"; see José I.

Cabezón, "Two Views on the Svātantrika-Prāsaṅgika Distinction in Fourteenth Century Tibet," in *The Svātantrika-Prāsaṅgika Distinction: What Difference Does a Difference Make?,* ed. Sara L. McClintock and Georges B. J. Dreyfus (Boston: Wisdom Publications, 2003), pp. 289–315.

9 Go rams pa uses *Dol bu ba* rather than the (more common) *Dol po pa.* We have used Dol po pa throughout the rest of the translation to conform to modern scholarly usage. On the life of Dol po pa Shes rab rgyal mtshan (1292–1361), see Cyrus Stearns, *The Buddha from Dolpo: A Study of the Life and Thought of the Tibetan Master Dolpopa Sherab Gyaltsen* (Albany: SUNY, 1999), which also contains an excellent overview of his doctrinal views, as well as translations of two important texts; also Jeffrey Hopkins, *Emptiness in the Mind-Only School of Buddhism: Dynamic Responses to Dzong-ka-ba's Essence of Eloquence I* (Berkeley: University of California Press, 1999), pp. 47–55. The collected works of Dol po pa have recently been found and published in India (see Introduction); Matthew Kapstein's introductory volume is especially valuable as a guide to this vast corpus. It is difficult to say which of Dol po pa's extensive writings Go rams pa used in compiling the following synopsis without more detailed research, although it would seem that they probably included the latter's monumental work, the *Ri chos nges don rgya mtsho* (RCNG), his shorter doctrinal condensation, the "Fourth Council," *Bka' bsdu bzhi pa* (KDZP), translated in Stearns, *Buddha from Dolpo,* and perhaps others of his Madhyamaka-related works, like the *Bden gnyis gsal ba'i nyi ma,* the *Nges don mthar thug de kno na nyid gsal byed,* and, of course, the *Lta ba mun gsal* and *Lta ba shan 'byed.* See also S. K. Hookham, *The Buddha Within: Tathāgatagarbha Doctrine According to the Shentong Interpretation of the Ratnagotravibhāga* (Albany: SUNY Press, 1991).

10 See, e.g., RCNG, 192ff. On the place of the three-nature doctrine in Dol po pa's thought, see Stearns, *Buddha from Dolpo,* pp. 254–55, n. 44. Jeffrey Hopkins, *Emptiness in the Mind-Only School,* pp. 55, 108–10, 129, 188, and 226, discusses and translates Tsong kha pa's criticism of Dol po pa's views on this matter.

11 See Dol po pa's "A Sun Clarifying the Two Truths," *Bden gnyis gsal ba'i nyi ma,* which deals extensively with this topic. Concerning Dol po pa's views about the relationship between the two forms of emptiness and the two truths, see KDZP, 366; Stearns, *Buddha from Dolpo,* p. 129.

12 Also called a "non-affirming negation," it is a negation that implies no positive thing in its wake. Dol po pa will maintain that the real ultimate truth is a form of emptiness that *does* imply something positive; on forms of negation, see Jeffrey Hopkins, *Meditation on Emptiness* (London: Wisdom Publications, 1983), pp. 721–27.

13 These characterizations of the emptiness of own nature *(rang stong)* are derived from the Kālacakra and its commentarial tradition. For an interesting gloss on the expressions "nihilistic" and "inanimate" emptiness in a passage from Red mda' ba's commentary to the Kālacakra, see Stearns, *Buddha from Dolpo,* pp. 58–59.

14 Dol po pa's discussion concerning which of the Buddha's teachings are definitive *(nges don)* and which provisional *(drang don)* is found, for example, in RCNG, 135, 173ff.; see also KDZP, 393–95; Stearns, *Buddha from Dolpo,* pp. 152–54. The early Dol po pa, it seems, follows the *Saṃdhinirmocana Sūtra,* which he cites at length in RCNG, on this issue. He says (RCNG, 177) that "in the second turning (i.e., in the Perfection of Wisdom Sūtras), for a special purpose *(dgos pa'i dbang gis),* what is not empty of self-nature (that is, the ultimate) is taught to be empty of self-nature. [In

that turning,] things are not well distinguished, the internal contradictions are not resolved. For these and various other reasons [the second turning] is said to be surpassable, temporary, provisional, and an object of dispute." It would seem, however, that Dol po pa changed his views by the time he wrote his later KDZP, since in that latter text he states that the second-turning sūtras teach principally the emptiness of other-nature *(gzhan stong).*

15 For a discussion of Nāgārjuna's philosophical works, see D. Seyfort Ruegg, *The Literature of the Madhyamaka School of Philosophy in India* (Wiesbaden: Otto Harrassowitz, 1981), pp. 4–47; and Cabezon, *Dose of Emptiness*, pp. 78–81, 430–32, nn. 182–97.

16 See, for example, RCNG, 82ff.

17 The four forms of purification are explained in the *Mahāyānasaṃgraha* (P vol. 112, 224) as follows, "Purification can be [related to] essence, to lack of stains, to the path, and to a referent. All pure objects can be subsumed into these four catgeories." *dag pa de ni rang bzhin dang/ dri ma med dang lam dang dmigs/ rnam par dag pa'i chos kyi rnams/ rnam pa bzhi pos bsdus pa yin/.* See also É. Lamotte, ed. and trans., *La somme du grand vehicule d'Asaṅga (Mahāyānasaṃgraha)* [Louvain: Université de Louvain, 1973], ch. II, para. 26 (vol. 1, p. 37ff.; vol. 2, p. 120ff.). According to Gung thang, the essential purity of things refers to their emptiness *(stong nyid)*; purity as the lack of stains refers to the truth of cessation *('gog bden)*; purity related to the path refers to the truth of the path *(lam bden)*; and that related to a referent refers to the Mahāyāna *piṭaka (theg chen gyi sde gnod)*; see his *Drang nges mchan,* in *The Collected Works of Gun-thang Dkon-mchog-bstan-pa'i-sgron me* (New Delhi: Ngawang Gelek Demo, 1972), 2, p. 873ff.

18 *Prajñāpāramitāpiṇḍārtha* (i.e., *Prajñāpāramitāsaṃgraha*), attributed to Dignāga, vv. 28b–29b. P vol. 146, 170. Toh no. 3809, Shes phyin *pha,* 293b. See G. Tucci, "Minor Sanskrit Texts on the Prajñāpāramitā," *Journal of the Royal Asiatic Society of Great Britain and Ireland* (1947): 53–75. The present citation corresponds to v. 29. See also E. Frauwallner, "Dignāga, Sein Werk und Seine Entwicklung," WZKSO 3 (1959): 142.

19 Dol po pa and his followers are not the only Tibetans to make such a claim. For example, it would appear that Cha pa (or Phya pa) Chos kyi seng ge (1109–69) adhered to a similar position, albeit for different reasons than Dol po pa. See Jeffrey Hopkins, *Maps of the Profound: Jam-yang-shay-ba's Great Exposition of Buddhist and Non-Buddhist Views on the Nature of Reality* (Ithaca, NY: Snow Lion Publications, 2003), p. 745ff.; Guy Newland, *The Two Truths in the Mādhyamika Philosophy of the Geluk-ba Order of Tibetan Buddhism* (Ithaca: Snow Lion, 1992), pp. 28–29, 90, and 276–77, n. 44.

20 The doctrine that the ultimate is empty of all other natures, but not empty of its own nature—the so-called *gzhan stong* doctrine—is of course one of Dol po pa's more controversial theses, treated in one form or another in many of his writings. See, e.g., RCNG 195: *kun brtags dang gzhang dbang gis stong pa'i chos nyid yongs grub don dam du yod par gsungs pa'i phyir don dam gzhang stong stong nyid du legs par grub po/*; "The real—that is, reality—which is empty of the imputed and the dependent, is taught to exist ultimately; that is why the ultimate exists as the emptiness of what is other." An interesting summary is also to be found in the Jo nang pa chapter of the *Thu'u bkwan grub mtha'* (Lan kru'u: Kan su'u mi rigs dpe skrun khang, 1989), 212–33; also available in *The Collected Works of Thu'u bkwan blo-bzang-chos-kyi-nyi-ma* (New

Delhi: Ngawang Gelek Demo, 1969), vol. II (*kha*), 242ff.; David Seyfort Ruegg, "A School of Buddhist Ontologists According to the *Grub mtha' śel gyi me loṅ*," *Journal of the Association of Oriental Studies* 83 (1963): 74ff. See also Seyfort Ruegg, *La théorie du Tathāgata-garbha et du Gotra* (Paris: École Française d'Extrême Orient, 1969), p. 325ff. and n. 142; Sgra tshad pa Rin chen rnam rgyal, DZGG, 166; Klong rdol bla ma, *Tibetan Buddhist Studies* (Mussoorie: Dalama, 1963) 1 237ff.; M. Broido, "The Jo-nang-pas on Madhyamaka: A Sketch," *Tibet Journal* 14.1 (1989); S. K. Hookham, *The Buddha Within*, p. 15ff.; Stearns, *Buddha from Dolpo*, p. 3ff.

21 Lists like these, which give synonyms of the *tathāgatagarbha*, are found throughout RCNG, e.g., 11, 14, 46–47, 59–60, 106, etc.; and throughout KDZP, e.g., 395; Stearns, *Buddha from Dolpo*, p. 154. The term "possessing the best of all qualities," *sarvākāravaropetā*, MVy 504, is, for example, found as the last of the 60 good qualities of the Buddha's speech; see also see P. L. Vaidya, ed., *Aṣṭasāhasrikā Prajñāpāramitā* (Darbhanga: Mithila Institute, 1960), p. 183; and RGV (I, 92) and (II, 11); Takasaki, *A Study*, pp. 264, 317.

22 MVy 119–28; RCNG, 51, quoting the *Mahānirvāṇa Sūtra*.

23 MVy 130–34; RCNG, 51, quoting the *Mahānirvāṇa Sūtra*.

24 MVy 235–67; RCNG, 199, quoting the *Mahānirvāṇa Sūtra*.

25 MVy 268–349; RCNG, 199; quoting the *Mahānirvāṇa Sūtra*.

26 This parable is found in chapter 22 of the *Avataṃsaka Sūtra* (LK, vol. 44, *nga*, f. 161b–163a). Bu ston, *Bde gshegs nying po gsal ba'i rgyan*, in *Collected Works*, ed. Lokesh Candra (New Delhi: International Academy of Indian Culture, 1965–1971), pp. 8–11, quotes the same sūtra. There he explains that the term *ri mo'i gzhi chen po* used in the sūtra was rendered by Rngog lo tsā ba as *dar yug chen po;* the passage is translated by Seyfort Ruegg, *Le traité sur le Tathāgatagarbha de Bu ston* (Paris: École Française d'Extrême Orient, 1973), p. 73ff. See also Lambert Schmithausen's discussion in "Zu D. S. Rueggs Buch *La Théorie du Tathāgatagarbha et du Gotra*," in WZKSO (1973), p. 131ff. Dol po pa mentions this as one of the similes of the intended meaning of the doctrine in KDZP, 397–98; Stearns, *Buddha from Dolpo*, pp. 156, 265, n. 111. See also RCNG, 48–51, where Dol po pa discusses the passage from *Ratnagotravibhāgavṛtti* related to this. For a translation of this portion of the *Ratnagotravibhāghavṛtti*, see Takasaki, *A Study*, pp. 189–92; for the Tibetan, Zuiryu Nakamura, ed., *Theg pa chen po rgyud bla ma'i bstan bcos kyi rnam par bshad pa thogs med gyis mdzad pa* in *Zō-Wa taiyaku Kukyō ichijō hōshōron kenkyū (Ratnagotravibhāga)* (Tokyo: Suzuki Gakujutsu Zaidan, 1967), 41, 43–45. In RCNG, 51–52, Dol po pa continues the discussion, relying this time on the *Mahānirvāṇa Sūtra*.

27 *Tathāgatagarbha Sūtra* (P vol. 36), 241–43; RGV (I, 96–97); Takasaki, *A Study*, p. 269ff. See also Seyfort Ruegg, *Le traité*, p. 71; and RCNG, 4–6.

28 An explanation of the *tathāgatagarbha* in terms of these and the following analogies, based on the *Mahāparinirvāṇa Sūtra*, is found in Dol po pa's RCNG, 46–47. See also Dol po pa's comments in KDZP, 375–77, 395; Stearns, *Buddha from Dolpo*, pp. 135–37, 154; and the *Gaṇḍavyūha* citation in Stearns, *Buddha from Dolpo*, p. 256, n. 51. On the use of these terms in the Pāli and Indian Sanskrit sources, see T.W. Rhys Davids, ed., *The Pāli Text Society's Pāli-English Dictionary* (London: Pāli Text Society, 1972), p. 85; and F. Edgerton, *Buddhist Hybrid Sanskrit Dictionary* (1953; repr., Delhi: Motilal Banasidass, 1972), p. 491. On permanent *(nitya)*, stable

(dhruva), and eternal *(śaśvata),* see Nakamura, *Rgyud bla ma'i rnam bshad,* pp. 53 and 54ff.; and MVy, nos. 7284–86. On the quality of unchangeablility *(a[vi]pariṇāmadharma),* see Nakamura, *Rgyud bla ma'i rnam bshad,* p. 41ff.; and MVy 7287.

29 The association of the *tathāgatagarbha* with the ultimate and with a self is found, e.g., in RGV (I, 35, and 37–38). Of course, claims such as this have brought charges that the view is non-Buddhist. This in turn has caused those who speak of "the perfection of the higher self," "pure self," "the sphere of the self," "great self," etc.—as Dol po pa, following RGV, does—to defend themselves against such charges; see, e.g., RCNG, 68–69, 76–78.

30 Concerning the scriptural sources on which Dol po pa relied, see Stearns, *Buddha from Dolpo,* pp. 178–79, nn. 12–13.

31 LK 148, vol. 57 (*da*), 299bff.; this text is part of the *'Phags pa de bzhin gshegs pa'i snying rje chen po nges par bstan pa,* Toh no. 147. See also Seyfort Ruegg, *Le traité,* p. 7.

32 In Toh no. 147. The work is cited, e.g., in RCNG, 19. See also Seyfort Ruegg, *Le traité,* p. 23.

33 Toh no. 92; the work is cited, e.g., in RCNG, 25.

34 Toh no. 258. This is the first sūtra cited in RCNG, 4, and is quoted extensively thereafter, e.g., 15, etc; for a discussion of the *Uttaratantra*'s use of this sūtra, see RCNG, 22–23. See also Ruegg, *Le traité,* p. 23.

35 Cited in RCNG, 32, 263, 298–99.

36 Toh no. 222. Cited, e.g., in RCNG, 24.

37 Toh no. 100.

38 Toh no. 91.

39 Toh no. 213. Dol po pa cites this sūtra extensively in RCNG, 54ff. and 181ff. See also Seyfort Ruegg, *Le traité,* p. 23.

40 Toh nos. 119–21. Cited extensively in RCNG, e.g., 6–7, 14, 21, 45, 51, 187. See also Seyfort Ruegg, *Le traité,* p. 24.

41 On the five works of Maitreya, see Stearns, *Buddha from Dolpo,* p. 179, n. 14. Dol po pa believed that the last three works of Maitreya *(Byams chos spyi ma gsum)* are the works that teach the real *(yongs grub)* to be a positive, true thing *(yāng dag pa).* Lists of the last three works vary in Tibetan philosophical literature. According to most Dge lugs pa sources, they are the *Uttaratantra,* mentioned here, the *Sūtrālaṃkāra,* and the *Abhisamayālaṃkāra;* see Cabezon, *Dose,* p. 421, n. 66. In Dol po pa, however, the *Abhisamayālaṃkāra* is replaced by the *Dharmadharmatāvibhaṅga.* In RCNG, 193–95, Dol po pa explains how the doctrine of the ultimate as empty of what is other is also found in the *Sūtrālaṃkāra,* in the *Dharmadharmatāvibhaṅga,* and in the *Madhyāntavibhaṅga.* If *this* is the list of Maitreya's three last works, however, it would seem to leave no room for the *Uttaratantra.* See Stearns, *Buddha from Dolpo,* pp. 146, 258, nn. 65–66; and S. K. Hookham, *The Buddha Within,* pp. 149–50, 268, 325–26, for an alternate list.

42 See, e.g., RCNG, 191, where Dol po pa states that "Ārya Asaṅga also advocates that the proper way of positing emptiness—in terms of the distinction between

self-emptiness and other-emptiness—is the Great Madhyamaka"; *rang stong dang gzhan stong du phye nas stong pa nyid legs par gtan la 'babs pa'i tshul 'di ni dbu ma chen po 'phags pa thogs med kyi zhal nas kyang gsungs te/.*

43 Dol po pa cites a variety of Madhyamaka works, including the *Dharmadhātustava,* at length, in RCNG, 57ff., in order to counter the objection of an opponent to the effect that "even though the *tathāgatagarbha* may be accepted as a [doctrine that is] definitive in meaning *(nges don),* Mādhyamikas do not accept this." The prefix "Madhyamaka" given by Go rams pa in the title of this work is an anomaly; the work is usually known usually as *Dharmadhātustava;* Toh no. 1118. See D. Seyfort Ruegg, "Le Dharmadhātustava de Nāgārjuna," in *Études Tibétains dédiées à la memoire de Marcelle Lalou* (Paris: Librairie d'Amerique et d'Orient, 1971), pp. 448–71. On Nāgārjuna's *stavas* generally, see Ruegg, *Literature of the Madhyamaka School,* pp. 31–32.

44 See Dol pa pa's comments in KDZP, 387–88; Stearns, *Buddha from Dolpo,* pp. 146–48.

45 *Abhidharmasamuccaya* (II, 1); P. Pradhan, ed., (Santiniketan: Visva Bharati, 1950), 40; Walpola Rahula, trans., *Le Compendium de la super-doctrine (philosophie) (Abhidharmasamuccaya) d'Asaṅga* (Paris: École Française d'Extrême-Orient, 1971), p. 65; P vol. 112, 252.31. *Chos mngon pa kun las btus pa, The Nyingma Edition of the sDe- dge Bka'-'gyur and bsTan-'gyur* (Oakland: Dharma Publishing, 1980), text no. 4049, vol. 80, 823. This passage from AS is found in the *Śūnyatā-nama-mahāsūtra;* vol. 38, 278. The Pāli version is found in the *Mahā-suñyatā-sutta, The Collection of the Middle Length Sayings, Majjhima Nikāya,* vol. III, trans. I. B. Horner (London: The Pali Text Society, 1959), p. 147 (Pali text no. 121). For Dol po pa's treatment of this passage see, e.g., RCNG, 87–88, and 191ff. See also G. Nagao, "What Remains in Śūnyatā: A Yogācāra Interpretation of Emptiness," in *Mahāyāna Buddhist Meditation: Theory and Practice,* ed. M. Kiyota and E. W. Jones (Honolulu: University of Hawaii Press, 1978), pp. 66–82. A similar passage is also to be found in the *Laṅkāvatāra Sūtra,* ed. Bunyiu Nanjio (Kyoto: Otani University Press, 1956), 75. See also Seyfort Ruegg, *Théorie,* pp. 319–46; L. Schmithausen, "The Definition of *Pratyakṣam* in the *AS,*" WZKSO 16 (1972): 155. For a Dge lugs pa interpretation of this passage, see Cabezón, *Dose,* pp. 46–47, 422, nn. 92–93.

46 *Abhidharmasamuccaya,* n. 45.

47 On the life and works of Tsong kha pa in Western language sources, see Rudolf Kaschewsky, *Das Leben des lamaistischen heiligen Tsongkhapa bLo-bzan-grags-pa (1357–1419) dargestellt und erläutert anhand seiner Vita "Quellort allen Glückes"* (Wiesbaden: Otto Harrassowitz, 1971), 2 vols; and Robert A. F. Thurman, ed., *The Life and Teachings of Tsong kha pa* (Dharamsala: Library of Tibetan Works and Archives, 1982). For a brief overview, see José I. Cabezón, "Tsong kha pa," in *Encyclopedia of Religion,* 2nd ed., forthcoming. Several of Tsong kha pa's Madhyamaka works are mentioned by Go rams pa. Not mentioned is the *vipaśyana (lhag mthong)* section of his *Lam rim chen mo* (LRCM), which has been translated in Tsong-kha-pa, *The Great Treatise on the Stages of the Path to Enlightenment: Lam rim chen mo,* vol. 3, ed. Joshua Cutler [ed. in chief, Guy Newland, and the Lamrim Chenmo Translation Committee] (Ithaca: Snow Lion, 2002–5). The secondary literature on Tsong kha pa's Madhyamaka views is extensive; see, for example, Helmut Tauscher, *Die Lehre von den zwei Wirklichkeiten in Tson kha pas Madhyamaka-Werken* (Wien: Arbeitskreis für Tibetische und Buddhistische Studien Universität Wien, 1995), a very useful work that, among other things, gives the complete *sa bcad* (divisions) for Tsong kha pa's major Madhyamaka

treatises; also G. Newland, *The Two Truths in the Mādhyamika Philosophy of the Geluk-ba Order of Tibetan Buddhism* (Ithaca: Snow Lion, 1992). D. Seyfort Ruegg, "On *pramāṇa* theory in Tson kha pa's Madhyamaka philosophy," in *Studies in the Buddhist Epistemological Tradition, Proceedings of the Second International Dharmakīrti Conference, Vienna, June 11–16, 1989*, ed. E. Steinkellner (Wien: Verlag der Österreichischen Akademie der Wissenschaften, 1991), 281–310; D. Seyfort Ruegg, *Two Prolegomena to Madhyamaka Philosophy: Candrakīrti's Prasannapadā Madhyamakavṛtti on Madhyamakakārikā I.1, and Tson kha pa Blo bzan grags pa / Rgyal Tshab Dar ma rin chen's Dka' gnad/gnas brgyad kyi zin bris: Annotated Translations* (Wien: Arbeitsekreis für Tibetische und Buddhistische Studien, Universität Wien, 2002). Also, Chizuko Yoshimizu, *Die Erkenntnislehre des Prāsaṇgika-Madhyamaka: nach dem Tshig gsal ston thun gyi tshad ma'i rnam bśad des 'Jam dbain bźad pa'i rdo rje: Einleitung, Textanalyse, Übersetzung* (Wien: Arbeitskreis für Tibetische und Buddhistische Studien, Universität Wien, 1996).

48 When applied to such figures as Nāgārjuna and Maitreya, this expression is meant to indicate the fact that they are the ones who reintroduced the teachings of the Buddha into the world (i.e., that they are the *shing rta srol 'byed*); see José I. Cabezón, *Buddhism and Language: A Study of Indo-Tibetan Scholasticism* (Albany: SUNY Press, 1994), p. 235, n. 25. When Go rams pa applies the expression to Tsong kha pa, however, it has a *double-entendre,* implying innovation on the part of Tsong kha pa, and therefore his departure from accepted tradition.

49 A complete translation of Tsong kha pa's commentary to the *Madhyamakakārikas,* the *Rtsa shes ṭīk chen,* is currently being completed by Jay Garfield and Ngawang Samten. For a translation of Nāgārjuna's root text, see Jay L. Garfield, *The Fundamental Wisdom of the Middle Way: Nāgārjuna's Mūlamadhyamakakārikā* (New York: Oxford, 1995). The full title of Tsong kha pa's commentary is *Dbu ma rtsa ba'i tshig le'ur byas pa shes rab ces bya ba'i rnam bshad rigs pa'i rgya mtsho* (Toh no. 5401), *Collected Works,* vol. *ba.* Portions of this work have already been translated by Jeffrey Hopkins, *Ocean of Reasoning* (Dharamsala: Library of Tibetan Works and Archives, 1974); and by William McGee, *The Nature of Things: Emptiness and Essence in the Geluk World* (Ithaca: Snow Lion, 1999).

50 Tsong kha pa's commentary to Candrakīrti's *Madhyamakāvatāra;* for a translation of Candrakīrti's text, see C. W. Huntington, *The Emptiness of Emptiness: An Introduction to Early Indian Mādhyamika* (Honolulu: University of Hawaii Press, 1989). The full title of Tsong kha pa's commentary is *Dbu ma la 'jug pa'i rgya cher bshad pa dgongs pa rab gsal* (Toh no. 5408), *Collected Works,* vol. *ma.* Portions of the work have been translated, and/or studied in Jeffrey Hopkins, *Compassion in Tibetan Buddhism* (London: Rider, 1980); Anne C. Klein, *Path to the Middle: Oral Mādhyamika Philosophy in Tibet* (Albany: SUNY Press, 1994); and Chizuko Yoshimizu, *Die Erkenntnislehre.*

51 *Drang nges legs bshad snying po* (Toh no. 5396), *Collected Works,* vol. *pha.* Complete English trans. in Robert A. F. Thurman, *Tsong kha pa's Speech of Gold in the Essence of True Eloquence* (Princeton: Princeton University Press, 1984). The first two volumes of Hopkins' translation and extensive study of this work have also now appeared: *Emptiness in the Mind-Only School of Buddhism: Dynamic Responses to Dzong-ka-ba's The Essence of Eloquence, Vol. 1* (Berkeley: University of California Press, 1999); and *Reflections on Reality: The Three Natures and Non-Natures in the*

Mind-Only School, Dynamic Responses to Dzong-ka-ba's The Essence of Eloquence, vol. 2 (Berkeley: University of California Press, 2002).

52 Of course, the claim that Tsong kha pa's exegesis was "unique" is, within the conservative scholastic worldview espoused by Go rams pa, an accusation rather than praise; see the Introduction.

53 Tsong kha pa, as a "hard doxographer," makes sharp distinctions between Svātantrikas and Prāsaṅgikas and claims that the former do not understand emptiness completely. As a soft doxographer who seeks to downplay these differences, Go rams pa will criticize Tsong kha pa. See Cabezón, "Two Views"; and C. Yoshimizu, "Tsong kha pa's Reevaluation of Candrakīrti's Criticism of Autonomous Inference," in McClintock and Dreyfus, *The Svātantrika-Prāsaṅgika Distinction,* pp. 257–88.

54 Nāgārjuna, *Śūnyatāsaptati,* Toh no. 3827, Dbu ma *tsa,* 26b; see also Chr. Lindtner, *Nagarjuniana, Studies in the Writing and Philosophy of Nāgārjuna* (Copenhagen: Akademisk Forlag, 1982), pp. 62–63. The relevant verse is quoted (with insignificant variations from the canonical version) by Tsong kha pa in various texts: LRCM, 657; TSTC, 32; LSN, 632; and GR, 178. From the wording, it would seem that Go rams pa is here paraphrasing the GR discussion of this verse.

55 Āryadeva, *Catuḥśataka* (XIV, 25); Vidhushekhara Bhattachārya, ed., *The Catuḥśataka of Āryadeva* (Calcutta: 1931); see also Karen Lang, *Āryadeva's Catuḥśataka: On the Bodhisattva's Cultivation of Method and Knowledge* (Copenhagen: Akademisk Forlag, 1986), pp. 134–35; and Geshe Sonam Rinchen and Ruth Sonam, *Yogic Deeds of Bodhisattvas: Gyel-tsap on Āryadeva's Four Hundred* (Ithaca: Snow Lion, 1994), p. 275. Tsong kha pa discusses the verse in LSN-mi, 462; Thurman, *Tsong kha pa's Speech,* p. 309. Tsong kha pa also discusses the last two lines of the verse in GR, 178; Klein, *Path,* p. 182. The verse is also discussed by Mkhas grub rje in Cabezón, *Dose,* pp. 246–47, where he cites the section of *Buddhapālita* that also quotes the verse (see Cabezón, *Dose,* p. 492, n. 818 for further references to the latter).

56 This is a paraphrase of *Catuḥśataka* VI, 10cd and 11ab; Lang, *Āryadeva's Catuḥśataka,* p. 66: *de phyir nyon mongs thams cad kyang/ gti mug bcom pas bcom par 'gyur/ rten cing 'brel bar 'byung ba ni/ mthong na gti mug 'byung mi 'gyur/.* The verse is cited and discussed by Tsong kha pa in GR, 178; Klein, *Path,* p. 182; and also in LSN-mi, 463–64; Thurman, *Tsong kha pa's Speech,* p. 310.

57 See GR, 178–79.

58 Go rams pa is here referring to what Tsong kha pa calls the *lam gyi dgag bya* (the "soteriological object-to-be-negated"), that is, the ignorance that stands as an obstacle to progress on the path. The notion that the object-to-be-negated must first be identified *(dgag bya ngos 'dzin)* before it can *be* negated is one of the cornerstones of Tsong kha pa's interpretation of the doctrine of emptiness. It is most extensively developed in his LRCM, 579ff.; Cutler, trans., vol. 3, p. 126ff. See also Mkhas grub rje, Cabezón, *Dose,* pp. 92, 441–42, nn. 286–88; LNMS, 187b–188b; and his explanation of the difference between the *lam gyi dgag bya* and the *rigs pa'i dgag bya* ("the logical object-to-be-negated"), Cabezón, *Dose,* pp. 127–28. See also Paul Williams, *Altruism and Reality: Studies in the Philosophy of the Bodhicāryāvatāra* (London: Curzon, 1998), part 4, for a critical discussion of one of the important Indian sources that the Dge lugs pas rely on to prove the necessity of identifying an object-to-be-negated.

59 On the importance of the notion of identifying the object-to-be-negated in the thought of Tsong kha pa, see Tauscher, *Die Lehre*, pp. 73–177; Elizabeth Napper, *Dependent Arising and Emptiness: A Tibetan Buddhist Interpretation of Mādhyamika Philosophy Emphasizing the Compatability of Emptiness and Conventional Phenomena* (Boston: Wisdom, 1989); and Jeffrey Hopkins, *Meditation on Emptiness* (London: Wisdom Publications, 1983), p. 54ff.; as well as his *Emptiness Yoga* (Ithaca: Snow Lion Publications, 1987), pp. 123–55.

60 Tsong kha pa discusses the measure, or extent, of the Svātantrika's object-to-be-negated in a variety of sources: GR, 175ff.; Klein, *Path*, pp. 167–70; also LSN–mi, 419ff.; Thurman, *Tsong kha pa's Speech*, pp. 265–87; but see LRCM, 660–61, where Tsong kha pa uses similar expressions to refer to the Prāsaṅgikas' object of refutation: e.g., 660, *blo'i dbang gis bzhag pa min par chos de rnams la rang rang gi ngos nas gnas tshul lam sdod thsul zhig yod pa.* One of the clearest expositions of this topic in Dge lugs pa literature is to be found in Mkhas grub rje's *Stong thun chen mo;* see Cabezón, *Dose*, pp. 139–47, 460, n. 469. Go rams pa also discusses the issue in TN-CW, 582ff. See also Donald S. Lopez, Jr., *A Study of Svātantrika* (Ithaca: Snow Lion, 1987), chap. 4; Hopkins, *Meditation on Emptiness*, pp. 436–37, 635–36; Hopkins, "A Tibetan Delineation of Different Views of Emptiness in the Indian Middle Way School," *Tibet Journal* 14.1 (1989): 10–43; and Hopkins, *Maps*, pp. 698–703, 737–39.

61 On "existence by virtue of own-characteristic" *(rang gi mtshan nyid kyis grub pa)*, see Yoshimizu, "Tsong kha pa's Reevaluation," pp. 275–76, which makes reference to her previous work on this topic. Also, Seyfort Ruegg, *Two Prolegomena*, pp. 168–202.

62 See GR, 175; Klein, *Path*, p. 169; LRCM, 620–21; and also, Cabezón, *Dose*, pp. 153, 155, 173, 179–80. According to the Dge lugs pa theory, from a Prāsaṅgika perspective, all of these seven terms are equivalent, and are objects-to-be-negated, constituting one of the major differences between Svātantrikas and Prāsaṅgikas, since the former, Tsong kha pa believes, differentiate between the seven terms. See Cabezón, *Dose*, p. 172, for a more extensive list of synonyms for the object-to-be-negated. See also Hopkins, *Maps*, pp. 825–27; and Ferdinand D. Lessing and Alex Wayman, eds. and trans., *mKhas-grub-rje's Fundamentals of the Buddhist Tantras* (The Hague: Mouton, 1968), pp. 90–93.

63 See GR, 162–70; also Cabezón, *Dose*, pp. 140, 173. This distinction is also treated in 'Jam dbyangs bzhad pa's commentary to the *Abhisamayālaṃkāra, Shes rab kyi pha rol tu phyin pa'i mtha' dypod 'khrul sel gang ga'i chu rgyun* (i.e., *Phar phyin mtha' dpyod*), in *The Collected Works of 'Jam-dbyangs.-bzad-pa*, vol.7 (*ja*) (New Delhi: Ngawang Gelek Demo, 1973), p. 88ff.

64 Tsong kha pa discusses this in LRCM, in *Collected Works*, vol. *pa* (New Delhi: Ngawang Gelek Demo, nd), 391b–396a; see also Cabezón, *Dose*, pp. 100–101, 162, 180–84.

65 Here Go rams pa is extrapolating from Tsong kha pa's writings for polemical advantage. The term *mngon par zhen pa* has both the more neutral connotation of "conceptualization" and the more loaded one of "attachment." Since for Tsong kha pa the real ultimate truth, emptiness, can be understood inferentially, it can be conceived; see Cabezón, *Buddhism and Language*, p. 116ff. It is true that for Tsong kha pa this conception should not be negated, since it serves as the basis for the meditative cultivation that leads to a direct understanding of emptiness; see, e.g., Tsong kha pa's remarks in LRCM 492bff., as well as his *Dbu ma'i lta khrid.* There are, however, three

senses in which, even for Tsong kha pa, the inferential conceptualization of emptiness *is* to be transcended. (1) If the conceptual understanding of emptiness is the result of critiquing the philosophical *(kun brtags pa'i)* views of, e.g., the realists—that is, if it is not being directed at one's own innate *(lhan skyes)* ignorance—then no amount of such conceptual understanding will have the desired soteriological effect. Thus, a conceptual understanding of emptiness in these terms must be "transcended" in favor of a more subtle one. (2) If a conceptual understanding of emptiness leads to the reification of emptiness—in which emptiness comes to be hypostasized into a real thing—then, once again, conceptualization has led one astray; for a discussion of this see, e.g., LRCM, 640ff. (3) Finally, even for Tsong kha pa, the conceptual understanding of emptiness must be transcended through the process of meditation, since the inferential (conceptual) understanding of emptiness only has the power to temporarily counteract the reification that grasps things to be true, that is, for as long as the force of that inference has not waned; see *Buddhism and Language*, pp. 137 and 250, nn. 36–39. For Tsong kha pa these are all dangers—or, in the latter case, an inherent limit—of the conceptual understanding of emptiness, but this in no way detracts from the ability of conceptual thought to come to a correct and proper understanding of emptiness: one that is not merely speculative, one that does not reify its object, and one that is used as a stepping stone to meditative appropriation. However, Go rams pa, being of the opinion that the conceptual understanding of emptiness that is the end result of rational analysis must itself be negated, is seeking here to set the stage for his subsequent critique of Tsong kha pa by using a term "conceptualization" *(mngon par zhen pa)* that has this *double-entendre* where one of its connotations, "attachment," is negative.

66 Discussed in a variety of works, e.g., LRCM, 600; see also 637–40. See Tauscher, *Die Lehre*, pp. 56–72, and especially pp. 67–69 and p. 69, n. 150. The passage is from the *Śālistambasūtra;* see P. L. Vaidya, ed., *Mahāyānasūtrasaṃgraha,* pt. 1 (Darbhanga: Mithila Institute, 1961), p. 115: *na san nāsanna sadasan na cāpy anubhayātmakaṃ*. The verse is also found in the *Jñānasārasamuccaya,* attributed to Āryadeva: *Ye shes snying po kun las btus pa,* Toh no. 3851, Dbu ma *tsha*, 27b; and C vol. 18, 27a.6: *yod min med min yod med min/ gnyis ka'i bdag nyid kyang min pas/.* See also K. Mimaki, *La réfutation Bouddhique de la permanence des choses (sthirasiddhidūṣana)* (Paris: Insitut de civilization indienne, 1976), pp. 186–89, 204ff. The passage is also cited in a variety of Madhyamaka polemical literature in Tibet; see, e.g., Cabezón, *Dose,* p. 93; Paṇ chen Blo bzang chos kyi rgyal msthan (1567–1662), *Sgra pa Shes rab rin chen pa'i rtsod lan lung rigs seng ge'i nga ro,* in *Miscellaneous Works of the First Paṇ chen Blo bzang Chos kyi rgyal mtshan,* reproduced from an incomplete mansucript collection from the Zangla khar (Rdzang la mkhar) (Gemur, H.P.: Topden Tsering, 1979), 381. For Dol po pa's interpretation of the *yod min med min* passages, see RCNG, 195–96; and Dol po pa Shes rab rgyal mtshan, *Lta ba shan 'byed yid kyi mun sel,* in *The 'Dzam thang Edition of the Collected Works (gsung-'bum) of Kun-mkhyen Dol-po-pa Shes-rab-rgyal-mtshan,* collected and presented by Matthew Kapstein (Delhi: Shedrup Books, 1992), vol. 5 *(ya)*: 792–93. Seyfort Ruegg also discusses the verse, and Go rams pa's interpretation, in *Three Studies,* pp. 203–4; see also Ruegg, *Three Studies,* p. 143 and n. 50, for a discussion of the Indian sources.

67 See Cabezón, *Dose,* pp. 106–7 for a discussion of the meaning of this verse; Mkhas grub rje's interpretation there varies from that attributed to Tsong kha pa in Go rams pa's account. He states: "Hence, the meaning is this: that existence does not truly

exist, nonexistence does not truly exist, a third alternative which is both does not truly exist, and a third alternative which is neither does not truly exist."

68 That the negation of non-*x* is *x*, or, in its more explicitly Tibetan version, that the repudiation of non-*x* forces one to accept *x*. This topic is discussed by Tsong kha pa in TSTC, 51ff. Go rams pa will challenge the law of double-negation below, just as he does explicitly in his *Dbu ma'i spyi don;* see BPD, 358.4.6. See also Cabezón, *Dose* p. 102ff., 448, n. 339. The repudiation of the law of double negation is also attributed to Stag tshang lo tsā ba by the first Paṇ chen bla ma; see his *Sgra pa Shes rab rin chen pa'i rtsod lan,* p. 380.

69 See Tsong kha pa's similar claim in LRCM, 773ff.; *Great Treatise,* 3: p. 331ff. On the views ascribed to the Chinese monk Hwa shang (Mahāyāna) in Tibet see the Introduction; also, David Seyfort Ruegg, *Buddha-nature, Mind and the Problem of Gradualism in a Comparative Perspective: On the Transmission and Reception of Buddhism in India and Tibet,* The Jordan Lectures in Comparative Religion 13 (London: School of Oriental and African Studies, 1989); Luis Gómez, "The Direct and the Gradual Approaches of Zen Master Mahāyāna"; and Jeffrey Broughton, "Early Ch'an Schools in Tibet," both in *Studies in Ch'an and Hua-yen,* ed. Robert M. Gimello and Peter N. Gregory (Honolulu: University of Hawaii Press/Kuroda Institute, 1983), pp. 69–167 and 1–68, respectively; G. W. Houston, *Sources for a History of the bSam yas Debate* (Sankt Augustin: VGH-Wissenschaftverlag, 1980); Paul Demieville, *Le Concile de Lhasa* (Paris: Impr. Nationale de France, 1952); Leonard W. J. van der Kuijp, *Contributions to Tibetan Buddhist Epistemology* (Wiesbaden: Franz Steiner, 1983), p. 45. Other Dge lugs pa sources on this issue include Mkhas grub rje, LNMS, 176a–178a, 193a; Cabezón, *Dose,* pp. 112–17, 266; and Klong rdol bla ma, on which see Cabezón, *Dose,* pp. 400–402, n. 33, for the reference and a translation of the relevant passage in *Dbu ma'i ming gi rnam grangs.*

70 This sentence is taken directly from Tsong kha pa's GR. See the note in the Tibetan edition of Go rams pa's text, in this volume. See also Klein, *Path,* p. 183.

71 Tsong kha pa and his followers are of the opinion that not all conceptual thought is a form of ignorance—that is, a form of the grasping at true existence—since there are many conceptual thoughts (e.g., the thought that understands composite things to be impermanent) that are valid. Therefore, not all conceptual thoughts are repudiated or negated by the reasoning of the Madhyamaka. See LRCM, 659–61; *Great Treatise,* 3: pp. 211–13. See also Cabezón, *Dose,* p. 114; and Klong rdol bla ma, cited in Cabezón, *Dose,* p. 401, n. 33.

72 Much—though not all—of the material contained in this section falls into the category of what has come to be known in Dge lugs pa literature as the "eight great difficult points" of Madhyamaka doctrine *(dka' gnad chen po brgyad).* For a list of the eight points, see GR, 277ff. A text by Tsong kha pa's disciple Rgyal tshab rje based on Tsong kha pa's teachings has been translated by D. Seyfort Ruegg, *Two Prolegomena,* section 2. See also Cabezón, *Dose,* p. 397, n. 23, which contains bibliographical references. Daniel Cozort's study of this subject is based principally on the treatment of the "difficult points" in 'Jam dbyangs bzhad pa and Lcang skya Rol pa'i rdo rje; D. Cozort, *Unique Tenets of the Middle Way Consequence School* (Ithaca: Snow Lion, 1998). An interesting list of twelve points that are the special tenets of the Prāsaṅgika is given in a lexicographical work of Lcang skya, *Dag yig mkhas pa'i 'byung gnas zhes bya ba las dbu ma'i skor* (photocopy of unidentified text, no bibliographical information, Hamburg, cat. no. MVI 610/2), 9b–10a: (1) non acceptance

of own-characteristic even at the nominal level, (2) a special way of dividing all afflictions, such as the grasping at true existence, into two levels of subtlety with two divisions each, (3) how they accept two subtle forms of selflessness, (4) that they identify mere imputation by conceptual thought as the meaning of interdependent (arising), (5) their special way of positing the self that is the basis of karma and its effects, (6) their special way of positing external objects, (7) their special way of not accepting the *ālaya, svasaṃvedana,* and *svatantras,* (8) their special way of positing the two obscurations, and how they are eliminated, (9) their acceptance of the fact that śrāvaka and pratyekabuddha āryans must understand the essencelessness of phenomena, (10) their acceptance of the fact that ordinary beings can have yogic direct perception, (11) their special way of positing the three times, (which involves), e.g., their accepting destruction to be a real entity, (12) their special (tenets concerning) the way in which the buddha understands phenomena. See also Seyfort Ruegg, *Two Prolegomena,* pp. 148–49; and Hopkins, *Maps,* pp. 927–46.

73 Although an important part of Tsong kha pa's Madhyamaka theory, this brief presentation of Tsong kha pa's theory of what it means for things to exist conventionally or nominally is not one of the "eight difficult points." Tsong kha pa discusses his views concerning the meaning of "conventional existence" in many of his works; see, e.g., LRCM, 626ff.; *Great Treatise,* 3, p. 177ff.; and Thurman, *Speech of Gold,* p. 366ff. See also Mkhas grub rje's explanation of his teacher's views in Cabezón, *Dose,* pp. 90–91, 101, 168–71, 176–77; see also Cabezón, *Buddhism and Language,* p. 161ff.

74 The foundation consciousness *(ālayavijñāna)*—posited, e.g., by the Mind-Only School—is the repository of karmic seeds, and therefore serves for this school as a mechanism for explaining the ripening of karma. Candrakīrti denies that such a mechanism is necessary to explain karma, and this leads him to deny the existence of the foundation consciousness. Tsong kha pa follows Candrakīrti on this matter, and therefore maintains that the ālaya does not exist even conventionally. On the foundation consciousness in general, see L. Schmithausen, *Alayavijñāna: On the Origin and Early Development of a Central Concept of Yogācāra Philosophy,* parts I and II, Studia Philologica Buddhica, Monograph Series IVab (Tokyo: International Institute for Buddhist Studies, 1989); and William S. Waldron, *The Buddhist Unconscious: The Ālaya-Vijñāna in the Context of Indian Buddhist Thought* (London: RoutledgeCurzon, 2003). Tsong kha pa, as just stated, believes that in the Prāsaṅgika Madhyamaka system the ālayavijñāna cannot be posited as existing *even conventionally;* although, see Sparham's remarks concerning a possible shift in Tsong kha pa's position on this issue, in his study of Tsong kha pa's *Yid dang kun gzhi'i dka' ba'i gnad rgya cher 'grel pa legs par bshad pa'i rgya mtsho,* Toh no. 5414, *Collected Works,* vol. *tsha;* Gareth Sparham, in collaboration with Shotaro Iida, *Ocean of Eloquence: Tsong kha pa's Commentary on the Yogācāra Doctrine of Mind* (Albany: SUNY Press, 1993), pp. 14–16, 18–22, 33–35, nn. 44–50. Sparham gives references to many of the important passages on the ālaya in a variety of Tsong kha pa's works. See LSN-mi, 455, and especially 468ff.; Thurman, *Tsong kha pa's Speech,* pp. 302 and 315ff. Also Seyfort Ruegg, *Two Prolegomena,* pp. 159–68. One of the most important discussions of this topic in post-Tsong kha pa Dge lugs pa literature is found in Mkhas grub rje, see Cabezón, *Dose,* pp. 314–24 and 504, n. 981, for other bibliographical references to both the primary and secondary literature on this subject. See also, Cozort, *Unique Tenets,* pp. 147–49, 235–37, 307–13, 435–38; and Hopkins, *Maps,* pp. 928–29.

75 This, of course, is one of the classic problems of Buddhist philosophy. In the Madhyamaka, it is treated as early as Nāgārjuna; see MMK (XVII, 6); Pras, 311. Walleser, trans., *Die Mittlere Lehre (Madhyamakaśāstra) des Nāgārjuna* (Heidelberg: 1911), p. 91; K. Inada, ed. and trans., *Nāgārjuna, a Translation of his Mūlamadhyamakakārikā with an Introductory Essay* (Tokyo: Hokuseido Press, 1970), p. 106; J. Garfield, *The Fundamental Wisdom,* pp. 233–34.

76 On *las kyi chud mi za ba* (Skt. *karma-avipraṇāśa*), see L. de la Vallée Poussin, trans., L. Pruden, English trans., *Abhidharmakośabhāṣyam* (Berkeley: Asian Humanities Press, 1988), 4: p. 1377, n. 157. For bibliographical references to a variety of other Sanskrit sources that deal with this notion see Cabezón, *Dose,* p. 504, n. 984. In Tsong kha pa, see TSTC, 356–60; and GR, 280ff. See also *Dose,* p. 315 for Mkhas grub rje's treatment of the issue; and Ruegg, *Two Prolegomena,* p. 159 passim, for Rgyal tshab/Tsong kha pa's treatment.

77 On *thob pa,* Skt. *prāpti,* see *Abhidharmakośa* (II, vv. 35–39); Swami Dwarikadas Shastri, ed., *Abhidharmakośam* (Varanasi: Bauddha Bharati, 1970), 1, pp. 209–24; and L. de la Vallée Poussin/ L. Pruden, trans., *Abhidarmakośabhāṣyam,* 1, pp. 206–19; also Cabezón, *Dose,* p. 315; Hopkins, *Maps,* pp. 239–40.

78 On *bag chags,* Skt. *vāsana,* and their relationship to the ālaya, see Schmithausen, *Ālayavijñāna,* 1: pp. 178–80; also Waldron, *The Buddhist Unconscious,* p. 218, n. 15. For the Dge lugs pa exposition of the Yogācāra doctrine of *bījas,* or "seeds," see Sparham, *Ocean,* p. 65; also Cabezón, *Dose,* p. 56, especially pp. 61–63.

79 Tsong kha pa attempts to solve the problem of how karma is preserved by positing an intermediary entity between the karmic cause and its effect that he calls "the destruction of the cause." See Candrakīrti's comments on this issue in MA (VI, 39–40), 126–30; MA-Fr, 317–20; Huntington, *Emptiness of Emptiness,* p. 162ff. Tsong kha pa believes that this "destruction" is not a permanent, unreal phenomenon *(dngos med),* as claimed by some schools, but a "thing" or "entity" *(dngos po)* that is momentary and evolves causally until it gives rise to its effect. This is the doctrine that Go rams pa is referring to here. For references to this theory in the works of Tsong kha pa, and a more detailed discussion of the problem, see Lobsang Dargyay, "Tsong Kha Pa's Concept of Karma"; and L. Schmithausen, "Critical Response," both in *Karma and Rebirth: Post Classical Developments,* ed. Ronald W. Neufeldt (Albany: SUNY Press, 1986), pp. 169–78 and 203–30, respectively. See also Mkhas grub rje's discussion in Cabezón, *Dose,* pp. 312–15; Cozort, *Unique Tenets,* pp. 349–67, 471–74; Hopkins, *Maps,* pp. 596–601, 933–38.

80 Hell beings, "hungry ghosts" (pretas), animals, humans, "demi-gods" (asuras) and gods, each of which see the cup as containing a different kind of fluid.

81 See Tsong kha pa, GR, 338–40; and Mkhas grub rje's extensive discussion in Cabezón, *Dose,* pp. 334–45. Both authors cite *Mahāyānasaṃgraha* VIII, 20 as their source for this doctrine; see full references in Cabezón, *Dose,* p. 509, nn. 1046–47. The doctrine that "destruction is an entity" is sometimes found in the list of the Prāsaṅgikas' unique tenets, and sometimes not. Even when it is not, however, it is sometimes treated in the context of the critique of the foundation consciousness; see Cozort, *Unique Tenets,* pp. 112–23; and Seyfort Ruegg, *Two Prolegomena,* pp. 143, 159–68.

82 Afflicted obscurations (Skt. *kleśāvaraṇa,* Tib. *nyon sgrib*) are obstacles that impede the attainment of emancipation *(mokṣa);* obscurations to omniscience (Skt.

jñeyāvaraṇa, Tib. *shes sgrib*) are obstacles to the attainment of the omniscience that is concomitant with full buddhahood. The latter term is explained in N. Dutt, ed., *Bodhisattvabhūmi* (Patna: K. p. Jayaswal Research Institute, 1966), 26.8: *jñeyejnānasya pratighāta āvaraṇam,* "obscurations in regard to what is to be known," that is, "obscurations that stand in the way of knowing [all that] is to be known"; a different definition is offered in *Bodhicaryāvatārapañjikā* IX, 55: *jneyam eva samāropita rūpatvād āvṛtiḥ,* "obscuration consisting in the objects known, given that all objects are falsely reified [by consciousness]"; P. L. Vaidya, ed., *Bodhicaryāvatāra of Śāntideva with the Commentary Pañjikā of Prajñākaramati* (Darbhanga: Mithila Insitute, 1960), p. 211. For Tsong kha pa's discussion, see LRCM, 651–56, 763–69; GR, 233–39; and TSTC, 34ff.; Thurman, *Tsong kha pa's Speech,* pp. 308–12. Mkhas grub rje discusses the topic in Cabezón, *Dose,* p. 127ff., and especially pp. 245–56; a bibliography of secondary literature on the topic is found in Cabezón, *Dose,* p. 491, n. 812. The topic is usually treated in discussions of the eight difficult points; see, e.g., Seyfort Ruegg, *Two Prolegomena,* pp. 234–50; and Cozort, *Unique Tenets,* pp. 243–48, 411–18, 463–69.

83 This appears to be a paraphrase of Tsong kha pa's comments on this subject in LRCM, 655–56.

84 MA, 393; for Tsong kha pa's comments see GR, 240; also LSN, 634. The passage is also cited and discussed by Mkhas grub rje in Cabezón, *Dose,* pp. 249–50.

85 See K. Mimaki, *Le Grub mtha',* p. 105; and Cabezón, *Dose,* p. 250.

86 This is not generally considered one of the eight difficult points. See Go rams pa, TN-CW, 66–67, where the subject is also treated. Tsong kha pa's discussion of the issue is found in, e.g., LSN, 625ff.; GR, 175ff.; LRCM, 662–64. An extensive discussion is also found in Cabezón, *Dose,* pp. 185–200.

87 The Dge lugs pas attribute this view to Bhāvaviveka on the basis of statements he makes in *Tarkajvāla,* C, Dbu ma *dza,* 80b; see also Cabezón, *Dose,* p. 479, n. 660 for references to this passage in the secondary literature; and Thurman, *Tsong kha pa's Speech,* p. 301ff.

88 See Hopkins, *Meditation on Emptiness,* p. 177; and 'Jam dbyangs bzhad pa's comments on the same topic in his *Grub mtha' rnam bshad,* Hopkins, *Meditation on Emptiness,* pp. 678–79, where relevant passages from Candrakīrti and Tsong kha pa are cited and discussed.

89 See LRCM, 661–62: *des na nang gi blo'i dbang gis bzhag pa min par rang gi ngo bo'i sgo nas yul gyi steng du grub pa de la bdag gam rang bzhin zhes zer la/ de nyid khyad par gyi gzhi gang zag gi steng du med pa ni gang zag gi bdag med dang/ mig sna la sogs pa'i chos kyi steng du med pa ni chos kyi bdag med du gsungs pas/ rang bzhin de gang zag dang chos kyi steng du yod par 'dzin pa ni bdag gnyis kyi 'dzin par shugs kyis rtogs par nus so/.* "Therefore, 'objective existence by virtue of self-nature, without being posited by the power of the mind *qua* inner thing' is what is meant by 'self' or 'essence.' The non-existence in the person of a substratum with these types of qualities is called the selflessness of the person. Its non-existence in phenomena like the eye, nose, and so forth, is called the selflessness of phenomena. From this, it is possible to indirectly understand that the [thought] that grasps at that essence as existing in the person and in phenomena is a grasping at the two selves." Tsong kha pa (LRCM, 661) also states, just prior to the cited passage, that the "anything else" in the expression "not depending on anything else" refers not to "causes and conditions"

(rgyu rkyen) generally, but rather, and more specifically, to the mind—that is, to the conventionally valid consciousness *(yul can tha snyad pa'i shes pa)*—in dependence on which Prāsaṅgikas believe all things are posited as existing.

90 This is usually considered one of the eight difficult points. This topic is treated by Tsong kha pa most extensively in GR, 60–76, 84; translated in Jeffrey Hopkins, *Compassion in Tibetan Buddhism,* pp. 150–81; see also *Legs bshad snying po* (Lhasa Zhol ed.), 73b–77b. The fact that Mkhas grub rje treats the subject very extensively in Cabezón, *Dose* (pp. 201–56, but see also the important discussion on pp. 195–96) indicates that there must have been (or that he perceived that there might in the future arise) controversy over Tsong kha pa's position of this issue. For more complete references to a variety of primary and secondary literature on the subject see Cabezón, *Dose,* p. 482, n. 706. See also Go rams pa, TN-CW, 32; and Rong ston pa's comments in BJN, 25–31. Cozort discusses and translates the view of later Dge lugs pa thinkers on the question in *Unique Tenets,* pp. 243–48, 411–18, 463–69.

91 Tsong kha pa grants that there *are* differences between Hīna- and Mahāyāna *philosophers*—e.g., between a Vaibhāṣika and a Prāsaṅgika—especially as regards their views of emptiness, but he believes that the same emptiness—the full-blown selflessness of phenomena—is taught in the scriptures of both vehicles, that there are Hīnayāna practitioners who come to understand that emptiness, and that, indeed, to achieve Hīnayāna "enlightenment," that is arhatship, it is *necessary* to understand the selflessness of phenomena. Go rams pa's comments here tend to somewhat oversimplify Tsong kha pa's position.

92 For Rong ston pa's comments on this point see BJN, 25; see also Mkhas grub rje's remarks in Cabezón, *Dose,* pp. 253–56; and Dkon mchog 'jigs med dbang po, in Mimaki, *Le Grub mtha',* p. 106; Sopa and Hopkins, *Cutting Through Appearances,* pp. 318–19.

93 See GR, 134ff.; the paragraph is a verbatim citation from GR, 58. Mkhas grub rje makes it quite clear (Cabezón, *Dose,* p. 254) that the division of the path of meditation into nine parts is a provisional teaching of the Buddha that cannot be taken literally. For a general explanation of the paths in Tsong kha pa's interpretation of the Prāsaṅgika, see Hopkins, *Meditation on Emptiness,* pp. 96–109. For historical background concerning the path structure in the Abhidharma, see E. Frauwallner, *Studies in Abhidharma Literature and the Origins of Buddhist Philosophical Systems,* trans. Sophie Francis Kidd (Albany: SUNY Press, 1995), chap. 7.

94 On the path of seeing (Skt. *darśanamarga*), see L. Schmithausen, "The Darśanamarga section of the *Abhidharmasamuccaya* and its Interpretation by Tibetan Commentators (with special reference to Bu ston Rin chen grub)," in *Contributions on Tibetan and Buddhist Religion and Philosophy,* ed. E. Steinkellner and H. Tauscher (Wien: Arbeitskreis für Tibetische und Buddhistische Studien, Universität Wien, 1983), pp. 259–74. On the paths of seeing and meditation in the *Abhisamayālaṃkāra,* see E. Obermiller, *Prajñāpāramitā in Tibetan Buddhism* (Delhi: Classics India Publications, 1988), pp. 32–38.

95 That is, the desire, form, and formless worlds (the *kāma, rūpa* and *ārūpya dhātus*).

96 For a listing of these sixteen aspects, see Obermiller, *Prajñāpāramitā,* pp. 16–17. See also Cozort, *Unique Tenets,* pp. 265–66, 342–43.

97 See BCA (IX, 45–49), 196–97; L. de la Vallée Poussin, *Bodhicaryāvatāra,* p. 121; Steinkellner, *Eintritt,* p. 128; Crosby and Skilton, *The Bodhicaryāvatāra,* pp. 119–20 (vv. 44–48). See also GR, 63–65. These verses are treated in an extensive fashion in Cabezón, *Dose,* pp. 217–21. On this point it is interesting that both Tsong kha pa and Mkhas grub rje see themselves as challenging the interpretations of two previous Tibetan scholars, namely Phya pa Chos kyi seng ge (1109–1169) and Brtseg/Rtsags Dbang phyug seng ge, a student of Phya pa.

98 On the foundation consciousness, see n. 74. The existence of external objects is usually considered one of the eight difficult points on its own; see Seyfort Ruegg, *Two Prolegomena,* pp. 202–7. Chiefly because Prāsaṅgikas seek to accord with worldly conventions, and because external objects are accepted in the world, Tsong kha pa follows Candrakīrti in maintaining the existence of external objects. The repudiation of reflexive awareness *(svasaṃvedana)* is also considered to be one of the eight difficult points on its own; see Ruegg, *Two Prolegomena,* pp. 220–26. Tsong kha pa discusses the topics that Go rams pa deals with in this section in GR, p. 279ff. and 338ff.; *Legs bshad snying po* (Lhasa Zhol ed.), 77b–81b; Thurman, *Tsong kha pa's Speech,* p. 312ff. For Mkhas grub rje's extensive treatment of the issue, see Cabezón, *Dose,* pp. 314–55; and for a brief overview of the issues involved in upholding the doctrine of reflexive awareness, with bibliographical references, especially to the Indian and secondary literature, see Cabezón, *Dose,* p. 511, n. 1066. For an extensive discussion of the relevant Sanskrit sources and Tsong kha pa's interpretation of them, see also Cozort, *Unique Tenets,* pp. 160–69, 370–89, 439–47. P. Williams, *The Reflexive Nature of Awareness: A Tibetan Madhyamaka Defence* (London: Curzon, 1998) is probably the most complete and interesting philosophical study of the subject of the Buddhist doctrine of reflexive awareness. See also Go rams pa, *Lta ngan mun sel,* 620ff.

99 The reference, of course, is to so-called Sautrāntika-Svātantrika-Mādhyamikas, like Bhāvaviveka; see, e.g., Dkon mchog 'jigs med dbang po, *Grub mtha',* K. Mimaki, ed., p. 97: *rang rig khas mi len zhing/ phyi don rang gi mtshan nyid kyis grub pa khas len pa'i dbu ma pa de...slob dpon legs ldan 'byed lta bu/;* Sopa and Hopkins, *Cutting Through Appearances,* pp. 283–84. See also Donald S. Lopez, Jr., *Study of Svātantrika,* part 2; and Hopkins, *Maps,* p. 704 passim.

100 Yogācāra-Svātantrika-Mādhyamikas, like Śāntarakṣita and Kamalaśīla; see Dkon mchog 'jigs med dbang po (Mimaki), *Grub mtha',* 97: *phyi don khas mi len zhing/ rang rig khas len pa'i Dbu ma pa de/...slob dpon zhi ba 'tsho lta bu/;* Sopa and Hopkins, *Cutting Through Appearances,* p. 283; Lcang skya, *Dag yig,* ff. 10b–11a. It is interesting that Go rams pa focuses on the difference concerning the foundation consciousness, whereas Dkon mchog 'jigs med dbang po focuses on reflexive awareness. Also Lopez, *Study of Svātantrika,* part 3; and Hopkins, *Maps,* p. 731 passim.

101 See above n. 98.

102 This is traditionally one of the eight difficult points. See LRCM, 672ff.; *Great Treatise,* p. 225ff.; Thurman, *Tsong kha pa's Speech,* p. 321ff. See Seyfort Ruegg's extensive treatment of Tsong kha pa's views in *Three Studies,* pp. 187–90, and Section III. See also Cabezón, *Dose,* pp. 257–85, 292, 297; for further references to secondary sources see Cabezón, *Dose,* p. 493, n. 834. For a treatment of the issues in some of the Sanskrit sources and in Tsong kha pa, focusing principally on the question of *prasaṅgaviparyaya,* see Tom J. F. Tillemans, "Tsong kha pa et al. on the Bhāvaviveka-Candrakīrti Debate," in *Tibetan Studies,* ed. Ihara Shoren and Zuiho Yamaguchi

(Narita: Naritasan Shinshoji, 1992), I: 315–26. For the views of Rong ston pa, see BTN, 28; BJN, 65. For those of Red mda' ba, see DSG, 185. The issue is also discussed by Go rams pa in BPD, 360.1.4. Cabezón has discussed the views of Rong ston pa on this issue in "Rong ston Shākya rgyal mtshan on Mādhyamika Thesislessness," in *Tibetan Studies,* ed. Helmut Krasser et. al. (Wien: Verlag der Osterreichischen Akademie der Wissenschaften, 1997), pp. 97–105. See also Cabezón, "Two Views"; Cozort, *Unique Tenets,* pp. 239–43, 369–70, 449–53; and Ruegg, *Two Prolegomena,* pp. 208–20.

103 See, LRCM, 705; *Great Treatise,* p. 261: "There are Mādhyamikas—such as the Master Bhāvaviveka—who accept that, conventionally, phenomena have essential or instrinsic character. The conventional existence of essential or intrinsic character is their reason for accepting autonomous reasons in their own system. Whether one posits autonomous reasons in one's own system finally depends upon what one posits as the extremely subtle object of refutation." The very same point is made by Mkhas grub rje in Cabezón, *Dose,* pp. 273–74.

104 Pras, 16; Toh no. 3860, Dbu ma *'a,* 4b. Cited by Tsong kha pa in LRCM, 677; *Great Treatise,* pp. 230–31. See also LRCM, pp. 690, 712; *Great Treatise,* pp. 245, 268; and Hopkins, *Meditation on Emptiness,* p. 475.

105 A summary of Tsong kha pa's position is found in LSN, 650; see also Mkhas grub rje's discussion in Cabezón, *Dose,* p. 272.

106 G.yag phrug (or G.yag ston) Sangs rgyas dpal (1348–1414), student of Sgra tshad pa Rin chen rnam rgyal (1318–1388), who was in turn one of the main students of Bu ston (see below; and GJL, 371). G.yag phrug's main teacher, however, was the great scholar of Sa skya, Brtson 'grus dpal, also a student of Bu ston. G.yag phrug was the main teacher of one of Go rams pa's own teachers, Rong ston Shes bya kun rig (1367–1449). In his time G.yag phrug was probably the greatest scholar of the monastery of Sa skya (see BA, 339; DN, 412–13); among his most important surviving works are his commentary on the *Uttaratantra* and his eight-volume *ṭīkā* on the *Abhisamayālaṃkāra; The Complete Yig-cha for the Study of the Prajñāpāramitā Literature* (Dehradun: Pal Evam Chodan Ngorpa Centre, 1985). The other figure mentioned is of course Red mda' ba Gzhon nu blo gros (1349–1412). See Seyfort Ruegg, *Three Studies,* 60ff. According to Thu'u bkvan, Red mda' ba "heard the Madhyamaka from Mkhan chen Byang sems" (GJL, TT: "Byang seng"). TT, 188, identifies this as one of the abbots of Jo mo nang. Shākya mchog ldan, however, states that his main Madhyamaka instructor was a certain "Mdog ldog pa." This perhaps refers to Mdog lo pa Mkhan chen Kun dga' dpal (that is, Nya dbon Kun dga' dpal), his ordination abbot; see TT, 194. Red mda' ba was one of Tsong kha pa's principal teachers, especially in the field of Madhyamaka, though, interestingly, his chief disciple in the area of Madhyamaka is listed by TT, 196, not as Tsong kha pa, but as a certain Gon g.yo Nyi ma grags. His commentary on the *Madhyamakāvatāra* survives (DSG); Jurgen Stoter-Tillman, and Acārya Tashi Tsering, trans., *Rendawa Shonnu Lodro's Commentary on the 'Entry into the Middle' Lamp which Elucidates Reality* (Sarnath: Central Institute of Higher Tibetan Studies, 1997), which includes a biography of Red mda' ba; see also M. Sato, "Die Madhyamaka-Philosophie der Sa skya pa-Schule—Red mda' ba gZon nu blo gros," in *Contributions on Tibetan and Buddhist Religion and Philosophy,* ed. Ernst Steinkellner and Helmut Tauscher, Proceedings of the Csoma de Körös Symposium, 2 vols (Wien: Arbeitskreis für Tibetische und Buddhistische Studien, Universität Wien, 1983), II: 43–58. Belonging to a generation

prior to Go rams pa, both figures—G.yag and Gzhon—had by Go rams pa's time probably already attained a status of somewhat mythical proportions. See David P. Jackson (in collaboration with Shunzo Onoda), ed., *Rong ston on the Prajñāpāramitā Philosophy of the Abhisamayālaṃkāra: His Subcommentary on Haribhadra's Sphuṭārtha* (Kyoto: Nagada Bunshodo, 1988), p. 1ff.; Thu'u bkvan Lo bzang chos kyi nyi ma, *Thu'u kvan grub mtha'* (Lan kru'u: Kan su'u mi rigs dpe skrun khang: 1989), 189ff.; Shākya mchog ldan, BB, 234; Ngor chen Dkon mchog lhun grub and Ngor chen Sangs rgyas phun tshogs, *A History of Buddhism, Being the Text of Dam pa'i chos kyi byun tshul legs par bshad pa bstan pa rgya mtshor 'jug pa'i gru chen zhes bya ba rtson 'phro kha skon bcas* (i.e., *Ngor chos byung*) (N. Delhi: Ngawang Tobgay, 1973), pp. 345–45; TT, 193–97. See also GJL: on G.yag phrug, 424–25 (the date of his birth is here given as 1350); and on Red mda' ba, 420–22. This latter work (GJL, 425; source = TT, 193–94) mentions an interesting tradition to explain the pairing of G.yag and Gzhon. It states that the two disciples of Bu and Dol (= Bu ston Rin chen grub, 1290–1364; and Dol po pa, see above) were Nya and Brtson (= Nya dpon/dbon Kun dga' dpal, fourteenth century; and Mkhan chen, or Mkhas dbang, Brtson 'grus dpal, fourteenth century), and that the two disciples of Nya and Brtson were G.yag and Gzhon. But if this saying is meant to imply two separate lineages (1. Bu-Nya-G.yag; and 2. Dol-Brtson-Gzhon), then this would seem wrong, since we know Nya dbon to have been one of the chief disciples of Dol po pa, and G.yag ston to have been one of the main disciples of Brtson 'grus dpal. More likely implied, therefore, are the lineages 1. Bu-Brtson-G.yag and 2. Dol-Nya-Gzhon. This leaves us with the result of having to include Red mda' ba in the lineage of Dol po pa, problematic because we know that Red mda' ba was one of the main critics of the *gzhan stong* views (as witnessed by Go rams pa's own citation of Red mda' ba to this effect in the *Lta ba'i shan 'byed;* see below). But TT (195–96) may resolve the situation for us by explaining a tradition that states that Red mda' ba at one point in his life turned from the Madhyamaka theories of Bu ston to those of Dol po pa, but that he became increasingly skeptical of the latter, and eventually renounced them. GJL, 425f., also includes Red mda' ba in the list of G.yag phrug's students.

107 The monastery founded by Rngog Legs pa'i shes rab (see following note); see also S. Onoda, "Abbatial Successions of the Colleges of Gsang phu sNe'u thog Monastery," in *Kokuritsu Minzokugaku Hakubutsukan Kenkyū* 15.4 (1990): 1049–71; Seyfort Ruegg, *Three Studies*, p. 28, n. 53; and Sde srid Sangs rgyas rgya mtsho, *Dga' ldan chos 'byung bai ḍūrya gser po* (Mtsho sngon: Mi rigs dpe skrun khang, 1991), 146ff.

108 Rngog lo tsā ba Blo ldan shes rab (1059–1109), student of Rngog Legs pa'i shes rab (eleventh century), who was his uncle. Legs pa'i shes rab was, in turn, one of the three chief disciples of Atiśa (982–1054) in Central Tibet (Dbus), and was also the founder of Gsang phu monastery. See TT, 112, for mention of some of his other teachers. Having studied among the pandits of Kashmir for seventeen years, Rngog Blo ldan shes rab returned to Tibet at age thirty-four, and began to teach and translate. He is perhaps best known as one of the first systematizers of philosophical studies (at Gsang phu, the abbacy of which he assumed in 1092), and for being the main source for the teachings of the "Svātantrika Madhyamaka" in Tibet. See Seyfort Ruegg, *Three Studies*, p. 28ff. A biography of Rngog in verse by his student Gro lung pa Blo gros 'byung gnas (1050–1130) is preserved in Patna, *'Jig rten mid gcig Blo ldan shes rab gyi rnam thar* (21ff.), bundle no. 545, work no. 1435; see D. Jackson, *The 'Miscellaneous Series' of Tibetan Texts in the Bihar Research Society, Patna: A Handlist*, Tibet and Indo-Tibetan Studies 2 (Stuttgart: Franz Steiner Verlag, 1989), p. 198; see also the later

biography by Shākya mchog ldan, *Rngog lo tsā ba chen po'i bstan pa ji ltar bskyangs pa'i tshul mdo tsam du bya ba ngo mtshar gtam gyi rol mo,* in *The Complete Works (gsungs-'bum) of gSer-mdog Paṇ-chen,* (Thimpu, Bhutan: Kunzang Tobgay, 1975), 16: 443–56. See also BA, 328ff.; DN, 399ff. On the transmission of the *Abhisamayālaṃkāra* through Rngog and eventually to Rong ston (Go rams pa's teacher) see Jackson, *Rong ston on the Prajñāpāramitā,* pp. ii, xxi. None of his strictly Madhyamaka writings are known to survive, though he is quoted or paraphrased in later Tibetan sources; see Cabezón, *Dose,* p. 89, where Mkhas grub rje sides with Rngog on the question of how to divide the Madhyamaka school; and pp. 143, 357–60, where his view "that the ultimate truth is not a knowable phenomenon" is criticized; also see Go rams pa, BPD, 361.3.4–361.4.5, where Go rams pa refutes a critic of Rngog on the same issue of the division of the Madhyamaka; and Stag tshang lo tsā ba, *Grub mtha' kun shes,* 205–6, where he criticizes Rngog. See also Shākya mchog ldan, BB, 223, 232 (where he traces Rngog's lineage, with a gap, upto G.yag ston), 234–35; there BB cites two verses from Rngog to show how he attempted to synthesize the Madhyamaka and Pramāṇika traditions; see also BB, 238f. His *bsdus don* commentaries on the *Uttaratantra* and on the *Abhisamayālaṃkāra* have been published with introductions by David Jackson, where additional bibliographical material is to be found; *Rgyud bla ma'i don bsdus (Theg chen rgyud bla ma'i don bsdus pa); Commentary on the Ratnagotravibhāga by Rnog Lotsaba Blo-ldan-śes-rab* (Dharamsala, H.P.: Library of Tibetan Works and Archives, 1993). See also van der Kuijp, *Contributions,* pp. 36–38; and Dung dkar rin po che, *Tshig mdzod,* 768.

109 Sa chen Kun dga' snying po (1092–1158); see GJL, 220–21; TT, 128ff; BA, 211; DN, 263–64. He became the third holder of the throne of Sa skya at age nineteen or twenty, in the year 1111. He studied the Madhyamaka under Khyung Rin chen grags (a direct disciple of Rngog lo tsā ba), under Ba ri lo tsā ba, and under Mes lhang tsher. Among his four sons, Kun dga' 'bar, Dpal chen 'od po, Bsod nams rtse mo (1142–1182) and Rje btsun Grags pa rgyal mtshan (1147–1216), it is especially the last two that are probably being referred to here; see David Jackson, "Madhyamaka Studies Among the Early Sa-skya-pas," *Tibet Journal* 10.2 (1985): 21ff. On Bsod nams rtse mo, GJL, 255–56, states that he studied the Madhyamaka and Prajñāpāramitā at Gsang phu under Phya pa (1109–1169) over a period of approximately eleven years, and that he became a renowned expert in these fields. He became responsible for Sa skya after his father's death, but appears to have preferred meditation and isolated retreat to the life of an administrator; see TT, 134. He was also a teacher to his half-brother, Rje btsun Grags pa rgyal mtshan (GJL, 258–60; TT, 134–35), the actual fourth throne holder (from 1172 on), and a teacher of the great Sa skya paṇḍita (1182–1251). See Seyfort Ruegg, *Three Studies,* pp. 56, 58.

110 Mar pa lo tsā ba (1012–1095), and his student Rje btsun Mi la ras pa (1040–1123); see GJL, 175–77, and 190–92, respectively; also TT, 84–87, and 90, respectively. Biographies in Western languages include J. Bacot, *La vie de Marpa le 'traducteur'* (1937; repr. Paris: P. Geuthner, 1976); Nalanda Translation Committee, trans., *The Life of Marpa the Translator* (Boulder: Prajna, 1980); W. Y. Evans-Wentz, *Tibet's Great Yogi Milarepa,* 2nd ed. (London: Oxford University Press, 1951); J. Bacot, *Milarepa—ses mefaits, ses preuves, son illumination,* 2nd ed. (1925; repr. Paris: P. Geuthner, 1971); and L. Lhalungpa, trans., *The Life of Milarepa* (London: Grenada Publishing, 1979). See also Seyfort Ruegg, *Three Studies,* p. 4, n. 5.

111 Born in 1055, he is the figure associated with the initial dissemination of the so-called "Prāsaṅgika Madhyamaka" teachings in Tibet. According to Stag tshang lo tsā ba, he

was the reincarnation of Candrakīrti and of Atiśa. See TT, 116. The latter, unable to introduce the Prāsaṅgika teachings into Tibet effectively, is said to have taken rebirth as Pa tshab in order to do so. He studied with pandits in Kashmir for 23 years and returned to Tibet to found a monastic study center in 'Phen yul where many of the works of Candrakīrti were translated into Tibetan. Apparently lacking disciples, he is said to have been given students by Sha ra ba (TT, 114). See GJL, 199; TT, 114–19; BA, 341ff.; DN, 415ff.; Shākya mchog ldan, BB, 233–34. His four main disciples (according to BB) were (1) Rma bya pa Byang chub brtson 'grus (GJL, 199; TT, 114; and BA, 343/DN, 417 all have Byang chub ye shes), (2) Gtsang pa Sar spros (GJL: spos; BA/DN: sbos; TT: Sa pa; Stag tshang in TT, 116: Gtsang pa 'Bre snur), (3) Dar yul ba Rin chen (GJL and BA/DN: Dar - yul ba - Yon tan grags; TT: Gangs po; Stag tshang in TT, 116, 119: Gangs pa She'u, also one of Rngog's chief students), and (4) Zhang (Thang sag/zag pa) 'Byung gnas ye shes (GJL and BA/DN: Ye shes 'byung gnas). BB, 234, states that it is through Zhang Thang sag pa that (ten generations later) the lineage of Pa tshab came to Dmar ston (= Thang sag pa'i sprul sku?) Gzhon nu rgyal mtshan, who then passed it on to Rong ston Shes bya kun rig (1367–1449), the teacher of Go rams pa. None of Pa tshab's works are known to survive, although he is cited and paraphrased by later scholars; see, e.g., Rong ston pa, BTN, 24f. (where Pa tshab is cited to the effect that Mādhyamikas reject positive theses, but not negative ones, so that there is no contradiction to their rejecting causality, and accepting that rejection), 152 (regarding the subject matter of the thirteenth chapter), and 331 (*mdzad byang* = colophon). See also Seyfort Ruegg, *Three Studies*, p. 44ff.

112 Student of Pa tshab (see previous note), and founder of Thang sag/zag monastery, where the Prāsaṅgika teachings were preserved at least until the time of Go rams pa. For a list of his known writings (none of which survive) and the abbatial succession of his monastery see BA, 343–44; and DN, 417–18. Zhang Thang sag pa seems to have been a controversial figure almost from the outset. BB, 233, states of Rma bya pa that he had expertise in both the words and the meaning of the doctrines of his master, Pa tshab; but of Zhang Thang sag pa (BB, 234) simply that he was "equal" *(cha mnyam pa)* in regard to both the words and meaning, but equally what? Interestingly, Stag tshang lo tsā ba, *Grub mtha' kun shes rnam bshad*, 244, attributes exactly the same quality of erudition to Rma bya pa, but states (quite bluntly) of Zhang that he *lacked* expertise in regard to both words and meaning (*gnyis ka la mi mkhas pa;* this same tradition is known to Mang thos, TT, 114)! And while the Prāsaṅgika Madhyamaka teachings of Zhang Thang sag pa seemed to have been flourishing at Thang sag at the time of the writing of DN and BB, Thu'u kvan (*Grub mtha'*, 189) cites Karma Dkon gzhon to the effect that had it not been for Red mda' ba, the very mention of the word "Madhyamaka" would have completely disappeared from Thang sag, since before Red mda' ba "there was nothing but the dead corpse of Madhyamaka left there" *(dbu ma shi ro gcig las gzhan med)*. Perhaps this shows, more than anything else, that what Thang sag pa considered to be the Madhyamaka was, at the very least, controversial; see Tauscher, *Die Lehre*, pp. 33–34, 165ff. This is witnessed as well by comments such as those of Lcang skya who, in his commentary on the *A ma ngos 'dzin* (offprint of xylograph, no bibliographical information), 8b, states that "except for Thang sag pa, the [Madhyamaka] interpretations of those [other] founding scholars accords with our own." Although Shākya mchog ldan mentions, curiously, that Thang sag pa composed many works "based on the notes *(mchan)* and subject headings *(sa bcad)*" of the teachings of his master, Pa tshab, none of his texts seem to have survived, nor do they seem to be cited by later scholars, as are the works of Pa tshab himself. Rong ston pa, BTN, 334, also mentions Zhang Thang sag pa,

and the special oral instruction *(man ngag)* lineage of the Madhyamaka that passes down from him; and both Rong ston pa and Go rams pa cite him in their respective texts, on which see below. See also Yoshimizu, "The Madhyamaka Theories Regarded as False by the Dge lugs pas," WZKSO 37 (1993): 207–9, 212–13, where other mentions of Thang sag pa in the works of Rong ston and Go rams pa are given; and Seyfort Ruegg, *Three Studies,* pp. 49–50.

113 One of the four chief disciples of Pa tshab lo tsā ba (see above). DN gives Rma bya Byang brtson's date of death as 1186 (BA, 329, mistranslates; DN, 400: *Phya pa sa mo glang* [= 1169] *la gshegs nas lo bcu bdun la Rma bya Byang brtson gshegs*); and states later that he was one of Phya pa's lions (see below), and a student of Jayānanda, and of the latter's student, Khu lo tsā ba (BA, 343; DN, 417), but DN lists the student of Pa tshab as Byang chub *ye shes.* A note (*mchan*) in TT, 117, states that Rma bya Byang ye dag pa might have been the student of Rma bya Byang brtson; and the text itself continues, "Yol lcags Rma bya Byang chub brtson taught the Madhyamaka to three (students): Rma bya Byang ye, Zhang thang zag and Gangs mnyan, the student of Gtsang pa Sa"; see also TT, 119. As does BA, Shākya mchog ldan (BB, 233) identifies Rma bya Byang brtson with Rma bya pa Rtsod pa'i seng ge, one of the eight lions of Phya pa Chos kyi seng ge (1109–1169), on which see GJL, 228–29. GJL, 281, identifies him as one of Sa skya paṇḍita's (1182–1251) teachers in the field of logic *(tshad ma),* but, given the approximate dates of Pa tshab, this, if true, could only have been for a short period in Sa pan's youth. BA, 147, also identifies him as a teacher of the great Rnying ma scholar-saint Rta ston Jo bo ye shes (1163–1230), on which see also GJL, 267–68. Although the author of several commentaries on Indian Madhyamaka texts (see BA, 343; DN, 417; and Seyfort Ruegg, *Three Studies,* p. 52), there survives only his magnificent commentary on the *Mūlamadhayamakakārikā,* the *Dbu ma rtsa ba shes rab kyi 'grel pa 'thad pa'i rgyan* (Gangtok: Rumtek, 1975); given the discrepancies concerning his name in the historical sources, it is worth mentioning that the colophon of *this* particular text gives the author's name as Byang chub brtson 'grus. See also Paul Williams, "Rma bya pa Byang chub brtson 'grus on Madhyamaka Method," *Journal of Indian Philosophy* 13 (1985): 205–25; Seyfort Ruegg, *Three Studies,* pp. 50–54; David Jackson, "Madhyamaka Studies," p. 24; and L. W. J. van der Kuijp, "Phya-pa Chos-kyi Seng-ge's Impact on Tibetan Epistemological Theory," *Journal of Indian Philosophy* 5 (1978): 366, n. 12.

114 Ngor chen, *Ngor chos byung,* 320, identifies a Bzad pa ring mo Dbang phyug as one of the four "scholarly" sons of Sa skya paṇḍita, but this would appear to be too late to be the present figure. Shākya mchog ldan, *Rngog lo tsā ba,* 451, identifies him as a student of Mnyal pa Dad pa bzang po.

115 BA, 344, and DN, 418, lists a Slob dpon Shes rab rdo rje as the third abbot of Thang sag after Zhang Thang sag pa. BA, 1025 (DN, 1194) mentions Lce sgom Shes rab rdo rje in the lineage of a certain Avalokiteśvara cycle.

116 It is because of expressions such as this that this view came to be known in Dge lugs pa circles as the "view that things are neither existent nor nonexistent" *(yod min med min gyi lta ba).* Consider, for example, Sum pa mkhan po's remarks in Sum pa mkhan po Ye shes dpal 'byor, *Chos 'byung dpag bsam ljong bzang* (Lan kru'u: Kan su'u mi rigs dpe skrun khang, 1992), 78: *rje yab sras ma byon khong du lta ba'i skor la bod 'dir ma dag pa mang du byung/... 'di yin 'di min gang du'ang bzungs med pa'i spros bral stong nyid yin zer ba dang/...yang chos thams cad btsal na mi rnyed pas yod pa'ang min zhing tha snyad 'khrul ngo tsam du yod pas med pa'ang min zhes zer ba dang/.* "Before the

Lord [Tsong kha pa] and his spiritual sons there arose in Tibet many errors in regard to the view [of emptiness]...[Like the view] that says that the freedom from proliferations, wherein nothing—'this is so,' 'this is not so'—is grasped at, is emptiness...and [the view that claims] that because no phenomenon is found when it is searched for, [phenomena] are not existent, and because they exist only within the purview of erroneous conventionality, they are not nonexistent." See also Cabezón, *Dose,* pp. 103, 113–17; LNMS, 176a–177a.

117 This is one of the classic forms of Madhyamaka reasoning: that things are not one, not many, not both, and not neither. See Hopkins, *Meditation on Emptiness,* p. 61ff.; Cabezón, *Dose,* pp. 147–49 and 464, n. 507; T. Tillemans, "The 'Neither One Nor Many' Argument for *śūnyatā* and its Tibetan Interpretations: Background Information and Source Materials," *Études de Lettres,* 3 (1982): 103–28; also found in *Contributions on Tibetan and Buddhist Religion and Philosophy,* ed. E. Steinkellner and H. Tauscher (Wien: Arbeitskreis für Tibetische und Buddhistische Studien, Universität Wien, 1983), pp. 305–20. Through statements like the one here, Go rams pa is making it clear that he is not repudiating the necessity of conceptual analysis as a stepping stone to the full understanding of emptiness. He will go on to say, however, that while such conceptual strategies are necessary, they are not sufficient for an understanding of full-blown emptiness, the real ultimate *(don dam mtshan nyid pa).*

118 We have already mentioned as puzzling the fact that Go rams pa considers Tsong kha pa a nihilist—puzzling because Tsong kha pa considers the Sa skya pa "neither existent nor nonexistent" position also to be a form of nihilism, since, as Tsong kha pa puts it in LRCM, such a view "refutes too much" *('gag bya khyab che ba).* Go rams pa is perhaps suggesting here that those who "grasp at emptiness" (i.e., Tsong kha pa and his followers) are giving something that is negative (i.e., emptiness) the status of an ultimate. Insofar as they are fixating on this negation, they are nihilists. This, at least, is one possible way of understanding Go rams pa's claim that Tsong kha pa is a nihilist.

119 GR, 178–79. See n. 65 above. In this passage, Tsong kha pa is making the point that the Madhyamaka critique does not destroy our ordinary conceptual understanding of the world: that the Madhyamaka deconstruction of the world, through its negation of the two forms of self-grasping, should not be seen as a critique of conceptuality in general. Contra a variety of Buddhist views that see conceptualization *itself* as the problem, for Tsong kha pa there are a plethora of conceptual understandings of the world that are valid and must be left intact—*including* the conceptual understanding of the ultimate truth, and of the Madhyamaka. But whether Tsong kha pa is making precisely that latter (and more specific point) in these lines, as Go rams pa is implying here, remains to be seen.

120 For similar critiques in Dge lugs pa sources, see Tsong kha pa's in *Legs bshad snying po,* Hopkins, *Reflections on Reality,* chaps. 16–17; also Mkhas grub rje, Cabezón, *Dose,* pp. 329–33; and 'Jam dbyangs bzhad pa in Hopkins, *Maps,* pp. 513–18.

121 On Red mda' ba, see note 106; a very brief biography in English is found in the preface to Jetsun Rendawa Shonnu Lodo, *Commentary to Āryadeva's 'Four Hundred Verses'* (Sarnath: Sakya Students' Union, 1974). A brief critique of Dol po pa—who, in fact, is never mentioned by name—can be found, e.g., in Red mda' ba's commentary on *Madhyamakāvatāra* (VI, 65); see DSG, 200–204; Stoter-Tillman and Tashi Tsering, *Commentary on the 'Entry into the Middle,'* pp. 211–15. Red mda' ba,

citing the *Laṅkāvatāra Sūtra,* claims that the teaching of the *tathāgatagarbha,* as it is literally taught in the scriptures followed by Dol po pa, is not even conventionally existent. It is, he states, a provisional teaching. Its true referent is emptiness. Finally, he claims that those who *do* take it as definitive, and as the ultimate purport of the Buddha, as Dol po pa does, have been misled. See also Red mda' ba's briefer statement in DSG, 13.

122 This passage is a paraphrase of Red mda' ba's position in DSG, 13. There Red mda' ba makes a reference to his "other book," in which he has given a detailed refutation of Dol po pa's interpretation of the Madhyamaka. This other book is probably his commentary on the *Uttaratantra,* the *Rgyud bla'i dka' 'grel dgongs zab snang ba,* which is unavailable to us. The section from Red mda' ba's *Rgyud bla ma* commentary relevant to the present passage has been quoted by 'Jam dbyangs bzhad pa in his *Grub mtha' chen mo;* see *The Collected Works of 'Jam-dbyang-bzhad-pa'i rdo-rje,* ed. Ngawang Gelek Demo (New Delhi, 1973), 14, pp. 665–66: *jo nang pa'i 'dod pa de bu ston rin po che dang rje btsun red mda' ba dang gnas rnying pa dang yar 'brog pa sogs du mas bkag pa'i rgyud bla'i dka' 'grel dgongs zab snang bar gang dag tshe 'dir sangs rgyas kyi bstan pa la zhugs su zin kyang...sngon chad rgya bod gsum gang du yang byung ba med do/;* Hopkins translates the entire passage in *Maps,* pp. 517–18.

123 See the *Abhidharmasamuccaya* citation discussed above in section 1.1.0.0.0, and n. 45. See also Luis Oscar Gómez, "Proto-Madhyamaka in the Pāli Canon," *Philosophy East and West* 26.2 (1976): 137–65.

124 The Vaibhāṣikas believe that there are fundamental elements—the *dharmas*—that substantially *(dravyasat)* exist. These constitute the fundamental building blocks of the universe. The five aggregates *(skandha)* that are the building blocks of the person, as dharmas, therefore, have real, substantial existence, even though they are the basis upon which a false self is imagined.

125 Similar expressions (e.g., *pratisamvid, pratyātmādhigama = so sor rang (gis) rig pa*) are found, for example, in *Laṅkāvatārasūtra.* See Lokesh Chandra, *Tibetan-Sanskrit Dictionary,* 2 vols. (Kyoto: Rinsen Book Co., 1976), II, pp. 2446, 2450; see also Shākya mchog ldan, BB, 215, for a division of the Madhyamaka based on the types of emptiness intuited, where the expression *so sor rang gis rig pa'i ye shes* is also found; and also Obermiller, *Prajñāpāramitā in Tibetan Buddhism,* p. 40, n. 2.

126 *Lokātītastava,* v. 2 and Lindtner, *Nagarjuniana,* 128; P vol. 46: 33. See also Fernando Tola and Carmen Dragonetti, "Nāgārjuna's Catustava," *Journal of Indian Philosophy* 13.1 (1985): 10, 20.

127 *Lokātītastava,* v. 3. Lindtner, *Nagarjuniana,* 128—which we follow in this translation—varies slightly (see the notes to the Tibetan text). The Skt. reads: *te 'pi skandhās tvayā dhīman dhīmadbyaḥ saṃprakāśitāḥ/ māyāmarīcigandharvanagarasvapnasaṃnibhāḥ//.*

128 See also Rong ston pa's comments in BTN, 287f. A similar division of the ultimate truth is found in some Dge lugs pa sources, e.g., in 'Jam dbyangs bzhad pa's *Grub mtha' 'khrul spong gdong lnga'i sgra dbyangs,* Daniel Cozort and Craig Preston, trans., *Buddhist Philosophy: Losang Gonchok's Short Commentary to Jamyang Shayba's Root Text on Tenets* (Ithaca NY: Snow Lion, 2003), p. 252; and in the latter's *Grub mtha' chen mo;* Hopkins, *Maps,* pp. 906–7. Despite use of similar nomenclature concerning the divisions of emptiness, however, Dge lugs pas' understanding of these different forms of emptiness is different from that being explained here.

129 Compare to Rong ston pa's comments in BTN, 226: *chos rnams kyi rang bzhin stong pa nyid ni gzhan sgra rtog las shes pa min te/ so sor rang gis rig pa'i mnyam bzhag gi ye shes kho nas mngon sum du rtogs bya yin pa'i phyir;* "Phenomena's emptiness of inherent [existence] is not something that is understood by other means—i.e., through words or conceptual thought. Why? Because it is something realized only in [an āryan's] own individual equipoise-gnosis."

130 See D. Seyfort Ruegg, "On the Knowability and Expressibility of Absolute Reality in Buddhism," *Journal of Indian and Buddhist Studies* 20 (1971): 495–99. On the general Dge lugs pa view concerning the claim of the ineffability of certain doctrines, which contrasts with Go rams pa's here, see Cabezón, *Buddhism and Language,* chapter 9.

131 That is, the emptiness of the self of persons, the metaphorical emptiness of phenomena, and the ineffable emptiness *qua* ultimate truth. The emptiness that Dol po pa accepts—an emptiness different from the three just mentioned—is of course the ultimate that is empty of everything that is other than it, but *not* empty of self-nature. It is an ultimate that is permanent, stable, pure, beginningless, and devoid of all conventionalities.

132 MMK (XIII, 7); Pras, 245–46. Toh no. 3824, Dbu ma *'a*, 8a. Inada, *Nāgārjuna,* p. 93; Garfield, *Fundamental Wisdom,* p. 211.

133 MMK (XIII, 8), Pras, 247. Toh ed. ibid. "The Victors have said that emptiness is the giving up of all views, but that those who have a *view* of emptiness will accomplish nothing." Inada, *Nāgārjuna,* p. 93; Garfield, *Fundamental Wisdom,* p. 212. An interpretation of this verse similar to the one offered here by Go rams pa is disputed by Mkhas grub rje in Cabezón, *Dose,* pp. 104–6.

134 There are various lists of Nāgārjuna's Philosophical Works. For an example of the classical Dge lugs pa sixfold list, see Cabezón, *Dose,* p. 78. For different ways of enumerating these texts in Sa skya pa sources, see Cabezón, *Dose,* p. 430, n. 182. Both Go rams pa and Dge lugs pa exegetes, however, agree, contra Dol po pa, that the purport of the philosophical and devotional works of Nāgārjuna is identical, even though they disagree as to what that purport is.

135 Dol po pa's exegesis on portions of Nāgārjuna's *Praises* can be found, e.g., in RCNG, 57ff.

136 A list of the three emptinesses is found in a variety of sources: e.g., in *Sūtrālaṃkāra* (XIV, 34), ed. S. Bagchi, (Darbhanga: Mithila Institute, 1970), 92: *abhāvaśūnyatāṃ jñātvā tathābhāvasya śūnyatāṃ/ prakṛtyā śūnyatāṃ jñātvā śūnyajña iti kathyate//.* Tib. in P vol. 108, Sems tsam *phi,* 22b.4: *med pa'i stong pa nyid shes shing/ de bzhin yod pa'i stong nyid dang/ rang bzhin stong pa nyid shes na/ stong pa shes pa zhes brjod do/*; the Tibetan P version mistakenly substitutes the word *yod pa* for *stong pa* in the third line. See also Sylvain Lévi, trans., *Mahāyāna-Sūtrālaṃkāra: Exposé de la doctrine du grand véhicule selon le système Yogācāra,* vol. II (Paris: Librairie Honoré Champion, 1907–11), p. 169. "Those who understand the emptiness of what is non-existent [that is, of the imaginary], who understand the emptiness of what does not exist as it [appears, that is, the dependent], and the emptiness of essence [that is, the kind of emptiness that is the real], understand emptiness." See also Nathmal Tatia, ed., *Abhidharmasamuccayabhāṣyam* (Patna: K. Jayaswal Research Institute, 1976), p. 52. Go rams pa's first emptiness, the "emptiness of own characteristic," is what in the *Sūtrālaṃkāra* passage is called "emptiness of what is nonexistent" *(abhavaśūnyatā,*

med pa'i stong pa nyid). Dol po pa (RCNG, 193–94) also cites this passage and gives his own interpretation.

137 This association of the three forms of emptiness with the three natures is found in the *Sūtrālaṃkārabhāṣyam* following the verse; see n. 136.

138 *Madhyāntavibhāga* (I, 2–3); P vol. 108, Sems tsam *phi*, 43b; S. Lévi, ed., *Madhyāntavibhāgaṭīkā* (Nagoya: Librairie Hajinaku, 1934), Skt. 10f, Tib. ed. 2f; R. C. Pandeya, ed., *Madhyanta-Vibhāga-Śāstra* (Delhi: Motilal Banarsidass, 1972), 9; T. Stcherbatsky, trans., *Madhyanta-vibhāga: Discourse on Discrimination Between Middle and Extremes*, Bibliotheca Buddhica 30 (1936; repr., Calcutta: Indian Studies Past and Present, 1971), 38ff; T. A. Kochmutton, *A Buddhist Doctrine of Experience: A New Translation and Interpretation of the Works of Vasubandhu the Yogācāra* (Delhi: Motilal Banarsidass, 1982), 29ff; S. Anacker, *Seven Works of Vasubandhu: The Buddhist Psychology Doctor* (Delhi: Motilal Banarsidass, 1986), pp. 211–12. See also G. Nagao, "From Mādhyamika to Yogācāra: an Analysis of MK, XXIV, 18 and MV. 1, 1–2," *JIABS* 2.1 (1979): 36. Tsong kha pa interprets these verses in LSN, 531–34; for Mkhas grub rje's interpretation see Cabezón, *Dose*, pp. 45 and 422, n. 88.

139 This position is similar to the position of Tsong kha pa, who also believes that in the Yogācāra or Cittamātra school the dependent is accepted as truly or substantially existing. See Tsong kha pa's remarks in LSN, 522ff., where he cites the *Viniścayasaṃgrahaṇī* and *Madhyāntavibhāga* (LSN, 531) as sources. The passage from *Viniścayasaṃgrahaṇī*, C, vol. 52, Sems tsam *zi*, 32a–32b reads: *mngon par brjod pa la yongs su goms pa rnam par bsal (bstsal) ba'i ming can gyi rnam par shes pa'i dmigs pa gzugs la sogs pa'i ming can gyi dngos po brjod du med pa'i bdag nyid gang gis yod pa de ni rdzas dang don dam pa gnyi gar yang de bzhin du yod par rig par bya'o//.*

140 This standard formula for expressing what might be termed "heresy"—that is, teachings that are non-authentic, not the word of the Buddha—is found as early as the *Mahāparinirvāṇasūtra*, ed. E. Waldschmidt (Kyoto: Rinsen Book Co. reprint, 1986), 238–39, where the full formulation is as follows: *sutre nāvataranti, vinaye na saṃdṛśyante, dharmatāṃ ca vilomayanti;* Tib. *mdo sde dang mi mthun/ 'dul ba la mi snang ste/ chos nyid dang 'gal/*. See also Ronald M. Davidson, "Appendix," in *Chinese Buddhist Apocrypha*, ed. Robert Buswell (Honolulu: University of Hawaii Press, 1990), pp. 291–325; and Cabezón, "Vasubandhu's *Vyākhyāyukti*."

141 Refutations of Dol po pa are to be found not only in the work of Red mda' ba, but also in the writings of Bu ston, and especially in those of his disciple Sgra tshad pa Rin chen rnam rgyal. See, for example, the latter's DZGG, 164ff. The same refutation is found in Tsong kha pa. *Legs bshad gser phreng = Shes rab kyi pha rol tu phin pa'i man ngag gi bstan bcos mngon par rtog pa'i rgyan 'grel pa dang bcas pa'i rgya cher bshad pa'i legs bshad gser phreng*, in *Tsong kha pa'i gsung 'bum (Collected Works)*, vols. *tsa* and *thsa*, (New Delhi: Ngawang Gelek Demo, nd), 524–25: *de'i phyir 'dus byas mtha' dag gis stong pa'i 'dus ma byas yongs grub don dam par grub pa byams chos phyi ma rnams dang sku mched kyi gzhung gi dgongs par 'dod pa blo rtsing rnams kyi mun sprul 'ba' zhig go/.*

142 JC: It has been suggested to me that the view being expressed here is not that of a generic defender of Dol po pa, but is rather Go rams pa's own position. If this is so, then Go rams pa is here critiquing Red mda' ba's refutation of Dol po pa. I grant that this reading is possible. If I opt to translate this portion of the text in such a way that it leaves the identity of Red mda' ba's challender ambiguous, it is because I believe

that Go rams pa himself means to. If nothing else, the discussion that follows shows that Sa skya pas were not univocal on the extent of Dol po pa's errors. At one end of the spectrum are thinkers like Red mda' ba, who believe that Dol po pa's views are tantamount to heresy. On the other, there are thinkers like Rong ston pa (see below) who believe that Dol po pa's views are superior to the views of the Cittamātra, falling just short of the Madhyamaka. While it can be argued that Go rams pa is more inclined to the former than the latter, nowhere does he actually say this. I try to capture this in my translation by leaving Go rams pa's own view as I believe he intended to portray it in this text: in a way that is occluded, if not necessarily ambivalent.

143 This refers especially to the *Saṃdhinirmocanasūtra;* on which see below.

144 The view expressed here is that in the hierarchy of different Buddhist philosophical tenets *(siddhānta)*, the views of Dol po pa fare rather well, since, like the Cittamātra, they serve as a stepping stone to the understanding of the highest view, that of the Madhyamaka. Hence, while granting that Dol po pa's is not the highest view, this supporter nonetheless (a) defends its inclusion in the Buddhist siddhānta scheme, and (b) makes a case for the fact that it deserves a relatively high position in such a scheme. On siddhānta classification as a hierarchical scheme, see Cabezón, "The Canonization of Philosophy," pp. 7–26.

145 The point is that there are, as it were, "advanced" Cittamātras who are close to understanding the Madhyamaka view (insofar as they have understood the truthlessness of the dependent), but still harbor tendencies to hypostasize the real. The advocate of Dol po pa is here claiming that these individuals are still Cittamātras, and hence that there are Cittamātras who hold that the dependent is truthless, the implication being that if such a class of Cittamātras exists, then there is no reason why Dol po pa cannot be considered among them.

146 Tibetan speculation concerning the division of Yogācāras, or Cittamātras, into those who accept true aspects (Skt. *ākāra*) and those who accept false aspects can be found in many works of the Tibetan siddhānta genre. See, for example, K. Mimaki, *Blo gsal grub mtha'*, 99ff. Also, 'Jam dbangs bzhad pa'i rdo rje, *Grub pa'i mtha' rnam par bzhags pa 'khrul spongs dgongs lnga'i sgra dbyangs,* Collected Works, vol. 14, ed. Ngawang Gelek Demo (New Delhi, 1973), 399f.; Cozort and Preston, *Buddhist Philosophy*, pp. 192–94. And Dkon mchog 'jig med dbang po, *Grub mtha'i rnam bzhag rin chen phreng ba*, ed. K. Mimaki, *Le Grub mtha'*, 89f.; H. Guenther, trans., *Buddhist Philosophy in Theory and Practice* (Baltimore: Penguin, 1971), pp. 104–7; Geshe L. Sopa and J. Hopkins, trans., *Practice and Theory of Tibetan Buddhism* (Bombay: B.I. Publications, 1977), pp. 107–9.

147 On Rong ston pa, see the Introduction; and also José I. Cabezón, "Madhyamaka Thesislessness," pp. 97–105.

148 In response to this, see DSG, 13, where Red mda' ba implies that there is a distinction between the Jo nang pas and "those who accept the final [wheel of the Buddha's] teachings to be of definitive meaning."

149 MMK (VII, 33); Pras, 176. Inada, *Nāgārjuna*, 70; Garfield, *Fundamental Wisdom*, p. 176.

150 Geshe Dargyay states: "The Sa skya scholar, Ven. Sherab Gyaltsen, has glossed *mnyam bzhag la zlo* as *mnyam bzhag bzhin pa'i skabs*, lit. 'during the period of equipoise,'" hence our translation, "within the context of equipoise."

151 *Vigrahavyāvartanī*, v. 24; P no. 5228, 24b; Skt. text ed. E. H. Johnston and A. Kunst in *The Dialectical Method of Nāgārjuna (Vigrahavyāvartanī)*, with Introduction and Notes by K. Bhattachārya (Delhi: Motilal Banarsidass, 1978), pp. 23–24; part II, pp. 26–27. See also the citation of this verse by an unidentified opponent, and Mkhas grub rje's response, in Cabezón, *Dose*, p. 257.

152 MMK (XXII, 11); Toh no. 3824, Dbu ma *tsa*, 13b; Pras, 444. Inada, *Nāgārjuna*, p. 134; Garfield, *Fundamental Wisdom*, p. 280.

153 The verse in question is most likely PV (I, 185); enumeration according to E. Steinkellner, *Verse-Index of Dharmakīrti's Works* (Wien: Arbeitskreis fur Tibetische und Buddhistische Studien, Universitat Wien, 1977), 41: *dngos med ngo bo med pa'i phyir/ ngo bo brjod pa dpyad bya nyid/ ma yin sgra ni de dag nyid/ rnam gcod rjod par byed par grub//.*

154 Go rams pa may here be referring to his contemporary Shākya mchog ldan, who was known to have held a view similar to the one being expressed here—at least during one period of his life. See Iaroslav Komarovski, trans., *Three Texts on Madhyamaka by Shākya Chokden* (Dharamsala: Library of Tibetan Works and Archives, 2000); and Tom J. F. Tillemans, and Toru Tomabechi, "Le *Dbu ma'i byung tshul* de Śākya mchog ldan," *Asiatische Studien/ Études Asiatiques*, 49.4 (1995): especially pp. 891–94. An interesting discussion of the similarities and differences between the Sa skya pa and Jo nang pa views is also to be found in Dpal ldan rdo rje, *Sa jo gnyis kyi lta ba'i gshan 'byed don la rang gi rtogs pa brjod pa*, TBRC W24129. In that text, the author makes it clear that it is principally in regard to the exposition of the conventional that the views of the two systems diverge: "Therefore, the real crux of the differences between the Sa skya and Jo nang views comes down to this: that [the former] claims that the view is a view that presumes that one will not abandon the appearances of the causal realm of conventionalities, while [the latter believes that the causal realm of conventionalities] *is* abandoned"; *des na sa jo gnyis kyi dgongs pa mi 'dra ba'i dngos gzhi/ rgyu kun rdzob gyi snang ba spong dang mi spong bar bzhed pa lta ba la lta ba zer ba yin no/*, ff. 2a–2b. It is interesting, then, that some scholars should have seen the major difference between the Sa skya pa and Jo nang pa views as lying not in their views of the ultimate (as Go rams pa clearly does in this section of the *Lta ba'i shan 'byed*), but rather in their respective treatment of the conventional. I am indebted to Gene Smith for providing me with the scanned images of this text, and it is to this TBRC edition that I make reference here.

155 Grags pa rgyal mtshan, *Mngon rtogs ljon shing = Mngon rtogs rgyud kyi mngon par rtogs pa rin po che'i ljon shing*, in *Grags pa rgyal mtshan bka' bum*, vol. 1, Bsod nams rgya mtsho, ed. *Complete Works of the Masters of the Sa skya Sect of Tibetan Buddhism* (Tokyo: Tōyō Bunko, 1968), 15.5ff.

156 It is clear that Go rams pa bases the comments that follow on Tsong kha pa's Madhyamaka works: works like GR, TSTC, and LSN. At the same time, Go rams pa does not directly quote those works, opting instead to paraphrase them. This has led later Dge lugs pa critics of Go rams pa—specifically, Se ra Rje btsun pa and Bde legs nyi ma—to fault him for misrepresenting Tsong kha pa.

157 Go rams pa's use of the words "thought construction" or "conceptual attachment" *(mngon par zhen pa)* here can be taken as an example of his misconstrual (or perhaps overstatement) of Tsong kha pa's position. In *Lam Rim chen mo*, ed. Ngawang Gelek Demo, part II, 208, Tsong kha pa states: *stong pa nyid du lta ba tsam la skyon*

yod pa'ang ma yin no.../; "There is no fault in merely viewing [things] in terms of emptiness." He then goes on to illustrate this with the following example: *dpe yang...nor med ces brjod pa'i tshe 'di la nor mi 'dug go snyam du dzin pa skyon ma yin gyi.../;* "For example, when [someone] states that he or she lacks wealth, there is no fault in thinking that [he or she] has no wealth." In other words, when we say that our pockets are empty, we are not thereby claiming that one should accept some real thing called "the emptiness of our pockets." Whereas Tsong kha pa uses fairly neutral terms like "viewing" and "understanding" in regard to the cognitive activity that is permissible in regard to emptiness, Go rams pa characterizes Tsong kha pa's position using a term with more negative connotations, namely, "thought construction," a term that is often used to imply a faulty cognitive process that brings with it hypostatization and attachment to an object.

158 Jñānagarbha, *Satyadvayavibhaṅgavṛtti,* C, vol. 28, Dbu ma *sa,* f. 5a; M. D. Eckel, *Jñānagarbha's Commentary on the Distinction Between the Two Truths* (Albany: SUNY Press, 1987), p. 159. This passage is found originally in the *Akṣayamatinirdeśa Sūtra.* The various versions present it in different forms. *Akṣayamatinirdeśa,* ed. J. Braarvig (Oslo: Solum Forlag, 1993), 114: *de la kun rdzob kyi bden pa gang zhe na/ 'jig rten gyi* tha snyad *dang yi ge dang* sgra *dang brdas bstan pa ji snyed pa'o//.* The Tun huang version (ibid. 278): *de la 'kund rdzob gyi bden ba gang zhe na/* gang *ji snyed du rjig rten gyi* rtsod pa *dang/ yi ge dang sgra dang/ brdas bstan pa'o//.* In Tun huang gang *ji snyed* for Skt. **yah kaścid/*ye kecid; tha snyad/rtsod pa* for Skt. *vyavahāra* and for Go rams pa's *tha snyad* gdag pa; Eckel, *Jñānagarbha's Commentary,* p. 121, n. 29, for *vyavahāra prajñapti.*

159 *Satyadvayavibhaṅgakārikā,* v. 7. Eckel, *Jñānagarbha's Commentary,* p. 159.

160 MA (VI, 23), 102; MA-Fr, 299, and n. 7 for the Skt. C. W. Huntington, *The Emptiness of Emptiness,* p. 160. For Mkhas grub rje's comments on this verse, see Cabezón, *Dose,* p. 363. See also K. Mimaki, *Blo gsal grub mtha',* 148ff; and Michael Broido, "Veridical and Illusive Cognition: Tsong-kha-pa on the Two Satyas," *Journal of Indian Philosophy* 16 (1988): 34–37.

161 *Bodhicaryāvatāra* (IX, 2); Bhattacharya, *Bodhicaryāvatāra,* 185; la Vallée Poussin, *Bodhicaryāvatāra,* p. 110; Steinkellner, *Eintritt,* p. 114; Crosby and Skilton, *The Bodhicaryāvatāra,* p. 115. See also M. Sweet, "*Bodhicaryāvatāra* (IX, 2) as a Focus for Tibetan Interpretations of the Two truths in the Prāsaṅgika Mādhyamika," *JIABS* 2.2 (1979): 79–89.

162 *rigs shes rjes dpag* should be understood as inferential valid cognition arising from logical reasoning, as pointed out in Go rams pa's TN-SK, 49.2.6: *rigs shes tshad ma ni rtags la brten pa'i rjes dpags yin pa'i phyir.*

163 Go rams pa appears to be at most paraphrasing, and not actually quoting Candrakīrti, since nowhere does the *Yuktiṣaṣṭikāvṛtti,* C, vol. 24 *(ya),* make this precise point. The closest one comes to the kind of notion being presented here is perhaps the discussion of the fact that an understanding of the two truths reinforces conventional morality; this is found in the commentary to vv. 30–31. See Cristina Anna Scherer-Schaub, *Yuktiṣaṣṭikāvṛtti: Commentaire à la soixantaine sur le raissonnement, ou, Du vrai enseignement de la causalité par le maître indien Candrakīrti* (Bruxelles: Institut belges des hautes études chinoises, 1991), pp. 72, 244–47. For a discussion of passages in Candrakīrti that are closer to the set of issues being discussed here, see

Guy Newland, *The Two Truths in the Mādhyamika Philosophy of the Ge-luk-ba Order of Tibetan Buddhism* (Ithaca: Snow Lion, 1992), pp. 87–89.

164 For a later Dge lugs pa response to this position, see 'Jam dbyangs bzhad pa's *Grub mtha' chen mo,* translated in Hopkins, *Maps,* pp. 906–7. See also Napper, *Dependent Arising,* pp. 429–39; Newland, *Two Truths,* pp. 161–62.

165 *Bodhicaryāvatāra* (IX, 8ab); Bhattachārya, *Bodhicaryāvatāra,* p. 186; Crosby and Skilton, *The Bodhicaryāvatāra,* p. 115; Steinkellner, *Eintritt,* p. 115.

166 MABh, 106; MA-Fr, 303. Toh no. 3862, Dbu ma *'a,* 254b. The full passage reads: "Those who suffer from an eye disease *(rab rib can)* perceive [various illusions]: entities like [nonexistent] hair, etc. But just as their [false perceptions] pose no challenge to the [validity of the consciousness] of those who *lack* the eye disease, likewise, the consciousnesses of ordinary beings, devoid of stainless wisdom, cannot challenge [the validity of] the stainless vision [of those who see reality]. Therefore, in such a way, worldly [beings' way of seeing things] poses no threat to the object [of āryan gnosis]." When the *context* of this passage (and those that follow) is taken into account, it is not a straightforward thing to see how precisely they bolster Go rams pa's argument that the emptiness that is the object of conceptual understanding is not a real ultimate. In the translations of these passages that follow we have adopted a policy of charity, offering translations that attempt to make Go rams pa's case, even while realizing that more accurate translations that take the context of the passages into account would in many instances have led to different translations that have little to do with the point Go rams pa is trying to prove.

167 *Satyadvayavibhaṅga,* 10cd; C vol. 28, Dbu ma *sa,* f. 6a; Eckel, *Jñānagarbha's Commentary,* p. 77, Tib. 161, where the second line varies from that found in Go rams pa's text: "It is reality *qua* object, but is not [real] reality."

168 *Prajñāpāramitāratnaguṇasaṃcayagāthā* (I, 9); A. Yuyama, ed., *Prajñā-pāramitā-ratna-guṇa-saṃṃcaya-gāthā* (Cambridge: Cambridge University Press, 1976), p. 160; LK vol. 34, Shes phyin *ka,* f. 189b. See also E. Conze's translation of the *Ratnaguṇa* in *The Perfection of Wisdom in Eight Thousand Lines and its Verse Summary* (Bolinas: Four Seasons Foundation, 1973), p. 10. For Tsong kha pa's discussion of this passage, see LRCM, 641; Cutler, *Great Treatise,* p. 193; and also A. Wayman, *Calming the Mind and Discerning the Real* (NY: Columbia University Press, 1978), p. 251.

169 *Pañcaviṃśatisāhasrikā-Prajñāpāramitā,* Toh no. 9. See *Pañcaviṃśatisāhsrikā-Prajñāpāramitā,* ed. Nalinakasha Dutt, Calcutta Oriental Series 28 (London: Luzac and Co, 1934), p. 139. The canonical version of this *Prajñāpāramitā* sūtra in Tibetan does not appear to have lines identical to those cited here; although for similar passages, see Toh. no 9, Nyi khri *ka,* 201b–202a, 204b. See also E. Conze, *The Large Sūtra on Perfect Wisdom with the Divisions of the Abhisamayālaṃkāra* (Berkeley: University of California Press, 1975).

170 *Abhisamayālaṃkāra* (III, 3ad); Go rams pa quotes only the first and fourth lines of this verse; Rāmaśaṅkaratripāṭhi, ed., *Abhisamayālaṃkaravṛttiḥ Sphuṭārtha* (Sarnath: Central Institute for Higher Tibetan Studies, 1977), Skt. 38, Tib. 69; the entire verse in that edition reads: *rūpādiskandhaśūnyatve dharmeṣu tyadhvageṣu ca/ dānādau bodhipakṣeṣu cāryāsaṃjñā vipakṣatā/; gzugs sogs phung po stong nyid dang/ dus gsum gtogs pa'i chos rnams dang/ sbyin sogs byang chub phyogs rnams la/ spyod pa'i 'du shes mi mthun phyogs//.* See also E. Obermiller, *Prajñāpāramitā in Tibetan Buddhism,* p. 68, where it is made clear that what is being spoken of is the relative inferiority of the

understanding of śrāvakas; also E. Conze, trans., *Abhisamayālaṃkāra Prajñāpāramitā* (Calcutta: Asiatic Society, 1954), p. 44. Go rams pa also cites this verse in *Lta ngan mun sel*, 588.

171 See *Abhisamayālaṃkāra* (I, 27–31); Conze, *Abhisamayālaṃkāra*, p. 14; Rāmaśaṅkaratripāṭhi, *Abhisamayālaṃkāravṛttih*, Skt. 13–15, Tib. 22–25.

172 MMK (XIII, 8); Toh no. 3824, Dbu ma *tsa*, 8a. Inada, *Nāgārjuna*, p. 93; Walleser, *Die Mittlere Lehre*, p. 75; Garfield, *Fundamental Wisdom*, pp. 36, 212–15. On Tsong kha pa's discussion of this verse, see LRCM 640–43; Cutler, *Great Treatise*, pp. 192–93. See also A. Wayman, *Calming the Mind*, p. 249.

173 MMK (XXII, 11); Toh. no 3824, Dbu ma *tsa*, 13b; Inada, *Nāgārjuna*, p. 134; Walleser, *Die Mittlere Lehre*, p. 139; Garfield, *Fundamental Wisdom*, pp. 61, 280. Go rams pa also cites this verse in *Lta ngan mun sel*, p. 588.

174 *Lokātītastava*, P vol. 46: 34.2.5; Lindtner, *Nagarjuniana*, pp. 136–37. The verse is also cited by Go rams pa in *Lta ngan mun sel*, p. 588.

175 MMK (XXVII, 30); Toh. no 3824, Dbu ma *tsa*, 18b; Pras, 592; Inada, *Nāgārjuna*, p. 171; Walleser, *Die Mittlere Lehre*, p. 176; Garfield, *Fundamental Wisdom*, pp. 83, 352.

176 MABh (Bhopal), 6. Toh no. 3862, Dbu ma *'a*, 22b.

177 MABh, 111, commenting on MA (VI, 29); Toh no. 3862, Dbu ma *'a*, 256a; MA-Fr, 307; Huntington, *The Emptiness of Emptiness*, pp. 233–34, n. 49.

178 *Satyadvayavibhaṅga* (v. 11a followed by an "intermediate verse" or *antaraśloka* that is *not* part of the root text); C, vol. 28, 61.5; Eckel, *Jñānagarbha's Commentary*, pp. 77, 162.

179 See Tsong kha pa's discussion concerning those who take emptiness to be a truly existent thing in LRCM, 639ff; Cutler, *Great Treatise*, 190ff. There he makes it clear that if the logic of the Madhyamaka requires that emptiness itself be repudiated, then the Madhyamaka is tantamount to realism: "If you disagree, and you refute the existence of emptiness which is the absence of intrinsic nature, then the absence of intrinsic nature would not exist. In that case, since essential or intrinsic nature *would* exist, it would be totally inappropriate to refute intrinsic nature"; Cutler, *Great Treatise*, p. 191. Note Tsong kha pa's commitment to the principle of double negation—that if *not-x* is repudiated, *x* is being affirmed—in this passage, something that Go rams pa will fault him on below. Viewed from a more psychological angle, we can say that Tsong kha pa believes that the conceptual thought that understands the emptiness of something—a sprout, say—does not automatically understand the *existence* of its emptiness. When this is so, it is for him a given that it—the very thought that understands emptiness—*cannot* grasp at the *true existence* of the emptiness. Neither the object of the understanding of emptiness (i.e., emptiness itself), nor the object of the subsequent thought that emptiness exists (i.e., the existence of emptiness) is for Tsong kha pa something that is to be repudiated by Mādhyamikas. Granted, says Tsong kha pa, the reification of emptiness can occur; emptiness can be grasped as if it were something real. However, this hypostatization of emptiness is not an intrinsic part of the conceptual thought that understands emptiness. When it *does* occur, says Tsong kha pa, then a separate form of reason—one that takes "emptiness" as its subject—must be employed to rid oneself of that reification. "When we refute the essential or intrinsic nature of a seedling, we have definite knowledge that the seedling does not intrinsically exist. Then, even if some other awareness apprehends that absence of intrinsic

nature as existing, reason does not refute the object of that other mind [i.e., the existence of the emptiness]. However, if that mind holds that emptiness exists essentially, then reason does refute that"; Cutler, *Great Treatise,* pp. 190–91 (my insertion).

180 The argument between Tsong kha pa and Go rams pa here hinges upon their respective interpretations of the so called "tetralemma" *(catuṣkoṭi, mu bzhi),* the fourfold analysis that Mādhyamikas use to deconstruct the world. Go rams pa takes the tetralemma as it is found in a variety of Madhyamaka sources at face value: (1) *x* is not existent, (2) *x* is not non-existent, (3) *x* is not both existent and nonexistent, and (4) *x* is not neither; and in Go rams pa's understanding, Mādhyamikas renounce the law of double negation (on which, see below). According to Tsong kha pa, the tetralemma cannot be posited in this fashion, for it would then violate the law of double negation, which he is loathe to do, and which he considers "an overly literal misunderstanding of Madhyamaka texts"; ŁRCM, 600; Cutler, *Great Treatise, vol. 3,* p. 147. For this reason, Tsong kha pa believes that what is being repudiated—i.e., in the first *koṭi*—is not "mere existence," but rather "*inherent* existence"; see LRCM, 637; and Cutler, *Great Treatise,* p. 189. But if this is true, says Go rams pa, then emptiness comes to be understood simply through the understanding of the first *koṭi,* making the other three unnecessary. For Go rams pa, understanding the first *koṭi* brings one to a kind of partial view of emptiness; but then, he believes, the tendency is to hypostasize that emptiness, and so there is a need for the second *koṭi,* which is a repudiation of emptiness.

181 Go rams pa is probably here refering to the eleventh rooth tantric vow "[insisting] on perceiving nameless dharmas using a logical mind" *(ming dang bral ba'i chos la rtog ges blos 'jal ba);* see Krang dbyi sun et. al. *Bod rgya tshig mdzod chen mo* (Beijing: Mi rigs dpe skrun khang, 1998), p. 2207. But see also the list of "root downfalls"—or serious transgressions—related to the *upatantra* given by Dudjom Rinpoche, the eleventh of which corresponds to "rejection of the Dharma"; see Dudjom Rinpoche, *Perfect Conduct: Ascertaining the Three Vows* (Boston: Wisdom, 1996). Interestingly, Tsong kha pa considers the position that Go rams pa is here maintaining equally heinous: "In brief, if you claim that the emptiness which is the absence of intrinsic existence is not the sublime emptiness taught by the Buddha and you refute it, then you will be reborn in a miserable realm due to having abandoned the true teaching"; LRCM, 600; Cutler, *Great Treatise,* vol. 3, p. 148.

182 An *analogue* of *x* is something that is concordant with—or analogous to—*x,* but not really *x.* In this case, the emptiness that can be expressed in language and understood conceptually is the *analogue* of the real ultimate truth that is beyond language and conceptual thought. Such an analogue to the ultimate—or, put another way, this quasi-ultimate—is an ultimate "in name only" *(rnam grangs pa'i don dam).* This doctrine has Indian origins; see Eckel, *Jñānagarbha's Commentary,* p. 112, n. 9.

183 For any syllogism to be valid, its "reason" *(rtags)* and "pervasion" *(khyab pa)* must be established for—that is, it must be acceptable to—the person who is being addressed. In the present instance, the reason ("it is not conventionally nonexistent") is accepted by Tsong kha pa. At the risk of over-simplifying, the pervasion is an "if-then" statement of the form "if reason, then predicate." In this case, it is: "If the pot is not conventionally nonexistent, then it must exist within the purview of the thought that is analyzing it." With regard to translating the Tibetan word *khyab,* which I have rendered here as "pervasion," see Kajiyama, *An Introduction to Buddhist Philosophy* (Kyoto University, 1966), p. 97; Stcherbatsky, *Buddhist Logic*

(New York, 1962), pp. 180, 186; E. Steinkellner has translated *khyab pa* as "nexus"; see his *Dharmakīrti's Pramāṇaviniścayaḥ Zweites Kapitel: Svārthānumānam, Teil II* (Wien: Verlag der Österreichischen Akademie der Wissenschaften, 1979), p. 83, n. 289.

184 One of the most famous philosophical debates in Buddhist history is that between the so-called Svātantrika and Prāsaṅgika Mādhyamikas. Both schools believe that Mādhyamikas can show their opponents the fallacious nature of their beliefs. For example, a Mādhyamika can show a follower of the Indian Sāṃkhya school that a sprout cannot arise from itself. (Sāṃkhyas believe that results are latent in their causes, and therefore that the sprout in some sense already exists at the time of the seed.) Do the Mādhyamikas and their opponents, however, share the same perspective on the different parts that make up the syllogism? For example, do they even share a common subject (the sprout), given that their presuppositions about the workings of causality are so different? Svātantrikas, who are said to hold to a strict form of formal logic, believe that such a common subject must appear *(chos can mthun snang)* to both parties in order for the syllogism to be valid and convincing. Prāsaṅgikas believe that this is not necessary—that logic can operate (and be convincing) without such rigid structures. Prāsaṅgikas therefore believe that Mādhyamikas can enter into successful arguments with their opponents even if they do not apprehend the terms of the argument (or the structures of reasoning) in the same way. In the present context, Go rams pa appears to be arguing that (from a Prāsaṅgika perspective at least) Mādhyamikas and Sāṃkhyas do not share a common subject because, in that context, Mādhyamikas possess no valid cognition that perceives the subject. (Whether he means that they possess no valid cognition of the subject *at all* or simply no valid cognition that perceives the subject the way that the Sāṃkhyas do is a question that he here leaves unanswered.) This is the background required to understand Go rams pa's challenge to Tsong kha pa. Now let us turn to the case at hand: a Mādhyamika is analyzing whether or not a pot truly exists. And Go rams pa asks Tsong kha pa: "When the Mādhyamika comes to the second *koṭi*—'not conventionally non-existent'—does the pot exist within the purview of the Mādhyamika's analysis?" Tsong kha pa, he implies, has only one answer: "It must exist, since it is not conventionally non-existent." But if this is Tsong kha pa's answer, Go rams pa continues, then that means that Mādhyamikas have valid cognitions of the subject during the time that they are engaged in analyzing the ultimate—that is, during time of the so-called "reasoning consciousness" *(rig[s] shes)*. If this is so, then it contradicts the *Prasannapadā's* statement to the contrary. In other words, Go rams pa is implying that Tsong kha pa has no rebuttal to the Svātantrika position (since that, after all, is what the *Prasannapadā* is attempting to do at this point: to rebut the Svātantrikas). The implication, of course, is that Tsong kha pa is therefore a crypto-Svātantrika himself. For a sampling of responses to some of the arguments Go rams pa is making here, see Cabezón, *Dose,* p. 100.

185 "Neither existence nor nonexistence" is not only a claim found in a variety of Madhyamaka sources, it is also the fourth *koṭi* of the *catuṣkoṭi.* As such, the Dge lugs pas, who are loathe to take such a claim literally, as we have seen, are required to offer an interpretation that preserves the law of double negation. Mkhas grub rje does precisely that in his reflections on the *catuṣkoṭi* in Cabezón, *Dose,* p. 106: "Hence, the meaning [of the *catuṣkoṭi*] is this: that existence does not truly exist, nonexistence does not truly exist, a third alternative which is both does not truly exist, and a third alternative which is neither does not truly exist." The last two *koṭis* are here formulated by Mkhas grub rje in such a way so as to prevent him from

falling into a contradiction. This is clear from a related passage in which he considers (and rejects) an alternative formulation that *does* culminate in contradiction: "One individual claims that [the *catuṣkoṭi* requires a simple qualifier—'ultimately'—to each of the four elements, yielding this:] (1) things are not ultimately existent, (2) not ultimately nonexistent, (3) not ultimately both existent and nonexistent, and (4) not ultimately neither existent nor nonexistent. But this does not free this individual from the fault of direct contradiction, for having advocated that things are not ultimately both, by claiming that they are ultimately neither, one is [in fact] advocating that they *are* ultimately both." The point is that Dge lugs pa scholars like Mkhas grub rje do not believe that the *catuṣkoṭi* should be interpreted as a simple negation of the true existence of the four *koṭis*—existence, nonexistence, and so forth—a position that Go rams pa is about to criticize.

186 MMK (VII, 33). Pras, 176; Inada, *Nāgārjuna*, p. 70; Garfield, *Fundamental Wisdom*, pp. 22, 176.

187 MMK (V, 6). Inada, *Nāgārjuna*, p. 58; Garfield, *Fundamental Wisdom*, pp. 15, 151.

188 See, for example, *Jñānasārasamuccaya*, *Ye shes snying po kun las btus pa*, attributed to Āryadeva, Toh no. 3851, Dbu ma *tsha*, 27b.

189 That is, if the *catuṣkoṭi* is to be interpreted such that the first *koṭi* = "*x* is not ultimately existent," and the second *koṭi* = "*x* is not conventionally non-existent," then the fourth *koṭi* should = "*x* is not neither ultimately existent nor conventionally nonexistent." A simple cancellation of the double negatives in this fourth *koṭi* yields what Go rams pa is claiming here. This is in fact precisely why Mkhas grub rje does *not* formulate the *catuṣkoṭi* in this fashion. See n. 185.

190 See M. Goldstein, *The New Tibetan-English Dictionary of Modern Tibetan* (Berkeley: University of California Press, 2001), p. 771.

191 The passage that follows is difficult, and the translation tentative. The words *rtags sal/bsal* can simply mean debate. But if considered separately, the *rtags* is the reason in a syllogism or reductio *(thal 'gyur)*, while the *sal/ bsal ba* is a technical term used to denote, in reductios like the one given here, that which in syllogisms is called the predicate *(bsgrub bya'i chos)*. Since what is being offered here is a reductio argument, there is, strictly speaking, no positive predicate, but only an absurd conclusion *(bsal ba)*; see Geshe Lobsang Tharchin, *The Logic and Debate Tradition of India, Tibet, and Mongolia* (NJ: Freewood Acres Howell, 1979), p. 135. Now if one were to take these terms in their more technical sense, then one might translate the present clause as follows: "Given that the reason's absurd predicate is in direct contradiction to what you accept."

192 Go rams pa is apparently quoting from Nāgārjuna's *Ratnāvalī* (I, 59); Rat, 25. See the note in the edition of the Tibetan text for variations. See also the translation by G. Tucci, "The Ratnāvalī of Nāgārjuna," *Journal of the Royal Asiatic Society of Great Britain and Ireland* (1934): 321: "If you object that by the refutation of its existence its non existence is logically implicit, why then does the refutation of non existence not imply existence?"

193 The implication, of course, is that the opponent to whom this verse is directed is someone like Tsong kha pa, who, by maintaining the law of double negation, believes that the negation of existence is tantamount to the upholding of nonexistence (and hence tantamount to nihilism).

194 See, e.g., Tsong kha pa's comments in LRCM, 643, 705; Cutler, *Great Treatise,* pp. 194, 260. Even after Tsong kha pa, there was a tradition among Dge lugs pa scholars of considering the *yod min med min* view to be tantamount to the views of Hwa shang, e.g., in the works of Se ra Rje btsun pa and Bde legs nyi ma. See *Lta ngan mun sel,* 172: *gzhan yang khyed kyis sher phyin gyi mdo dang/ dkon brtsegs/ mngon rtogs rgyan/ 'phags pa yab sras kyi gzhung rnams kyi don gnas lugs bsgom pa'i tshe/ yod med yin min bden par yod med sogs gang du yang mi 'dzin pa yin gyi bdag med pa'i don bsgoms na yang chad pa'i mthar lhung bar bzung 'dug pa 'di ni hwa shang gi lugs yin gyi dbu ma'i dri tsam yang mi bro ste/.* And 183: *yod med yin min sogs gang du yang mi 'dzin pas grol ba 'thob na gnyid 'thug po log pas kyang yod med dang yin min sogs gang du mi 'dzin par mtshungs pa'i phyir.* This issue is much elaborated in the *Lta ngan mun sel,* but restrictions with regard to space do not allow for a further discussion of this controversy. Hwa shang's doctrinal position is discussed in the following publications: Paul Demieville, *Le Concile de Lhasa;* Houston, *Sources;* D. Seyfort Ruegg, *Buddha Nature.* See also the following note.

195 Most notably in his *Bhāvanākramas.* See Gyaltsen Namdrol, *Bhāvanā-krama* (Sarnath: Institute of Higher Tibetan Studies, 1985); G. Tucci, *Minor Buddhist Texts,* Serie Orientale Roma, 9.2 (Rome: IsMeo, 1956–58); Luis O. Gómez, "Primer Tratado de Cultivo Graduado," *Dialogos* 11.29–30 (1977).

196 Bla ma Dbu ma pa ("Madhyamaka Lama") Dpa' bo rdo rje (fourteenth century; exact dates unknown) was a figure that Tsong kha pa initially relied on to "channel" Mañjuśrī when Tsong kha pa had questions concerning emptiness. The traditional hagiographies of Tsong kha pa state that this became unnecessary when Tsong kha pa began to have visions of Mañjuśrī himself. That many of these works also claim that Tsong kha pa's principal Madhyamaka teacher was Red mda' ba (and not Bla ma Dbu ma pa) is probably indicative of the fact that Dge lugs pas were at some level uncomfortable with Tsong kha pa's connection to the latter. Go rams pa is far from being the only figure in Tibetan history to claim that Bla ma Dbu ma pa misled Tsong kha pa. See, Kaschewsky, *Das Leben,* pp. 98–104. See also Yoshimizu, "Madhyamaka Theories," pp. 218–19, n. 43.

197 This is not a direct quote, but rather a paraphrase of Tsong kha pa's *Gsang ba'i rnam thar,* which reads: *nged kyi lta ba 'di thal rang gang yin zhus pas gang yang min gsung/ de dus rje 'di'i thugs la yang khas len ci yang med cing/ gang du'ang bzung mi nyan par lta ba de thugs la bde ba tsam yod par 'dug go/.* See *Rje rin po che'i gsang ba'i rnam thar...rin po che'i snye ma* by Mkhas grub rje, in *The Collected Works of Rje-tsong-kha-pa,* vol. *ka,* ed. Gelek Demo (New Delhi, n.d.), 171.1–2. Similar lines are also found in Mkhas grub rje's other biography, the *Dad pa'i 'jug ngog,* in *Collected Works,* Lhasa Zhol ed., vol. *ka,* 31a: *de'i tshe rje 'di'i thugs yul na yang khas len ci'ang med cing gang yang rang lugs la bzhags med par gzhan ngo 'ba' zhig la skyel ba'i dbu ma'i lta ba de cung thugs la bde bar yod pas/ bdag gi dbu ma'i lta ba 'di thal rang gang gi lta ba yin zhus pas/ gang gi'ang min zhes gsung zhing.*

198 On Zhang thang sag pa Ye shes 'byung gnas, see above, n. 112. See also L. Dargyay, "Tsong-kha-pa's Understanding of Prāsaṅgika Thought," *JIABS* 10.1 (1987): 59; BA, 343; Padma dkar po, *Chos 'byung bstan pa'i pad ma rgyas pa'i nyin byed* (blockprint, no bibliographical information), 118.5.

199 In point of fact Mkhas grub rje, the "author" in question, does not use the words Go rams pa attributes to him; see n. 197 for the Tibetan. Instead he says that at this point in time Tsong kha pa held the view that "nothing whatsoever is to be accepted...and

that nothing whatsoever was to be grasped at," a view "that [Mādhyamikas] posited nothing whatsoever in their own system, but only when confronting others." Nowhere in this context does he mention the view of "neither existence nor nonexistence," nor the name of Zhang Thang sag pa.

200 Compare to the position of Mi pham in John Pettit, *Mipham's Beacon of Certainty* (Boston: Wisdom Publications, 1999), p. 387.

201 See the section, "Those who claim that the freedom from extremes is the Madhyamaka" below.

202 In this section, Go rams pa attempts to show that Tsong kha pa has misunderstood what the Indian scriptures and treatises mean when they say that things are only a "conventional designation"—that they can only be posited as something labeled by words and thought. The scriptural sources use both of these terms—"words" and "thought"—to designate that on the basis of which the world is posited or constructed. Go rams pa will claim that Tsong kha pa emphasizes the "word" portion of this formula, and hence that he gives a more linguistic interpretation, ending up as a nominalist. Following Jñānagarbha, Go rams pa opts for emphasizing the "thought" portion of the scriptural passages. Even when the texts claim that the things of the world are "mere names," he says, what they *really* mean—given that words originate in the mind—is that they are "mere mental constructs." Of course, offering this more mentalistic picture of the world is consistent with Go rams pa's general view that the Yogācāra and Madhyamaka are compatible, a stance that has led Cabezón to label him a "soft doxographer"; see Cabezón, "Two Views of the Svātantrika-Prāsaṅgika Distinction," pp. 289–315. On Madhyamaka nominalism, see Cabezón, *Buddhism and Langauge,* chapter 8. See also Paul Williams, "Tsong-kha-pa on *kun-rdzob bden-pa,*" in *Proceedings of the 1979 Oxford Symposium on Tibetan Studies,* ed. M. Aris and A. Suu Kyi (Warminster: Aris and Phillips, 1981).

203 Go rams pa is here paraphrasing Tsong kha pa's *Legs bshad snying po,* where he says that there is nothing that is not established through linguistic designation and that even the two truths, and saṃsāra and nirvāṇa, are all established in this way. Tsong kha pa sees his exposition as being in line with Nāgārjuna's intention, as interpreted by Buddhapālita and Candrakīrti. Tsong kha pa states in LSN, 627: *'on kyang mchod sbyin no// mig go zhes pa sogs kyi tha snyad kyang nges par bya dgos pas tha snyad kyi dbangs gis ma bzhag pa'i ngo bo med pa dang/ tha snyad kyi dbang gis yod par bzhag pa la 'khor 'das kyi rnam gzhag thams cad ches shin tu 'thad pa'i bden pa gnyis kyi rnam gzhag 'di ni sang rgyas bskyang dang zla ba'i zhabs kyis 'phags pa yab sras kyi dgongs pa bkral ba 'grel pa gzhan las khyad zhugs pa'i khyad chos bla na med pa 'o//.* Tsong kha pa cites the *Dharmasaṃgīti Sūtra* and *Śūnyatāsaptati* in support of his position. But Go rams pa asserts that the meaning of those texts is contrary to what Tsong kha pa is attempting to prove, and Go rams pa in fact uses the same sources to argue for his own interpretation.

204 Go rams pa's quotation differs from the *'Phags pa chos yang dag par sdud pa (Dharmasaṃgīti Sūtra)* as given in LK vol. 65 (*dza*), 65b. For the Sanskrit, see Vaidya, *Bodhicaryāvatāra Pañjikā,* 274; Vaidya, *Sikṣasamuccaya,* p. 140. Chinese trans. in *Lokasannive̒śa,* Taisho no. 761, 627a.

205 C vol. 28, Dbu ma *sa,* 5a; Eckel, *Jñānagarbha's Commentary,* p. 158.

206 *Śūnyatāsaptati* v.1. Toh. no. 3827, Dbu ma *tsa,* 110a; Lindtner, *Nagarjuniana,* pp. 34–35.

207 C vol. 28, Dbu ma *sa*, 5a. See Eckel, *Jñānagarbha's Commentary*, pp. 158, 74, and p. 121, n. 29. We have followed Eckel's lead in the translation of this passage.

208 Thus Go rams pa follows Jñānagarbha in maintaining that the conventionalism of the Mādhyamikas is not a linguistic conventionalism as much as a cognitive conventionalism. Or, more precisely, that "according with the language of the world" is the result of a logically and temporally antecedent "accordance with the thought of the world." See Eckel, *Jñānagarbha's Commentary*, passim for more on this topic.

209 And, in fact, Tsong kha pa believes that Jñānagarbha, the author of the text that Go rams pa is quoting here, is a Svātantrika, although see Eckel's astute observations concerning Tsong kha pa's position in this regard; *Jñānagarbha's Commentary*, pp. 27–31.

210 MA (VI, 54cd), 145; MA-Fr, 333. Huntington, *Emptiness of Emptiness*, pp. 163 and 240, n. 81.

211 MA (VI, 53), 144; MA-Fr, 332. Huntington, *Emptiness of Emptiness*, p. 163. "The three" being spoken of here refers to the mind *(manas)*, the object *(dharma)* and the mental consciousness *(manovijñāna)*; see Huntington, *Emptiness of Emptiness*, p. 240.

212 MA (VI, 29a), 109; MA-Fr, 305. Huntington, *Emptiness of Emptiness*, p. 160.

213 MABh, 110; MA-Fr, 306. Toh no. 3862, Dbu ma *'a*, 255b.

214 On Tsong kha pa's concept of *zhig pa dngos po ba* see GR, 283–85; TSNS, 218–28, 353–69; and LSN, 640. For further discussion, see L. Dargyay, "Tsong-kha-pa's Concept of Karma," pp. 169–78.

215 MA (VI, 32), 114; MA-Fr-309; Huntington, *Emptiness of Emptiness*, p. 161: "Worldly people merely sow the seed, and yet they claim, 'I produced that boy,' or they imagine 'That tree was planted [by me].' Therefore production from another is not viable even by the standards of mundane existence."

216 See Tsong kha pa's remarks in GR, 254–55.

217 See above, n. 76.

218 See above, n. 77. Also, Dkon mchog 'jigs med dbang po, *Grub mtha' rin chen phreng ba*, Mimaki, 79f.; Sopa and Hopkins, *Practice and Theory*, p. 76.

219 A more detailed discussion of this issue is found in Go rams pa's TN-CW, 524ff.

220 The actual MA lines (VI, 39) read "no foundation [consciousness]" *(kun gzhi med)* rather than "no real destruction" *(zhig dngos med)*. Huntington, *Emptiness of Emptiness*, p. 162: "No [action] is terminated through its intrinsic nature, and consequently one must understand that even without any repository for its efficacy, and despite the lapse of a considerable period of time following the termination of the action, the fruit [of that action] will materialize somewhere"; see also pp. 235–36, n. 57.

221 For example, in MMK (XVII, 6); Pras, 311. Inada, *Nāgārjuna*, p. 106; Garfield, *Fundamental Wisdom*, p. 233:

> If until the time of ripening
> Action had to remain in place, it would have to be permanent.
> If it has ceased, then having ceased,
> How will a fruit arise.

222 As mentioned above, Go rams pa offers a more extensive critique of Tsong kha pa's theory of the workings of karma in TN-CW, 524ff. Go rams pa also develops his own thought regarding karma in his commentary to MMK, *Dbu ma rtsa ba'i shes rab kyi rnam par bshad pa yang dag lta ba'i 'od zer, The Complete Works of Go-ram* (sic)*-bsod-nams-seng-ge,* vol. 2 (Tokyo, 1969), pp. 329–33. A brief rejection of Tsong kha pa's theory regarding the workings of karma is also found in his *Nges don rab gsal,* 369–70. Se ra Rje btsun Chos kyi rgyal mthsan has responded to Go rams pa's refutation of Tsong kha pa's karma theory in *Lta ngan mun sel,* 264–74.

223 The scenario is this. Imagine a cup full of what human beings call "water." When "hungry spirits" (pretas) sees this, they do not see water, but rather pus and blood; when hell beings see it, they may see molten metal. Gods see nectar, and so forth. The beings in each realm see what it is their karmic predisposition to see.

224 On *dngos po stobs zhugs (kyi rjes dpag),* see D. Jackson, *The Entrance Gate for the Wise (Section III),* vol. II (Wien: Arbeitskreis für Tibetische und Buddhistische Studien, Universität Wien, 1987), pp. 428–30.

225 On *log pa'i kun rdzob,* see *Bodhicaryāvatāra Pañjika,* Vaidya, 171. Tsong kha pa, and the Dge lugs pas generally, maintain that the distinction between true and false conventionalities *(yang dag kun rdzob/ log pa'i kun rdzob)* is a uniquely Svātantrika tenet that is rejected by the Prāsaṅgikas; see Cabezón, *Dose,* pp. 368–69.

226 MA (VI, 71), 164; MA-Fr, 318. Huntington, *Emptiness of Emptiness,* p. 165: "[The mechanism involved when] hungry ghosts experience cognition of a river flowing with pus is identical to that of the visual organ afflicted with opthalmia. Our meaning here must be understood as follows: Just as there is no object of knowledge, there is no cognition." See also GR, 338ff.

227 Go rams pa uses Kaśyapa and Purāṇa as the names of two different persons in his example, but usually they are part of a single name "Purāṇa-kaśyapa."

228 *dbang gis phyug pa dag ma gtogs.* The implication seems to be that only a god-like being would presume to make such an absurd claim and hope to get away with it.

229 Tsong kha pa's understanding of "the bowl filled with water" is also discussed by Go rams pa in his TN-SK, 60.2, where he quotes from GR and then argues against its interpretation. The later Dge lugs pa polemicists Se ra Rje btsun pa and Bde legs nyi ma, in turn, criticized Go rams pa for *his* views; see, e.g., *Lta ngan mun sel,* 316–38.

230 Go rams pa is claiming that his view is the more intuitive and therefore that it is the one that accords with the Prāsaṅgika imperative to accept things as they are posited in the world. He is further arguing that Tsong kha pa, precisely because his position is so *counter*intuitive, is resorting to a form of philosophical speculation that is a breach of the Prāsaṅgika mandate to abide by what the world accepts. At issue here, of course, is where one draws the line between what is acceptable and unacceptable metaphysical speculation in the Prāsaṅgika system.

231 Regarding the obscurations to omniscience, see the above section, "[How Tsong kha pa] identifies the two obscurations."

232 MMK (XVIII, 5); Pras, 350. Inada, *Nāgārjuna,* p. 114; Garfield, *Fundamental Wisdom,* p. 248. Rong ston explains this verse in his MMK commentary (BTN, 212) as follows: *las dang nyon mongs pa ni...rnam par rtog pa las byung ste...rnam par rtog pa de dag ni spros pa las byung ste.../*; "karma and the afflictions come from misconcep-

tion...[and misconceptions] come from proliferations." See also E. Frauwallner, *Die Philosophie des Buddhismus* (Berlin: Akademie Verlag, 1969), p. 186.

233 *Śūnyatāsaptati,* v. 64; Toh no. 3827, Dbu ma *tsa,* 26b; Lindtner, *Nagarjuniana,* pp. 62–63, where the variants found in the canonical versions are given.

234 See *Catuḥśataka* (XIV, 25); Lang, *Āryadeva's Catuḥśataka,* pp. 134–35: *srid pa'i sa bon rnam shes te/ yul rnams de yi spyod yul lo/ yul la bdag med mthong na ni/ srid pa'i sa bon 'gag par 'gyur;* "Consciousness is the seed of existence, and objects are what it manipulates. But those who see that objects lack a self will bring an end to the seed of existence" (our translation). See Tsong kha pa's interpretation of this passage in, e.g., LRCM, 778; Cutler, *Great Treatise,* p. 335.

235 The seven limbs of dependent origination that are results are:
1. consciousness *(rnam par shes pa)*
2. name and form *(ming gzugs)*
3. the (six) sense fields *(skye mched)*
4. contact *(reg pa)*
5. feeling *(tshor ba)*
6. birth *(skye ba)*
7. old age and death (rga shi)

See Klong rdol bla ma Ngag dbang blo bzang, *Klong rdol bla ma rin po che ngag dbang blo bzang gi gsung 'bum: Tibetan Buddhist Studies of Klong rdol bla ma ngag dbang blo bzang,* edited from the Lhasa xylograph by Ven. Dalama, vol. 1 *(nya)* (Mussoorie: Dalama, 1963–64), p. 214.

236 The five limbs of dependent origination that are causes are:
1. ignorance *(ma rig pa)*
2. karmic formations *('du byed)*
3. craving *(sred pa)*
4. grasping *(len pa)*
5. becoming or existence *(srid pa)*

However, there are different understandings concerning where "consciousness" should be listed. Klong rdol bla ma, for instance, categorizes consciousness as only a cause; see his *Gsung 'bum,* vol.1 *(nya),* 214. In general, however, there are two kinds of "consciousness" *(rnam par shes pa)*: "consciousness at the time of the cause" *(rgyu dus kyi rnam shes),* and "consciousness at the time of the effect" *('bras dus kyi ram shes).* See Gung thang Dkon mchog bstan pa'i sgron me, *Rten 'brel gyi rnam bzhag lung rigs bang mdzod,* in *The Collected Works of Gung-thang,* vol. 3, (New Delhi: Ngawang Gelek Demo, 1972), 51.

237 *Ratnāvalī* (I,35). Rat, 15; John Dunne and Sara McClintock, trans., *The Precious Garland: An Epistle to a King* (Boston: Wisdom, 1997), p. 14.

238 See the above section, "[Tsong kha pa's] exposition of emptiness, the ultimate" and n. 55.

239 The two kinds of conceptualization (i.e., *gzung rtog* and *'dzin rtog*) are mentioned in AA (I, 34–35, 72); *Abhisamayālaṃkāra-Prajñapāramitā-Upadeśa-śastra: The Work of the Bodhisattva Maitreya, Part I, Introduction, Sanskrit text and Tibetan Translation,* ed. T. Stcherbatsky and E. Obermiller (1929; repr., Delhi: Sri Satguru Publicatons, 1992), Skt., 6, 10–11, and Tib. 10, 19; E. Conze, *Abhisamayālaṃkāra,* Serie Orientale Roma, VI (Rome: IsMEO, 1954), pp. 16, 29; Rāmaśaṅkaratripāṭhi, ed., *Abhisamayālaṃkāravṛttiḥ Sphuṭārtha,* 28–29, 47–48. Here *'dzin pa* refers to the self or

"I"—i.e., to the object of the notion "I"; *gzung ba* refers to the objects "enjoyed by" the I—that is, to phenomena. Tsong kha pa, *Legs bshad gser phreng*, 396, states: *gzung ba ni rdzas btags kyi bdag gis spyad par bya ba ste bza' bya'o// 'dzin pa ni de la spyod par byed pa ste za ba po'o//*; "'What is grasped' *(gzung ba)* refers to what is consumed, that is, what is enjoyed by a self that is imputed/labeled as a substance. What grasps *('dzin pa)* refers to the consumer, that is, to what does the enjoying." In Go rams pa's system both *gzung rtog* and *'dzin rtog* are seen as obscurations to omniscience. That is why śrāvakas and pratyekabuddhas cannot remove them. This position has been challenged by Tsong kha pa in *Legs bshad gser phreng*, 397.

240 *Mahāyanottaratantraśāstra* (= *Ratnagotravibhāga*) (I, 56); E. H. Johnston and T. Chowdhury, eds., *Ratnagotravibhāga Mahanottaratantraśāstra* (Patna: Bihar Research Society, 1950), p. 42f.; Toh no. 4024, Sems tsam *phi*, 57a. J. Takasaki, *A Study*, p. 236.k

241 *Mahāyanottaratantraśāstra* (V, 14ab); Johnston and Chowdhury, ed., *Ratnagotravibhāga*, p. 117; Toh. no. 4024, Sems tsam *phi*, 72b. Takasaki, *A Study*, p. 383. Per Takasaki, *A Study*, p. 383, n. 28, the "three misconceptions" refer to the "three aspects of activity," e.g., giver, receiver, and gift.

242 *gzung rtog (grāhyakalpa)*, abbreviation for *gzung ba'i rnam par rtog pa*, which are conceptualizations particularly attached to objects. This object-directed form of conceptualization *(gzung rtog)* is divided into two categories: (a) afflicted *(kun nyon gzung rtog)*, and (b) pure *(rnam byang gzung rtog)*. Haribhadra's commentary to the *Abhisamayālaṃkāra*, the *Sphuṭārtha*, Rāmaśaṅkaratripāṭhi, ed., *Abhisamayālaṃkāravṛtti*, 28, states: *gzung bar rnam par rtog pa kun nas nyon mongs pa'i gzhi'i rten can dang/ gnyen po'i rten can nyid kyis rnam pa gnyis;* "Conceptualization that is object-directed is of two kinds: (a) that which possesses an afflicted basis, and (b) that which possesses a basis *qua* antidotes." 'Jam dbyangs bzhad pa, *Phar phyin mtha' spyod*, 456, explains: *rang gi dmigs yul gzung ba la dmigs nas longs spyad bya'i rigs su bden par bzung ba'i cha nas bzhag pa'i bden 'dzin de shes sgrib gzung rtog gi mtshan nyid;* "The definition of an object-directed conceptualization that is an obscuration to omniscience is: "A form of grasping at truth that focuses on its own objective referent object, and posits it—from the object-aspect—as something that is true [while taking it simultaneously] as something that is to be enjoyed/manipulated." See also Conze, *Abhisamayālaṃkāra*, p. 16 and n. 108.

243 *'dzin rtog*, an abbreviation for *'dzin pa'i rnam par rtog pa*, refers to conceptualization that is particularly attached to the side of the subject. Subject-directed conceptualization *('dzin rtog)* is divided into two categories: (a) substantializing *(rdzas 'dzin rtog pa)*, and (b) nominalizing *(btag 'dzin rtog pa)*. The *Sphuṭārtha*, Rāmaśaṅkaratripāṭhi, *Abhisamayālaṃkāravṛtti*, 29, states: *gang zag rdzas su yod pa dang skyes bu btags par yod pa la dmigs pa'i 'dzin pa'i rnam par rtog pa yang rnam pa gnyis yin la/;* "It is of two kinds: the subject-directed conceptualization (a) that focuses on the person as a substance, and (b) that focuses on the individual as an imputation/label." For a more extensive discussion, see 'Jam dbyangs bzhad pa, *Phar phyin mtha' spyod*, 457. Also, Mimaki, *Le Grub mtha'*, p. 100; Sopa and Hopkins, *Practice and Theory*, p. 129; Guenther, *Buddhist Philosophy*, p. 134.

244 *Catuḥśatakavṛtti*, commentary to *Catuḥśataka* (XIV, 25).

245 Tsong kha pa discusses Bhāvaviveka's stance—citing the same lines that Go rams pa cites here—in his *Legs bshad snying po, Collected Works*, Lhasa Zhol ed., vol. 4 *(pha)*, 71aff. See also Thurman, *Tsong kha pa's Speech*, pp. 301–2. See also Mkhas grub rje's

defense of Tsong kha pa's claim that Bhāvaviveka believes that the mental consciousness is an instantiation or exemplification *(mtshan gzhi)* of the self—i.e., that it *is* the self—in Cabezón, *Dose,* pp. 186–87, where he in fact cites the same passage from the *Tarkajvāla* that Go rams pa cites in support of *his* position!

246 Go rams pa distinguishes between the self's *gdags gzhi* (the basis for designating the self) and its *mtshan gzhi* (an instantiation of the self). Thus he claims that Bhāvaviveka accepts consciousness as the basis for designating the self, but *not* as an instantiation of the self. See also TN-SK, 67ff. The *Tarkavjālā* passage can be found in C, vol. 19, 80b; and in Toh no. 3856, Dbu ma *dza,* 80b. See also Shotaro Iida, *Reason and Emptiness: A Study in Logic and Mysticism* (Tokyo: Hokuseido Press, 1980), p. 180.

247 In other words, those individuals go too far who believe that not finding the self in an analysis of the type described in the previous paragraph implies that the self does not exist even at the level of worldly conventions *in general.*

248 MA (VI, 162), 281; MA-Fr, 323. Huntington, *The Emptiness of Emptiness,* pp. 177 and 261, nn. 196, 198.

249 See n. 250.

250 The views of Rong ston Shes bya kun rig have also been discussed by Go rams pa in his TN-SK, 34.4ff. Go rams pa's interpretation of Rong ston pa's text has been critiqued by Se ra Rje btsun pa in *Lta ngan mun sel,* 135.

251 Tsong kha pa believes that the "mere I" is the ordinary, conventional conception of the self as this is accepted in the world. Since Prāsaṅgikas maintain that conventional reality is coterminous with what the world accepts—with worldly usage—they must assert the conventional existence of the "mere I." But then Go rams pa asks: What happens when this "mere I"—not the object of innate ignorance, which is clearly nonexistent, but the conventional self—is subjected to the Madhyamaka critique? Is there anything to be found? Does the conventional self "withstand" such an analysis? If so, says Go rams pa, then it must truly exist. The implication, of course, is that (as with other examples of Tsong kha pa's philosophical categories examined previously, like *destruction qua entity*), Tsong kha pa—at least in Go rams pa's view—is reifying a phenomenon, in this case the self *qua* "mere I." It would seem, therefore, that Go rams pa is implying that Tsong kha pa in the end accepts some notion of a real self, the so-called "mere I." In response to Go rams pa's argument a Dge lugs pa might reply that in Tsong kha pa's view the "mere I" is precisely the self as it is accepted in the world, i.e., *without analysis.* It becomes impossible, then, in Tsong kha pa's view, to subject the "mere I" to the Madhyamaka dialectic—that is, to subject it to what Tsong kha pa calls "an ultimate analysis"—since by definition the "mere I" is the *un*analyzed, conventionally accepted self.

252 *nyer len* (Skt. *upādāna*) may refer to the act of appropriating as well as to what is appropriated. In the present context, this allows for its identification both with karma—the action that leads to the appropriation of the aggregates—as well as with the aggregates that are appropriated. See also Go rams pa, TN-SK, 71.3.4f.: *bdag dang phung sogs la 'ang nye bar len pa po dang nye bar blang bya sogs kyi tha snyad ma dpyad pa'i blo ngor grub.* "Within the purview of a mind that does not analyze [or seek to find the referents of] linguistic terms like 'what appropriates' and 'what is appropriated,' the self and the aggregates are established."

253 MABh, 281; MABh (Bhopal), 216; MA-Fr, 323. In the MABh the five aggregates are identified with action *(las)*. See also GR, 456: *las su bya ba phung po lnga'o//;* "What is acted out are the five aggregates."

254 See MA (VI, 151), 271–72; MA-Fr, 316; Huntington, *Emptiness of Emptiness,* p. 176. The chariot (1) is not different from its parts; (2) is not the same as the parts, (3) does not possess the parts; (4) is not in the parts; (5) nor are the parts in it; (6) is not the mere composite of its parts; (7) is not the shape of those parts.

255 MABh, 288; MA (VI, 167cd). Huntington, *Emptiness of Emptiness,* pp. 177–78. The entire verse, in Huntington's translation, reads: "Qualities, parts, clinging, distinguishing characteristics, fuel, and so on; [in addition to] a possessor of qualities or parts, a base for clinging or for distinguishing characteristics, fire, and so on: Such things do not exist according to the seven alternatives when, after the manner of the carriage, they are subjected to analysis. On the other hand, they do exist insofar as they are taken for granted in the context of everyday experience."

256 This refers to the Vātsīputrīyas. See Cabezón, *Dose,* pp. 260 and 478, n. 650 for references to the views of this school in other Indian and Western sources.

257 *Catuḥśatakavṛtti,* commenting on (XIV, 25), for example, states: *de nyid kyi phyir rnam par shes pa dngos po'i rang gi ngo bo lhag par sgro 'dogs par byed pa nyon mongs pa can gyi mi shes pa'i dbang gis dngos po rnams la chags pa dang ldan zhing 'khor ba 'jug pa'i sa bon du gyur pa.* "Therefore, it is by virtue of consciousness' reification [of things] in terms of own-nature—it is by virtue of afflicted ignorance—that one becomes attached, and [this in turn] becomes the seed of entrance [i.e., the seed of future rebirth] in saṃsāra."

258 Based on the discussion that follows, the implication seems to be that when the *Catuḥśatakavṛtti* makes this claim, it is claiming that the self of phenomena is a grasping at truth *(bden 'dzin)*.

259 See Pras 350.13–15: *te ca vikalpā...prapañcād upajāyante.*

260 MMK (XVIII, 5). Pras, 350; Inada, *Nāgārjuna,* p. 114; Garfield, *Fundamental Wisdom,* p. 248.

261 Perhaps referring to the treatment of the topic in another section of the *Lta ba'i shan 'byed* itself; see below.

262 Tsong kha pa claims that śrāvakas and pratyekabuddhas understand the essencelessness of person *and* the essencelessness of phenomena; see GR, 60–76; and also Go rams pa's exposition of Tsong kha pa's views above. Go rams pa's critique of Tsong kha pa on this point is similar to Bhāvaviveka's position. Bhāvaviveka criticizes Buddhapālita's interpretation in his commentary in MMK, chapter VII, claiming that if the śrāvakas and pratyekabuddhas could acquire a correct understanding of the essencelessness of all dharmas, the Mahāyāna teaching would become meaningless. See also TN-SK, 32f; and GR, 84.

263 See *Abhisamayālaṃkāra,* (I, 25–27); Stcherbatsky and Obermiller, *Abhisamayālaṃkāra,* Skt. 4–5, Tib. 7–8; Conze, *Abhisamayālaṅkāra,* pp. 12–13. Rāmaśaṅkaratripāṭhi, *Abhisamayālaṃkāra Sphutarta,* Tib. 20–23.

264 *klu sgrub yab sras.* It is usually only Āryadeva who is considered Nāgārjuna's "spiritual son" *(sras)*, but Go rams pa implies elsewhere in the *Lta ba'i shan 'byed* that Candrakīrti should also be so considered.

265 *Lokātītastava*, v. 65. Lindtner, *Nagarjuniana*, pp. 138–39, which provides the Skt. The verse is also cited and discussed by Mkhas grub rje (see Cabezón, *Dose*, p. 206), who clearly realizes that it represents an impediment to the plausibility of Tsong kha pa's views on this matter.

266 *anyatīrthika;* Edgerton, *Buddhist Hybrid Sanskrit Dictionary*, p. 41, renders this as "heretic(s)."

267 *Ratnāvalī* (I, 79); Rat, 33. See also Tucci, "The Ratnāvalī of Nāgārjuna," pp. 237–52, 423–35; Michael Hahn, *Nāgārjuna's Ratnāvalī* (Bonn: Indica et Tibetica Verlag, 1982), 1:33; and Jeffrey Hopkins, *The Precious Garland and The Song of the Four Mindfulnesses* (New York: Harper and Row, 1975), p. 28; Dunne and McClintock, *Precious Garland*, p. 21.

268 *Ratnāvalī* (IV, 96); Rat, 131. Tucci "The Ratnāvalī," p. 434; Hopkins, *Precious Garland*, p. 76; Dunne and McClintock, *Precious Garland*, p. 71: "He taught to some a Dharma not based on duality. And to some, he taught a profound Dharma that terrifies the timid: its essence is emptiness and compassion, and it is the means to attain awakening." But see below, where the meaning of this verse appears to be understood differently by Go rams pa.

269 MABh, 31; MABh (Bhopal), 26–27; *Madhyamakāvatārabhāṣya*, Toh. no. 3862, Dbu ma *'a*, 230b.

270 MABh, 22–3; MABh (Bhopal), 20; *Madhyamakāvatārabhāṣya*, Toh no. 3862, 227b.

271 Tib. *khu 'phrig;* Skt. *bhīru* ("fearful, timid.") The Tibetan word *khu 'phrig* varies in its meaning according to different sources. According to Chos grags's *Dictionary* (Dharamsala: Damchoe Sangpo, 1980), it is synonymous with: (a) *rnam rtog za ba*, "to doubt, to be superstitious about," and (b) *brtag dpyad byed pa*, "to investigate." The *Bod rgya tshig mdzod chen mo*, 230, renders it similarly *dogs pa'am rnam rtog*, "doubt or superstition." Go rams pa, however, appears to give the word a more positive connotation. For example, he glosses the word in another work as follows: *rtogs pa po'i khyad par stong nyid la bag chags bzhag pa'i khu 'phrig yod pas;* "the characteristic of the one who realizes it is that s/he has apprehensions *(khu 'phrig)*, which are the latent propensities for [understanding] emptiness"; *Nges don rab gsal*, 349.2.3f. Ajitamitra's (Mi pham bshes gnyen's) commentary on the *Ratnāvalī*, the *Rin po che'i phreng ba'i rgya cher bshad pa*, glosses the word as "one who possesses it as an object": *khu 'khrig can de dmigs pa can.../*; C, vol. 93, olio 170b; Y. Okada, *Die Ratnāvalī des Ajitamitra*, Nāgārjuna's Ratnāvalī vol. 2 (Bonn: Indica et Tibetica Verlag, 1990), p. 133.

272 This line and the one immediately preceding it appear to contradict the meaning of the original *Ratnāvalī* passage, which states that it is precisely those who are apprehensive who *do not* realize or understand the profound doctrine of emptiness.

273 MA (VI, 4), 78; MA-Fr, 275–76. Toh no. 3862, 204a. The verse is preserved in Sanskrit; see Huntington, *Emptiness of Emptiness*, pp. 157 and 226, n. 6.

274 MMK (XVIII, 5); Pras, 349–50; Inada, *Nāgārjuna*, p. 114. Garfield, *Fundamental Wisdom*, p. 248.

275 MK (XIII, 8); Pras, 247; Inada, *Nāgārjuna*, p. 93. Garfield, *Fundamental Wisdom*, p. 212.

276 By way of comparison, see Pettit, *Beacon,* pp. 278–79, for Klong chen pa's and Mi pham's position on this issue.

277 This is a line from the second of the two passages from MABh just cited by Go rams pa.

278 For Go rams pa, the individuals who are depicted in MA (VI, 4)—who react to the teachings of emptiness by shedding tears, etc.—are Mahāyānists. Their response to the teachings appears to be for Go rams pa a result of the fact that the form of emptiness they are hearing is a more profound form of emptiness (an emptiness of all four extremes) that is taught only in the Mahāyāna, a form of emptiness that is *not* taught in the Hīnayāna, and not fathomed even by arhats. Thus, according to Go rams pa, Tsong kha pa is hard-pressed to explain why only Mahāyānists react to emptiness with tears, given that Tsong kha pa believes that both śrāvakas and bodhisattvas have access to emptiness. For Tsong kha pa's understanding of MA (VI, 4), see Anne Carolyn Klein, *Path to the Middle: Oral Mādhyamika Philosophy in Tibet* (Albany: SUNY Press, 1994), p. 157. There it becomes clear that Tsong kha pa does not take the next line in MA (VI, 5)—"the seed of a perfect Buddha's awareness lies within such a person"—as referring to the fact that the person of the previous verse has "awakened their Mahāyāna lineage" (as Go rams pa claims), but instead as implying that "Such [persons] have the seed of realizing emptiness."

279 The "three cycles" of giving are the giver, the gift, and the person to whom the gift is given.

280 If the perception spoken of here were a perception of true existence, says Go rams pa, then it would be utterly nonexistent, and not, as the passage states, a truth of the conventional world.

281 This very objection is first raised by Bhāvaviveka. It is answered by Candrakīrti in MABh. Tsong kha pa gives a synopsis of Candrakīrti's reasons in GR; see Hopkins, *Compassion in Tibetan Buddhism,* pp. 172–76.

282 See Hopkins, *Compassion in Tibetan Buddhism,* p. 119.

283 MABh, 23; MABh (Bhopal), 20.

284 The position being described here is of course that of Tsong kha pa and his followers. See, for example, Tsong kha pa's remarks in GR, 77ff.; see also Mkhas grub rje's comments on the topic, which reiterate and expand on Tsong kha pa's views, in Cabezón, *Dose,* pp. 206–7, 237–38.

285 According to Go rams pa's interpretation of MABh, Tsong kha pa should admit that Mahāyānists are less intelligent than śrāvakas because they need a detailed proof for understanding emptiness, while the śrāvakas can come to an understanding of emptiness through the use of an abbreviated form of reasoning. But Tsong kha pa has explained in GR that Mahāyānists resort to more extensive forms of reasoning because their goal is to develop a more comprehensive understanding of emptiness, so as to remove the obscurations to omniscience. By contrast, śrāvakas do not need such detailed proofs because their goal is to remove only the afflicted obscurations, thus requiring a less extensive understanding of emptiness. GR, 87, states: *nyan rang rnams ni nyon mongs tsam spong ba'i phyir brtson pa yin la/ de la ni de kho na nyid kyi don mdor bsdus pa de tsam zhig rtogs pas chog go/ theg chen pa shes sgrib spong ba lhur len pas/ de la de kho na nyid la shes rab mched nas blo shin tu rgyas pa zhig dgos pa yin no//;* "śrāvakas and pratyekabuddhas strive to eliminate only the afflictions, and [to

accomplish] this it is permissible [for them] to realize the meaning of reality in only an abbreviated fashion. Mahāyānists, [on the other hand], strive to eliminate the obstacles to omniscience, and [to accomplish] this they need an extremely extensive mind that has a profound knowledge of reality."

286 Of course, from Go rams pa's perspective the reason that śrāvakas move more swiftly through the path is not so much because they use abbreviated forms of reasoning, but because the form of emptiness that they cognize is more coarse.

287 See, e.g., *Pramāṇavārttika* (I, 239); Raniero Gnoli, ed., *The Pramāṇavārttikam of Dharmakīrti: The First Chapter with the Autocommentary* (Rome: IsMEO, 1960), p. 120, where the autommentary states: *tad apare 'py anuvadantīti nirdayākrāntabhuvanaṃ dhig vyāpakaṃ tamaḥ/;* "fie upon the pervading darkness that has cruelly befallen the world." See also Rgyal tshab Dar ma rin chen, *Tshad ma rnam 'grel gyi rnam bshad (Thar lam gsal byed),* in *Gsung 'bum, (Collected Works),* reprinted from impressions of the old Tashi lhunpo blocks, vol. *cha* (New Delhi: Ngawang gelek demo, 1980–1981); *Thar lam gsal byed,* Collected Works (Dharamsala: Shes rig par khang, 1984), vol. *cha,* 106a. There he explains this verse as follows: *dpyod pa ba chos can/ log rtog ngan pa'i mun pas khyab par thal/ dam bca' dang sgrub byed ltar snang 'di la'ang 'di kho na bzhin no/ zhes rjes su brjod pa yod cing zhen pa des na'i phyir/;* "This analysis is pervaded with the darkness of evil misunderstandings because, while the thesis and the proof (i.e., reason) are wrong, they claim them and become attached to them as if they were right."

288 Tsong kha pa makes clear his view in GR, 58, that the tenet that "the nine Bodhisattva stages are antidotes to the nine obscurations to omniscience" is not a Prāsaṅgika tenet. According to the AA, the path of meditation is divided into nine parts, each of which serves as an antidote to one of the nine obscurations to omniscience (small-small, small-medium, small-big, medium-small, medium-medium, etc.). AA (II, 30) states: *mṛdumṛdvādiko mārgaḥ śuddhir navasu bhūmiṣu/ adhimātrādhimātrāder malasya prātapakṣataḥ/*; Tib. *sa dgu la ni chen po yi/ chen po la sogs dri ma yi/ gnyen po chung ngu'i chung ngu la/ sogs pa'i lam ni dag pa yin/;* Stcherbatsky and Obermiller, *Abhisamayalaṅkara,* Skt., 15, Tib., 27; Conze, *Abhisamayālaṃkāra,* pp. 42–43. For a Dge lugs pa response to Go rams pa on this issue, see Se ra Rje btsun pa, *Lta ngan mun sel,* 93–97.

289 Actually a line of the *Pramāṇavārttika* (IV, 46); Toh. no. 4210, Tshad ma *ce,* 141a: *nan gyis khyod 'di 'dod ces pa/ gsal par dbang phyug spyod pa yin/.* "You say that you [nonetheless] accept this point insistently, but this is clearly like the analysis carried out by a [petulant] god."

290 It is widely accepted that Asaṅga and Vasubandhu interpreted the *Prajñāpāramitā* sūtras from a Cittamātra perspective, but there are no extant commentaries of either author on the AA. Haribhadra, mentions both of these figures in the introductory verses of his *Sphuṭārtha;* see Rāmasaṅkaratripāṭhi, *Abhisamayālaṃkāravṛttiḥ Sphuṭārtha,* Skt., 3f. See also Obermiller, *Prajñāpāramitā,* pp. 10–11.

291 Regarding *sbas don,* see Obermiller, *Prajñāpāramitā,* p. 6.

292 Tsong kha pa, of course, considers the AA to be a Svātantrika-Madhyamaka work.

293 Go rams pa is here attacking Tsong kha pa for a position that he takes in the context of his interpretation of five verses of the *Bodhicaryāvatāra* (IV, 45–49); that discussion is found in GR, 63–65.

294 The four aspects of the truth of cessation—four of the sixteen aspects of the four noble truths—are given in *Bod rgya nang don rig pa'i tshig mdzod* (Si khron: Mi rigs dpe skrun khang, 1993), I: 277: *nyon mongs pa dang sdig pa'i las rnams spangs te mi 'byung bas 'gog pa dang/ sdug bsngal ci yang mi 'byung bas zhi ba/ phyis kyang khams gsum du skye zhing sdug bsngal myong bar mi 'gyur bas gya nom pa/ 'khor ba las thar te myan 'das kyi gnas bde bar phyin pas nges 'byung bcas bzhi'o//*; "*Cessation,* because the afflictions and sinful action are abandoned and will no longer arise; *peace,* because no suffering whatsoever will arise; *sublime,* because one will never again be reborn into the three realms, and experience suffering [therein]; *deliverance* because one has become free from saṃsāra, and has gone to the bliss of the state of nirvāṇa."

295 Rta thul (i.e., Aśvajit), one of the five monks *(pañcavaggiyābhikkhū)* who Śākyamuni addressed in his first sermon; Edgerton, *Buddhist Hybrid Sanskrit Dictionary,* p. 81.

296 MABh, 71; MABh (Bhopal), 58. Toh. no. 3862, Dbu ma *'a,* 243b.

297 See Go rams pa, TN-SK, 35.3.3, where he discusses the meaning of the relevant *Bodhicaryāvatāra* passages.

298 BCA (IX, 47cd), 197.; L. de la Vallée Poussin, *Bodhicaryāvatāra,* pp. 121–22; Steinkellner, *Eintritt,* p. 122; Crosby and Skilton, *The Bodhicaryāvatāra,* p. 120.

299 For Mkhas grub rje's remarks on this topic, see Cabezón, *Dose,* p. 219.

300 Śāntarakṣita, *Madhyamakālaṃkāravṛtti;* C, vol. 28 *(sa),* 56b; Masamichi Ichigō, *Chūkan sōgenron no kenkyū: Shāntarakushita no shisō* (Tokyo: Buneidō, 1985), p. 14: *dngos po'i rnam pa ma brtags gcig pu na dga' ba ma lus pa gzugs brnyan la sogs pa lta bur / yang dag par na rang bzhin med par rtogs na...* The point of citing this verse and the ones that follow is to show that, contra Tsong kha pa, the Svātantrikas' formulation of emptiness is no different from that of the Prāsaṅgikas. See also Cabezón, "Two Views"; Malcolm David Eckel, "The Satisfaction of No Analysis: On Tsong kha pa's Approach to Svātantrika-Madhyamaka," in McClintock and Dreyfus, *The Svātantrika-Prāsaṅgika Distinction,* pp. 173–203.

301 Jñānagarbha, *Satyadvayavibhaṅga,* v. 20; Eckel, *Jñānagarbha's Commentary,* Tib., p. 174; trans., pp. 88–89.

302 Jñānagarbha, *Satyadvayavibhaṅga,* v. 21ab; Eckel, *Jñānagarbha's Commentary,* Tib., p. 175; trans., pp. 88–89.

303 Jñānagarbha, *Satyadvayavibhaṅgavṛtti;* Eckel, *Jñānagarbha's Commentary,* Tib., p. 175; trans., p. 89.

304 Bhāvaviveka, *Prajñāpradīpamūlamadhyamakavṛtti* (XXII, 8ab); C, vol. 18 *(tsha),* 222a.: *'ba' zhig ces bya ba ni ngo bo nyid med pa ste / ngo bo nyid kyi dri tsam gyis kyang ma bsgos pa dag yin no//;* "'Isolated' refers to the lack of a nature, and so it is pure, unstained even by the trace odor of essentialism."

305 Rāmasaṅkaratripāṭhi, *Abhisamayālaṃkāravṛttiḥ Sphuṭārtha,* 115.

306 Go rams pa maintains that there are two different conceptions of *ālayavijñāna* in circulation in the Indian tradition: one in the Cittamātra/Yogācāra sources, and the other among Mādhyamikas; see TN-SK, 55–56. This view has been criticized by Se ra Rje btsun pa in *Lta ngan mun sel,* 294–305.

307 According to Tsong kha pa and his followers, the Prāsaṅgika school does not accept the *ālayavijñāna* even on the conventional level; see *Dka' gnad brgyad kyi zin bris,* in

Tsong kha pa *Gsung 'bum* (Delhi: N. Gelek Demo, n.d.) vol. *ba,* 568. Go rams pa's point here is that Prāsaṅgikas *ought to* accept some notion of the *ālayavijñāna* because this is the view advocated by Nāgārjuna himself. In support of this, Go rams pa looks to three verses from *Bodhicittavivaraṇa,* vv. 33–35; Lindtner, *Nagarjuniana,* p. 196; see Go rams pa, TN-SK, 56. See also L. Dargyay, "Tsong-kha-pa's Understanding," pp. 62–63.

308 That Svātantrikas and Prāsaṅgikas differ in this regard—that is, over whether or not conventionally things exist by virtue of their own characteristics—is a well-known aspect of Tsong kha pa's Madhyamaka theory, found throughout his writings. See, for example, Cabezón, "Two Views," pp. 296–98; Thurman, *Tsong kha pa's Speech,* pp. 266ff., 296. See also four articles of Chizuko Yoshimizu, "Rang gi mtshan nyid kyis grub pa ni tsuite I," *Naritasan Bukkyō Kenkyūshu Kiyō* (1992) 15: 609–56; Yoshimizu, "Rang gi mtshan nyid kyis grub pa ni tsuite II," *Indogaku Mikkyōgaku Kenkyū, Essays in Honor of Dr. Y. Miyasaka on His Seventieth Birthday* (Kyoto: Hōzōka, 1993), 971–90; "On raṅ gi mtshan ñyid kyis grub pa III. Introduction and Section I," *Naritasan Bukkyō Kenkyūshu Kiyō* (1993) 16: 91–147; and "On raṅ gi mtshan ñyid kyis grub pa III. Section II and III," *Naritasan Bukkyō Kenkyūshu Kiyō* (1994) 17: 295–354. See also Lopez, *A Study of Svātanrika,* passim.

309 The argument that follows must have been well-known as a critique of the Dge lugs pas' views on this matter, since it is found in sources that predate Go rams pa. Mkhas grub rje, for example, cites the argument and responds to it in his *Stong thun chen mo;* see Cabezón, *Dose,* pp. 173–80.

310 The *Lta ba'i shan 'byed* is one of the few instances in classical Tibetan literature where an author gives the precise folio number of the work he is citing. It is not surprising that the enumeration does not correspond to that of the Lhasa Zhol edition of Tsong kha pa's *Collected Works,* published at the end of the nineteenth century, where the passage is found on folio 91a of vol. *pha.* It is, however, difficult to imagine how the passage could occur on a folio 48 of *any* edition unless (a) the folio pages contained twice as much material as the pages of the standard long-page *(dpe ring)* texts known to us today, or (b) the work was originally published in two volumes (unlikely, given that it is a relatively short work). See also below for another instance in which a folio enumeration of Tsong kha pa's texts are given.

311 LSN, 666. The Dge lugs pas claim that there are many ways of characterizing the type of false or reified existence, the negation of which is emptiness. Mkhas grub rje lists these in Cabezón, *Dose,* p. 172: true existence *(bden par grub pa),* ultimate existence *(don dam par grub pa),* existence by virtue of own characteristic *(rang gi mtshan nyid kyis grub pa),* and so forth. Tsong kha pa and his followers believe that the Prāsaṅgikas negate *all* of these forms of reified existence, but they claim that the Svātantrikas' critique is not as thorough-going. In particular, they hold that Svātantrikas believe that things exist by virtue of their own characteristic, at least at the level of conventions *(tha snyad du).* That does not mean, however, that the Dge lugs pas believe that the Svātantrikas are realists *(dngos smra ba),* for they do negate many, even if not all, of the forms of false existence mentioned in the above list. For example, Svātantrikas are said to negate true existence *(bden par grub pa).* Lcang skya rol pa'i rdo rje (1717–1786) puts it this way, "Even those Mādhyamikas [the Svātantrikas] who assert existence by way of its own character *(svalakṣaṇa, rang mtshan)* conventionally do not, in any way, assert that phenomena are truly established"; Lopez, *Study of Svātantrika,* p. 278. Or, as Mkhas grub rje states (*Dose,* p. 173), "Svātantrikas...believe that if something exists

by virtue of its own characteristic, it need not truly exist." See also Seyfort Ruegg, *Prolegomena*, pp. 57–58, n. 62.

312 LSN, 638.

313 See MA (VI, 201–215), 316–17, for Candrakīrti's discussion of specific or distinguishing characteristics, and the emptiness of such characteristics *(svalakṣaṇaśūnyatā)*; Huntington, *Emptiness of Emptiness*, pp. 181–82. And for Tsong kha pa's commentary on these verses, see GR, 519f.

314 On autonomous (Skt. *svatantra*, Tib. *rang rgyud*) forms of reasoning, see LMS, 58; M. Sprung, *Lucid Exposition of the Middle Way* (London: Routledge and Kegan Paul, 1979), p. 278; Cabezón, *Buddhism and Language*, chapter 7; and Dreyfus and McClintock, *The Svātantrika/Prāsaṅgika Distinction*, passim.

315 Tsong kha pa believes that the Svātantrikas' use of autonomous syllogisms is a reflection of the fact that they uphold a certain subtle form of reified existence, "existence by virtue of own characteristic." However, it is *not* the case that Tsong kha pa believes that *it is the function* of autonomous syllogisms and reasons *to prove* that things exist by virtue of their own characteristic.

316 In Dharmakīrti's system, "particulars," or "self-characterized phenomena" *(svalakṣaṇa, rang mtshan)* are synonymous with "thing" (Skt. *vastu*, Tib. *dngos po*); universals (Skt. *sāmānya*, Tib. *spyi*) are therefore "non-things" *(dngos med)*. See, for example, Dharmakīrti's comments on PV (I, 112); Gnoli, *The Pramāṇavārttikam*, p. 58. On the concept of *sāmānya* in Dharmakīrti's thought, see Dreyfus, *Recognizing Reality*, chapters 6–10; Anne C. Klein, *Knowing, Naming and Negation: A Sourcebook on Tibetan Sautrāntika* (Ithaca: Snow Lion, 1991), pp. 54–74. See also Stcherbatsky, *Buddhist Logic*, II: p. 40, n. 4.

317 The syllogism being spoken of here presumably looks something like this: "*Subject:* Generally characterized phenomena. *Predicate:* are unreal (or "lack thingness"). *Reason:* because they do not function efficaciously." Generally characterized phenomena *(spyi mtshan)* are precisely those phenomena that are not specifically characterized *(rang mtshan)*. Go rams pa seems to be claiming that since the subject, predicate, and thesis (the combination of subject and predicate) all belong to the realm of generally characterized, unreal, phenomena, they cannot be specifically characterized phenomena. He then plays on the grammar of the expression "established by virtue of their own (or specific) chararacteristic" *(rang gi mtshan nyid kyis grub pa)* to assert that these various parts of the syllogism cannot be so established because they are not specifically characterized phenomena. In response to this, Tsong kha pa might argue—as indeed he has in LSN and elsewhere—that the *rang mtshan* spoken of by the logicians (e.g., when they claim that generally characterized phenomena are unreal/non-things) is not the same as the *rang mtshan* rejected by Prāsaṅgikas in the expression *rang gi mtshan nyid kyis ma grub pa*. See Tsong kha pa, *Legs bshad snying po, Collected Works*, Lhasa Zhol ed., vol. *pha*, 32a; see also Mkhas grub rje's remarks on this topic in Cabezón, *Dose*, pp. 176–77.

318 The classical Indian locus for the discussion concerning the appropriateness of the use of autonomous *(svatantra)* forms of reasoning is MMK, and especially MMK (I, 1). The issue concerns the type of argumentation permissible in the Madhyamaka, especially in light of Buddhapālita's comments on this verse. Bhāvaviveka criticizes Buddhapālita's understanding of the type of argument that Nāgārjuna is leveling against the Sāṃkhyas here, and Candrakīrti, in turn, criticizes Bhāvaviveka and

defends Buddhapālita's interpretation. David Seyfort Ruegg has published a translation of Candrakīrti's *Prasannapadā* commentary on this verse in *Two Prolegomena,* pp. 1–135. Tsong kha pa's treatment of this topic can be found in TSTC, 31bff; LRCM, 672–719; Cutler at al, *Great Treatise,* chapters 18–21. See also Tsong kha pa, *Drang nges legs bshad snying po,* in *Collected Works,* Lhasa Zhol ed., 81b. Rong ston discusses the issue in BTN, 11ff.; BJN, 87ff. For Mkhas grub rje's analysis, see Cabezón, *Dose,* p. 290ff. Chos dbang grags pa'i dpal has also commented on the topic in *Dbu ma rtsa ba'i 'grel pa tshig gsal gyi mtha' bzhi skye 'gog pa'i stong thun,* Mādhyamika Text Series, vol. 1 (Delhi: Lha mkhar yongs 'dzin, 1972), 473–506. See also Hopkins, *Meditation on Emptiness,* pp. 469–98; Cabezón, *Buddhism and Language,* chapter 7; and T. Tillemans, "Tsong kha pa *et al.* on the Bhāvaviveka-Candrakīrti Debate," in *Tibetan Studies,* Proceedings of the 5th Seminar of the International Association of Tibetan Studies (Narita: Naritasan Shinshoji, 1992), I: 315–26.

319 Buddhapālita, *Mūlamadhyamakavṛtti, Dbu ma rtsa ba'i 'grel pa.* Toh no. 3842, Dbu ma *tsa,* 161b. See also M. Sprung, *Lucid Exposition,* p. 36; Seyfort Ruegg, *Two Prolegomena,* p. 25.

320 Bhāvaviveka, *Prajñāpradīpamūlamadhyamakavṛtti.* C, vol.18 *(tsa),* 49a; Toh no. 3853, Dbu ma *tsha,* 49a.; Seyfort Ruegg, *Two Prolegomena,* p. 26.

321 *gzhan la grags pa* or *gzhan grags (paraprasiddha),* "the reason accepted by the other party [i.e., by the opponent]." See Seyfort Ruegg, *Literature of the Madhyamaka School,* p. 79. For the views of Rong ston pa and Go rams pa concerning the difference between "inference based on what is acceptable to others" *(gzhan la grags pa'i rjes dpag)* and *svatantra* forms of inference, see Cabezón, "Two Views," pp. 298–306.

322 See Gerald James Larson, *Classical Sāṃkhya: An Interpretation of Its History and Meaning,* 2nd revised ed. (Delhi: Motilal Banarsidass, 1979). The Sāṃkhya accepts the doctrine of *satkāryavāda:* that the effect (the sprout) exists in a latent or unmanifest way within the cause (the seed), and that therefore when a thing arises from its cause, it is actually arising from an aspect, albeit an unmanifest aspect, of itself. See Pras, 16ff.; Tib. in *Dbu ma rtsa she'i 'grel pa tshig gsal* (Bhopal: 1968), 12ff.

323 Pras, 17; Tib. Bhopal ed., 12.

324 Pras, 15; Tib. Bhopal ed., 11.

325 For the relevant passage in *Prasannapadā,* where Candrakīrti quotes the *Catuḥśataka* and the *Vigrahavyāvartanī,* see Pras, 16; Tib. Bhopal ed., 11–12.

326 The relevant line in *Prasannapadā* reads (Pras, 16; Tib. Bhopal ed., 11.): *na ca mādhyamikasya svataḥ svatantramanumānaṃ kartuṃ yuktaṃ pakṣāntarābhyupagamābhavāt; dbu ma pa yin na ni rang gi rgyud kyi rjes su dpag par bya ba rigs pa ma yin te/ phyogs gzhan khas blangs pa med pa'i phyir ro/;* "If one is a Mādhyamika, it is incorrect for one to resort to autonomous inference because one lacks a belief in the other's position." See Go rams pa's comments in BPD, 408.2.4, where he also takes issue with Tsong kha pa's position that "lacking a belief in the other's position" means "lacking a belief in existence by virtue of own-characteristic."

327 See Rong ston Shes bya kun rig, BTN, 38.

328 Go rams pa takes a similar stance in regard to his teacher's interpretation in BPD.

329 Go rams pa is questioning his teacher's (Rong ston Shes bya kun rig's) interpretation of the lines from *Prasannapadā*—that is, he doubts Rong ston's justification for the

rejection of the use of autonomous syllogisms. According to Rong ston pa, *svatantra* forms of inference are to be rejected because Mādhyamikas do not accept the opposite of the position held by the opponent—that is, because they reject not only self-arising, but also the arising of one thing from another. Rong ston pa believes that accepting the opposite of a position being rejected in the Madhyamaka tetralemma—in this case the arising of one thing from another as the opposite of arising from itself—commits one to accepting *svatantra* forms of inference. Go rams pa is claiming that it is not correct to posit the Madhyamaka rejection of "the arising of one thing from another" as the reason for the rejection of autonomous inference. In other words, Go rams pa seems to hold that the use of autonomous syllogisms in the refutation of "self-arising" stands or falls on other grounds, without any need to refer to the Mādhyamika rejection of the arising of one thing from another, which occurs in the *next* section of the *Prasannapadā*. For more discussion of this point, see Cabezón, "Two Views," pp. 304–6.

330 See the relevant note in the Tibetan edition. The translation reflects the emendation.

331 See Pras, 19; Tib., Bhopal, 13. On the definition of proponent *(snga rgol)* and opponent *(phyi rgol)*, see Klong rdol bla ma, *The Collected Works of Longdol Lama* (New Delhi: International Academy of Indian Culture, 1973), I: 389: A proponent is a person who agrees to undertake a proof [of his thesis]; *snga rgol ni/ sgrub byed 'god par khas len pa'i gang zag/*. An opponent is a person who agrees to express a criticism [of someone else's position]; *phyi rgol ni sun 'byin brjod par khas len pa'i gang zag/*.

332 See Pras, 34; Tib., Bhopal, 24.

333 As regards the two terms in question, 'Jam dbyangs bzhad pa, in his MA commentary, gives the following explanation of "[their] own inference" and "inference acceptable to the other party"; *Dbu ma 'jug pa'i mtha' dpyod lung rig gter mdzod,* in *The Collected Works of 'Jam-dbyangs-bzad-pa'i-rdo-rje* (New Delhi: Ngawang Gelek Demo, 1973), 418: *rang grags kyi rtags dang/ de'i rjes dpag dang/ gzhan grags kyi rtags dang/ de'i rjes su dpag pa rnams don gcig...snga rgol dbu ma pas phyi rgol dngos smra la dngos po bden med sgrub tshe phyi rgol rang nyid la grags pas na rang grags dang/ snga rgol las gzhan pa'i phyi rgol la grags pas na gzhan grags zhes bshad pa'i phyir/;* "As regards 'a reason acceptable to [them]selves, and the inference it [generates],' and 'a reason acceptable to the other party, and the inference that it [generates]': these are synonymous. When it is the Mādhyamika *qua* proponent who is proving to a realist that things are truthless, since [the Mādhyamika is using reasoning] acceptable to the [realist] opponent [them]selves, it is called 'acceptable to [them]selves.' When [the Mādhyamika uses reasoning] acceptable to an opponent who is different from the proponent, it is called 'acceptable to the other party.'"

334 *rang ngos nas gzhal na tshad mas kyang grub la.* This is the crux of the passage, the interpretation of which makes or breaks Go rams pa's claim that Tsong kha pa has contradicted himself. If the expression *rang ngos nas* is interpreted, as Go rams pa interprets it, as refering to the Mādhyamika proponent ("from *our* own side"), then Tsong kha pa would seem to be upholding the position that Go rams pa claims he does: that even the Mādhyamika must ascertain the various parts of the syllogism by means of a valid cognition (though it still remains to be seen whether that form of ascertainment is of the same kind as that advocated by the opponent, and therefore whether the subject, predicate, etc., are held in common). If, however, *rang ngos nas* refers to the realist opponent ("from *their* own side"), then Tsong kha pa is making a different claim—namely, that it is not enough for the opponents to merely

accept—that is, to merely pay lip-service to—the various parts of the syllogism, but that they must actually establish these through the use of valid cognition *(tshad ma)*—i.e., that these must be for them *actual* beliefs. That Tsong kha pa means to imply the latter is evident from the rest of the passage. However, we have attempted to translate the passage in such a way that the ambiguity is somewhat preserved, and this so as to give greater plausibility to Go rams pa's reading.

335 See LSN, 665.

336 The ambiguity of the word *chos,* which can mean both phenomena *qua* existing thing, and property *qua* quality, is important here and in the passages that follow. Since there is no single English word that possesses both connotations, I have opted for the infelicitous "phenomena/properties" in the present context.

337 See BPD, 404.1.1: *de rang gi mtshan nyid kyis skye ba med par bsgrub pa'i skabs yin pa'i phyir ro//.* Go rams pa's point is this: since the refutation of arising from self is the first step in the proof of non-arising, it is a part of a proof of emptiness; it is therefore absurd to claim that what is actually being proved is that things exist by virtue of their own characteristic—the opposite of emptiness.

338 The topic of discussion, the question of whether or not there exists in syllogisms a common subject for Mādhyamikas and their opponents *(chos can mthun snang)*, is one of the most important in Tibetan Madhyamaka exegesis. Classical Buddhist logic dictates that for syllogisms to be valid, there must be a common subject—that is, Mādhyamikas and their opponents have to, in some sense, be focusing their discussions on the same thing. But this of course is problematic, given that Mādhyamikas and realists have such radically different presuppositions concerning the nature of phenomena—the former claiming that nothing exists by virtue of its own characteristic, and the latter claiming that things *must* exist by virtue of their own characteristic. Go rams pa is arguing for the fact that the *Prasannapadā*'s position is that what makes something a *svatantra*—and what makes it unacceptable to Prāsaṅgikas—is the requirement that there be a subject in common for both parties. For a lucid treatment of the issue in a Dge lugs source, see Cabezón, *Dose,* p. 277ff.

339 In this context the opponent and proponent are reversed, and it is the Madhyamaka who is the opponent. See BPD, 410.1.5: *legs ldan 'byed rang nyid la gzhi ma grub pa'i phyogs kyi skyon dang gtan tshigs kyi skyon du 'gyur te/ rang gis don dam par mig la sogs pa'i skye[d] mched khas ma blangs pa'i phyir ro//,* and 410.2.2: *pha rol pos mig sogs kun rdzob pa khas ma blangs pas.* Pras, 27: *paramārthataḥ svataścakṣurādyāyatanānām anabhyupagamāt,* and ibid., 28: *parair vastusatāmeva cakṣurādīnām abhyupagamāt prajñaptisatāmanabhyupagamāt parato 'siddhādhāraḥ pakṣadoṣaḥ syād.* Tib., Bhopal, 19.

340 See Pras, 27 ff; Tib., Bhopal, 19ff.

341 On the meaning of "wanes" in the present context, see the citation from the *Prasannapadā* that follows.

342 Pras, 29; Tib., Bhopal, 20. 'Jam dbyangs bzhad pa glosses this passage in his MA commentary, *Dbu ma 'jug pa'i mtha' dpyod lung rig gter mdzod,* 450, as follows: *de kho nar zhes pa yan chad kyis rigs shes kyi ngo'i de kho nar skye ba bkag pa bsgrub bya'i chos yin pa'i tshe zhes bshad/ de'i rten chos can zhes pas bsgrubs bya'i khyad gzhi 'am rtsod gzhi bstan/ phyin ci log tsam gyis zhes pas yul can phyin ci log shes pa 'khrul pa tsam gyis zhes bstan/ rang gi ngo bo zhes pas chos can rang gi ngo bo zhes bstan pa'i phyir/.* According

to his explanation, then, *phyin ci log,* "mistaken or false," refers to a mistaken thought or consciousness *(yul can* or *shes pa).* See also LSN, 657; and Cabezón, *Dose,* p. 280.

343 Pras, 30; Tib., Bhopal, 20–21. See also Cabezón, *Dose,* pp. 280, 282.

344 With regard to the exegesis of these *Prasannapadā* passages, Tsong kha pa argues that those who accept the concept of "existence by virtue of own characteristic" *(rang gi mtshan nyid kyis grub pa)* have no choice but to accept *svatantras;* see LSN, 649–50. Go rams pa, as we have seen, considers the two concepts to be independent, so that someone who accepts *svatantras* need not necessarily accept "existence by virtue of own-characteristic"; see above. It is for this reason that the passages under discussion are interpreted in such different ways.

345 Jñānagarbha, *Satyadavayavibhaṅgavṛtti,* C, vol. 28, f. 9b–10a; Eckel, *Jñānagarbha's Commentary,* Tib. 173–74; trans. p. 88.

346 Go rams pa is here following Rong ston pa, who offers a similar threefold typology of "thesis"—mere theses, *svantantras,* and *prasaṅgas* (or *reductios*)—in BTN, 30–31; see also Cabezón, "Rong ston," p. 104.

347 Jñānagarbha, *Satyadavayavibhaṅgakārika,* vv. 18–19a; C, vol. 28, 2b; Eckel, *Jñānagarbha's Commentary,* Tib. 173, trans. p. 88.

348 Pras, 15; Tib. Bhopal, 11

349 MA (I, 9cd), 24; MA-Fr, 273. Huntington, *Emptiness of Emptiness,* pp. 150, 152, and 220, n. 15. Hopkins, *Compassion in Tibetan Buddhism,* p. 183. Go rams pa's point appears to be that this represents a case of a Prāsaṅgika (Candrakīrti) using an autonomous syllogism. Together with the lines that follow, this shows that for Go rams pa, autonomous syllogisms are ordinary, "innocuous" syllogisms. Following Zhang Thang sag pa, Go rams pa believes that such autonomous inferences are valid in all conventional contexts, but *in*valid when one is analyzing reality.

350 Go rams pa identifies the *Daśabhūmikasūtra* as Candakīrti's source, but the quotation actually occurs in the *Daśadharmakasūtra;* LK, vol. 36 *(kha),* 274a.

351 *phyir mi ldog pa'i rtags* (Skt. *avaivartikaliṅgāni*): the AA mentions forty-four such marks or signs *(rtags)*; they are classified into three groups: (a) twenty associated with the path of preparation (Tib. *sbyor lam;* Skt. *prayogamārga*); AA (IV, 40–45); Stcherbatsky and Obermiller, Skt. 23–24, Tib. 43–44; Rāmasaṅkaratripāṭhi, *Abhisamayālaṃkāravṛttih Sphuṭārtha,* 105–7; (b) sixteen associated with the path of seeing *(mthong lam; darśanamārga)*; AA (IV, 47–51); Stcherbatsky and Obermiller, Skt. 24–25; Tib., 44–45; Rāmasaṅkaratripāṭhi, *Abhisamayālaṃkāravṛttih Sphuṭārtha,* 108–110; (c) eight associated with the path of meditation *(sgom lam; bhāvanāmārga);* AA (IV, 52–59); Stcherbatsky and Obermiller, Skt., 25–26, Tib., 45–47; Rāmasaṅkaratripāṭhi, *Abhisamayālaṃkāravṛttih Sphuṭārtha,* 116–17.

352 Zhang thang sag pa's work is no longer extant, but the same quotation is found in Rong ston's BTN, 35.

353 Rong ston pa (BTN, 31) states: *de la thal 'gyur bas rang rgyud kyi dam bca' mi 'thad par gsungs pa ni/ don dam dpyod pa'i dbang du byas pa yin la/ tha snyad rnam par 'jog pa'i tshe ni/ rang rgyud kyi dam bca' dang rtags yod pa'i tshul 'og nas 'chad do//.* "But what about the claim that Prāsaṅgikas repudiate autonomous theses? This is [only true] in the context of the analysis of the ultimate. When one is positing the conventional, there *are* autonomous theses and reasons, as will be explained below"; see

also BTN, 35–36. Sera Rje btsun pa and Bde legs nyi ma have responded to this claim—that Prāsaṅgikas accept autonomous forms of inference on the conventional level—in *Lta ngan mun sel,* 206ff.

354 The main points of divergence between Prāsaṅgika and Svātantrika are investigated by Rong ston pa in his BJN, 74ff.

355 *rang ldog = rang ma yin las sdog pa'am log pa.* In this context it means that the being of an entity is "turned away" from the being of other entities that are not it. The being of an entity, when turned away from the being of others, is the entity *itself.* See *Tshig mdzod chen mo: rang ldog rang dang tha dad las log pa'i chos te/.../ bum pa'i rang ldog bum pa rang nyid yin pa lta bu 'o/;* "The *rang ldog* of *x* refers to the phenomenon that is the opposite of those things different from *x*...(for example), the *rang ldog* of the pot is the pot itself."

356 See Cabezón, "Rong ston," pp. 97–105.

357 Go rams pa here turns to the epistemo-logical tradition of Dignāga and Dharmakīrti to make sense of the workings of logic in the Madhyamaka tradition. In Dharmakīrti, language and conceptual thought are said to engage their objects in a negative way that permits for specificity in the ascertainment of those objects, honing in on a specific quality or property. Direct perception, on the other hand, perceives an object as an undifferentiated whole, such that all of the qualities of the object appear simultaneously and *en masse.* See Cabezón, *Buddhism and Language,* chapter 6. The term *sel 'jug* is defined by 'Jam dbyangs bzhad pa in *Bsdus chen gyi rnam bzhag rigs lam gser gyi sgo 'byed* (in *The Collected Works of 'Jam-dbyangs-bzhad-pa,* vol. 15, 445) as follows: *rang yul la 'dod pa'i dbang gis 'jug pa de sel 'jug gi mtshan nyid/;* "Engaging [an object] negatively is defined as 'engaging one's object through a desire [to be selective].'" See also Rgyal tshab rje, *Tshad ma rnam 'grel gyi rnam bshad (Thar lam gsal byed), Collected Works,* vol. *cha,* 50a.; and *Tshig mdzod chen mo: yul can gyis yul la 'jug tshul gyi khyad par zhig ste/ yul can sgra dang rtog pas rang rang yul la sel ba'am cha shes su phye nas dgag pa dang/ bcad pa'i rnam pas 'jug pa/ dper na/ bum pa zhes brjod pa'i sgra dang bum 'dzin rtog pas bum pa bzung ba na/ bum pa shes bya yin pa mi rtag pa yin pa dang dbyibs dang kha dog la sogs pa'i bum pa'i khyad par ram cha shes du ma yod pa gzhan rnams bsal nas bum pa yin pa'i cha kho na brjod pa dang 'dzin pa lta bu'o//;* "[The 'negative engagement of an object'] is one of the specific ways in which subjects [i.e., the minds of beings] engage objects; as in when language and conceptual thought *qua* subjects engage their respective objects in a negative way through [first] dividing them up into their parts, and then refuting or negating [everything that is not the object itself]. For example, when the word 'pot' or the conceptual thought that thinks 'pot' grasps [the object] pot, they negate [all of the other qualities] of the pot—like the fact that it is a phenomenon, the fact that it is impermanent, or all of the other specific qualities or parts that the pot may have—[and only through such a negation do speech and conceptual thought] express or grasp the mere aspect of its being a pot."

358 The term *sgrub 'jug* is defined by 'Jam dbyangs bzhad pa in *Bsdus chen gyi rnam bzhag,* (in *The Collected Works,* vol. 15, 445) as follows: *rang yul la dngos dbang gis 'jug pa de sgrub 'jug gi msthan nyid/ rang yul la dngos dbang gis 'jug pa dang snang ba'i dbang gis 'jug pa dang/ sgrub 'jug rnams don gcig/;* "'Engaging [an object] in a positive way is defined as engaging the object through its thingness. Engaging an object through its thingness, engaging it through appearance, and engaging it positively are all synonymous." *Tshig mdzod chen mo* defines it as follows: *yul can.../ rtog med kyi shes pa*

rang yul la cha shes su mi phye bar rang yul du bsgrubs nas 'jug pa/ dper na bum 'dzin mig shes kyis bum pa bzung ba na bum pa'i steng gi byas mi rtag la sogs pa'i kyad par ram cha shes gcig kyang phar ma bsal bar thams cad tshogs pa'am 'dres pa'i sgo nas tshur rang gi yul du byas nas 'jug pa lta bu'o//; "[Engaging an object positively] refers to the way in which a subject…a nonconceptual consciousness, positively engages its own object, i.e., without dividing the object up into its parts. For example, the eye-consciousness apprehending the pot engages the pot *qua* object passively as the composite of all [its qualities] in such a way that [those qualities] are all mixed together; that is, it does not actively select out a specific aspect or part [of the pot] like the pot's compositeness, its impermanence, and so forth."

359 *chos thams cad kyi gnas lugs mngon sum du rtogs pa.* The word *chos (dharma)* may refer to "phenomenon." If so, we would have to translate the phrase in question "understands directly the reality of all phenomena." In that case, Go rams pa may mean to imply that directly understanding the reality of one phenomenon *leads to* the effortless understanding of the reality of all other phenomena in subsequent moments. On the other hand, if the word *chos* refers to a specific "property" of an object—our interpretation here—he would seem to be implying that the direct understanding of the emptiness of a pot brings with it the simultaneous understanding of all of the pot's qualities or properties, a problematic—though not an absurd—claim. Some gloss of this kind would seem to be necessary, since on face value it appears absurd to claim that the direct understanding of the reality of one phenomenon is the equivalent of the direct understanding of the reality of all phenomena. Presumably, only a Buddha is capable of the latter.

360 For example, during the time that he was studying with Bka' brgyud pa and Sa skya pa masters; see Cabezón, "Tsong kha pa" (forthcoming).

361 See n. 196.

362 *Ratnaguṇasaṃcayagāthā* (XXI, 2–3). *Prajña-pāramitā-ratna-guṇa-saṃcaya-gāthā (Sanskrit Recension A),* ed. Akira Yuyama (Cambridge: Cambridge University Press, 1976), p. 179; Conze, *Perfection of Wisdom in Eight Thousand Lines,* p. 49.

363 Go rams pa also deals with the topic of the two kinds of candidates of the Madhyamaka teachings in BPD, 354.3.1ff.

364 That is, the Vaibhāṣikas and Sautrāntikas. On the sources of Buddhist atomism, see Fernando Tola and Carmen Dragonetti, *el idealismo budista: la doctrine de 'solo-la-mente'* (Tlahuapan, Puebla: Premia, 1989), pp. 134–35, n. 69; see also their translation of, and commentary on, Dignāga's *Ālambanaparikṣa* (I, 1), in *el idealismo,* pp. 31–32, 44–45.

365 See, for example, the arguments found in Vasubandhu's *Viṃsatika;* Thomas A. Kochumuttom, *A Buddhist Doctrine of Experience,* pp. 174–81; Stefan Anacker, *Seven Works of Vasubandhu,* pp. 167–70; Tola and Dragonetti, *el idealismo,* p. 87ff.

366 See Go rams pa, BPD, 354.4.3 and 392.4.6; Mkhas grub rje, *Dose,* pp. 147–51; and Tillemans, "The 'Neither One Nor Many' Argument."

367 MA (VI, 4), 78; see above.

368 *Ratnāvalī* (IV, 96), see above.

369 Go rams pa, it would seem, believes that Mādhyamikas can have a variety of visions of the conventional world. For example, he suggests that believing that external

objects do not exist, and that everything is of the nature of mind—a belief of the Cittamātras—does not disqualify one from being a true Mādhyamika. Tsong kha pa, by contrast, believes that holding to the idealism of the Yogācāras runs counter to the principle that Mādhyamikas should "accord with worldly conventions," since the world in fact accepts the existence of external objects. Thus, for Tsong kha pa, holding a Yogācāra or Cittamātra view of the conventional world as being "mind-only" precludes one's being a true Mādhyamika (by which of course he means a Mādhyamika of the Candrakīrti variety). Go rams pa, on the other hand, appears to be claiming that Candrikīrti's represents only one option as regards the way in which the conventional world may be understood in the Madhyamaka. See Cabezón, *Dose,* pp. 325–27.

370 See, for example, MA (VI, 14–21), 87, and especially (VI, 15–17) where the example of different types of seeds giving rise to their own unique types of sprouts is found; MA-Fr, 287ff. Huntington, *Emptiness of Emptiness,* 158ff.

371 The term *sgrub byed*—which usually means "proof"—has a broader meaning in the present context, carrying a sense of "speculative theory" or "speculative justification."

372 If the effect comes into contact (or connects) with the cause, then the effect would have to exist at the time of the cause, and so the effect would be unchanging from one moment to the next, making it permanent. See, for example, MMK (X, 6–7), (XIV, 1–3), and (XVII, 6).

373 If effects need have no connection or contact with their causes, then any effect could arise from any cause. See previous note.

374 This demonstrates that the speculative theories of the realists are the result of going beyond the merely conventional validity of things; see Go rams pa, TN-CW, 52–55.

375 The expression *skyo ma snga btsan* appears to be a legal term. It is explained by Dge bshes Chos grags in his *Dictionary,* 57: *sngar phra ma 'am 'thab rtsod pa'i tshe phyir de ltar mi rtsod pa'i btsam po'i chad pas bcad pa'i don/.* According to *Tshig mdzod chen mo,* 167: *snga dus khrims sar zhu gtug sngon la byed mkhan de bden pa che ba yod skad/,* implying a principle whereby greater credence was given to a position presented earlier.

376 Go rams pa, TN-CW, 552ff.

377 BCA (IX, 25–26), 191; la Vallée Poussin, *Bodhicaryāvatāra,* p. 116; Steinkellner, *Eintritt,* p. 118; Crosby and Skilton, p. 117.

378 *Dharmadhātustava,* v. 64; P vol.46, 32.4.3; David Seyfort Ruegg, "Le Dharmadhātustava," p. 469.

379 *sgra don 'dres 'dzin,* the definition of conceptual thought *(rtog pa).* Instead of seeing its referent clearly, as does direct perception *(mngon sum),* conceptual thought is an erroneous *('khrul pa)* form of consciousness that mixes up the word and its meaning (the generic image = *don spyi*).

380 The five ways of reasoning are mentioned as early as MMK (XXII, 1 and 8); see also Go rams pa, BPD, 393.1.6ff. For a very detailed explanation see 'Jam dbyangs bzhad pa, *Phar phyin mtha' dpyod,* 91 ff; and for Mkhas grub rje's treatment, see Cabezón, *Dose,* pp. 147–58, 290–306. See also Hopkins, *Meditation on Emptiness,* p. 639ff.

381 See Hopkins, *Meditation on Emptiness,* pp. 57–59.

382 MA (VI, 150f), 271; MA-Fr, 315. Huntington, *Emptiness of Emptiness*, p. 176. See also 'Jam dbyangs bzhad pa, *Phar phyin mtha' dpyod*, 91ff.; Hopkins, *Meditation on Emptiness*, p. 677ff.

383 As mentioned above, the word *zhen pa* has a double sense that is difficult to capture with a single English word. It can have the more neutral sense of "conceptual construction," and the more loaded—and negative—connotation of "attachment."

384 Go rams pa identifies the *Yuktiṣaṣṭikā* as source of this quotation, but the passage is actually found in the *Vigrahavyāvartanī*, v. 26; see Lindtner, *Nagarjuniana*, p. 79; Bhattachārya, *The Dialectical Method of Nāgārjuna*, p. 20.

385 Go rams pa's retort here is arguably less than satisfactory, for the context of the passage from Nāgārjuna, which is making a claim about essencelessness or emptiness—to wit, that its repudiation requires the acceptance of its opposite, essentialism—is not at all an analysis of the conventional, but rather of the ultimate. Now because emptiness is here being treated in the medium of conceptual thought and language, Go rams pa might claim that this does not represent an instance of "reasoning that is engaged in an analysis of the *real* ultimate truth" *(don dam mtshan nyid pa'i dpyod pa'i rigs pa)*, but this is a dangerous move to make, for—given that all analysis is, by definition, linguisitc/conceptual—it would mean that there could then be no analysis of the real ultimate, no analysis of reality; or, put another way, no context within which the law of double negation could be violated.

386 The terms *rnam grangs pa'i don dam (pāryaya paramārtha)* and *rnam grangs min pa'i don dam (aparyāya paramārtha)* have their origin in Indian "Svātantrika" texts. In BPD, 381.3.5, Go rams pa states: *rang rgyud pa dag/ yul can gyi blo'i sgo nas rigs shes tshad mas spros pa bkag pa'i don dam pa dang/ 'phags pa'i mnyam bzhag gis myong ba mngon du gyur pa'i don dam gnyis las snga ma ni rnam grangs pa dang/ phyi ma ni rnam grangs ma yin par bzhed do/;* "The Svātantrikas [classify] the ultimate into two [subdivisions] from the viewpoint of mind *qua* subject: (1) the ultimate that has negated proliferations by means of a valid cognition *qua* reasoning consciousness, and (2) the ultimate that becomes manifest [when] experienced by āryans' equipoise. The first of these is an ultimate in name only. The latter is an ultimate *not* in name only—[that is, it is a real ultimate]"; see also BPD, 383.1.6ff. Also, Kennard Lipman, "A Controversial Topic from Mi-pham's Analysis of Śāntarakṣita's *Madhyamakālaṃkāra*," in *Wind Horse* (Berkeley, 1981), p. 43. See Also Seyfort Ruegg, *Literature of the Madhyamaka School*, p. 64, concerning of the use of the term *paryāya* in the *Madhyamakārthasaṃgraha*.

387 Dharmakīrti, *Pramāṇavārttika* (II, 214d), Steinkellner enumeration of the Tibetan verses; Swami Dwarikadas Shastri, ed., *Pramāṇavārttika of Achārya Dharamakīrti with the Commentary of Achārya Manorathanandin* (Varanasi: Bauddha Bharati, 1968), 75.

388 Dharmakīrti, *Pramāṇavārttika* (III, 213cd), Steinkellner enum.; Shastri, ed., *Pramāṇavārttika*, 164.

389 Śrāvakayāna, Pratyekabuddhayāna, and Mahāyāna.

390 Go rams pa must mean here the second in each of the first two categories—that is, (1) the real ultimate *qua* emptiness of truth, and (2) the real ultimate *qua* emptiness of the four extremes.

391 "This system," it would seem, refers to the Prāsaṅgikas. See BPD, 433.1.6: *bdag med 'di ni 'gro ba rnams dgrol phyir* [MA (VI, 179a), 301] *zhes pa'i 'grel par nyan rang la...chos kyi bdag med rtog pa yod kyi.../.*

392 The original division (see above) is called "the union of the two accumulations" *(tshogs gnyis zung 'jug)*, but this is simply a question of nomenclature, for, in fact, the two accumulations are those of method and wisdom. See BPD, 433.2.5ff.

393 For a detailed Dge lugs pa treatment of this topic, which, as we have seen, differs from that presented by Go rams pa here, see Cabezón, *Dose,* pp. 245–56.

394 The discussion begins at *Uttaratantra* (II, 6–7); Johnston and Chowdhury, *The Ratnagotravibhāga,* 80ff.; Takasaki, *A Study,* p. 315ff.

395 See MABh, 304ff.

396 See the previous discussion of the *Uttaratantra* passage in the section, "The analysis of (Tsong kha pa's views concerning) the identification of the two obscurations]."

397 See Cabezón, *Dose,* pp. 251–53, for Mkhas grub rje's understanding of the obscurations to omniscience.

398 See Cabezón, *Dose,* pp. 249–51, for Mkhas grub rje's understanding of "afflicted obscurations."

399 There are six basic (i.e. root) mental defilements, and twenty secondary ones; see Herbert V. Guenther and Leslie Kawamura, *Mind in Buddhist Psychology* (Emeryville, CA: Dharma Publishers, 1975), pp. 64, 82; Lati Rinbochay and Elizabeth Napper, *Mind in Tibetan Buddhism* (Valois, NY: Gabriel/Snow Lion), pp. 37–38.

400 The Vaibhāṣikas and the Sautrāntikas are known as the two schools of the śrāvakas. As 'Jam dbyangs bzhad pa, *Grub mtha' chen mo,* 283, states: *bye mdo gnyis thos kyi sde snod tsam khas blangs pas/ der bshad pa'i grub mtha' smra ba yin pas na nyan thos par bzhag la/.* "Because the Vaibhāṣikas and the Sautrāntikas accept only the *piṭaka* of the hearers, and because they advocate philosophical positions explained therein, they are called 'śrāvaka [schools]'."

401 Dkon mchog 'jigs med dbang po, *Grub mtha' rin chen phreng ba,* K. Mimaki, 95 (III, 4.3); Sopa and Hopkins, *Cutting Through Appearances,* pp. 272–77.

402 In the Dge lugs pa doxographical literature, this distinction is elaborated in the context of their treatment of the Svātantrika. The Yogācāra-Svātantrika-Mādhyamikas, they claim, believe that the śrāvakas and pratyekabuddhas differ in regard to both their theory of reality *and* their view of what is abandoned by these two types of adepts. Dkon mchog 'jigs med dbang po, *Grub mtha' rin chen phreng ba,* Mimaki, 100: *des na lugs 'di la nyan rang gnyis spang bya dang/ rtogs rigs mi 'dra ba'i dbang gis thob bya'i 'bras bu la'ang mchog dman yod do//;* "In this [Yogācāra-Svātantrika-Madhyamaka] system, śrāvakas and pratyekabuddhas are [considered] lower and higher, respectively, with reference to the result that they obtain, and this by virtue of the differences in the obscurations that they abandon, and the differences in the kinds of understanding [used to abandon them]." See also Sopa and Hopkins, *Cutting Through Appearances,* pp. 290–92. The Sautrāntika-Svātantrika-Mādhyamikas, however, see no difference at all between the two; Mimaki, 101; Sopa and Hopkins, *Cutting Through Appearances,* pp. 298–99.

403 The *bar chad med lam (ānantārya mārga)* are the meditative equipoises that serve as the actual antidotes to specific afflications and obscurations. They are called "uninterrupted" because once they begin, they continue unimpeded until the given affliction or obscuration is eradicated from the mind. See Lati Rinbochay, et al., *Meditative States in Tibetan Buddhism* (Boston: Wisdom, 1983), p. 144; E. Obermiller, *Prajñāpāramitā,* p. 35; Sopa and Hopkins, *Practice and Theory,* p. 84. The uninterrupted path being spoken of here is that of the path of seeing, which is the initial absorption into the direct experience of emptiness.

404 The terms *rang sangs rgyas* and *rang rgyal* are used interchangeably in the Tibetan literature, and we have here translated both as pratyekabuddha so as to avoid confusion.

405 It is not clear whether it is Rong ston pa who is being referred to here as "the incomparable Dharma Lord," but for Rong ston pa's position on this issue, see BJN, 25ff.

406 *Daśabhūmika Sūtra,* Vaidya, ed., (Darbhanga: Mithila Institute, 1967), 39; Toh no. 44, Phal chen *kha,* 234a. For a full translation of the passage and its interpretation in Dge lugs pa sources, see Hopkins, *Compassion in Tibetan Buddhism,* p. 145ff.; and Cabezón, *Dose,* p. 201ff. The full passage reads: "Oh children of the Conqueror, it is like this. Take, for example, the case of the prince who is born into the family of a king and who possesses the marks of royalty. As soon as he is born he surpasses in status all of the assembly of ministers by virtue of his being royalty, but not from the viewpoint of his intellectual prowess. But when he has grown up, he generates his own intellectual prowess and greatly supercedes all of the activities of the ministers. Oh Children of the Conqueror, likewise, the bodhisattva, as soon as he has generated the [awakening] mind, surpasses all of the śrāvakas and pratyekabuddhas because of the greatness of his superior intention *(lhag pa'i bsam pa),* but not from the viewpoint of his intellectual prowess. But the bodhisattva who abides in the seventh bodhisattva stage utterly supercedes all of the activities of the śrāvakas and pratyekabuddhas because of the greatness of the understanding of his object."

407 Go rams pa's interpretation of this passage from the *Daśabhūmika-Sūtra* has been criticized by Se ra Rje btsun pa in *Lta ngan mun sel,* 82–83.

408 *Daśabhūmika Sūtra,* Vaidya ed., 39.24 states: *asyāṃ tu saptamyāṃ bodhisattvabhūmau sthito bodhisattvaḥ svaviṣayajñānaviśeṣamāhātmyāvasthitvāt sarvaśrāvakapratyekabuddhakriyāmatikrānto bhavati/.* P vol. 58, 116 differs from the wording of the passage in Go rams pa's text.

409 AA (I, 27); Scherbatsky and Obermiller, ed., Skt. 14, Tib. 8; Conze, *Abhisamayālaṅkāra,* pp. 13–14.

410 AA (IV, 26); Scherbatsky and Obermiller, Skt. 21, Tib. 39; Conze, *Abhisamayālaṅkāra,* p. 61.

411 This interpretation is criticized by Se ra Rje btsun pa in *Lta ngan mun sel,* 85ff.

412 Go rams pa has explained this topic in BPD, 445.1.5ff.

413 The word "even" is found in Go rams pa's text, but missing in the canonical editions.

414 Jñānagarbha, *Satyadvayavibhaṅgavṛtti,* commentary on verse 9ab; Eckel, Tib. 161; trans., 76.

415 Śāntarakṣita, *Madhyamakālaṃkāra;* C, vol. 28 *(sa),* 55b.

416 Śāntarakṣita, *Madhyamakālaṃkāravṛtti;* C, vol. 28 *(sa),* 73a; Toh no. 3885, Dbu ma *sa,* 73a; Masamichi Ichigō, *Chūkan sōgenron no kenkyū: Shāntarakushita no shisō,* p. 230.

417 See above, n. 163.

418 Literally, "son of a god", or "a god," meaning an individual of noble descent.

419 The words "an object of" are missing from Go rams pa's text, but are found in the MABh itself.

420 Although similar claims about the ultimate are found in Atiśa's *Satyadvayāvatāra,* this is not the source of the present quote, which appears to come from a sūtra. See *The Complete Works of Atiśa, Śrī Dipaṃkara Jñāna, Jo-bo-rje,* trans. Richard Sherburne, S.J. (New Delhi: Aditya Prakashan, 200), pp. 352–55, for a similar notion. The same sūtra passage is cited in *Madhyamakāvatārabhāṣya,* Toh no. 3862, Dbu ma *'a,* 255b–256a. This is most likely Go rams pa's source.

421 Go rams pa's wording differs in several respects from that found in the canonical versions of this text, as well as from the version found in Pras. See the relevant note in the edition of the Tibetan text. See also *Kaśyapaparivarta,* A. freiherr von Stael-Holstein, ed. (Shanghai: Commercial Press, 1926), p. 64; and also Pras, p. 248.

422 *Nyi khri,* i.e., *Shes rab kyi pha rol tu phyin pa stong phrag nyi shu lnga pa (Pañcaviṃśatisāhasrikā-Prajñāpāramitā),* Toh no. 9, Nyi khri *ka,* 164b. *Pañcaviṃśatikasāhasrikā,* N. Dutt, ed., Calcutta Oriental Series no. 28 (London: Luzac and Co., 1934), p. 119 and n. 4. See also E. Conze, *The Prajñāpāramitā Literature* (The Hague: Mouton, 1960), p. 37ff.

423 *'Bum,* i.e., *Shes rab kyi pha rol tu phyin pa stong phrag brgya pa (Śatasāhasrikā-Prajñāpāramitā),* Toh no. 8. See E. Conze, *The Prajñāpāramitā Literature,* p. 40ff.

424 Such a work is not listed in Toh.

425 See Nāgārjuna, *Ratnāvalī* (I, 43–45); Go rams pa, BPD, 358.1.6 ff; Hahn, *Nāgārjuna's Ratnāvalī,* pp. 18–19; Dunne and McClintock, *The Precious Garland,* p. 15.

426 *Ratnagotravibhāga* (IV, 53–56), Johnston and Chowdhury, p. 42; Takasaki, *A Study,* p. 368.

427 See Introduction.

428 See Introduction.

429 This also appears as "thirteenth."

430 The Earth Male Rat year falls mostly in 1428, but because we know that the text was written in the twelfth lunar month, we know that the date of composition actually falls in 1429.

Bibliography

The first section lists Buddhist canonical works in Tibetan. Entries from the *bka' 'gyur* (sūtras) are listed by title, those from the *bstan 'gyur* (śāstras) by author. The second section lists all other works, in Tibetan, Sanskrit, and Western languages, by author, editor, or translator.

A. Buddhist Canonical Works in Tibetan

I. Sūtras

Blo gros mi zad pas bstan pa zhes bya ba theg pa chen po'i mdo; Akṣayamatinirdeśa-nāma mahāyāna sūtra.
N no. 175, vol. 22, ff. 782–974.
Toh no. 175, Mdo sde vol. *ma,* ff. 79–175.
P no. 842, Mdo sde vol. *bu,* ff. 82–180.
C no. 815, Mdo sde vol. *ma,* ff. 88–205.
LK no. 176, Mdo mang vol. *pha,* ff. 122–270.

Chos bcu pa zhes bya ba theg pa chen po'i mdo; Daśadharmaka nāma mahāyāna sūtra.
N no. 53, vol. 15, ff. 864–905.
Toh no. 53, Dkon brtsegs vol. *kha,* ff. 164–84.
P no. 760, Dkon brtsegs vol. *dzi,* ff. 183–206.
C no. 1029, Dkon brtsegs vol. *kha,* ff. 192–216.
LK no. 53, Dkon brtsegs vol. *kha,* ff. 268–303.

Chos yang dag par sdud pa zhes bya ba theg pa chen po'i mdo; Dharmasaṃgīti nāma mahāyāna sūtra.
N no. 238, vol. 24, ff. 1–198.
Toh no. 238, Mdo sde vol. *zha,* ff. 1–100.
P no. 904, Mdo sde vol. *wu,* ff. 1–107.
C no. 877, Mdo sde vol. *zha,* ff. 1–113.
LK no. 239, Mdo mang vol. *dza,* ff. 1–154.

Das Mahāparinirvāṇasūtra: Text in Sanskrit und Tibetisch verglichen mit dem Pāli nebst einer Übersetzung der chinesischen Entsprechung im Vinaya der Mūlasarvāstivādins. Edited by Ernst Waldschmidt. Berlin: Akademie-Verlag, 1950–1951. Reprint, Kyoto: Rinsen Book Co., 1986.

De bzhin gshegs pa'i snying po zhes bya ba theg pa chen po'i mdo; Tathāgatagarbha nāma mahāyāna sūtra.
N no. 258, vol. 24, ff. 1099–1127.
Toh no. 258, Mdo sde vol. *za,* ff. 245–59.
P no. 934, Mdo sde vol. *zhu,* ff. 259–74.
C no. 897, Mdo sde vol. *za,* ff. 274–89.
LK no. 260, Mdo mang vol. *zha,* ff. 1–24.

De bzhin gshegs pa'i snying rje chen po nges par bstan pa zhes bya ba theg pa chen po'i mdo; Tathāgatamahākaruṇā nirdeśa nāma mahāyāna sūtra.
N no. 147, vol. 21, ff. 880–1082.
Toh no. 147, Mdo sde vol. *pa,* ff. 142–243.
P no. 814, Mdo sde vol. *nu,* ff. 102–204.
C no. 787, Mdo sde vol. *pa,* ff. 96–212.
LK no. 148, Mdo mang vol. *da,* ff. 153–319.

Gtsug na rin po ches zhus pa zhes bya ba theg pa chen po'i mdo; Ratnacūḍa paripṛcchaa nāma mahāyāna sūtra.
N no. 91, vol. 17, ff. 418–508.
Toh no. 91, Dkon brtsegs vol. *cha,* ff. 210–55.
P no. 760, Dkon brtsegs vol. *'i,* ff. 204–57.
C no. 1029, Dkon brtsegs vol. *cha,* ff. 221–73.
LK no. 91, Dkon brtsegs vol. *cha,* ff. 350–418.

Lha mo dpal phreng gi seng ge'i sgra zhes bya ba theg pa chen po'i mdo; Śrīmālādevī siṃhanāda nāma mahāyāna sūtra.
N no. 92, vol. 17, ff. 508–554.
Toh no. 92, Dkon brtsegs vol. *cha,* ff. 255–78.
P no. 760, Dkon brtsegs vol. *'i,* ff. 257–85.
C no. 1029, Dkon brtsegs vol. *cha,* ff. 273–98.
LK no. 92, Dkon brtsegs vol. *cha,* ff. 418–54.

Mdo chen po stong pa nyid ces bya ba; Śūnyatā nāma mahāsūtra.
N no. 290, vol. 26, ff. 498–505.
Toh no. 290, Mdo sde vol. *sha,* ff. 250–53.
P no. 956, Mdo sde vol. *lu,* ff. 274–78.
C no. 929, Mdo sde vol. *sha,* ff. 294–99.
LK no. 293, Mdo mang vol. *ra,* ff. 476–82.

Mdo chen po stong pa nyid chen po zhes bya ba; Mahā Śūnyatā nāma mahāsūtra.
N no. 291, vol. 26, ff. 505–22.
Toh no. 291, Mdo sde vol. *sha,* ff. 253–62.
P no. 957, Mdo sde vol. *lu,* ff. 278–87.
C no. 930, Mdo sde vol. *sha,* ff. 299–309.
LK no. 294, Mdo mang vol. *ra,* ff. 482–95.

'Od srungs kyi le'u mdo; Kaśyapaparivarta nāma mahāyāna sūtra, in *Dkon mchog brtsegs pa chen po'i chos kyi rnam grangs le'u stong phrag brgya pa; Mahāratnakūṭa dharmaparyāya śatasāhasrika grantha.*
N no. 87, vol. 15, ff. 237–302.
Toh no. 87, Dkon brtsegs vol. *cha,* ff. 119–52.
P no. 760, Dkon brtsegs vol. *'i,* ff. 100–138.
C no. 1029, Dkon brtsegs vol. *cha,* ff. 125–61.
LK no. 87, Dkon brtsegs vol. *cha,* ff. 211–60.

Prajñā-pāramitā-ratna-guṇa-saṃcaya-gāthā: Sanskrit recension A. Edited with an introduction, bibliographical notes, and a Tibetan version from Tunhuang. Edited by Akira Yuyama. Cambridge, New York: Cambridge University Press, 1976.

Rnga bo che chen po'i le'u zhes bya ba theg pa chen po'i mdo; Mahābherīhāraka parivarta nāma mahāyāna sūtra.
N no. 222, vol. 23, ff. 779–864.
Toh no. 222, Mdo sde vol. *dza,* ff. 84–127.
P no. 888, Mdo sde vol. *tshu,* ff. 88–134.
C no. 861, Mdo sde vol. *dza,* ff. 117–72.
LK no. 223, Mdo mang vol. *tsa,* ff. 141–208.

Rta skad byang chub sems dpa'i zhus pa'i mdo; not listed in N, Toh, or P.

Sa bcu'i le'u; Daśabhūmika sūtra, in *Sangs rgyas phal po che zhes bya ba shin tu rgyas pa chen po'i mdo; Buddhāvataṃsaka nāma mahāvaipulya sūtra.*
N no. 44, vol. 13, ff. 1114–1348.
Toh no. 44, Phal chen, chap. 31.
P no. 761, Phal chen vol. *li,* ff. 49–168.
C no. 1030, Phal chen, chap. 31.
LK no. 94, Phal chen, chap. 31.

Sangs rgyas phal po che zhes bya ba shin tu rgyas pa chen po'i mdo; Buddhāvataṃsaka nāma mahāvaipulya sūtra.
N no. 44, vol. 13, f. 1–vol. 14, f. 3115.
Toh no. 44, Phal chen vol. *ka,* f. 1–vol. *'a* f. 363.
P no. 761, Phal chen vol. *yi,* f. 1–vol. *hi,* f. 253.

C no. 1030, Phal chen vol. *ka,* f. 1–vol. *cha,* f. 284.
LK no. 94, Phal chen vol. *ka,* f. 1–vol. *cha,* f. 341.

Sangs rgyas thams cad kyi yul la 'jug pa'i ye shes snang ba'i rgyan zhes bya ba theg pa chen po'i mdo; Sarvabuddhaviṣayāvatāra jñānālokālaṃkāra nāma mahāyāna sūtra.
N no. 100, vol. 18, ff. 550–609.
Toh no. 100, Mdo sde vol. *ga,* ff. 276–305.
P no. 768, Mdo sde vol. *khu,* ff. 301–34.
C no. 741, Mdo sde vol. *ga,* ff. 334–66.
LK no. 103, Mdo mang vol. *ga,* ff. 483–535.

Shes rab kyi pha rol tu phyin pa sdud pa tshigs su bcad pa; Prajñāpāramitāsaṃcayagāthā.
N no. 13, vol. 12, ff. 1181–1218.
Toh no. 13, Sher phyin vol. *ka,* ff. 1–20.
P no. 735, Sher phyin vol. *tsi,* ff. 1–22.
C no. 1002, Sher phyin vol. *ka,* ff. 1–21.
LK no. 17, Sher phyin vol. *ka,* ff. 189–215.

Shes rab kyi pha rol tu phyin pa stong phrag brgya pa; Śatasāhasrikā prajñāpāramitā.
N no. 8, vol. 6, f. 1–vol. 9, f. 9406.
Toh no. 8, Sher phyin 'bum, vol. *ka,* f. 1–vol *'a,* f. 395.
P no. 730, Sher phyin stong phrag brgya pa, vol. *ra,* f. 1–vol. *ji,* f. 320.
C no. 999, Sher phyin stong phrag brgya pa, vol. *ka,* f. 1–vol. *ma,* f. 299.
LK no. 9, Sher phyin 'bum, vol. *ka,* f. 1–vol. *na,* f. 521.

Shes rab kyi pha rol tu phyin pa stong phrag nyi shu lnga pa; Pañcaviṃśatisāhasrikā prajñāpāramitā.
N no. 9, vol. 10, ff. 1–2306.
Toh no. 9, Sher phyin nyi khri vol. *ka,* f. 1–vol. *ga,* f. 381.
P no. 731, Sher phyin nyi shu lnga pa vol. *nyi,* f. 1–vol. *di,* f. 282.
C no. 1000, Sher phyin nyi khri vol. *ka,* f. 1–vol. *nga,* f. 308.
LK no. 10, Sher phyin nyi khri vol. *ka,* f. 1–vol. *ga,* f. 537.

Sor mo'i phreng ba la phan pa zhes bya ba theg pa chen po'i mdo; Aṅgulimālīya nāma mahāyāna sūtra.
N no. 213, vol. 23, ff. 250–412.
Toh no. 213, Mdo sde vol. *tsha,* ff. 126–207.
P no. 879, Mdo sde vol. *tsu,* ff. 133–215.
C no. 852, Mdo sde vol. *tsha,* ff. 146–243.
LK no. 214, Mdo mang vol. *ma,* ff. 196–315.

Yongs su mya ngan las 'das pa chen po'i mdo; Mahāparinirvāṇa mahā sūtra.
N no. 119, vol. 19–20, ff. 1185–2544.
Toh no. 119, Mdo sde vol. *nya,* f. 1–vol. *ta,* f. 339.
P no. 787, Mdo sde vol. *ju,* f. 1–vol. *nyu,* f. 355.
C no. 760, Mdo sde vol. *nya,* f. 1–vol. *ta,* f. 383.
LK no. 368, Myang das vol. *ka,* f. 1–vol. *kha,* f. 529.
Yongs su mya ngan las 'das pa chen po'i mdo; Mahāparinirvāṇa sūtra.
N no. 121, vol. 20, ff. 976–980.
Toh no. 121, Mdo sde vol. *tha,* ff. 151–53.
P no. 789, Mdo sde vol. *tu,* ff. 157–59.
C no. 762, Mdo sde vol. *tha,* ff. 169–71.
LK no. 123, Mdo mang vol. *nya,* ff. 222–25.
Yongs su mya ngan las 'das pa chen po theg pa chen po'i mdo; Mahāparinirvāṇa nāma mahāyāna sūtra.
N no. 120, vol. 20, ff. 677–976.
Toh no. 120, Mdo sde vol. *tha,* ff. 1–151.
P no. 788, Mdo sde vol. *tu,* ff. 1–157.
C no. 761, Mdo sde vol. *tha,* ff. 1–169.
LK no. 122, Mdo mang vol. *nya,* ff. 1–222.

II. Śāstras

Ajitamitra. *Rin po che'i phreng ba'i rgya cher bshad pa; Ratnāvalīṭīkā.*
N no. 4159, vol. 93, ff. 1153–1231.
Toh no. 4159, Spring yig vol. *ge,* ff. 126–65.
P no. 5659, Spring yig vol. *nge,* ff. 152–98.
C no. 4126, Spring yig vol. *ge,* ff. 135–74.
Āryadeva. *Bstan bcos bzhi brgya pa zhes bya ba'i tshig le'ur byas pa; Catuḥśataka.*
N no. 3846, vol. 68, ff. 565–99.
Toh no. 3846, Dbu ma vol. *tsha,* ff. 1–19.
P no. 5246, Dbu ma vol. *tsha,* ff. 1–20.
C no. 3812, Dbu ma vol. *tsha,* ff. 1–18.
———. *The Catuḥśataka of Āryadeva.* Edited by Vidushekhara Bhattacharya. Calcutta: Visva-Bharati 2.2, 1931 (Tibetan and Sanskrit).
———. *Ye shes snying po kun las btus pa; Jñānasārasamuccaya.*
N no. 3851, vol. 68, ff. 613–616.
Toh no. 3851, Dbu ma *tsha,* ff. 26–28.
P no. 5251, Dbu ma *tsha,* ff. 29–31.

C no. 3817, Dbu ma *tsha,* ff. 26–27.
Asaṅga. *Chos mngon pa kun las btus pa; Abhidharmasamuccaya.*
N no. 4049, vol. 80, ff. 759–911.
Toh no. 4049, Sems tsam vol. *ri,* ff. 44–121.
P no. 5550, Sems tsam vol. *li,* ff. 51–141.
C no. 4016, Sems tsam vol. *ri,* ff. 44–121.
———. *Rnal 'byor spyod pa'i sa rnam par gtan la dbab pa bsdu ba; Yogācārabhūmi Viniścayasaṃgrahaṇī.*
N no. 4038, vol. 79, ff. 113–940.
Toh no. 4038, Sems tsam vol. *zhi,* f. 1–vol. *zi,* f. 127.
P no. 5539, Sems tsam vol. *zi,* f. 1–vol. *'i,* f. 143.
C no. 4005, Sems tsam vol. *zhi,* f. 1–vol. *zi,* f. 128.
———. *Theg pa chen po bsdus pa; Mahāyānasaṃgraha.*
N no. 4048, vol. 80, ff. 675–759.
Toh no. 4048, Sems tsam vol. *ri,* ff. 1–44.
P no. 5549, Sems tsam vol. *li,* ff. 1–51.
C no. 4015, Sems tsam vol. *ri,* ff. 1–44.
———. *Theg pa chen po rgyud bla ma'i bstan bcos kyi rnam par bshad pa; Mahāyānottaratantraśāstravyākhyā.*
N no. 4025, vol. 77, ff. 137–247.
Toh no. 4025, Sems tsam vol. *phi,* ff. 74–129.
P no. 5526, Sems tsam vol. *phi,* ff. 74–135.
C no. 3992, Sems tsam vol. *phi,* ff. 69–124.
———. *Theg pa chen po rgyud bla ma'i bstan bcos kyi rnam par bshad pa thogs med gyis mdzad pa.* Edited by Zuiryu Nakamura in *Zō-Wa taiyaku Kukyō ichijō hōshōron kenkyū (Ratnagotravibhāga).* Tokyo: Suzuki Gakujutsu Zaidan, 1967 (Tibetan, Sanskrit, Chinese, and Japanese).
Bhāvaviveka. *Dbu ma'i rtsa ba'i 'grel pa shes rab sgron ma; Prajñāpradīpa-mūlamadhyamakavṛtti.*
N no. 3853, vol. 68, ff. 651–1079.
Toh no. 3853, Dbu ma vol. *tsha,* ff. 45–259.
P no. 5253, Dbu ma vol. *tsha,* ff. 53–326.
C no. 3819, Dbu ma vol *tsha,* ff. 45–263.
———. *Dbu ma'i snying po'i 'grel pa rtog ge 'bar ba; Madhyamaka hṛdaya vṛtti tarkavjālā.*
N no. 3856, vol. 68, ff. 1217–1795.
Toh no. 3856, Dbu ma vol. *dza,* ff. 40–329.
P no. 5256, Dbu ma vol. *dza,* ff. 43–380.

C no. 3822, Dbu ma vol. *dza,* ff. 41–329.
Buddhapālita. *Dbu ma rtsa ba'i 'grel pa buddhapālita; Buddhapālita mūlamadhyamakavṛtti.*
N no. 3842, vol. 68, ff. 313–558.
Toh no. 3842, Dbu ma vol. *tsa,* ff. 158–281.
P no. 5242, Dbu ma vol. *tsa,* ff. 178–317.
C no. 3808, Dbu ma vol. *tsa,* ff. 154–278.
Candrakīrti. *Dbu ma la 'jug pa; Madhyamakāvatāra.*
N no. 3861, vol. 70, ff. 539–75.
Toh no. 3861, Dbu ma vol. *'a,* ff. 201–20.
P no. 5262, Dbu ma vol. *'a,* ff. 245–64.
C no. 3827, Dbu ma vol. *'a,* ff. 198–217.
———. *Dbu ma la 'jug pa'i bshad pa; Madhyamakāvatārabhāṣya.*
N no. 3862, vol. 70, ff. 575–831.
Toh no. 3862, Dbu ma vol. *'a,* ff. 220–348.
P no. 5263, Dbu ma vol. *'a,* ff. 264–411.
C no. 3828, Dbu ma vol. *'a,* ff. 217–349.
———. *Dbu ma la 'jug pa'i tshig le'ur byas pa; Madhyamakāvatārakārikā.*
P no. 5261, Dbu ma vol. *'a,* ff. 225–45.
———. *Dbu ma la hjug pa ran hgrel.* Bhopal: The Tibetan Publishing House, 1968.
———. *Dbu ma rtsa ba'i 'grel pa tshig gsal ba; Mūlamadhyamakavṛtti prasannapadā.*
N no. 3860, vol. 70, ff. 141–539.
Toh no. 3860, Dbu ma vol. *'a,* ff. 1–201.
P no. 5260, Dbu ma vol. *'a,* ff. 1–225.
C no. 3826, Dbu ma vol. *'a,* ff. 1–198.
———. *Madhyamakāvatāra par Candrakīrti.* Traduction tibétaine publiée par Louis de La Vallée Poussin. Bibliotheca Buddhica 9. St. Petersburg: Imprimerie de l'Academie impériale des Sciences, 1907–12.
———. *Rigs pa drug cu pa'i 'grel pa; Yuktiṣaṣṭikāvṛtti.*
N no. 3864, vol. 70, ff. 833–91.
Toh no. 3864, Dbu ma vol. *ya,* ff. 1–30.
P no. 5265, Dbu ma vol. *ya,* ff. 1–33.
C no. 3830, Dbu ma vol. *ya,* ff. 1–29.
Dharmakīrti. *Tshad ma rnam 'grel gyi tshig le'ur byas pa; Pramāṇavārttikakārikā.*
N no. 4210, vol. 94, ff. 183–297.

Toh no. 4210, Tshad ma vol. *ce,* ff. 94–152.
P no. 5709, Tshad ma vol. *ce,* ff. 190–250.
C no. 4177, Tshad ma vol. *ce,* ff. 94–152.

Dignāga. *Shes rab kyi pha rol tu phyin ma bsdus pa'i tshigs le'ur byas ba; Prajñāpāramitā piṇḍārtha (Prajñāpāramitā saṃgrahakārikā).*
N no. 3809, vol. 67, ff. 583–87.
Toh no. 3809, Sher phyin vol. *pha,* ff. 292–94.
P no. 5207 [5870 duplicate text], Sher phyin vol. *pha,* ff. 333–36.
C no. 3775, Sher phyin vol. *pha,* ff. 293–301.

Haribhadra. *Shes rab kyi pha rol tu phyin pa'i man ngag gi bstan bcos mngon par rtogs pa'i rgyan zhes bya ba'i 'grel pa; Abhisamayālaṃkāranāma prajñāpāramitopadeśaśāstra vṛttiḥ (Sphuṭārtha).*
N no. 3793, vol. 65, ff. 43–167.
Toh no. 3793, Sher phyin vol. *ja,* ff. 78–140.
P no. 5191, Sher phyin vol. *ja,* ff. 93–161.
C no. 3759, Sher phyin vol. *ja,* ff. 83–147.

Jayānanda. *Dbu ma la 'jug pa'i 'grel bshad / Madhyamākavatāraṭīkā.*
N no. 3870, vol. 70–71, ff. 1581–2308.
Toh no. 3870, Dbu ma vol. *ra,* ff. 1–365.
P no. 5271, Dbu ma vol. *ra,* ff. 1–443.
C no. 3836, Dbu ma vol. *ra,* ff. 1–268.

———. *Dbu ma la 'jug pa'i 'grel bshad / Madhyamākavatāraṭīkā.* Sde dge 3870. Asian Classics Input Project, Release IV, TD3870-1/2.

Jñānagarbha. *Bden gnyis rnam par 'byed pa'i 'grel pa; Satyadvayavibhaṅgavṛtti.*
N no. 3882, vol. 72, ff. 5–29.
Toh no. 3882, Dbu ma *sa,* ff. 3–15.
P not found.
C no. 3849, Dbu ma *sa,* ff. 3–15.

———. *Bden pa gnyis rnam par 'byed pa'i tshig le'ur byas pa; Satyadvayavibhaṅgakārikā.*
N no. 3881, vol. 72, ff. 1–5.
Toh no. 3881, Dbu ma *sa,* ff. 1–3.
P not found.
C no. 3848, Dbu ma *sa,* ff. 1–3.

Kamalaśīla. *Bsgom pa'i rim pa; Bhāvanākrama.*
N no. 3915–17, vol. 73, ff. 42–135.
Toh no. 3915–17, Dbu ma vol. *ki,* ff. 22–68.
P no. 5310–12, Dbu ma vol. *a,* ff. 22–74.

C no. 3882–84, Dbu ma vol. *ki,* ff. 22–70.

———. *First Bhāvanākrama,* edited by Giuseppe Tucci in *Minor Buddhist Texts part II.* Serie Orientale Roma, v. IX, 2. Roma: Istituto Italiano per il Medio ed Estremo Oriente, 1958 (Sanskrit and Tibetan text).

———. *Slob-dpon Kamalaśīlas mdzad pa'i Bsgom rim thog mtha' bar gsum zhugs so / Ācāryakamalaśīlapraṇītaḥ Bhāvanākramaḥ.* Edited by Namdol Gyaltsen. Sāranātha, Vārāṇasī: Kendrīya Ucca Tibbatī-Śikshā-Saṃsthānam, 1985 (Edited in Tibetan, Sanskrit, and Hindi).

Maitreyanātha. *Abhisamayālaṃkāra-Prajñāpāramitā-Upadeśa-śāstra: The Work of Bodhisattva Maitreya.* Edited by Theodor Ippolitovich Stcherbatsky and Evgenii Obermiller. Bibliotheca Buddhica 23. Leningrad: 1929. Reprint, Delhi, India: Sri Satguru Publications, 1992 (Sanskrit and Tibetan).

———. *Chos dang chos nyid rnam par 'byed pa; Dharmadharmatā vibhaṅga.*
N no. 4022, vol. 77, ff. 87–93.
Toh no. 4022, Sems tsam vol. *phi,* ff. 46–50.
P no. 5523, Sems tsam vol. *phi,* ff. 48–51.
C no. 3989, Sems tsam vol. *phi,* ff. 43–47.

———. *Dbus dang mtha' rnam par 'byed pa'i tshig le'ur byas pa; Madhyāntavibhaṅgakārikā.*
N no. 4021, vol. 77, ff. 77–87.
Toh no. 4021, Sems tsam vol. *phi,* ff. 40–46.
P no. 5522, Sems tsam vol. *phi,* ff. 43–48.
C no. 3988, Sems tsam vol. *phi,* ff. 38–43.

———. *Shes rab kyi pha rol tu phyin pa'i man ngag gi bstan bcos mngon par rtogs pa'i rgyan zhes bya ba'i tshig le'ur byas pa; Abhisamayālaṃkāra nāma prajñāpāramitopadeśa śāstra kārikā.*
N no. 3786, vol. 63, ff. 1–25.
Toh no. 3786, Sher phyin vol. *ka,* ff. 1–14.
P no. 5184, Sher phyin vol. *ka,* ff. 1–15.
C no. 3752, Sher phyin vol. *ka,* ff. 1–14.

———. *Theg pa chen po mdo sde'i rgyan zhes bya ba'i tshig le'ur byas pa; Mahāyānasūtrālaṃkāraḥ nāma kārikā.*
N no. 4020, vol. 77, ff. 1–77.
Toh no. 4020, Sems tsam vol. *phi,* ff. 1–40.
P no. 5521, Sems tsam vol. *phi,* ff. 1–43.
C no. 3987, Sems tsam vol. *phi,* ff. 1–38.

———. *Theg pa chen po rgyud bla ma'i bstan bcos; Mahāyanottaratantra-śāstra (Ratnagotravibhāga).*
N no. 4024, vol. 77, ff. 99–137.
Toh no. 4024, Sems tsam vol. *phi,* ff. 54–74.
P no. 5525, Sems tsam vol. *phi,* ff. 54–74.
C no. 3991, Sems tsam vol. *phi,* ff. 51–69.

Nāgārjuna. *Chos kyi dbyings su bstod pa; Dharmadhātustava.*
N no. 1118, vol. 37, ff. 125–133.
Toh no. 1118, Bstod tshogs vol. *ka,* ff. 63–67.
P no. 2010, Bstod tshogs vol. *ka,* ff. 73–77.
C no. 1066, Bstod tshogs vol. *ka,* ff. 72–76.

———. *Dbu ma rtsa ba'i tshig le'ur byas pa shes rab ces bya ba; Prajñā nāma mūlamadhyamakakarikā.*
N no. 3824, vol. 68, ff. 1–37.
Toh no. 3824, Dbu ma vol. *tsa,* ff. 1–20.
P no. 5224, Dbu ma vol. *tsa,* ff. 1–22.
C no. 3790, Dbu ma vol. *tsa,* ff. 1–20.

———. *'Jig rten las 'das par bstod pa; Lokātītastava.*
N no. 1120, vol. 37, ff. 135–37.
Toh no. 1120, Bstod tshogs vol. *ka,* ff. 68–69.
P no. 2012, Bstod tshogs vol. *ka,* ff. 79–80.
C no. 1068, Bstod tshogs vol. *ka,* ff. 77–79.

———. *Nāgārjuna's Ratnāvalī, Vol. 1, The Basic Texts (Sanskrit, Tibetan, and Chinese).* Edited by Michael Hahn. Bonn: Indica et Tibetica Verlag, 1982.

———. *Rgyal po la gtam bya ba rin po che'i phreng ba; Rājaparikathāratnāvalī.*
N no. 4158, vol. 93, ff. 1115–53.
Toh no. 4158, Spring yig vol. *ge,* ff. 107–26.
P no. 5658, Spring yig vol. *nge,* ff. 129–52.
C no. 4125, Spring yig vol. *ge,* ff. 116–35.

———. *Rtsod pa bzlog pa'i tshig le'ur byas pa; Vigrahavyāvartanī kārikā.*
N no. 3828, vol. 68, ff. 50–55.
Toh no. 3828, Dbu ma vol. *tsa,* ff. 27–29.
P no. 5228, Dbu ma vol. *tsa,* ff. 30–34.
C no. 3794, Dbu ma vol. *tsa,* ff. 27–29.

———. *Stong pa nyid bdun cu pa'i 'grel pa; Śūnyatāsaptativṛtti.*
N no. 3831, vol. 68, ff. 216–38.
Toh no. 3831, Dbu ma vol. *tsa,* ff. 110–21.

P no. 5231, Dbu ma vol. *tsa,* ff. 126–38.
C no. 3797, Dbu ma vol. *tsa,* ff. 109–19.
———. *Stong pa nyid bdun cu pa'i tshig le'ur byas pa; Śūnyatāsaptatikārikā.*
N no. 3827, vol. 68, ff. 44–50.
Toh no. 3827, Dbu ma vol. *tsa,* ff. 24–27.
P no. 5227, Dbu ma vol. *tsa,* ff. 27–30.
C no. 3793, Dbu ma vol. *tsa,* ff. 24–27.
Śāntarakṣita. *Dbu ma rgyan gyi tshig le'ur byas pa; Madhyamakālaṃkārakārikā.*
N no. 3884, vol. 72, ff. 104–11.
Toh no. 3884, Dbu ma vol. *sa,* ff. 53–56.
P no. 5284, Dbu ma vol. *sa,* ff. 48–52.
C no. 3851, Dbu ma vol. *sa,* ff. 52–56.
———. *Dbu ma'i rgyan gyi 'grel pa; Madhyamakālaṃkāravṛtti.*
N no. 3885, vol. 72, ff. 111–66.
Toh no. 3885, Dbu ma vol. *sa,* ff. 56–84.
P no. 5285, Dbu ma vol. *sa,* ff. 52–84.
C no. 3852, Dbu ma vol. *sa,* ff. 56–83.
Śāntideva. *Bodhicaryāvatāra.* Edited by Vidushekhara Bhattacharya. Bibliotheca Indica 280. Calcutta: The Asiatic Society, 1960 (Sanskrit and Tibetan).
———. *Bslab pa kun las btus pa; Śikṣāsamuccaya.*
N no. 3940, vol. 73, ff. 718–1101.
Toh no. 3940, Dbu ma vol. *khi,* ff. 3–194.
P no. 5336, Dbu ma vol. *ki,* ff. 3–225.
C no. 3907, Dbu ma vol. *khi,* ff. 3–196.
———. *Byang chub sems dpa'i spyod pa la 'jug pa; Bodhisattvacaryāvatāra.*
N no. 3871, vol. 71, ff. 549–627.
Toh no. 3871, Dbu ma vol. *la,* ff. 1–41.
P no. 5272, Dbu ma vol. *la,* ff. 1–45.
C no. 3837, Dbu ma vol. *la,* ff. 1–39.
Sthiramati. *Dbus dang mtha' rnam par 'byed pa'i 'grel bshad; Madhyāntavibhaṅgaṭīkā.*
N no. 4032, vol. 77, ff. 885–1143.
Toh no. 4032, Sems tsam vol. *bi,* ff. 189–318.
P no. 5534, Sems tsam vol. *tshi,* ff. 19–171.
C no. 3999, Sems tsam vol. *bi,* ff. 189–317.

———. *Madhyāntavibhāgaṭīkā; exposition systématique du Yogācāra-vijñaptivāda.* Edited by M. Sylvain Lévi. Nagoya: Librairie Hajinkaku, 1934. Reprint, Tokyo: Suzuki Foundation, 1966 (Sanskrit, Tibetan, and Chinese).

Vasubandhu. *Rnam par bshad pa'i rigs pa; Vyākhyāyukti.*
N no. 4061, vol. 81, ff. 264–475.
Toh no. 4061, Sems tsam vol. *shi,* ff. 29–134.
P no. 5562, Sems tsam vol. *si,* ff. 31–156.
C no. 4028, Sems tsam vol. *shi,* ff. 28–138.

B. Other Scholarly Works: Sanskrit, Tibetan, and Western Languages

Agassi, Joseph. *The Gentle Art of Philosophical Polemics: Selected Reviews and Comments.* La Salle, IL: Open Court, 1988.

Anacker, Stephen. *Seven Works of Vasubandhu: The Buddhist Psychology Doctor.* Delhi: Motilal Banarsidass, 1986.

Asad, Talal. *Genealogies of Religion: Disciplines and Reasons of Power in Christianity and Islam.* Baltimore: The Johns Hopkins University Press, 1993.

Atiśa (as treasure-revealer) [Jo bo A ti śas gter nas bton pa]. *Bka' chems ka khol ma.* Lan chou: Kan su'u mi rigs dpe skrun khang, 1989.

Aung, Shwe Zan and Caroline Augusta Foley Rhys Davids, trans. *Points of Controversy (Kathāvatthu).* Pali Text Society Translation Series no. 5. London: Luzac 1915. Reprint, Oxford: The Pali Text Society, 1993.

Bacot, Jacques. *La vie de Marpa le 'traducteur'.* 1937. Paris: P. Geuthner, 1976.

———. *Milarepa: ses mefaits, ses preuves, son illumination,* 2nd ed. Paris: P. Geuthner, 1971.

Bagchi, Sitansusekhar, ed. *Mahāyānasūtrālaṃkāraḥ.* Buddhist Sanskrit Texts Series 13. Darbhanga: Mithila Institute, 1970.

Bakhtin, Mihail M. *The Dialogic Imagination: Four Essays by M. M. Bakhtin.* Edited by Michael Holquist, translated by Caryl Emerson and Michael Holquist. Austin: University of Texas Press, 1981.

Batchelor, Stephen. *A Guide to the Bodhisattva's Way of Life.* Dharamsala: Library of Tibetan Works and Archives, 1979.

Beckwith, Christopher. "The Medieval Scholastic Method in Tibet and the West." In *Reflections on Tibetan Culture: Essays in Memory of Turrell V. Wylie,* Studies in Asian Thought and Religion, 12, edited by Lawrence Epstein and Richard F. Sherburne. Lewiston: The Edwin Mellen Press, 1990.

Berzin, Alex. "Eliminating the Two Sets of Obscurations in Sutra and Highest Tantra According to the Nyingma and Sakya." http://www.berzin-archives.com/tantra/eliminating_2_sets_obscurations.html

Bhattacharya, Kamaleswar. *The Dialectical Method of Nāgārjuna (Vigrahavyāvartanī).* New Delhi: Motilal Banarsidas, 1978.

Bhattacharya, Vidushekhara, ed. *Bodhicaryāvatāra.* Bibliotheca Indica 280. Calcutta: The Asiatic Society, 1960 (Sanskrit and Tibetan).

———, ed. *The Catuḥśataka of Āryadeva.* Calcutta: Visva-Bharati 2.2, 1931 (Sanskrit and Tibetan).

Bjerken, Zeff. "Exorcising the Illusion of Bon Shamanism: A Critical Genealogy of Shamanism in Tibetan Religions." *Revue d'Études Tibetains* 6 (2004): 4–60.

Bod pa sprul sku Mdo sngags bstan pa'i nyi ma. *Lta grub shan 'byed gnad kyi sgron me'i rtsa 'grel.* Khreng tu'u: Si khron Mi rigs dpe skrun khang, 1996.

Braarvig, Jens, ed. *Akṣayamatinirdeśasūtra.* Oslo: Solum Forlag, 1993.

Brauen, Martin. *The Dalai Lamas: A Visual History.* Zurich: Ethnographic Museum of Zurich, 2005.

Broido, Michael. "The Jo-nang-pas on Madhyamaka: A Sketch." *The Tibet Journal* 14.1 (1989): 86–90.

———. "Veridical and Illusive Cognition: Tsong-kha-pa on the Two Satyas." *Journal of Indian Philosophy* 16 (1988): 34–37.

———. "Sa-skya Paṇḍita, the White Panacea and the Hva-shang Doctrine." *Journal of the International Association of Buddhist Studies* 10.2 (1987): 27–68.

———. "A Note on dGos-'brel." *The Journal of the Tibet Society* 3 (1983): 5–19.

Broughton, Jeffrey. "Early Ch'an Schools in Tibet." In *Studies in Ch'an and Hua-yen,* edited by Robert M. Gimello and Peter Gregory, 1–68. Honolulu: University of Hawaii Press/Kuroda Institute, 1983.

Bsod-nams-rgyal-mtshan, Sa-skya-pa Bla-ma Dam-pa, and Per K. Sørensen. *The Mirror Illuminating the Royal Genealogies: Tibetan Buddhist Historiography: An Annotated Translation of the XIVth Century Tibetan Chronicle: Rgyal-Rabs Gsal-Ba'i Me-Long.* Asiatische Forschungen, Bd. 128. Weisbaden: Harrassowitz, 1994.

Bu ston Rin chen grub. *Bde gshegs nying po gsal ba'i rgyan.* In *Gsung 'bum; Collected Works,* ed. Lokesh Candra. New Delhi: International Academy of Indian Culture, 1965–71.

———. *Bu ston chos 'byung.* Mtsho sngon: Krung go'i bod kyi shes rig dpe skrun khang, 1988.

———. *History of Buddhism,* translated by E. Obermiller. Heidelberg: In Kommission bei O. Harrassowitz, 1932.

Cabezón, José Ignacio. "Tsong kha pa," in *Encyclopedia of Religion,* 2nd ed., forthcoming.

———. "Two Views of the Svātantrika-Prāsaṅgika Distinction in Fourteenth Century Tibet." In *The Svātantrika-Prāsaṅgika Distinction: What Difference Does a Difference Make?,* edited by G. B. J. Dreyfus and S. L. McClintock, pp. 289–315. Boston: Wisdom, 2003.

———. "Toward A History of Sera Monastery: The Early Years." Paper presented at the meeting of the International Association of Tibetan Studies, Oxford, 2003.

———. "Rong ston Shākya rgyal mtshan on Mādhyamika Thesislessness." In *Tibetan Studies,* Proceedings of the International Conference on Tibetan Studies (Graz, Austria), vol. 1, edited by H. Krasser, et. al., 97–105. Wien: Verlag der Osterrichischen Akademie der Wissenschaften, 1997.

———. "On the *sGra pa Rin chen pa'i rtsod lan* of Paṇ chen bLo bzang chos rgyan." *Asiatische Studien/Études Asiatiques* 49.4 (1995): 643–69.

———. *Buddhism and Language: A Study of Indo-Tibetan Scholasticism.* Albany: State University of New York Press, 1994.

———. *A Dose of Emptiness: An Annotated Translation of the Stong thun chen mo of mKhas grub Dge legs dpal bzang.* Albany: State University of New York Press, 1992.

———. "Vasubandhu's Vyākhyāyukti on the Authenticity of the Mahāyāna Sutras." In *Texts in Contexts: Traditional Hermeneutics in South Asia,* edited by J. Timm. Albany: SUNY Press, 1992.

———. "The Canonization of Philosophy and the Rhetoric of *Siddhānta* in Indo-Tibetan Buddhism." In *Buddha Nature: A Festschrift in Honor of Minoru Kiyota,* edited by P. J. Griffiths and J. Keenan, 7–26. San Francisco: Buddhist Books International, 1990.

The Cambridge Dictionary of Philosophy. General Editor Robert Audi. Cambridge: Cambridge University Press, 1999.

Chag lo tsā ba and others. *Sngags log sun 'byin kyi skor.* Thimpu, Bhutan: Kunsang Topgyel and Mani Dorje, 1979.

Chandra, Lokesh. *Materials for a History of Tibetan Literature.* Kyoto: Rinsen Book Co., 1981.

———. *Tibetan-Sanskrit Dictionary,* 2 vols. Kyoto: Rinsen Book Co., 1976.

Conze, Edward. *The Perfection of Wisdom in Eight Thousand Lines and its Verse Summary.* Bolinas: Four Seasons Foundation, 1973.

———. *Abhisamayālaṅkāra.* Introduction and Translation from original text, with Sanskrit-Tibetan Indexes. Serie Orientale Roma VI. Roma: Istituto Italiano per il Medio ed Estremo Oriente, 1954.

Cozort, Daniel. *Unique Tenets of the Middle Way Consequence School.* Ithaca: Snow Lion, 1998.

Crosby, Kate, and Andrew Skilton. *Śāntideva's Bodhicāryāvatāra.* Oxford and New York: Oxford University Press, 1995.

Dargyay, Eva. "Srong-btsan sgam-po of Tibet: Bodhisattva and King." In *Monks and Magicians: Religious Biographies of the East,* edited by Phyllis Granoff and K. Shinohara. Ontario: Mosaic Press, 1988.

———. *The Rise of Esoteric Buddhism in Tibet.* Delhi: Motilal Banarsidass, 1979.

Dargyay, Lobsang. "What is Non-Existent and What is Remanent in Śūnyatā." *Journal of Indian Philosophy* 18 (1990): 81–91.

———. "Tsong-kha-pa's Understanding of Prāsaṅgika Thought." *Journal of the International Association of Buddhist Studies* 10.1 (1987): 55–65.

———. "Tsong Kha Pa's Concept of Karma." In *Karma and Rebirth: Post Classical Developments,* edited by Ronald W. Neufeldt, 169–78. Albany: SUNY Press, 1986.

Davidson, Ronald M. "Gsar ma Apocrypha: The Creation of Orthodoxy, Gray Texts, and the New Revelation." In *The Many Canons of Tibetan Buddhism,* PIATS 2000, edited by Helmut Eimer and David Germano, 203–24. Leiden: Brill, 2002.

———. "Reflections on the Maheśvara Subjugation Myth: Indic Materials, Sa-skya-pa Apologetics, and the Birth of Heruka." *Journal of the International Association of Buddhist Studies* 14.2 (1991): 197–7235.

———. "Appendix." *Chinese Buddhist Apocrypha,* edited by Robert Buswell, 291–325. Honolulu: University of Hawaii Press, 1990.

Dbal mang Dkon mchog rgyal mtshan. *Bden gtam snying rje'i rol mtsho las zur du phyung ba sa rnying bka' brgyud sogs kyi khyad par 'go smos tsam mu to'i rgyangs 'bod kyi tshul du bya gtong snyan sgron bdud rtsi'i bsang gtor.* In *Dgag lan phyogs bsgrigs,* ed. by Rin chen tshe ring, 647–743. Khreng tu'u: Si khron mi rigs dpe skrun khang, 1997.

Della Santina, Peter. *Madhyamaka Schools in India: A Study of the Madhyamaka Philosophy and of the Division of the System into the Prāsaṅgika and Svātantrika Schools.* Delhi: Motilal Banarsidass, 1986.

Demiéville. Paul. *Le Concile de Lhasa.* Paris: Imprimerie Nationale de France, 1952.

Dge 'dun chos 'phel. *Dbu ma'i zab gnad snying por dril ba'i legs bshad klu grub dgongs rgyan.* In *Dge 'dun chos 'phel gyi gsung rtsom,* ed. by Hor khang Bsod nams dpal 'bar, vol. 2, 271–376. Lha sa: Bod ljongs bod yig dpe snying dpe skrun khang, 1990.

Dhongthog, T. G. Rinpoche. *Byang phyogs thub pa'i rgyal tshab dpal ldan Sa-skya-pa'i bstan pa rin po che ji ltar byung ba'i lo rgyus rab 'byams zhing du snyan pa'i sgra dbyangs zhes bya ba bzhugs so: A History of the Sa-skya-pa Sect of Tibetan Buddhism.* New Delhi: Dhongthog, 1977.

Dignāga. *Prajñāpāramitāpiṇḍārtha (Prajñāpāramitāsaṃgraha).* In Tucci, Giuseppe, "Minor Sanskrit Texts on the *Prajñāpāramitā*," *Journal of the Royal Asiatic Society of Great Britain and Ireland* (1947): 53–75.

Doctor, Andreas. *The Tibetan Treasure Literature: Revelation, Tradition and Accomplishment in Visionary Buddhism.* Ithaca: Snow Lion, 2006.

Dol po pa Shes rab rgyal mtshan. *Bden gnyis gsal ba'i nyi ma.* In *The 'Dzam thang Edition of the Collected Works (gsung-'bum) of Kun-mkhyen Dol-po-pa Shes-rab-rgyal-mtshan,* vol. 5, 811–849. Delhi: Shedrup Books, 1992.

———. *The 'Dzam thang Edition of the Collected Works (gsung-'bum) of Kun-mkhyen Dol-po-pa Shes-rab-rgyal-mtshan,* collected and presented by Matthew Kapstein. Delhi: Shedrup Books, 1992.

———. *Bka' bsdu bzhi pa,* in *The Collected Works (gSung 'bum) of Kun-mkhyen Dol-po-pa Śes-rab-rgyal-mtshan (1292–1361), reproduced from eye copies of prints from the Rgyal-rtse Rdzong blocks preserved at Kyichu Monastery in the Paro valley, Bhutan,* vol. 1, 363–417. Paro: Lama Ngodrup and Sherab Drimay, 1984.

———. *Ri chos nges don rgya mtsho.* Delhi: Dodrup Sangyey, 1976.

Dondrub, Sampe. "A Dispute of Jangzhon." *Jangzhon* 4 (1992): 1–4.

Don rdor and Bstan 'dzin chos grags, compilers, *Gangs ljongs lo rgyus thog go grags can mi sna.* Lha sa: Bod ljongs mi dmangs dpe skrun khang: 1993.

Dreyfus, Georges B. J. *The Sound of Two Hands Clapping: The Education of a Tibetan Buddhist Monk.* Berkeley: University of California Press, 2003.

———. "The Shuk-Den Affair: Origin of a Controversy." *Journal of the International Association of Buddhist Studies* 21.2 (1998): 227–70. http://www.tibet.com/dholgyal/shugden-origins.html#_ftn1 (revised).

———. *Recognizing Reality: Dharmakīrti's Philosophy and Its Tibetan Interpretations.* Albany: SUNY Press, 1997.

Dreyfus, Georges B. J. and Sara L. McClintock. *The Svātantrika/Prāsaṅgika Distinction: What Difference Does a Difference Make?* Boston: Wisdom Publications, 2003.

Dudjom Rinpoche. *Perfect Conduct: Ascertaining the Three Vows.* Boston: Wisdom, 1996.

Dudjom Rinpoche and Jikdrel Yeshe Dorje. *The Nyingma School of Tibetan Buddhism: Its Fundamentals and History.* Boston: Wisdom, 1991.

Dung dkar Blo bzang 'phrin las. *Mkhas dbang dung dkar blo bzang 'phrin las mchog gis mdzad pa'i bod rig pa'i tshig mdzod chen mo shes bya rab gsal zhes bya ba bzhugs so (Dung dkar tshig mdzod chen mo).* Beijing: Krung go'i bod rig pa'i dpe skrun khang, 2002.

Dunne, John, and Sara McClintock, trans. *The Precious Garland: An Epistle to a King.* Boston: Wisdom, 1997.

Dutt, Nalinakasha, ed. *Bodhisattvabhūmi.* Patna: K. P. Jayaswal Research Institute, 1966.

———, ed. *Pañcaviṃśatisāhasrikā-Prajñāpāramitā.* Calcutta Oriental Series 28. London: Luzac and Co, 1934.

Dwarikadas Shastri, Swami, ed. *Abhidharmakośam; Svopajñabhāṣyasahitam. Ācāryavasubandhu-viracitam. Ācāryayaśomitrakṛta-sphuṭārthāvyākhyopetam.* Varanasi: Bauddha Bharati, 1970–73.

———, ed. *Pramāṇavārttikam Ācāryaśrīdharmakīrttiviracitā; Ācāryamanorathanandivṛttiyutam.* Varanasi: Bauddha Bharati, 1968.

Dze smad rin po che Blo bzang dpal ldan bstan 'dzin yar rgyas. *Dge 'dun chos 'phel gyi dgag lan,* in *Collected Works of Kyabje Zemey Rimpoche: Journal of Teachings Received and Assorted Lecture Notes,* ed. by Geshe Thupten Jinpa, vol. 3, 1–270. Mundgod, Karnataka State: Zemey Labrang, Gaden Shartse Monastic College, 1997.

Dzongsar Khyentse Rinpoche. *Introduction to the Middle Way: Chandrakirti's Madhyamakaratara. With commentary by Dzongsar Jamyang Khyentse Rinpoche,* http://www.khyentsefoundation.org/publications.html.

Eckel, Malcolm David. "The Satisfaction of No Analysis: On Tsong kha pa's Approach to Svātantrika-Madhyamaka." In *The Svātantrika/Prāsaṅgika*

Distinction: What Difference Does a Difference Make?, edited by G. B. J. Dreyfus and S. L. McClintock, pp. 289–315. Boston: Wisdom, 2003.

———. *Jñānagarbha's Commentary on the Distinction Between the Two Truths*. Albany: SUNY Press, 1987.

Edgerton, Franklin. *Buddhist Hybrid Sanskrit Dictionary*. 1953. Delhi: Motilal Banasidass, 1972.

Evans-Wentz, Walter Yeeling. *Tibet's Great Yogi Milarepa*, 2nd ed. London: Oxford University Press, 1951.

Ferrari, Alfonso. *mKhyen brTse's Guide to the Holy Places of Central Tibet*, Serie Orientale Roma 16. Rome: IsMEO, 1958.

Frauwallner, Erich. *Studies in Abhidharma Literature and the Origins of Buddhist Philosophical Systems*. Trans. Sophie Francis Kidd. Albany: SUNY Press, 1995.

———. *Die Philosophie des Buddhismus*. Berlin: Akademie-Verlag, 1969.

———. "Dignaga, Sein Werk und Seine Entwicklung." *Wiener Zeitschrift für kunde Sud-und Ostasiens* 3 (1959), 83–164.

Gardiner, Michael. *The Dialogics of Critique: M.M. Bakhtin and the Theory of Ideology*. London: Routledge, 1992.

Garfield, Jay L. *The Fundamental Wisdom of the Middle Way: Nāgārjuna's Mūlamadhyamakakārikā*. New York: Oxford, 1995.

Germano, David. "Architecture and Absence in the Secret Tantric History of the Great Perfection *(rdzogs chen)*." *Journal of the International Association of Buddhist Studies* 17.2 (1994): 315–24.

Gimello, Robert M. and Peter N. Gregory, ed. *Studies in Ch'an and Hua-yen*. Honolulu: University of Hawaii Press/Kuroda Institute, 1983.

Gnoli, Raniero, ed. *The Pramāṇavārttikam of Dharmakīrti: The First Chapter with the Autocommentary*. Serie Orientale Roma, v. XXIII. Roma: Istituto Italiano per il Medio ed Estremo Oriente, 1960.

Goldstein, Melvyn C. *The New Tibetan-English Dictionary of Modern Tibetan*. Berkeley: University of California Press, 2001.

Gómez, Luis O. "The Direct and the Gradual Approaches of Zen Master Mahāyāna." In *Studies in Ch'an and Hua-yen*, edited by Robert M.

Gimello and Peter N. Gregory, 69–167. Honolulu: University of Hawaii Press/Kuroda Institute, 1983.

———. "Primer Tratado de Cultivo Graduado." *Dialogos* 11.29–30 (1977): 177–224.

———. "Proto-Madhyamaka in the Pali Canon." *Philosophy East and West* 26.2 (1976): 137–65.

Gonchok, Losang. *Buddhist Philosophy: Losang Gonchok's Short Commentary to Jamyang Shayba's Root Text on Tenets.* Translated by Daniel Cozort and Craig Preston. Ithaca, NY: Snow Lion, 2003.

Goodwin, David. "Distinction, Argumentation and the Rhetorical Construction of the Real." *Argumentation and Advocacy* 27 (1991): 141–58.

Go rams pa Bsod nams seng ge. *Lta ba'i shan 'byed.* Together with Mkhan chen Bsod nams lhun grub. *Rtags kyi bzhag rigs lam gsal ba'i sgron me.* Sarnath: Sakya Students' Union, 1988.

———. *Lta ba'i shan 'byed.* Cyclostat in the collection of the library of the Institut für Kultur und Geschichte Indiens und Tibets, Hamburg, access number MIV 345/6, catalogued 1968, most likely printed in Buxador, India in the early 1960s, 42 folios.

———. *Lta ba'i shan 'byed.* In *Sa skya pa'i bka' 'bum: The Complete Works of the Great Masters of the Sa skya Sect of Tibetan Buddhism,* compiled by Bsod nams rgya mtsho, vol. 13. Tokyo: The Tōyō Bunko, 1968.

———. *Rgyal ba thams cad kyi thugs kyi dgongs pa zab mo dbu ma'i de kho na nyid spyi'i ngag gis ston pa nges don rab gsal (Dbu ma'i spyi don).* In *Sa skya pa'i bka 'bum: The Complete Works of the Great Masters of the Sa skya Sect of Tibetan Buddhism,* compiled by Bsod nams rgya mtsho, vol. 12. Tokyo: The Tōyō Bunko, 1968.

———. *Dbu ma la 'jug pa'i dkyus kyis sa bcad pa dang gzhung so so'i dka' ba'i gnas la dpyad pa lta ba ngan sel (Lta ba ngan sel).* In *Sa skya pa'i bka 'bum: The Complete Works of the Great Masters of the Sa skya Sect of Tibetan Buddhism,* compiled by Bsod nams rgya mtsho, vol. 13. Tokyo: The Tōyō Bunko, 1968.

———. *Dbu ma la 'jug pa'i dkyus kyis sa bcad pa dang gzhung so so'i dka' ba'i gnas la dpyad pa lta ba ngan sel (Lta ba ngan sel).* In *The Collected*

Works of Kun-mkhyen Go-rams pa bSod-nams-seng-ge, edited by Lama Sherab Gyaltsen, vol. 5 *(ca),* ff. 511–751. Kangra: Dzongsar Institute, n.d.

———. *Zhugs gnas kyi rnam gzhag skyes bu mchog gi gsal bye; Illuminating the Holy Saints: Stages of Entrance and Attainment.* Sakya Centre, n.d.

'Gos lo tsa ba Gzhoṇ nu dpal. *Deb ther sngon po,* 2 vols. Ch'eng tu: Si khron mi rigs dpe skrun khang: 1985.

Grags pa rgyal mtshan. *Mngon rtogs rgyud kyi mngon par rtogs pa rin po che'i ljon shing (Mngon rtogs ljon shing).* In *Grags pa rgyal mtshan bka' bum,* ed. by Bsod nams rgya mtsho, vol. 1. *Sa skya pa'i bka 'bum: Complete Works of the Masters of the Sa skya Sect of Tibetan Buddhism.* Tokyo: The Tōyō Bunko, 1968.

Griffiths, Paul J. *An Apology for Apologetics: A Study in the Logic of Interreligious Dialogue.* Mayknoll: Orbis, 1991.

Gro lung pa Blo gros 'byung gnas. *Bde bar gshegs pa'i bstan pa rin po che la 'jug pa'i lam gyi rim pa rnam par bshad pa.* Asian Classics Input Project, Release IV, SL0070-1/2.

Guenther, Herbert V. *Buddhist Philosophy in Theory and Practice.* Baltimore: Penguin, 1971.

Guenther, Herbert V., and L. Kawamura. *Mind in Buddhist Psychology.* Emeryville: Dharma Publishing, 1975.

Gun thang Dkon mchog bstan pa'i sgron me. *Rten 'brel gyi rnam bzhag lung rigs bang mdzod.* In *The Collected Works of Gun-thang Dkon-mchog-bstan-pa'i-sgron me,* reproduced from prints from the Lha-sa blocks by Ngawang Gelek Demo, vol 3. New Delhi: Ngawang Gelek Demo, 1972.

———. *Drang nges rnam 'byed kyi dka' 'grel.* In *The Collected Works of Gun-thang Dkon-mchog-bstan-pa'i-sgron me,* reproduced from prints from the Lha-sa blocks by Ngawang Gelek Demo, vol. 2, 403–723. New Delhi: Ngawang Gelek Demo, 1972.

Gu ru bkra shis, Ngag dbang blo gros Stag sgang mkhas mchog. *Gu bkra'i chos 'byung.* Pe cin: Krung go'i bod kyi shes rig dpe skrun khang, 1990.

G.yag ston (G.yag phrug) Sangs rgyas dpal. *The Complete Yig-cha for the Study of the Prajñāpāramitā Literature (g.Yag ston sher phyin ṭīka).* Manduwala, Dehradun: Pal Evam Chodan Ngorpa Centre, 1985.

Gyaltsen, Namdol, ed. *Slob-dpon kamalaśīlas mdzad pa'i bsgom rim thog mtha' bar gsum zhugs so/ Ācāryakamalasīlapraṇītaḥ Bhāvanākramaḥ.* Sarnath: Central Institute of Higher Tibetan Studies, 1985 (Tibetan and Sanskrit with Hindi translation).

Gyatso, Janet. "Drawn from the Tibetan Treasury: The gTer ma Literature." In *Tibetan Literature,* edited by Jose Cabezón and Roger Jackson, 170–86. Ithaca, NY: Snow Lion, 1996.

Hahn, Michael, ed. *Nāgārjuna's Ratnāvalī. Vol. 1. The Basic Texts (Sanskrit, Tibetan, and Chinese).* Bonn: Indica et Tibetica Verlag, 1982.

Hookham, Shenphen. K. *The Buddha Within: Tathagatagarbha Doctrine According to the Shentong Interpretation of the Ratnagotravibhaga.* Albany: SUNY Press, 1991.

Hopkins, Jeffrey. *Maps of the Profound: Jam-yang-shay-ba's Great Exposition of Buddhist and Non-Buddhist Views on the Nature of Reality.* Ithaca, NY: Snow Lion, 2003.

———. *Emptiness in the Mind-Only School of Buddhism: Dynamic Responses to Dzong-ka-ba's The Essence of Eloquence: I.* Berkeley: University of California Press, 1999.

———. "A Tibetan Delineation of Different Views of Emptiness in the Indian Middle Way School." *Tibet Journal* 14.1 (1989): 10–43.

———. *Emptiness Yoga.* Ithaca, NY: Snow Lion, 1987.

———. *Meditation on Emptiness.* London: Wisdom Publications, 1983.

———. *Compassion in Tibetan Buddhism.* London: Rider, 1980.

———. *The Precious Garland and The Song of the Four Mindfulnesses.* New York: Harper and Row, 1975.

———. *Ocean of Reasoning.* Dharamsala: Library of Tibetan Works and Archives, 1974.

Horner, Isaline B., trans. *Mahā-suññyata-sutta, The Collection of the Middle Length Sayings, Majjhima Nikāya,* vol. III, Pali text no. 121. London: The Pali Text Society, 1959.

Horvath, Z. "Structure and Content of the Chad-ma rigs-pa'i gter, an epistemological Treatise of Saskya Paṇḍita." *Tibetan and Buddhist Studies* 29.1 (1984): 267–302.

Houston, Gary W. *Sources for a History of the bSam yas Debate.* Sankt Augustin: VGH-Wissenschaftverlag, 1980.

Hugon, Pascale. "Continuity and Rupture in the Development of Tibetan Espistemology." Paper presented at the Princeton Graduate Student Conference, 2005.

Huntington, C. W., Jr. "A Lost Text of Early Indian Madhyamaka." *Asiatische Studien/Études Asiatiques* 59.4 (1999): 693–767.

Huntington, C. W. Jr. with Geshé Namgyal Wangchen. *The Emptiness of Emptiness: An Introduction to Early Indian Madhyamika.* Honolulu: University of Hawaii Press, 1989.

Iaroslav, Komarovski, trans. *Three Texts on Madhyamaka by Shākya Chokden.* Dharamsala: Library of Tibetan Works and Archives, 2000.

Ichigō, Masamichi. *Chūkan sōgenron no kenkyū: Shāntarakushita no shisō.* Tokyo: Buneidō, 1985.

Iida, Shotaro. *Reason and Emptiness.* Tokyo: Hokuseido Press, 1980.

Imaeda, Yoshiro. "Documents Tibétains de Touen-houang Concernant le Concile du Tibet." *Journal Asiatique* (1975): 125–46.

Inada, Kenneth K., ed. and trans. *Nāgārjuna, a Translation of His Mūlamadhyamakakārikā with an Introductory Essay.* Tokyo: Hokuseido Press, 1970.

Jackson, David P. *A Saint in Seattle: The Life of the Tibetan Mystic Dezhung Rinpoche.* Boston: Wisdom Publications, 2004.

———. *Enlightenment by a Single Means: Tibetan Controversies on the "Self-Sufficient White Remedy" (Dkar po chig thub).* Wien: Verlag der Österreichischen Akademie der Wissenschaften, 1994.

———. "Sa-skya Paṇḍita the 'Polemicist': Ancient Debates and Modern Interpretations." *Journal of the International Association of Buddhist Studies* 13.2 (1990): 17–116.

———. *The Early Abbots of 'Phan-po Ne-len-dra: The Vicissitudes of a Great Tibetan Monastery in the 15th Century.* Wien: Arbeitskreis für Tibetische und Buddhistische Studien, Universität Wien, 1989.

———. *The 'Miscellaneous Series' of Tibetan Texts in the Bihar Research Society, Patna: A Handlist,* Tibet and Indo-Tibetan Studies 2. Stuttgart: Franz Steiner Verlag, 1989.

———. *The Entrance Gate for the Wise.* Wien: Arbeitskreis für Tibetische und Buddhistische Studien, Universität Wien, 1987, 2 vols.

———. "Madhyamaka Studies among the Early Sa-skya-pas." *The Tibet Journal* 10.2 (1985): 20–34.

———. "Commentaries on the Writings of Sa skya Paṇḍita." *Tibet Journal* 8.2 (1983): 3–23.

Jackson, David P. and Shunzo Onoda, *Rong-ston on the Prajñāpāramitā Philosophy of the Abhisamayalaṃkara: His Sub-commentary on Haribhadra's 'Sphuṭarthā'.* Kyoto: Nagata Bunshodo, 1988.

Jackson, Roger R. "Sa-skya Paṇḍita's Account of the bSam yas Debate: History as Polemic." *Journal of the International Association of Buddhist Studies* 5.2 (1982): 89–99.

'Jam dbyangs bzhad pa' rdo rje. *Shes rab kyi pha rol tu phyin pa'i mtha' dypod 'khrul sel gang ga'i chu rgyun (Phar phyin mtha' dpyod).* In *gSung 'bum, The Collected Works of 'Jam-dbyangs-bźad-pa,* reproduced from prints from the Bkra shis 'khyil blocks by Ngawang Gelek Demo, vol. 7 *(ja).* New Delhi: Ngawang Gelek Demo, 1973.

———. *Grub mtha' rnam bshad chen mo.* In *gSung 'bum, The Collected Works of 'Jam-dbyangs-bźad-pa,* reproduced from prints from the Bkra shis 'khyil blocks by Ngawang Gelek Demo, vol. 14, 33–1091. New Delhi: Ngawang Gelek Demo, 1973.

———. *Grub pa'i mtha' rnam par bzhags pa 'khrul spongs dgongs lnga'i sgra dbyangs.* In *gSung 'bum, The Collected Works of 'Jam-dbyangs-bźad-pa,* reproduced from prints from the Bkra shis 'khyil blocks by Ngawang Gelek Demo, vol. 14. New Delhi: Ngawang Gelek Demo, 1973.

———. *Dbu ma 'jug pa'i mtha' dpyod lung rig gter mdzod.* In *gSung 'bum, The Collected Works of 'Jam-dbyangs-bźad-pa,* reproduced from prints from the Bkra shis 'khyil blocks by Ngawang Gelek Demo, vol. 9, 3–885. New Delhi: Ngawang Gelek Demo, 1973.

'Jam dbyangs dga' ba'i blo gros. *Lta ba ngan pa thams cad tshar gcod pa'i bstan bcos gnam lcags 'khor lo zhes bya ba go bo bsod nams seng ge zhes bya ba'i dge ba'i bshes gnyen la gdams pa.* In *Dgag lan phyogs bsgrigs,* ed. by Rin chen tshe ring, pp. 519–605. Khreng tu'u: Si khron mi rigs dpe skrun khang, 1997.

Jasper, James M. "The Politics of Abstractions: Instrumental and Moralist Rhetorics in Public Debate." *Social Research* 59.2 (1992): 315–44.

Johnston, Edward Hamilton, and Arnold Kunst, eds. *The Dialectical Method of Nāgārjuna: Vigrahavyāvartanī, translated from the original Sanskrit with introduction and notes by Kamaleswar Bhattacharya.* Delhi: Motilal Banarsidass, 1978.

Johnston, Edward Hamilton, and T. Chowdhury, eds. *Ratnagotravibhāga Mahāyānottaratantraśāstra.* Patna: Bihar Research Society, 1950.

Jorden, Ngawang. "Buddha-Nature: Through the Eyes of Go rams pa Bsod nams seng ge in Fifteenth-Century Tibet." Ph.D. diss., Harvard University, 2003.

Kajiyama, Yuichi. *An Introduction to Buddhist Philosophy.* Kyoto: Kyoto University, 1966.

Kalupahana, David J. *Nāgārjuna: The Philosophy of the Middle Way, Mūlamadhyamakakārikā.* Albany: SUNY Press, 1986.

Kamalaśīla. *Third Bhāvanākrama.* In *Minor Buddhist Texts part III,* ed. by Giuseppe Tucci. Serie Orientale Roma, vol. XLIII. Roma: Istituto Italiano per il Medio ed Estremo Oriente, 1971.

———. *First Bhāvanākrama.* In *Minor Buddhist Texts part I,* ed. by Giuseppe Tucci. Serie Orientale Roma, vol. IX, 2. Roma: Istituto Italiano per il Medio ed Estremo Oriente, 1958 (Sanskrit and Tibetan).

Kapstein, Matthew. *The Tibetan Assimilation of Buddhism: Conversion, Contestation, Memory.* Oxford: Oxford University Press, 2000.

———. "The Purifactory Gem and Its Cleansing: A Late Tibetan Polemical Discussion of Apocryphal Texts." *History of Religions* 28.3 (1998): 217–44.

———. "gDams ngag: Tibetan Technologies of the Self." In *Tibetan Literature,* edited by Jose Cabezón and Roger Jackson, 275–90. Ithaca, NY: Snow Lion, 1996.

———. *The 'Dzam thang Edition of the Collected Works of Kun-mkhyen Dol-po-pa Shes-rab-rgyal-mtshan: Introduction and Catalogue.* Delhi: Shedrup Books, 1992.

Karmay, Samten G. *The Arrow and the Spindle: Studies in History, Myths, Rituals and Belief in Tibet.* Kathmandu: Mandala Book Point, 1998.

———. *The Great Perfection: A Philosophical and Meditative Teaching of Tibetan Buddhism.* Leiden: E. J. Brill, 1988.

Kaschewsky, Rudolf. *Das Leben des lamaistischen heiligen Tsongkhapa bLo-bzan-grags-pa (1357–1419) dargestellt und erläutert anhand seiner Vita "Quellort allen Gluckes,"* 2 vols. Wiesbaden: Otto Harrassowitz, 1971.

Kawamura, Leslie. *Nāgārjuna and Lama Mipham, Golden Zephyr, bShes-spring gi mchan-'grel padma-dkar-po'i phreng-ba, the Garland of White Lotus Flowers: A Commentary on Nāgārjuna's "A Letter to a Friend."* Emeryville: Dharma Press, 1975.

Keeble, N. H. "The Autobiographer as Apologist: Reliquiae Baxterianae (1696)." In *The Literature of Controversy: Polemical Strategies from Milton to Junius,* edited by Thomas N. Corns. Totowa, NJ: Frank Cass, 1987.

Klein, Anne C. *Path to the Middle: Oral Mādhyamika Philosophy in Tibet.* Albany: SUNY Press, 1994.

———. *Knowing, Naming, and Negation: A Sourcebook on Tibetan Sautrāntika.* Ithaca: Snow Lion, 1991.

Klong rdol bla ma Ngag dbang blo bzang. *Klong rdol bla ma Rin po che ngag dbang blo bzang gi gsung 'bum: Tibetan Buddhist Studies of Klong rdol bla ma ngag dbang blo bzang.* Edited from the Lhasa xylograph by Ven. Dalama. Mussoorie: Dalama, 1963–64.

———. *The Collected Works of Longdol Lama.* Śatapiṭaka, vol 100. New Delhi: International Academy of Indian Culture, 1973.

Kochumuttom, Thomas A. *A Buddhist Doctrine of Experience: A New Translation and Interpretation of the Works of Vasubandhu the Yogacarin.* Delhi: Motilal Banarsidass, 1982.

Kong ston Dbang phyug grub, *Rje bla ma'i rnam par thar pa ngo mtshar rin po che'i phreng ba (Kun mkhyen Bsod nams sen ge'i rnam thar, The Biography of Kun-mkhyen Go-rams-pa Bsod-nams Sengge),* ed. by T. G. Dhongthog. Delhi: Dhongthog, 1973.

Ko zhul Grags pa 'byung-gnas, and Rgyal ba Blo bzang mkhas grub. *Gang can mkhas grub rim byon ming mdzod (Ming mdzod).* Lan chou: Kan su'u Mi rigs dpe skrun khang, 1992.

Krang dbyi sun et al. *Bod rgya tshig mdzod chen mo.* Beijing: Mi rigs dpe skrun khang, 1998.

Kristeva, Julia. "Word, Dialogue, and the Novel." In *The Kristeva Reader,* edited by Toril Moi. New York: Columbia University Press, 1986.

Lamotte, Étienne, ed. and trans. *La somme du grand vehicule d'Asanga (Mahāyānasaṃgraha).* Louvain: Université de Louvain, 1973.

Lang, Karen. *Āryadeva's Catuḥśataka: On the Bodhisattva's Cultivation of Method and Knowledge.* Copenhagen: Akademisk Forlag, 1986.

Larson, Gerald James. *Classical Sāṃkhya: An Interpretation of Its History and Meaning,* 2nd revised ed. Delhi: Motilal Banarsidass, 1979.

Lati Rinbochay, et al. *Meditative States in Tibetan Buddhism.* Boston: Wisdom, 1983.

Lati Rinbochay and Elizabeth Napper, *Mind in Tibetan Buddhism.* Valois, NY: Gabriel/Snow Lion, 1980.

La Vallée Poussin, Louis de . *Abhidharmakośabhāṣyam.* Translated into English by Leo Pruded. Berkeley, California: Asian Humanities Press, 1988.

———."Madhyamakāvatāra: introduction au traité du milieu de l'ācārya Candrakīrti, avec le commentaire de l'auteur." *Le Muséon* 8 (1907): 249–317; 11 (1910): 271–358; 12 (1911): 235–328.

———, ed. *Mūlamadhyamakakārikās de Nāgārjuna avec la Prasannapadā Commentaire de Candrakīrti.* Bibliotheca Buddhica 4. St. Petersburg: Imprimerie de l'Academie impériale des Sciences, 1903–13.

Lcang lung paṇḍita Ngag dbang blo bzang bstan pa'i rgyal mtshan. *Grub pa dang rnal 'byor par rlom pa rnams kyi de nyid gsal byed.* In *gSung 'bum, the Collected Works of lCan-lun pandi ta nag-dban-blo-bzan-bstan-pa'i-rgyal-mtshan.* Delhi: Mongolian lama Gurudeva, 1975–85.

Ldan ma Blo bzang chos dbyings. *Rtsod lan blo dman snying gi gdung sel ga bur thig pa'i spun zla: A Refutation of the Views of 'Jam mgon 'Ju Mi pham rgya mtsho in the Series of Polemical Writings on the Nature of Śūnyatā and Mādhyamika Philosophy.* Paṇ chen Bsod nams grags pa literature series, vol. 40. Mundgod: Drepung Loseling Library Society, 1985.

Ldan ma Blo bzang rdo rje, and others. *Three Texts Reflecting the Views of Pha-bong-kha-pa Bde-chen-snying-po on the Questions of Heresies and Intersectarian Relations in Tibet.* New Delhi: Ngawang Tobgay, 1977.

The Leiden project. "Thinking Differences." http://website.leidenuniv.nl/~hettematl/Onderzoek/thinkdif-pap.html

Lessing, F. D. and Alex Wayman, eds. and trans. *mKhas-grub-rje's Fundamentals of the Buddhist Tantras.* The Hague: Mouton, 1968.

Lévi, Sylvain, trans. *Mahāyāna-Sūtrālaṃkāra: Exposé de la doctrine du grand véhicule selon le système Yogācāra,* vol. II. Paris: Librairie Honoré Champion, 1907–11.

Lhalungpa, Lobsang, trans. *The Life of Milarepa.* London: Grenada Publishing, 1979.

Lindtner, Christian. *Nagarjuniana, Studies in the Writing and Philosophy of Nāgārjuna.* Copenhagen: Akademisk Forlag, 1982.

Lipman, Kennard. "A Controversial Topic from Mi-phams's Analysis of Śāntarakṣita's *Madhyamkālaṃkāra.*" In *Wind Horse: Proceedings of the North American Tibetological Society,* edited by Ronald M. Davidson. Berkeley: Asian Humanities Press, 1981.

Lopez, Donald S. "Polemical Literature *(dGag lan).*" In *Tibetan Literature: Studies in Genre,* edited by José I. Cabezón and Roger R. Jackson, 217–28. Ithaca: Snow Lion, 1996.

———. *A Study of Svātantrika.* Ithaca, NY: Snow Lion, 1987.

Maher, Derek Frank. "Knowledge and Authority in Tibetan Middle Way Schools of Buddhism: A Study of the Gelukba (dGe lugs pa) Epistemology of Jamyang Shayba ('Jam dbyangs bzhad pa) in its Historical Context." Ph.D. diss., University of Virginia, 2003.

Makransky, John. *Buddhahood Embodied: Sources of Controversy in India and Tibet.* Albany: SUNY Press, 1997.

Mang thos Klu grub rgya mtsho. *Bstan rtsis gsal ba'i nyin byed tha snyad rig gnas lnga'i byung tshul blo gsal mgrin rgyan.* Lha sa: Bod ljong mi dmangs dpe skrun khang, 1987.

Martin, Dan. *Unearthing Bon Treasures: Life and Contested Legacy of a Tibetan Scripture Revealer.* Leiden: Brill, 2001.

———. "Beyond Acceptance and Rejection? The Anti-Bon Polemic in the Thirteenth-Century *Single Intention* (Dgong-gcig Yig-cha) and Its Background in Tibetan Religious History." *Journal of Indian Philosophy* 25 (1997): 263–64.

Matsumoto, Shirō. "Chibetto no Chūgan Shisō—Toku ni 'rihen chūgan setse' wo chūsin ni shite" (Tibetan Mādhyamika thought, with a special focus on the theory of 'freedom from extremes as the middle view'). *Tōyō Gakujutsu Kenkyū* 21.2 (1982): 161–78.

———. "sTag tshang pa no Tsong kha pa Hihan ni tsuite" (On sTag tshang pa's criticism of Tsong kha pa). *Report of the Japanese Association for Tibetan Studies* 28 (1982): 11–14.

———. "Mādhyamika Philosophy in Tibet—on the mTha' bral dbu ma'i lugs." *Journal of Oriental Studies* 21.2 (1982).

Mayer, Robert. "Were the Gsar-ma-pa Polemicists Justified in Rejecting Some Rnying-ma-pa Tantras?" In *Tibetan Studies,* edited by Helmut Krasser, et. al., II: 618–32. Wien: Verlag der Osterreichichen Akademie der Wissenschaften, 1997.

McGee, William. *The Nature of Things: Emptiness and Essence in the Geluk World.* Ithaca, NY: Snow Lion, 1999.

Mi bskyod rdo rje, Eighth Karma pa. *Dbu ma la 'jug pa'i rnam bshad dpal ldan dus gsum mkhyen pa'i zhal lung dwags brgyud grub pa'i shing rta,* in *gSung 'bum* (Collected Works) ed. by Karma bde legs, v. 14, 1–975. Lhasa: Tsadra, 2004.

Mimaki, Katsumi. *bLo gsal grub mtha'*. Kyoto: Zinbun Kagaku Kenkyusyo, 1982.

———. "Le *Grub mtha' rnam bzag rin chen phren ba* de dKon mchog 'jigs med dban po (1728–1791)." *Zinbun* 14 (1977): 55–112.

———. *La réfutation Bouddhique de la permanence des choses (sthirasiddhi-dūṣaṇa)*. Paris: Institut de civilization indienne, 1976.

Mkhas grub Dge legs dpal bzang po. *Lam ngan mun sel sgron ma*. In *gSung 'bum, reprinted from a set of impressions of the old Tashilhunpo blocks,* vol. *ta*. Dharamsala: Sherig Parkhang, 1997.

———. *Phyin ci log gi gtam gyi sbyor ba la zhugs pa'i smra ba ngan pa rnam par 'thag pa'i bstan bcos gnam lcags 'khor lo*. In *Dgag lan phyogs bsgrigs,* ed. by Rin chen tshe ring, 1–68. Khreng tu'u: Si khron mi rigs dpe skrun khang, 1997.

———. *Rje btsun bla ma Tsong kha pa chen po'i ngo mtshar rmad du byung ba'i rnam par thar pa dad pa'i 'jug ngog*. Asian Classics Input Project, Release IV, S5259.

———. *Tsong kha pa'i ngo mtshar rmad byung rnam thar (Rje btsun bla ma tsong kha pa chen po'i ngo mtshar rmad du byung ba'i rnam par thar pa dad pa'i 'jug ngog),* in *Gsung 'bum,* vol. *ka*. New Delhi: Ngawang Gelek Demo, 1983.

———. *Rje rin po che'i gsang ba'i rnam thar rgya mtsho lta bu las cha shas nyung ngu zhig yongs su brjod pa'i gtam rin po che'i snye ma*. In *Gsung 'bum,* vol. *ka*. New Delhi: Ngawang Gelek Demo, 1983.

———. *sTon thun chen mo of mKhas-grub dGe-legs-dpal-bzang and Other Texts on Madhyamika Philosophy,* ed. by Lha mkhar yongs 'dzin Bstanpa rgyal mtshan. Madhyamika Text Series, vol. 1. New Delhi, 1972.

Nagao, Gadjin M. "From Mādhyamika to Yogācāra: an Analysis of MK, XXIV/18 and MV. I /1-2." *Journal of the International Association of Buddhist Studies* 2.1 (1979): 29–43.

———. "What Remains in Śūnyatā: A Yogācāra Interpretation of Emptiness." In *Mahāyāna Buddhist Meditation: Theory and Practice.* Edited by M. Kiyota and E. W. Jones, 66–82. Honolulu: University of Hawaii Press, 1978.

Ṅag-dbaṅ-blo-bzaṅ-rgya-mtsho, Dalai Lama V. *The History of Tibet by the Fifth Dalai Lama of Tibet.* Translated from Tibetan by Zahiruddin Ahmad. Bloomington: Indiana University, Research Institute for Inner Asian Studies, 1995.

Nagel, Thomas. *The View from Nowhere.* NY: Oxford University Press, 1986.

Nakamura, Zuiryu ed. *Zō-Wa taiyaku Kukyō ichijō hōshōron kenkyū (Ratnagotravibhāga).* Tokyo: Suzuki Gakujutsu Zaidan, 1967 (Japanese and Tibetan, with Sanskrit and Chinese).

Nalanda Translation Committee, trans. *The Life of Marpa the Translator.* Boulder: Prajna, 1980.

Namdrol, Gyaltsen. *Bhāvanā-krama.* Sarnath: Institute of Higher Tibetan Studies, 1985.

Nance, Richard. *Models of Teaching and the Teaching of Models:: Contextualizing Indian Buddhist Commentaries.* Doctoral dissertation. University of Chicago, 2004.

Nanjio, Bunyiu, ed. *Laṅkāvatāra Sūtra.* Bibliotheca Otaniensis, vol. 1. Kyoto: Otani University Press, 1956.

Napper, Elizabeth. *Dependent Arising and Emptiness: A Tibetan Buddhist Interpretation of Madhyamika Philosophy Emphasizing the Compatability of Emptiness and Conventional Phenomena.* Boston: Wisdom, 1989.

Naughton, Alex. *The Buddhist Path to Omniscience.* Ph.D. diss., University of Wisconsin—Madison, 1989.

Neufeldt, Ronald W., ed. *Karma and Rebirth: Post-Classical Developments.* Albany: SUNY Press, 1986.

Neumaier-Dargyay, E. K. *The Sovereign All-Creating Mind: The Motherly Buddha.* Albany: State University of New York Press, 1992.

Newland, Guy. *The Two Truths in the Mādhyamika Philosophy of the Geluk-ba Order of Tibetan Buddhism.* Ithaca: Snow Lion, 1992.

Ngor khri chen the Tenth, Dkon mchog lhun grub, and Ngor khri chen the Twenty-fifth, Sang rgyas phun tshogs. *A History of Buddhism: Being the Text of Dam pa'i chos kyi byung tshul legs par bshad pa bstan pa rgya mtshor 'jug pa'i gru chen zhes bya ba rtsom 'phro kha skong bcas (Ngor pa'i chos byung)*. New Delhi: Ngawang Topgey, 1973.

Obermiller, Evgenii. *Prajñāpāramitā in Tibetan Buddhism*. Acta Orientalia 11, 1932. Reprint, Delhi: Classics India Publications, 1988.

———, ed. *Prajñā-pāramitā-ratna-guṇa-saṃcaya-gāthā, Sanskrit and Tibetan text*. Hague: Mouton and Co, 1937. Reprint, *Indo-Iranian Journal*, vol. V, 1960. Reprint, Delhi: Sri Satguru Publications, 1992.

Okada, Yukihiro. *Nāgārjuna's Ratnāvalī. Vol. 2. Die Ratnāvalī des Ajitamitra*. Bonn: Indica et Tibetica Verlag, 1990.

Ong, Walter J. *Fighting for Life: Context, Sexuality, and Consciousness*. Amherst: The University of Massachusetts Press, 1981.

———. *The Presence of the Word*. New Haven: Yale University Press, 1967.

Onoda, Shunzo. "Bsdus grwa Literature." In *Tibetan Literature: Studies in Genre*, edited by José I. Cabezón and Roger R. Jackson, 187–201. Ithaca: Snow Lion, 1996.

———. *Monastic Debate in Tibet: A Study of the History and Structures of Bsdus grwa Logic*. Wien: Arbeitskreis für Tibetische und Buddhistische Studien, Universität Wien, 1992.

———. "Abbatial Successions of the Colleges of Gsang phu sNe'u thog Monastery." *Kokuritsu minzokugaku Hakubutsukan Kenkyu* 15.4 (1990): 1049–71.

O rgyan gling pa. *Bka' thang sde lnga*. Pe cin: Mi rigs dpe skrung khang, 1986.

Padma dkar po. *Chos 'byung bstan pa'i pad ma rgyas pa'i nyin byed*. Blockprint, no bibliographical information.

Paṇ chen Blo bzang chos kyi rgyal msthan. *Sgra pa shes rab rin chen pa'i rtsod lan lung rigs seng ge'i nga ro*. In *Miscellaneous Works of the First Paṇ chen Blo bzang chos kyi rgyal msthan*. Reproduced from an incomplete manuscript collection from Zangla Khar. Gemur, H.P.: Topden Tsering, 1979.

Paṇ chen Bsod nams grags pa. *Deb ther dmar po gsar ma*. In *Deb ther dmar po gsar ma: Tibetan Chronicles by bSod-nams-grags-pa*, ed. by Giuseppe

Tucci. Serie Orientale Roma, v. XXIV. Roma: Istituto Italiano per il Medio ed Estremo Oriente, 1971.

Pandeya, Ram Chandra, ed. *Madhyānta-vibhāga-śāstra, Containing the Kārikās of Maitreya, Bhāṣya of Vasubandhu, and Ṭīkā by Sthiramati.* Delhi: Motilal Banarsidass, 1972.

Peirce, Charles Sanders. *Collected Papers,* edited by Charles Hartshorne, et al. Cambridge, MA: Harvard University Press, 1931.

Perdue, Daniel E. *Debate in Tibetan Buddhism.* Ithaca: Snow Lion, 1992.

Pettit, John Whitney. *Mipham's Beacon of Certainty: Illuminating the View of Dzogchen, the Great Perfection.* Boston: Wisdom Publications, 1999.

Phuntsho, Karma. "The Position of Mipham in the Indo-Tibetan Debate on Emptiness." Doctoral dissertation, University of Oxford, 2003.

Phur lcog Blo bzang tshul khrims byams pa rgya mtsho. *Tshad ma'i gzhung don 'byed pa'i bsdus grwa dang blo rtags kyi rnam bzhag rigs lam 'phrul gyi lde mig.* Lan kru'u: Kan su'u mi rigs dpe skrun khang, 1982.

Phur lcog Ngag dbang byams pa. *Stag tshang lo tstsha ba'i brgal lan rdo rje'i gzegs ma.* In *Collected Works (gSung 'bum) of Phur-bu-lcog Nag-dbang-byams-pa reproduced from a set of tracings from the prints from the Phur-bu-lcog Hermitage blocks,* vol. 1, 272–353. New Delhi: Ngawang Sopa, 1973.

Phya pa chos kyi seng ge. *Dbu ma shar gsum gyi stong thun,* ed. by Helmut Tauscher. Wien: Arbeitskreis für Tibetische und Buddhistische Studien, Universität Wien, 1999.

Pradhan, Pralhad, ed. *Abhidharmasamuccaya.* Santiniketan: Visva Bharati, 1950.

Rahula, Walpola, trans. *Le Compendium de la super-doctrine (philosophie) (Abhidharmasamuccaya) d'Asaṅga.* Paris: École Française d'Extrême-Orient, 1971.

Rakra Rinpoche. "The Consequential Dispute Caused Either by Zurkharpa Lodoe Gyalpo's Failure in Conducting Proper Analysis on the Root text of Tibetan Poetry or His Upholding Others' Misinterpretation." *Jangzhon* 3 (1991): 1–23.

Rāmaśaṅkaratripāṭhi, ed. *[Prajñāpāramitopadeśaśāstre ācāryaharibhadraviracitā] Abhisamayālaṃkāravṛttiḥ Sphuṭārtha.* Sarnath: Central Institute for Higher Tibetan Studies, 1977.

Red mda' ba Gzhon nu blo gros. *Dbu ma la 'jug pa'i rnam bshad de kho no nyid gsal ba'i sgron ma.* Sarnath: Sakya Students' Union, 1983.

———. [Rendawa Shonnu Lodo]. *Commentary to Āryadeva's "Four Hundred Verses" (Dbu ma bzhi brgya pa'i 'grel pa).* Sarnath: Sakya Students' Union, 1974.

Rgyal tshab Dar ma rin chen. *Tshad ma rnam 'grel gyi rnam bshad (Thar lam gsal byed).* In *Gsung 'bum* (Collected Works), vol. *cha.* New Delhi: Ngawang Gelek Demo, 1980–81.

Rhys Davids, Thomas William, ed. *The Pali Text Society's Pali-English Dictionary.* London: Pali Text Society, 1972.

Rhys Davids, Thomas William, and William Steade. *Pali-English Dictionary.* Delhi: Motilal Banarsidass, 2003.

Rin chen tshe ring, ed. *Dgag lan phyogs bsgrigs.* Khreng tu'u: Si khron mi rigs dpe skrun khang, 1997.

Rma bya ba Brtson grus seng ge. *Dbu ma rtsa ba śes rab gyi 'grel ba 'thad pa'i rgyan.* Rumtek: Dharma Chakra Center, 1975.

Rngog Lo tsā ba Blo ldan shes rab. *Mngon rtogs rgyan gyi don bsdus pa (Lotsaba chen po'i bsdus don bzugs so); Commentary on the Abhisamyalamkara by Rnog Lotsaba Blo-ldan-śes-rab; with an introduction by the 81st abbot of Śar-rtse Grwa-tshang, 4th A-mchog Rinpoche, Blo-bzaṅ-mkhyen-rab-rgya-mtsho and David Jackson.* Dharamsala: Library of Tibetan Works and Archives, 1993.

———. *Rgyud bla ma'i don bsdus (Theg chen rgyud bla ma'i don bsdus pa); Commentary on the Ratnagotravibhāga by Rnog Lotsaba Blo-ldan-śes-rab; with an introduction by David P. Jackson.* Dharamsala: Library of Tibetan Works and Archives, 1993.

Roccasalvo, Joseph F. "The Debate at Bsam yas: Religious Contrast and Correspondence." *Philosophy East and West* 30.4 (1980): 505–20.

Roerich, Georges N. *The Blue Annals.* Delhi: Motilal Banarsidass, 1976.

Rong ston Shes bya kun rig. *Dbu ma rtsa ba'i rnam bshad zab mo'i de kho na nyid snang ba.* Sarnath: Sakya Students' Union, 1975. Reprint 1988.

———. *Dbu ma la 'jug pa'i rnam bshad nges don rnam nges.* In *Two Controversial Madhyamaka Treatises.* New Delhi: Trayang and Jamyang Samten, 1974.

———. *Dbu ma rigs tshogs kyi dka' ba'i gnad bstan pa rigs lam kun gsal.* Photo reproduction of xylograph with no bibliographical information.

Rong zom Chos kyi bzang po. *Rong zom chos bzang gi gsung 'bum.* Khreng tu'u: Si khron mi rigs dpe skrun khang, 1999.

———. *Rang byung ye shes chen po'i 'bras bu rol pa'i dkyil 'khor du blta ba'i yi ge.* In *Rong zom chos bzang gi gsung 'bum,* vol. 2, 111–30. Khreng tu'u: Si khron mi rigs dpe skrun khang, 1999.

Ruegg, David Seyfort. *Two Prolegomena to Madhyamaka Philosophy: Candrakīrti's Prasannapadā Madhyamakavṛttiḥ on Madhyamakakārikā I.1, and Tson kha pa bLo bzang Grags pa/ Rgyal tshab Dar ma rin chen's dKa' gnad/gnas kyi zin bris, Annotated translations,* Studies in Indian and Tibetan Madhyamaka Thought, Part 2. Wien: Arbeitskreis für Tibetische und Buddhistische Studien Universität, Wien, 2002.

———. *Three Studies in the History of Indian and Tibetan Madhyamaka Thought, Studies in Indian and Tibetan Madhyamaka Thought, Part 1.* Wien: Arbeitskreis für Tibetische und Buddhistische Studien, Universität Wien, 2000.

———. "On *Pramana* Theory in Tsoṅ kha pa's Madhyamaka philosophy," *Studies in the Buddhist Epistemological Tradition, Proceedings of the Second International Dharmakīrti Conference, Vienna, June 11–16, 1989,* edited by E. Steinkellner, 281–310. Wien: Verlag der Österreichischen Akademie der Wissenschaften, 1991.

———. *Buddha-Nature, Mind and the Problem of Gradualism in a Comparative Perspective: On the Transmission and Reception of Buddhism in India and Tibet,* The Jordan Lectures in Comparative Religion 13. London: School of Oriental and African Studies, 1989.

———. "A Kar ma bKa' brgyud Work on the Lineages and Traditions of the Indo Tibetan Dbu-Ma (Madhyamaka)." In *Orientalia Iosephi Tucci*

Memoriae Dicata, Serie Orientale Roma 56, vol. 3, edited by G. Gnoli and L. Lanciotti, 1249–80. Rome: IsMeo, 1988.

———. "Thesis and Assertion in the Madhyamaka/dBu ma." In *Tibetan and Buddhist Studies Commemorating the 200th Anniversary of the Birth of Alexander Csoma de Körös,* edited by Ernst Steinkellner and Helmut Tauscher, II: 205–41. Budapest: Akademias Kiado, 1984.

———. "Autour du *Lta ba'i khyad par* de Ye shes sde (version de touenhouang, Pelliot Tibetain 814)." *Journal Asiatique* 269 (1981): 207–29

———. *The Literature of the Madhyamaka School of Philosophy in India.* Wiesbaden: Harrassowitz, 1981.

———. *Le traité sur le Tathāgatagarbha de Bu ston.* Paris: École Française d'Extrême Orient, 1973.

———. "Le Dharmadhātustava de Nāgārjuna." In *Études Tibétains dédiées à la memoire de Marcelle Lalou,* 448–71. Paris: Librairie d'Amerique et d'Orient, 1971.

———. "On the Knowability and Expressibility of Absolute Reality in Buddhism." *Journal of Indian and Buddhist Studies* 20 (1971): 495–99.

———. *La Theorie du Tathagata-garbha et du Gotra.* Paris: École Française d'Extrême Orient, 1969.

———. "The Jo-nang-pas: A School Of Buddhist Ontologists According to the *grub-mtha' sél-gyi me-long.*" *Journal of the American Oriental Society* 8.2 (1963): 73–91.

Sakaki, Ryōzaburō, ed. *Mahāvyutpatti.* Tōkyō: Suzuki Gakujutsu Zaidan, Shōwa 37, 1962 (reprint of the 1916 ed.).

Sakya Pandita Kunga Gyaltsen. *A Clear Differentiation of the Three Codes: Essential Distinctions among the Individual Liberation, Great Vehicle and Tantric Systems,* translated by Jared Douglas Rhoton. Albany: State University of New York Press, 2002.

Śāntideva. *Bodhicaryāvatāra: introduction à la pratique des futurs Bouddhas/ poème de Çantidéva; traduit du sanscrit et annoté par Louis de La Vallée.* Paris: Librarie Bloud et Cie, 1907.

Sa skya Paṇḍita. *Skyes bu dam pa rnams la spring yig.* In *Paṇḍita Kun dga' rgyal mtshan gyi bka' 'bum (The Complete Works of Paṇḍita Kun dga' rgyal mtshan)*, compiled by Bsod nams rgya mtsho; *Sa skya pa'i bka' 'bum, The Complete works of the Great Masters of the Sa skya sect of Tibetan Buddhism*, vol. 5, 330–33. Tokyo: The Tōyō Bunko, 1968.

———. *Tshad ma rigs gter gyi rtsa ba daṅ raṅ grel: The Root Text and Autocommentary of Tshad ma rigs gter, Fundamental Work on Buddhist Logic.* Dehradun, U. P.: Sakya Centre, 1985.

Sa skya yongs 'dzin Ngag dbang chos grags. *Bod kyi mkhas pa snga phyi dag gi grub mtha'i shan 'byed mtha' dpyod dang bcas pa'i 'bel ba'i gtam skyes dpyod ldan mkhas pa lus rgyan rin chen mdzes pa'i phra tshom bkod pa (Pod chen drug gi 'bel gtam).* Thim-phu: Kunsang Tobgyel and Mani Dorje, 1979.

Sato, M. "Die Madhyamaka-Philosophie der Sa skya pa-Schule—Red mda' ba gZon nu blo gros." In *Contributions on Tibetan and Buddhist Religion and Philosophy,* Proceedings of the Csoma de Körös Symposium, 2 vols, edited by Ernst Steinkellner and Helmut Tauscher. II: 243–58. Wien: Arbeitskreis für Tibetische und Buddhistische Studien, Universität Wien, 1983.

Scherer-Schaub, Cristina Anna. *Yuktiṣaṣṭikāvṛtti: Commentaire à la soixantaine sur le raissoment ou Du vrai enseignement de la causalité par le Maître indien Candrakīrti.* Bruxelles: Institut Belges des Hautes Études Chinoises, 1991.

Schmithausen, Lambert. *Ālayavijñāna: On the Origin and Early Development of a Central Concept of Yogācāra Philosophy,* parts I and II, Studia Philologica Buddhica, Monograph Series IVab. Tokyo: International Institute for Buddhist Studies, 1989.

———. "Critical Response." In *Karma and Rebirth: Post Classical Developments,* edited by Ronald W. Neufeldt, 202–30. Albany: SUNY Press, 1986.

———. Zur Liste der 57 "kleineren Fehler" in der Ratnāvalī und zum Problem der Schulzugehoerigkeit Nāgārjunas. *Studien zur Indologie und Iranistik Heft* 11/12 (1986): 203–32.

———."The Darśanamarga Section of the *Abhidharmasamuccaya* and Its Interpretation by Tibetan Commentators (With Special Reference to Bu ston Rin chen grub)." In *Contributions on Tibetan and Buddhist Religion and Philosophy,* edited by E. Steinkellner and H. Tauscher, 259–74.

Wien: Arbeitskreis fur Tibetische und Buddhistische Studien, Universitat Wien, 1983.

———. Zu D. Seyfort Rueggs Buch "La theorie du tathāgatagarbha et du gotra." *WZKSO* 17 (1973): 123–60.

———."The Definition of *Pratyakṣam* in the *Abhidharmasamuccaya.*" *WZKSO* 16 (1972): 153–63.

Schwabland, Peter A. "Direct and Indirect Cognition and the Definition of Prāmaṇa in Early Tibetan Epistemology." *Asiatische Studies/Études Asiatiques* 49.4 (1995): 793–816.

Sde srid Sangs rgyas rgya mtsho. *Dga' ldan chos 'byung baiḍurya gser po.* Pe cin: Krung go'i bod kyi shes rig dpe skrun khang, 1991.

Sells, Michael A. *Mystical Languages of Unsaying.* Chicago: University of Chicago Press, 1994.

Se ra rje btsun Chos kyi rgyal mtshan. *Zab mo stong pa nyid kyi lta ba la log rtog 'gog par byed pa'i bstan bcos lta ba nga ngan pa'i mun sel (Go shak gnyis kyi dgag lan).* Delhi: Champa Chogyal, 1969. The same text is to be found in Se ra rje btsun Chos kyi rgyal mtshan and Paṇ chen Bde legs nyi ma, *Zab mo stong pa nyid kyi lta ba la log rtog 'gog par byed pa'i bstan bcos lta ba ngan pa'i mun sel.* In *Dgag lan phyogs bsgrigs,* ed. by Rin chen tshe ring, part I, *Chen po Shāk mchog pa'i rtsod lan,* 178–385, and part II, *Go bo rab 'byams pa'i rtsod lan,* 385–514. Khreng tu'u: Si khron mi rigs dpe skrun khang, 1997.

———. *Gsung lan klu sgrub dgongs rgyan.* In *Dgag lan phyogs bsgrigs,* ed. by Rin chen tshe ring. Khreng tu'u: Si khron mi rigs dpe skrun khang, 1997.

Sgom sde shar chen Nam mkha' rgyal mtshan. *Byang chub sems 'grel gyi rnam par bshad pa'i zhar byung 'brug pa mi pham padma dkar pos phyag chen rgyal ba'i gan mdzod ces par rje tsong kha pa la dgag pa mdzad pa'i gsung lan.* In *Dgag lan phyogs bsgrigs,* ed. by Rin chen tshe ring. Khreng tu'u: Si khron mi rigs dpe skrun khang, 1997.

Sgra tshad pa Rin chen rnam rgyal. *Bde bzhin gshegs pa'i snying po'i mdzes rgyan gyi rgyan.* In *The Collected Works of Bu ston,* vol. 28. New Delhi: International Academy of Indian Culture, 1965–71.

Shākya mchog ldan, Gser mdog Paṇ chen. *Rngog lo tsā ba chen po'i bstan pa ji ltar bskyangs pa'i tshul mdo tsam du bya ba ngo mtshar gtam gyi rol mo.* In *The Complete Works (gsungs-'bum) of Gser-mdog Paṇ-chen Śākya-mchog-ldan,* ed. by Kunzang Topgay, reprint of the Pha jo sdings 'og ma gnyis pa edition, vol. 16, 443–56. Thimpu, Bhutan: Kunzang Topgay, 1975.

———. *Dbu ma'i byung tshul rnam par shes pa'i gtam yid bzhin lhun po,* in *Collected Works,* reprint of the Pha jo sdings 'og ma gnyis pa edition, vol. 4, 209–48. Delhi: Ngawang Tobgyal, 1988.

Sherburne, Richard, S. J., trans. *The Complete Works of Atisa, Śrī Dipaṃkara Jñāna, Jo-bo-rje.* New Delhi: Aditya Prakashan, 2000.

[Dge bshes] Shes rab rgya mtsho. *Rtsod yig rigs pa'i gad rgyangs la rnam par dpyad pa bskal pa'i me dpung,* in *Rje btsun shes rab rgya mtsho 'jam dpal dgyes pa'i blo gros kyi gsung rtsom,* vol. I: 137–309. Zi ling: Mtsho sngon mi rigs dpe skrun khang, 1982.

Shing bza' paṇḍita Skal bzang chos kyi rgyal mtshan. *Bod sog chos 'byung.* Gangs can rig brgya'i sgo 'byed lde mig, vol. 18. Pe chin: Mi rigs dpe skrun khang, 1993.

Smith, E. Gene. *Among Tibetan Texts: History and Literature of the Himalayan Plateau.* Boston: Wisdom Publications, 2001.

Sog bzlog pa Blo gros rgyal mtshan. *Gsang sngags snga 'gyur la bod du rtsod pa snga phyir byung ba rnams kyi lan du brjod pa nges pa don gyi 'brug sgra.* Khreng tu'u: Si khron mi rigs dpe skrun khang, 1998.

Sonam Rinchen, Geshe, and Ruth Sonam. *Yogic Deeds of Bodhisattvas: Gyel-tsap on Aryadeva's Four Hundred.* Ithaca: Snow Lion, 1994.

Sopa, Lhundup and Jeffrey Hopkins. *Cutting Through Appearances: Practice and Theory of Tibetan Buddhism.* Ithaca: Snow Lion, 1982.

———. *Practice and Theory of Tibetan Buddhism.* Bombay: B.I. Publications, 1977.

Sparham, Gareth, and Shotaro Iida. *Ocean of Eloquence: Tsong kha pa's Commentary on the Yogacara Doctrine of Mind.* Albany: SUNY press, 1993.

Sprung, M. *Lucid Exposition of the Middle Way.* London: Routledge and Kegan Paul, 1979.

Staël-Holstein, Alexander Freiherr von, ed. *The Kāçyapaparivarta, a Mahāyānasūtra of the Ratnakūṭa class.* Shanghai: Commercial Press, 1926.

Stcherbatsky, Theodor Ippolitovich, trans. *Madhyanta-vibhāga: Discourse on Discrimination Between Middle and Extremes,* Bibliotheca Buddhica 30 (1936). Calcutta: Indian Studies Past and Present, 1971.

———. *Buddhist Logic.* New York: Dover Publications, 1962.

Stcherbatsky, Theodor Ippolitovich and Evgenii Obermiller, eds. *Abhisamayālaṃkāra-Prajñāpāramitā-Upadeśa-śāstra: The Work of Bodhisattva Maitreya.* Bibliotheca Buddhica 23. Leningrad: 1929. Reprint, Delhi, India: Sri Satguru Publications, 1992 (Sanskrit and Tibetan).

Stearns, Cyrus. *The Buddha from Dolpo: A Study of the Life and Thought of the Tibetan Master Dolpopa Sherab Gyaltsen.* Albany: SUNY Press, 1999.

———. "Dolpo-pa Shes-rab rgyal-mtshan and the Genesis of Gzhan stong Position in Tibet." *Asiatische Studien/Études Asiatiques* 49.4 (1995): 829–54.

Steinkellner, Ernst. *Śāntideva: Eintritt in das Leben zur Erleuchtung.* Dusseldorf: Diederichs, 1981.

———. *Verse-Index of Dharmakīrti's Works.* Wien: Arbeitskreis fur Tibetische und Buddhistische Studien, Universität Wien, 1977.

———. *Dharmakīrti's Pramāṇaviniścayaḥ Zweites Kapitel: Svārthānumānam, Teil II.* Wien: Verlag der Österreichischen Akademie der Wissenschaften, 1979.

Sthiramati. *Madhyāntavibhāgaṭīkā; exposition systématique du Yogācāravijñaptivāda.* Ed. by M. Sylvain Lévi. Nagoya: Librairie Hajinkaku, 1934. Reprint, Tokyo: Suzuki Foundation, 1966 (Sanskrit, Tibetan, and Chinese).

Stoter-Tillman, Jurgen, and Acarya Tashi Tsering, trans., *Rendawa Shonnu Lodro's Commentary on the "Entry into the Middle" Lamp Which Elucidates Reality.* Sarnath: Central Institute of Higher Tibetan Studies, 1997.

Streng, Frederick John. *Emptiness, A Study in Religious Meaning.* NY: Abingdon Press, 1967

Sweet, Michael J. "Bodhicaryāvatāra (IX, 2) as a Focus for Tibetan Interpretations of the Two Truths in the Prāsaṅgika Mādhyamika." *Journal of the International Association of Buddhist Studies* 2.2 (1979): 79–89.

Takasaki, Jikido. *A Study of the Ratnagotravibhāga (Uttaratantra), Being a Treatise on the Tathāgatagarbha Theory of Mahāyāna Buddhism.* Serie Orientale Roma, 33. Rome: IsMEO, 1966.

Talmage, Frank E. *Apples of Gold, Settings of Silver: Studies in Medieval Jewish Exegesis and Polemics,* edited by Barry Dov Walfish. Toronto: Pontifical Institute of Mediaeval Studies, 1999.

Tanselle, Thomas G. "Books, Canons and the Nature of Dispute." *Common Knowledge* 1:1 (1992): 78–91.

Tatia, Nathmal, ed. *Abhidharmasamuccayabhāṣyam.* Patna: K. P. Jayaswal Research Institute, 1976.

Tauscher, Helmut. *Die Lehre von den zwei Wirklichkeiten in Tson kha pas Madhyamaka-Werken.* Wien: Arbeitskreis fur Tibetische und Buddhistische Studien, Universität Wien, 1995.

———. "Paramārtha as an Object of Cognition—Paryāya- and Aparyāya-Paramātha in Svātantrika-Madhyamaka." In *Tibetan Studies: Proceedings of 4th Seminar of the International Association for Tibetan Studies,* edited by Helga Uebach and Jampa L. Panglung. München: Kommission für Zentralasiatische Studien, Bayerische Akademie der Wissenschaften, 1988.

Taylor, Mark C. *Nots.* Chicago: University of Chicago Press, 1993.

Tenzin Gyatso. *The Key to the Middle Way,* translated by Jeffrey Hopkins and Lati Rinpoche. London: Allen and Unwin, 1975.

Tharchin, Lobsang. *The Logic and Debate Tradition of India, Tibet, and Mongolia.* NJ: Freewood Acres Howell, 1979.

Thondup, Tulku. *Hidden Teachings of Tibet: An Explanation of the Terma Tradition of the Nyinma School of Buddhism,* edited by Harold Talbott. London: Wisdom Publications, 1986.

Thurman, Robert A. F. *Tsong khapa's Speech of Gold in the Essence of True Eloquence: Reason and Enlightenment in the Central Philosophy of Tibet.* Princeton, New Jersey: Princeton University Press, 1984.

———, ed. *The Life and Teachings of Tsong kha pa.* Dharamsala: Library of Tibetan Works and Archives, 1982.

Thu'u bkwan Blo bzang chos kyi nyi ma. *Grub mtha' shel gyi me long (Thu'u bkwan grub mtha').* Lan kru'u: Kan su'u mi rigs dpe skrun khang, 1984.

———. *gSung 'bum, The Collected Works of Thu'u bkwan blo-bzang-chos-kyi-nyi-ma.* Edited and reproduced from the Lhasa Zhol par khang edition by Ngawang Gelek Demo. New Delhi: Ngawang Gelek Demo, 1969.

Tillemans, Tom J. F. "Tibetan Philosophy." In *Routledge Encyclopedia of Philosophy.* Edited by E. Craig. London: Routledge, 1998. http://www.rep.routledge.com/article/F003.

———. "Tsong kha pa et al. on the Bhāvaviveka-Candrakīrti Debate." In *Tibetan Studies: Proceedings of the 5th Seminar of the International Association For Tibetan Studies, Narita 1989,* vol. 1, edited by Ihara Shoren and Yamaguchi Zuiho, 315–26. Narita: Naritasan Shinshoji, 1992.

———."The 'Neither One Nor Many' Argument for *Śūnyatā* and its Tibetan Interpretations: Background Information and Source Materials." *Études de Lettres* 3 (1982): 103–28.

Tillemans, Tom J. F., and Toru Tomabechi. "Le *dBu ma'i byung tshul* de Śākya mchog ldan." *Asiatische Studien/Études Asiatiques* 49.4 (1995): 891–918.

Tola, Fernando and Carmen Dragonetti. *El idealismo budista: la doctrine de 'solo-la-mente.'* Tlahuapan, Puebla: Premia, 1989.

———. "Nāgārjuna's Catustava." *Journal of Indian Philosophy* 13.1 (1985): 1–54.

Toulmin, Stephen. *Cosmopolis: The Hidden Agenda of Modernity.* Chicago: The University of Chicago Press, 1990.

Trichen, Chobgye. *The History of the Sakya Tradition: A Feast for the Minds of the Fortunate.* Translated by Jennifer Scott. Bristol: Ganesha Press, 1983.

Tshe brtan phun tshogs Chab spel and Nor brang O rgyan, eds. *Bod kyi lo rgyus rags rim g.yu yi phreng ba.* Lha sa: Bod ljongs dpe snying dpe skrun khang, 1989–91.

Tsong-kha-pa, *The Great Treatise on the Stages of the Path to Enlightenment: Lam rim chen mo,* trans. by the Lamrim Chenmo Translation Committee, edited by Joshua Cutler, 3 vols. Albany: Snow Lion, 2000–2004.

Tsong kha pa Blo bzang grags pa. *Bstan bcos chen po dbu ma la 'jug pa'i rnam bshad dgongs pa rab gsal.* In *Gsung 'bum,* vol. *ma.* New Delhi: Ngawang Gelek Demo, 1975–81.

———. *Dbu ma rtsa ba'i tshig le'ur byas pa shes rab ces bya ba'i rnam bshad rigs pa'i rgya mtsho (Rtsa shes ṭik chen).* In *Gsung 'bum,* vol. *ba.* New Delhi: Ngawang Gelek Demo, 1975–81.

———. *Byang chub lam rim che ba.* Zi ling: Mtsho sngon mi rigs dpe skrun khang, 1985.

———. *Drang ba dang nges pa'i don rnam par phye ba'i bstan bcos legs bshad snying po.* In *Rje tsong kha pa chen po'i gsung 'bum,* vol. *pha.* Zi ling: Mtsho sngon mi rigs dpe skrun khang, 1987.

———. *Drang ba dang nges pa'i don rnam par phye ba'i bstan bcos legs bshad snying po.* In *Gsung 'bum,* vol. *pha.* New Delhi: Ngawang Gelek Demo, 1975–81.

———. *Dbu ma'i lta khrid.* In *Gsung 'bum,* vol. *tsha.* New Delhi: Ngawang Gelek Demo, 1975–81.

———. *Dka' gnad brgyad kyi zin bris.* In *Gsung 'bum,* vol. *ba.* New Delhi: Ngawang Gelek Demo, 1975–81.

———. *Lam rim chen mo.* In *Gsung 'bum,* vol. *pa.* New Delhi: Ngawang Gelek Demo, 1975–81.

———. *Drang nges legs bshad snying po.* In *Collected Works,* vol. *pha.* Lhasa: Zhol ed., 1897. Asian Classics Input Project, Release IV, S5396.

———. *Shes rab kyi pha rol tu phin pa'i man ngag gi bstan bcos mngon par rtog pa'i rgyan 'grel pa dang bcas pa'i rgya cher bshad pa'i legs bshad gser phreng (Legs bshad gser phreng).* In *Gsung 'bum,* vols. *tsa* and *tsha.* New Delhi: Ngawang Gelek Demo, 1975–81.

Tsukamoto, Keishō, trans. *The Cycle of the Formation of Schismatic Doctrines.* BDK English Tripiṭitaka 61–VI, 76–1. Berkeley: Numata Center for Buddhist Translation and Research, 2004.

Tucci, Giuseppe. "The Ratnāvalī of Nāgārjuna." *Journal of the Royal Asiatic Society of Great Britain and Ireland* (1934): 307–25; (1936): 237–52, 423–35.

Vaidya, P. L., ed. *Daśabhūmikasūtram.* Buddhist Sanskrit texts no. 7. Darbhanga: Mithila Institute, 1967.

———, ed. *Mahāyānasūtrasaṃgrahaḥ.* Buddhist Sanskrit texts no. 17. Darbhanga: Mithila Institute, 1961

———, ed. *Aṣṭasāhasrikā Prajñāpāramitā.* Buddhist Sanskrit texts no. 4. Darbhanga: Mithila Institute, 1960.

———, ed. *Sikṣāsamuccayaḥ.* Buddhist Sanskrit texts no. 11. Darbhanga: Mithila Institute, 1960.

———, ed. *Bodhicaryāvatāraḥ of Śāntideva with Pañjikā of Prajñākaramati.* Buddhist Sanskrit texts no. 12. Darbhanga: Mithila Institute, 1960.

van der Kuijp, Leonard W. J. *Contributions to the Development of Tibetan Buddhist Epistemology from the Eleventh to the Thirteenth Century,* Alt- und neu-indische Studien, 26. Wiesbaden: Franz Steiner Verlag, 1983.

———. "Phya-pa Chos-kyi Seng-ge's Impact on Tibetan Epistemological Theory." *Journal of Indian Philosophy* 5 (1978): 355–69.

———. "An Early Tibetan View of the Soteriology of Buddhist Epistemology: The Case of 'Bri-gung 'Jig-rten mgon-po." *Journal of Indian Philosophy,* 15 (1987): 57–70.

Vitali, Roberto. *Records of Tho.ling: A Literary and Visual Reconstruction of the "Mother" Monastery in Gu.ge.* Dharamsala: High Asia, 1999.

Vostrikov, A. I. *Tibetan Historical Literature,* translated by H. Chandra Gupta. Soviet Indology Series no. 4. Calcutta, Indian Studies: Past and Present, 1970.

Waldron, William S. *The Buddhist Unconscious: The Ālaya-Vijñāna in the Context of Indian Buddhist Thought.* London: RoutledgeCurzon, 2003.

Waldschmidt, Ernst, ed. *Das Mahāparinirvāṇasūtra: Text in Sanskrit und Tibetisch verglichen mit dem Pāli nebst einer Übersetzung der chinesischen Entsprechung im Vinaya der Mūlasarvāstivādins.* Berlin: Akademie-Verlag, 1950–51. Reprint, Kyoto: Rinsen Book Co. 1986.

Walleser, Max. *Die Mittlere Lehre des Nāgārjuna (Mādhyamikaśāstra).* Heidelberg: Carl Winters Universitätsbuchhandlung, 1911.

Wayman, Alex. *Calming the Mind and Discerning the Real: Buddhist Meditation and the Middle View from the Lam rim chen mo of Tsong-kha-pa.* New York: Columbia University Press, 1978.

Williams, Paul. *Buddhist Thought: A Complete Introduction to the Indian Tradition.* London: Routledge, 2000.

———. *Altruism and Reality: Studies in the Philosophy of the Bodhicaryāvatāra.* Surrey: Curzon, 1998.

———. *The Reflexive Nature of Awareness: A Tibetan Madhyamaka Defence.* London: Curzon, 1998.

———. "Rma bya pa Byang chub brtson 'grus on Madhyamaka Method." *Journal of Indian Philosophy* 13 (1985): 205–25.

———. "A Note on Some Aspects of Mi bskyod rdo rje's Critique of dGe lugs pa Madhyamaka." *Journal of Indian Philosophy* 11 (1983): 125–45.

———. "Tsong-kha-pa on *kun-rdzob bden-pa.*" In *Proceedings of the 1979 Oxford Symposium on Tibetan Studies,* edited by M. Aris and A. Suu Kyi. Warminster: Aris and Phillips, 1981.

Yoshimizu, Chizuko. "Tsong kha pa's Reevaluation of Candrakīrti's Criticism of Autonomous Inference." In *The Svātantrika-Prāsaṅgika Distinction: What Difference Does a Difference Make?* Edited by G. B. J. Dreyfus and S. L. McClintock, pp. 257–88. Boston: Wisdom, 2003.

———. *Die Erkenntnislehre des Prāsaṅgika-Madhyamaka: nach dem Tshig gsal ston thun gyi tshad ma'i rnam bśad des 'Jam dbaṅs bźad pa'i rdo rje: Einleitung, Textanalyse, Übersetzung.* Wien: Arbeitskreis für Tibetische und Buddhistische Studien, Universität Wien, 1996.

———. "On raṅ gi mtshan ñid kyis grub pa III. Section II and III." *Naritasan Bukkyō Kenkyūshu Kiyō* (1994) 17: 295–354.

———. "Rang gi mtshan nyid kyis grub pa ni tsuite II." In *Indogaku Mikkyōgaku Kenkyū, Essays in Honor of Dr. Y. Miyasaka on His Seventieth Birthday,* 971–90. Kyoto: Hōzōka, 1993.

———. "On raṅ gi mtshan ñid kyis grub pa III. Introduction and Section I." *Naritasan Bukkyō Kenkyūshu Kiyō* (1993) 16: 91–147.

———. "The Madhyamaka Theories Regarded as False by the dGe lugs pas." *WZKSO* 37 (1993): 201–27.

———. "The Distinction between Right and Wrong in the Conventional *(kun rdzob, saṁvṛti)* According to Tsong kha pa and mKhas grub rje." In *Tibetan Studies: Proceedings of the 5th Seminar of the International Association For Tibetan Studies, Narita 1989,* vol. 1, edited by Ihara Shoren and Yamaguchi Zuiho, 335–40. Narita: Naritasan Shinshoji, 1992.

———. "Rang gi mtshan nyid kyis grub pa ni tsuite I." *Naritasan Bukkyō Kenkyūshu Kiyō* (1992) 15: 609–56.

Yuyama, Akira, ed. *Prajñā-pāramitā-ratna-guṇa-saṃcaya-gāthā: Sanskrit Recension A / Edited with an Introduction, Bibliographical Notes, and a Tibetan Version from Tunhuang.* Cambridge: Cambridge University Press, 1976.

Zhang Zhung Chos dbang grags pa. *Dbu ma rtsa ba'i 'grel pa tshig gsal gyi mtha' bzhi skye 'gog pa'i stong thun.* In *sTon thun chen mo of mKhas-grub dGe-legs-dpal-bzang and Other Texts on Madhyamika Philosophy,* ed. by Lha-mkhar yongs-'dzin Bstanpa rgyal mtshan. Madhyamika Text Series, vol. 1. New Delhi, 1972.

Zurmang Drungpa Tulku Choekyi Gyatso, "A Letter of Criticism," *Jangzhon* 7 (1994): 41–42.

Index

A
A mdo, 31
Abandoning the Four Attachments, 39
Abhidharma, 35, 38
  and explanation of five aggregates, 177
  and path structure, 292n93
  specific and general characteristics in, 91
Abhidharmasamuccaya (Asaṅga), 77
Abhidharmasamuccayabhāṣya (Asaṅga), 251–52n40, 301–2n136
Abhisamayālaṃkāra (Maitreya), 40, 295–96n108, 315n239, 321n290, 321n292, 328n351, 334n409, 334n410
  bodhisattva path in, 169–71, 195, 227, 321n288, 328n351
  and Cittamātra, 321n290
  and emptiness of aggregates, 121
  Go rams pa's commentary on, 35, 37
  G.yag phrug's *ṭīkā* on, 294–95n106
  Haribhadra's commentary on and conceptualization, 316n242
  and *Madhyamakāvatāra,* 171
  as provisional, 169
  on śrāvaka vs. bodhisattva realization, 223
  as Svātantrika-Madhyamaka work according to Tsong kha pa, 169, 321n292
  and three forms of enlightenment, 278n7
  transmission through Rnog Blo ldan shes rab to Rong ston, 295n108
  and truthlessness, 223
  and two conceptualizations, 147
  and ultimate as empty of other, 282n41
abstract truth, 15
accumulation, path of, 157
accumulations, two, 159, 165
ad hominen attacks, 17
adversarial speech *(rgol ngag),* 12
advice *(nasīha),* 253n51
afflicted obscuration, 143–45, 147, 290–91n82
afflictions
  and craving, 173
  critique of Tsong kha pa regarding, 171–73
  and grasping at the self, 219
  and meditative equipoise, 334n403
  and obscurations to omniscience, 149, 219
  śrāvakas' removal of, 320–21n285
Agassi, Joseph, 5
aggregates, 99, 109, 219
  and action/karma, 153, 155, 318n253
  appropriation of, 153, 317n252
  emptiness of, 121
  existence of for Vaibhāṣikas, 97, 300n124
  and existence of the self, 151
  and selflessness of person, 99, 213
  and specific and general characteristics, 177
  and śrāvaka schools, 221, 223
  truthlessness of in Madhyamaka, 221
agonistic rhetoric, 3
Akṣayamatinirdeśa Sūtra, 305n158
Akutobhayā (Nāgārjuna), 253–54n56
ālayavijñāna (foundation consciousness), 288–89n72, 290n81, 293n98
  as basis for karma and its results, 137–39, 175, 313n220

does not exist for Tsong kha pa or Candrakīrti, 89–91, 289n74
and Go rams pa's view of Cittamātra, 322n306
as repository of karmic seeds, 83–85, 289n74
altruism, 15, 87
analogue, 125–27, 308n182
analysis, rational
of the conventional, 207–9
existence of things as long as not subjected to, 153, 173–75, 318n255
as necessary prerequisite to understanding reality, 54
of the real ultimate or reality, 332n385
of reality and conceptuality, 215
and truthlessness of persons and phenomena, 213
See also reasoning
Aṅgulimāliya Sūtra, 75
animals, as characterization of polemicists' opponents, 13, 17
antidotes that eliminate obscurations, 221–27, 334n403
Anūnatvāpurṇatvanirdeśa Sūtra, 75
apologetics, 252n41
apophatic discourse
as ideal-typical category, 3–4, 251–52n40
and knowledge, 2
polemics as discourse of, 3, 4, 6
and Tibetan Buddhist literature, 11
Aquinas, Thomas, 250n32
arhat, 167, 292n91
See also śrāvakas and Śrāvakayāna; pratyekabuddhas
argumentation
adequate, 193
and entering Madhyamaka directly, 205
arising from self, refutation of, 179–81, 213, 325–26n329, 327n337
arising via four alternatives, 213
Aristotle, 254n58
Āryadeva, 237, 318n264
Āryadhāraṇīśvararāja Sūtra, 75
Āryasatyadvayāvatāra, 231
Asad, Talal, 15, 253n51
Asaṅga
and *Abhisamayālaṃkāra,* 321n290
and Dol po pa, 51, 97, 99–101, 105, 107
and emptiness of other, 75, 282–83n42
and existence of the dependent, 103
and three emptinesses, 101
See also *Abhidharmasamuccaya*; *Cittamātra* (Yogācāra) school
ascertaining consciousness, 197, 237
aspects, true and false, 105, 303n146
Aṣṭasāhasrikāpiṇḍārtha (Dignāga), 73
Aśvajit, Ārya, 173
Atiśa (982–1054), 22, 26, 257n86
and Legs pa'i shes rab, 295–96n108
and Pa tshab Nyi ma grags, 296–97n111
atoms, 205
attraction between those who argue, 244n10
Audi, Robert, 254n58
audience, 15
autonomous beliefs, 181
autonomous reasons, 55, 85, 91–93, 177, 288–89n72, 324n315
accepted by Go rams pa in conventional contexts, 193–95, 328n349
in argumentation, 179–81
critique of, 177–91
and existence by virtue of own characteristics, 185, 328n344
inappropriate because no subject in common, 185–87
and Prāsaṅgika-Svātantrika distinction, 197–201, 213, 328–29n353–4
and Prāsaṅgikas, 195–97
and "reasoning acceptable to other party," 185
and Svātantrikas, 197, 199, 213
and unmistaken vs. mistaken thoughts, 187, 327–28n342
and unspecified subject, 187
use of in conceptual contexts only, 328n349
autonomous theses, 191. *See also* theses
Avataṃsaka Sūtra, 75, 281n26
Avatāra. See *Madhyamakāvatāra* (Candrakīrti)

Avatārabhāṣya. See *Madhyamakāvatārabhāṣya* (Candrakīrti)

B

Ba ri lo tsā ba, 296n109
Bakhtin, Mikhail, 247n20
Baxter, Richard, 248n24
Bcom ldan rig ral (b. thirteenth century), 258n96, 259n98
  and discovery of *Guhyagarbha*, 24
  and periodization of history, 260n121
Bde legs nyi ma. *See* Paṇ chen Bde legs nyi ma
Bdud 'joms *Chos 'byung*, 259n100
Bdud 'joms rin po che, 24, 259n100
beliefs, 113
Bhāvanākrama (Stages of Meditation) (Kamalaśīla), 20–21, 256n76
Bhāvaviveka, 87, 175, 187, 291n87
  acceptance of external objects, 175
  and autonomous reasons, 91, 185, 294n103, 324–25n318
  finds faults in Buddhapālita's refutation of self-arising, 179
  and Hīnayāna vs. Mahāyāna view of essencelessness, 318n262, 320n281
  acceptance of self as consciousness, 149–50, 316–17n245, 317n246
bhūmis, 87–89
Bjerken, Zeff, 255n70
Bka' brgyud pas, 7, 25, 27, 31, 330n360
  challenge to doctrines of, 25
  and Dge lugs/Stag tshang debate, 263n145
  and Mahāmudrā, 27
  and White Panacea doctrine, 248–49n27
  See also Shangs pa bka' bgryud pas
Bka' dus bzhi pa (Dol po pa), 279n9, 279n11, 279–80n14, 281n21, 281n26, 281n28, 283n44
Bka' thang sde lnga, 20
Bka' Bstan (Tibetan Buddhist canon), 253n54
Bkra shis lhun po monastery, 42, 44
Bla ma Dbu ma pa ("Madhyamaka Lama") Dpa' bo rdo rje (fourteenth–fifteenth century), 131, 199, 274n240, 311n196
Blo bzang chos grags (b. seventeenth century), 264n150
Blue Annals, The (Deb sngon) ('Gos lo tsā ba Gzhon nu dpal), 24, 294n106, 295–96n108, 296n109, 297–98nn111–13, 311n198
Bodhicaryāvatāra (Śāntideva), 264n148, 278n5, 285n58, 293n97, 322n298, 331n377
  and ignorance, 211
  on an individual who has not obtained path of seeing, 89, 171–73, 293n97, 321n293
  and ultimate as not an object of mind, 117
  and yogi's apprehension of reality, 119
Bodhicaryāvatārapañjikā (Prajñākaramati), 290–91n82
Bodhicittavivaraṇa (Nāgārjuna), 175, 322–23n307
bodhisattvas, 15, 159, 163, 201, 221
  attributes of, adduced through inference, 193–95
  and irreversibility in *Abhisamayālaṃkāra,* 195, 328n351
  and nine levels of obscurations to omniscience, 169, 321n288
  stages of arhat entering Mahāyāna, 167–69
  surpassing śrāvakas and pratyekabuddhas, 225–27
Bon, 7, 16, 254n57, 255n71
  and anti-Buddhist polemic, 18–19, 255n71
  and mixed-genre polemics, 249–50n31
  Western academic writing on, 19, 255n70
"Books, Canons and the Nature of Dispute" (Tanselle), 56
Brag dkar sprul sku (1866–1928), 30
'Bras spungs monastery, 42
'Bras yul Skyed tshal monastic college, 34, 35, 267n172
Brgal lan nyin byed snang ba (Mi pham), 264n148

brgal lan (rebuttal), 12, 251–52n40
'Bri gung pa Dpal 'dzin (c. fourteenth century), 258n96, 260n120
Brtseg/Rtsags Dbang phyug seng ge, 293n97
Bsam yas debate, 19–20
Bsdus chen gyi rnam bzhag ('Jam dbyangs bzhad pa), 329n357, 358–59n358
Bsod nams chos kyi kun dga' bkra shis rgyal mtshan dpal bzang po, 267–68n184
Bsod nams grags pa (1478–1554), 44, 271n216
Bsod nams rtse mo (1142–82), 25, 273n232
Bstan rim chen mo (Gro lung pa Blo gros 'byung gnas), 261n124
Bu ston chos 'byung (Bu ston), 251–52n40, 258n95
Bu ston Rin chen grub (1290–1364), 23, 24, 246–47n16, 251–52n40, 252n46, 256n83, 258n95, 258n96, 260n121, 281n26, 294–95n106, 300n122, 302n141
  on the negative motivations of polemicists, 14
  periodization of history, 260n121
  purpose in writing polemics, 15, 252n46
  refutation of Dol po pa, 302n141
  and soteriological knowledge, 251–52n40
  and Ye shes 'od, 256–57n83
Buddha from Dolpo, The: A Study of the Life and Thought of the Tibetan Master Dolpopa Sherab Gyaltsen (Stearns), 279n9, 293–94n102
Buddha, Gautama, 69, 123, 141–43, 173, 253n53, 277n1
  enlightenment of, 71, 278n7
  and linguistic conventions, 133–35
  and understanding of phenomena, 288–89n72
Buddhapālita, 29, 312n203, 318n262
  and autonomous forms of reasoning, 177–79, 324–25n318
  and inferences, 181–83
buddhas, polemics addressed to, 15
Buddhism and Language (Cabezón), 81, 286n65, 301n130, 329n357
"Buddhology," 28, 262n138
'Bum phrag gsum pa (1432/33–1504), 40
Byams chen rab 'byams pa Sangs rgyas 'phel (1411–85), 34, 35, 43, 48, 267n172
Byang chub 'od (eleventh century), 258n95
Byang Ngam ring monastery, 35

C
Cabezón, José Ignacio, 246–47n16, 247n18, 302–3n142, 306n166, 332n385
  on Go rams pa and Rong ston pa as "soft doxographers," 278–79n8, 312n202
  See also *Buddhism and Language; Dose of Emptiness*
Cakrasaṃvara, 35
Candrakīrti, 117, 177, 187, 324n313, 296–97n111
  on arising from another, 209, 331n370
  on essenceless phenomena in Hīnayāna, 320n281
  and freedom from dualistic extremes, 123
  Go rams pa's allegiance to, 49
  Go rams pa's commentary on *Madhyamakāvatāra*, 37
  on grasping at truth of phenomena, 149
  on karma, 211, 290n79
  on karma and foundation consciousness, 139, 289n74, 313n220
  on linguistic designation, 312n203
  Madhyamakāvatāra of, 77, 284n50
  as Nāgārjuna's spiritual son, 157, 264n264
  and nominal existence of "I," 151, 153
  Phya pa's critique of, 26, 253n53
  rebuttal of by Svātantrikas, 189–91
  rejection of autonomous reasons and theses, 91, 177–79, 181, 185–87, 193–95n349, 197, 324–25n318

Tsong kha pa's view of, 29
and the two natures of perception, 117
and two truths, 117–19, 305–6n163
view of the conventional, 207, 330–31n369
See also *Catuḥśatakaṭīkā; Madhyamakāvatāra; Madhyamakāvatārabhāṣya; Yuktiṣaṣṭikavṛtti*
Canon
Bka' 'gyur, 15–16, 23, 253n54
collected works of saints as example of, 253n54
experiential, 253n55
See also Bka' Bstan
caricature of opponents, 8, 9
causal interdependencies, five, 147, 315n236
cataphatic discourse, 2, 3, 11, 244n6, 249n28, 251–52n40
in Christian mysticism, 244n9
as ideal type, 3–4, 251–52n40
Catuḥśataka (Āryadeva), 36, 79, 181, 285n55, 285n56, 318n264, 325n325
grasping at truth of phenomena in, 145–47, 149, 315n234
Catuḥśatakaṭīkā (Candrakīrti), 155, 316n244, 318n257, 318n258
catuṣkoṭi. *See* four alternatives
cause and effect, 175
censorship, 31–32
cessation, four aspects of truth of, 171–73, 322n294
Cha pa Chos kyi seng ge. *See* Phya pa Chos kyi seng ge
Chab spel Tshe brtan phun tshogs, 273–74n238
Chag lo tsā ba Chos rje dpal (1197–1264), 23, 251n37, 38, 257n90
and criticisms of Pha Dam pa sang rgyas, 24–25
on the purpose of writing polemics, 14–15, 252n45
Ch'an's similarity to White Panacea, 28
characteristics
specific and general, 175, 177
and *svatantras*, 177, 185, 199, 324n315, 328n344
things existing by virtue of their own, 131, 173, 175–77, 323–24n311
chariot, example of, 153, 318n254
Chinese-Indian Buddhist doctrinal conflict, 19–20
Chobgye Trichen Rinpoche, 267n182, 269n201
Chos grags, Dge bshes, 331n375
Chos kyi bstan pa shan 'byed (Distinguishing the Teachings of Dharma) (Rong ston pa), 255n71
Chos log sun 'byin (Bu ston), 258n95
Christianity, 244n6, 9
Chu mig pa (thirteenth century), 261n125
Cittamātra (Yogācāra) school
and *Abhisamayālaṃkāra*, 169, 321n290
and *ālayavijñāna*, 83–85, 289n74
and atoms, 205
compatibility with Madhyamaka, 312n202
and conventional appearances, 207, 330–31n369
and Dol po pa, 105–7
and existence, 302n130
and karmic "seeds," 83–85, 290n78
and nonduality, 217, 221
as one of the four philosophical schools, 71, 277n4
and Rong ston, 105–7
and *Saṃdhinirmocana Sutra*, 107
tenets of compared with Dol po pa's, 51, 107, 303n145, 303n144.105
those who accept true or false aspects as subschools of, 105, 303n146
and views of enlightenment in Mahāyāna and Hīnayāna, 221
Clearing Away the Darkness of Bad Views (Dol po pa), 46, 272n222
close lineage *(nye brgyud)*, 253n55
codyamparihāra (rebuttal), 251n40
cogitation, improper, 147
Collected Topics (bsdus grwa) literature, 11
commentary
annotations as a form of *(mchan 'grel)*, 11

and Tibetan scholastic tradition, 15
Vasubandhu's rules regarding, 18
compassion, 87, 163, 235
Compassion in Tibetan Buddhism (Hopkins), 284n50, 292n90, 320n281, 320n282, 328n349, 334n406
Compassionate Lake of Straightforward Speech, A (Bden gtam snying rje'i rol mtsho) (Dbal mang Dkon mchog rgyal mtshan), 263n143
Complete Works of Atiśa, Śrī Dipaṃkara Jñāna, The, 335n420
composite entities, 107, 109–11, 127
conceptual thought, 95, 215, 299n119
cannot realize ultimate truth, 119–21, 306n166
and Hwa shang, 129
imputation by, 288–89n72
mixes up words and meaning, 213, 215, 331n379
not all is form of ignorance, 288n71
not sufficient for Go rams pa, 93, 299n117
and relationship to speech and negation, 111
conceptualization, 147, 149, 223–25, 227, 315–16n239, 316n243
engages its object in negative way, 199, 329n357
of objects as both afflicted and pure, 149, 316n242
of truth or emptiness, 81, 286–87n65
consciousness, 91
Cittamātrins' residual grasping at, 205
and limbs of dependent origination, 315n235, 236
mental, and the self, 149–51, 316–17n245
as seed of existence, 79, 145, 147
conventional, 83, 113, 117, 135, 137, 187, 207, 289n73, 312n202, 330–31n369
differences between in Sa skya and Jo nang schools, 304n154
in Dol po pa, 73
and essences, 215, 332n385
existing by virtue of own characteristics, 131, 173, 175–77, 323–24n311
Go rams pa's examination of Tsong kha pa's views of, 54–55, 133–37
Go rams pa's exposition of, 207–11
how understood in world, 209
and "I" or self, 153, 317n251
is as it appears until analyzed, 173–75
and karma and its effects, 137
and linguistic conventions, 133, 135, 141
and "neither existence nor nonexistence" doctrine, 215, 332n385
posited by appearance to the mind, 153
in Prāsaṅgikas and Svātantrikas, 175, 193–95
true and false, 141, 314n225
yogi's use of, 119
corpses, magical manipulation of, 22
countering/overturning an argument *(rtsod spong, rtsod bzlog),* 12
Cozort, Daniel, 288n72, 289n74, 292n90
craving, 173
critical analyses *(mtha' dpyod),* 275n242
criticism, polemical, 4–6
criticism *(naqd),* 253n51
Critique of the False Tantras (Sngags log sun 'byin) (Rin chen bzang po), 257n90
critique/repudiation *(sun 'byin),* 12
Cycle of the Formation of Schismatic Doctrines, The (Vasumitra), 254n61

D

Dalai Lama, *See* Fifth Dalai Lama; Tenzin Gyatso; Dge 'dun grub; Dge 'dun rgya mtsho
Dar yul ba Rin chen, 296–97n111
Daśabhūmikasūtra, 195, 225, 227, 328n350, 334nn406–8
Daśadharmakasūtra, 328n350
Davidson, Ronald, 253n53, 257–58n91
Dbal mang Dkon mchog rgyal mtshan (1764–1853), 28, 263n143
Dbu ma dgongs pa rab gsal (Tsong kha pa), 285n54, 285nn55–57, 286n60, 286nn62–63, 288n70, 288n72,

290n76, 290n81, 291n82, 291n84, 291n86, 292n90, 292n93, 293n97, 293n98, 299n119, 304n156, 313n214, 313n216, 314n226, 314n229, 318n253, 318n262, 320n281, 320nn284–85, 321n288, 321n293, 324n313

Dbu ma la 'jug pa'i rnam bshad de kho na nyid gsal ba'i sgron me (Red mda' ba), 293–94n103, 294–95n106, 299–300n121, 300n122, 303n148

Dbu ma la 'jug pa'i rnam bshad nges don rnam neges (Rong ston), 292n90, 292n92, 294n102, 325n318, 329n354, 334n405

Dbu ma rigs tshogs kyi dka' gnad bstan pa rigs lam kun gsal (Rong ston), 227nn1–2, 278n6, 278n8

Dbu ma rtsa ba'i rnam bshad zab mo de kho na nyid snang ba (Rong ston), 278n8, 294n102, 297n111, 297n112, 300n128, 301n129, 314n232, 325n318, 325n327, 328n346, 328nn352–53

Dbu ma rtsa ba shes rab kyi 'grel pa 'thad pa'i rgyan (Rma bya Byang brtson), 298n113

Dbu ma shar gsum (Phya pa chos kyi seng ge), 26, 260n123

Dbu ma thal rang gi shan 'byed (Ngag dbang chos grags), 271n218

Dbu ma'i byung tshul (Shākya mchog ldan), 295n106, 296n108, 297nn111–13, 300n125

Dbu ma'i spyi don (Go rams pa), 288n68, 293–94n102, 295–96n108, 325n326, 325n328, 327n337, 327n339, 330n363, 330n366, 331n380, 332n386, 333n391, 333n392, 334n412, 335n425

Deb ther sngon po ('Gos lo tsā ba Gzhon nu dpal). See *Blue Annals*

debate, 12, 32, 251n39
- art of and Dge lugs *Collected Topics* literature, 11
- rules of and *rtsod yig,* 243n4
- *See also* oral debates

Demiéville, Paul, 255n72

demons, possessing opponents, 129

dependent
- existence of, 103, 105, 302n139, 303n145
- as truthless according to Dol po pa, 105

dependent arising, 85, 145, 213, 315n235, 236

"destruction *qua* entity"
- and karma, 85, 211, 290n79, 290n81
- not real according to Go rams pa, 54
- real according to Tsong kha pa's Prāsaṅgika, 137–39, 288–89n72, 290n79

devotion
- polemics as act of, 6, 246–47n16
- to spiritual master, 28

Dga' ldan monastery, 42

Dga' ldan pas, 28, 43, 44, 47, 247n19
- criticism of, 25, 260n116
- *Distinguishing the Views* as repudiation of, 52–56
- and efforts to control opposing religious institutions, 31
- and interpretation of Dharmakīrti, 26
- major monasteries of, 42
- status at time of writing of *Distinguishing the Views,* 41–42
- *See also* Dge lugs school; Tsong kha pa

Dgag lan phyogs bsgrigs (Rinchen Tshering), 249n29

Dge 'dun chos 'phel (1903–51), 32–33

Dge 'dun grub (First Dalai Lama) (1391–1474), 42, 44, 269n204, 271n216

Dge 'dun rgya mtsho (Second Dalai Lama) (1475–1572), 269n204

Dge lugs school, 28
- and *Collected Topics* literature, 11, 247n18
- and conflict with Sa skya pas, 44
- efforts to control rivals, 31–32
- on false or reified existence, 323–24n311
- on the ineffability of certain doctrines, 301n130
- and "neither existence nor nonexistence," 309–10n185

and Shugs ldan affair, 247n17
on śrāvakas vs. pratyekabuddhas' realizations, 223, 333n402
on the two obscurations, 333n393
on the understanding of emptiness, 300n129
See also Dga' ldan pas
Dgon po dbang phyug, Chos rje, 48
Dhammacakkapavattana Sutta, 256n81
Dharmadharmatāvibhaṅga (Maitreya), 282n41
dharmadhātu, 235. *See also* emptiness; reality
Dharmadhātustava (Nāgārjuna), 75, 211–13, 283n43, 331n378
dharmakāya, 75
Dharmakīrti (600–660), 246–47n16
interpretation of in Dga' ldan school, 26
logic of and Madhyamaka, 29, 262n142
on "particulars" or "self-characterized phenomena," 324n316
on speech and conceptual thoughts, 111, 329n357
Vādanyāya, 248n25
dharmas according to Vaibhāṣikas, 97, 300n124
Dharmasaṃgīti Sūtra, 133, 312n203
Dhongthog Rinpoche, T.G., 266n168
dialogical nature of polemics, 8, 247n20
diamond-sliver, 213
Differentiating the Three Vows (Sdom gsum rab dbye) (Sa skya Paṇḍita), 23, 27, 50, 250n34, 258n95
Dignāga, 107, 280n18, 329n357, 330n364
disciple. *See* student
disputational document or record *(rtsod yig),* 12, 251n39
distinguishing quality or character, 179, 324n313
Distinguishing the Philosophical Tenets (Grub mtha'i rnam dbye) (Byang chub 'od), 258n95
Distinguishing the Views: Clearing Away Mental Darkness (Dol po pa), 46–47, 272n225
Distinguishing the Views and Practices (Lta sgrub shan 'byed) (Bod pa sprul sku), 56
Distinguishing the Views (Lta ba'i shan 'byed) (Go rams pa), 2, 28, 35, 36, 37, 44–45, 49, 237, 264n148, 270n208
as both offensive and defensive work, 45
"commitment to compose," 69, 277n3
continuing influence of, 56
and critics of Dol po pa, 30
Dge lugs tradition's response to, 55–56
exposition of middle way in, 203–37
individuals influencing, 237
and intertextuality, 46–47
motivation for composition of work, 69, 277n2
and Nāgārjuna's version of Madhyamaka, 273–74n238
other works with similar names, 47, 271n218
as polemic, 2, 50
printing of, 32
refutation of Dol po pa in, 45, 51–52, 97–114
refutation of Tsong kha pa in, 45, 52–56, 115–201
scholars who followed, 93
socio-political background of composition of, 41–45
and Stag tshang lo tsā ba, 52, 275n245
structure and contents of, 48–50
texts compiled from, 61
Dkon mchog 'jigs med dbang po, 293n100
Dkon mchog lhun grub Ngor chen (1497–1557), 266n168
Dkon mchog 'phel (1445–1514), 36, 40
Dmar ston (= Thang sag pa'i sprul sku?) Gzhon nu rgyal mtshan, 296–97n111
doctrinal controversies, 16, 25–33, 50
doctrine, definition of, 260n117

dogmatics, 16
Dol po pa Shes rab rgyal mtshan (1292–1361), 28–29, 271n218
as author of two minor polemic tracts, 30, 45–46
on Cittamātra, 107
compared to Tsong kha pa, 28–29
and criticism of Sa skya interpretation of Madhyamaka, 43, 45, 46–47
critics of, 29–30, 263n144, 302n141
on the dependent, 103
emptiness accepted by, 101, 301n131
as founder of a successful institution, 42
Go rams pa's evaluation of in hierarchy of Buddhist philosophy, 105, 303n144
Go rams pa's summary of views of in *Distinguishing the Views,* 71–77
historical study of, 279n9
and last works of Maitreya, 75, 282n41
and Perfection of Wisdom sūtras, 279–80n14
refutation of in *Distinguishing the Views,* 51–52, 97–114
Sa skya pas not univocal on, 302–3n142
suppression of his works, 45, 279n9
theory of Madhyamaka, 71–77, 93–95, 262n141
Don drub rdo rje, 44, 270n211, 213
Dose of Emptiness, A: An Annotated Translation of the Stong thun chen mo of mKhas grub Dge legs dpal bzang (Cabezón), 278–79n8, 285n55, 288n69
on the *ālayavijñāna,* 289n74
on autonomous reasons and theses, 91–93, 293–94n102, 294n105
on bodhisattvas surpassing śrāvakas and pratyekabuddhas, 334n406
critique of alternative views in, 263n143
on the four negations, 287–88n67
and Go rams pa arguments regarding "reasoning consciousness," 309n184
use of invective in, 17, 254n60
on "karmic inexhaustibility," 290n76
on karmic propensity, 290n81
on Nāgārjuna's philosophical works, 301n134
on "neither existent nor nonexistent" view, 298–99n116
on objects to be abandoned and realized, 292n90
on path of meditation in nine parts, 292n93
on Rngog Blo ldan shes rab, 295–96n108
and Rong ston pa, 255n71
on syllogisms and common subject, 327n338
on the two obscurations, 290–91n82, 291n84, 85, 333n393
on the two selves, 291n86
and *Vigrahavyāvartanī,* 304n151
on Yogācāra doctrine of *bījas* or seeds, 290n78
See also Mkhas grub Dge legs dpal bzang; *Stong thun chen mo*
double negation, 81–83, 288n68, 332n385
and analysis of Madhyamaka, 129, 310n192, 193
Dge lugs scholars upholding of, 309–10n185
and Dol po pa, 47
Go rams pa's repudiation of, 54
and Nāgārjuna, 129, 310n192
and reasoning consciousness, 215
Tsong kha pa's vs. Go rams pa's views of, 307–8n179, 308n180
and Tsong kha pa's repudiation of Sa skya pas, 45
See also fourfold negation
doxography, 278–79n8, 285n53, 312n202
Dpa' ri(s) Blo bzang rab gsal (b. 1840), 30
Dpal ldan rdo rje (1411–82), 36, 271n218
Dragonetti, Carmen, 330n364
Drang ba dang nges pa'i don rnam par phye ba'i bstan bcos legs bshad snying po (Tsong kha pa), 324n317
Dṛḍhādhyaśayaparivarta Sūtra, 75

Dreyfus, Georges, 15, 27, 266n166, 266n170, 324n316
Drung chen Nor bu bzang po, 267–68n184
dualistic appearances, 117
Dudjom Rinpoche, 255n72, 308n181
Dung dkar Rin po che, 273n237
Dunhuang texts, 18, 20, 255–56n73
'Dzam thang, 31
Dze smad rin po che Blo bzang dpal ldan bstan 'dzin yar rgyas (1927–68), 33
Dzongsar Khyentse Rinpoche, 269n190

E

early dissemination period *(snga dar),* 1, 18–19, 19–20, 259n101, 260n121
Eckel, Malcolm David, 313n209
eight great difficult points *(dka' gnad chen po brgyad),* 55, 83–85, 288–89n72, 291n86
  and autonomous reasons and theses, 91–93, 293–94n102
  and existence of external objects, 89–91, 293n98
  and objects to be abandoned and realized, 292n90
Eighth Karma pa Mi bskyod rdo rje (1507–54), 30
eisegesis, 16
elements, 99
Eliade, Mircea, 244n6
Elimination the Darkness of Bad Views (Lta ba ngan pa'i mun sel) (Se ra Rje btsun Chos kyi rgyal mtshan and Paṇ chen Bde legs nyi ma), 30, 265n154
Eloquent Disquisition Aimed at Destroying Another's Adversarial Claim, An (Rig 'dzin Chos kyi grags pa), 13
Elucidation of the Definitive and Provisional (Tsong kha pa), 77, 175–77, 284–85n51, 323n310
  and *Prasannapadā,* 189, 318n344
  See also *Drang ba dang nges pai'i don*; *Essence of Eloquent Discourse*
emetics *(skyug sman)* as metaphor, 252n42
emptiness, 1, 2, 205, 217, 235
  arising by virtue of own characteristic, 327n337
  arrived at through rational analysis, 50, 99, 117
  being attched to 233, 235
  can be conceived for Tsong kha pa, 29, 45, 81, 125, 286–87n65, 307–8n179, 308n181
  in Cittamātra, 217, 221
  conceptual understanding of is not ultimate truth, 52–53, 119, 306n166
  different uses of term according to Go rams pa, 217
  in Dol po pa, 29, 73, 101, 301n131
  of essence, 101, 301–2n136
  existence of, 307–8n179
  extinguishes proliferations, 155, 161
  of form, 121
  grasping of, according to Tsong kha pa, 52
  Hīnayāna vs. Mahāyāna understanding of, 87, 97, 161, 161–63, 165, 217, 227, 292n91, 321n286
  "in name only" *(rnam grangs pa),* 99
  mystical realization of, 50, 52–53, 99
  and object-to-be-negated, 79, 285n58, 286n59
  of own characteristic, 101, 301–2n136
  of own nature, 73, 279n11
  and permanence, 97
  of proliferation of four extremes, 161, 217
  as renunciation of all views, 121–23
  of self of the person or phenomena, 97–99, 213, 217
  signs that an individual is ripe to be taught it, 161, 163, 320n278
  three kinds of in Maitreya texts, 101–3
  of truth, 161, 213, 217
  Tsong kha pa's exposition of according to Go rams pa, 79–83
  two kinds of according to Go rams pa, 50
  as utter negation, 29, 117–19
  of what is nonexistent, 301–2n136

See also dharmadhātu; reality
Emptiness in the Mind-Only School of Buddhism: Dynamic Responses to Dzong-ka-ba's Essence of Eloquence I (Hopkins), 279n9, 10
"emptiness of what is other" *(gzhan stong)*, 29, 101, 262n141, 279–80n14
and Dol po pa, 75, 280–81n20, 282n41, 282–83n42
not compatible with Nāgārjuna, 101
Rong ston pa's criticism of, 270n208
and Shākya mchog ldan, 51–52, 269n207
as trademark of Jo nang pas, 49
enlightenment, 1, 221–23
and Cittamātra school, 221
and freedom from proliferations of four extremes, 221
Mahāyāna and Hīnayāna understandings of, 221–23
and White Panacea doctrine, 28, 261–62n135
Enlightenment by a Single Means (Jackson), 245n13, 251n37, 256n79, 261nn133–34
entitiness, 223–25
epistemology, 3
Go rams pa's writings on, 38
and Gsang phu monastery, 26
and Tsong kha pa and Dharmakīrti, 29, 262n142
Epistle to the Holy Beings, An (Skyes bu dam pa rnams la spring yig) (Sa skya Paṇḍita), 251n37
equipoise
and correct perception, 117
and freedom from extremes, 109–11, 217, 334n403
Essence of Eloquent Discourse, The (Legs bshad snying po) (Tsong kha pa), 30, 285nn54–56, 286n60, 289n74, 291n84, 291n86, 294n105, 302nn138–39, 304n156, 312n203, 313n214, 323n311, 324n312, 324n317, 327n335, 328n342, 328n344
essentialism, 175, 215, 322n304
eternalism, 1, 69, 71, 111
and Asaṅga and Vasubandhu, 103
Dol po pa's claim to be free of, 75–77
attributed to the Jo nang pas, 48
and nonexistence, 129, 235, 310n192
realists falling into extreme of, 71, 278n6
See also extremes, four
exegesis, 16
existence
of emptiness, 307–8n179
existence by virtue of own characteristic and *svatantras*, 91–93, 177, 199, 328n344, 324n315
extreme of, 113
false or reified, 175–77, 323–24n311
inherent vs. mere, 180n180
repudiation of in Go rams pa, 50
ultimate, 46, 272n226
See also conventional; extremes, four
experiential canon, 253n55
expository commentary, 3
"expression of humility," 246–47n16
external objects. *See* objects, external
extremes, four, 107–9, 113, 197
elimination of, 215, 217
emptiness of proliferation of, 161, 217
not seeing things in terms of, 117
and realization of Madhyamaka view, 129
extremes, thirty-two, 121
eye, as metaphor for subject, 185–87
eye consciousness, 139–43, 211
Eye-Lamp of Dhyāna (Bsam gtan mig sgron), 21

F
false practices *(log spyod)*, 22
Fifth Dalai Lama, Ngawang Losang Gyatso (1617–82), 28, 31, 247n19, 252–53n47, 270n213
on the meeting of Ngor chen and Nor bzang pa, 271n216
and Sa skya Paṇḍita's criticism of Mahāmudrā, 28
and unified culture under Dga' ldan pa hegemony, 247n19
five ancillary points, 55
form, 121

foundation consciousness. See *ālaya-vijñāna*
four extremes. *See* extremes, four
four noble truths
  and cessation, 171–73
  sixteen aspects of, 89, 157, 293n96
fourfold alternatives *(catuṣkoṭi),* 123, 309n184
  Mkhas grub rje's formulation of last two *koṭis,* 309–10n185
  negation of, 127, 309–10n185
  and "neither existence nor nonexistence" view,125, 127–29, 309–10n185, 310n189
  and Rong ston pa, 325–26n329
  taken literally by Go rams pa, 50, 52, 53
  and transcending of analysis, 54
  and truth, 213
  Tsong kha pa vs. Go rams pa's interpretation of, 125, 308n180
  Tsong kha pa's explanation of, 81–83
Frauwallner, Erich, 292n93
"freedom from proliferations" or "extremes," 47, 217
  and *Abhisamayālaṃkāra,* 227
  and bodhisattva surpassing pratyakebuddhas and śrāvakas, 225–27
  difference in understanding of in the three vehicles, 165
  and elimination of obscurations to omniscience, 223
  and emergence of welfare of sentient beings, 235
  Go rams pa's explication of, 203–37
  history of expression in India and Tibet, 48, 273n237
  and Pa tshab, 49
  summary of in *Distinguishing the Views,* 93–95
  scriptural evidence for, 231–35
  three subdivisions of, 203
  as trademark for Go rams pa's lineage of Madhyamaka, 48–49
  as understanding of selflessness of phenomena, 227

G
Gangs mnyan, 298n113
Garland of Jewels: An Open Letter to the Holders of the Teachings (Dus kyi 'khor lo'i spyad pa las brtsams te bstan 'dzin rnams la 'phrin du gsol ba nor bu'i phreng ba) (Red mda' ba), 270n209
Gdong thog Bstan pa'i rgyal mtshan, 48
Gendun, Lama, story of a dge bshes's debate with, 32
General Exposition of Madhyamaka (Dbu ma 'i spyi don) (Go rams pa), 249n30
generally characterized phenomena, 177, 324n317
Gentle Art of Philosophical Polemics, The (Agassi), 5
Glang dar ma, 21
Glo bo mkhan chen Bsod nams lhun grub (1456–1532), 41, 269n200
gnosis *(ye shes),* 29, 119
  accumulation of, 163
  compared to conceptual analysis of reality, 215, 332n286
  and emptiness that is mystically realized, 52, 99, 301n129
  and freedom from proliferations of four extremes, 125, 217
  and understanding of the ultimate and buddhahood, 46
Go bo rab 'byams pa Shes rab dpal, 33–34
Go rams pa. *See* Gorampa Sönam Sengé
Golden Doctrines of the Shangs pas, 25
Gon g.yo Nyi ma grags, 294–95n106
Gorampa Sönam Sengé (Go rams pa) (1429–89), 15, 16
  banning of his works, 30, 31–32
  and Dge lugs pas, 32
  disciples of, 40–41
  his founding of Rta nag gser gling monastery, 35, 267n182
  life of, 33–36, 39–40
  his literal reading of Indian sources, 49–50

major esoteric works of, 36–39
and Ngor monastery, 36, 268n187
ordination of, 34, 267n176
and relationship to Shākya mchog ldan, 269n202
and Rin spungs court, 40
and Rngog Blo ldan shes rab, 295–96n108
his *Rtsom phro* commentary, 249n28
and Skyed tshal monastery, 35
as soft doxographer, 278–79n8, 312n202
as systematizer and defender of Sa skya tradition, 41, 43
and Thub bstan rnam rgyal monastery, 36, 40
and title *rab 'byams pa,* 34
as visionary, 39
See also *Distinguishing the Views (Lta ba'i shan 'byed)*
'Gos Khug pa lhas btsas (b. eleventh century), 23, 251n37, 258n93
and *Guhyagarbha Tantra,* 24
on the purpose of writing polemics, 252n45
'Gos lo tsā ba Gzhon nu dpal (1392–1481), 24
gradualist *(rim gyis pa)* position, 19, 261–62n135
grasping at extremes, 129
grasping at self of persons, 213, 219, 221. *See also* emptiness of self of persons
grasping at self of phenomena, 55, 149
and grasping of signs, 155
See also emptiness of self of phenomena
grasping at things to be true, 79, 87–89, 95, 109, 125, 165, 223,
and Cittamātra, 105
and conceptualization, 95, 147, 299n119
gives rise to grasping at "I," 167
and grasping at aggregates and self, 147, 225
and obscuration to omniscience, 89, 143–49
relationship to afflicted obscuration, 143–45, 149
as root of cyclic existence, 79
and Śrāvakayāna vs. Mahāyāna, 165–67
two levels of for Prāsaṅgika, 288–89n72
See also fourfold negation
Great Perfection *(rdzogs chen),* 259n101, 260n120, 263n143, 273–74n238
claims for superiority of, 259n101
controversy regarding, 25, 248–49n27
Great Seal. *See* Mahāmudrā
Great State of the Buddha (Sangs rgyas kyi sa chen po) (Rong zom Chos kyi bzang po), 257n88
Great Treatise on the Philosophical Schools ('Jam dbyangs bzhad pa Ngag dbang brtson 'grus), 30
Great Treatise on the Stages of the Path (Lam rim chen mo) (Tsong kha pa), 45
Griffiths, Paul J., 244n6
Gro lung pa Blo gros 'byung gnas (eleventh century), 261n124
Grub mtha' kun shes (Stag tshang lo tsā ba), 52, 263n145, 270n210, 295–96n108, 297n112
Gsang phu ne'u thog monastery, 26–27, 42, 93, 295n107
and lineage of Madhyamaka, 49, 274n239
Gsang sngags snga 'gyur la bod du rtsod pa snga phyir byung ba rnams kyi lan du brjod pa nges pa don gyi 'brug sgra (Blo gros rgyal mtshan), 249n29
Gsang sngags snga 'gyur la bod du rstod pa snga phyir byng ba rnams kyi lan (Sog bzlog pa), 257–58n91, 258n93
Gtsang, 31, 42, 43–44, 270n211
Gtsang nag pa (late twelfth century), 261n125
Gtsang pa Sar spros, 296–97n111, 298n113
Gtsang smyon Heruka (1452–1507), 245–46n15
Gu ru bkra shis (b. eighteenth century), 24, 271n216

Gu ru Chos dbang (1212–70), 258n93
Guhyagarba Tantra, 23–24, 257n85
Gung ru Shes rab bzang po (1411–75), 34–35, 267n178
  his encouragement to Go rams pa to write *Distinguishing the Views,* 35, 48, 237
  as polemicist, 48, 270n210
  and tantric works, 270n210
Gung thang Dkon mchog bstan pa'i sgron me (1762–1823), 280n17
G.yag ston (G.yag phrug) Sangs rgyas 'phel (1348–1414), 93, 237, 274n240, 294–95n106
G.yag ston Sangs rgyas dpal (1367–1449), 245n15
G.yung pa tshe dbang, 267–68n184
'Gyur med tshe dbang mchog grub (1761–1829), 14
Gzad pa (= Bzad pa?) ring mo, 93, 274n240, 298n114
Gzhan phan mtha' yas (b. 1800), 56
Gzhan phan 'od zer gyi rtsod spong (Go rams pa), 39
gzhan stong. See "emptiness of what is other" *(gzhan stong)*
Gzhi kha ba [Rin spungs pa], 39

H
Haribhadra, 37, 175, 316n242, 321n290
"heresy," Buddhist, 103, 302n140
heterodox, 3, 157, 161
Hevajra Tantra, 25, 268n188
Hīnayāna
  and difference from Mahāyāna on emptiness, 85, 87, 161–63, 157–73, 165, 227, 292n91, 321n286
  and Do pol pa, 51, 97
  and eternalism and nihilism, 235
  and obscurations, 87–89
  and perception of things as true, 163
  and selflessness of phenomena, 320n284
  and signlessness, 159–61
  understand ultimate truth according to Tsong kha pa's Prāsaṅgikas, 217
  view of enlightenment, 221–23
  See also Sautrāntika; śrāvakas and Śrāvakayāna; Vaibhāṣika
Hinduism, 16
History of Buddhism (Bu ston), 246–47n16
History of the Nyingma (Bdud 'joms rin po che), 24, 255n71, 259n100, 259n105, 259n107, 260nn113–15,
Ho shang Mo ho yen. *See* Hwa shang Mahāyāna
Hopkins, Jeffrey, 279n9, 279n10, 279n12, 284n49, 284n50, 284n51, 286n59, 286n60, 291n88, 292n90, 292n93, 299n120, 300n122, 334n406
Hor Dpal 'byor bzang po, 271n216
Houston, G. W., 255n72
Hugon, Pascale, 261n125
Huizinga, Johan, 2
human sacrifice, 22
"humility, expression of," 246–47n16
Hwa shang Mahāyāna
  and Bsam yas debate, 19–20
  and four extremes, 81–83, 288n60
  and Go rams pa, 129, 311n194
  as paradigmatic "other," 21
  and *yod min med min* view, 54

I
"I"
  existence of and Madhyamaka critique, 317n251
  Go rams pa's criticism of Tsong kha pa's view of, 151–55
  and grasping at aggregates, 147, 151
  grasping at truth gives rise to grasping at, 167
  referent of, 315–16n239
  Prāsaṅgika acceptance of nominal existence of, 55, 87, 151, 317n251
ideal types, 3–4, 251–52n40
Idealismo budista (Toda and Dragoneeti), 330n364
identity-formation via polemics, 6, 8
ignorance, 1, 315n236
  as afflicted obscuration, 145, 147
  and grasping at things to be true, 79
  as obscuration to omniscience, 145, 147

and twelve links, 145, 149
imaginary, 101, 103
improper cogitation, 147
impure stages, seven, 167
inconceivability of reality, 163. *See also* ultimate truth
Indian Buddhism
chosen over Chinese, 1
rarely an object of polemical critiques, 26
polemics in, 18, 254n61, 62, 64
and Tsong kha pa, 29
as *traditio franca,* 15, 253n53
Indian-Chinese debate at Bsam yas, 19–21, 254n66
ineffability, 301n130
inference
and autonomous syllogisms, 195
and theses, 191
See also reasoning; syllogism
inference acceptable to others
Go rams pa on, 183–85, 189–91
'Jam dbyangs bzhad pa on, 326n333
and valid cognition, 183, 326–27n334
vs. *svatantra,* 325n321
inference acceptable to one's own side, 326n333
informal fallacies, 17
insult in polemical literature, 17–18
inter and intrasectarian polemics, 6–7, 247n19
interdependent arising, 288–89n72. *See also* dependent arising
Intermediate Mother [Perfection of Wisdom Sūtra], 121
intertextuality, 45–47, 272–73n230
intimidation, rhetoric of, 25
Introduction to the Mahāyāna Method (Theg pa chen po'i tshul la 'jug pa) (Rong zom Chos kyi bzang po), 257n88
irenic tone, 3
Islam, Tibetan, 7
Islamic criticism, 253n51
"isolated," 175, 322n304

J
Jackson, David, vii, ix, 28, 32, 49, 245n13, 245–46n15, 256n79, 261n128, 261n133, 265n158, 267n171, 267n178, 267n179, 268n185, 269n195, 269n202, 270n210, 271n217, 273n237, 273n238, 274n239, 294–95n106, 295–96n108, 296n109, 314n224
'Jad Thub bstan yangs pa can monastery, 41
'Jam dbyangs bzhad pa Ngag dbang brtson 'grus (1648–1721), 28, 30, 300n128, 326n333
on the eight great difficult points, 288–89n72
on the five forms of reasoning, 331n380
on negative vs. positive engagement of an object, 329n357, 329–30n358
on object-directed conceptualization, 316n242
his response to *Distinguishing the Views,* 55–56
and Vaibhāṣikas and Sautrāntikas, 333n400
'Jam dbyangs kun dga' chos bzang (1433–1503), 40
Jambudvīpa, 169
Jasper, James, 273n236
Jayānanda, 298n113
'Jig rten mgon po (1143–1217), 27
'Jigs med gling pa (1729/30–98), 24
Jñānagarbha, 49, 229, 312n202, 313n208, 313n209
Jñānālokālaṃkāra Sūtra, 75
Jñānasārasamuccaya, 127
Jo nang school
compatability with Sa skya views, 111, 304n154
creation of their own identity, 43, 44
criticisms of by Tsong kha pa and followers, 269n207
and Dol po pa, 28
persecution and preservation of, 31
polemics against opponents, 47
and those who accept *Saṃdhinirmocana Sūtra,* 303n148

at time of writing of *Distinguishing the Views,* 41–42
on whether their view is Buddhist, 51, 282n29
See also Dol po pa
Jokhang temple, 22
Jorden, Ngawang, 266n168, 267n171, 267n176, 267n182, 267–68n184, 268n186, 268n191, 268n193, 269n198

K
Kālacakra, 270n209
Kamalaśīla
and Bsam yas debate, 19–21, 256n79
as paradigmatic defender of faith, 21
and repudiation of Hwa shang, 129
Kapstein, Matthew, 45, 245n15, 248–49n27, 253n55, 258n95, 259n108, 279n9
karma, 209, 290n75, 288–89n72
acceptance of and avoidance of nihilism, 235
aggregates cannot be doer of, 155
arises from misconception, 145, 147
and cause and effect, 175
faulty explanations for, 209–11
Go rams pa's examination of Tsong kha pa's view of, 137–39, 314n222
Go rams pa's own views of, 314n222
and "I" as nominally doer and experiencer of, 153
and "inexhaustibility," 83, 137–39, 290n76
realists' view of, 211
Tsong kha pa on how it can give rise to effect, 83–85, 91, 137–39, 290n79
Karma Dkon gzhon, 274n240, 297–98n112
Karma pa controversy, 247n17
Karma pa Pakshi Rangjung Dorje (1204–83), 245–46n15
Karma Phuntsho, 254n66
Kaśyapa, 141–43, 233
Kaśyapaparivarta, 233
Khams, 31, 32, 33, 35, 42
'Khon Dkon mchog rgyal po (1034–1102), 256n80
Khri srong lde'u btsan, 1, 19
Khu lo tsā ba, 298n113
Khug pa lhas btas, *See* 'Gos Khug pa lhas btsas
Khyung Rin chen grags (eleventh–twelfth centuries), 296n109
killing rites, 252n42
Klong chen rab 'byams pa Dri med 'od zer (1308–64), 24, 259n101
Knowledge of All Philosophical Systems (Grub mtha' kun shes) (Stag tshang lo tsā ba Shes rab rin chen), 263n145
Kong ston Dbang phyug grub (b. fifteenth century), 40, 269n197
Kristeva, Julia, 47, 272–73n230
Kun dga' 'bum, 33, 266n169
khyab pa (pervasion), 308–9n183

L
La stod Dmar po, 258n93
label (linguistic), 54
Lam 'bras. *See* Path and Its Result *(lam 'bras)*
Lam ngan mun sel sgron ma (Go rams pa), 285n58, 288n69, 298–99n116
Lam rim chen mo (Tsong kha pa), 283n47, 284n54, 285n58, 286n60, 286n62, 286n64, 286–87n65, 287n66, 288n69, 288n71, 289n73, 291n82, 291n83, 291n86, 291n89, 293n102, 294n103, 294n104, 299n118, 304–5n157, 306n168, 307n172, 307n179, 308n180, 380n181, 311n194, 315n234, 325n318
Lamp that Dispels the Darkness of Bad Views, The (Lam ngan mun sel sgron ma) (Mkhas grub Dge legs dpal bzang), 263n143
Laṅkavatāra Sūtra, 299–300n121
Larson, Gerald James, 325n322
later dissemination period *(phyi dar),* 1–2, 6, 19, 21, 257n88
Lcang lung paṇḍita (1770–1845), 30
Lcang skya Rol pa'i rdo rje (1717–1786), 288–89n72, 297–98n112, 323–24n311
Lce sgom Shes rab rdo rje, 93, 231, 274n240, 298n115

Ldan ma Blo bzang chos dbyings (b. nineteenth century), 30
Legs bshad snying po (Tsong kha pa). See *Essence of Eloquent Discourse*
Leiden project on religious polemics, 244n6
Letter Offered to All of the Buddhas and Bodhisattvas of the Ten Directions, A (Phyogs bcu'i sangs rgyas dang byang chub sems pa rnams la phul ba 'i yi ge) (Sa skya Paṇḍita), 251n37
Lha bla ma Ye shes 'od. *See* Ye shes 'od
linguistic designation, 133, 312n203
links, twelve, 85, 145
Lobsang Dargyay, Geshe, vii–xiv, 243n1, 290n79, 303n150
Lokātītastava (Nāgārjuna), 99, 300n126, 300n127, 307n174, 319n265
Lopez, Donald S., and polemical literature, 248n27
Lta ba ngan sel (Go rams pa), 286n60, 291n86, 292n90, 305n162, 313n219, 314n229, 317n252, 318n262, 322n297, 322n306, 323n307, 321n374, 331n376
Lta ba'i khyad par (Ye shes sde), 271n218
Lta ba'i shan 'byed (Go rams pa). See *Distinguishing the Views (Lta ba'i shan 'byed)*
Lta ba'i shan 'byed (Ye shes de), 271n218
Lta ba shan 'byed yid kyi mun sel (Dol po pa Shes rab rgyal mtshan), 271n218
Lta grub shan 'byed (Bod pa sprul sku Mdo sngags bstan pa'i nyi ma), 249n30

M

Madhyamaka, 26, 48, 69, 207, 227, 277n2, 277n4
called Niḥsvabhāvavāda by other schools, 71
decision to propagate in Tibet, 1
doctrine of according to Go rams pa, 207–29
Dol po pa's criticism of Sa skya pa views of, 43
Dol po pa's theory of, 29, 71–77
early Tibetan works on, 28
emergence as distinct field of Tibetan philosophy, 1–2
Go rams pa's major writings on, 37
and Mahāmudrā, 261–62n135
and Mkhas grub Dge legs dpal bzang, 263n143
as one of four philosophical schools, 71
path of according to Go rams pa, 219–27
of Sa skya Paṇḍita, 273–74n238
Tsong kha pa's repudiation of Sa skya views of, 42
Tsong kha pa's theory of, 29, 77–93
and three vehicles, 235
two truths in, 207–17
use of term *emptiness* in, 217
See also Prāsaṅgika Madhyamaka; Svātantrika Madhyamaka
"Madhyamaka Thesislessness" (Cabezón), 303n147
Madhyamakālaṃkāravṛtti (Śāntarakṣita), 173
Madhyamakāvatāra (Candrakīrti), 77, 135–37, 139, 151, 193–95, 284n50, 290n79, 291n84, 305n16, 306n166, 307n177, 313nn210–13, 313n220, 314n226, 317n248, 318nn253–55, 319n273, 320n278, 324n313, 328n349, 330n367, 331n370, 332n382, 333n391
and *Abhisamayālaṃkāra,* 169, 171
on the bodhisattva path, 169
on causality, 331n370
'Jam dbyangs bzhad pa's commentary on, 326n333
and nominal existence of "I," 151–53
Red mda' ba's commentary on, 264–65n106
and selflessness of person, 213
Tsong kha pa's commentary on, 95, 299n119
Madhyamakāvatārabhāṣya (Candrakīrti), 85, 153, 159, 161,

306n166, 307nn176–77, 313n213, 318n253, 318n255, 319nn269–70, 320n277, 320n281, 320n283, 320n285, 322n296, 333n395, 335n420, 335n419
Go rams pa's explanation of, 163–65
and obstacles to omniscience, 219
and truth of cessation, 173
Madhyāntavibhaṅga (Maitreya), 103, 105, 282n41, 302n138, 304n139
magic, 22
Mahābherī Sūtra, 75
Mahābrahma, 173
Mahākāla, four-faced *(Gdong bzhi pa),* 39
Mahāmudrā, 27, 261–62n135, 263n143
Mahāparinirvāṇa Sūtra, 75, 302n140
Mahāyāna, 97, 163, 235
bhūmis of, 88–89
and compassion, 235
critique of Tsong kha pa's views of differences from Hīnayāna, 157–73, 318n262
and difference from Hīnayāna on emptiness, 89, 227, 292m91
extensive explanation of emptiness in, 165, 217, 320–21n285
and four forms of signlessness, 150–61, 157
and freedom from dualism, 225, 235
vs. Hīnayāna regarding the path, 165–69, 321n286
vs. Hīnayāna regarding views of enlightenment, 221–23
and obscurations, 88–89
signs of having lineage of, 163, 195, 320n278
surpassing Hīnayāna through understanding, 157
Mahāyānasaṃgraha (Asaṅga), 105, 280n17, 290n81
Mahāyānottaratantra (Maitreya). See *Uttaratantra*
Maher, Derek, 252–53n47
Maitreya, 147, 169, 223, 273–74n238, 284n48
and afflicted obscurations, 221
and Dol po pa, 51, 105
and existence of the dependent, 103
last works of, 75, 282n41
and three emptinesses, 101
See also *Abhisamayālaṃkāra*; *Dharmadharmatāvibhaṅga*; *Madhyāntavibhaṅga*; *Sūtrālaṃkāra*; *Uttaratantra*
Makransky, John, 262n138
Man ngag mnyam med dbang po'i rdo rje lta bu (Dkha' bzhi 'dzin pa Rin chen rdo rje), 263n144
Mañjuśrī, 17, 69, 131, 199
Mar pa Chos kyi blo gros (d. 1097), 27, 49, 99, 296n110
Māra, 201
Martin, Dan, ix, 248n26, 255n69, 259n111, 263n144, 270n209
and criticism of polemics, 10, 248n23
and early Bon-Buddhist dialectic, 18, 254n66
Mdog lo pa Mkhan chen Kun dga' dpal (Nya dbon Kun dga' dpal), 294–95n106
means, practice of, 261–62n135
measure of object-to-be-negated, 79, 286n60
meditation, path of, and division into nine parts, 89, 292n93
meditative equipoise of āryans, 109–11, 217, 334n403
mental consciousness
as phenomenon and not person, 151
and the self, 149–51, 316–17n245
mental defilements, 333n399
mere "I." *See* "I"
merit, 261–62n135
Meru, Mount, 233
Mes lhang tsher (1142–82), 296n109
metaphors, used in titles of polemicists tracts, 13–14
Mgon po dbang phyug (fifteenth century), 237
Mi bskyod rdo rje (1507–54), 30
Mi la ras pa (1052–1135), 27, 49, 93, 296n110
Mi pham rgya mtsho (1846–1912), 30, 56, 264n148, 265n165, 312n200, 320n276, 332n386

middle way, 273n236
as structural device for *Distinguishing the Views,* 48–49
Middle Way. *See* Madhyamaka
"Middle Way *qua* freedom from extremes" *(mtha' bral dbu ma),* 46. *See also* "freedom from proliferations" or "extremes"
mind
and construction of conventional world, 135, 153, 207, 312n202
and correct perception, 117
dichotomizing filter of, 53–54
nondual, 123
and reality, 217
and White Panacea doctrine, 28, 261–62n135
Mind-Only school. *See* Cittamātra (Yogācāra) school
Ming mdzod, 266n168, 169
misconception, 145, 147, 205
and mental proliferations, 155, 161
three, 147, 316n241
mistaken and unmistaken thought, 187
Mkhan chen Byang sems, 294–95n106
Mkhan chen Kha phyar ba, 34
Mkhas dbang, Brtson 'grus dpal (fourteen century), 294–95n106
Mkhas grub Dge legs dpal bzang (1385–1438), 17, 245–46n15, 285n55
on afflicted obscurations, 333n398
on *ālayavijñāna,* 289n74
on catuṣkoṭi, 287–88n67, 309–10n185, 310n189
on craving and afflictions, 322n299
his defense of Tsong kha pa's theory of karma, 290n79
on emptiness, 301n131
on false existence, 323–24n311
on the five forms of reasoning, 331n380
on the intrinsic character of phenomena, 294n103
on mental consciousness as self, 316–17n245
on "neither existence nor nonexistence" doctrine, 311–12n199
on objects, 285n58, 292n90, 323n309
on obscurations to omniscience, 333n398
on the path of meditation of nine parts, 292n93
on Rngog Blo ldan shes rab, 295–96n108
role in the creation of Dga' ldan pa identity, 42, 247n18, 263n143
on selflessness of phenomena, 320n284
on Svātantrika/Prāsaṅgika distinction, 279n8, 323–24n311
See also *Dose of Emptiness; Stong thun chen mo*
Mnga' ris Paṇ chen Padma dbang rgyal (1487–1542), 24
Mnyal pa Dad pa bzang po, 298n114
Mongol Yuan dynasty in China, 43
motivations for writing polemics, 14–15
Mueller, Max, 2
Mūlamadhyamakakārikā (Nāgārjuna), 101, 107, 197, 290n75, 301n132, 301n133, 303n149, 304n152, 307n172, 307n173, 307n175, 310n186, 310n187, 313n221, 314n222, 314n232, 318n260, 318n262, 319n274, 324–25n318, 331n372, 331n380
and *Akutobhayā,* 253n56
and autonomous forms of reasoning, 324–25n318
and Candrakīrti's arguments against autonomous syllogisms, 197
commentary on by Go rams pa, 37, 249n28
and extinguishing of proliferation, 155
and karma and the afflictions, 139, 145, 147, 313n221
Rma bya Byang chub brtson 'grus commentary on, 298n113
Tsong kha pa's commentary on, 77
See also *Prajñāmūla*
Mus chen Dkon mchog rgyal mtshan (1388–1469), 34, 35, 39, 267n176, 177
influence on *Distinguishing the Views,* 48, 237
Mus chen Sangs rgyas rin chen (1450–1524), 40

Mus chen Thugs rje dpal bzang (b. fifteenth century), 40–41

N

Nāgārjuna, 69, 101, 107, 147, 149, 157–59, 215, 231, 237, 273–74n274, 284n48, 301n134
and afflicted obscurations, 221
and *Akutobhayā,* 253–54n56
and autonomous forms of reasoning, 324–25n318
and Bsam yas debate, 19
devotional works of, 75
and Dol po pa, 29, 51, 101
and double negation, 129, 310n192
and emptiness, 99–101, 121–23
and foundation consciousness, 175
and grasping at signs, 155
and linguistic designation, 312n203
and "neither existence nor nonexistence [doctrine]," 131
philosophical works of, 301n134
and selflessness of phenomena, 227
and truthlessness, 223
and Tsong kha pa, 29
See also *Mūlamadhyamakakārikā*; *Ratnāvalī*; *Śūnyatāsaptati; Vigrahavyāvartanī*; *Yuktiṣaṣṭikā*
Naiyāyikas, 248n25, 254n64
Nalendra Monastery, 34, 40, 267n178, 271n217
name only, 125–27, 308n182
natures, three, 101, 302n137
according to Dol po pa, 73, 279n10
negation, 52
and aphophatic discourse, 3
conceptualization of emptiness via, 53, 79, 115, 121, 213, 286–87n65
nonaffirming or simple absolute, 73, 279n12
See also double negation; fourfold negation
negationist branch of Madhyamaka, 29
"neither existent nor nonexistent" *(yod min med min)* view, 45, 125, 127–29, 271n219, 309–10n185, 309–10n185, 310n189
does not apply at conventional level, 209, 215
Go rams pa's summary description of, 93, 298–99n116
and quietism or Hwa shang, 54
Tsong kha pa on, 52, 131, 311n197
"neither one nor many" form of reasoning, 93, 205, 330n366, 299n117
Neumaier, Eva, vii–viii, xi–xiv, 285n95
New Red Annals (Deb ther dmar po gsar ma) (Bsod nams grags pa), 44
new translations *(gsar ma)* schools, 24–25, 28
Ngag dbang chos grags (1572–1641), 271n218
Nges shes rin po che sgron me (Mi pham), 264n148, 265n156, 275n249, 312n200, 320n276
Ngor chen Kun dga' bzang po (1382–1456), 25, 34, 35, 44, 260n116, 271n216
Ngor chen Sang rgyas phun sthogs (1649–1705), 266n168
Ngor E vam chos ldan monastery, 34, 36, 40, 44, 268n186, 187
nihilism, 1, 52, 71, 103, 113, 129, 235
Dol po pa's claim to be free of, 77
equated with Dga' ldan pa's view, 48
Middle Way eliminates extremes of, 69
and Tsong kha pa, 45, 52, 95, 299n118
See also extremes, four
noncomposite entities, 107, 109–11, 127
nonexistence, extreme of. *See* nihilism
nongrasping of clarity and emptiness *(gsal stong 'dzin med),* 263n143, 273–74n238
nonsectarian *(ris med)* movement, 33, 265n165
Nor brang O rgyan, 273–74n238
Nor bu bzang po (d. 1466), 44, 270n213, 271n216
Nya dpon/dbon Kun dga' dpal (1345–1439), 43, 269n207, 294–95n106
Nya phrug Kun dga' dpal (d. 1379?), 263n144

Nyang (or Myang) Nyi ma 'od zer (1136–1204), 255–56n73
Nyingma. *See* Rnying ma

O

O rgyan Rin chen dpal (1230–1309), 24
"object conceptualization," 149, 316n242
object-to-be-negated, 285n58
  and composite and noncomposite things, 109–11
  identificationor measure of, 79, 285n58, 286n59, 286n60
  rough, 93–95
  subtle and autonomous reasons, 91, 294n103
  subtle vs. rough, 81
objects, external, 53–55, 79, 83, 85, 199, 207, 223, 329n357, 330n359
  Tsong kha pa's acceptance of, 85, 89–91, 175, 293n98
obscurations
  afflicted, 143–44, 221, 290–91n82, 333n398
  antidotes that eliminate two, 221–27, 334n403
  differences between Hīnayāna and Mahāyāna, 87–89
  and grasping at self of phenomena, 219
  identification of two to be eliminated, 85–87, 219–21, 288–89n72, 290–91n82
obscurations to omniscience, 89, 143–49, 333n397
  and grasping at truth of phenomena, 145–47, 219
  Hīnayāna vs. Mahāyāna on, 167, 223
  Mahāyāna process of elimination of, 23, 320–21n285
  manifest and latent, 219–21
  and nine stages of bodhisattva path, 169, 321n288
  and pratyekabuddhas, 223
  and thought that conceptualizes three cycles, 219
Omniscience in Tenets (Grub mtha' kun shes) (Stag tshang lo tsa ba), 270n210
one and many, being devoid of, 213
Ong, Walter, 244n10, 245n11
Onoda, Shunzo, 245n15, 249n31, 267n171, 294–95n106, 295n107
opponent in logical argumentation, 8–9, 183, 326n331
oral debates/disputation
  in Indian Buddhism, 18, 254n61
  and polemical exchanges, 12–13
  records of, 243n1
ordinance *(bka' shog)*, 12
Ordinance (Lha bla ma Yeshes 'od), 21–22, 258n95
Ordinance (Zhi ba 'od), 23, 25, 257–58n91, 258n95
Ornament to the Intention of Nāgārjuna: A Response to Honorable Speech (Gsung lan klu sgrub dgons rgyan) (Rje btsun Chos kyi rgyal mtshan), 30
Ornaments to the Purport of Nāgārjuna (Klu grub dgongs rgyan) (Dge 'dun chos 'phel), 250n34

P

Pa tshab Nyi ma grags (b. 1055), 49, 93, 296–97n111, 298n113
Pad ma dkar po (1527–92), 264n149
Paṇ chen Bde legs nyi ma (sixteenth century), 30, 265n154
  and autonomous forms of inference, 328–29n353
  critique of Go rams pa, 304n156
  and perception of water, 314n229
Paṇ chen I, Blo bzang chos kyi rgyal mtshan (1570–1662), 30, 288n68
Path and Its Result *(lam 'bras)* instruction, 34, 36, 267n177
path of accumulation, 157
patrons, 42, 44
  for Go rams pa, 267–68n184, 270n213
perception
  correct, 117
  criticism of Tsong kha pa's view of, 54–55, 139–43
  engages its object in positive way, 199, 358–59n358

of cup of water across world spheres, 54–55, 139–43, 211
Perdue, Daniel, 250
Perfection of Wisdom sūtras, 73, 91, 169, 269, 279–80n14
works by Go rams pa on, 37–38
See also Prajñāpāramitā
pervasion. See *khyab pa*
permanence, and emptiness, 97. *See also* eternalism
persecution, 31–32
Pha bong kha Bde chen snying po (1878–1941), 23
Pha Dam pa sangs rgyas (b. 11th century), 24–25, 258n93
Phag mo gru pas, 43–44, 270n211
'Phags pa Blo gros rgyal mtshan (1235–80), 273n232
phenomena, 1, 330n359
arising by themselves, 179–81
exist only to extent that one does not analyze them, 131
generally characterized *(spyi mtshan),* 177, 324n317
reasoning that proves the selflessness of, 213–15
self of, 87, 155, 318n257, 258
selflessness of, 89, 159, 161, 171
specifically characterized *(rang mtshan),* 324n317
Pho brang Zhi ba 'od (second half of the eleventh century), 23, 251n37
Phur lcog Ngag dbang byams pa (1682–1762), 30
Phya pa (or Cha pa) Chos kyi seng ge (1109–69), 26, 260n123, 261n125, 280n19
and Bsod nams rtse mo, 296n109
and critique of Candrakīrti, 253n53
and individual who has not obtained path of seeing, 293n98
and Rma bya Byang chub rtson 'grus, 298n113
Sa skya Paṇḍita's criticism of, 27
Phyogs bcu'i sangs rgyas dang byang chub sems dpa' thams cad la phul ba'i yi ge (Sa paṇ), 253n48
Pierce, Charles Sanders, 2
pilgrimage, 27, 261n132
Pod chen drug gi 'bel gtam (Ngag dbang chos grags), 271n218
"Polemical Document" *(rtsod yig),* 263n145
polemics, 2–33, 56–57, 243n4
as an act of devotion, 6, 246–47n16
as apophatic literary discourse, 3, 4, 6
audience of, 15
Buddhist theory of, 248n25
as a controlled genre, 9
counterproductive variety of, 10, 56, 248n24
creates clarity, 56–57
and criticism, 4–6
criticism of the field of, 10, 248n23
as dialogue, 8–9, 13
dignified variety of genre, 10, 248n25
as a discipline in general, 2–10
history of Tibetan, 18–33, 62, 64, 254n61
initiatory vs. responsive, 12–13
intra and inter-sectarian, 6–7
motivations of writers of, 14–15
pain caused by, 4-6
popularity of, 4, 6, 17
as proportion of Tibetan literature, 12, 250n34
public nature of, 5
role in the formation of identity, 6, 8
scholarly treatment of religious, 244n6
self-assurance of writers of, 6, 245–46n15
in Tibet centers on practice, texts, and doctrines, 16
Tibetan works as cataphatic vs. apophatic, 11
titles of Tibetan works of, 13–14, 252n42
as vilification or insult, 17–18
"Politics of Abstractions, The" (Jasper), 273n237
Popper, Karl, 5
positivist tradition, 29
pot, analogies of, 125, 183, 186, 308–9n183, 309n184

Prajñāmūlamadyamakakārikas. See *Mūlamadyamakakārikā*
Prajñāpāramitā in One Hundred Thousand [Lines], 235
Prajñāpāramitāsūtras (phar phyin), 35, 37–38, 235, 262n138. *See also* Perfection of Wisdom sūtras
pramāṇa. *See* valid cognition
Pramāṇavārttika (Dharmakīrti), 27, 40, 217, 246–47n16, 304n153, 321n287, 321n289, 324n316
  Go rams pa's commentary on, 38
Pramāṇikas, 254n64
prasaṇga. See *reductio* argument
prasaṇgavipāryaya, 293–94n102
Prāsaṅgika Madhyamaka, 143, 314n230
  and acceptance of "I" as nominally existing, 151, 317n251
  ālayavijñāna does not exist for, 289n74, 322–23n307
  and autonomous reasons and theses, 55, 91–93, 177, 193–95
  belief in external objects, 173, 314n230, 317n251
  and bodhisattva stages and obscurations to omniscience, 169, 321n288
  Candrakīrti as exponent of, 26, 49
  five forms of reasoning of, 213
  Go rams pa's identity vis a vis, 49
  Pa tshab Nyi mag grags as exponent of, 296–97n111
  reductio arguments of, 191, 205
  regarding commonality with opponents vis a vis the parts of syllogisms, 309n184
  and specifically characterized phenomena, 324n317
  and Thang sag/zag monastery, 297–98n112
  as trademark for Dge lugs pa's Madhyamaka, 49
  as Tsong kha pa's theory of Madhyamaka, 29, 49, 77–79
  twelve special tenets of, 288–89n72
  and ultimate truth, 117
Prāsaṅgika/Svātantrika Madhyamaka distinction, 271n218
  and adequate argumentation, 193
  and autonomous syllogisms, 197
  and the conventional, 175
  and distinction between two truths, 193–201
  and emptiness, 173–75, 322n300
  Go ram pa's views of, 278–79n8, 285n53
  and the nature of construction, 135
  and objects-to-be-negated as subtle vs. rough, 55, 63, 79–81, 286n62, 323–24n311
  and Rngog Blo ldan shes rab, 295–96n108
  and rules of logical argumentation, 309n184
  and theses, 191
  and things existing by virtue of own nature, 175, 323n308
  Tsong kha pa on, 77–79, 278n8, 285n53
Prasannapadā (Candrakīrti), 127, 177–79, 290n75, 294n104, 301nn132–33, 303n149, 304n152, 307n175, 309n184, 310n186, 313n221, 314n232, 318nn259–60, 319nn274–75, 325nn322–26, 325–26n329, 326nn321–32, 327nn339–40, 327n342, 328n343, 328n348, 335n421
  and argumentation, 193
  and autonomous reasons inappropriate, 185
  and discussion of Prāsaṅgikas vs. Svātantrikas, 191
  and inference, 183–85
  Tsong kha pa's exegesis of, 157, 161, 189, 328n344
pratyekabuddhas, 55, 223–25, 225–27, 278n7, 334n404
  and emptiness of persons and phenomena, 157, 217, 225, 288–89n72, 318n262
  removal of afflictions, 320–21n285
  and śrāvaka view of enlightenment, 221
preparation, path of, 157
pretas, 85, 141, 211, 290n80
proliferations

and self of phenomena, 155
See also extremes, four; "freedom from proliferations"
proponent in logical argumentation, 183, 326n331
purification, four forms of, 73, 280n17

Q
quasi-ultimate truth, 215, 332n286
quietism, 54

R
Ra lo Rdo rje grag (1016–1198), 252n42
Ras chung pa (= Rdo rje grags pa?, 1085–1161), 258n93
rab 'byams pa, 34
Ratification of the True Principles of the Great Vehicle of Sudden Awakening (Tun wu ta cheng cheng li chueh) (Wang Hsi), 20
rationalism, 18
Ratnacūda Sūtra, 75
Ratnāvalī (Nāgārjuna), 147, 157–59, 235, 310n192, 315n237, 319nn267–68, 272
Rdo rje shugs ldan, 247n17, 266n166
Rdo rje tho ba (Dkha' bzhi 'dzin pa Rin chen rdo rje), 263n144
Rdo rje thog chen (Dkha' bzhi 'dzin pa Rin chen rdo rje), 263n144
Rdzogs chen. *See* Great Perfection *(rdzogs chen)*
realist schools, 71, 177, 217, 277n4, 331n374
and Dol po pa, 105, 107
and karma, 155, 211
indiviauls who are converted from to Mahāyāna, 203, 205
reality
analysis of, 332n386
and autonomous syllogisms, 197–201, 328–29n353
descriptions of by Dol po pa, 75
and freedom from all four extremes, 217
not emptiness of truth, 213
not empty of self-nature, 75
as term for ultimate truth, 1
understood differently in three vehicles, 165
See also dharmadhātu; emptiness
reasoning
emptiness established by means of, 117, 131, 213, 305n162
five forms of, 213, 331n380
and the "ultimate in name only," 125–27, 308n182
See also inference; syllogism
reasoning consciousness, 215
rebirth, 167
rebuttal *(brgal lan),* 12, 251–52n40
record of a refutation *(dgag yig),* 12
Red mda' ba Gzhon nu blo gros (1349–1412), 43, 47, 93, 231, 270n209, 303n148
and Go rams pa's critique of Dol po pa, 51, 97–105, 299–300n121
identity of challenger of in *Distinguishing the Views,* 302–3n142
lineage of, 294–95n106
as Prāsaṅgika, 273–74n238
and resuscitation of Madhyamaka, 274n240, 297–98n112
reductio argument, 191, 193, 197, 205
reflexive awareness
Dkon mchog 'jigs med dbang po on, 293n100
Tsong kha pa's repudiation of, 89, 293n98
refutation *(dgag pa),* 12, 243n5
Refutation of the False Tantras (Sngas log sun 'byin), 258n95
reifications, thirty-two, 121
rejection *(pratikṣepamukha),* 251–52n40
religious experience, 16, 253n55
replies to questions *(dris lan, zhus lan),* 12, 251n38
Reply to 'Brug ('Brug lan) (Sgom sde Nam mkha' rgyal mtshan), 264n149
Reply to Go, The, (Go lan) (Se ra Rje btsun Chos kyi rgyal mtshan and Paṇ chen Bde legs nyi ma), 30, 265n154
Reply to Shāk, The (Shāk lan) (Se ra Rje btsun Chos kyi rgyal mtshan

and Paṇ chen Bde legs nyi ma), 30, 265n154
Response to a Refutation, A: A Necklace for Those Who Preach Scripture and Reasoning (Rig 'dzin Chos kyi grags pa), 13
response to a refutation *(dgag lan,* honorific *gsung lan),* 12, 243n5
Response to Questions Concerning the Tantra Corpus (Rgyud 'bum dri lan) ('Jigs med gling pa), 24
resultant interdependencies, seven, 147, 315n235
Rgod tshang pa, 273n237
Rgyal ba sman, 33
Rgyal rong Nam mkha' lhun grub (b. seventeenth century), 264n150
Rgyal rtse Dpal 'khor chos sde monastery, 32
Rgyan ro Byang chub 'bum, 258n96
Ri chos nges don rgya mtsho (Dol po pa), 279n9, 279n10, 279n14, 280n16, 280n20, 281–82nn21–29, 282nn32–36, 282–83nn39–43, 283n45, 287n66, 301n135, 301–2n136
Rig 'dzin Chos kyi grags pa (1595–1659), 13
Rin chen bzang po (958–1055), 23, 257n90, 257–58n91, 258n95
Rin chen rdo rje, Bka' bzhi pa or Dka' bzhi 'dzin pa, (fourteenth century), 263n143, 269n207
Rin spungs court, 40, 43–44, 270n211, 271n217
ris med (nonsectarian) movement, 33, 265n165
Rje btsun Chos kyi rgyal mtshan. *See* Se ra rje btsun Chos kyi rgyal mtshan
Rje btsun Grags pa rgyal mtshan (1147–1216), 33, 111, 231, 273n232, 274n240, 296n109
and criticism of Jo nang pa–like views, 52
Rma bya pa Byang chub brtson 'grus (d. 1185), 93, 274n240, 296–97n111, 297–98n112, 298n113
Rma bya pa Rtsod pa'i seng ge. *See* Rma bya Byang chub brtson 'grus
Rma Rin chen mchog, 258n93
Rnam rgyal grags pa, 35
Rngog Legs pa'i shes rab (tenth century), 26, 274n121, 295n107, 295–96n108
Rngog lo tsā ba Blo ldan shes rab (1059–1109), 26, 49, 93, 261n125, 281n26, 295–96n108, 296n109, 296–97n111
Rngog Nyi ma seng ge (twelfth century), 25
Rnying ma, 7, 25, 257n85
Sog bzlog pa's defense of, 22, 257n85
Rnying ma dang bon gyi rnam gzhag (Spyan snga Blo gros rgyal mtshan), 255n70
Rnying ma tantras, 23–24, 251n37, 259n100
critiques regarding authenticity, 23–24, 248–49n27, 261n129
Rong ston Shes bya kun rig (1367–1449), 35, 41–43, 199, 245–46n15, 267n171, 270n208, 303n147
and autonomous reasons and theses, 181, 195, 223–25, 278n6, 273n238, 293–94n102, 325–26n329, 328n346, 328–29n353
and defense of Bon, 255n71
and Dol po pa's views, 51, 105–7, 302–3n142
and emptiness, 270n208, 300n128, 301n129
Go rams pa's study with, 34
and inference based on what is acceptable to others, 325n321
and karma and afflictions, 314–15n232
lineage from Pa tshab Nyi ma grags, 296–97n111
and nominal existence of the "I," 153, 317n250
and obscurations to omniscience, 292n92
and Rngog Blo ldan shes rab, 295–96n108
as student of G.yag phrug, 294–95n106

and Zhang Thang sag pa, 297–98n122
Rong zom Chos kyi bzang po (b. eleventh century), 257n88
rough object-to-be negated, 93–95
Rta nag gser gling monastery
  curriculum set up by Go rams pa at, 41
  destruction of during Chinese Cultural Revolution, 40
  founding of, 35, 36, 44, 267n182, 267–68n184
  and political power struggles, 271n217
  writing of *Distinguishing the Views* while being built, 44–45, 48
Rta skad byang chub sems dpa'i zhus pa'i mdo, 235
Rta ston Jo bo ye shes (1163–1230), 298n113
Rtsa shes ṭīk chen (Tsong kha pa), 284n54, 288n68, 290n76, 290–91n82, 304n156, 324–25n318
rtsod yig, 243n4. *See also* disputational document or record
Ru tsha Zhang skyabs, 33
Ruegg, D. Seyfort, 19–20, 243n2, 244n9, 255n72, 255–56n73, 265n74, 257n88, 260n122, 262n139, 262n140, 262n142, 271n218, 275n246, 280n15, 281n20, 281n26, 27, 282n31, 282n32, 282n34, 283n43, 283n45, 284n47, 286n60, 287n66, 288n69, 288–89n72, 289n74, 290n76, 290n81, 291n82, 293n98, 293n102, 294n106, 295n107, 295n108, 301n130, 311n194, 324n311, 324–25nn318–21, 332n386
Rygal sras Thogs med pa (1295–1369), 35
Rgyal tshab rje (1364–1432), 288–89n72

S

Sa bzang Ma ti paṇ chen (1294–1376), 43
Sa chen Kun dga' snying po (1092–1158), 25, 93, 273n232, 296n109
Sa jo gnyis kyi lta ba shan 'byed don la rang gi rtogs pa brjod pa (Dpal ldan rdo rje), 271n218
Sa paṇ. *See* Sa skya Paṇḍita Kun dga' rgyal msthan (Sa paṇ)
Sa skya College in Dehra Dun, India, 41
Sa skya monastery, 39–40, 41, 269n201, 294–95n106
Sa skya school, 7, 25, 31–32, 42, 47, 256n80
  Go rams pa and, 34, 35, 237
  political hegemony of, 43, 44
  styles of Madhyamaka in, 273–74n238
Sa skya Paṇḍita Kun dga' rgyal msthan (Sa paṇ) (1182–1251), 5, 15, 27, 245n14, 251n37, 258n96, 261–62n135, 273–74n238
  on the authenticity of Rnying ma tantras, 261n129
  challenge to Gsang phu epistemological tradition, 27
  critique of White Panacea, 256n79
  on the date of death of Buddha, 253n53
  and Gzad pa ring mo, 298n114
  and Hwa shang Mahāyāna's teachings, 255–56n73
  on Phya pa's interpretation of Dharmakīrti, 27
  on right practice of polemics, 248n25
  and Rje btsun Grags pa rgyal mtshan, 296n109
  and Rma bya Byang chub rtson 'grus, 298n113
  use of term "freedom from proliferations," 273n237
  See also *Treasury of Valid Reasoning*
Saṃcayagāthā sūtra, 121, 201
Saṃdhinirmocanasūtra, 105, 107, 279–80n14, 303n143
Sāṃkhyas, 179, 185, 309n184, 324–25n318, 325n322
Samten Gyaltsen Karmay, 243n4, 249, 256n82, 257n85, 257n88
Śāntarakṣita, 229–31
Śāntideva, 29, 278n5, 291n82. See also *Bodhicaryāvatāra*

Satyadvayavibhaṅga (Jñānagarbha), 49, 115, 119, 123–25, 173–75, 193, 305n159, 306n167, 307n178, 322n301, 322n302, 335n420
Satyadvayavṛtti (Jñānagarbha), 115–16, 135, 189–91, 305n158, 322n303, 334n414
Sautrāntika, 71, 83, 221, 277n4, 333n400
  and emptiness, 97, 217
Sautrāntika-Svātantrika Mādhyamikas, 89–91, 100, 293n99, 333n402
Sbyin bzang (Bka' bcu pa), 34
Schmithausen, Lambert, vii, viii, xiii, xiv, 281n26, 283n45, 289n74, 290n78, 290n79, 292n94
scriptural evidence
  and division of ultimate, 229–31
  and freedom from proliferations of four extremes, 231–35
Sdom gsum rab dbye (Sa skya Paṇḍita), 35
Sdom gsum rnam nges (Mnga' ris Paṇ chen Padma dbang rgyal), 24
Se ra monastery, 42
Se ra Rje btsun Chos kyi rgyal mtshan (1469–1544/46), 30, 55–56, 264n151, 314n229, 321n288, 328–29n353, 334n407, 411
  and defense of Tsong kha pa, 263n143
  and Go rams pa's misrepresentation of Tsong kha pa, 304n156
  and nominal existence of "I," 317n250
  and Tsong kha pa's karma theory, 314n222
  and two conceptions of *ālayavijñāna,* 322n306
Secret Mantra or Vajra Vehicle, 199
sectarian identity-formation and polemics, 6, 7–8
seeds, 137, 290n78, 313n215
  and grasping at truth of existence, 79, 145, 315n234
seeing, path of, 89, 121, 292n4
  and elimination of four extremes simultaneously, 217
  of Mahāyāna and freedom from extremes, 223
  and obscurations to omniscience, 149
  and understanding of reality, 157
  uninterrupted path of, 223, 334n403
self, 85, 87, 149–55, 153, 288–89n72, 291n86, 291–92n89, 317n246, 317n251
  associated with tathāgatagarbha and the ultimate, 282n29
  as basis of karma and its effects, 288–89n72
  cannot withstand rational analysis, 153, 155
  mental consciousness and label of, 149–51, 316–17n245
  of phenomena, 155, 318n257, 258
  two forms of, 85, 87, 149–55,
  See also "I"
self-arising, autonomous reasons necessary to repudiate, 179–81, 325–26n329
selflessness, 165, 227
  and freedom from proliferations, 227
  of person, 213
  of phenomena, 213, 331n380
Sells, Michael A., 244n6
sense fields, internal, 181
Sgam po pa (1079–1153), 28
Sgom sde Nam mkha' rgyal mtshan (1532–92), 264n149
Sgra tshad pa Rin chen rnam rgyal (1318–88), 294–95n106, 302n2141
Sha ra ba (1070–1141), 296–97n111
Shākya mchog ldan (1428–1507), 30, 51, 258n96, 270n210, 271n218, 274n238, 275n241,
  criticism of Tsong kha pa, 264n147, 269n207
  and emptiness, 275n241, 300n125
  on the compatibility of Jonang and Sa skya views, 111, 304n154
  philosophical affiliations of, 273–74n238
  and Red mda' ba, 294–95n106
  relationship to Go rams pa, 51–52, 269n202
  and Rgog Blo ldan shes rab, 295–96n108
  and Rma bya Byang chub rtson' grus, 298n113

suppression of works of, 32
and Thang sag pa, 297–98n112
Shangs pa bka' brgyud school, 25
Sherab Gyaltsen, 303n150
Sherburne, Richard, 335n420
Shes bya kun rig. *See* Rong ston
Shes rab rgya mtsho, Dge bshes (1884–1968), 33
Shugs ldan. *See* Rdo rje shugs ldan
siddhānta classification, 303n144
sign of truth, 159–61
signlessness, 157, 159–61
signs
elimination of all apprehension of, 227
grasping of, 155, 163
preoccupation with, 121
silk cloth, metaphor of, 75
simulacrum, 244n9
simulataneist *(cig car ba)* view, 19, 21, 261–62n135
Smith, E. Gene, 27, 249n27, 255n70, 255n71, 263n145, 304n154
smoke, 195
Sngags log sun 'byin kyi skor (Chag lo tsā ba), 251n38, 252n45, 258n93, 258n95
Sngon mo rdzong monastery, 40
Sog zlog pa Blo gros rgyal mtshan (1552–1624), 22, 24, 249n29, 251n38, 257n84, 257n85, 257–58n91, 258n93, 258n96, 259n98, 259n104,
soteriological knowledge, 251–52n40
sound, metaphor of, 187
Sparham, Gareth, 289n74, 290n78
specifically characterized phenomena, 324n317
speculative justification, 209, 331n371
speech and conceptual thought, 111
Sphuṭārtha (Haribhadra), 37, 316n242, 321n290
spiritual master, devotion to, 28
sprout analogy, 127, 197, 199, 209, 309n184
arising of and autonomous reasons, 197–99
and different kinds of seeds, 209, 331n370
and existence by virtue of own characteristics, 185, 325n322
Spyan snga Blo gros rgyal mtshan (1402–72), 255n70
śrāvakas and Śrāvakayāna, 55, 71, 157, 159–61, 217
and aggregates, 221, 223, 225, 306–7n170
and brief explanation of emptiness, 165, 320–21m285
difference in realization from pratyekabuddhas, 223, 333n402
and elimination of afflicted obscuration, 87
and enlightenment, 221
and essencelessness, 157, 163, 223–25, 288–89n72, 318n262
must realize selflessness of the person, 225
speed of moving through path, 165–69, 321n286
surpassed by bodhisattva's understanding, 225–27
and uninterrupted path, 223, 334n403
Śrīmālādevīsiṃhanāda Sūtra, 75
Stag tshang lo tsā ba, 270n210, 275n245, 288n68, 297–98n112
criticisms of Tsong kha pa, 30, 52, 251n39, 263n145
and Pa tshab Nyi ma grags, 296–97n111
and Rgog Blo ldan shes rab, 295–96n108
Stearns, Cyrus, 252n43, 262n141, 269n206, 269n207, 272n223, 275n243, 279n9, 279n11, 279n13, 279n14, 281n20, 281n21, 281n26, 281n28, 282n30, 282n41, 283n44, 293–94n102
Steinkellner, Ernst, 264n150, 278n5, 284n47, 292n94, 293n97, 295n106, 299n117, 304n153, 305n161, 306n165, 306n183, 322n298, 331n377, 332n387, 332n388
Stong thun chen mo (Mkhas grub Dge legs dpal bzang), 263n143, 278–79n8, 286n60, 323n309. See also *Dose of Emptiness*

student
 realists who become Mādhyamikas, 203–4
 those who are steadfastly Mādhyamikas, 203, 205–7
subject, common
 and adequate argumentation, 193
 and validity of syllogisms, 183, 185–87, 326–27n334, 327n338
 See also autonomous reasons
subject/object duality, 127–29
subject, waning of in equipoise, 187
Sum pa mkhan po (1704–88), 24, 298–99n116
Summa Theologiae (Aquinas), 250
Śūnyatāsaptati (Nāgārjuna), 79, 133–34, 145, 147, 285n54, 312n203, 312n206, 315n233
Sūtrālaṃkāra (Maitreya), 282n41, 301–2n136
Sūtrālaṃkārabhāṣyam, 302n137
svasaṃvedana, 288–89n72
svatantra See autonomous reasons
Svātantrika Madhyamaka, 26, 49
 acceptance of autonomous reasons, 91, 177, 189–91, 197, 205, 213, 324n315
 acceptance of true and false conventionalities, 314n225
 acceptance of true existence, 175, 323–24n311
 adherence to strict logic, 309n184
 Bhāvaviveka's view of mental consciousness, 87, 291n87
 and foundation consciousness and external objects, 89–91, 293n99, 100
 and measure of object-to-be-negated, 55, 79, 286n60
 and mind as creator of conventional world, 135
 and phenomena existing by virtue of own characteristics, 131, 173, 175, 323–24n311
 and Rngog Blo ldan shes rab, 295–96n108
 and two truths, 117, 332n386
 See also Prāsaṅgika-Svātantrika Madhyamaka distinction
Sword of Wisdom that Refutes the False Tantras (Sngags log sun 'byin shes rab ral gri) (Chag lo tsā ba), 23, 258n93, 258n95
syllogism, 127, 308–9n183, 309n184
 and unreality of generally characterized phenomena, 324n317
 See also autonomous reasons; subject, common; trimodal criteria; reasoning

T

Tai situ Byang chub rgyal mtshan (1302–64), 43
Talmage, Frank E., 244n6
Tanselle, G. Thomas, 56–57
tantras, 36
 critique of practices and texts of, 16, 22–27, 257n90
 Indian, and Mahāmudrā, 261–62n135
 Ye shes 'od's views of, 22, 256–57n83, 257n85
tantric priests *(sngags pa),* 22
Tāranātha (1575–1634), 31
Tarkajvālā (Bhāvaviveka), 151, 316–17n245
Tathāgatagarbha Sūtra, 75
tathāgatagarbha, 281n21, 281–82n28, 282n29, 283n43, 299–300n121
Tauscher, Helmut, 260n123, 264n150, 283n47, 286n59, 287n66, 292n94, 294n106, 297n112, 299n117
Taylor, Mark C., 244n9
Tenzin Gyatso (fourteenth Dalai Lama), 7–8
Testament of the Pillar (Bka' chems ka khol ma), 22–23, 25, 257n86
tetralemma. See fourfold alternatives
Thang sag/zag monastery, 297–98n112
theses, 55, 85, 91–93, 296–97n111
 differences between Prāsaṅgikas and Svātantrikas on, 191
 autonomous, 179–81
Tho ling monastery, 23
Thornbush, The: A Treatise Refuting the Hevajra and Lam 'Bras [Traditions] (Dgyes ndor dang lam 'bras

'gog pa'i bstan bcos gze ma ra mgo) (Rngog Nyi ma seng ge), 25
"thought construction," 115, 304–5n157, 312n202
three cycles of giving, 259, 263, 320n279
three enlightenments, 71, 278n7
three times, 288–89n72
three vows, 38–39
Thub bstan rnam rgyal monastery, 36, 40, 270n213
Thu'u bkwan Blo bzang chos kyi nyi ma (1737–1802), 24, 255n69, 255n70, 273–74n238, 294–95n106, 297–98n112
Thu'u bkwan grub mtha' (Thu'u bkwan), 255n69, 280n20
Tibet, 7–8
  adoption of Buddhism in, 1, 21–22
  Madhyamaka as distinct field in, 1–2
Tibetan Buddhist Resource Center (TBRC), 12, 250n34
Tillemans, Tom J. F., ix, 243n2, 248n25, 293–94n102, 299n117, 304n154, 325n318, 330n366
titles of Tibetan literary works, 13–14, 252n42
Tola, Fernando, 330n364
Toulmin, Stephen, 15
treasures *(gter ma)*, 23, 24
Treasury of Valid Reasoning (Tshad ma rigs gter) (Sa skya Paṇḍita), and polemics, 27, 38, 40, 248n25
trimodal criteria, 193
true existence, negation of, 53, 54, 55, 323–24n311
truth
  beyond mental objectification, 116–17
  conventional and Prāsaṅgikas and Svātantrikas, 193–95
  conventional and ultimate, 81, 117–19, 286–87n65
  emptiness of, 131, 213–15, 217
  Dol po pa on, 75
  not abstract for Tibetans, 15
  quasi-ultimate, 215, 332n286
  and reasoning consciousness, 215
  terms that designate ultimate, 1
  two senses of word, 113
  union of two, 207–17
  See also conventional; ultimate truth
truthlessness, 119
  and conceptualization of entitiness, 223–25
  as negation, 213
  understood by śrāvakas and pratyekabuddhas, 223
Tshad ma rigs gter. See *Treasury of Reasoning* (Sa skya Paṇḍita)
Tshad ma'i gzhung don 'byed pa (Blo bzang tshul khrims byams pa rgya mtsho), 250n32
Tsong kha pa Blo bzang grags pa (1357–1419)
  and autonomous reasons, 177, 324n315, 328n344
  on Bhāvaviveka and mental consciousness, 316–17n245
  on conceptual thought, 81–83, 288n71
  creation of infrastructure for successful institution, 42
  Dge 'dun chos 'phel's critique of, 32
  and Dol po pa, 28, 30
  and emptiness understood in Hīnayāna, 163, 320n278
  on external objects, 89–91, 293n98
  and foundation consciousness and reflexive awareness, 89–91, 289n74
  Go rams pa's summary of his Madhyamaka system, 77–93
  as hard doxographer, 285n53
  on individual who has not obtained path of seeing, 89, 171–73, 293n97, 321n293
  and Jo nang pas, 47, 269n207, 272n229
  on karma, 83–85, 290n79
  on law of double negation, 45
  life and works of, 77, 199, 283–84n47
  on the objects to be abandoned and realized, 85, 87–88, 157–73, 318n262
  polemics defending and attacking, 29–30, 30, 45, 247n19, 263n143, 264n149
  repuditation of "neither existence nor

nonexistence" doctrine, 45, 131, 271n219
repudiation of Sa skya pas' philosophical views, 42, 45, 47
self-identifies as Prāsaṅgika, 29, 49
and Stag tshang lo tsā ba, 251n39
as student of Red mda' ba, 294–95n106
and Svātantrikas not understanding the ultimate truth, 77–79, 285n53
on the two obscurations, 85–87, 290–91n82
and two selves, 85, 87, 149–55, 291n86, 291–92n92
on valid cognition, 183, 326–27n334
visions of Mañjuśrī, 17

Tsong kha pa Blo bzang grags pa (1357–1419), Go rams pa's refutation of in *Distinguishing the Views,* 52–56, 115–201, 304n156, 304–5n157
on *ālayavijñāna,* 322–23n307
on the conventional, 54–55, 133–37
on the distinctions between Mahāyāna and Hīnayāna, 157–73
on emptiness, 52–53, 115, 161–63
on external objects and the foundation consciousness, 173–77
on how karma gives rise to its effects, 137–39
on the identification of the two selves, 149–55
on nominal existence of "I," 151
on perception of objects, 139–43
and Svātantrikas and autonomous syllogisms, 199
system not in accordance with sūtra and tantras, 199–201
and thought constructions, 115
Tsong kha pa as crypto-Svātantrika, 309n184
Tsong kha pa's commentary on *Bodhicaryāvatāra,* 322n297
Tsong kha pa's tenets falsely derived from tutelary deity *(yi dam),* 199–201
on the ultimate, 115–33
on why no autonomous reasons and theses, 177–91

Tucci, Giuseppe, 20, 256n76, 270n211
tutelary deity (*yi dam*), 199–201
Twenty-Five-Thousand-Line Prajñāpāramitāsūtra, 233
two accumulations, 261–62n135

U

ultimate truth, 55, 217
beyond all speech, 217, 231–33
and destruction *qua* real entity, 137
differences in three vehicles concerning, 165
Dol po pa's treatment of, 73, 75
Go rams pa's treatment of, 211–17
as freedom from proliferations, 55, 217, 231
in name only, 125–27
vs. quasi-ultimate, 215, 332n386
Tsong kha pa's views of as examined by Go rams pa, 79–83, 115–31
uninterrupted path, 223, 334n403
universals, 177
Uttaratantra (Maitreya), 39, 75, 211, 219, 221, 227n1, 239, 281n21, 281n27, 282n29, 282n34, 282n41, 295–96n108, 333n394, 333n396
G.yag phrug's commentary on, 294–95n106
identifies improper cogitation as an obscuration to omniscience, 147
Red mda' ba's commentary on, 300n122

V

Vādanyāya, 248n25
Vaibhāṣikas
and aggregates, 97, 221, 300n124
doctrine of "karmic inexhaustibility," 83, 137, 290n76
and emptiness, 97, 217, 292n91
as one of four philosophical schools, 71, 277n4
as śrāvaka school, 333n400
Vaiśeṣika school, 139
valid cognition *(pramāṇa),* 27, 35, 183, 205, 326–27n334
and adequate argumentation, 193
and autonomous theses, 191

and Go rams pa's understanding of conventional, 207–9
van der Kuip, Leonard, 260n123, 261n131, 266n168, 267n172, 267n173, 268n192, 273n235, 288n269, 296n108, 298n113
Vasubandhu, 18, 103, 251n40, 321n290
  Dol po pa's views on, 51, 105
  and emptiness, 75, 101
  See also *Vyākhyāyukti*
Vasumitra, 254n61
Vātsīputrīyas, 31n256, 155
"view that things are neither existent nor nonexistent." *See* "neither existence nor nonexistence" view
Vigrahavyāvartanī (Nāgārjuna), 107–9, 111, 181, 254n64, 304n151, 325n325, 332n384
Vijñapti[mātra], 103
vilification of opponent, 17–18
village religion, 22
Vinaya, 35, 38, 40
vows, three *(sdom gsum skor),* 38–39
Vyākhyāyukti (The Science of Exegesis) (Vasubandhu), 251–52n40, 277n2

W
Wang Hsi, 20
water, as example of object perceived differently by different beings, 54–55, 139–43, 211
Weber, Max, 3–4
Wheel of Thunderbolts, The (Phyin ci log gi gtam gyi sbyor ba la zhugs pa'i smra ba ngan pa rnam par 'thad pa'i bstan bcos gnam lcags 'khor lo) (Mkhas grub Dge legs dpal bzang), 263n143
White Panacea *(dkar po chig thub)* doctrine, 27–28, 256n79
  Sa skya Paṇḍita's rejection of, 27–28, 248–49n27, 261–62n135
Williams, Paul, 243n2, 264n151, 285n58, 298n113, 312n202
wisdom, 261–62n135. *See also* gnosis
word-commentary *(tshig 'grel),* 11
words and construction of the world, 312n202

Y
Yamāntaka, 25, 260n116
Ye shes 'od, 21, 22, 23, 256–57n83, 257n85
yod min med min. See "neither existence nor nonexistence" view
Yogācāra-Svātantrika Mādhyamikas
  and external objects and foundation of consciousness, 89–91, 293n100
  and śrāvakas and pratyekabuddhas, 333n402
yogic direct perception, 288–89n72
Yol lcag Rma bya Byang chub brtson, 298n113
Yoshimizu, Chizuko, 263n143, 264n147, 284n47, 284n50, 285n53, 286n61, 298n112, 311n196, 323n208
Yuan dynasty in China, 43
Yuktiṣaṣṭikā (Nāgārjuna), 215, 332n384
Yuktiṣaṣṭikavṛtti (Candrakīrti), 117–19, 163, 231, 305n163
Yum don rab gsal (Go rams pa), 35

Z
Zhang thang sag/zag pa Ye shes 'byung gnas (b. eleventh century), 93, 131, 195, 263n143, 274n249, 296–97n111, 297–98n112, 298n113
  and "neither existence nor nonexistence [doctrine]," 131, 311–12n199
  and use of autonomous inferences in conventional contexts, 328n349
Zhang Tshal pa (1123–93), 28
Zhi ba 'od, 257–58n91, 258n95

About the Translators

José Ignacio Cabezón is the XIVth Dalai Lama Professor of Tibetan Buddhism and Cultural Studies at the University of California Santa Barbara. He studied at Sera Monastery in India and got his Ph.D. from the University of Wisconsin–Madison. Cabezón is the author or editor of eleven books and dozens of articles on various aspects of Tibetan religion and religious studies.

The late Geshe Lobsang Dargyay was trained at Drepung Monastery in Tibet. He got his doctorate in Buddhist and Tibetan Studies from the Ludwig Maximilians Universität and held teaching and research positions in Vienna, Hamburg, and Calgary. Among his many publications is *Die Legende von den sieben Prinzessinen,* published in Vienna.

About Wisdom

Wisdom Publications, a nonprofit publisher, is dedicated to making available authentic works relating to Buddhism for the benefit of all. We publish books by ancient and modern masters in all traditions of Buddhism, translations of important texts, and original scholarship. Additionally, we offer books that explore East-West themes unfolding as traditional Buddhism encounters our modern culture in all its aspects. Our titles are published with the appreciation of Buddhism as a living philosophy, and with the special commitment to preserve and transmit important works from Buddhism's many traditions.

To learn more about Wisdom, or to browse books online, visit our website at www.wisdompubs.org.

You may request a copy of our catalog online or by writing to this address:

Wisdom Publications
199 Elm Street
Somerville, Massachusetts 02144 USA
Telephone: 617-776-7416 • Fax: 617-776-7841
Email: info@wisdompubs.org • www.wisdompubs.org

The Wisdom Trust

As a nonprofit publisher, Wisdom is dedicated to the publication of Dharma books for the benefit of all sentient beings and dependent upon the kindness and generosity of sponsors in order to do so. If you would like to make a donation to Wisdom, you may do so through our website or our Somerville office. If you would like to help sponsor the publication of a book, please write or email us at the address above.

Thank you.

Wisdom is a nonprofit, charitable 501(c)(3) organization affiliated with the Foundation for the Preservation of the Mahayana Tradition (FPMT).

Other titles in the Studies in Indian and Tibetan Buddhism Series

Among Tibetan Texts
History and Literature of the Himalayan Plateau
E. Gene Smith
Edited by Kurtis Schaeffer
384 pages, cloth, ISBN 0-86171-179-3, $39.95

Approaching the Great Perfection
Simultaneous and Gradual Methods of Dzogchen Practice in the Longchen Nyingtig
Sam Van Schaik
448 pages, ISBN 0-86171-370-2, $29.95

Foundations of Dharmakīrti's Philosophy
John D. Dunne
512 pages, ISBN 0-86171-184-X, $39.95

Luminous Lives
The Story of the Early Masters of the Lam 'bras Tradition in Tibet
Cyrus Stearns
320 pages, ISBN 0-86171-307-9, $34.95

Mipham's Beacon of Certainty
Illuminating the View of Dzogchen, the Great Perfection
John Whitney Pettit
592 pages, ISBN 0-86171-157-2, $28.95

Reason's Traces
Identity and Interpretation in Indian and Tibetan Buddhist Thought
Matthew T. Kapstein
480 pages, ISBN 0-86171-239-0, $34.95

Scripture, Logic, Language
Essays on Dharmakīrti and His Tibetan Successors
Tom J.F. Tillemans
320 pages, ISBN 0-86171-156-4, $32.95

The Svātantrika-Prāsaṅgika Distinction
What Difference Does a Difference Make?
Edited by Georges Dreyfus and Sara McClintock
384 pages, ISBN 0-86171-324-9, $34.95

Vajrayoginī
Her Visualizations, Rituals, and Forms
Elizabeth English
608 pages, ISBN 0-86171-329-X, $34.95